Transitional Justice, Distributive Justice, and Transformative Constitutionalism

Transitional Justice, Distributive Justice, and Transformative Constitutionalism

Comparing Colombia and South Africa

Edited by

DAVID BILCHITZ AND RAISA CACHALIA

With

MAGDALENA INÉS CORREA HENAO AND NATHALIA BAUTISTA PIZARRO

OXFORD
UNIVERSITY PRESS

OXFORD
UNIVERSITY PRESS

Great Clarendon Street, Oxford, OX2 6DP,
United Kingdom

Oxford University Press is a department of the University of Oxford.
It furthers the University's objective of excellence in research, scholarship,
and education by publishing worldwide. Oxford is a registered trade mark of
Oxford University Press in the UK and in certain other countries

First Edition published in 2023

Published in the United States of America by Oxford University Press
198 Madison Avenue, New York, NY 10016, United States of America

British Library Cataloguing in Publication Data

Data available

Library of Congress Control Number: 2023946845

ISBN 978–0–19–288762–7

DOI: 10.1093/oso/9780192887627.001.0001

Printed and bound by
CPI Group (UK) Ltd, Croydon, CR0 4YY

In Memoriam for Jeffrey Cohen-Dorfman
To a unique, authentic friend and scientist committed to the dignity and equality of all, an explorer who loved the engagement between countries and cultures, who left the earth too soon
David Bilchitz

For my precious newborn daughter, Talia
Raisa Cachalia

Preface

In September 2016, the government of Colombia and the FARC rebels signed a landmark peace agreement ending a long-standing armed conflict. The atmosphere in the crowd was electric, with participants dressed all in white and witnessing long-standing enemies committing to a future founded upon dialogue rather than violence. The celebrations at this momentous event felt very similar to the elation experienced when all South Africans—irrespective of skin colour—stood in queues together for the first time to cast their vote in the first democratic election in South Africa in 1994. That was followed by South Africans from all backgrounds uniting in great joy at the spine-tingling victory of South Africa over New Zealand in rugby, a sport previously emblematic of apartheid South Africa. These truly euphoric moments have sadly been followed by the colossal challenges both countries have faced in moving beyond a past characterised by stark divisions, injustice, and conflict to create a stable future society based on liberty, equality, democracy, and constitutionalism.

Whilst there are many similarities between South Africa and Colombia, there have been very few books that have sought to examine their trajectories in a comparative light. Indeed, this is part of a wider problem of limited academic engagement between Africa and Latin America due, amongst other factors, to language differences and geographical distance. That said, we strongly believe that the rich intellectual possibilities offered by such an exchange require that greater attention and resources should be devoted to similar comparative engagements. It is this belief that motivated this book.

Of course, beliefs can remain inchoate without action. We are grateful for the many individuals who not only thought this project worthwhile but committed resources and energy to making it a reality. Projects such as this begin with individual connections and relationships—and those can best be formed in person. The two visits we made respectively to Colombia in 2016 were deeply enriching on a personal and professional level but also led us to build friendships and connections not possible in a purely virtual world. Those relationships led us to sign a memorandum of agreement between the University of Johannesburg and Universidad Externado de Colombia. In many instances, such agreements are simply a formality and expression of good will. However, the Rector of the Universidad Externado de Colombia at the time, Professor Juan Carlos Henao Perez, himself an esteemed jurist and inspirational individual, pressed upon all participants the need to ensure the collaboration would result in concrete connections and outputs. The initial participants in this discussion were mostly lawyers though we immediately recognised the need for perspectives that were not confined to law itself. That led us to brainstorm together and decide on a comparative project focused on linking three normative concepts together that we regarded as central to the shift taking place in our societies: transitional justice, distributive justice, and transformative constitutionalism.

Such an approach required us to reach out to authors with different forms of expertise. The concept could easily have remained just that if the excellent academics we approached had not agreed to contribute to the project. Doing so was not a simple matter: it involved reaching out across time zones, language differences, and geography to build relationships and create high quality academic papers. We are deeply grateful for the commitment of our authors over several years. The papers were presented in a workshop that helped refine the ideas and were further worked on in several iterations after editorial engagement. In between, we had the COVID-19 pandemic which disrupted the lives of our authors as well as posing significant challenges to our societies. Only once we were confident in the quality of the pieces did we approach a publisher. We were delighted that the hard work and commitment of each author paid off with Oxford University Press accepting the edited collection in May 2022.

Ensuring the successful completion of this project required leadership in both Colombia and South Africa. Whereas we took on this mantle in South Africa, we are deeply grateful to Magdalena Inés Correa Henao and Nathalia Bautista Pizarro for their management of this work in Colombia. We greatly appreciate their warmth and friendship throughout, as well as the spirit of collaboration in which all our endeavours have been undertaken. We all equally designed this project but, due to our mutual decision to publish in English, it was agreed that we would take on the primary editorial role in relation to preparing the chapters for publication, developing the book proposal, and navigating the publication process. The important contribution of Magdalena and Nathalia is recognised through their designation as adjunct editors of this book.

We are deeply grateful to the University of Johannesburg's Faculty of Law and the Dean at the time, Professor Letlhokwa Mpedi, for their support of this project and providing the venue and resources for the conference. The project itself was led under the research centre of the Faculty of Law at the University of Johannesburg which David Bilchitz directs and in which Raisa Cachalia was a researcher—the South African Institute for Advanced Constitutional, Public, Human Right and International Law (SAIFAC). We wish to thank colleagues, both junior and senior, for their support and particularly Naomi Hove for her administrative assistance. David Bilchitz, during the period of work on this book, also joined the University of Reading part-time and he would like to thank colleagues there for their support. Some of the work for this project also took place during David Bilchitz's sabbatical, when he was based in Berlin, and he expresses gratitude to the Humboldt

Foundation for the award of a Georg Forster Research Fellowship which enabled this productive academic period in his life.

The Universidad Externado de Colombia is thanked also for their support and sponsoring academics to come to the initial conference. In particular, we thank the Rector, Professor Juan Carlos Henao Pérez for his infectious enthusiasm, commitment, and tremendous hospitality when we visited. We are deeply grateful to the Konrad Adenauer Foundation, both in South Africa and Colombia, for helping to sponsor the initial conference and travel of many participants.

We are most grateful to the staff at Oxford University Press who have worked with us in a professional and productive manner. Brian Stone was the wonderful commissioning editor who conducted the review process and has helped shepherd this book through the initial stages of its existence. We also are extremely grateful to Lane Berger, the outstanding project editor who worked with us so attentively in ensuring an efficient process for entering production. Finally, we would like to express our gratitude to Shenbagarajan Subramani, our production project manager, for his efficient and smooth running of the production process.

On a personal level, David Bilchitz is deeply grateful for the friendship and hospitality shown to him in Colombia on his various visits. A highlight of his life was attending the signing of the peace agreement between the Colombian government and the FARC rebels in September 2016—the elation of that moment has maintained his enthusiasm and belief in this project throughout. David would like to thank his wonderful group of supportive friends, family, and colleagues who have nurtured him during the writing of this book. In particular, David would like to mention his two nephews Gavriel and Shalev who, he hopes, will share a commitment to healing the wrongs of the past and creating more just societies. It is hard to find the words to express his appreciation for the continued love and support of his parents—Ruven and Cynthia Bilchitz—as well as the visceral sense of opposition to injustice they inculcated in himself and his brother Leonard (who, together with his wife Lara, are creating a similar foundation for his nephews). His husband, Dr Ruvi Ziegler, is a constant source of intellectual engagement, companionship, and love—editing this volume has been much easier thanks to his support and belief that it would come to fruition.

Raisa Cachalia would also like personally to thank our Colombian colleagues for inviting her to the administrative law and peace conference in August–September 2016, which took place in the build-up to the signing of the historic peace agreement later in that year. At this conference she had the pleasure of meeting Julián Pimiento Echeverri and Irit Milkes, who were warm and welcoming to her. She is grateful to these colleagues for giving of their time to introduce her to Bogotá, showing her many of its fascinating attractions, and to the organisers for giving Raisa and her husband an opportunity to visit Colombia's most romantic city—Cartagena. It was also at this conference that she presented the early ideas of the chapter that would become her contribution to this book and which moved her to collaborate with Julian and Irit on questions of procedural justice, peacebuilding, and democratic consolidation. A special acknowledgement goes to her parents, Leila Patel and Azhar Cachalia, who have always encouraged Raisa and her sister, Ammara to contribute to building a better world. And, finally, to her husband Luc Spiller and her cherished children—Zia, Ara, and Talia—who inspire her in all that she does.

David Bilchitz
Raisa Cachalia
October 2022

Contents

Theme 8: The Role of International Law in Advancing Transitional Justice

List of Figures

List of Contributors

Editors

Primary Editors

David Bilchitz is a Professor of Fundamental Rights and Constitutional Law at the University of Johannesburg (UJ) and a Professor of Law at the University of Reading. He is also the Director of the South African Institute for Advanced Constitutional, Public, Human Rights and International Law (SAIFAC), a centre of UJ. He is a member of the Academy of Sciences of South Africa and Vice-President of the International Association of Constitutional Law. In 2017, he was awarded a research fellowship from the Humboldt Foundation. He publishes widely including his latest monograph *Fundamental Rights and the Legal Obligations of Business* (2022).

Raisa Cachalia is an LLD Candidate at Stellenbosch University, a Research Associate in the Faculty of Law at the University of Johannesburg and an editor of the *Constitutional Court Review*. Her research interests are broadly in the fields of constitutional law and administrative law with her current doctoral project being focused on the legal regulation of state contracts in South Africa. She was previously a lecturer at the University of Johannesburg (UJ) and, before that, a researcher at SAIFAC (a centre of UJ) where she dedicated a significant portion of her time there to working on this project. Prior to that, she served as a law clerk of the Constitutional Court of South Africa.

Adjunct Editors

Magdalena Inés Correa Henao is a Professor of Constitutional Law at the Universidad Externado de Colombia. She has a Master's degree in public administration from the University of Antwerp and a PhD in law from Carlos III of Madrid University. She has worked as director of the Constitutional Law Department at the Universidad Externado de Colombia, assistant magistrate at the Colombian Constitutional Court, and an expert hired by the Inter-American Commission on Human Rights. Her areas of interest are especially in the economic aspects of constitutionalism and socio-economic rights.

Nathalia Bautista Pizarro is a Professor of Criminal Law and Philosophy of Law, researcher of the Centro de Investigación en Filosofía y Derecho, and member of the Gender Office (Unidad de Género) at the Universidad Externado de Colombia. She has been a scholar of the German Service of Academic Exchange (DAAD), the Ernst und Anna Landsberg Foundation of Switzerland, and Universidad Externado de Colombia. Her research fields are focused on the theory of crime, legitimacy questions of criminal law, transitional justice, as well as the philosophy of law of the modern state, and its debates surrounding pluralism.

She has also edited and translated many publications on criminal law, international criminal law, and the philosophy of law. She has been invited as a guest researcher, professor, and lecturer in Germany, Perú, Chile, Bolivia, and South Africa.

Authors

Theme 1

Thaddeus Metz is a Professor of Philosophy at the University of Pretoria. He has previously been a Distinguished Professor of Philosophy at the University of Johannesburg and a Professor at the University of the Witwatersrand. He received his PhD from Cornell University. He publishes widely, his latest monograph being *A Relational Moral Theory: African Ethics in and Beyond the Continent.*

Nathalia Bautista Pizarro—as above under Editors

Theme 2

Kim Berman is a Professor in Visual Art at the University of Johannesburg and Executive Director of Artist Proof Studio, a community-based printmaking centre in Newtown, Johannesburg. Her books include *Finding Voice: A Visual Approach to Engaging Change.*

Michelle LeBaron is a Professor at the Allard School of Law, University of British Columbia, Canada. Her work explores how arts help to bridge worldview differences and transform conflict. Michelle's five books include the 2018 *Changing Our Worlds: Art as Transformative Practice.*

Yolanda Sierra León is a Research Professor at the Department of Constitutional Law and the Faculty of Cultural Heritage, and Director of the Cultural Rights Group: Derecho, Arte y Cultura (Law, Arts and Culture) at Universidad Externado de Colombia. She has also been the Director of the Citizen Pedagogy Program for Students in Bogotá's Institute for Educational Research and Pedagogical Development, a monument and historical archives restorer, and Secretary-General at Bogotá's Cultural Institute.

Theme 3

Emilia Potenza is the curator of exhibitions and education at the Apartheid Museum in Johannesburg. She has a BA and a Higher Diploma in Education (University of the Witwatersrand). Through the museum's exhibitions and public programmes, she creates opportunities for a range of audiences to engage with South Africa's history, and to draw on the crucial lessons that this offers.

Adriénne van den Heever is a curatorial assistant at the Apartheid Museum. She has a BA Hons (Fine Arts) and a Postgraduate Diploma in Arts and Culture Management (University of the Witwatersrand). Her focus is on using tangible heritage and contemporary art to explore the past and create dialogue with the present and future.

Nancy Rocío Rueda Esteban is the Academic Coordinator in the Tourism and Hotel Management Faculty at the Universidad Externado de Colombia. She has a Master's degree in Planning and Management of Tourism from the Universidad Externado de Colombia and a Master's degree in Tourism and Heritage from the Université Lumière Lyon 2, and a PhD in Cultural Heritage at the University of Birmingham. Her research interests lie in tourism, culture, and heritage.

Theme 4

David Bilchitz—as above under Editors

Magdalena Inés Correa Henao—as above under Editors

Theme 5

Meghan Finn is a lecturer in the Department of Public Law of the University of Johannesburg. Meghan is an admitted advocate of the High Court of South Africa, and previously practised at the Johannesburg Bar. She has served as a law clerk of the Constitutional Court of South Africa and is also an editor of the *Constitutional Court Review*.

Andrés Mauricio Gutiérrez Beltrán is a Professor of Constitutional Law at the Universidad Externado de Colombia. Currently, he is a deputy justice of the Colombian Constitiutional Court. He holds a PhD in Constitutional Law from the Universidad Autónoma de Madrid and was awarded the Nicolás Pérez Serrano Prize for the best doctoral dissertation on Constitutional Law in 2016.

Theme 6

Sindiso MnisiWeeks is Associate Professor in Legal and Political Science at the University of Massachusetts, Amherst, and Adjunct Associate Professor in Public Law at the University of Cape Town. She received her DPhil from the University of Oxford's Centre for Socio-Legal Studies, as a Rhodes Scholar, and previously clerked for then Deputy Chief Justice of the Constitutional Court of South Africa, Dikgang Moseneke.

Diana Carolina Rivera-Drago is a Researcher and Professor of the Civil Law Department at the Universidad Externado de Colombia. She completed her Master's degree in Law at Queen Mary University of London and her PhD in Law at the University of Turin, Italy.

She has also worked at the Colombian Constitutional Court and as a consultant in different prior consultation processes with many Indigenous communities across the country.

Filipo Ernesto Burgos Guzman is a Professor and Researcher at the Universidad Externado de Colombia. He completed his legal training at the Sorbonne University, Paris II; his LLM in Management and Administration from the Sorbonne University, Paris I; and is a PhD candidate at Universidad Externado de Colombia.

Theme 7

Raisa Cachalia—as above under Editors

Julián Andrés Pimiento Echeverri is a Professor in Administrative Law at Universidad Externado de Colombia, and has held visiting professorships at institutions such as the Universidad Católica de Chile, and the Universidad de Barcelona. Julián was awarded a post-doctoral research fellowship at the University of Barcelona and has worked in legal practice at Colombia's Bar as well as an auxiliary magistrate in Colombia's Conseil d'Etat.

Irit Milkes is a Research Assistant in the Department of Administrative Law at the University Externado of Colombia. She has a Master's degree in Public Law and Digital Public Administration at the Sorbonne University (Panthéon-Sorbonne Paris I). She is currently a PhD candidate in Law and Political Science at the University of Barcelona. She also works as a consultant in public and administrative law.

Theme 8

Mispa Roux is Senior Research Officer in the SARChI Chair for International Constitutional Law, Faculty of Law, University of Pretoria. She was previously a senior lecturer in Public International Law and Human Rights at the Law Faculty of the University of Johannesburg (UJ). She was also Head of the Sexual and Gender-Based Violence Unit and Deputy Director at the South African Institute for Advanced Constitutional, Public, Human Rights and International Law (SAIFAC), a centre of UJ. She is also an editor of the *Constitutional Court Review*.

Natalia Silva Santaularia is a researcher and lecturer at the Research Centre for Philosophy and Law of the Universidad Externado de Colombia and a consultant at the Special Jurisdiction for Peace. She is currently a PhD candidate at the University of Cologne (Germany). She has previously worked at the Special Jurisdiction for Peace (Colombia), in the Office of the Director of Public Prosecutions (Colombia), and in the Max Planck Institute for Foreign and International Criminal Law (Germany). She also interned at the International Criminal Tribunal for the Former Yugoslavia (Netherlands).

1

Developing a Conceptual Framework for Global South Comparisons

Colombian and South African Contributions

David Bilchitz and Raisa Cachalia

Colombia and South Africa are two societies struggling to move beyond a history of injustice and violent conflict amongst their peoples. Both societies, at formative moments, developed progressive constitutions that sought to provide the institutional framework for building a better future where conflicts are mediated through the institutions of law and respect for individual rights is entrenched. These constitutions were ambitious: they sought not only to develop the architecture of democracy but also to address entrenched socio-economic deprivation and chart the course towards a future of greater internal economic equality.

These two societies might be seen as emblematic of a model of social change in the Global South which includes three dimensions: the first is what may be grouped under the broad term 'transitional justice' and involves calibrating one's response to past injustice in a way that addresses that difficult history but does not inhibit the establishment of a new order; the second is a commitment to 'transformative constitutionalism', a law-governed model of social change that is rooted in a progressive constitution; and the third is 'distributive justice', which recognises the economic inequalities that have resulted from past wrongs and pursues greater socio-economic equality through measures that, initially at least, address dire poverty. There is a vast literature on each of these concepts. In Section 1 of this chapter, we sketch the conceptual foundations of this book by articulating our understanding of the three concepts, their importance in the context of Global South societies and, importantly, the interconnections between them.

Section 2 contends that this conceptual framework is particularly apposite to comparisons in the Global South. It then narrows in on the examples of Colombia and South Africa, explaining why they are ripe for comparison and why the three dimensions of this conceptual framework are particularly apt for examining these two contexts. Section 3 engages with our approach to addressing some of the challenges of conducting Global South comparisons of the kind conducted in this book. These challenges emerge both from the current hierarchies of knowledge

David Bilchitz and Raisa Cachalia, *Developing a Conceptual Framework for Global South Comparisons* In: *Transitional Justice, Distributive Justice, and Transformative Constitutionalism.* Edited by: David Bilchitz and Raisa Cachalia, with Magdalena Inés Correa Henao and Nathalia Bautista Pizarro, Oxford University Press. © David Bilchitz and Raisa Cachalia 2023.
DOI: 10.1093/oso/9780192887627.003.0001

production as well as from practical considerations. This discussion naturally leads into our explanation and justification for the specific methodology adopted in this book. It includes the identification of specific themes on which authors write chapters on their own contexts and then a joint reflection about what emerges from considering the comparison between them. Section 4 outlines the different segments of the book. We delineate the themes around which the chapters are organised and then provide a brief summary of the key arguments made by the authors. Whilst any one book is limited in the dimensions that can be analysed, we hope that this contribution will be a catalyst for more in depth South-South comparisons in the future.

1. Connecting the Dots: Three Interrelated Dimensions

A. Transitional Justice

Whilst across history societies have shifted from one order to another, the distinct domain of transitional justice developed in the late 1980s and sought to address two critical and sometimes conflicting ends.[1] The first relates to the meaning and understanding of justice in the context of societies trying to transition from a history of colonialism, long-standing conflict, and widespread violations of human rights.[2] Transitional justice sought to examine what particular approaches might be adopted to try and assist societies in leaving behind histories of violent conflict. In so doing, it involves the idea that, without addressing the past, it would come to haunt the present and compromise the peace and democratic stability of the societies in question. Addressing the past was thus important for future peacebuilding efforts of transitional societies[3] and necessary for reconciliation after long-standing conflict.[4]

[1] See P Arthur, 'How "Transitions" Reshaped Human Rights: A Conceptual History of Transitional Justice' (2009) 31 Human Rights Quarterly 321, 355–57, who provides a history of the transitional justice idea and suggests there are two normative aims: 'providing some measure of justice to those who suffered under repressive regimes'; and 'facilitating an exit from authoritarianism and shoring up a fragile democracy'. See also A Boraine, 'Transitional Justice: A Holistic Interpretation' (2006) 60 Journal of International Affairs 26.

[2] See, in general, R Teitel, *Transitional Justice* (OUP 2000). See also R Teitel, 'Transitional Justice Genealogy' (2003) 16(69) Harvard Humans Rights Journal 69 stating that, 'Transitional justice can be defined as the conception of justice associated with periods of political change, characterized by legal responses to confront the wrongdoings of repressive predecessor regimes'.

[3] See C Goetze, *The Distinction of Peace: A Social Analysis for Peacebuilding* (University of Michigan Press 2017) where she favours a broad conception of peacebuilding as 'a catch-all term to describe efforts ... to restore or construct a peaceful society in the wake—or even in the midst—of conflict'. See further CT Call and SE Cook 'On Democratization and Peacebuilding' (2003) 9 Global Governance 233–46, 235, where the authors see peacebuilding as pertaining to the 'postconflict social and political reconstruction activities aimed at avoiding "a relapse into conflict"'. In this way, peacebuilding ought to be seen as a facet of the broader field of transitional justice.

[4] Boraine (n 1) 22–23.

In response, this field sought to examine possible institutional responses to engaging with the past through the development of novel structures (such as truth commissions, to assist in finding out the truth about past wrongs pertaining to, for instance, murders, kidnapping, and disappearances). Also relevant in this regard is the question whether such attempts should be complemented or replaced by the punitive force of criminal law for perpetrators of gross violations of fundamental rights. These attempts to address the past often conflict with the question of how to ensure a stable transition to a democratic future founded on fundamental rights and the rule of law. Prosecutions, for instance, could threaten the stability of societies with armed forces being unwilling to support the transition—and potentially scuppering attempts to create a new order—without a guarantee of amnesty for past violations.[5] The tension between a backward-looking perspective, focused on holding perpetrators to account for serious wrongs and a forward-looking perspective, focused on creating the foundations for a peaceful and stable democratic order are central to the distinct field of transitional justice.[6]

It is useful conceptually to distinguish between a narrower and broader conception of transitional justice.[7] A narrower approach focuses largely on legal and institutional changes required to address past violations and move the society forward through, for example, prosecutions, truth-telling, transformation of the state security apparatus and compensation for harms committed. This approach, for instance, is encapsulated in the quoted definition of transitional justice put forward by Roth-Arriaza as pertaining to 'that set of practices, mechanisms and concerns that arise following a period of conflict, civil strife or repression, and that are aimed directly at confronting and dealing with past violations of human rights and humanitarian law'.[8] That approach raises vital questions about justice for past wrongs but has been criticised for conceptualising the wrongs of the past too narrowly—in terms of, for instance, violations of civil and political rights rather than the serious undermining of socio-economic rights.[9] That failure can in turn undermine a country's ability to establish the new society on a stable footing and 'haunt post conflict peace initiatives'.[10]

[5] See Arthur (n 1) 353–54, for a discussion of early debates in this regard amongst intellectual leaders in the field.

[6] L Laplante, 'Transitional Justice and Peace Building: Diagnosing and Addressing the Socioeconomic Roots of Violence through a Human Rights Framework' (2008) 2 International Journal of Transitional Justice 331, 333.

[7] See A Cahill-Ripley, 'Foregrounding Socio-Economic Rights in Transitional Justice: Realising Justice for Violations of Economic and Social Rights' (2014) 32 Netherlands Quarterly of Human Rights 183, who makes this distinction.

[8] N Roht-Arriaza, 'The New Landscape of Transitional Justice' in N Roht-Arriaza and J Mariezcurrena (eds), *Transitional Justice in the 21st Century—Beyond Truth Versus Justice* (CUP 2006) 2.

[9] Cahill-Ripley (n 7) 192–96.

[10] I Muvingi, 'Sitting on Powder Kegs: Socioeconomic Rights in Transitional Societies' (2009) 3 International Journal of Transitional Justice 163, 167.

A broader approach to transitional justice conceives of it as grappling in a wider way with how to achieve justice when moving away from a past characterised by historical wrongs to a flourishing society where peace, stability, democracy, and human rights are respected. Such a conception requires an understanding of the past wrongs that are ripe for investigation by various institutional mechanisms as including harm to the socio-economic rights of individuals as well as systemic and structural injustices.[11] However, it goes beyond a focus on legal institutional mechanisms alone—such as truth commissions or prosecutions—to include a broader set of measures required to address the wrongs of the past.[12] Justice, for instance, could also partially be achieved through memorialisation in museums and art works that grapple with the past and instantiate a new ethos.[13] Broader policy attempts to address the legacy of past injustice (for instance, through ensuring decent education for all marginalised groups) would also form part of transitional justice based on this wider conception.

It is also useful to consider the temporal dimension of transitional justice, which is often linked to the broader/narrower distinction discussed above. The narrower approach would often focus on the period immediately after the conflict subsides, during which prosecutions take place or truth commissions operate. The broader approach would see transition as a continuing process that is not linear or focused on a moment in time[14] and does not end with the report of a truth commission or conviction of violators of human rights. It recognises the long-standing impact of past injustice and sees transitional justice as a continual struggle to overcome the past. Societies on the latter conception may still be in transition a long time after the formal end of historical injustices and the questions of justice that arise require continual alertness to the legacy of the past.[15]

There are merits to a narrower focus for a field but, in our view, one of the important lessons from the Global South is the need to adopt a wider conception of transitional justice. The legacies of the past—division, hierarchy, exclusion, and psychological harm—remain long after the end of formal processes of truth-gathering and prosecutions. These effects continue to cast a shadow over the goal of creating a flourishing future for the society in question. To achieve the latter aim, the wider legacy of past injustice needs to be confronted in a way that is not time-limited to specific institutions or processes and that provides a continuous

[11] Laplante (n 6) 333.

[12] See K Mcevoy, 'Letting Go of Legalism: Developing a 'Thicker' Version of Transitional Justice' in K Mcevoy and L Mcgregor (eds), *Transitional Justice from Below: Grassroots Activism and the Struggle for Change* (Hart 2008) 29, who argues for the need to understand the limits of law and embed justice within communities affected by violence and conflict.

[13] Themes 2 and 3 of this book explore these possibilities.

[14] See, for instance, K Mcevoy and L Mcgregor, 'Transitional Justice from Below: An Agenda for Research, Policy and Praxis' in K Mcevoy and L Mcgregor (n 12) 6.

[15] E Schmid and A Nolan, 'Do No Harm?' Exploring the Scope of Economic and Social Rights in Transitional Justice' (2014) 8 The International Journal of Transitional Justice 362, 374–75, who argue that this applies both to violations of civil and political rights as well as economic and social rights.

understanding of how the past colours the present. Moreover, the continuing harms of the past are often not only the terrible trauma of losing a loved family member but a deeper legacy of socio-economic deprivation and exclusion. Only this expanded frame can identify these issues and ensure the goals of the transition are met. The wider frame naturally leads us to think not just about specific institutional responses to past harms but also about how to create an enduring framework for a different and better society and the appropriate methodology for effecting change. It is to this question that 'transformative constitutionalism' offers a response.

B. Transformative Constitutionalism

The notion of transformative constitutionalism (TC) can be traced back to a seminal article by Karl Klare. His definition of the notion included two aspects which are important for our purposes: the first relates to a methodology of social change. TC 'connotes an enterprise of inducing large-scale social change through nonviolent political processes grounded in law'.[16] Typically, such change occurs through the enactment and utilisation of a post-conflict constitution to effect transitional goals—in Klare's words, the commitment is to a 'long-term project of constitutional enactment, interpretation and enforcement'.[17] The second aspect relates to the substance or goal of the transition: for Klare, this involves 'transforming a country's political and social institutions and power relationships in a democratic, participatory and egalitarian direction'.[18] Klare identifies six aspects of the South African constitution that are transformative in character: the existence of social rights and a substantive conception of equality; positive state duties; the application of the constitution to non-state actors; participatory governance; multiculturalism and a celebration of diversity; and a historical self-consciousness. It is clear that TC was conceptualised to relate to a particular society in transition, namely South Africa. In this context, a post-conflict constitution was seen to be part of the social compact that seeks to use law to heal the past and create a different and better future.

After the publication of Klare's important academic contribution, the concept itself has been applied beyond South Africa to many countries in the Global South—such as India, Brazil, and Colombia—grappling with similar questions and demonstrating faith in law-governed processes.[19] The concept has also, more

16 K Klare, 'Legal Culture and Transformative Constitutionalism' (1998) 14 South African Journal on Human Rights 146, 150.

17 ibid.

18 ibid.

19 See, for instance, O Vilhena, U Baxi, and F Viljoen (eds), *Transformative Constitutionalism: Comparing the Apex Courts of Brazil, India and South Africa* (Pretoria University Law

recently, been argued to apply to Global North societies that have embarked on similar processes of transition.[20] Why has the concept had such purchase for comparative studies?

We would argue that TC helps to describe a framework for achieving transitional justice, broadly conceived. That framework requires understanding the central wrongs of the past as well as identifying the normative goals the society sets itself for the future. It then adopts a particular methodology to achieve that future—through the framework of a constitution and utilisation of the law. A constitution here is designed to change the status quo in the direction of the normative goals identified though placing certain constraints on political actors. As such it is a particular method of enacting transitional justice (broadly conceived) that continually comes under pressure as the constraints of law are in tension with the demand to enact rapid and visible social change. Amongst other reasons, TC may be defended as seeking to enshrine sustainable social change and peace. Without the processes of law, transitions are quickly hijacked, corrupted, and subverted by elites or those with the strongest guns often under the pretence of enacting radical social change.

The exact normative goals specified by Klare may differ from society to society. Interestingly, there is a significant overlap between the features he identifies in South Africa and those in many other societies of the Global South that adopted constitutions after the collapse of the Soviet Union. One of the most important features of these constitutions has been the inclusion not just of civil and political rights, but also socio-economic rights. This brings in the dimension of distributive justice to which we now turn.

C. Distributive Justice

It is no accident that one of the features of Global South constitutions is the inclusion of socio-economic rights. The long-standing historical injustices that are the subject of transitional justice processes often resulted from skewed distributions of resources between various groups. The conflicts that emerged may have been related at least partially to the socio-economic relations between different groups in society.[21] The wrongs that were done included denials of equal education and

Press 2013); A von Bogdandy (ed), *Transformative Constitutionalism in Latin America: The Emergence of a New Ius Commune* (OUP 2017); D Bonilla, *Constitutionalism in the Global South* (CUP 2013).

[20] M Hailbronner, 'Transformative Constitutionalism: Not Only in the Global South' (2017) 65 American Journal of Comparative Law 527–65.

[21] This is certainly true in Colombia. See, for instance, M Palacios, *Between Legitimacy and Violence: A History of Colombia* (R Stoller tr, Duke University Press 2006), prologue esp xii and RA Berry, 'Reflections on Injustice, Inequality and Land Conflict in Colombia' (2017) 42 Canadian Journal of Latin American and Caribbean Studies 277–97.

health care and consigning groups of the population to lives of poverty. In transitioning to a new order, there are thus significant expectations that these issues will be addressed.

It is possible that some transitional justice processes and mechanisms—relating to the narrow conception articulated above—can include an examination of the wrongs done in the socio-economic dimensions discussed above.[22] Reparation can be made to those who suffered from gross human rights violations.[23] Yet, in many societies, it is not possible to pursue the matter of socio-economic deprivation simply on the basis of compensation to individuals wronged in the past. The harms are often too widespread and deeply entrenched. A wider approach is thus required to engage with questions of distributive justice more generally.

Distributive justice relates to the allocation of resources in society and seeks to examine what constitutes a just distribution. There is a vast literature identifying principles of distributive justice from ensuring the 'greatest benefit to the least-advantaged members of society',[24] equality of resources,[25] to the protection for individual capabilities.[26] Some theorists such as Robert Nozick reject such general 'patterned principles' but argue for inclusion of a principle of rectification for past historical wrongs in their understanding of distributive justice.[27] However, Nozick concedes that, given the complexity of correcting for widespread individual wrongs, it might be necessary to adopt a patterned principle of distributive justice (such as those suggested by other theorists) as a 'rule of thumb' to rectify past injustices, such as ensuring the greatest benefit to the least advantaged.[28]

At the centre of transitions in the Global South context is the question of how to address the widespread socio-economic harms caused by past wrongs and to ensure everyone has access to at least a sufficient level of resources. That question has led the foundational documents of those societies to address distributive justice questions, at least to some extent, through the entrenchment of socio-economic rights.[29] These rights have raised many debates and tensions. For example, there is an important question about what exactly they guarantee: are they meant simply to ensure every individual has access to a minimum level of resources, an adequate

[22] Cahill-Ripley (n 7) 201–07, for instance, considers the engagement of truth commissions with socio-economic rights.

[23] Boraine (n 1) 24–25.

[24] J Rawls, *Justice as Fairness: A Restatement* (E Kelly ed, Belknap Press 2001) 42–43.

[25] R Dworkin, *Sovereign Virtue: The Theory and Practice of Equality* (Harvard University Press 2000) 65 ff.

[26] M Nussbaum, *Women and Human Development* (CUP 2000) 74–75.

[27] R Nozick, *Anarchy State Utopia* (Basic Books 1974) 123. He prefers not to use the term distributive justice but rather 'justice in holdings' (at 121). See further T Roux, 'Land Restitution and Reconciliation in South Africa' in F Du Bois and A Du Bois-Pedain (eds), *Justice and Reconciliation in Post-Apartheid South Africa* (CUP 2008), where he explores the meaning of this concession in the context of land reform in South Africa.

[28] Nozick ibid 171.

[29] D Bilchitz, 'Constitutionalism, the Global South and Economic Justice' in D Bonilla (n 19) 51.

standard of living, or to ensure a wider form of equality between people?[30] Given they involve the significant outlay of economic resources, should the judiciary have the final say in giving effect to them or should they largely be the preserve of political institutions?[31] These rights, in some sense, test the limits of law and the ability of transformative constitutionalism to bring about the social change it desires.

D. Connecting the Three Concepts

These three concepts are interconnected but have developed separately and often in different domains without an adequate exploration of the intersections between them.[32] Only relatively recently, for instance, has the literature started considering specifically the relationship between transitional justice and socio-economic rights, as well as distributive justice more generally.[33] We have already begun the process of charting their relationships above but here we produce a summary of how we see their interconnections. In doing so, we set the scene for a deeper analysis of the contexts of Colombia and South Africa in the discussion in Section 2.

As mentioned, we conceive of transitional justice as speaking to the importance of addressing past wrongs in a way that enables a new society to emerge. In doing so, transitions, in our view, should not be conceptualised as having a finite ending. Transformative constitutionalism provides an approach to transitional justice thus conceived through utilising constitutional structures and the law to bring about the desired change. Indeed, many of the specific institutional mechanisms for addressing past injustice are themselves rooted in new constitutions or constitutional amendments.[34] The question of transition, however, goes beyond the establishment of truth commissions or special tribunals: it is about creating the democratic architecture for a society including, for instance, enshrining a separation of powers with an independent judiciary, and developing strong institutions that ensure the participation of the citizenry and accountability for state institutions (for instance, in matters relating to the public purse and corruption). This architecture is the foundation for developing a considered response to addressing past injustice and for the creation of a promising future.

[30] See, for instance, D Bilchitz, *Poverty and Fundamental Rights* (OUP 2007); S Liebenberg and B Goldblatt, 'The Interrelationship Between Equality and Socio-Economic Rights and South Africa's Transformative Constitution' (2007) 23 South African Journal on Human Rights 335–61.

[31] Bilchitz (n 30) 102–34; M Pieterse, 'Coming to Terms with the Judicial Enforcement of Socio-Economic Rights' (2004) 20 South African Journal on Human Rights 383–417.

[32] Schmid and Nolan (n 15) 363 fn 4, who contend that some of the seminal texts in the transitional justice field, for instance, have very little to say about socio-economic questions.

[33] See, for instance, Muvingi (n 10), Cahill-Ripley (n 7), and Schmid and Nolan (n 15).

[34] See *Azanian Peoples Organisation v President of the Republic of South Africa* [1996] ZACC 16; 1996 (4) SA 672 (CC) ('*AZAPO*'), for an analysis of the provisions of the South African Interim Constitution in this regard; and in Colombia, the Constitutional Amendments pursuant to the recent Peace Agreements such as Legislatives Acts 1/2012, 1/2016, and 1/2017.

The correction of past wrongs, however, requires specific attention to the socio-economic harms caused by past injustice. Experience in many countries across the world—particularly in the Global South—suggests that a successful transition to a stable democratic society based upon the rule of law cannot be achieved without considering questions of distributive justice. Large-scale inequality continually threatens to undermine the gains achieved unless it is addressed. It is for this reason that transformative constitutions have sought to deal with distributive questions through the inclusion of an important set of provisions, particularly those relating to socio-economic rights. Doing so serves the dual purpose of correcting the wrongs of the past and establishing a new, more egalitarian society.[35] A degree of distributive justice must thus be achieved in order to realise the very aims of transitional justice, namely, correcting past wrongs and establishing a stable future. Transformative constitutionalism requires that the processes of law be utilised to attain a change in the allocation of resources. Socio-economic rights thus provide constitutional protection for a basic level of well-being for everyone and enable judicial intervention in this regard. The legislature and executive are tasked with developing the institutional architecture to provide for the socio-economic well-being of all and ensuring adequate budgetary allocations are made. The relationship between these concepts could be investigated further. However, for purposes of this chapter, these linkages are sufficient to establish a framework for the ensuing comparison of Colombia and South Africa.

2. Global South Comparisons: Examining Colombia and South Africa

The three dimensions discussed above and the interconnections between them are particularly relevant to transitions occurring in the Global South.[36] Indeed Dann, Riegner, and Bönnemann, in their recent edited collection, write insightfully about what is distinctive about constitutionalism in the Global South. They argue that Southern countries have often been shaped by colonialism, which has continuing effects on the global geo-political asymmetries that persist.[37] We could reframe this point to argue that these countries remain in processes of transition and are still struggling to shake off the legacy of colonialism. In doing so, these authors argue that Southern constitutionalism has been characterised by distinctive themes. The first of these is that 'constitutions and constitutional law in the Global South

[35] See Bilchitz, Chapter 11 in this book on the dual aims of including socio-economic rights in constitutions.

[36] For an exploration of the use of the term Global South, see P Dann, M Riegner, and M Bönnemann 'The Southern Turn in Comparative Constitutional Law: An Introduction' in P Dann, M Riegner, and M Bönnemann (eds), *The Global South and Comparative Constitutional Law* (OUP 2020) 5–7.

[37] ibid 15–18.

are conceived as symbols and instruments of fundamental social transformation, aimed at dismantling socio-economic hierarchies and inequalities'.[38] The second theme they identify relates to the struggle to build stable and effective democratic state institutions and the final theme is about enabling access to justice and the emancipatory power of the law.[39] The conceptual architecture discussed above is consistent with the analysis of these authors. We could reframe or expand their analysis to recognise how transformative constitutionalism in the Global South context seeks to achieve both transitional and distributive justice.

If these dimensions are emblematic of Global South constitutionalism, then they should be reflected across countries that fit this designation. However, in moving beyond their abstract content to understand the more detailed contours of these concepts, the dilemmas they raise as well as their application in practice, it is necessary to provide a more thorough analysis of each context. To understand the strengths and weaknesses of the approaches that have been adopted towards giving effect to these ideas, comparison is useful particularly between countries that share several distinctive features. Whilst there are many countries to compare, we believe that Colombia and South Africa offer a particularly fruitful opportunity for examining these concepts and their operationalisation. We now briefly outline the relevant context of each of these societies and then summarise some core dimensions that render the comparison between them meaningful.

A. Colombia

Colombia has been fuelled by violent conflict for more than fifty years. The conflict has roots in strong divisions between liberals and conservatives, urban and rural populations, as well as between the rich and the poor.[40] Its armed conflict, more recently, did not take the form of a classic civil war but rather clashes between the government and the guerrilla and right-wing paramilitary groups that had formed. Factors driving the conflict included drug trafficking[41] and territorial control as well as a sense of political exclusion by ordinary people.[42] Given the multifaceted nature of the conflict and despite efforts by various governments to defeat the guerillas and right-wing paramilitary groups, no military victory was possible. As a result, there have been several attempts to reach peace agreements and embark upon transitional justice processes.

[38] ibid 20.

[39] ibid 23–30.

[40] Comisión para el Esclarecimiento de la Verdad, la Convivencia y la No Repetición, *Hay futuro, si hay verdad*, Hallazgos y Recomendaciones (2022) 492 ff.

[41] ibid 311 ff.

[42] ibid 87 ff, 91 ff, 499 ff.

The first notable and participative process took place in advance of the negotiation of the 1991 Constitution, which represented an attempt to address the armed conflict and end hostilities with certain guerilla groups—the M19 in particular.[43] There were great hopes placed on the new Constitution and it was indeed transformative in nature—seeking to instantiate a law-based process of social change. The Constitution gave priority to civil and political rights but also included socio-economic rights in recognition of the distributive justice questions that in many respects animated the past conflicts. The Constitution also included a number of important legal innovations, most particularly the tutela action, which offers a quick remedy for those who have had their fundamental rights violated.[44] The remedy appeared to be designed only to address violations of civil and political rights. Yet, Colombia has a pioneering Constitutional Court, which has sought to be more widely accessible to ordinary people and to deal with wide-ranging circumstances of vulnerability. The Court has thus effectively extended the availability of the tutela to socio-economic rights with the effect that ordinary people have a powerful remedy available to them when their rights are violated.[45] Its interventions in that regard have made legal remedies accessible to individuals; yet, it has also sought to tackle serious structural impediments to the realisation of these rights through declaring, in several circumstances, an 'unconstitutional state of affairs' which must be remedied in more comprehensive ways. Such a declaration has, for instance, sought to improve the socio-economic conditions of the most vulnerable—such as internally displaced persons[46]—and also to bring about improved conditions in the health care sector[47] and for prisoners.[48]

Sadly, the conflict was not resolved in 1991 and armed hostilities continued between the government and the Revolutionary Armed Forces of Colombia (FARC) rebels. Many atrocities were committed particularly against rural populations including killings, disappearances, and rape.[49] Whilst the FARC was significantly weakened through military action, there was still no real victory for the government over the guerillas. Thus, in 2016, there was an attempt to reach an agreement between the government and the FARC. The peace agreement reached between them in 2016[50] needed to accomplish a number of goals including ending the violent conflict; punishing those responsible for serious atrocities; developing a

[43] ibid 100 ff. See also D Villamizar, *Las guerrillas en Colombia. Una historia desde los orígenes hasta los confines* (Penguin Random House 2017) 559–89.

[44] The tutela was enshrined in art 86 of the Constitution.

[45] See T-406/92, T571/92, T-116/93, which articulate the doctrine that they are fundamental rights by connection and T-760 of 2008, which recognises they are fundamental rights of a provisional character.

[46] See T-025 of 2004.

[47] T-760 of 2008.

[48] T-153 of 1998 and T-388 of 2013.

[49] Comisión para el Esclarecimiento de la Verdad, la Convivencia y la No Repetición (n 40) 121 ff.

[50] Final Peace Agreement, 12 November 2016 https://www.cancilleria.gov.co/sites/default/files/Fotos2016/12.11_1.2016nuevoacuerdofinal.pdf accessed 3 October 2022.

historical record of what transpired; and addressing the underlying causes of the conflict so it would not happen again.

In realising these goals, the peace agreement created several innovative mechanisms of transitional justice. These included a truth commission; a tribunal known as the Special Jurisdiction for Peace for trying perpetrators involved in serious crimes committed during the armed conflict (with innovative and limited punishments); and a special institution for determining what happened to people who disappeared. Since the peace agreement was reached in a global context that rejected impunity for war crimes and crimes against humanity—with Colombia being a signatory to the Rome Statute establishing the International Criminal Court (ICC)—a simple amnesty for violent crimes would not have been acceptable.[51] The peace agreement and the institutions it creates—such as the Special Jurisdiction for Peace—attempt to balance the need to move forward with some measure of punishment for those who were responsible for various atrocities.

Transitional justice in Colombia thus has both restorative and retributive elements. It was enacted through a political process and a series of constitutional amendments, thus solidifying the connection with constitutionalism. Moreover, far-sightedly, the peace agreement recognised that it had to deal with the underlying socio-economic determinants of the conflict. Unusually, the peace agreement has segments dealing with agrarian reform and the autonomy of Indigenous peoples. Colombia's current peace agreement thus forms part of a long-standing attempt to heal the cleavages in Colombian society, which require attending both to the serious violence of the past but also current socio-economic deprivation. A vibrant yet imperfect society has emerged: the commitment to peace remains fragile with much back-tracking in the past administration and an upsurge once again of violence. The COVID-19 pandemic set back economic development further and socio-economic inequality remains extremely high.

B. South Africa

South Africa transitioned to constitutional democracy in 1994, ending a long period of White minority rule. The apartheid system in South Africa sought to keep Black and White people separate and to entrench structurally the inferiority of Black people in society. It was intimately tied to the desire to create an economic under-class who would perform manual labour and help fuel the growth of wealth by the minority White population.[52] Without a strong army, the liberation movements could not defeat the apartheid government. Strong international sanctions,

[51] This is explored by Silva Santaularia, Chapter 24 in this book.

[52] H Wolpe, 'Capitalism and Cheap Labour-Power in South Africa: From Segregation to Apartheid' (1972) 1 Economy and Society 425 ff.

internal resistance, the end of the Cold War, and the looming threat of civil war led the apartheid government to conclude that the status quo could not continue. Once again, there was no victory to be had but, rather, a negotiated settlement.[53] Over a period of five years, a transitional constitution was negotiated—the 1993 Interim Constitution—which was explicit about being a transformative constitution. In the postamble it expressly described itself as a 'historic bridge between the past of a deeply divided society characterised by strife, conflict, untold suffering and injustice and a future founded on recognition of human rights, democracy, peaceful co-existence and development opportunities for all South Africans irrespective of colour, race, class belief or sex'.[54] This Constitution also referenced the need for important transitional justice mechanisms. In meeting this mandate, the Truth and Reconciliation Commission was established. It heard emotional testimony from victims of gross human rights violations, providing a historical record of the atrocities committed by the apartheid government and, in some cases, the liberation movements. It also included a structure that would grant perpetrators of serious crimes amnesty if they confessed the truth of what they had done. This would at least allow victims to know, for instance, what had happened to loved ones who had disappeared. Unlike Colombia, these mechanisms were set up before the ICC and thus there was no requirement on South Africa to set up punitive mechanisms.[55]

After the first democratic elections were held, a Constituent Assembly was created which drafted the Final Constitution of the country. Once again, this document is, on its face, transformative in nature, recognising the need to 'heal the divisions of the past and establish a society based on democratic values, social justice and fundamental human rights'.[56] South Africa's Final Constitution also recognised the importance of addressing the economic legacy of apartheid. Its attention to matters of distributive justice can be seen through the entrenchment of a set of justiciable socio-economic rights in the Bill of Rights.[57] Its weak property clause also places a duty on the government to address the legacy of Black people having been dispossessed of their land and allows for expropriation with limited (and possibly no) compensation.[58] Whilst reparations to those directly harmed by

[53] See C Ramaphosa, 'Negotiating a New Nation: Reflections on the Development of South Africa's Constitution' in P Andrews and S Ellmann (eds), *The Post-Apartheid Constitutions: Perspectives on South Africa's Basic Law* (Ohio University Press 2001).

[54] 'National Unity and Reconciliation' postamble in Constitution of the Republic of South Africa Act 200 of 1993.

[55] See, in general, du Bois and du Bois-Pedain (n 27). This is also explored by Roux, Chapter 23 in this book.

[56] Preamble to Constitution of the Republic of South Africa Act 108 of 1996.

[57] These are included in sections 26–29 of the Constitution.

[58] The property clause is section 25 of the Constitution and is widely seen as a compromise after heavy negotiation. See, in this regard, H Klug, 'Decolonisation, Compensation and Constitutionalism: Land, Wealth and the Sustainability of Constitutionalism in Post-Apartheid South Africa' (2018) 34(3) South African Journal on Human Rights 469–91.

the violence of the apartheid government has been limited, the approach adopted in South Africa has been to advance distributive justice as a means of responding collectively to the wrongs of the past. That approach has been recognised as a legitimate one by the Constitutional Court.[59]

The Constitutional Court of South Africa has adopted innovative approaches to adjudicating socio-economic rights disputes. For example, its jurisprudence on housing evictions has sought to strengthen the rights of unlawful occupiers to housing by allowing evictions only where, generally, alternative accommodation can be provided.[60] It has also required the government to engage meaningfully with vulnerable people before evicting them, thus re-balancing the power relationships somewhat in society.[61] The Court has sought to adjudicate socio-economic rights on a programmatic basis and enhance the accountability of governmental bodies, requiring their programmes to meet a reasonableness standard.[62] It has powerfully required the provision of HIV/AIDS medication, which has saved hundreds of thousands of lives.[63] Furthermore, it has ordered the appointment of a special administrator to oversee land claims.[64]

Despite these developments, the Court has also been criticised for a socio-economic rights jurisprudence that is rather complex and inaccessible to the poor.[65] There is a lack of an easy remedy such as the tutela in Colombia which would enable much greater access to justice. Whilst the socio-economic conditions of many Black people have advanced since democracy, large numbers remain in a state of grinding poverty. The COVID-19 pandemic has exacerbated this situation, posing a threat to South Africa's political stability. The growth of inequality has exposed fault-lines in South Africa's transition and led to a questioning of the very constitutional settlement upon which it was founded.[66]

This situation was exacerbated with the strong assault on state institutions in the form of widespread corruption that was enabled and encouraged during President Zuma's reign. A commission has detailed the extent of malfeasance that has affected many sectors of the South African economy, including its energy security (with rolling electricity blackouts), its tourism (with severe harm to its national

[59] See *Azapo* (n 34) para 44.

[60] See, for instance, *Port Elizabeth Municipality v Various Occupiers* [2004] ZACC 7; 2005 (1) SA 217(CC) and *City of Johannesburg v Blue Moonlight Properties* [2011] ZACC 33; 2012 (2) SA 104 (CC).

[61] See *Occupiers of 51 Olivia Road, Berea Township and 197 Main Street Johannesburg v City of Johannesburg* [2008] ZACC 1; 2008 (3) SA 208 (CC).

[62] *Government of the Republic of South Africa v Grootboom* [2000] ZACC 19; 2001 (1) SA 46 (CC).

[63] *Minister of Health v Treatment Action Campaign* [2002] ZACC 13; 2002 (5) SA 721 (CC).

[64] *Mwelase v Director-General for the Department of Rural Development and Land Reform* [2019] ZACC 30; 2019 (6) SA 597 (CC).

[65] See, eg, Bilchitz (n 30) and S Wilson and J Dugard, 'Constitutional Jurisprudence' in M Langford and others (eds), *Socio-Economic Rights in South Africa: Symbols or Substance?* (CUP 2013).

[66] See, eg, J Modiri, 'Introduction to Special Issue: Conquest, Constitutionalism and Democratic Contestations' (2018) 34 South African Journal on Human Rights 295–99, and other articles cited in this series.

airline carrier), and its railways and ports.[67] That, together with a lack of skills in the public sector, has led to widespread government incapacity to perform basic state functions. The institutions established by the 1996 Constitution have, however, played an important role in preserving South Africa's democracy. For example, the Public Protector during Jacob Zuma's reign fearlessly exposed corruption and the courts have retained their independence and vital role in upholding the rule of law and promoting a culture of good governance in the public decision-making practices of the state.[68] South Africa has unquestionably built a vibrant democracy with important independent institutions but remains a fractured, profoundly unequal, and politically unstable society struggling to overcome the divisions and injustices of the past.

C. Why Compare Colombia and South Africa?

This book seeks to offer the first deep scholarly comparison between Colombia and South Africa in relation to the conceptual framework we have articulated: transitional justice, transformative constitutionalism, and distributive justice. This section articulates the reasons why this comparison is likely to be productive whilst also recognising the differences between the contexts of these countries.

(i) Transitional justice

Both countries offer a rich context in which to investigate transitions from a troubled past beset by violence and inequality to a society founded on a commitment to equality, dignity, and the fundamental rights of all. The narrower approach to transitional justice we identified above focuses on formal legal mechanisms of transition. Both countries have interesting and innovative histories worthy of analysis in this regard. South Africa created a Truth and Reconciliation Commission, which provided a vehicle for victims to testify but also granted amnesty in return for truth. Colombia, in its 2016 peace agreement, similarly adopted a Truth Commission but also a Special Jurisdiction for Peace (SJP) to ensure that there would be some (albeit limited) punishment for serious crimes. The two societies adopted models that have similarities but also interesting contrasts that require further explanation and engagement. This helps us understand why these approaches were adopted, whether they are connected to particular features of these societies, and also, perhaps, to evaluate which is normatively more desirable. For instance, as is explored in the last theme of this book (Theme 8), Colombia's processes occurred more than

[67] See the Final Reports of the Commission of Inquiry into State Capture <https://www.statecapture.org.za/site/information/reports> accessed 3 October 2022.

[68] See, in this regard, *Economic Freedom Fighters v Speaker of the National Assembly; Democratic Alliance v Speaker of the National Assembly* [2016] ZACC 11; 2016 (3) SA 580 (CC).

twenty years after South Africa's and in a context where amnesty for international crimes was no longer acceptable. That difference partially explains the SJP but also raises important questions about the relationship between international legal developments and the resolution of conflicts in the domestic sphere.

As we have already discussed, we understand the term 'transitional justice' in a broader manner as an enduring process of societal reconstruction and democratic consolidation. That affects what temporal period is considered by the authors in this book relating to the processes in the two countries. For example, in the case of Colombia, the contributions to this book do not limit their focus to the events surrounding the 2016 peace agreement but extend to developments in the country since the enactment of the 1991 Constitution. Similarly, in the South African context, many of the contributions to this book extend their analysis beyond the events culminating in the 1996 Constitution (and its aftermath) to more recent socio-economic and political developments. Theme 7, for instance, explores the importance of procedural justice not only in the immediate aftermath of transition but as a continuing mode of preventing a recurrence of conflict in these societies.

This wider frame requires us to consider, beyond the formal legal mechanisms, how societies heal in light of traumatic pasts. Law cannot be the full answer and it is thus of great importance to engage with the role of non-legal processes and their relationship to more formal legal processes in both contexts. On the one hand, it is critical that any initiatives and formal mechanisms connect with values deeply embedded in these societies. As is argued in the first theme of this book, the deep values of many oppressed people in Colombia and South Africa suggest the need to move away from a retributive focus to one that is more restorative in nature. How these values have been expressed—or fail to be included—in the various formal mechanisms of justice is an important question raised in these contributions. Moreover, there are also important initiatives in both societies where art and memory have been utilised as methods to heal the wounds of the past. In this regard, Themes 2 and 3 compare and contrast these initiatives offering opportunities both for learning and evaluation when considered side by side.

(ii) Transformative constitutionalism

Both countries have sought to utilise the structures of law to address the legacy of the past and build a different future. The model that has been adopted is the one of 'transformative constitutionalism'[69] discussed above. The faith in the law and constitutionalism, is a clear similarity between the societies, even though it was often the source of oppression.

Both Colombia and South Africa adopted constitutions that had an activist goal of shifting society to a new order. To this end, they also enshrined a bill of

[69] Klare (n 16).

rights, democratic structures, a strong form of judicial review, and the separation of powers. Of course, they have not always adopted identical structures and the functioning of those structures and particular institutional design is also useful to compare. In this regard, Theme 5 considers certain legal innovations such as class actions and remedies and Theme 6 explores the impact of new constitutional structures on Indigenous communities and their difficult interaction with existing structures of authority. Both societies have, for various reasons, serious structural flaws in the operation of the democratic branches of government that have resulted in strong judicial interventions. The various features of post-conflict constitutionalism are thus of great interest to analyse. The uses and limits of law in shifting society also require investigation in each society and the extent to which law is capable of adequately advancing the goals of both transitional and distributive justice.

(iii) Distributive justice

The respective histories of Colombia and South Africa are deeply connected to a present which embodies deep-seated economic inequality. Levels of absolute poverty are high in both countries with many people lacking the most basic necessities. Indeed, these are two of the most unequal societies in the world (measured by Gini-coefficient).[70] The failure to address these conditions imperils the transition to a different society and perpetuates the legacies of past injustice in these countries. It is thus important to consider the manner in which the attempt to create a semblance of distributive justice has been integrated into the structures created by the constitutions of these countries.

One of the major features of transformative constitutionalism has been the constitutional entrenchment of socio-economic rights, which, in turn, has become a central object of study. Major questions arise about the legal approach adopted in each society towards advancing these rights and whether those approaches can address the devastating economic legacies of the past. The relationship between transitional and distributive justice in the jurisprudence on the right to housing is engaged, for instance, in Theme 4. The relative roles of the political branches and the judiciary have also been strongly debated. The comparison of the two societies can not only identify differences but also encourage a normative evaluation of which approaches are better at realising these rights and achieving a level of distributive justice.

In each of the concepts we have analysed and the interconnections between them, we have argued that both Colombia and South Africa adopted measures which are ripe for analysis and comparison. We now turn to consider the challenges that arise in South-South comparisons of this kind and the methodology we have adopted in this book.

[70] See https://data.worldbank.org/indicator/SI.POV.GINI?locations=CO accessed 3 October 2022.

3. South-South Comparisons and the Approach of this Book

A. South-South Comparisons—Challenges

One of our motivations in developing this book was to engage in a deep comparison between two Global South contexts, Colombia and South Africa. We also sought to consider the thematic intersections of relevance to the Global South and the reasons why there have been limited attempts at South-South comparisons of this kind. In this latter regard, the fact that there are a limited number of similar projects relates to complex dynamics within the academy as well as some very practical issues. In this section, we briefly highlight some of these issues as well as our approach to addressing them.

Bonilla, in an illuminating analysis, argues that there is a hierarchy in legal academia with the scholarship emerging from the Global South being placed at a very low tier. He refers to 'background unstated assumptions that govern the production, circulation and use of legal knowledge'.[71] We focus on two that are relevant here. The first of these is what he calls the 'production well'.[72] This assumption involves the idea that it is the Global North which is the source of original and innovative theory and that the production of knowledge in the Global South ultimately applies the theory generated in the North or is derived from it. The second is 'protected geographic indication',[73] which suggests that knowledge produced in the Global South is usually assumed to be inferior to that produced in the North. Global South scholarship thus requires the confirmation of its quality by those in the North to be taken seriously.

In relation to the production well, we have sought in this work to invite authors not only to draw on paradigms created in the North but to utilise their own understandings of their respective societies to create new theory relevant to their chapters. We recognise that we are all embedded in a global academy which entrenches the power dynamics articulated by Bonilla. That means that many of us have connections or training in the Global North and some of us situate our contributions in conversation with those theories. We do not think that knowledge should be bifurcated along a strong binary between the Global North and Global South and, given the interconnections between them, that would be impossible in any event. None of us can also claim to be situated in a hermetically sealed world of the Global South. Nevertheless, we have sought in this work to encourage authors to be inspired by the contexts of Colombia and South Africa and to develop their analysis accordingly, and where necessary, to forge new theoretical paradigms or show the

[71] D Bonilla, 'Towards a constitutionalism of the global south' in D Bonilla (n 19) 11.
[72] ibid 12.
[73] ibid 12–13.

limits of existing ones. An awareness of these power dynamics at least allows us to be conscious of what we are doing and our influences.

In relation to the second assumption, we hope that the content produced in these chapters will speak for themselves, demonstrating the quality of scholarship that can emerge from the Global South. We recognise that our choice to publish with Oxford University Press does involve embracing a publisher whose origins are in the Global North and which, in some sense, places a 'Northern' stamp of quality on this work. We believe our choice is nevertheless justified for the reasons given below.

Ultimately, we do not believe it is desirable to stratify academia into a binary opposition between the Global North and Global South. As such, we are heartened by the growing list of titles from publishers such as Oxford University Press that relate to the Global South. Apart from the need to respond constructively to the ordinary review process—which is designed to enhance the quality of this work—our publisher has not sought to control in any way the contents of what we publish. We thus view our publishing with a press of this esteem as empowering and enabling rather than constraining. In some sense, support for projects such as ours from power publishers in the North with full academic freedom can be seen as a form of correction to some of the dynamics of knowledge production identified by Bonilla. Moreover, our choice of press can also contribute to the diffusion of scholarship about and from the Global South. Of course, we hope that there will be many more projects of this kind supported by presses such as Oxford University Press as well as greater support for, and the development of, such projects within Global South presses and institutions.

Apart from these global dynamics, we also believe there are practical reasons why very few have embarked on similar projects. Comparisons of this nature create obstacles that require resources and creativity to overcome. First, part of the reason for the lack of similar comparative projects has been the lack of strong institutional ties between universities, for instance, in Colombia and South Africa. This project has its origins in the development of academic relationships between the individual editors (mentioned briefly in the preface) which provided the foundation for the establishment of a formal collaboration between two universities—the University of Johannesburg and the Universidad Externado de Colombia—that sought to develop these ties and provide them with institutional backing. To avoid the collaboration being simply formal, we identified a joint comparative project that would render it meaningful, some of the fruits of which can be seen in this book. We believe that further South-South collaborations need to be developed, nurtured, and given strong institutional support.

Secondly, there is the practical question of geography. Colombia and South Africa are far apart and there is no direct air-travel connection between them. Travelling between the two countries often takes over a day and is extremely expensive. The lack of South-South connectivity itself inhibits connections and renders collaboration difficult. To produce this book, we organised a workshop in Johannesburg where some Colombian academics were sponsored by our institutions to attend the meeting and others joined online. Hopefully, the rise of virtual conferences will encourage more connections, though these too lack the personal, human dimension that is so valuable to interactions of this kind.

Thirdly, there is the question of language. The lingua franca in South Africa is English whilst in Colombia it is Spanish. Most of the South African contributors could not speak Spanish whilst only some Colombians could speak English. Writing in a language that is not your own also poses serious difficulties. The decision was made to publish in English to encourage wider dissemination across the world, which has had an impact on how we have structured the editorial tasks. We have agreed that the South African editors (David Bilchitz and Raisa Cachalia) would be primarily responsible for managing and editing this book, given their being native English speakers. The Colombian leaders of the project (Magdalena Ines Correa Henao and Nathalia Bautista Pizarro) are recognised as adjunct editors for their work with Colombian authors and in helping make this book a reality. We are grateful to the institutions to which we belong for providing some translation services that have enabled Colombian authors who had difficulty writing in English still to produce excellent chapters.

B. Our Approach to Comparison

In building a comparative project of this kind, one is immediately confronted by several methodological questions. We consider two: first, what should be the focus of the comparative work; and second, how should the comparison be organised and effected? We recognise that there are choices to be made in this area and here we seek to explain our approach.

In terms of focus, it is quite clear that Colombia and South Africa are complex societies and there are multiple dimensions that could be compared. We started with an attempt to identify a conceptual framework linked to our disciplines and of relevance to our societies: the interconnections between transitional justice, distributive justice, and transformative constitutionalism suggested themselves as important fields of enquiry. These three topics raise multiple issues which exceed the possibilities for comprehensive treatment in one book. We thus held engagements with academics in the two countries, identifying relevant themes. We immediately recognised that, in relation to these topics, there was an interconnection between legal and non-legal dimensions, which explains the multidisciplinary nature of this book. We sought to match individuals in both countries to the identified themes in relation to their areas of interest. We then encouraged the authors focusing on each theme to meet one another online and to discuss what they wished to write on. After a period of writing, we brought the authors together (some personally, some virtually) in a conference to discuss the various contributions and receive feedback.

This collaborative approach naturally led to an answer to the second question of how the comparison was to be organised and effected. In relation to the themes, each author initially engaged with their own context and sought to make a thoughtful and original contribution. Prior to the conference, we asked the authors to read each other's papers and to provide a brief discussion of what aspects were of interest in situating the two contexts against one another. That naturally led to the current structure of this book.

The book is designed around eight thematic contributions (which we have grouped into three parts). In relation to each theme, we have a chapter from Colombia and a chapter from South Africa. These chapters allow for a deeper engagement with each context in relation to specific themes. It is also important to recognise that our interest has not been in simple descriptions of the developments or jurisprudence in each country. Each author of the project was requested to be ambitious and to think through how the context of each country could help advance the thinking in this area. After outlining each context separately, the Colombian and South African authors wrote a joint reflection about what emerged from the comparison between them. We hope that this structure enables both a deeper understanding of each of the contexts and that the joint reflections provides an informative and enlightening comparative engagement with the themes of the book.

We recognise that some authors challenge this idea of how comparison should be effected.[74] Other choices were possible, including asking authors from both countries to write joint contributions from the start. We did experiment with this approach and found, in general, the results to be less satisfying. Such an approach often led to a truncation of the discussion of the individual contexts and an immediate move to comparison which was insufficiently grounded and often quite shallow as a result. We preferred a deep engagement with each context to set up a genuinely interesting basis for comparative reflection. Whilst focusing on their context, some of our authors, however, have included some comparative dimension already in their chapters and then utilised their analysis to produce an even more insightful joint reflection.

[74] See, for instance, J Reitz, 'How to Do Comparative Law' (1998) 46 The American Journal of Comparative Law 617, 634.

4. The Structure and Synopsis of the Book

A. Part I: Innovative Ways of Conceiving and Implementing Transitional Justice

Part I of the book involves three perspectives from disciplines other than law. In addition to transitional justice, the contributions themselves also speak to distributive justice and also recognise the need for transformative constitutionalism in such societies to be supported by extra-legal initiatives and projects. Theme 1 begins with a philosophical reflection on how transitional justice is conceived in Colombia and South Africa. That sets the grounding for an engagement with novel and innovative attempts to instantiate this understanding in law and society. Metz, in his chapter, tackles the important question of how to effect reconciliation in these deeply divided societies with a practical focus on the distribution of economic goods. His approach is rooted in the relational value of harmonious co-existence, which is deeply embedded in indigenous value systems in Colombia and South Africa. Restoring the harmony in the relationships between people after terrible wrongs have been committed requires, in Metz's view, that the perpetrators of the wrongs undergo burdens in such a way that improves the socio-economic living conditions of the victims by, for example, donating a portion of their salary or assisting them to till the land. Metz argues that the Colombian final peace agreement better instantiates this ideal than South Africa's transitional justice processes did.

In a similar vein, Bautista Pizarro examines the philosophical underpinnings of practices of reconciliation adopted in South Africa through the value of *ubuntu* as well as in three Colombian communities—the *Misak* Indigenous people of Cauca, the *Afroatratenian* community of *Chocó* and the urban community *Agroarte* of *Medellín*. In doing so, the study shows how the practices within these communities provide the real-life instantiation of a restorative rather than retributive justice approach to dealing with conflict. That approach is less individualistic and more communitarian but, importantly, is focused on restoring interpersonal relationships within those communities. As such, differences and past wrongs are dealt with through dialogues, narratives, art, and other innovative methodologies.

The joint reflection considers how Metz's *ubuntu*-based reconciliatory approach to reparations might be relevant to Colombia in ways that he did not consider, after which it reflects on how the kinds of communitarian practices Bautista advances might be relevant to South Africa and strengthen its transitional justice model. The authors argue that these cross-applications are revealing, pointing out how economic compensation in Colombia should plausibly be influenced by cultural factors, and how considerations of cultural redress in South Africa call for compensation beyond economic factors.

Theme 2 then turns to the role of art in the process of healing from past wrongs, examining the social foundation for peace and stability as well as how art can function as a non-legal form of accountability. Berman and LeBaron consider how public engagement with art, and art-making processes, can further transitional justice after trauma and violence. They articulate two important concepts, 'aesthetic negotiation' and 'artefactual agency', which together help to capture the way in which art functions and contributes towards symbolic reparation within these communities. The authors then apply these concepts to particular examples where, for instance, South African artworks have been censored, covered up, removed, defaced, or intentionally burnt. The authors explore the contested nature of these artworks and argue for a dialogical approach that seeks to address hurt, uncover complexity, and be alive to diverse perspectives, thereby playing a meaningful role in creating more just societies.

Sierra León also recognises the significant role that artistic and cultural practices can play in overcoming the devastating effects of the Colombian armed conflict. She, however, prefers to utilise the concept of 'aesthetic litigation', indicating how art can, in a sense, place the actions of the past and certain key actors on trial and, societally if not legally, achieve a form of symbolic reparation. In this way, art can provide an alternative means of achieving transitional justice other than through traditional legal processes. In particular, the author focuses on the experience of *Hip-Hop Agrario*, a rap group from Medellín, which she utilises as an illustrative case study of how aesthetic litigation works and can further the objectives of peace and transitional justice in Colombia. The chapter also makes proposals for ways in which the Colombian Truth Commission could incorporate aesthetic litigation into its mandate and, thus, foster new ways of receiving, processing, and transmitting the truth after more than five decades of armed conflict.

The joint reflection considers the similarities and differences between the two concepts introduced in the two chapters, namely, 'aesthetic negotiation' and 'aesthetic litigation'. A reflection on these terms highlights differences in the context of both these societies and also offers an opportunity to consider in more depth the role of art in advancing transitional justice.

Theme 3 considers the question how we remember the past and the role that plays in transitional justice and supporting transformative constitutionalism. Potenza and van den Heever conducted an empirical survey of visitor expectations before they visited a special exhibition on Truth and Reconciliation at the Apartheid Museum in South Africa, which was set up to address the history of apartheid and its demise. The visitors were also asked to reflect on their feelings on leaving the museum. Based on this research, the authors investigate the role that museums can play in advancing the goals of transitional justice and the benefits and disadvantages of particular approaches to memorialising the past.

Rueda Esteban, in her chapter, was faced with the difficulty that Colombia currently has no dedicated museum that comprehensively deals with Colombia's violent past and the peace processes it has undergone. The exhibitions that do exist record specific examples of regional violence and represent a specific construction of memory processes limited to those territories. Parallel to the South African chapter, she conducted empirical research in two different museums on visitor expectations and knowledge: the Museo Nacional de Colombia in Bogotá, and the Centre of Memory, Peace and Reconciliation of Bogotá. Based on the outcomes of this research, the chapter reflects on the need for museums and their role in transitional justice processes.

The joint reflection draws out common themes emerging from the empirical research on museums from both Colombia and South Africa and arrives at a series of broader insights concerning the role of museums in advancing transitional justice. The comparative analysis focuses on how the restorative and transitional justice processes in Colombia and South Africa have been curated and the findings on visitors' feelings, experiences, and expectations. In so doing, the reflection seeks to understand the extent to which museum exhibitions can be used as proactive tools to further the understanding of difficult histories and bring about a deeper process of societal healing as a result.

B. Part II: Socio-Economic Rights and the Relationship between Transitional and Distributive Justice

Part II of the book places the relationship between transitional and distributive justice at the centre of the analysis. In addition, the inclusion in both constitutions of a set of socio-economic rights speaks to transformative constitutionalism and how the constitutional legal framework can be utilised to advance greater socio-economic equality.

Theme 4 analyses directly the explicit role of history and transitional justice in the jurisprudence of the highest courts of Colombia and South Africa on socio-economic rights. Bilchitz argues that historical justice can provide both an independent justification for these rights as well as important context in which to construct the content of these rights and their path to implementation. His chapter focuses on housing rights and then analyses the ways in which history has explicitly influenced the jurisprudence of the South African Constitutional Court in this area. The chapter finds that the Court often expressly references South Africa's history of injustice and that this does appear to have influenced the approach it adopts towards these rights. Following from South Africa's negotiated transition, there is a preference expressed by the Court for individuals and institutions to sort out the problems between them through a process of continuing negotiation. There are also obligations placed on private parties to address the legacies of the past in an approach that appears aimed very much at restoring relationships that have been ruptured between people in society—mirroring what Metz and Pizarro have identified as reflective of traditional values in Africa and Latin America.

Parallel to Bilchitz's chapter, Correa Henao investigates the role of historical injustice in the jurisprudence of the Constitutional Court in Colombia. The author immediately recognises that the historical injustices of Colombia are different to those in South Africa and relate to the entrenchment of serious socio-economic exclusions and inequalities relating to particular groups such as Indigenous communities, peasants, and women. The massive problem of internally displaced persons as a result of armed conflict has aggravated the prior existing situation of land concentration, inequity, and economic under-development of this population. After examining the case law of the Colombian Constitutional Court on the right to housing relating to victims of forced displacement—much of which is highly progressive—the author finds that, strangely, there is very little reference to historical injustice in its jurisprudence. Instead, the court has emphasised the current situation (or 'present injustice') of vulnerable persons.

The joint reflection offers explanations for the clear difference in the courts' approach to past injustice emerging from the prior two chapters. Possible reasons for this difference are analysed, which raise a number of fascinating questions concerning, for instance, the usefulness of historical consciousness in transitional societies and the role of judges in this context.

Theme 5 considers novel approaches by litigants and courts—such as class actions and structural interdicts—to advancing wider distributive equality in a transitional context. Finn explores the development of a new procedural mechanism—the class action—which has developed in post-apartheid South Africa to allow groups to bring litigation before the courts. Finn argues that such a procedural innovation in South African law serves the purposes of both transitional and distributive justice. In relation to transitional justice, the harms of the past were often perpetrated against groups of individuals. It is thus necessary in correcting them, to address these harms collectively. In relation to distributive aspects, Finn argues that access to courts is itself a scarce resource that requires a fair allocation amongst persons: class actions enable individuals to access courts in an efficient manner where they may have not been able to if they had to bring individual actions.

Instead of those who bring actions, Gutiérrez Beltrán focuses on a major collective remedial intervention by the Colombian Constitutional Court to address the disempowerment of a large class of persons. T-025 of 2004 declared the existence of an 'unconstitutional state of affairs' relating to the situation of the internally displaced people who had to flee their homes due to the armed conflict in Colombia. This chapter grapples with how to assess the effectiveness of this ambitious judgment and focuses on the extent to which it brought about real changes in the living conditions of the victims. It argues that limited benefits have been achieved from this perspective, which casts doubt on the ability of courts to bring about major socio-economic changes without the support of the political branches and strong political mobilisation.

The joint reflection considers what can be learnt from considering the South African and Colombian experiences in relation to collective mechanisms for the advancement of social rights. In this context, the authors begin by discussing the role of the courts and judicial activism in crafting novel processes and remedies and then contrast the procedures available for litigation for collective ends in Colombia and South Africa. They move on to consider the participatory dimensions of both structural judgments and class actions, which they argue can allow for rights that might not otherwise be represented through democratic processes to be vindicated. Finally, they explore the symbolic effects of the forms of collective action, as well as the limits of law—and particularly, of litigation—in securing meaningful social change in their respective jurisdictions.

C. Part III: The Role of Novel Legal Structures in Realising Transitional and Distributive Justice

In continuing the thematic focus on transformative constitutionalism, Part III considers a number of novel legal structures adopted in the respective countries and their relationship to transitional and distributive justice.

Theme 6 considers the legal regimes that have been developed to address the suffering of Indigenous peoples who were particularly affected by past injustices. MnisiWeeks analyses the socio-legal situation of traditional peoples in post-apartheid South Africa subsequent to the country's transition. The focus of the chapter is on access to land rights and security of tenure for traditional communities. The chapter evaluates whether the South African Constitution has enhanced these rights whilst also considering the impact of the political economy that has persisted and unfolded after apartheid. The argument presented is that, twenty-five years after the formal end of apartheid, traditional communities have experienced limited land rights protection and material security under the post-apartheid regime. The transition has thus not succeeded in fundamentally contributing towards greater distributive justice for these groups.

Rivera-Drago and Burgos Guzman focus on the effects of the peace agreement between the FARC and the government on the position of the Indigenous peoples of Colombia. The peace agreement expressly addresses the plight of Indigenous peoples through land reform and compensation for the damages they suffered during the armed conflict. The chapter considers both aspects: whether the framework established by the agreement has been adequate in leading to greater access to land for Indigenous peoples and the extent to which it has managed to compensate them for the enormous losses they experienced due to the conflict. The conclusions are pessimistic. Sadly, leaders of the Indigenous groups do not consider their interests to have been adequately protected and the damage that was inflicted upon them remains uncompensated.

The joint reflection analyses the commonalities and differences between the consequences of transition to a post-conflict order for the Indigenous groups in Colombia and traditional peoples in South Africa. It also explains how indigenous movements have contributed to the construction of peace and the advancement of transitional and distributive justice in both countries. Lessons are drawn from the comparison to understand what each country could do differently to enhance the tenure security of these groups that were previously dispossessed of their land.

Theme 7 considers the relationship between procedural justice in public decision-making and transitional justice. Cachalia explores the constructive role that procedural values can play in consolidating peace and democracy in South Africa. This theme is developed against the backdrop of the high levels of violent protest action in South Africa arising, at least in part, from a feeling of dissatisfaction with the quality of governance in the post-apartheid context. The chapter analyses the role that three procedural values—such as participatory governance, impartiality and justified decision-making—can play in dissuading citizens from resorting to violence as the modality for compelling government responsiveness. The crux of the argument is that if one of the causes of violence is that citizens feel unheard and unacknowledged, then it is incumbent on public officials to demonstrate their commitment to procedural justice as a means of deterring violent protest action by discontented citizens.

Pimiento Echeverri and Milkes focus on the role of public participation in implementing the 2016 peace agreement signed between the Colombian government and the FARC. The chapter begins by locating public participation within the goals of transitional justice. The authors argue that participation ensures that victims are central to peace processes and, in so doing, it acts as an essential component for guaranteeing the non-repetition of violence. The chapter then explores the paradoxes that exist within the participation principle. The negative outcome of the 2016 Plebiscite showed how public participation can run counter to the goal of achieving peace. The chapter argues that what is needed is a 'meaningfulness' standard to guide the process of involving citizens in the peacebuilding decisions of the Colombian state. This standard entails a balancing of diverse and at times competing constitutional mandates to ensure the effective implementation of the peace agreement and the creation of a peace that is stable and lasting in Colombia.

The joint reflection argues that procedural values can both *support* and *undermine* peace, depending on how they are conceptualised and applied. In order to support rather than undermine peace, Cachalia and Milkes argue that the emphasis must be placed on the proper purpose of involving citizens in the transitional justice project as well as the quality of involvement of the stakeholders. In short, they argue that the purpose of involving citizens in peacebuilding is not to acquire citizen consent or agreement with decisions impacting on the peace and stability of a nation but, rather, to ensure meaningful political inclusion of *all* stakeholders in these processes.

Lastly, Theme 8 considers the impact of international law—and, in particular, the advent of the Rome Statute—on the model of transitional justice that was adopted in each of the societies. Roux starts her chapter by considering South Africa's negotiated settlement in the early 1990s, where the explicit decision was made not to prosecute apartheid as a crime against humanity or a gross violation of fundamental rights. Instead, the Truth and Reconciliation Commission was established, which was empowered to grant amnesty to perpetrators in return for full disclosure of their crimes. The South African settlement was achieved before the advent of the ICC. More recently, South Africa has expressed the intention to withdraw from membership of the ICC on the grounds that the inability to grant immunity from prosecutions hampers South Africa's peacebuilding efforts on the African continent. This chapter argues that this approach is mistaken and that the recent decision continues a legacy of overlooking the *erga omnes* obligation to prosecute international crimes through prioritising peace over justice.

Silva Santaularia considers the implications of the fact that the recent Colombian peace agreement, unlike that in South Africa, took place in the era of the ICC and a situation of complete amnesty for international crimes was not viable. In Colombia, the ICC has not opened a formal investigation and has sought to promote a constructive dialogue with the Colombian government and institutions created by the peace agreement such as the Special Jurisdiction for Peace (SJP). This chapter focuses on the idea that transitional justice contexts require a flexible understanding of the principle of complementarity, and shows that the ICC can work together with a state to achieve lasting peace after an armed conflict. It provides examples of such processes, for instance, the submission of an amicus curiae brief by the ICC to the Constitutional Court and the latter's responsiveness to it. Silva Santaularia argues that the positive interaction between the ICC and a state not only encourages national peacebuilding efforts, but also helps to alleviate the workload of the ICC.

The joint reflection considers the central tension in transitional justice between punishment for past wrongs and establishing a stable peace and how that has been affected by the coming into being of the ICC. Prior to the ICC, South Africa's transitional arrangements initially allowed for blanket amnesties in return for truth-telling. Given Colombia is a signatory to the Rome Statute, such an approach was not possible in the 2016 peace agreement, leading to its innovative institutional architecture. The joint reflection recognises that the South African approach was drawn from a different era and is no longer acceptable or desirable. However, it challenges a purely retributive approach to addressing past crimes and suggests an important evolution is taking place in the role of the ICC—whilst pushing for accountability for past wrongs, it is also working in a dialogical and collaborative manner with domestic jurisdictions to support and empower their own transitional justice processes.

5. Conclusion

As has been mentioned, there is no in-depth edited volume comparing Colombia and South Africa in relation to the three interrelated concepts we have articulated above: namely, transitional justice, distributive justice, and transformative constitutionalism. We hope this book will fill a major gap and in so doing, advance South-South scholarship more broadly. We also hope it will deepen the global understanding of the challenges afflicting these countries and stimulate greater engagement with and between these two contexts which, as this book demonstrates, have much to learn from each other. It is also hoped that the project will highlight productive courses and corrections that can heal the wounds of the past and establish the foundation for thriving constitutional democracies that are respectful of fundamental rights. Since the major questions of transitional and distributive justice and their instantiation in legal processes remain of vital importance more broadly, the book will also be of interest in other contexts where transitions from prior unjust regimes are taking place. The shadows from a difficult past loom large over the futures of all these societies—a comparative project of this kind hopefully improves our knowledge and understanding and can provide resources for continuing discussion and innovation on how to build a fairer and more just future.

PART I

INNOVATIVE WAYS OF CONCEIVING AND IMPLEMENTING TRANSITIONAL JUSTICE

THEME 1

RE-CONCEIVING RECONCILIATION AS RELATIONSHIPS: THE ROLE OF AFRICAN AND LATIN AMERICAN VALUES

2

The Role of Economic Goods in National Reconciliation

Evaluating South Africa and Colombia

Thaddeus Metz

1. Introducing Transitional Justice, Economic Goods, and Indigenous Values

South Africa's institutional reflection about how to engage in transitional justice took place largely in the 1990s, even if the process has yet to be concluded. More than twenty years after South Africa's Parliament authorised the Truth and Reconciliation Commission to make recommendations about how to effect reparations to apartheid-era victims, the executive branch of the government has yet to put them meaningfully into effect.[1]

In contrast, it was only at the end of 2016 that the outlines of a transitional justice pact in Colombia appeared. In this chapter I focus specifically on what was titled the 'Final Agreement' (sometimes also called the 'Peace Agreement') of 24 November 2016,[2] meant to provide a definitive framework for peace between the state and the FARC rebels. The Final Agreement proposes a way to compensate victims with economic goods that, I argue, is compelling from a certain understanding of national reconciliation and merits being upheld as a model. Although there has been a Victim's Law in Colombia since 2011,[3] the Final Agreement would involve wrongdoers themselves making socio-economic reparations to victims in a way that I contend is morally important. Although the Final Agreement has the status of law,[4] its reparative measures have not yet been put into practice systematically.

[1] Ra'essa Pather, 'Ramaphosa under Pressure to Support Reparations for Apartheid Victims', *Mail & Guardian* (17 December 2018) <https://mg.co.za/article/2018-12-17-ramaphosa-under-pressure-to-support-reparations-for-apartheid-victims> accessed 3 October 2022.

[2] <https://www.peaceagreements.org/viewmasterdocument/1845> accessed 3 September 2023. I rely on this English translation of the Final Agreement, but note that the original Spanish version is here: <https://www.jep.gov.co/Normativa/Paginas/Acuerdo-Final.aspx> accessed 3 September 2023.

[3] Victims and Land Restitution Law of 2011 (Law 1448).

[4] See Constitutional Amendment 1 of 2017, Chapter IV, as well as Gonzalo Ramírez-Cleves, 'The Colombian Constitutional Court Rules that the Peace Agreement is Mandatory for Three Presidential Terms' <http://www.iconnectblog.com/the-colombian-constitutional-court-rules-that-the-peace-agreement-is-mandatory-for-three-presidential-terms/> accessed 26 September 2023.

Thaddeus Metz, *The Role of Economic Goods in National Reconciliation* In: *Transitional Justice, Distributive Justice, and Transformative Constitutionalism*. Edited by: David Bilchitz and Raisa Cachalia, with Magdalena Inés Correa Henao and Nathalia Bautista Pizarro, Oxford University Press. © Thaddeus Metz 2023. DOI: 10.1093/oso/9780192887627.003.0002

In this chapter, I argue that they should be. Specifically, I provide reason to believe that, in the light of a certain conception of national reconciliation, the agreement is attractive when it comes to the way the Colombian government is to allocate economic goods. It is much more attractive than what South Africa has achieved to date and even compared to what its salient policy had prescribed back in 1998, when South Africa's Truth and Reconciliation Commission issued its report.[5] Scholars have recently compared the transitional justice processes of Colombia and South Africa in some respects,[6] but there has yet to be a thorough moral-philosophical evaluation of them and, specifically, regarding the way they have sought to allocate property—especially land and money—as well as opportunities such as access to education and job training. I maintain here that the Final Agreement's approach to economic reparation constitutes an advance relative to South Africa's attempts at transitional justice.

The conception of national reconciliation that I advance is informed by an ethic of harmonious relationship, which, broadly understood, is a value salient in the worldviews of many Indigenous peoples in both sub-Saharan Africa and South America.[7] By this conception, national reconciliation is largely a matter of co-operative participation in projects expected to benefit formerly conflicting parties in combination with the disavowal of respects in which parties had flouted the value of harmony in the past. Although I believe this conception of reconciliation follows from relational ethical perspectives prominent in the Global South (though I do not contend they are ubiquitous there or exclusive to those societies), many readers will find the approach to reconciliation intuitively appealing even if they do not adhere to such an ethic. I argue that, given this plausible account of reconciliation, Colombia's proposed manner of allocating property and opportunities is much better than what the South African government has done and even what

[5] Truth and Reconciliation Commission of South Africa, *Truth and Reconciliation Commission of South Africa Report* (Truth and Reconciliation Commission 1998) <http://www.justice.gov.za/trc/report/> accessed 3 October 2022.

[6] Nadiehezka Paola Palencia Tejedor, 'The Role of Constitutional Courts in Transitional Justice: Colombia and South Africa' (2016) 9 Criterio Jurídico Garantista 14; Allen Weiner, 'Ending Wars, Doing Justice: Colombia, Transitional Justice, and the International Criminal Court' (2016) 52 Stanford Journal of International Law 211; Héctor Olasolo and others, 'Have the Colombian Government and the FARC Learnt the Lessons of the South African Truth and Reconciliation Commission as to the Need to Clearly Define and Prioritize the Main Goals of a Truth Commission?' (2017) Harvard Human Rights Journal--Online Symposium on Transitional Justice <https://journals.law.harvard.edu/hrj/2017/10/online-symposium-on-transitional-justice/> accessed 26 September 2023; Jerónimo Delgado Caicedo and Juliana Andrea Guzmán Cárdenas, 'Rethinking the Colombian Transition to Peace through the South African Experience' in Fabio Andres Diaz Pabon (ed), *Truth, Justice and Reconciliation in Colombia* (Routledge 2018) 189.

[7] For some broad comparisons between Indigenous African and South American philosophies, see Johannes Waldmüller, '"Corazonar", "Ubuntu", "Self-Transformation": From Western Universality to Global Pluriversality?', Paper presented at the Human Development and Capabilities Association International Conference on Human Development in Times of Crisis: Renegotiating Social Justice in Athens, Greece (2014); and Thaddeus Metz, 'Political Philosophy in the Global South: Harmony in Africa, South America, and East Asia' in Uchenna Okeja (ed), *Routledge Handbook of African Political Philosophy* (Routledge 2023).

its Truth and Reconciliation Commission sought to do, though I acknowledge that Colombia has yet to implement fully the economic dimensions of the Final Agreement. In both countries, there is a large gap between institutional thought and practice, but I argue that Colombia's thought is at least close to the proper aim, particularly because it requires offenders to undergo burdensome ways of improving their victims' socio-economic quality of life.

In the following, I presume that the reader is familiar with the essentials of the conflicts that took place in South Africa and Colombia, and instead begin by advancing the conception of national reconciliation that I use to appraise South Africa's and Colombia's proposed allocations of economic goods pertaining to transitional justice (Section 2). I show that this construal of reconciliation complements a harmonious ethic that is broadly shared amongst these countries' Indigenous populations, how it differs in plausible ways from other, influential conceptions of reconciliation, and what the favoured conception entails for the distribution of property and opportunities. On this score, I highlight the fact that those guilty of injustice should be the ones to provide property to, and to facilitate opportunities for, their victims. Assuming that it would be morally ideal to have the guilty labour for the sake of those whom they have wronged, particularly by improving their economic standing, I then show that what South Africa has done and even had proposed to undertake do not conform to the key tenets of this conception of what justice requires. South Africa has focused on certain kinds of restorative, retributive, and distributive justice that have not approximated national reconciliation of a particularly attractive sort when it comes to allocating goods such as property and opportunities (Section 3). In the last major section, I argue that Colombia's Final Agreement better approximates the reconciliatory ideal (Section 4), after which I conclude by briefly suggesting why different political factors in both countries have prevented proper economic reconciliation from being realised in practice (Section 5).

2. A Conception of National Reconciliation

I ultimately want to know how a state should allocate opportunities, including education and jobs, as well as property, such as money and land, in order to effect transitional justice in a country. To make that project manageable, I presume that central to (if not exhaustive of) transitional justice is national reconciliation, and I consider the degree to which South Africa's and Colombia's different approaches to the allocation of economic goods have fostered it. In this section I advance an account of national reconciliation that would, upon reflection, have broad appeal in at least Colombia and South Africa, applying it only in the following sections to the ways the two countries have proposed to distribute opportunities and property in respect of transitional justice. Specifically, in this section I first briefly sketch a relational value of harmony that is salient in the worldviews of people indigenous to both countries (Section 2A), after which I draw on it to advance a conception of national reconciliation (Section 2B), contrast it with salient alternatives (Section 2C), and bring out what it entails for how to allocate economic goods (Section 2D).

A. Harmony as an Indigenous Value

Beyond WEIRD (western, educated, industrialised, rich, and democratic) societies, which have a disproportionately large share of influence over globally influential principles and policies, some conception of harmonious relationship is widely taken to be the 'mother of all values'.[8] In particular, harmony is salient in the ethical perspectives of the Indigenous peoples of (particularly southern) Africa and South America.[9] Instead of deeming autonomy, rationality, independence, self-reliance, desire-fulfilment, satisfaction, pleasure, authenticity, uniqueness, or other individualist values to be central, these peoples tend to prize relationality.

In drawing on harmony as a value that is salient amongst indigenous worldviews of those in South Africa and Colombia, I do not aim to provide a detailed account of the worldviews in these countries, let alone their continents, or even of how harmony is understood in them. My goals are merely to point out a broad ethical perspective shared by victims of historical injustice in both societies, and to utilise it to ground a philosophical ideal of reconciliation that may be drawn on to evaluate the transitional justice measures undertaken in them.

In the case of southern Africa, often the relational values associated with harmony (or community) are captured with the terms '*ubuntu*' and '*botho*', the Nguni and Sotho-Tswana terms (respectively) for humanness. The broad ethical perspective is that one should develop one's humanness, which can be achieved insofar as one honours harmonious (or communal) relationships with others, which are the core normative aspects of the ubiquitous maxim, 'A person is a person through other persons'.[10] Such an ethic counts as 'African' insofar as it has been salient in the cultures of many peoples indigenous to the continent. Note that there is no suggestion that it is the only value that has been held by them, or even that it is utterly unique to that part of the world.

As for what harmony (communion) involves in at least the southern African tradition, consider remarks such as these from South African intellectuals: 'Harmony is

[8] In the words of Daniel A Bell and Yingchuan Mo, 'Harmony in the World 2013: The Ideal and the Reality' (2014) 118 Social Indicators Research 797.

[9] See n 7 and discussion in the rest of this section. Consider, too, East Asia, where different conceptions of harmony are central to Daoism and Confucianism, for two examples.

[10] See, eg, Reuel Khoza, *Ubuntu, Botho, Vumunhu, Vhuthu, African Humanism* (Ekhaya Promotions 1994) 3; Mluleki Mnyaka and Mokgethi Motlhabi, 'The African Concept of *Ubuntu/Botho* and Its Socio-moral Significance' (2005) 3 Black Theology 218.

achieved through close and sympathetic social relations within the group';[11] 'I participate, I share ... Harmony, friendliness, community are great goods. Social harmony is for us (Africans--ed.) the *summum bonum*—the greatest good ... Anger, resentment, lust for revenge, even success through aggressive competitiveness, are corrosive of this good';[12] 'If you asked *ubuntu* advocates and philosophers: What principles inform and organise your life? ... the answers would express commitment to the good of the community in which their identities were formed, and a need to experience their lives as bound up in that of their community'.[13]

In these and other characterisations of how to relate, two distinct properties are mentioned.[14] On the one hand, there is being close, participating, and experiencing life as bound up with others. Here, one enjoys a sense of togetherness with others and engages in cooperative projects with them. On the other hand, there is mention of sympathy, sharing, and being committed to the good of others, where such ways of relating involve doing what is likely to meet others' needs (including their need to realise their own humanness), doing so out of sympathy and for their own sake, and, where feasible, doing so reciprocally.

These ways of relating harmoniously on the face of it ground several salient practices amongst Indigenous African peoples that are intuitively appealing, including (amongst other things[15]): collective harvesting and building, not leaving individuals to fend for themselves; resolving political disputes by giving all affected a voice and seeking consensus amongst them (or at least popularly appointed elders), not resting content with majority rule that would exclude a minority; enjoying a family far extended beyond the nuclear structure whose members care for one another's children; distributing wealth as to avoid great inequalities that would leave people hungry and risk fostering attitudes of envy and distance; and seeking reconciliation, and not so much retribution, after wrongdoing and more generally conflict.

Turning to South America, there the ethic of harmony tends to go under the heading of the Spanish phrase '*buen vivir*', which means living well or good living. As one commentator from Colombia remarks, 'Similar to the concept of *ubuntu* from South Africa, it (*buen vivir*--ed.) holds that an individual's wellbeing can only be achieved through harmonious relationships with the wider community—including people, the environment, other living beings, their ancestors and the

[11] Yvonne Mokgoro, '*Ubuntu* and the Law in South Africa' (1998) 1 Potchefstroom Electronic Law Journal 17.

[12] Desmond Tutu, *No Future Without Forgiveness* (Random House 1999).

[13] Gessler Muxe Nkondo, '*Ubuntu* as a Public Policy in South Africa: A Conceptual Framework' (2007) 2 International Journal of African Renaissance Studies 91.

[14] First reconstructed in Thaddeus Metz, 'Toward an African Moral Theory' (2007) 15 Journal of Political Philosophy 321.

[15] For these and other respects in which an ethic of communion grounds recurrent ways of life amongst 'traditional' sub-Saharan peoples, see Thaddeus Metz, *A Relational Moral Theory: African Ethics in and Beyond the Continent* (OUP 2022) 128–36.

cosmos.'[16] The ethic of *buen vivir* 'seeks to establish a harmonious relationship between mankind and nature and a social equilibrium within societies'.[17] Note the two key ideas in this remark and many others summing up *buen vivir*, such as that its aim is to achieve 'harmony between human beings, and also between human beings and nature'.[18]

Harmony between humans is of course the central concept when it comes to reconciliation consequent to *social* conflict. Here, the idea is of relating to other people in mutually supportive ways to achieve an objectively decent quality of life, one that is neither consumerist nor competitive. In part *buen vivir* involves 'acting in concert with others in a community with reciprocity as key element and the aim of living well, but not necessarily living better than others'.[19] Another scholar remarks that '[i]n opposition to Western concepts of exclusivity, categorization, competition, subjectification, etc., Buen Vivir puts emphasis on key values such as solidarity, generosity, reciprocity and complementarity'.[20]

While there are surely differences to be teased out between *ubuntu* and *buen vivir*—which has yet to be done systematically in the literature—I focus on the patent similarities, so as to articulate an ethical perspective that can be used to evaluate the approaches to the distribution of economic goods that have been taken in the two post-conflict societies of South Africa and Colombia. For both, harmony involves: being inclusive, as opposed to viewing some as inferior or other; participating, instead of remaining isolated; cooperating, instead of subordinating or being fiercely competitive; helping others, rather than leaving them to fend for themselves, let alone harming them for gain to oneself; engaging in mutual aid in ways that are objectively good for people, rather than seeking to promote their desires or pleasures; and aiming to help others for their own sake, and not merely one's long-term self-interest. What then does this cluster of values mean for how to respond properly to serious social conflict, that is, to discordant ways of relating that run counter to an ethos that many of those indigenous to South Africa and Colombia seek to promote?

16 Dimitri Selibas, 'Buen Vivir: Colombia's Philosophy for Good Living' *BBC* <https://www.bbc.com/travel/article/20210207-buen-vivir-colombias-philosophy-for-good-living> accessed 3 October 2022. See also Martha Chaves and others, 'Radical Ruralities in Practice: Negotiating *Buen Vivir* in a Colombian Network of Sustainability' (2018) 59 Journal of Rural Studies 153. I do not here consider the debate about how the values associated with the Quechua phrase '*sumak kawsay*', prominent in Bolivia and Ecuador, relate to *buen vivir* as understood in Colombia and elsewhere in South America. For one discussion, see Javier Cuestas-Caza, 'Sumak Kawsay Is Not Buen Vivir' (2018) 5 Alternautas 51.

17 Ana Agostino and Franziska Dübgen, '*Buen Vivir* and Beyond: Searching for a New Paradigm of Action', Degrowth Conference Venice 2012, 6 <https://www.degrowth.info/en/catalogue-entry/buen-vivir-and-beyond-searching-for-a-new-paradigm-of-action/> accessed 3 October 2022.

18 Eduardo Gudynas quoted in Oliver Balch, '*Buen Vivir*: The Social Philosophy Inspiring Movements in South America', *The Guardian* (4 February 2013) <https://www.theguardian.com/sustainable-business/blog/buen-vivir-philosophy-south-america-eduardo-gudynas> accessed 3 October 2022.

19 Agostino and Dübgen (n 17) 6.

20 Johannes Waldmüller, 'Buen Vivir, Sumak Kawsay, "Good Living": An Introduction and Overview' (2014) 1 Alternautas 21.

B. Reconciliation as Valuing Harmony

If relating harmoniously is a high value, then some kind of reconciliation, the repair of discordant relationships, is the natural response to social conflict. Prizing harmony on the face of it would rule out not only responding retributively to wrongdoing, that is, imposing 'an eye for an eye' without the essential expectation of any good to come of it, but also imprisoning offenders so as to prevent them from committing crime again, without concern for what they do during their removal from society. Instead, valuing harmony prescribes expressing the attitude that offenders had wrongfully prized the opposite of discord, while doing what is likely to ameliorate the harm they did and improve their relationships with their victims and the broader society.

More specifically, I submit that an attractive form of reconciliation is one in which parties to a conflict disavow respects in which the value of harmony was flouted and come to relate in a somewhat harmonious way, namely, on a cooperative basis that is, at least down the road, expected to be good for all sides.[21] There are two distinct features to clarify.

One part is a familiar feature of reconciliation, namely, the idea that parties interact in positive ways, and specifically by coordinating behaviour towards mutual aid. Reconciliation is not akin to divorce, meaning that some kind of cohesion is instead essential. My favoured view focuses on people's behaviour, that is, how they act in respect of each other, and not so much their feelings, beliefs, desires, or emotions.

A second part of the preferred view includes disavowal, that is, expressing disapproval and related negative attitudes towards wrongful discord. Treating harmony as important calls for a critical response to it when it has been objectionably undermined, or, more concretely, treating victims with respect means acting as though they should not have been mistreated. In the first instance, such action ought to come from offenders. They should express remorse for what they have done, including by apologising for it, striving to make up for harm they caused as part of their offence, and working to make it clear they will not reoffend. All of these are normal ways for a person to distance himself from immoral ways in which he has treated others.

However, at least if offenders are not willing to engage in these practices, then the political community ought to step in and perform some of these functions. It should in that case (though probably not only in it) express the judgement that what the offender did was wrong, perhaps with informed reports and symbolic

[21] First articulated and defended in Thaddeus Metz, 'The Reach of Amnesty for Political Crimes: Which Extra-Legal Burdens on the Guilty Does National Reconciliation Permit?' (2011) 3 Constitutional Court Review 243, and Thaddeus Metz, 'A Theory of National Reconciliation: Some Insights from Africa' in Claudio Corradetti and others (eds), *Theorizing Transitional Justice* (Ashgate 2015) 119.

memorials, compel the offender to make up for the harm caused, step in to make compensation if he cannot, and work to ensure that the offender will not do it again. And where the state itself was guilty, perhaps of not having stopped offenders when it could have, then, it, too, must express remorse.

Notice that it would intuitively not genuinely express disapproval merely to say the words 'I am sorry' or 'That was wrong'. Instead, in cases of serious discord, doing so plausibly requires burdens to be willingly undertaken by the offender, or imposed on him by the state. However, the burdens should be productive ones that help to repair the broken relationship, namely by serving the functions of compensating victims and rehabilitating offenders.[22] By this approach, accountability is inherent to reconciliation; it is not enough to shake hands and act as though nothing happened. Offenders should undergo hard treatment, albeit forms of it that express disapproval of what they did and specifically in ways that improve victims' well-being and offenders' character.

Both parts, namely, the realisation of some facets of harmony and the disavowal of prior discord, are essential for a plausible account of reconciliation. Mere disavowal of a wrong might not be sufficient for something to count as reconciliation at all, which probably requires more cohesion than that. For instance, it would be difficult to speak of 'reconciliation' if all that happened were for a state verbally to criticise offenders and pay compensation to victims on their behalf; offenders should really be involved and in ways at least likely to result in improved relationships with their victims. Conversely, mere cohesion without disavowal would not be a particularly attractive kind of reconciliation. For example, if victims elected simply to forget how they were mistreated, offenders did not express any remorse for what they had done, but both sides moved forward with cooperative projects of mutual aid, that would be a form of reconciliation, but one that would not be as desirable as one that included moral disavowal of the past.[23]

C. Contrasts with Rival Conceptions of Reconciliation

Unlike many other conceptions of reconciliation, the one I advance is behavioural. For this conception, what matters is what people do and what is expressed by their actions, even if they themselves lack certain attitudes such as remorse, forgiveness, and sympathy. Although such emotions are commonly associated with talk of 'reconciliation', I maintain that they are not essential to an attractive sort of it.

[22] Some ideas here are borrowed from Thaddeus Metz, 'Reconciliation as the Aim of a Criminal Trial' (2019) 9 Constitutional Court Review 113.

[23] For a fuller defence of these claims, see Thaddeus Metz, 'Why Reconciliation Requires Punishment but Not Forgiveness' in Krisanna Scheiter and Paula Satne (eds), *Conflict and Resolution: The Ethics of Forgiveness, Revenge, and Punishment* (Springer 2022) 265.

The first choice would of course be for offenders themselves to feel sorry. The best form of reconciliation would be for offenders to have this sort of mental state and to mean it when they apologise and the like. However, a good enough sort of reconciliation, I submit, would be for them to do what signifies a remorseful state of mind even if they lack it—for example, by making restitution.[24]

For another respect in which attitudes are not essential to reconciliation, note that forgiveness, understood as including the dissipation of negative emotions, is not essential to the conception I propose. Some South African thinkers, particularly those in the Christian tradition,[25] have held that reconciliation requires forgiveness on the part of victims. While emotions must change enough in order for people to engage in cooperative projects expected to be mutually beneficial in the long run, that does not necessarily mean there are no lingering resentments. Entirely letting go of those would be desirable from the perspective of a fully harmonious relationship, but reconciliation is normally viewed as a stepping-stone or a bridge to an ideal, rather than a social ideal itself.

Similarly, I deny that reconciliation essentially involves empathy,[26] let alone 'a spiritual sense of belonging and community that draws people towards a fullness of humanity through others'.[27] Probably the best possible form of reconciliation, or a full-blown harmony, would include such mental states, but that would be a tall order for a state to promote between, say, an apartheid agent and the family of a non-violent black activist he murdered. It would count as reconciliation enough, and quite an amazing one, if the agent sent a large amount of his paycheque to them for the rest of his life and the family let him visit their son's grave from time to time.

D. From National Reconciliation to the Allocation of Economic Goods

I have suggested that valuing harmony means seeking reconciliation as a central response to discord, where the proper form reconciliation should take includes the political community, if not offenders, disavowing the unjust discord that occurred. Such disavowal, in turn, means that offenders must undergo burdensome ways of both reforming themselves so as not to reoffend and compensating their victims. It

[24] For discussion of how one can express an attitude without having it oneself, see Thaddeus Metz, 'The Nature of Reactive Practices' (2008) 3 South African Journal of Philosophy 49.

[25] For just one example, see Tutu (n 12).

[26] For a contrary view, see Patrick Lenta, 'In Defence of AZAPO and Restorative Justice' in Wessel le Roux and Karin van Marle (eds), *Law, Memory and the Legacy of Apartheid* (Pretoria University Law Press 2007) 162, 172.

[27] In the words of Charles Villa-Vicencio, 'Reconciliation: A Thing that Won't Go Away' in Fanie Du Toit and Erik Doxtader (eds), *In the Balance: South Africans Debate Reconciliation* (Jacana Media 2010) 165.

is the compensatory facet of reconciliation that is relevant to the way a state should allocate property and opportunities so as to advance transitional justice.

Insofar as reconciliation requires offenders to undertake labour or other kinds of sacrifice in order to make up for wrongful harm done to their victims, it is distinct from two related sorts of justice. First, it is different from retributive justice, the point of which is to respond to past injustice with a proportionate burden placed on an offender, one that is not inherently meant to produce any future economic benefit to the victim. Victims might happen to feel satisfied upon knowing those who wronged them have been made to suffer, but that would be an unintended side-effect of retribution and would of course do nothing in respect of property and opportunities.

Whereas retributive justice would have offenders suffer harm simply because they deserve it, without any forward-looking aim such as improving victims' economic standing, distributive justice is squarely concerned with the allocation of economic goods. Apart from libertarian views, according to most other accounts of distributive justice, the state should do what it can to improve its people's quality of life, particularly those who have become economically badly off through no fault of their own. However, distributive justice does not prescribe promoting economic benefits essentially as a way of responding to past injustice, let alone with any burden placed on those responsible for that. Instead, it is conceived as a morally required response to distributions that have become inappropriate without specifiable guilt. For example, distributive justice might involve providing financial support to those who have lost their jobs due to automation, or enabling those born into poor families to attend university.

In contrast to both retributive and distributive justice, reconciliation (or, more narrowly, compensatory justice) includes the idea that offenders should express remorse by undergoing burdensome ways of making reparations to their victims. Like retributive justice and unlike distributive justice, it involves responding to past injustice and doing so by placing burdens on wrongdoers, but, unlike retributive justice and like distributive justice, it involves doing what is expected to improve people's quality of life.

Offenders are in the first instance responsible for compensating their victims. For offenders to reconcile by disavowing their injustice, they must perform actions that express remorse, which, in turn, means (amongst other things) undergoing labour or some other burden in order to do what will improve their victims' socio-economic conditions. Although compensation merely for the sake of moving forward together need not involve hard treatment of an offender, compensation in order to disavow a crime plausibly must. If an offender were truly sorry and wanted to demonstrate his guilt, he would be willing to place hardship on himself as a way to display those emotions, where the greater his wrongdoing and the stronger his apt emotional reactions to it, the heavier the hardship—but a hardship that is expected to improve the situation of his victim. Normally, the burden on an offender that would compensate his victim would have an economic dimension, since property and opportunities are central to a victim's life going well. Improving socio-economic conditions would be a particularly important way to compensate victims in cases of large-scale social conflict of the kinds that transpired in South Africa and Colombia; for the nature of the wrongful harm done to victims there characteristically included taking property such as land and reducing opportunities for education/jobs.

So, for example, an offender might offer financial compensation to his victim. Where the wrongdoer is rich, that is not all he or she would do, since merely writing a cheque might then not be enough to express contrition. However, in the case where giving up money would mean a noticeable shift in lifestyle for someone not so well off, it could be enough to express remorse, depending on the nature of the wrongdoing.

There are additional ways that a wrongdoer might undergo a burden in order to improve his victim's economic standing, which do not involve a transfer of money. Those who have unjustly taken land in the past should return it, or at least large parts of it, along with a time-consuming transfer of capital and skills needed to make the land productive. Possibly someone who has unjustifiably taken the life of a breadwinner should help farm with his hands, providing sustenance to the victim's family, or he could help build a school so that the victim's children can get an education.

However, the state (or other political community) also has a role to play in effecting compensation. For one, at least in cases where offenders are disinclined to effect reparations in burdensome ways, the state should express its disapproval of their behaviour by making them do so. That is, it should subject them to judicial proceedings to establish guilt, and, upon it having been established in a fair way, impose hard treatment on the guilty that will serve the function of making restitution to victims. For another, sometimes offenders make a mess bigger than they could ever clean up on their own. Where they have caused more wrongful harm than they can repair with their money, labour, and other contributions, the state should step in to 'top up' as it can afford.[28] Both engagements would be ways for the state to disavow the injustice.

[28] Compensatory justice is not the only form of justice, and it can come into conflict with a state's ability to advance distributive justice. Urgent needs for compensation, eg to repair severe injury, take priority over meeting non-urgent needs for distribution, say, for internet access. Similarly, urgent needs for distribution, eg for food and water, take priority over meeting non-urgent needs for compensation, say, provision of stolen land where the victim had retained quite a lot of similar land. Beyond such norms, it is difficult at this stage for me to provide guidance about how to make trade-offs between the two kinds of justice. For a South African Constitutional Court case on the related matter of how to balance an interest in retributive justice with forward-looking concerns such as compensatory and distributive justice, see *AZAPO v President of the Republic of South Africa* [1996] ZACC 16; 1996 (4) SA 671 (CC).

It is worth asking just how much of a productive burden may be demanded of an offender. The principle that the worse the crime, the greater the burden that is appropriate does not indicate which limits there might be to the burdens the state may rightly place on a criminal. At this point, all I can say is that a strict proportionality between the nature of the crime and the sort of hardship imposed on the criminal would probably be too much in some cases. The death penalty would normally be ruled out because it usually would not serve the function of compensating a killer's victims (or reforming his character). However, suppose that a criminal has tried to kill an innocent party and in so doing has fatally injured her liver, where the only way for the latter to survive would be to obtain the former's healthy liver, foreseeably leading to his death. May the state engage in forcible organ transfer if necessary and sufficient for the offender to make his victim whole? While the offender should offer to give up his liver at the cost of his own life in order to save hers, I baulk at the idea that the state may force him to do so, even if necessary to save the life of his victim. Expressing respect for victims must be done in a way that does not fail to express respect for offenders, who invariably retain some human rights despite their misdeeds.

3. South Africa's Approach to Economic Goods in the Light of Reconciliation

In the rest of this chapter I take for granted the conception of reconciliation advanced in the previous section, and use it to evaluate South Africa's and Colombia's economic approaches to transitional justice. More specifically, I consider how the two countries have allocated, or principally considered allocating, property and opportunities, and consider the extent to which they measure up when it comes to the reconciliatory principle that offenders should undergo burdensome forms of compensating their victims.

In this section I argue that while South Africa has advanced certain kinds of restorative, retributive, and distributive justice since the transition to democracy in 1994, it has fallen far short of reconciliation, or roughly compensatory justice, so construed. Basically, the Truth and Reconciliation Commission proposals about reparations were not implemented by the government (Section 3A), while large-scale economic programmes that the government did adopt either were forms of distributive justice or were reparative schemes limited in both the benefits to victims and the burdens placed on those responsible for (or even who gained from) apartheid (Section 3B).

A. Truth and Reconciliation Commission Recommendations

As is well known, one major way that South Africa responded to the injustice of apartheid was with its Truth and Reconciliation Commission (TRC), set up in the mid-1990s to investigate human rights abuses during the apartheid era. It heard testimony from more than 21,000 victims, and more than 7,000 people applied for amnesty,[29] whereby those who fully disclosed their political crimes were freed from both criminal and civil prosecution. Those who did not reveal the truth about their apartheid-era misdeeds could be, and sometimes (albeit rarely) were, prosecuted through normal legal channels. These procedures were reasonably effective at publicising what happened during apartheid, and so in that respect they did advance a part of reconciliation or a kind of restorative justice.

However, victim compensation, let alone offender burden to effect it, have been inadequate, from the reconciliatory perspective advanced in the previous section. The TRC was not empowered to award any sorts of damages, and was limited to making recommendations to the government about how to do so. On this score, the TRC did make substantial recommendations regarding compensation, but virtually none of them was ever adopted by the South African government.

On the one hand, in the late 1990s the TRC suggested large-scale redistributive mechanisms to transfer wealth from those responsible for apartheid, or rather more often from those who benefitted from it, to those who were victims of it, including at the community level. For example, it suggested a wealth tax, a percentage donation from companies listed on the stock exchange, the disbursement of a special insurance fund covering political risk to which business had contributed, and a retrospective surcharge on both profits earned by corporations and 'golden handshakes' given to civil servants.[30] None of these proposals was implemented by the post-apartheid government,[31] which even fought the attempt of activists and apartheid-era victims to sue multinational corporations who had done business with the apartheid government.[32]

On the other hand, the TRC also proposed the payment of reparations by the government to thousands of individual victims of human rights abuses. Some

[29] Truth and Reconciliation Commission of South Africa, *Truth and Reconciliation Commission of South Africa Report, Volume One* (Truth and Reconciliation Commission 1998) 12, 34 <http://www.justice.gov.za/trc/report/finalreport/Volume%201.pdf> accessed 3 October 2022.

[30] South African Press Association, 'Wealth Tax Proposed by TRC' (29 October 1998) <http://www.justice.gov.za/trc/media%5C1998%5C9810/s981029t.htm> accessed 3 October 2022.

[31] Adam Yates, 'Justice Delayed: The TRC Recommendations 20 Years Later', *Daily Maverick* (5 September 2018) <https://www.dailymaverick.co.za/article/2018-09-05-justice-delayed-the-trc-recommendations-20-years-later/> accessed 3 October 2022.

[32] Isaac Mangena, 'Mbeki's Big Blunder: Apartheid Reparations', *Thought Leader* (9 March 2012) <https://thoughtleader.co.za/readerblog/2012/03/09/mbekis-big-blunder-apartheid-reparations/> accessed 3 October 2022; Rebecca Davis, 'US Corporations Can't Be Sued for Apartheid, Court Rules', *Daily Maverick* (22 August 2013) <https://www.dailymaverick.co.za/article/2013-08-22-us-corporations-cant-be-sued-for-apartheid-court-rules/> accessed 3 October 2022.

people did receive payment, but it was much less than the TRC had suggested, and it came many years later.[33] As I write, there is about 1.5 billion rand (approximately 100 million US dollars) in the President's Fund earmarked for reparative purposes that has yet to be paid out.[34] Beyond the fact that specific persons who particularly suffered from apartheid injustice have not been compensated (with some having died in the interim), it is noteworthy that South Africa would have the government, and not those responsible for the suffering, make the compensation—thereby using taxes collected from millions of black people, that is, those who were victims of apartheid or are their offspring.

B. South African Government Policies

In the late 1990s and early 2000s the government took three major measures to effect redress. One was the implementation of land reform. Apartheid-era laws had prevented black people from owning a large majority of South African land and had also forcibly excluded them from living in choice areas. The new, post-apartheid government quickly began a process of land reform, in 1994 adopting a law that allowed for those who had been dispossessed of land to claim it back.[35]

Although tens of thousands of claims have been settled and millions of hectares of land have been transferred, no source suggests that the government has achieved its 2014 goal of having 30 per cent of the farmland owned by black people.[36] Instead, there is ongoing debate about how far short of that percentage the government has come and why. Three widely cited explanations for the failure to reach that target are: first, that the relevant government departments have been short-staffed and could not oversee such a massive project; secondly, that the government had initially sought to buy land from white farmers at market-related prices that it could not afford; and, finally, that it had transferred the land to black people without having provided the capital, skills, and the like needed to run farms, only to become wary of the land becoming unproductive.[37] Regardless of the reasons,

[33] Jasmina Brankovic, 'Questioning the Model: Transitional Justice in South Africa after the TRC' in James Stormes and others (eds), *Transitional Justice in Post-Conflict Societies in Africa* (Hekima Institute of Peace Studies and International Relations 2016) 136–39.

[34] Pather (n 1).

[35] Restitution of Land Rights Act 22 of 1994, with several amendments, including in 1997 and 2003.

[36] Ben Cousins, 'South Africa's Land Debate Is Clouded by Misrepresentation and Lack of Data' *The Conversation* (8 March 2018) <https://theconversation.com/south-africas-land-debate-is-clouded-by-misrepresentation-and-lack-of-data-93078> accessed 3 October 2022.

[37] Lungisile Ntsebeza and Ruth Hall, 'Introduction' in Lungisile Ntsebeza and Ruth Hall (eds), *The Land Question in South Africa* (HSRC Press 2007) 8–9; South African History Online, 'Land Restitution in South African since 1994'. <https://www.sahistory.org.za/article/land-restitution-south-africa-1994> accessed 3 October 2022; South African History Online, 'Timeline of Land Dispossession and Restitution in South Africa 1995–2013' <https://www.sahistory.org.za/topic/timeline-land-dispossession-and-restitution-south-africa-1995-2013> accessed 3 October 2022.

the bottom line is that a good portion of the transfer of land came with compensation for white farmers, and a large majority of South Africa's farmland remains in the hands of white people, without many black people having been otherwise compensated.

A second reparative measure undertaken by the post-apartheid government has been affirmative action, or what is more often called 'equity' in the South African context. By law since 1998, organisations have been required to give preference to black people when hiring,[38] and, indeed, universities, sports teams, firms, and governments have systematically used numerical goals and sometimes even quotas to do so.[39]

However, as less than 9 per cent of the population is white, there has been only so much good that affirmative action could have achieved for the much larger black population. Additionally, it is well known that much of the white population remains decently employed because of its skills (although not so much in government departments). Educational facilities were much better for whites than for blacks during apartheid, with white parents able to pass on better schooling, greater cultural capital, and the like to their offspring, with the white unemployment rate far lower than the black one.[40]

The third major reparative policy that the post-apartheid government adopted was Black Economic Empowerment (BEE).[41] Initially it involved companies being required to have a certain percentage of black shareholders, which led to their making a very small minority of black people very rich. It was then amended so that the benefits would be spread more widely. For example, there are schemes in which black South Africans can obtain shares in major companies at a reduced rate and in which governments and firms are to give preference to black suppliers.

Although the more recent versions of BEE have spread the wealth somewhat more broadly, no one maintains that it has reached a majority of black South Africans. Those who have managerial skills, own businesses, can afford to buy shares, and enjoy related kinds of economic standing have likely benefitted, but the very large majority of black South Africans without them have not.[42] More than half the country lives in poverty, with more than 90 per cent of poor people being

[38] Employment Equity Act 55 of 1998, and Employment Equity Amendment Act 47 of 2013.

[39] For an important South African Constitutional Court case affirming the legitimacy of equity in hiring, see *South African Police Service v Solidarity obo Barnard* [2014] ZACC 23; 2014 (6) SA 123 (CC).

[40] BusinessTech, 'White vs Black Unemployment in South Africa' <https://businesstech.co.za/news/general/96887/white-vs-black-unemployment-in-south-africa/> accessed 3 October 2022.

[41] Broad-Based Black Economic Empowerment Act 53 of 2003, and Broad-Based Black Economic Empowerment Amendment Act 46 of 2013.

[42] Gwen Ngwenya, 'B-BBEE Proves that When One Black Person Prospers, Others Do Not Necessarily Benefit by Proxy', *BusinessDay* (4 August 2018) <https://www.businesslive.co.za/bd/opinion/2018-08-04-b-bbee-proves-that-when-one-black-person-prospers-others-do-not-necessarily-benefit-by-proxy/> accessed 3 October 2022.

black,[43] and the unemployment rate for African people is between 30 and 40 per cent, depending on the definition.[44]

Beyond these reparative measures, the post-apartheid government has adopted many welfare programmes to provide opportunities and resources to South Africans, including: child support grants, old age grants, sickness/disability grants, unemployment insurance, job training (SETAs), and loans for tertiary education. The extent of support is substantial, with more than a quarter of South Africans benefitting from at least one of the grants and more people receiving a grant than are employed.[45]

Even so, these programmes have been far removed from what transitional justice, and specifically national reconciliation, would prescribe, in that they have been available to all South Africans, without a focus on victims, and none of the programmes has been primarily financed by apartheid-era offenders. The grant systems have been part of South Africa's attempt to advance distributive justice, but that is of course not a reaction towards injustice in the past. One might suggest that reconciliation would have been advanced more in South Africa, had economic policies improved black people's quality of life more substantially, and they were not so reliant on meagre grants. That might be true, in one, purely future-oriented sense of 'reconciliation' focused on overcoming extant racial animosity. However, the account of reconciliation I have defended includes a requirement to disavow respects in which harmony had been flouted, that is, to honour those who were victimised in the past. That requires the transfer or other provision of economic goods as a burdensome way for offenders to express remorse for their past misdeeds or at least for the state to make an effort to impose such burdens on offenders. That simply did not happen systematically in South Africa.

4. Colombia's Approach to Economic Goods in the Light of Reconciliation

The TRC in South Africa made some sensible recommendations in respect of economic goods, from the perspective of the reconciliation favoured here, but the government did not implement them. Although these recommendations targeted mostly those who benefitted from apartheid, and not so much those who

[43] Kate Wilkinson, 'South Africa's Official Poverty Numbers', *Africa Check* (15 February 2018) <https://africacheck.org/factsheets/factsheet-south-africas-official-poverty-numbers/> accessed 3 October 2022.

[44] Kate Wilkinson, 'Ramaphosa Right about "Big Difference" between Black & White Unemployment in SA', *Africa Check* (20 February 2018) <https://africacheck.org/spot-check/ramaphosa-right-about-big-difference-between-black-white-unemployment-in-sa/> accessed 3 October 2022.

[45] BusinessTech, 'There Are Officially More South Africans on Social Grants than Working' (21 June 2017) <https://businesstech.co.za/news/business/180503/there-are-officially-more-south-africans-on-social-grants-than-people-who-work-irr/> accessed 3 October 2022.

were responsible for it (which would have been ideal), they would at least have been better than what the government actually did, which was to adopt redress programmes that benefitted mainly those black people who already enjoyed competitive economic advantages and that came at virtually no cost to the white beneficiaries, let alone the architects of apartheid.

Colombia has had the chance to do things differently. In particular, its policy is even more attractive than what the TRC had recommended (and than what the South African government has done, of course) when it comes to effecting compensation for victims at the expense of offenders. Colombia's proposed way forward, even though not its systematic practice yet, includes the ideal that 'victim compensation should be at the core of any agreement'[46] and that the 'rights of the victims of the conflict are non-negotiable'.[47] Colombia's approach is more oriented towards not only benefitting victims, but also doing so at the expense of offenders, and thereby advancing the favoured conception of reconciliation. There are two major facets of the Final Agreement that propose such compensatory justice, one concerning reform in rural areas (Section 4A) and another about victim reparation more generally (Section 4B).

A. Comprehensive Rural Reform

The first chapter of the Final Agreement between the Colombian government and the FARC is titled 'Towards a New Colombian Countryside: Comprehensive Rural Reform' (abbreviated 'CCR').[48] Since much of the conflict was occasioned by a distribution of land that the FARC had perceived to be unjust, it makes good sense to see the Final Agreement begin with the countryside.

There are many proposals in the Final Agreement about how to effect CCR, many of which pertain to distributive justice. Of relevance to the present discussion, though, are the principles expressing a demand for compensatory justice. First off, the agreement 'prioritises the territories most affected by the conflict, poverty and neglect'[49] and aims to 'reverse the effects of the conflict, to achieve restitution for the victims of dispossession and forced displacement and the restoration of land rights to communities'.[50] These are clear reparative goals.

Furthermore, as to where the land will come from, the very first proposal made is to deploy 'legal cessation of ownership in favour of the Nation ... with a view to reversing the unlawful concentration of land ownership'.[51] In other words, those

[46] Final Agreement (n 2) 9.
[47] ibid 132; see also 154.
[48] ibid 10.
[49] ibid 11.
[50] ibid 18; see also 13, 16, 22.
[51] ibid 15.

with unjust possession of land will undergo the burden of being deprived of it for the sake of those they had deprived. That is not the only source of land that the Final Agreement proposes to distribute to the landless, for there is also mention of unoccupied public land, donated land, and the like,[52] but, from the perspective of reconciliation, it is welcome that it is included. It is a way for the government to express disapproval of past injustice, and for those responsible for the injustice at least to act in ways that express remorse for it.

Finally, the CCR is specific about how to realise its reparative aims beyond simply the provision of land. It does not merely state an intention to compensate in the abstract, but is fairly concrete about what should be done in order for compensation to be realised. For instance, the agreement says, 'Although the aforesaid access to land is a prerequisite for transformation of the countryside, on its own it is insufficient; national plans financed and promoted by the state must be set up with a view to achieving the comprehensive rural development that will provide public services and goods'.[53] The agreement includes details of the kinds of training and resources that should be provided (presumably as an essential 'top up' from the state beyond what offenders could muster), so that the land would be genuinely expected to improve victims' quality of life.

Lately, much of the South African populace has become enthusiastic about speeding up the pace of land reform, exhibiting less patience with great racial inequalities in the distribution of land and other kinds of property, indeed to the point of protest and invasion of land. In addition, the government has finally, in the past ten years or so, worked to enable black beneficiaries of land reform to make productive use of it, with some success.[54] Colombia ideally would not wait so long in order to make effective redress when it comes to land.

B. Comprehensive System for Truth, Justice, Reparations and Non-Recurrence

The fifth chapter of the agreement is about responding to victims of the conflict, with the agreement prescribing what is labelled a 'Comprehensive System for Truth, Justice, Reparations and Non-Recurrence'. It includes a wide and intricate array of mechanisms designed to honour victims, including searching for those who disappeared during the conflict, obtaining the truth about what happened to victims during it, assuring victims that they are safe from further attacks, and imposing long sentences of imprisonment on those guilty of the most serious human

52 ibid 15.
53 ibid 11, 16, 24–30, 195.
54 Cousins (n 36).

rights violations. Of interest to the present discussion are the reparative mechanisms that are also discussed.

First, as with the CCR, there are clearly stated aims of compensating victims: 'These measures seek to ensure the comprehensive reparation of the victims, including the rights to restitution, indemnification, rehabilitation, realisation and non-recurrence; and the collective reparation of the territories, the populations and the communities most affected by the conflict'.[55] Notice the two dimensions, of the individual and the social. In terms of the agreement, it is not just persons who are entitled to redress, but also networks of them, that is, communities that were broken up and otherwise wrongfully harmed.

As to who it is that is to compensate individuals and communities, the agreement proposes that it should be offenders in the first instance, with the use of the compelling phrase 'restorative sanctions':[56] 'In the context of these [reparation] plans, stress will be laid on acknowledging the responsibility of the state, the FARC-EP, paramilitaries and any other group, organisation or institution that caused harm or injury during the conflict'.[57] Those responsible are to be sanctioned in part according to their revelation of truth about serious crimes, where the 'sanctions will have the overall aim of realising the rights of victims and consolidating peace. They will need to have the greatest restorative and reparative function in relation to the harm caused'.[58] Such an approach is precisely what I have argued that a plausible form of reconciliation prescribes: instead of improving the lives of victims while letting offenders off the hook, and instead of punishing offenders without regard for improving the lives of victims, Colombia's agreement would see at least some offenders burdened in ways that serve the function of improving the lives of victims. In particular, they would be put to work for the sake of victims in ways that provide victims property and opportunities. This form of accountability is much of what has been intuitively missing from South Africa's approach to transitional justice.

Such an approach is not completely novel, having been undertaken to some degree in Rwanda, in response to the 1994 genocide. The country had flirted with the idea of a *Fonds d'indemnisation* (FIND), a compensation fund into which those convicted of genocide were supposed to pay.[59] While that did not materialise, the famous Gacaca courts did sentence more than 100,000 offenders to perform community service.[60]

[55] Final Agreement (n 2) 138; see also 154.

[56] ibid 175. Compare this phrase with 'reconciliatory sentencing' in Metz, 'Reconciliation as the Aim of a Criminal Trial' (n 22).

[57] Final Agreement (n 2) 191; see also 137, 145, 189.

[58] ibid 174.

[59] For discussion, see Paul Christoph Bornkamm, *Rwanda's Gacaca Courts: Between Retribution and Reparation* (OUP 2012).

[60] Penal Reform International, *Eight Years On ... A Record of Gacaca Monitoring in Rwanda* (2010) <https://cdn.penalreform.org/wp-content/uploads/2013/05/WEB-english-gacaca-rwanda-5.pdf> accessed 3 October 2022.

Finally, the Colombian agreement is specific about the ways that offenders could be put to work for the sake of improving their victims' socio-economic conditions. Included amongst a list of restorative sanctions are: repairing infrastructure, building houses and schools, engaging in waste disposal, growing crops, fixing roads, and improving access to water/electricity.[61] The document includes an awareness of the need to obtain permission from a community in order to have offenders in its presence, and to undertake reparative labour in ways that respect community cultures.

At least in theory and law, even if not yet implementation, Colombia has the makings of an approach to economic goods that would truly compensate victims while simultaneously holding offenders accountable, thereby manifesting an intuitively appealing kind of reconciliation.

5. Conclusion: Political Explanations of the Limits to Reconciliation

I close this chapter with a brief suggestion about why the favoured approach to economic goods was not adopted in South Africa and has also been contested in Colombia. My suspicion is that, whereas in South Africa politics forbade imposing retribution on offenders, or indeed holding them accountable in any real sense, in Colombia politics has required retribution as a form of accountability, with restorative sanctions (as well as amnesties and pardons) viewed as insufficient. Although in some ways these are opposite forces, what they both have in common are departures from the reconciliatory sentences that I have argued would be ideal.

In previous sections, I pointed out how reconciliation, of a sort that would include hard, but productive, treatment of offenders, was not approximated in South Africa. However, the TRC in combination with the economic policies weakly oriented towards redress *might* have been the best that South Africa could do. Perhaps democracy and distributive justice could not have been achieved without offering amnesty in exchange for truth and thereby forgoing the disavowal of facets of reconciliation that would have included restorative sanctions. According to one commentator citing several historical analyses of South Africa, 'The vast majority of accounts of the amnesty negotiations concur that in the absence of agreement on amnesty, negotiations would have faltered, with the likely result that the violent struggle would have continued, and more lives would have been lost'.[62]

In contrast, in Colombia it has been precisely the demand for punitive disavowal that is one major explanation of why the Final Agreement's non-retributive facets have been challenged. The agreement does say that the most serious crimes,

[61] Final Agreement (n 2) 183–84.
[62] Lenta (n 26) 158–59.

including crimes against humanity, are to be dealt with by normal criminal legislation or at least some heavy sentences of imprisonment.[63] However, that has not been enough to assuage a notable proportion of the public, which voted against the Final Agreement in a referendum. One commentator remarked, 'Colombians are culturally accustomed to war ... Justice is seen as an eye for an eye, a tooth for a tooth'.[64] Similar sentiments have also moved the President to challenge facets of the agreement.[65]

Given the account of reconciliation advanced in this chapter, South Africa's institutional approach was too soft on offenders, while some of the Colombian public and executive are being too hard on them. South Africa should have had the architects of apartheid undergo heavy burdens that served the function of improving victims' socio-economic livelihoods, rather than get off scot free with their time and booty. Colombia should have those members of the government and the FARC who engaged in gross human rights violations do the same, rather than simply rot in jail. That would advance an attractive kind of reconciliation grounded on the values of harmony salient in the Indigenous cultures of both countries.

[63] Final Agreement (n 2) 158, 161, 307, 311, 317, 319.

[64] Pedro Piedrahita Bustamante quoted in Joe Parkin Daniels, 'Colombia's Polarised Election Raises Fears for Fragile Peace', *The Guardian* (16 June 2018) <https://www.theguardian.com/world/2018/jun/16/colombias-election-peace-ivan-duque-gustavo-petro> accessed 3 October 2022.

[65] Lally Weymouth, 'Colombia's President on a Wobbly Peace with the FARC', *The Washington Post* (27 September 2018) <https://www.washingtonpost.com/outlook/colombias-president-on-a-wobbly-peace-with-the-farc/2018/09/27/d501197e-c1f9-11e8-a1f0-a4051b6ad114_story.html> accessed 3 October 2022.

3

Building Peace and Restoring Law upon the Ethos

A Comparison Between South Africa and Colombia

Nathalia Bautista Pizarro

1. Introduction

Defining principles of justice and mechanisms to give effect to them within a peacebuilding process of a society that has endured serious human rights violations for many decades, as has been the case of South Africa and Colombia, is a very complex task. In scenarios such as these, the ordinary system of justice is pushed to its limits. This precipitates unexpected questions which serve to highlight the need to develop new ways of resolving societal conflicts and particularly the shaping of prosecution and reparation systems. However, for many societies, it is difficult to take on this challenge because the sense of justice has often been understood to require retribution, even in times of transition.

In contrast, the ancestral and cultural values of some communities that have suffered the pain of war teach us that a peacebuilding process implies renouncing the satisfaction of our individual interests in order to recognise the interests of others. This is the foundation of a robust process of restoring a sense of order and healing in such societies.

In this chapter, I seek to explore the contribution of social philosophies that have proven to be effective in the preservation of a peaceful order at a community level and that could, therefore, assist in offering new ways of resolving societal conflicts. Whilst there have been studies about the usefulness of values such as *ubuntu* in the South African case,[1] this chapter will primarily build upon the studies conducted

[1] Thaddeus Metz, 'A Theory of National Reconciliation. Some Insights from Africa' in Claudio Corradetti, Nir Eisikovits, and Jack Volpe Rotondi (eds), *Theorizing Transitional Justice* (Ashgate 2014) 119–35; Thaddeus Metz, 'South Africans Truth Reconciliation Commission in the Light of Ubuntu: A Comprehensive Appraisal' in Mia Swart and Katrin van Marle (eds), *The Limits of Transition: The South African Truth and Reconciliation Commission 20 Years on* (Brill Nijhoff 2017) 221–52; Namia Bohler-Muller, 'Beyond Legal Metanarratives: The Interrelationship between Storytelling, Ubuntu and Care' (2007) Stellenbosch Law Review 133–60; the consideration of peaceful social philosophies in peacebuilding processes has also been observed in other peoples in Africa, however, not only as a proper theme of justice, but as a broader strategy for the prevention of violence. Negasa Gelana Debisa,

Nathalia Bautista Pizarro, *Building Peace and Restoring Law upon the Ethos* In: *Transitional Justice, Distributive Justice, and Transformative Constitutionalism.* Edited by: David Bilchitz and Raisa Cachalia, with Magdalena Inés Correa Henao and Nathalia Bautista Pizarro, Oxford University Press.
DOI: 10.1093/oso/9780192887627.003.0003

by scholars in Colombia that recognise the meaning and importance of cultural values in human rights reparation proceedings.[2] In essence, I contend that by moving away from retributive models of justice we can begin to reimagine new and better ways of doing justice in transition and contributing to a peacebuilding process.

This is in line with the Colombian Peace Agreement of 2016 which is characterised precisely by innovations in the responses to the crimes and damages committed during the armed conflict. Indeed, its transitional justice system has been shaped upon principles of restorative justice providing measures that not only focus on the prosecution of persons responsible for perpetrating the most serious crimes (by granting punitive benefits), but also on the active participation of victims in the proceedings, their reparation, the recognition of the truth, the commitment to non-repetition of the armed conflict, and the guarantee of co-existence within Colombian society.[3] In other words, this transitional justice system contains measures that also seek to build a long-lasting peace.[4]

In order to develop this idea, this study will explain, first, the difficulty of overcoming armed conflict and building peace based upon a retributive idea of justice as well as the necessity of considering alternative approaches (Section 2). Subsequently, the influence of *ubuntu* in the South African peace process will be presented (Section 3) to lay the foundations for a comparative reflection (Section 4) on the social philosophies of three Colombian communities having different ethnic and cultural characteristics: the Indigenous *Misak* people of Cauca, the *Afroatratenian* community of Chocó, and the urban community *Agroarte* of Medellín. This analysis highlights the cultural diversity of the communities that experienced the internal armed conflict in Colombia (Indigenous, Afro-descendants,

'Building Peace by Peaceful Approach: The Role of Oromo Gadaa System in Peace-Building' (2022) 8(1) Cogent Social Sciences 1–17.

[2] Yolanda Sierra León, 'Relaciones entre el arte y los derechos humanos' (2014) 32 Derecho del Estado 77–100; see also multiple references to the influence of cultural values and arts in the field of human rights law in Colombia, Latin America, and the Inter-American System of Human Rights in Yolanda Sierra León (ed), *Reparación Simbólica: Jurisprudencia, cantos y tejidos* (Universidad Externado de Colombia 2018); Yolanda Siera León, *Teoría general de la reparación simbólica* (Universidad Externado de Colombia, Ejército Nacional de Colombia 2021).

[3] Colombian Final Peace Agreement 2016, Chapter 5.

[4] Scholars recognise the term peacebuilding as a robust process that does not necessarily involve addressing transitional justice. This concept refers to any activity that seeks to prevent conflict, diminish violence, and create conditions for peaceful governance. See Molly M Melin, *The Building and the Breaking of Peace: Corporate Activities in Civil War Prevention and Resolution* (OUP 2021) 32. In this regard, the Colombian Peace Agreement of 2016 contains a large number of measures that seek to address the causes of the Colombian conflict and guarantee peaceful co-existence such as a land and political participation reform programmes (Chapters 1 and 2). But its transitional justice system has also been shaped in order to avoid the repetition of the conflict and to enable co-existence in the territories. Its focus is not only directed towards the past, but also towards the future. This normative framework reflects the understanding of the relationship between transitional justice and peacebuilding as set out in this chapter.

peasants and mestizos) and examines their particular approaches to repair the damage they suffered and to build peace, and how they emerged from their different environments (rural and urban) and value systems.

2. Restoring Law upon the Ethos

A. Crime and Punishment

The peace agreement signed by the Colombian government and the former rebel group FARC-EP[5] is a comprehensive attempt to end an armed conflict that existed for more than five decades and left in its wake millions of victims. Chapter 5, which contains the principles of restorative justice, envisages a Comprehensive System of Truth, Justice, Reparation and Non-Repetition.[6] In order to guarantee the recognition of truth, the non-repetition of violence, and also an end to the armed conflict, this transitional justice system offers certain benefits, such as amnesties and pardons for political crimes and their related offences for the members or enablers of the FARC-EP, as well as those who have committed minor offences during social demonstrations.[7] It also contains a pardoning system for state agents who have perpetrated crimes 'due to, in occasion or in direct or indirect relation to the armed conflict'[8] and the imposition of special sanctions for serious violations of human rights and breaches of international humanitarian law (IHL) committed before 1 December 2016, as long as they are selected by the case prioritisation system of the Special Jurisdiction for Peace.[9] The type of sanction to be imposed depends on the

[5] 'Fuerzas Armadas y Revolucionarias de Colombia—Ejército del Pueblo' (Revolutionary Armed Forces of Colombia—People's Army), currently as the political party 'Fuerza Alternativa Revolucionaria del Común' (Revolutionary Alternative Force of the Common).

[6] Regulated mainly in the Constitutional Amendments 1/2016 and 1/2017, the Decrees 588/2017, 589/2017, and 902/2017 and the Statutory Law for the Special Jurisdiction for Peace 1957/2019 and the Act 1922/2018.

[7] Final Peace Agreement 5.1.2, 40 and the Amnesty Act 1820 of 30 December 2016, arts 2, 15, 16, 23, and 24: Political crimes are political demonstrations against the government executed by use of force or violence, such as rebellion or sedition. Related crimes are those that are committed in order to enable, to support and to finance the rebel actions and those that could be normally perpetrated during a protest and do not represent major damages, for example, small injuries (in a person or its assets), 'obstruction of public roads', 'disorderly conduct in public transportation'. Conduct that implies a serious violation of human rights or a breach to international humanitarian law (IHL) or those committed with 'ferocity, brutality or any equivalent' cannot be considered political crimes (arts 10, 23, and 30), see also Colombian Constitutional Court decision C-007/2018.

[8] Final Peace Agreement 5.1.2, 44; Amnesty Act 1820/2016, arts 45 and 46; Act 1957/2019, art 45. Accordingly, the pardoning system for state agents cannot be applied when the conduct has no relation with the armed conflict, or when it represents a serious violation of a human right or a breach of IHL, or it represents a misconduct against the service, discipline, interest, honour, or security of the Public Forces, as provided in the Military Penal Code, in the case of military members.

[9] Constitutional Amendment 1/2017, transitory art 7; the persons that, without being combatants, have engaged in conduct 'on occasion, due to, or in direct or indirect relation to the armed conflict' (the so-called third parties), can apply to the sanction system, if they voluntarily participate. See C-674 of 2017.

degree of cooperation in the elucidation of truth and the recognition of individual liability. There is a sliding scale of penalties identified which include, first, an order that detention take place in a location different from a prison and the prisoner is required to accomplish restorative tasks (such as projects to improve infrastructure or to eradicate illicit crops) for a five- to eight-year period (proper sanction of the Special Jurisdiction for Peace). A more serious second sanction is to order five to eight years of imprisonment (alternative sanction) and, in the worst case scenario, imprisonment of fifteen to twenty years is a possibility (ordinary sanction).[10] The idea of replacing imprisonment with detention in other regional locations and a substantial reduction of time served—considering that the ordinary punitive system provides for imprisonment from forty to sixty years for serious human rights violations—were some of the main grounds which led to the rejection by a slim margin of the initial peace agreement referendum held on 2 October 2016. Consequently, a new negotiation with the political opposition was necessary, and the Final Peace Agreement was signed on 24 November 2016 and approved by Congress on 1 December 2016. Since the main aspects of this sanction system remain in force, there is still tension between the system's proponents and those who opposed the terms of the peace agreement.

Behind the arguments of the detractors of the peace process lies the common idea of retribution. Many citizens expect the imposition of punishment as the strongest mechanism of justice to address serious human rights violations caused during the armed conflict. This flows from a legal culture that prioritises the idea of retribution, an idea that is central to the understanding of much of what lies behind the national and international criminal legal system. Indeed, the modern liberal legal tradition conceives of punishment as an exclusive power of the state that can be triggered when the perpetrator transgresses the freedom of others.[11] In this way, a logical correlation between crime and punishment has been established. In this sense, Kant, for example, understood punishment as a categorical imperative that has to be followed in order to compensate for the value of justice breached by the crime[12] and, for Hegel, punishment is also a question of balance between the crime and the breached normative order, it is the 'negation of the negation of law'.[13] At present, besides the many functions that have been recognised for punishment by philosophy and criminal law theory, its relationship to crime remains an important

[10] Final Peace Agreement 5.1.2., 60, and *List of Sanctions*; Statutory Law for the Special Jurisdiction for Peace Act 1957/2019, arts 125–143; it is also possible to admit for the term of punishment to be reduced from two to five years when the degree of contribution to the crime is not decisive, see Final Peace Agreement 5.1.2., 60, Act 1957/2019, art 129.

[11] cf Thomas Vorbaum, *Einführung in die moderne Strafrechtsgeschichte* (Springer 2009) 39–43.

[12] Immanuel Kant, *Die Metaphysik der Sitten* (first published 1797, Surhkamp 1977)A 195 196/B 225 226–A 204/B 234; cf Rainer Zaczyk, 'Zur Begründung der Gerechtigkeit menschlichen Strafens' in Jörg Arnold and others (eds), *Menschengerechtes Strafrecht: Festschrift für Albin Eser zum 70. Geburtstag* (C.H. Beck 2005) 207 ff.

[13] Georg Wilhelm Friedrich Hegel, *Grundlinien der Philosophie des Rechts* (first published 1821, Surhkamp 1986) ss 97–103.

facet of the dominant societal approach.[14] This idea is also supported by international criminal law, since, in order to guarantee world peace, punishment has become an imperative and the strongest mechanism to address the harm caused to victims of serious human rights violations.[15] Thus, the central question is whether the imposition of a retributive punishment does in fact respond adequately to the magnitude of the damage caused during an internal armed conflict, such as that which occurred in Colombia, or whether it is necessary to introduce other ways of conceiving justice.

B. Criminal Justice in Times of War

To answer this question, first, it is necessary to acknowledge that criminal justice, as well as the entire legal system, has been conceived to operate in ideal conditions of stability. This stems from the fact that peace and general security are the minimal conditions to guarantee co-existence and the full enjoyment of freedoms.[16] An atmosphere of stability liberates the individual from the burden of a permanent calculation of risks related to their existence and instead allows them to focus on the realisation of their life projects.[17] To achieve this, it is necessary to concentrate the use of force solely in the state, in order to prevent the dangers of the State of Nature—that is, an internal war—and to give birth to a civil community.[18]

In this regard, a situation of widespread instability, which arises from the fact that several members of the community are failing to comply with societal norms, as in the case of the long internal armed conflict in Colombia, is a big challenge for a legal system that was conceived to operate only in times of peace. The question is whether the state is able to confront this challenge relying only on the ordinary organs of justice. In Colombia, it was necessary to activate every institution of the criminal justice system to prosecute the crimes committed by armed groups and, moreover, to resort to the most forceful mechanism: the national armed forces. A war ensued as a result.

Nevertheless, conducting war as a means of securing the entire normative order, in order to protect individual freedoms and to support the operation of the

[14] Tatjana Hörnle, *Straftheorien* (Mohr Siebeck 2011) 15 ff; Günther Jakobs, *System der strafrechtlichen Zurechnung* (Vittorio Klostermann 2012) 14, crime is a 'discourse' and punishment its 'answer'; see also Urs Kindhäuser, 'La lógica de la construcción del delito' (2009) RAE Jurisprudencia 503 f.

[15] Gerhard Werle, 'Menschenrechtsschutz durch Völkerstrafrecht' (1997) Zeitschrift für die gesamte Strafrechtswissenschaft 814 ff; Katrin Gierhake, *Begründung des Völkerstrafrechts auf der Grundlage der Kantischen Rechtslehre* (Duncker & Humblot 2005) 245 ff, 255 ff, 266; Robert Cryer and others, *An Introduction to International Criminal Law and Procedure* (CUP 2014)28 ff, 56 ff.

[16] I here draw on contractarian theories of the state, Hobbes, *Leviatán* (Losada 2004), 132 ff; John Locke, *Segundo Tratado sobre el Gobierno Civil. Un ensayo acerca del verdadero origen, alcance y fin del Gobierno Civil* (Carlos Mellizo ed, Alianza 2004) 36 ff, 46 ff.

[17] Michael Pawlik, *Das Unrecht des Bürgers* (Mohr Siebeck 2012), 104 ff.

[18] Hobbes (n 16) 163 ff; Locke (n 16) 102 ff.

criminal justice system, is questionable from different points of view. First, doing so reduces law to the use of force, since war seeks to silence the voices of a great number of dissidents, instead of offering spaces to discuss the motives that led them to disregard the law in a widespread manner. In this respect, it is important to clarify that a normative order that is grounded in the idea of freedom must ensure strong and harmonious interpersonal bonds through the assent of individual recipients, rather than by the coercive imposition thereof.[19]

Modern and democratic societies have understood that the formation of this bond implies equal recognition of the members of the community as subjects of rights and duties,[20] particularly with access to private property as a mechanism that allows the realisation of individual life projects.[21] Likewise, this recognition entails the consideration of individual or collective identity and, with it, particular life aspirations, which can in fact clash with the classical liberal model of a citizen.[22] In this sense, normative bonds are built in an environment of inclusion, in which the state has the task of at least enabling and facilitating the materialisation of every one of these individual and collective life projects. When this is done, citizens will feel bound and identified with the state and its normative system which, by these means, is accepted without resorting to a culture of coercive enforcement.[23] Consequently, the display of disobedience to the law, on the part of a considerable number of recipients during a long period of time, indicates that the democratic and liberal project is massively failing.

In this regard, inequality and social exclusion have been recognised in the Final Peace Agreement as one of the main causes of the Colombian armed conflict. For many ex-combatants, joining the rebel armed groups represented a minimal livelihood or, at least, the only 'occupation' they could find in the desolate landscape of their territories, historically abandoned by society and the state. In this situation, the punitive judgment must yield to make way to the benefits of amnesty and pardon[24]—at least partially—and condition its grant to the compliance with other compensatory measures, in order to satisfy the rights of victims. This is the model of Colombian transitional justice, which provides a sanction system less drastic than the ordinary one and that places a greater value on the reparation of victims,

[19] Michael Pawlik, 'Kants Volk von Teufeln und sein Staat' (2006) 14 Jahrbuch für Recht und Ethik 287 ff; Günther Jakobs, 'Zur Genese von Rechtsverbindlichkeit' in Gerhard Höver (ed), *Verbindlichkeit unter den Bedingungen der Pluralität* (THEOS 1999)5 ff, 36 ff; Nathalia Bautista Pizarro, *Das erlaubte Vertrauen im Strafrecht. Studie zu dogmatischer Funktion und Grundlegung des Vertrauensgrundsatzes im Strafrecht* (Baden-Baden 2017)208 ff, 212 ff.

[20] See, eg, Hegel (n 13) s 36; Martha C Nussbaum, *Las fronteras de la justicia. Consideraciones sobre la exclusión* (Paidós 2007) 29 ff (44 ff).

[21] Locke (n 16) 55 ff; Hegel (n 13) ss 41 ff.

[22] Charles Taylor, 'The Politics of Recognition' in Charles Taylor (ed), *Multiculturalism. Examining the Politics of Recognition* (PUP 1994) 25 ff. See also Nussbaum (n 20) 29 ff.

[23] Pawlik (n 19) 280, 287 ff (289); Jakobs, 'Zur Genese von Rechtsverbindlichkeit' (n 19) 5 ff, 37.

[24] This leads to the question of legitimacy of punishment in the special context of unequal societies. See Jesús-María Silva Sánchez, *Mallum passionis. Mitigar el dolor del Derecho penal* (Atelier 2018)67 ff.

the judicial and collective recognition of the truth, as well as preventing the repetition of the cycle of violence.

On the other hand, it is important to take into account that war itself brings terrible excesses, as can unfortunately be observed in the Colombian case, where there are a considerable number of cases in which the rules of IHL were breached.[25] Trying to enforce an order that seeks to guarantee the minimum respect among citizens by creating situations that increase the risk of mutual interference is, therefore, contradictory. The war cannot end with the conducting of a war.

Lastly, alongside the mentioned foundational reasons, I share the argument that from a pragmatic point of view, considering the complexity of the armed conflict, the expectations of justice and reparation of the victims cannot be satisfied by means of the ordinary criminal justice system and that it seems inevitable that the challenges associated with the achievement of these goals will endure for a very long time.[26]

In conclusion, achieving equilibrium by relying exclusively on the principles of retributive justice in a situation of widespread instability (ie by activating the ordinary criminal justice system backed by the military forces) produces an incoherence in the liberal and democratic legal system: the protection of individual freedom by the mere use of force is an endeavour that is doomed to fail.[27] Consequently, it is necessary to rethink the traditional way of resolving conflicts in the context of social, economic, political, and cultural differences and to configure mechanisms that enable peacebuilding which is accepted by the norm recipients.[28] In this regard, the consideration of social philosophies emanating from particular communities is useful since they illuminate in a bottom-up manner how these communities conceive of developing and sustaining the vital normative bonds I have discussed in this section. I now turn to consider some of these philosophies in South Africa and Colombia.

[25] See the *Report on the Human Rights Situation in Colombia 2013–2017* from the International Office for Human Rights—Action Colombia (OIDHACO) <https://reliefweb.int/report/colombia/report-human-rights-situation-colombia-2013-2017-coordination-groups-and> accessed on 27 September 2023.

[26] Yesid Reyes Alvarado, 'Víctimas, fin y necesidad de la pena en el Derecho penal y en la llamada justicia transicional' in Elena Maculan and Alicia Gil Gil (eds), *La influencia de las víctimas en el tratamiento jurídico de la violencia colectiva* (Dykinson 2017) 188 ff, 201 ff.

[27] A different reflection would be to question whether punishing in ideal conditions of peace is always desirable. This is a deep discussion in criminal law science, which varies from the voices in favour of abolitionism to those who recognise different functions of punishment from classic retribution. Nevertheless, developing this discussion lies beyond the purposes of this chapter.

[28] Nathalia Bautista Pizarro, 'Die Bedeutung der Strafe im Rahmen eines Friedensverfahrens. Überlegungen am kolumbianischen Beispiel' (2017) 7–8 Zeitschrift für Internationale Strafrechtsdogmatik 363 ff.

3. *Ubuntu* and the South African Peace Process

The South African transitional experience represents an interesting paradigm, since it was conceived on the basis of amnesty in exchange for truth, guided ultimately by the communitarian principle of *ubuntu*. As the South African Interim Constitution (Act 200 of 1993) acknowledges, 'there is a need for understanding but not for vengeance, a need for reparation but not for retaliation, a need for ubuntu but not for victimization'. Therefore, the question of how a social philosophy became so important for a country that sought to overcome a troubled past must be examined.

A. *Ubuntu* as a National Reconciliation Model

Ubuntu is known as an African philosophy of the sub-Saharan Indigenous communities that is grounded in the recognition of interpersonal relationships between people and, therefore, on the values of reciprocity and solidarity.[29] As Archbishop Desmond Tutu, Nobel Prize winner and former Chairperson of the Truth and Reconciliation Commission (TRC), observed:

> *Ubuntu* is very difficult to render into a Western language. It speaks of the very essence of being human. When we want to give high praise to someone we say, '*Yu, u nobuntu*' Hey, so-and-so has *ubuntu*'. Then you are generous, you are hospitable, you are friendly and caring and compassionate. You share what you have. It is to say, 'My humanity is caught up, is inextricably bound up, in yours'. We belong in bundle of life. We say, 'A person is a person through other persons'. It is not, 'I think, therefore I am'. It says rather: 'I am human because I belong. I participate. I share'.[30]

The members of the Khulumani Support Group in Sharpeville have also described *ubuntu* as 'respect and behaving well to another'; as 'creating and recreating yourself through your connections with other people'; 'helping each other and just caring'; and 'so, if you have *ubuntu*, you have all the things that a human should have, respect, faith, understanding, to treat one another in a good manner'.[31] Based on these values, *ubuntu* has been recognised as providing the basis for a national reconciliation model by Thaddeus Metz.[32] In his opinion, *ubuntu* is a

[29] Metz, 'A Theory of National Reconciliation' (n 1) 119–35; Metz, 'South Africans Truth Reconciliation Commission in the Light of Ubuntu' (n 1) 223–26.

[30] Desmond Tutu, *No Future Without Forgiveness* (Doubleday 1999)ch 1.

[31] Interview carried on 27 April 2018 in Sharpeville for the purposes of this research.

[32] Metz, 'A Theory of National Reconciliation. Some Insights from Africa' (n 1) 122 ff; Metz, 'South Africans Truth Reconciliation Commission in the Light of Ubuntu: A Comprehensive Appraisal' (n 2) 226 ff.

communitarian way of life founded on the values of 'identity and solidarity', which can be seen as being in contrast with the Euro-American model of social ethics developed on a 'Kantian, utilitarian, contractual, egoistic or divine-command theory' basis.[33] Furthermore, according to the *ubuntu* philosophy, the individual realises what is most important about herself by relating harmoniously, by sharing a way of life with others, and caring for their quality of life. This means adjusting individual goals in order to achieve not merely peace, but also integration, into the community.[34] Consequently, *ubuntu* is a value that can guide a reconciliation model focused on restoring harmonious relationships between people and that, therefore, puts aside a simple need for retaliation.

B. *Ubuntu*, the TRC, and the Struggle for Recognition

The influence of the *ubuntu* philosophy in the fundamental choices made in the South African peace process can be observed. As is known, the transitional justice model focused on the work of the TRC, which was tasked to build collective memory through the retelling and recollection of individual stories and experiences of gross violations of human rights perpetrated under the apartheid system of racial segregation from 1948 to 1994.[35] The TRC also had to evaluate whether amnesty should be granted based on whether the perpetrator committed the crimes 'with a political purpose' and 'ha[d] made a full disclosure of all relevant facts', that is, whether they had disclosed the truth.[36] Furthermore, the TRC had to draw up recommendations for the government concerning reparations and rehabilitation for the victims of such violations.[37] According to this model, the values of truth, victims' reparation, and the construction of an egalitarian and democratic society were more important than retributive justice, that is, through the imposition of punishment in the criminal sense.[38] As the former TRC commissioner Mary Burton explains, the most important contribution of the TRC was to provide a space for the victims, in which they could 'tell their stories in their own words' and thereby alter the prevailing version of the truth to accommodate their experience.[39] A further goal was to clarify that human rights activists were no longer to be regarded as criminals, but rather to be seen as social leaders, 'freedom fighters'.[40]

[33] Metz, 'A Theory of National Reconciliation. Some Insights from Africa' (n 1) 123.

[34] Metz, 'South Africans Truth Reconciliation Commission in the Light of Ubuntu: A Comprehensive Appraisal' (n 1) 224 ff.

[35] Mary Ingouville Burton, *The Truth and Reconciliation Commission* (Jacana 2016)13 ff.

[36] ibid 29 ff, 30 f.

[37] ibid 82 ff.

[38] ibid 62: 'Amnesty was the price that had to be paid for the transition to the 1994 general election and installation of president Mandela . . . '.

[39] Tutu (n 30) 19; Burton (n 35) 33 ff; see also Metz, 'South Africans Truth Reconciliation Commission in the Light of Ubuntu' (n 1) 234–37.

[40] Burton (n 35) 66.

In this regard, the transitional justice model adopted in South Africa seems to be closer to the philosophy of *ubuntu* than to the meaning of retributive justice characteristic of the western legal tradition.

Additionally, it is also often thought that the *ubuntu* philosophy played an important role in the enactment of the Constitution of 1996. In this sense, former TRC commissioner Fazel Randera states that *ubuntu* is not only about reconciliation but also 'dignity ... human rights ... recognising the worth of every other person'.[41] In his opinion, the recognition of equality among all humans in South Africa, regardless of their ethnic origin or skin colour, is the biggest victory of the transition and in this way is clearly related to the philosophy of *ubuntu*, in the sense of 'reciprocal recognition' of persons as other persons. The victory was achieved symbolically through the liberation and election of President Mandela and the enactment of the final South African Constitution in 1996.[42] This interpretation is also reminiscent of the renowned idea of Hegel, the so-called 'struggle for recognition',[43] which refers to overcoming hierarchical social relations of serfdom or slavery.[44]

C. *Ubuntu* and Overcoming a Troubled Past through Narratives

Finally, *ubuntu*, within the context of South Africa's transition, has also been associated with traditional African modes of oral storytelling by providing victims with opportunities to overcome their troubled and hurtful past by sharing their personal stories.[45] Through these narratives, people are able to communicate, distance themselves from the pain, and, ultimately, to elucidate the truth and reconstruct memory, thereby beginning the process of healing the wounds of the past.[46] These kinds of victim-centred processes are also considered to be a special form of justice, referred to as a 'jurisprudence of care'.[47] In this regard, the members of the Sharpeville Khulumani Support Group refer to a similar way of reconstructing memory in their own processes.[48] Their meetings, for example, include a time for

41 Interview of 24 April 2018 in Johannesburg.

42 ibid.

43 Hegel (n 13) ss 36, 57; the reciprocal recognition theory dates back to Fichte's epistemological starting point: 'a human is a human through other humans' ('Ein Mensch ... wird nur unter Menschen ein Mensch') Johann Gottlieb Fichte, *Grundlage des Naturrechts nach Principien der Wissenschaftlehre* (first published 1796, Walter de Gruyter 1971) 39.

44 For this reason, contemporary political philosophy has appealed to this term to explain diverse emancipation movements at a global level. Axel Honneth, *Kampf um Anerkennung. Zur moralischen Grammatik sozialer Konflikte* (Suhrkamp 2014) 11 ff; Taylor (n 22) 5 ff; Jürgen Habermas, 'Struggles for Recognition in the Democratic Constitutional State' in Charles Taylor (ed), *Multiculturalism. Examining the Politics of Recognition* (PUP 1994) 107 ff.

45 Bohler-Muller (n 1) 133 ff.

46 ibid 140.

47 ibid 134 ff. She states that these kinds of proceedings allow us 'to situate others and ourselves and to ensure that rights and values' not as 'abstract rules or rigid legal formulations' (134).

48 Interview of 27 April 2018 in Sharpeville.

storytelling in that they remember the events of the Sharpeville Massacre of 21 March 1960, which is then complemented by a theatre play and a campfire on the annual anniversary of the incident. In this way, children and young people are also given an opportunity to learn about South Africa's painful history. The collective memory can, therefore, be saved through these cultural expressions and the community can experience a sense of reciprocal support, especially those who have not been recognised as victims or been compensated by the state. *Ubuntu* has, in conclusion, the power to join people together and to bring about a feeling of harmony and proximity between the members of a community. However, according to Burton, the effectiveness of *ubuntu* principles as a reconciliation tool may be more limited where people have been affected by intense transgressions of their rights.[49] Nevertheless, the feeling of being supported and listened to by others makes the difficult moments of confronting the troubled past easier in some ways, as the Khulumani members have explained.

From this analysis, it is possible to discern a relation between the philosophy of *ubuntu*—and its ethos of living together harmoniously in community—and the origin of non-traditional mechanisms of solving conflicts, which were applied in the transition to peace after the existence of an oppressive state. Indeed, this transitional process drew on the spirit of solidarity that characterises interpersonal relations in traditional communities. Thus, the achievements of peace and reconciliation as objectives of a national political programme reflected a communitarian sense of living. This mentality enabled greater importance to be given to jointly building a new South Africa, rather than following the path of retaliation. The aforementioned can be observed in the model of justice applied, which featured the creation and intervention of the Truth Commission, as well as the practice of ancestral oral rituals during the proceedings ('a jurisprudence of care'). Hence, transitional justice in this case is defined effectively to entail a form of restorative justice[50] that restores relations as a basis for peaceful future social interactions.

4. Social Philosophies and Building Peace in Colombia

Bearing in mind the multiple ways in which the *ubuntu* philosophy has infused the South African peace process, in this chapter, I have tried to find similar social philosophies in the Colombian context, not only in order to be taken as a reconciliation model as Metz articulates, but also as a source of knowledge to construct alternative mechanisms for the restoration of law and peacebuilding in times of transition. For that purpose, this research analyses three kinds of communities: the *Misak* Indigenous people, the *Afroatratenian* community, and the urban community of

[49] Burton, Interview of 18 April 2018 in Cape Town; Burton (n 35) 16 ff.
[50] Regarding this aspect, see Metz, Chapter 2 in this book.

Agroarte. In this framework, the concept of 'emotional communities' created in a study about the *Naya* territory is alluded to.[51] The presentation of the *Misak* and *Agroarte* communities is the result of specific fieldwork research undertaken for this particular study and the descriptions of the *Afroatatenians* coincide with the research conducted by anthropologist Quiceno[52] with some references to the work of anthropologist Arocha.[53]

A. The *Misaks'* Peaceful Way of Living Around the Nakuk

The *Misak* people are an Indigenous community that occupied the territory of Guambía in Cauca, a region that suffered continuous episodes of violence during the armed conflict and, even more so, since the days of the Spanish conquest.[54] Like the African notion of *ubuntu*, the *Misaks'* social philosophy is also founded on the value of reciprocal recognition in community relationships. The difference consists in the fact that nature and natural beings are also subjects: 'I cannot recognise myself without thinking about everything, the Nature, our territory', as Jefferson Chirimuscay explains.[55] *Misaks* are, like many Indigenous people in Colombia, deeply connected to the territory, both the Earth and Nature. Their meaning of life is 'to be connected with everything that surrounds us', 'the Earth is our mother and we are all part of the territory', 'our bodies are a territory', and that 'we all are connected by our footing, that is, the Earth'.[56] In this sense, they recognise the main principle of the *Misaks*: 'to live always and forever as people within our surroundings' (*Mananasrønkurri mananasrønkatik Misak Misak waramik*).

As the community healer Myriam Aranda explains, the connection to family, community, and the entire territory is practised in the *nachak* (the kitchen) around the *nakuk* (the stove with fire), which is where the children are born and where they learn their ancestral traditions.[57] Furthermore, in order to preserve consciousness of, and respect for, the territory and Nature, children grow up next to their parents, seeing how they take care of the plants, the woods, and how they weave. They learn

[51] Myriam Jimeno, Daniel Varela, and Angela Castillo, 'Violence, Emotional Communities, and Political Action in Colombia' in Morna Macleod and Natalia Di Marinis (eds), *Resisting Violence. Emotional Communities in Latin America* (Palgrave Macmillan 2018) 23–52.

[52] Natalia Quiceno, *Vivir sabroso. Luchas y movimientos afroatrateños en Bojayá, Chocó, Colombia* (Universidad del Rosario 2016).

[53] Jaime Arocha, *Ombligados de Ananse. Hilos ancestrales y modernos en el Pacífico colombiano* (Universidad Nacional de Colombia 1999).

[54] See the report related to the impact of the armed conflict and the structural perpetuation of violence since colonial times on Indigenous communities Centro Nacional de Memoria Histórica and Organización Indígena de Colombia, *Tiempos de vida y muerte. Memorias y luchas de los pueblos indígenas en Colombia* (2019).

[55] Interview of 10 June 2018.

[56] ibid with Esperanza Aranda, member of the circle of the administration of justice.

[57] Interview of 10 June 2018.

that each *Misak* is responsible for caring for the territory. For this reason, *Misaks* include in their concept of 'family' not only their human relatives, such as their parents, siblings, or children, but also the picture of sitting around the *nakuk* and being inextricably connected to trees, the river, the garden, animals, the sky, the sun, and the clouds.[58]

The importance of the *nakuk* infiltrates the entire community and informs their peaceful way of resolving differences. During social gatherings, the *nakuk* is surrounded by people and when somebody needs to solve a problem, this is discussed and done within the broader group.[59] Around the *nakuk*, diverse acts of solidarity arise, which resemble the *ubuntu* philosophy as a model of reconciliation. This is the case, for example, of the institution of the *minga* (*alik*), which is the meeting of the members of the community in order to accompany others in times of celebration or misfortune. It is about 'being together, sharing as equals'.[60] A *minga* can, for example, be organised when somebody dies. The entire community assists the affected family during the celebration of the funeral and helps to collect firewood for the *nakuk* or to prepare meals for everybody, as observed during the fieldwork research (see Figure 3.1). These kinds of activities are upheld by two ethical principles, the *Mayailei* law ('there is no place for selfishness', 'there is something for everyone') and also the *lata lata* principle ('equal equal' for everybody), which requires everyone to be treated as equal, avoiding preferential treatment of one person over another.[61]

The fact that differences are resolved by means of dialogue is one of the key ways in which the traditions of the *Misak* can inform a model of reconciliation that is motivated by restorative, rather than retributive, justice. The *Misak* people have never had military or police forces, since they do not believe in the use of force as a mechanism to resolve disputes.[62] Consequently, *Misaks* fully support the Colombian peace process led by former President Juan Manuel Santos.[63]

Their justice system is also grounded in this idea that social transgressions must be resolved with reference to the principles of generosity, reciprocity, and consensus, and thereby acknowledge the value of restorative measures such as those that draw on supernatural and religious principles.[64] However, in cases of serious

[58] Focus group activity of 9 and 10 June 2018 in Mamá Manuela School in Silvia – Cauca.

[59] Interview of 9 June 2018 with Luis Enrique Uyundé Aranda, chairperson for the education policies in Guambía.

[60] ibid 411.

[61] ibid.

[62] Interview of 9 June 2018 with Luis Enrique Uyundé Aranda, chairperson for the education policies in Guambía.

[63] Interview of 11 June 2018 with the governor of Guambía, Heriberto Tunubalá Paja.

[64] Herinaldi Gómez Valencia and Pueblos Indígenas de Colombia, *Justicias indígenas de Colombia: reflexiones para un debate cultural, jurídico y político* (Consejo Superior de la Judicatura 2015) 201, 412 ff; in this respect, it has been also established that the Colombian Indigenous communities could contribute to conceptualising and developing alternatives proceedings even in the ordinary criminal justice system, see Marzia Dalto, 'El aporte del derecho indígena a la construcción de las

Figure 3.1 Minga in a funeral, Guambía, Cauca, 2018 (Courtesy of the author)[a]
[a]Picture taken by Nathalia Bautista Pizarro, Guambía 2018.

misconduct (eg murder) the imposition of more punitive measures, such as imprisonment, has been accepted in some cases.[65] Nevertheless, this practice has been attributed to the *Misaks*' adaptation and assimilation into the ordinary legal system of Colombia, rather than a deliberate choice to use this non-restorative mode of conflict resolution.[66]

On the other hand, several weaving activities conducted by women from the *Misak* and the neighbouring Indigenous community, the *Nasa* people, have been documented, which seek to represent, in their ancestral pieces of clothing (*chumbes*), violent acts against women, which occurred during the armed conflict, thus, starting a female emancipation movement.[67] Recourse to aesthetic expressions as ways of approaching episodes of violence constitutes a mechanism of personal transformation and an efficient peacebuilding process, as has been reported in several cases.[68]

políticas criminales' in Thomas Mathiesen and others (eds), *Política criminal y libertad* (Universidad Externado de Colombia 2014) 239 ff.

[65] Gómez Valencia and Pueblos indígenas de Colombia (n 64) 412 ff.

[66] ibid 201.

[67] Gestoras de memoria histórica del Resguardo de Jambaló, *Hilando Memorias para tejer resistencias: Mujeres indígenas en lucha contra las violencias* (Impresol Ediciones 2015).

[68] Sierra León, 'Reparación simbólica, litigio estético y litigio artístico: reflexiones en torno al arte, la cultura y la justicia restaurativa en Colombia' in *Reparación Simbólica: Jurisprudencia, cantos y tejidos* (n 2) 19 ff.

To conclude, the *Misaks*' communitarian way of life offers several insights that could be significant for the Colombian peace process. First, their ancestral peaceful tradition of resolving conflicts can be highlighted. This demonstrates the prevalence of the means of dialogue and renouncing the use of force, which is manifested in the ancestral ritual of gathering around the fire. This takes place together with the active accompaniment of the members of the community that require care. Hence, the peaceful mentality of the *Misaks* together with their solidarity, on the one hand, can legitimate the peace process itself, which seeks to end the national armed conflict, as occurred with the *ubuntu* philosophy in South Africa. On the other hand, its model of resolving conflicts could be beneficial in restorative processes that include the participation of the community, victims, and ex-combatants. Indeed, the construction of narratives in communitarian spaces, in order to elucidate the different sides of the causes and history of war under respectful conditions of dialogue and even through ancestral aesthetic practices, could become, over time, solid processes of memory building and a step by step guarantee of healthy co-existence.

B. The *Afroatratenians* and the *vivir sabroso* Philosophy

The *Afroatratenian* community[69] also believes in values of peaceful co-existence and solidarity. Similar to *ubuntu* and the *Misaks*' conception of the good, the *Afroatratenian* moral system is also grounded in the recognition of the individual as a member of a territory and a community. This Afro-descendant population lives in the Atrato river basin of the department of Chocó, in the Pacific Coast region. In the 1990s, rebels and far-right paramilitary groups, as well as drug traffickers and miners, took over this area. The most emblematic tragedy took place on 2 May 2002, when the rebel group of the FARC-EP used improvised explosives, without regard for civilian casualties, to attack a far-right paramilitary group (AUC) and in so doing massacred the people that had been taking shelter in Bellavista's town church during the war in the Bojayá region. Anthropologist, Quiceno travelled to this territory in order to understand how the community was able to deal with this kind of violence and discovered that community had a particular philosophy that she called *vivir sabroso*, which means to live lusciously.[70] This social philosophy means 'keeping the balance between temperature, movement and distance'. It is about living in a way that acknowledges how to handle 'danger, risk, tension and conflict' but which does not endorse 'the use of force or the extermination of the other'.[71] *Vivir sabroso* is also 'a process' in the sense that it offers 'the possibility to

69 Quiceno (n 52) 16 ff.
70 ibid 4.
71 ibid.

embark, to put in motion, to activate and balance life in an autonomous manner, without any militarisation of the territories, without having fear and imposing ways of living that conduce to stalling or being stuck'.[72]

The *vivir sabroso* philosophy is embodied in African ancestral traditions, such as the way people connect to their territory, their music, and its use as an accompaniment of many social activities as well as the way they understand the relationship between the world of the dead and the world of the living.[73] As with the *Misak* people, for the *Afroatratenians* the connection to the territory and Nature is central to the way this community exists in the world. As Arocha explains, it begins with a ritual performed with the umbilical cord,[74] a widespread practice of many Afro-descendant communities in Chocó that demonstrates their bond to the cultural traditions of their African ancestry.[75] When babies are born, the umbilical cord, after going through a healing process, is buried with the tree that her pregnant mother planted in their terrace, a tree that the child will know as his 'belly button'.[76] Additionally, the community is founded upon the notion of *compadrazgo* (joint fatherhood), which is about creating a big family, connected in the territory by the rivers, where communitarian activities such as farming take place.[77] In this environment, the way of leading their lives is grounded in a strong feeling of solidarity and care for each other, which also allows the construction of relationships based on respect and political cooperation with the *Embera* Indigenous community, with whom they share their territory.[78] In this regard, a peaceful co-existence between many Afro-descendant and Indigenous communities has been demonstrated, not only in the areas of Atrato but also in San Juan and Baudó in Chocó[79] (see Figure 3.2).

On the whole, the *Afroatratenian* community lived peacefully since the enactment of the Constitution of 1991 and the later issued Act 70/1993, which recognised the territories of the Afro-descendant population as a collective property with political and administrative autonomy.[80] However, peace was jeopardised with the arrival of armed groups, companies, and drug traffickers that aimed to exploit their natural resources and thereby destroy the balance with Nature and their everyday life.[81] Nevertheless, Quiceno observed that their strong feeling of

[72] ibid 5.
[73] ibid 159 ff, 164 ff.
[74] ibid 108 ff, 111 ff.
[75] Arocha (n 53) 13 ff, in particular, by using the metaphor of the *ombligados de Ananse*, meaning, those whose umbilical cord was treated to bond with *Ananse*, the spider goddess who dominates chaos, and in whom most of the Indigenous people of the Afro-American communities and the communities in the Bay of Benin (Africa) believe.
[76] ibid.
[77] Quiceno (n 52) 29 ff, 59 ff.
[78] ibid 65 ff, 68 ff, 70 ff, 80 ff.
[79] Arocha (n 53) 127 ff, 141 ff.
[80] Arocha (n 53) 127 ff; Quiceno (n 52) 65 ff, 70 ff, 83 ff.
[81] Quiceno (n 52) 70 ff.

Figure 3.2 Atrato River in Quibdó, Chocó (Courtesy of the author)[b]
[b]Picture taken by Nathalia Bautista Pizarro, Quibdó 2019.

solidarity helped them to remain resilient and to resist the violence. For example, like the *Misaks*, the *Afroatratenians* are especially generous and compassionate in the case of a death of a member, since the ordinary routine of the entire community is immediately suspended as everybody assists the affected family with the process of leading the deceased into the world of the dead.[82] This commonly begins with raising funds to cover funeral expenses, including drinks, meals, and cigarettes for the attendees that come to pray.[83]

Furthermore, as Quiceno explains, the *Afroatratenians* have resisted resorting to violence by denouncing certain victimising acts through their saints, such as Santo Ecce Homo and the Virgen del Carmen.[84] Indeed, she observed that after the massacre in Bellavista's church and the subsequent episode of violence, the people publicly denounced this violence during religious celebrations by performing acts such as crossing the rivers with rafts and creating sculptures of their saints (*balsadas*), in which the saints, but not the people themselves, were the ones who expressed the

[82] ibid 164 ff.
[83] ibid 167 ff.
[84] ibid 135 ff.

magnitude of the damage caused in their territories by the conflict.[85] Moreover, the way of singing to their saints, the *alabados*, helped them to compose protest songs against the victimising acts, such as the *alabado* of the Cristo Mutilado de Bojayá, who became a new saint, embodied in the remains of the sculpture of Jesus that survived the massacre in Bellavista's church. This is an object that helps to keep alive the memory of this tragic day.[86] These ways of dealing with, and trying to overcome, an intense episode of violence show us the power of aesthetic expressions to publicly recognise the victimising acts, and to build memory through the narratives of music and religious rituals.[87] In this regard, the *vivir sabroso* philosophy can also be taken as an alternative philosophical approach to resolve conflicts in times of transition. Additionally, it represents the possibility of restoring order through solidarity and collective intervention.

C. *Agroarte* and the Return to the Land

Another interesting case that can be useful for the conception of restorative measures in transition and a broader peacebuilding process is that found in *Agroarte*, an urban community who were also victims of serious violations of human rights perpetrated by the national armed forces and far-right paramilitary groups in Medellín's Comuna 13 (District 13). These armed groups took over this area as part of a programme of extermination of rebel militias, which started a series of military interventions in 2002 that ended with the so-called *Operación Orión* (Orion Operation) executed in October of that year.[88] Many civilians disappeared, some were massacred, and others were forced to leave their homes due to death threats. *Agroarte*'s resistance against these acts of violence has endured for more than seventeen years.[89] Its main objective is to preserve the truth and memory of the

[85] ibid 146 ff; this kind of practice is similar to Yolanda Sierra León's concept of 'aesthetic litigation' discussed in León, Chapter 6 in this book and in Sierra León, 'Reparación simbólica, litigio estético y litigio artístico: reflexiones en torno al arte, la cultura y la justicia restaurativa en Colombia' in *Reparación Simbólica: Jurisprudencia, cantos y tejidos* (n 2) 25–30.

[86] Quiceno (n 52) 151 ff; the *alabados* became a common way to express and denounce the violence recognised in the country by artist Juan Manuel Echavarría in his collection, *Bocas de Ceniza* <https://jmechavarria.com/es/work/bocas-de-ceniza/> accessed 1 September 2020.

[87] Quiceno (n 52) 151 ff, 141 ff; in this sense see also Sierra Léon, 'Reparación simbólica, litigio estético y litigio artístico: reflexiones en torno al arte, la cultura y la justicia restaurativa en Colombia' in *Reparación Simbólica: Jurisprudencia, cantos y tejidos* (n 2) 19 ff.

[88] See in this regard the report of the Group on Historical Memory of the National Commission for the Reparation and Reconciliation (Grupo de Memoria Histórica de la Comisión Nacional de Reparación y Conciliación), *La huella invisible de la guerra. Desplazamiento forzado en la Comuna 13* (2011).

[89] See Sandra Milena Álvarez Ramírez, *La Escombrera: entre la memoria y la impunidad. La búsqueda política de las mujeres por la vida, la verdad y la justicia*, Degree Thesis, Faculty of Social and Human Sciences, Universidad de Antioquia, 2010; Juan Sebastián Martínez Rincón, *Por debajo de la tierra van creciendo las raíces. Un encuentro con Agroarte en las Comunas 13 y 3 de Medellín*, Degree Thesis, Faculty of Anthropology, Universidad de Los Andes, 2018.

victims of the aforementioned crimes through the participation of people of all ages in different cultural activities that have become testimonies of the serious violations of human rights that, up until now, the Colombian state has yet to recognise and respond to satisfactorily.[90]

Behind this artistic movement, there is a concrete social philosophy that operates in a similar way to the spirit of solidarity and reciprocity of *ubuntu*. *Agroarte* was founded by women that wanted to change the cycle of violence in the Comuna 13 territory, where the effects of the armed conflict have been felt especially strongly.[91] These women invited young people and children to plant vegetables—and sow ornamental vegetables—near their homes and, in this way, to begin to rediscover their cultural identities. The inhabitants of this sector came mostly from the countryside as victims of forced displacement and many planted what they cultivated in their former homes. As they began to talk about the violence, they were able to confront their personal feelings of pain and commemorate the victims. Over the years, a social philosophy was born around planting, cooking, and eating together; accompanying families to the funerals of young people who had been murdered in the midst of urban violence; and composing hip-hop music.[92] As an organisation, it is also part of the common action led by many artistic and cultural groups that build peace in the territories of Medellín, called *Unión entre Comunas* (Union between Districts). Hip-hop music, which embodies the flow of rhythms and rhymes in the lyrics of a song, demonstrates the power of music to transform the personal lives of many people, especially the young who have suffered from violence and the terrible effects of drug-trafficking in these areas.[93]

As with the *Misak* and the *Afroatratenian* communities, *Agroarte* is based on the connection of the people to the territory. They think that 'every violence inflicted in our territories, is also inflicted on the bodies of all their members'.[94] The

[90] Considering the large number of human rights violations, there are few decisions against these perpetrators. On the one hand, there are several decisions and proceedings against ex members of far-right paramilitary groups such as the Decision of 6 February 2008 of the Juzgado Tercero Penal Especializado de Medellín against the higher commander of the Cacique Nutibara Front, Diego Fernando Murillo, alias 'Don Berna', and some references to the context of violence in the Comuna 13 in other cases, as the one against Fredi Alonso Pulgarín Gaviria, alias '*La Pulga*', before the Tribunal Superior de Medellín, Sala de Justicia y Paz, Reporting Judge María Consuelo Rincón Jaramillo, Decision of 9 September 2016 and in the decision against some members of the Bloque Héroes de Granada, Tribunal Superior de Medellín, Sala de Justicia y Paz, Reporting Judge Juan Guillermo Cárdenas Gómez, 21 February 2019. On the other hand, retired General Mario Montoya, one of the military commanders during the interventions in the Comuna 13, signed a document to submit himself, on 17 October 2018, to the Special Jurisdiction for Peace and has been formally linked to Case 03 'Deaths illegally presented as casualties in combat by state agents'—JEP Communication 014, 11 February 2020—the most famous precedent comes from international tribunals, *Yarce y otras v Colombia* CIDH 22 November 2016.

[91] Interviews with EL AKA of 4 March 2018 and Wilmar Botina of 26 August 2017 in Medellín.

[92] Interviews with Wilmar Botina of 26 August 2017 and Ghido Alma and El Metan-o of 2 March 2018 in Medellín.

[93] Interviews with DJ Wam of 27 August 2017 and the young rappers of the AK-47 hip-hop band of 2 August 2017 in Medellín.

[94] Interview Wilmar Botina of 26 August 2017 in Medellín and EL AKA of 11 September 2017 in Bogotá.

Figure 3.3 Urban gardening of Agroarte in San Javier 'Galerías Vivas', Comuna 13, Medellín (Courtesy of the author)[c]

[c]Picture taken by Nathalia Bautista Pizarro, Medellín 2017.

evocation of this idea and their rural life is present in their cultural and artistic activities—especially in the symbolic planting (see Figure 3.3) and their performance *Cuerpos Gramaticales* (Grammatical Bodies). As EL AKA, one of the hip-hop singers (and a leader of the community) explains, territorial connection through artistic expression helps these people to overcome their feelings of dislocation and alienation and find catharsis.[95] In this regard, the members of *Agroarte* assert that they 'are staying above the streets, streets made of asphalt, but under the asphalt is the Earth, and we all come from the Earth'.

Even though *Agroarte* shares some values with the Colombian communities, such as the connection to the territory and the foundation of their relations based on solidarity rather than egoism and individuality, it distinguishes itself by being a community built by members from diverse cultural origins. *Agroarte* is about forming a community based on the goal of resistance against violence, the necessity of preserving memory, having solidarity with all who suffered during the conflict, and then reuniting those who share these ideals in order to create a sense of ownership of their territories and of community involvement in the process of healing and peacebuilding.

[95] Interviews with EL AKA of 4 March 2018 in Medellín.

In this regard, the formation of similar communities in Colombia has been observed subsequently. This can be seen in the *Naya* community in the Southwest of the country, which was affected by the incursion of far-right paramilitary groups during the Holy Week of 2001, where more than forty people were murdered. Thereafter, several families from various ethnic backgrounds created a new community based on emotional identification.[96] In this regard, the members of the community (composed of Indigenous people, Afro-descendants, and peasants) organised meetings to commemorate the victims, which contributed to the start of a conversation about the victimising acts.[97] According to expert opinion, these meetings have been shown to have transformative potential[98] because through the narratives, the *Naya* build social bonds, grounded in 'emotions' and 'mutual-identification' as victims of rights violations.[99] Consequently, it is not necessary to have the same ethnic origin in order to build communities based on identity and solidarity between people who have suffered the pain of the war, a fact that can also be useful for the configuration of restorative measures in transition and building a diverse and peaceful Colombian political community more generally.

5. Conclusion and Final Considerations

This chapter has sought to illustrate the ways in which ancestral and cultural philosophical values of particular communities can contribute to building a restorative conception of transitional justice, which contrasts with the typical retributive mechanisms of justice of modern society. The studies related to *ubuntu* in South Africa and the selected cases of the Colombian communities teach us, first, that it is possible to resolve disputes without resorting only to punishment and retaliation but also by emphasising communitarian values such as solidarity and mutual respect between members of a community. The essential premise is that once someone is part of a community, that person will never be alone and will always be accompanied with care, love, and consideration, through good and bad times. This way of thinking and acting enables the application or creation of mechanisms to overcome the complexity of the damage caused by war, conflict, and oppression. Consequently, different ways of seeing life lead to different ways of understanding justice.

Likewise, we can observe that a wide variety of mechanisms already exist in the practices of these communities, which approach the conception of justice from a restorative point of view: the differences and conflicts can be resolved by dialogue,

96 Jimeno, Varela, and Castillo (n 51) 23 ff.
97 ibid 24 ff.
98 ibid 24.
99 ibid 24 ff.

narrative, consent, or advice. Additionally, the ideas of 'belonging to each other' and 'taking care of each other' bring people together. In such an atmosphere, a process of reflection about difficult moments of violence can develop naturally. On this basis, the role of justice is different from the one that is often applied in individualistic contexts, since the stakeholders and the community can participate in more common and open spaces, in order to develop a sense of closure from the terrible victimising acts. This approach is also of importance in the treatment of former *combatants*, to support the process of finding their place as members of their communities and society, that is, as civilians.

Accordingly, the chapter goes beyond documentating these alternative approaches and suggests the desirability of including mechanisms of justice that reflect the cultural diversity of the communities that make up large political communities such as those in Colombia and South Africa. Traditional legal institutions are often presented as abstract concepts, imposed through a certain hierarchy by officials.[100] However, there is in fact no universal model of reparation, since every territory suffers the effects of war in different ways and every community has its own expectations and norms about appropriate responses. Consequently, reparation has to be configured in such a way that makes sense for the people involved, according to their traditions or ways of living, introducing, for example, cultural and artistic activities. Furthermore, the normative bond between people can be built this way as a matter of identity and provide the basis for a sustainable peace.

In this sense, the restorative measures of the Colombian peace agreements in fact impressively embody some of these ideas by recognising the reality of the communities and their social norms. Colombia applies concepts such as a differential approach, and encourages a more active participation of the victims in the proceedings, and the creation of scenarios of social fabric reconstruction, attending to the particularities of the territories, including the contribution of liable agents.[101] If implemented properly then, it provides the hope of restoring relationships between people and building the foundations for not only the absence of conflict, but strong communal bonds.

[100] See, eg, Natalia Cardona Berrío, Orlando Arroyave Álvarez, and Luis Ramirez, 'Procesos de reparación, entre la reparación estatal y la recuperación comunitaria' (2019) El Ágora USB 387–403.

[101] See, eg, the reparations chapter, Final Peace Agreement 5.1.3. and the sanction system Act 1957/2019, arts 126 and 141; see also the agreement between Indigenous communities and the Comprehensive System of Truth, Justice, Reparation and Non-Repetition regarding the cooperation in activities within the peace process *Diversidad étnica y cultural, pluralismo jurídico y consulta previa. Instrumentos de coordinación y articulación entre los pueblos indígenas y el sistema integral de verdad, justicia, reparación y no repetición (SIVJRNR)* (2019) <https://www.jep.gov.co/DocumentosJEPWP/protocolo.pdf> accessed on 1 September 2020, and the Protocol signed between Afro Colombian communities and the Special Jurisdiction for Peace *Protocolo de Relacionamiento entre la JEP y los pueblos negros, afrocolombianos, raizal y palenqueros* (2021) <https://www.jep.gov.co/Infografas/participacion/Protocolo%20Relacionamiento%20JEP%20y%20pueblos%20NARP%209%20febrero%202021%20pag.pdf> accessed on 27 July 2022.

4

Joint Reflection: Economic Goods and Communitarian Values

Thaddeus Metz and Nathalia Bautista Pizarro

1. Introduction

The prior contributions by us, Bautista Pizarro and Metz, address the proper way to respond to gross human rights violations in the light of certain values prevalent in South America and Africa. Specifically, considering the histories of Colombia and South Africa and some of the moral beliefs of a few ethnic or victims' communities with diverse cultural origins, we develop non-individualist and non-retributive approaches to the major conflicts that have taken place in our respective countries. Broadly speaking, we both advocate relational and constructive forms of transitional justice that make victim compensation central.

Specifically, according to Bautista Pizarro, it is important not merely to rely on legal strategies, but also to draw on the values, cultures, and traditions of local peoples, in order to resolve conflict.[1] She highlights respects in which those from three different Colombian societies believe in communitarian ways of 'restoring the normative bond' between former enemies as well as the social fabric, destroyed by the war, approaches that the state ought to consider when making reparations. Metz appeals to communal/harmonious values frequently associated with the South African Indigenous philosophy of *ubuntu* (and the Colombian Indigenous worldview of *buen vivir*) to construct an account of reconciliation, and he brings out what reconciliation entails for how to make economic restitution in a post-conflict society.[2] He maintains that offenders ought to undergo burdensome ways of providing property and opportunities to their victims so as to improve the socio-economic quality of their lives.

In this chapter, we consider how Metz's largely *ubuntu*-based reconciliatory approach to reparations might be relevant to Colombia in ways that he did not consider, after which we reflect on how the kinds of communitarian practices Bautista Pizarro advances might be relevant to South Africa and strengthen its transitional justice model. We conclude that these cross-applications are revealing, pointing

[1] Nathalia Bautista Pizarro, Chapter 3 in this book.
[2] Thaddeus Metz, Chapter 2 in this book.

Thaddeus Metz and Nathalia Bautista Pizarro, *Joint Reflection: Economic Goods and Communitarian Values* In: *Transitional Justice, Distributive Justice, and Transformative Constitutionalism.* Edited by: David Bilchitz and Raisa Cachalia, with Magdalena Inés Correa Henao and Nathalia Bautista Pizarro, Oxford University Press. © Thaddeus Metz and Nathalia Bautista Pizarro 2023. DOI: 10.1093/oso/9780192887627.003.0004

out how economic compensation in Colombia should plausibly be influenced by cultural factors, and how considerations of culture in South Africa call for compensation beyond economic factors.

2. Applying *Ubuntu* to Colombia

According to the concept of compensatory justice developed by Metz, the restoration of law after an intense period of violence should include the allocation of economic goods as an important manifestation of harmony and a vital component of transitional justice. Having offenders provide property and opportunities to their victims not merely would be a way of improving the latter's quality of life, but also could and should have symbolic meaning. Indeed, following this perspective, those who have caused pain to others should compensate for damages, not necessarily via financial compensation, but perhaps by executing material compensatory acts such as building a school or working on a farm, as a way to express remorse. Part of the relational value of reconciliation would thereby be nurtured and encouraged. Taking this approach into account, we reflect on the potential role of economic goods in Colombian communities, and propose a culturally sensitive interpretation of the meaning of Metz's concept of compensatory justice for these cases.

Economic goods are a material means of configuring peoples' lives and their relations with others. Even more, they are a way to be related to the 'things' of the world, a way to materialise or realise a project that could exist only in an abstract, purely psychological manner.[3] For that reason, each community needs economic goods in order to operate according to its particular understanding of the world and configure its individual and common life in accordance with that viewpoint.

In the case of the *Misak* people, discussed in Bautista Pizarro's chapter, material well-being is closely associated with access to 'territory' and simultaneously with the bonds that develop between the land, all natural beings (including humans, whose bodies are also a territory), and, in fact, the entire cosmos. Each *Misak* has the duty to care for their territory in order to maintain the balance between all beings in that locale and beyond. In this regard, one should understand that damage caused to a member of the community or a part of the territory has larger implications for the entire community, in terms of its order. In this case, as mentioned, the appropriate compensatory measures do not correspond to the meaning of retribution or indeed any other individualist ethic, but involve performing restorative

[3] Georg Wilhelm Friedrich Hegel, *Grundlinien der Philosophie des Rechts* (first published in 1821, Surhkamp 1986) § 41.

actions that can include spiritual tasks meant to restore balance throughout society and nature.[4]

Yet, the question regarding how an agent liable for damages could comply with these restorative ends of special justice is something that has to be defined by the Indigenous communities on a case by case basis, since they are, or at least should be, autonomous.[5] In general, the recognition of damages inflicted on 'the peoples, communities, their members, authorities, as well as on the ancestral territory and its spirituality' has been demanded.[6] Likewise, the reparation must be 'transformative' in regards to these dimensions of the damages, taking into account that these are peoples, cultures, and territories that have been 'historically violated in their material and immaterial dimension'.[7] Thus, reparations must also aim to strengthen self-determination of peoples and the elimination of 'frameworks of discrimination and marginalisation' as possible causes of victimising acts.[8]

A wrongdoer who is not from the community could have some difficulties in fulfilling these tasks due to cultural differences. However, taking into account the cooperation between Indigenous communities and state organs within the framework of the peace process, liable agents could at least undertake logistical tasks or provide resources for members of the community so that they can carry them out. The aforementioned would also conform to the sanction with a restorative function of the Special Jurisdiction for Peace and the measures of reparation of the Final Peace Agreement.[9] In this sense, there are cases in which the community itself has expressed the need for external support to conduct restorative actions, as was the case, in fact, of a group of *Misak* and *Nasa* women, who sought the help of several organisations to make 'memory weaves' in response to the violence inflicted against women.[10]

A second major way that culture should probably influence economic reparation, beyond facilitating healing ceremonies and collective actions, would be to return stolen land. Economic compensation for the *Misaks*, as for all the ethnic communities in Colombia, should involve guaranteeing free access to their

[4] For broadly similar views amongst Indigenous African peoples, see Egbeke Aja, 'Crime and Punishment: An Indigenous African Experience' (1997) 31 Journal of Value Inquiry 353.

[5] The autonomy of the Laws of Origin and Nature, the Word of Life, the Major Law, or the Special Law of Indigenous peoples shall be recognised in all the proceedings and stages of the Special Jurisdiction for Peace. *Diversidad étnica y cultural, pluralismo jurídico y consulta previa. Instrumentos de coordinación y articulación entre los pueblos indígenas y el sistema integral de verdad, justicia, reparación y no repetición (SIVJRNR)* (2019) 11 <https://www.jep.gov.co/DocumentosJEPWP/protocolo.pdf> accessed 1 September 2020.

[6] ibid 12, numeral 5 'Transformative reparation' (*Reparación Transformadora*).

[7] ibid.

[8] ibid.

[9] Act 1957/2019, arts 128 and 141; Final Peace Agreement 5.3.1, eg, Plans for collective reparation with a territorial approach 5.1.3.3.2.

[10] Gestoras de memoria histórica del Resguardo de Jambaló, *Hilando Memorias para tejer resistencias: Mujeres indígenas en lucha contra las violencias* (Centro Nacional de Memoria Histórica 2016).

ancestral territories, which is of utmost importance, as their meaning of life is determined by their material and spiritual connections to their respective lands. That is the reason why *Misaks* think that the period of violence for them began with the Spanish conquest, when free access to their territory was blocked by the process of colonisation. Consequently, next to the recognition of their cultural identity and political autonomy, land reform is one of the main issues to be considered when compensating an Indigenous community in Colombia and contexts similar to it. Considerations of culture arguably should shape the form of economic restitution, with land being central and unable to be substituted with, say, the provision of money or education. The right way to show remorse and to improve the quality life of Indigenous Colombian communities, such as the *Misaks*, is at least partly by considering what they find important. That means attending to their spiritual and material relation to their territory and Nature as well as applying restorative measures such as guaranteeing free access to the land.

The point also applies to Afro-descendant communities in Colombia, whose ancestors were taken from Africa and brought as slaves to the Americas, and who have an interest in recovering ways of life that had been suppressed. They suffered harm in that they were forced to learn a foreign language and to try to forget their religious and cultural origins. An apt form of compensation would enable Afro-descendants to retain and develop their ancestral customs and related practices, which, in turn, would also mean according them their own territory.

Recalling the case of the *Afroatratenian* community from Bautista Pizarro's prior chapter, as with the *Misaks*, the meaning of economic goods for them is defined by the connection to their territory and Nature. The territory is inhabited not only by the living, but also by the dead and other spirits, with whom the living must stay in contact. Furthermore, according to the *vivir sabroso* philosophy, the community needs to be in motion to exist, and, thus, the construction of personal relations increases through the extension of the rivers. Free access to their territory, in particular, freedom of movement, was impeded by the presence of armed groups. Many members of the community were, and still are, being murdered and forcefully displaced. In this regard, compensating this Afro-descendant community should be defined through the meaning of being connected to a specific territory, sharing it with the dead and the spirits, and being able to move through a land that is connected by the rivers. In this sense, Colombian constitutional case law has in fact recognised the Atrato river as a subject of rights and has publicly called for its protection.[11] This is an important precedent not only to accept its channel as a stage where the memory of the damages of war is depicted, but also to acknowledge the rightful actions of their inhabitants to resist.[12] Likewise, the community

[11] Constitucional Court T-622/2016.

[12] Pilar Riaño-Alcalá and Natalia Quiceno, 'Presencias, sensibilidades y políticas cotidianas del habitar en el Atrato' (July–December 2020) 56(2) Revista Colombiana de Antropología 7–17.

gained state support to commemorate, in November 2019, the funerals of the victims of the 2 May 2001 massacre according to their ancestral practices—this is an important issue in order to overcome the episodes of violence, bearing in mind their special relation with the dead.[13]

We observe again that economic goods acquire a special meaning for Colombian ethnic communities: the material side of reparation has to respond to their spiritual identities and, vitally, to acknowledge the centrality of land to the pursuit of transitional justice in Colombia. In other words, it is not only about compensating through money or employment, important as these would be, but also about materially guaranteeing the restoration of breached rights in a way that is respectful of the cultures and traditions of affected communities and that recognises the way that land is integral to the identities of Indigenous peoples. Compensating in this way is essential for human rights violators to express remorse, or for the state to express its disapproval of the way they treated their victims.

However, there are other peoples in Colombia for whom the abilities to undertake healing practices or obtain access to a certain territory are not so important. For them, economic compensation should take a different form, although issues of culture remain relevant in principle.

In the case of the urban community of *Agroarte*, constituted by people with diverse cultural origins, the meaning of economic goods—at least as a matter of compensation in a transitional justice process—seems similar to the one in modern western society. However, there is also a demand for justice in a symbolic horizon, and, in this sense, it could be supported by Metz's conception of compensatory justice. *Agroarte* was born in an area of Medellín where people have serious challenges such as access to property, health care, and education. As mentioned in Bautista Pizarro's chapter, this community suffered a particularly intense episode of violence during a military intervention in the area in 2002, in which people lost their relatives or were displaced through force. From the perspective of a symbolic horizon, *Agroarte*, as a philosophy that speaks in the name of the victims, 'of those who do not have voices',[14] demands the complete elucidation of the truth of those who have participated in this armed intervention. In one of their songs, members of *Agroarte* also demand their 'remorse' as a condition to 'forgive them'.[15] In addition, they believe in restorative processes and the power of joining people especially

[13] ibid 15–16; Diana Camila Orjuela Villanueva, '¿Qué hacemos con tanto muerto junto? Tratar la muerte violenta y masiva en el Medio Atrato' (July–December 2020) 56(2) Revista Colombiana de Antropología 7–17.

[14] Interview with El Metan-o on 2 March 2018 in Medellín.

[15] '*No soñamos con matar a quien nuestra gente mató, pues buscamos la verdad estando lejos del rencor, no hay perdón por lo que hicieron, pues no olvidamos nada de aquello que sucedió, escucha amigo mío, no es posible perdonar al que perdón nunca pidió*' ('We don't dream of killing the one who killed our people, since we search for the truth being away from bitterness, there is no forgiveness for what they've done, as we don't forget what happened, listen to me my friend, it isn't possible to forgive someone who has not asked for it'), Cuerpos Gramaticales, Hip Hop Agrario.

through recovering their connection to the territory by symbolic planting and arts. Economic resources should be spent on revealing the truth about what transpired as well as fostering cultural responses to it.

The *Agroarte* points to the need for recognition of the inhabitants of the hills of Medellín as equals, especially by reinforcing the pride of belonging to the neighbourhood, as their song *Mi Barrio* alludes. In addition, in their song *Cuerpos Gramaticales*, they demand from the government the right to free education instead of conscription. In this respect, the compensation for damages to this urban community has to be defined in terms of not only the significance of truth and symbolism, but also a materially better life for the victims, on which Metz mainly focuses in his contribution. The situation of inequality of the inhabitants of these impoverished areas of Medellín has to be considered, particularly since poverty has been regularly used as an excuse or motivation to commit human atrocities in Colombia. However, it is not merely about compensating according to the economic situation of each victim, calculating the damage caused to the individual at the moment of the human rights violation, but also about understanding the victim's relative economic situation in society, before and after the violation. For this reason, the peace agreement[16] and the Statutory Law of the Special Jurisdiction for Peace 1957/2019[17] have created a differential approach in order to capture the special gravity of particular human rights violations that considers the vulnerability of the person (eg being a member of Indigenous or Afro-descendant communities, or being a woman, child, or elder) and specifically taking into account the fact of their being amongst the worst off. This approach could also be applied in the case of the aforementioned ethnic communities.

To sum up, while Metz in his chapter maintains that a just response to human rights violations requires offenders to compensate their victims with economic goods, his analysis is one-sided, failing to take account of how an *ubuntu* communitarianism plausibly means that culture should influence the allocation of these goods. Upon reflection, we have suggested in this chapter that the relevant economic goods depend at least partially upon a given community's self-conception, which in some cases will mean a focus on providing resources that would facilitate spiritual healing and reconnection with land.

3. Applying Colombian Communitarianism to South Africa

African societies have mainly been the ones known for featuring reconciliation as a way to respond to large-scale social conflict. Although South Africa's Truth and Reconciliation Commission (TRC) is the best known, also influential have

[16] 5.1.2., I, 7.
[17] Art 13.

been reconciliatory processes in Sierra Leone, Zimbabwe, and Rwanda. These approaches grew out of Indigenous value systems that prize relational values such as a sense of togetherness, cooperation, mutual aid, and compassion. Bautista Pizarro's chapter reveals that similar values pertaining to harmony or community have been salient amongst Indigenous Colombian peoples[18] and that they have also tended to ground a broadly reconciliatory approach to human rights violations.

Of particular interest are Bautista Pizarro's discussions of the *Misak* and *Afroatratenian* communities. The former focuses on reciprocal recognition, an inclusive and egalitarian relationship meant to include not merely human beings, but also the natural world as a whole, while the latter is centred on *vivir sabroso* (meaning living lusciously or well) and idealises balance or harmony between human beings, ancestral spirits, and the environment. Bautista Pizarro traces the way that both communitarian value systems have grounded responses to the Colombian conflict that are not retributive and are instead focused on repairing broken relationships, where doing so includes addressing people's identities and hence their religions, aesthetic orientations, senses of place, and, particularly, their relationships to land.

The relevance of people's identities for reconciliation had not been particularly visible in either the South African reconciliation processes or the normative reflections on them in the literature, at least until recently with the rise of the 'decolonial' and FeesMustFall movements in 2015. The practical and theoretical focus, at least in respect of South Africa's TRC and other policies adopted at the end of apartheid, had largely been on obtaining the truth about past misdeeds and then allocating money, land, and similar kinds of resources expected to improve socio-economic conditions. However, Bautista Pizarro's analysis of the way that culture should be considered relevant to effecting reconciliation in Colombia is pertinent to the (South) African context and can make sense of the movements mentioned in Section 2. If reconciliation of the right sort includes an expression of remorse on the part of the offender, which, in turn, means undertaking labour that will improve the quality of his victims' lives, then he ought to attend to all the major ways he has harmed them. And harm from human rights violations are often not merely socio-economic in a narrow sense, but can also involve impairments to, and degradations of, people's self-understandings developed through the cultures in which they have been embedded.

For a first example in the South African context, consider that it is typical of Indigenous black peoples to believe in what are often called the 'living-dead'. That is, they tend to think that people survive the deaths of their bodies and continue

[18] For the suggestion that harmony is typically foundational for small-scale or non-western peoples, see George Silberbauer, 'Ethics in Small-scale Societies' in Peter Singer (ed), *A Companion to Ethics* (Basil Blackwell 1991) 14, and Daniel A Bell and Yingchuan Mo, 'Harmony in the World 2013' (2014) 118 Social Indicators Research 797.

to reside on Earth (at least for a certain amount of time), perhaps in a certain animal or at a particular place. Some of the living-dead count as 'ancestors', those who significantly influenced the clan and have the task of continuing to provide moral guidance to it. In the words of a black South African woman who went to court to be able to visit the grave of her dead son located on land held by a white farmer:

> [I]t is our custom and religious belief that when a member of our family passes away, he/she gets only physically separated from us but spiritually that person will always be with us and is capable of sharing a day to day life with us though in a different form. It is against this background that a graveyard to us is not only a place to bury our deceased, but a second home for those of us who live in the world of spirits.[19]

When, therefore, Indigenous peoples in South Africa were systematically deprived of land, they lost out not merely on an important economic resource, but also on what they understood to be access to their family members. The hardship of being unable to relate to family merits its own kind of compensation, or at the very least is arguably an additional consideration to factor in when effecting land reform. Even if, for example, a farmer who had obtained a large tract of land as a result of colonial era policies were allowed to retain it, say, for the sake of food productivity, he ought at least to be required to allow people to visit a gravesite or other territory where they believe the spirits of their family members continue to reside.

A second respect in which identity or culture is relevant to reconciliation in a South African context has to do with epistemic considerations. Part of who people are is a function of how they interpret the world, with one kind of injustice being a violation of their ability to use their own epistemic categories. Colonial powers in Africa routinely treated Indigenous people's attempts to understand themselves and their environment as inferior to the models provided by Christianity and modern science. One need not be a relativist who maintains that all belief systems are equally justified in order to find it wrong, for instance, not to teach any African philosophy in South African public universities and instead to instruct only western philosophy.[20] Plausibly that is wrong, regardless of whether staff are prohibited by a colonial government from teaching African worldviews or whether the post-colonial culture still inclines instructors, most of whom are of European descent, to disregard them. Decolonial theorists in South Africa have described

[19] *Nkosi and Another v Bührmann* [2001] ZASCA 98 [6].

[20] Indeed, it is only in the past five or ten years that the African ethic of *ubuntu* has begun to be systematically taught in South African universities.

such epistemic domination as 'spiritual genocide',[21] 'cultural violence',[22] 'symbolic castration',[23] and 'epistemicide'.[24]

Making reparations in the light of cultural harm, then, would need to include redress for ways in which people were wronged in regard to their abilities to interpret the world. It is not merely tangible goods that need to be considered when expressing remorse for, and disapproval of, apartheid in South Africa, but also intangible belief systems—which would require some provision of money, labour, and related resources to investigate, enrich, and transmit them.

Concretely, this might mean that South Africa's National Research Foundation or National Institute for the Humanities and Social Sciences prioritises support for projects that focus on indigenous perspectives. It could also involve the Department of Higher Education and Training or the Council on Higher Education urging public universities to Africanise their teaching and research, expecting them to report to the government on how they have done so. In addition, individual lecturers and scholars—and ideally those who in the past had denigrated or neglected African sources—could use them in their classrooms and journal articles, and, furthermore, could do the work of finding ways to share them with members of the broader public who cannot attend university.

We submit that the involvement of government bodies in seeking epistemic redress need not involve the micromanagement of academics, and could instead be a matter of request and negotiation of sorts that would allow lecturers and researchers to Africanise in their own ways, thereby respecting values such as institutional autonomy and academic freedom. In addition, the inclusion of under-represented African perspectives need not mean treating anything non-African as anathema: cross-cultural dialogue would be possible and presumably welcome.

4. Conclusion

In sum, taking some kind of reconciliation for granted as the proper way to respond to large-scale social conflict, reflection on the Colombian context reveals some respects in which South Africa's TRC and related post-apartheid programmes were limited, at least for a long while. As Bautista Pizarro puts it, in a peace process, the mechanisms of justice must be improved in a way that accommodates the cultural

[21] HW Vilakazi, 'Education Policy for a Democratic Society' in Sipho Seepe (ed), *Black Perspective(s) on Tertiary Institutional Transformation* (Vivlia Publishers and the University of Venda 1998) 76.

[22] Catherine Odora Hoppers, 'African Voices in Education' in Philip Higgs and others (eds), *African Voices in Education* (Juta 2000) 5.

[23] Catherine Odora Hoppers, 'Indigenous Knowledge Systems and Academic Institutions in South Africa' (2001) 19 Perspectives in Education 74.

[24] J Teboho Lebakeng and others, 'Epistemicide, Institutional Cultures and the Imperative for the Africanisation of Universities in South Africa' (2006) 13 Alternation 70.

diversity and identity of the communities.[25] Running with this plausible communitarian approach, we have suggested that, applied to South Africa, a full reconciliation would involve attending to what land means to victims beyond a focus on narrowly material considerations as well as effecting redress for respects in which their epistemic ways of life were suppressed. In his preceding chapter, Metz had pointed out that the beneficiaries of apartheid and the South African state have generally done a poor job of effecting reparations of property and opportunities; unfortunately, the reflection here indicates that the failure to make compensation is even greater, for having also left victims' culture and unique epistemic and spiritual relationships to the world around them largely out of the picture.

[25] Bautista Pizarro, Chapter 3 in this book.

THEME 2

ART AND TRANSITIONAL JUSTICE

5

Aesthetic Negotiation and Artefactual Agency

Key Processes for Symbolic Repair in Transitional Justice

Kim Berman and Michelle LeBaron

1. Introduction

Art provokes. It poses questions even if it is silent. It unsettles 'givens' and resists singular interpretations. Art invites the eyes and the whole bodies of viewers and makers, in dialogue with others, to perceive, sense, and feel multiple dimensions. Art is one of the most potent ways to approach healing in the face of unrightable wrongs and associated memories so deep and damaging that they are beyond comprehension or expression in words. It draws attention to what has been hidden or unnoticed. As Gabeba Baderoon writes, in *Regarding Muslims*, '[a]rt can shift] what *can be seen* … [challenging] what is normative and central, and what is marginal and insignificant'.[1]

Art practices are potent in addressing schisms in society born out of contested histories and unresolved traumas because the arts enable crossing boundaries, discovering commonalities, living in dynamic and porous ambiguities, curiosity, presence beyond language, and conscious connection.[2] They resurface what has been covered over and bring us into aesthetic, often deeply felt, engagement with each other. For this engagement, we use the term aesthetic negotiation. Aesthetic negotiation, defined in the following section, can engage citizens in critical reflection, building the capacities required for active participation in rebuilding democracy. Elmarie Costandius, who has long worked with the arts in enhancing social responsibility and citizenship, stresses that the arts enable the expression of feelings in indirect and metaphoric ways. She writes: 'Through these personal expressions,

[1] Gabeba Baderoon, *Regarding Muslims: From Slavery to Post-Apartheid* (Wits UP 2014) 16.

[2] Cynthia Cohen, 'Creative Approaches to Reconciliation' in Mari Fitzduff and Chris Stout (eds), *The Psychology of Resolving Global Conflicts: From War to Peace* (Bloomsbury Academic 2005) <https://www.brandeis.edu/ethics/pdfs/publications/Creative_Approaches.pdf> accessed 3 October 2022.

Kim Berman and Michelle LeBaron, *Aesthetic Negotiation and Artefactual Agency* In: *Transitional Justice, Distributive Justice, and Transformative Constitutionalism.* Edited by: David Bilchitz and Raisa Cachalia, with Magdalena Inés Correa Henao and Nathalia Bautista Pizarro, Oxford University Press.
DOI: 10.1093/oso/9780192887627.003.0005

we come to realise multiple interpretations to the same issue as well as the intricacy involved when dealing with complex issues.'[3]

The multiple functions of art and art-making are vitally important in the aftermath of violent conflict. The arts foreground that which has been hidden, suppressed, or attacked, and can be as important as truth-telling, such as was evident in the South African Truth and Reconciliation Commission (TRC). The arts are critical to a society re-finding its capacity for resilience, for regaining a sense of coherence in the face of trauma, loss, and pain, and for symbolic reparations. Indeed, in transitional South Africa, questions of identity (who are we now?), freedom (for whom and in which forms?), voice (whose voice is heard and whose voice counts?), and fairness (how do structural and systemic reforms fulfil aspirational visions?) are more compelling than ever.

Addressing these questions involves a social, political, and economic process that must extend beyond commissions and policy papers. Courts and legislatures cannot impose solutions, as they ultimately cannot operate sustainably without the active engagement and support of civil society. When civil society has been torn apart, it cannot be rewoven without social healing. Social healing, we maintain, is a process that can only be achieved over time and with the broadest and most multivalent engagement possible. The arts are vital in transitional justice because they accent commonalities and pay careful attention to humanising processes rather than assuming adversarial approaches.

We begin this chapter by defining the concepts of aesthetic negotiation and artefactual agency and continue by grounding these concepts in three case studies. Each case study focuses on one piece of artwork, all resting in the context of a transitioning South Africa. We aim to show how aesthetic negotiation and artefactual agency are two potent ways to achieve symbolic reparations, restore the rule of law, and minimise the harmful effects of past injustices. They help us think about, design, implement, and evaluate programmes, initiatives, and processes across a wide spectrum of transitional justice settings in South Africa. They also assist us in considering how transitional justice and distributive justice go hand-in-hand in furthering the long journey of reconciliation.

2. Defining Aesthetic Negotiation and Artefactual Agency

Aesthetic negotiation refers to reciprocal processes of artist- or community-generated works that open possibilities towards change. Whether artists instigate the work, or community leaders invite others into a project, aesthetic negotiation is

[3] Elmarie Constandius, 'Citizenship Project Helps Students Address Social Issues through Art and Creates Research Opportunities at Visual Arts Department' (2010) 6 Newsletter of the Faculty of Arts and Social Sciences 14.

always relational. Just as negotiation involves two or more people coming together to find an agreement, aesthetic negotiation involves people working through the arts to open new paths going forward. The focus is on felt and sensed experience. Just as commercial or family negotiation aims for integrative outcomes that work for all involved, aesthetic negotiation as a process foregrounds aesthetics in reaching for constructive social change, appealing to multiple intelligences and diverse groups. Just as fairness and procedural satisfaction are intricately interwoven and interdependent with desired material outcomes in legal negotiations, aesthetic negotiation foregrounds the process of art-making and responding to art, which are both collaborative activities. Here, art-making is not limited to one moment in time but involves an ongoing dialectic with ripples extending out in unpredictable ways from its creation. Just as international negotiation admits nuances of meaning and optimally improves relations amongst those involved, aesthetic negotiation includes strengthening relational bonds within its purview. Of those who participate in it, aesthetic negotiation asks respect for dynamism, comfort with emergence, and an awareness of complexity. It also asks that those involved open themselves to arts processes and outcomes as legitimate ways of mobilising change. This takes us to our second main concept, artefactual agency.

Artefactual agency is a term that links material objects to mobilisation and action. As Deborah Johnson and Merel Noorman write, artefactual agency emphasises 'the role of objects in constituting the material [and, we would add, relational] world[s]'.[4] As Nathi Mthethwa, then-South African minister of arts and culture proclaimed in 2014, 'creative arts bring us closer together, being a force of social cohesion and nation-building'.[5] At the same time, because products of artistic endeavours (visual art, theatre, dance) have agency in the sense referenced below, they can be resisted or attacked just as human actions can. Thus, artefacts of artistic processes spawn ongoing engagement as those who encounter them contest their meanings by protesting, defending, critiquing, or acquiescing.

Artefactual agency draws our attention to the nuances and complexity of artefacts, and also to their dynamic natures. Artefacts are not inert, neutral, or passive. Always a part of ongoing relational dances, they are compelling and often controversial. Thus, whether we encounter artist-produced works or design opportunities for non-artists to engage in co-creation, we are giving form to things that touch and move us; we are encountering beauty. As Elaine Scarry has argued, beauty ignites liveliness, engagement, and attention.[6] Exploring what constitutes

[4] Deborah G Johnson and Merel Noorman, 'Artefactual Agency and Artefactual Moral Agency' in Peter Kroes and Peter-Paul Verbeek (eds), *The Moral Status of Technical Artefacts* (Springer 2014) 143 <https://link.springer.com/chapter/10.1007/978-94-007-7914-3_9> accessed 8 September 2023.

[5] Brenda Schmahmann, 'Embroidering Controversy. The Politics of Visual Imaging' in Christopher Ballantine and others (eds), *Living Together, Living Apart? Social Cohesion in a Future South Africa* (University of KwaZulu-Natal Press 2017) 122.

[6] Elaine Scarry, *On Beauty and Being Just* (Princeton University Press 1999) 80.

beauty, and what is or is not redemptive in the wake of violence and trauma, similarly motivates people to engage. The aesthetic negotiation involved in deciding which objects should be displayed and how the new 'we' should be represented is often fractious, unpredictable, and messy. The selection of modes of engagement, or curatorial decisions about which objects are displayed, are not only practically but symbolically significant. The agency of humans who have made artefacts, as well as how an object's agency itself is observed, arises as another aspect of aesthetic negotiation.

A. Applying Artefactual Agency

Since its transition to democracy, South Africa has seen contestations in many places about symbolic objects. Arguably, artefactual agency has been repeatedly invoked as statues have been toppled, visual art destroyed, and portraits of white male leaders displaced. Brenda Schmahmann recalls her 2008 initiative to move photographs of white male former vice-chancellors and chairs at Rhodes University from their prominent position in the council chamber.[7] A heated conflict followed, during which arguments that the photographs should remain were tied to a fear that all contributions by white male scholars would be eradicated from the university. Had those in the university met the conflict not via a heated and binary debate, but using aesthetic and dialogical modes of engagement, different and more nuanced exchanges might have been possible. What would have happened if those involved had been invited to represent their views by selecting or contributing music to a 'listening wall', or via storytelling in circle processes, or by making prints that conveyed their feelings? The example of *Paper Prayers*, described later in this chapter, is one possible approach that can be used in such settings.

Strangely, universities, sites of learning, often turn away from pedagogical values in the face of intense conflict. Yet gathered pedagogical wisdom shows us that the *process* of engagement matters. As Raisa Cachalia writes in this book, legal processes are often important in reducing violence.[8] But legal processes themselves are limited, given their formality, rules of evidence, and limited available causes of action. Do we choose war as the metaphor that is ubiquitously paired with conflict (yet is more likely to escalate trouble than solve it), or do we find more nuanced ways of remembering or responding?

Artefactual agency shines a light not only on the *how* but also the *what* of remembering. Inclusive imagery, multiple versions of narratives, and modern visual art are amenable to many interpretations—all these are useful in pedagogically invoking artefactual agency.

[7] Schmahmann (n 5) 130.

[8] See Raisa Cachalia, Chapter 20 in this book.

While artefactual agency can be engaged in a pedagogical way, an intention to do so is often lacking. Contested meanings are not new; what can be new is to step back from heated conflict, deliberately designing an aesthetic negotiation process that admits multiple meanings, effects, and symbols. As Costandius asserts, '[e]xperience cannot be separated from our learning, and what happened in the past still has an effect on many facets of the social psyche, like self-esteem, for instance'.[9]

How can we use the artefactual agency of artworks as a pedagogical strategy for repair, healing, and social justice, given their contested meanings? We maintain that, precisely because concepts like what constitutes transitional justice are contested, artworks and processes are fertile resources for communities to navigate the aesthetic negotiation that will yield new social consensus.[10] For this to happen, effective leadership and dialogical exchange via the arts are essential. At the same time, it is important to emphasise that arts processes and products are not merely tools to be used or applied. Respecting the artistic intention of artists and the integrity of works is important even as the works themselves may be seized upon as symbols to advance particular agendas. South Africa offers several powerful examples of aesthetic negotiation over contested meanings, some of which are detailed below.

Before examining South African examples of aesthetic negotiation and artefactual agency, we pause to examine the place and potency of the symbolic domain in conflict. Conflict, after all, is an essential part of human and natural existence. Without it, life stops—not only bloodshed and suffering but also well-being and progress. Indeed, though we know that without cooperation humans would long ago have become extinct, competition still figures into biological and evolutionary development and into social and political institutions.[11] The key to conflict fluency—the ability to embrace or at least manage even the most threatening conflicts—is to understand it as a force that brings change. The type of change conflict brings depends on how we engage it: resisting conflict almost never makes it disappear. It is often more useful to approach conflict indirectly than directly. Even in cultures where direct communication is the norm, confrontation can evoke fight or flight impulses and escalate trouble.

B. Artefactual Agency, Aesthetic Negotiation, and Conflict

One way to think about conflict is via three concentric circles, each including the previous ones. At the centre is relationship. All conflict involves *relationships*: even

[9] Constandius (n 3) 14.
[10] John Paul Lederach, *The Moral Imagination: The Art and Soul of Building Peace* (OUP 2005).
[11] Mary E Clark, *In Search of Human Nature* (Routledge 2002).

inner conflict is a struggle between different parts of the psyche. Because all conflict is relational, effective approaches to analysis and intervention must also be relational and process-oriented. Thus aesthetic negotiation is centred in relationship.

The second concentric circle signifies the *symbolic*. Struggles over resources or political systems are tied up with identity, worldviews, and perceptions. The symbolic domain includes identity and collective self-image, human needs for security and belonging, and sacred meanings and values. The complexity of the symbolic realm can be seen in any intractable conflict. In South Africa, a racist political system not only wrought unspeakable material wrongs, it also violated the sacredness and dignity of human life and fundamental values including equality, justice, and freedom. When sacred meanings or transgressions against what is held precious and sacrosanct are part of a conflict, it will be much harder to address because relational or material actions will be amplified and 'charged' with symbolic meanings. For this reason, attempted social healing in the aftermath of intractable conflicts must incorporate the symbolic dimension. Aesthetic negotiation is thus valuable as a creative strategy in South Africa's transition to a new society because it combines sensory, emotional, and physical approaches with analytical problem-solving in negotiating symbolic meanings.

Proceedings before the South African TRC illustrate symbolic aspects of transitional justice. As it heard testimony from perpetrators and victims, the TRC provided a social space for painful narratives that were both visceral and deeply emotional. In one hearing, a former Western Cape security policeman Jeff Benzien, seeking amnesty for torture, demonstrated the 'wet bag' method to those present at the insistence of African National Congress (ANC) MP Tony Yengeni.[12] Yengeni had been tortured by Benzien himself. In this powerful moment, the material act of torture came together with the relational indignities suffered; the symbolic resonance of the truth was both vivid and powerful.

A visual response to this story was explored by co-author Kim Berman in a series titled 'Playing Cards of the Truth Commission' (depicted below). In this series, Berman, a printmaker, drew recognisable portraits of thirteen apartheid perpetrators, linked to spades in a pack of cards and portrayed as forces of evil. She used a layered printing process in which the first layer depicts an accurately rendered portrait using the printmaking technique of mezzotint, which starts as a darkened and grained surface created by an aquatint on a metal plate. The surface is then scratched and burnished to reveal the light and form emerging from the dark ground. This plate is then printed in black ink and finally layered with two additional engraved plates containing text and colour which are printed on top of the portrait (see Figures 5.1 and 5.2). Her artist statement explains:

[12] 'Cop Demonstrates "Wet Bag" Torture' *Mail & Guardian* (14 July 1997) <https://mg.co.za/article/1997-07-14-cop-demonstrates-wet-bag-torture> accessed 3 October 2022.

This technique became a metaphor of finding the light from the darkness, a search for discovering their humanity. I struggled to reconcile the brutality in the testimonies of the victims with the denial of their perpetrators. I added layers onto the images, first tinting them with a toxic colour, and then aggressively scratching and scribbling over the finely worked surfaces with a sharp tool. The effect was therapeutic and another layer was added to the delicately worked portraits with fragments of texts from their victims. The process represented my attempt to seek my own reconciliation with the TRC and attempt to let go of the bitterness.[13]

Figures 5.1 and 5.2 Fig. 5.1. Kim Berman's *Playing Cards of the Truth Commission: An Incomplete Deck . . .*, inside cover page (*left*); Fig. 5.2. Jeffrey Benzien's *Seven of Spades* (*right*) (Photographs by and with permission of Kim Berman)

Source: Kim Berman, *Playing Cards of the Truth Commission: An Incomplete Deck . . .* (A Portfolio of 13 Portraits, inside title page, 1999, mezzotint with drypoint and surface roll); Jeffery Benzien, *Seven of Spades* in Berman *Playing Cards of the Truth Commission* (1999, mezzotint with dry point and surface roll).

Numerous other artistic, literary, and theatrical responses to the TRC process attempted to interpret and process multiple underlying and embedded meanings. Generally, they used symbolic representations to engage obliquely with the horrific accounts being broadcast daily. In doing so, these artistic responses framed justice

[13] Kim Berman Artist Statement (1989); further reference to this series: Christine Mullen Kraemer (ed), *Inscribing Meaning: Writing and Graphic Systems in African Art* (National Museum of African Art 2006).

as a potentially restorative process alongside calls for distributive justice. The arts have the capacity to synthesise and integrate differences and dislocations amongst diverse people in transitional justice contexts. Arguably, the most iconic performative piece based on TRC hearings was the Handspring Puppet Company's 1997 production of *Ubu and the Truth Commission* directed by William Kentridge. The play by French playwright, Alfred Jarry featured a nineteenth-century licentious character Ubu Roi for whom torture, murder, sex, and food were all aspects of a single gross appetite. Jane Taylor rewrote the script, casting Ubu as a South African policeman with similar appetites. Ubu thus became a symbol for a large cast of characters whose violence had torn apart not only families and communities but a nation.

Symbolic aspects of conflict are vitally important because they are often what keep conflicts stuck. Warring parties may refuse to sign a peace treaty and let a war-weary country transition despite its being beneficial for each of them. The reason for their intransigence is because of the meaning the parties make of the conflict and the treaty terms. This has been powerfully illustrated in Colombia in recent years.[14] In South Africa, substantial legal and constitutional changes have supplanted apartheid with democracy. Expectations of resulting fairness and justice symbolically clashed with President Zuma's lavish lifestyle, leading to his 2018 resignation. Similarly, the *Rhodes Must Fall* movement targeted Cecil John Rhodes' statue at the University of Cape Town (UCT) in an action that rippled far beyond the campus.[15] Thus the symbolic realm of conflict has a multiplier effect: when a symbolic nerve is touched, the effects can be far greater than anticipated. For this reason and many others, art is a powerful way of negotiating conflict.

The final dimension on the outer of the three concentric circles is the *material*. This circle is about the tangible things in a conflict, such as land or resources. A lot of work on negotiation has focused on how to improve efficiency and material outcomes. Phrases like 'expand the pie' and 'win/win' focus on increasing the possibilities in conflict to yield complementary gains. Much progress in this area arose from game theory, popularised in the successful book *Getting to Yes*.[16] While these ideas are helpful, symbolic and relational dimensions of intractable conflicts and transitional justice contexts may be untouched or even worsened by materially-focused interventions. While ameliorating poor living conditions is an essential focus in transitional societies, for example, it is helpful to have both relational and symbolic aspects also in mind. Too many examples from international and community development projects illustrate the pitfalls of 'experts' deciding on

[14] 'Colombia Referendum: Voters Reject FARC Peace Deal' *BBC News* (3 October 2016). <http://www.bbc.com/news/world-latin-america-37537252> accessed 3 October 2022.

[15] Roseanne Chantiluke, Brian Kwoba, and Athinangamso Nkopo (eds), *Rhodes Must Fall: The Struggle to Decolonise the Racist Heart of Empire* (Zed Books 2018).

[16] Roger Fisher, William Ury, and Bruce Patton, *Getting to Yes: Negotiating Agreement without Giving In* (Houghton Mifflin 1981).

poverty reduction measures that are actually unresponsive to local conditions.[17] Few scholars have explored how fundamental—between a relational foundation and the material outcomes—is the mediating layer of the symbolic.[18] Though it is less visible and measurable, its value is significant.

All three of these circles have fuzzy boundaries and overlapping areas. Focusing on any one or two of them and excluding another from social healing will make efforts more likely to fail. The slow progress in improving material conditions expected after democratic elections in South Africa, for example, casts doubt on the sincerity of politicians and others tasked with leading the 'rainbow nation'. Symbolic and ceremonial actions, visionary statements, and inspiring speeches lose their potency when material results are lacking. Similarly, the most rational negotiating framework in the world may not work if people do not feel their personal and group identities are acknowledged and recognised. When people are in conflict over issues with deep, symbolic, emotional valences like land, failing to understand the symbolic meanings of land to each party may doom a process. Symbolic dimensions, as indicated earlier, can have a multiplier effect when ignored, escalating conflict beyond the material aspects of its genesis.

Aesthetic negotiation spans all three of these dimensions. Intimate with symbols, the arts surface stories in relational ways, conveying multiple meanings. Intricately material, artwork brings the elements of earth, fire, air, and water into new relations, yielding creative syntheses and generative possibilities. Art and creativity are always relational, even if they are composed in solitude. Every artist draws on her own experience in creating work and shares it in various forms with others. Artists, often on the edge of social institutions and conventions, bring perspective, independence, and new ways of thinking to communities. Thus creative strategies are important in transitional South Africa, where new ways of addressing the aftermath of apartheid are urgently needed. In the next section of this chapter, we illustrate aesthetic negotiation and artefactual agency with examples.

3. Artefactual Agency, Aesthetic Negotiation, and Transformation

We begin with Artist Proof Studio (APS), an art centre in the inner city of Johannesburg, where the focus is on printmaking that is understood as a democratic medium because of its accessibility. Established in 1991 after Nelson Mandela's release from prison, APS opened its doors to talented artists unable to access tertiary institutions due to economic or educational inequalities. The centre sought to provide excellent subsidised training and facilities, enabling artists to make a living

[17] Ram Babu Singh (ed), *Sustainable Urban Development* (Concept Publishing Company 2006).
[18] Bernard S Mayer, *Beyond Neutrality: Confronting the Crisis in Conflict Resolution* (Wiley 2004).

from the sale of their work. At APS, printmaking as a nexus of aesthetic negotiation crosses the three concentric circles of the relational, symbolic, and material. In the centre, or inner circle, relationships are centred around learning and exchange, as well as intense struggles with understanding technical and social dynamics that support visual voice. This is surrounded by the circle of the symbolic, in which young artists grapple with individual and collective identity formation as represented in their work. In this dimension, artists come to terms with creating images of themselves and their environments. The outer circle, the space of material outcomes and resources, is intricately interwoven with the other two. APS' vision is to provide aspiring artists with the skills and capacities to achieve a measure of self-sufficiency through generating income. Thus the material realm also includes tangible recognition, potency, material successes, disappointments, and conflict.

Aesthetic negotiation is framed through the studio's values or 'habits of mind'.[19] The APS motto 'ISEE-U', stands for 'innovation, self-awareness, engagement, excellence through ubuntu'. The mission of the studio promotes the values of *ubuntu*, or humanity towards others, through excellence, innovation, and internal and external engagement. APS encourages artists to push beyond printmaking conventions to find their own visions and to derive inspiration through collaboration and community engagement. Through its programmes and its mindfulness of the interconnected relational, symbolic, and material circles, APS aims to foster transformation not only in the lives of students but in radiating bands of influence across wider social circles (see Figure 5.3).

APS positioned itself as a microcosm of South Africa's new democracy since its establishment. It contributed through various interventions and portfolios to, among others, the following: transitional justice during the drafting of the new constitution; social justice campaigns including advocating testing, treatment, and access to medical care during the height of the HIV/AIDS epidemic; advocacy for gender justice and ending violence against women and children; and the fight against xenophobia. Community interventions, participatory arts-based processes, murals, and workshops were all used in promoting aesthetic negotiation as an important way to actualise active citizenship and positive social change.

A powerful example of APS' work can be found in the Paper Prayers campaign, which used accessible printmaking approaches to create awareness of social issues, especially among those without access to advanced education or art materials. The Paper Prayers method arose from the Japanese tradition of using prayer-inscribed papers as a vehicle for healing and well-being. The Paper Prayers AIDS awareness campaign is one example of Paper Prayers, and it also illustrates artefactual agency.

[19] 'Habits of mind' is a unifying framework first coined by John Dewey (1859–1952) in the early twentieth century. Adopted by APS from its development by the Boston Arts Academy, it promotes the values that enhance learning capacities and helps fulfil social justice goals. See Linda Nathan, *The Hardest Questions Aren't on the Test: Lessons from an Innovative Urban School* (Beacon Press 2010).

Figure 5.3 APS students collaborate in a group woodcut print that promotes values of Ubuntu (Photograph by S Antonopoulo courtesy of Artist Proof Studio)

Source: Published in Janis P Sarra and Kim Berman, 'Ubuntu as a Tool for Resilience: Arts, Microbusiness and Social Justice' (2017) 34 Conflict Resolution Quarterly 455, 471.

This campaign involved employing a simple printmaking technique as a way to motivate testing for HIV/AIDS during a time of high death rates in South Africa. Given widespread misinformation and the stigma associated with a positive HIV/AIDS diagnosis, many South Africans, particularly in rural areas, had not been tested. Yet cultural taboos about direct discussions of sexual relations and condoms made intervention challenging. The Paper Prayers AIDS awareness campaign met participants where they were; many of them had never experienced art-making. By applying inks or paints onto found objects like leaves, or corrugated iron, and then rubbing and transferring the impressions onto paper, they created powerful pieces. As they did so, their perceptions of agency, and of what could be publicly expressed, shifted.

One female participant chose a piece of wire fencing—for her, a symbol of protection and unity in the face of HIV/AIDS. After inking up the fencing and transferring it onto a strip of paper, her artwork gained artefactual agency, amplifying the importance of the symbol for her by its transformation into something tangible and beautiful (see Figure 5.4). She and other participants came to understand this 'praying with paper' as having the potency to save another's life because it amplified the importance of HIV testing without addressing it directly.[20] Participation in the

[20] ibid 161.

Figure 5.4 Matshidiso Spagelo's Paper Prayer artwork with artistic narrative statement (Photograph by S Sellschop and reproduced by permission from artist)

Source: Reproduced in Michelle LeBaron and Janis Sarra (eds), *Changing our Worlds: Art as Transformative Practice* (Sun Press 2018) 95.

campaign also gave community participants new printmaking skills which contributed to their self-sufficiency. Thus artefactual agency conferred tangible, embodied meaning on objects and their associated symbols. In this way, artefactual agency became a powerful catalyst for transformative change on human rights or social issues.

As Paper Prayers were made in response to HIV/AIDS and testing, gender rights, and other human rights issues, participants experienced newly found agency. Through participation and activism, Paper Prayers (as well as other modes of aesthetic negotiation including visual mapping, collective mural-making, and Photovoice) have proven effective as a way of enhancing voice and strengthening advocacy.[21] All of these modes accented and anchored the physical catharsis involved in making; the relational experience of participants creating together

[21] The Paper Prayers Campaign developed into a programme to track the impact of arts-based approaches in community craft initiatives such as the Phumani Paper projects. This impact is extensively documented in Kim Berman, *Finding Voice. A Visual Arts Approach to Engaging Social Change* (University of Michigan Press 2017) 135–77.

strengthened their sense of belonging and shared responsibility. Thus Paper Prayers connected and attached agency to relational, symbolic, and material aspects of intangible constructs like justice, fairness, and progress.

Another example of artefactual agency comes from a rural community experiencing a high number of AIDS-related deaths. In 2005, South Africans were dying at the rate of 900 per day and only 12 per cent knew their HIV status. Over 330,000 preventable deaths occurred while former South African President Thabo Mbeki denied the relationship between HIV and AIDS.[22] For many, being HIV positive was a death sentence; the silence and stigma around this epidemic were destroying communities. During the peak pandemic period between 2005 and 2009, APS and the University of Johannesburg initiated the *Cultural Action for Change* project. Phumani Paper and Paper Prayers were two facets of the project, spawning sixteen hand-papermaking craft projects around South Africa. After its completion, handmade paper was used in Paper Prayers educational workshops facilitated by trained AIDS educators and counsellors. The artwork became the way of sharing awareness of the importance of testing, as well as breaking the silence and stigma associated with HIV/AIDS. It also helped extend knowledge into wider circles as participants took their Paper Prayers home and into their communities (see Figure 5.5).

Kgomotso Oordira 2007

Black colour: I was in darkness not knowing my status and afraid to it. I attended a workshop about HIV/Aids, they taught me.
I said why do other people leave their family with HIV/Aids, I can't leave my kids alone. I see green grass, sit on it I see birds flying and singing. Then I told myself that HIV/Aids is not death but a challenge! Live to keep your loved one happy and warm. Let us know our status and live a healthy life, especially we mothers, otherwise our kids will be without parents.

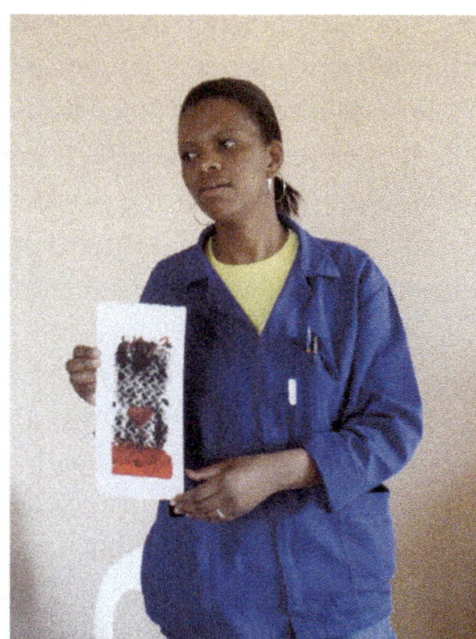

Figure 5.5 Kgomotso Oodira's Paper Prayer artwork with artistic narrative statement (Photograph by Kim Berman and reproduced by permission from artist)

Source: Kim Berman, *Finding Voice. A Visual Arts Approach to Engaging Social Change* (University of Michigan Press 2017) 106–97 (ref plate 17).

[22] 'Mbeki Aids Policy "Led to 330,000 Deaths"', *The Guardian* (South Africa, 27 November 2008) <https://www.theguardian.com/world/2008/nov/27/south-africa-aids-mbeki> accessed 3 October 2022.

The image and narrative in Figure 5.5 are from one community participant who explained her choice of a symbol and its meaning. The colours of her Paper Prayer symbolise the darkness of dying, as well as the hope of new knowledge that could prevent her children from becoming orphans. Her Paper Prayer poignantly proclaims her vision for a future in which she and others can flourish so their children will have parents.

A follow-up evaluation found that 85 per cent of the members from the sixteen craft groups had gone for testing and had referred others in their families to test.[23] Thus the intervention contributed to artefactual agency and constituted a process of aesthetic negotiation. The visual artefact of this woman and many others underscores the potency of both artefactual agency and aesthetic negotiation, and evidences the transformational change in her and others' lives. The programme ended only in 2011 when, with the introduction of anti-retroviral drugs at the end of the Mbeki regime, the mortality rate decreased exponentially.[24]

These examples illustrate how community-generated art relates to our two key concepts. We now look at South African artist-generated processes in relation to aesthetic negotiation and artefactual agency. Three artistic works have played significant roles in surfacing ethical and moral aspects of trauma and repair, important to aesthetic negotiation—*The Spear* by Brett Murray, Willie Bester's sculpture of Sarah Baartman, and *The Blue Dress* by Judith Mason. Below, we explore their continued potency in provoking activist responses and civic debates about a range of justice issues. These include questions surrounding freedom of expression, how dignity is constituted for those deprived of respect in the past, and how multiple meanings can be legible from a single work leading to diverse political mobilisation. Given that the works themselves became focal points onto which different values, political positions, and social orders are projected, they illustrate what we mean by aesthetic negotiation.

A. Artefactual Agency, Aesthetic Negotiation, and Aesthetic Litigation

In her companion piece in this book, Colombian colleague Yolanda Sierra León refers to the term 'aesthetic litigation' in which work by artists has provoked change in the midst of transitional justice. We prefer the term aesthetic negotiation as

[23] Berman (n 21) 142.

[24] South Africa has the biggest HIV epidemic in the world, with 18.9 per cent HIV positive or 7.1 million living with HIV in 2016. South Africa has the largest anti-retroviral treatment (ART) programme in the world with nearly 86 per cent of people knowing their status. AIDS-related deaths have fallen by 48 per cent since the peak in 2005. By 2015, 3.5 million people had died from HIV-related causes. 'At a Glance: HIV in South Africa' (2021) <https://www.avert.org/professionals/hiv-around-world/sub-saharan-africa/south-africa> accessed 3 October 2022.

it encompasses work made by artists and community members, and it does not carry the more adversarial connotation of litigation. In litigation, of course, there are winners and losers, and a presiding official makes a decision. Also, litigation processes tend to borrow from the metaphor of war, most often playing out as a no-holds-barred contest in which the winner takes all, even if 'all' means inflicting debilitating damage on the 'loser'. Where art is concerned, there is no official closure, and we at least aspire to ongoing generative engagement that negotiates the meanings of diffuse concepts such as identity and justice in the dynamic contexts where we live. Thus, in our view, the term aesthetic negotiation seems a better fit to describe the way that art functions in symbolic reparations.

In South Africa, artworks have provoked political controversy as part of the ongoing negotiations that underline their symbolic potency. In some instances, violent protests have resulted, including the toppling of the Rhodes statue at the UCT, and the burning of the artworks there.[25] These aesthetic negotiations were characterised by hostility and outrage, leading to the destruction, removal, and censorship of various artworks on the campus. The students clearly prevailed in the negotiation, as their actions led the Vice Chancellor to remove approximately seventy-four works of art from the University's collection by some of the country's acclaimed artists 'on the grounds of their vulnerability to potential damage' or because 'some members of the campus community have identified certain works of art as offensive to them—for cultural, religious or political reasons'.[26] Ivor Powell observes that these responses by the UCT administration were not about art or learning. He equates the conflict more to war than negotiation; perhaps this is an instance when aesthetic negotiation gave way to Sierra León's 'aesthetic litigation'. When underlying motivations and observable actions are clearly drawn from the more draconian and win-lose mindset, aesthetic litigation may supersede aesthetic negotiation. As can be seen from the unsatisfying stalemate following the student protests, aesthetic litigation may have the effect that many lawsuits have—stopping the potential for dialogue. Powell writes:

> The narrative engaged by UCT's student militants is bluntly, brutally and convulsively political in ways that have more in common with the conventions of warfare than they do with parliamentary processes. This is about a struggle for the control and ownership of resources, a winner-takes-all model in which the old is obliterated and a tabula rasa is created on which to inscribe the new.[27]

[25] See image of protesters in February 2016 carrying work on UCT campus for burning in Natalie Pertsovsky, 'Here is the List of Art Destroyed on UCT' *GroundUp* (9 June 2017) <https://www.groundup.org.za/article/here-list-art-destroyed-uct/> accessed 3 October 2022.

[26] Ivor Powell, 'Behind UCT's Removed Art: The Writing on the Wall' *Art Times* (2 August 2017) <http://arttimes.co.za/behind-ucts-removed-art-writing-wall-ivor-powell/> accessed 3 October 2022.

[27] ibid.

These are not examples of symbolic repair and healing: they illustrate what can happen when parties to aesthetic negotiation use competitive tactics that brook no respect for their counterparts. As with nations negotiating a peace treaty who instead turn to warfare, the outcome can be tragic and destructive. In the UCT case, the students' and university workers' anger and frustration resulted in violence and destruction of property. The protesting students used the symbolic potency of artwork as a negotiating demand to force the hand of the University to provide 'free' and 'de-colonised' education. Unsatisfied with the University's actions, they turned to violence. UCT thus lost the negotiation when, rather than finding a more transformative mode of engagement, they were met with litigation-like warfare. As a party in litigation may act to conserve threatened assets, the UCT administration closed down possibilities for continued aesthetic negotiation when they removed artworks from public display.

If both parties had been open to aesthetic negotiation instead of aesthetic litigation, there might have been more integrative and satisfying outcomes for both sides. In many instances, artworks continue to renegotiate their meanings and agency as contexts change. This durable artefactual agency can emerge from the artwork's symbolic power and may be independent of artists' intentions. A good example of this is Willie Bester's sculpture of Sarah Baartman, described below.

(i) Sarah Baartman

In 2000, UCT acquired the sculpture of Sarah Baartman by Bester, a mixed-race artist whose political work frequently features steel objects welded together. The sculpture, with chains at her feet, became known as 'the Hottentot Venus', a reference to a derogatory term used for Khoisan people by European settlers in South Africa. This life-sized mechanical, machine-like figure made of an assemblage of industrial debris communicates Bester's critique of scientific racism. 'Saartjie' Baartman was taken on a ship and exhibited as a subject of curiosity in nineteenth-century France, and is thus an iconic symbol of extreme objectification, indignity, and degradation. It was not until 2002 that the South African government repatriated Baartman's remains and buried her in the Eastern Cape as a measure towards restoring her dignity.

According to Bester, the work raises issues of identity: first, for the suffering and racism that occurred in the colonial and post-colonial contexts, and second, as he put it in an interview, 'so that [we] can confront who we are ... [We] fought for everyone to be acceptable with whatever deficiency they have, or what is seen as a deficiency'.[28] With these comments, Bester seeks to participate in the ongoing

[28] Quoted in Natalie Pertsovsky, 'Sarah Baartman Sculptor Speaks Out Against Art Censorship' *GroundUp* (5 June 2017) <https://www.groundup.org.za/article/sara-baartman-sculptor-speaks-out-against-art-censorship/> accessed 3 October 2022.

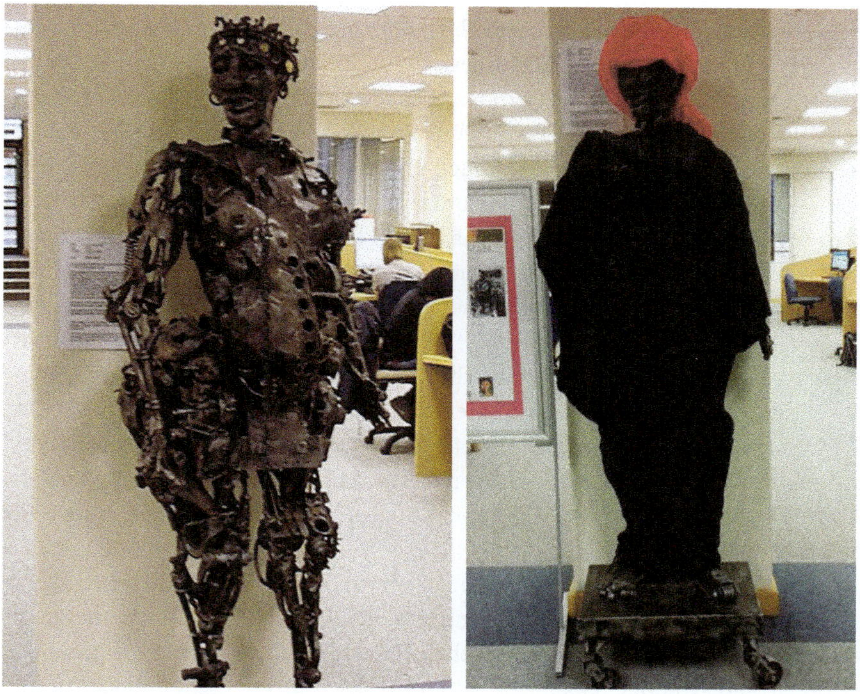

Figures 5.6 and 5.7 Photographs of Willie Bester's Saartjie Baartman sculpture at UCT Library. Fig. 5.6. Sculpture presented as intended, UCT Library (*left*); Fig. 5.7. Same sculpture after it was covered up (*right*) (Photographs cropped and reproduced by permission from GroundUp)

Source: Natalie Pertsovsky, 'Sarah Baartman Sculptor Speaks Out Against Art Censorship' *GroundUp* (5 June 2017) <https://www.groundup.org.za/article/sara-baartman-sculptor-speaks-out-against-art-censorship/>.

aesthetic negotiation. His voice is not determinative, but one among many. The aesthetic negotiation continued when, during the student protests of 2015 and again in 2016, Bester's sculpture was wrapped in cloth (see Figures 5.6 and 5.7). The Black Academic Caucus (BAC) Womxn's Collective at UCT took responsibility for this action. They claimed that the label 'Hottentot Venus' 'continue[d] to haunt our memory of Sarah Baartman'. They saw the sculpture as a symbol instrumentalising Sarah's body that had 'become symbolic, representing a significant majority of women at UCT and beyond'.[29] The sculpture remained robed for about two years.

29 BAC Womxn's Collective, 'The Place of Sarah Baartman at UCT' *University of Cape Town* (20 March 2018) <https://www.news.uct.ac.za/article/-2018-03-20-the-place-of-sara-baartman-at-uct> accessed 3 October 2022.

The aesthetic negotiation continued. In March 2018, William Daniels, the senior UCT librarian and a white American, admitted to uncovering the sculpture of Sarah Baartman. Bester wrote to Daniels thanking him, as he viewed the cover-up of the work as censorship.[30] David Goldblatt, similarly, offended by the robing wrote: 'Head to toe, as though a shameful object, it was hidden under cloth, grotesquely demonstrating the university's trashing of freedom of expression'.[31] Daniels responded, insisting that '[c]ensorship is anathema to the library profession and a grave violation of South African and international codes of professional ethics for librarians, not to mention a scandal to academic freedom and to the Constitution of South Africa'.[32] In their reply, members of the womxn's collective asserted that the sculpture should be engaged symbolically and critically because she represents the experience of many of the black women at UCT and beyond. 'It is not just a sculpture; it is not just a piece of cloth—it is centuries of trauma ... [t]aking the robes off so unceremoniously is to shame all of us, reminding us once again, how black women's bodies easily become the repository for violent histories'.[33]

As the Baartman aesthetic negotiation illustrates, artistic works and actions have artefactual agency that can provoke and trouble historical legacies. As the quest for transitional justice unfolds in South Africa, there is much need for material, relational, and symbolic repair. Ahmed Bawa asks 'how we might use our constitutional democratic framework to mobilise the energy of the tension to make decisive strides toward socio-economic justice'.[34] Tension and energy at the heart of transitional struggles can lead to destructive or constructive results; this relates in part to the quality and velocity of energy that is mobilised. For some women students, the artefactual agency of Bester's sculpture became a locus of tension onto which they hooked their struggle for greater gender justice within UCT. How and from whose point of view do we assess their tactics and whether they crossed the line between aesthetic negotiation into aesthetic litigation or war? Aesthetic negotiation can foster meaningful conflict engagement, encompassing material and relational dimensions in its symbolic potency when done with respect and openness to dialogue. In this case, each side's actions further escalated conflict in the absence of dialogue. While opportunities for increased understanding across these divides

[30] Quoted in Natalie Pertsovsky and others, 'Quarrel Over Sarah Baartman Sculpture at UCT' *GroundUp* (2 March 2018) <https://www.groundup.org.za/article/quarrel-over-sarah-baartman-sculpture-uct/> accessed 3 October 2022.

[31] ibid.

[32] ibid.

[33] BAC Womxn's Collective (n 29).

[34] Ahmed Bawa, 'Dialogue and Debate: Human Rights and Sustainable Democracy' in J Jordaan (ed), *Art of Human Rights: A Collection of Arts and Poems for Human Rights* (Art for Humanity 2015) 10.

at UCT were missed, publicity attending the aesthetic negotiation catalysed conversations in the wider public.

Powell supports this understanding of the symbolic power of art: 'It is precisely through engagement with human consciousness that art works become part of the intellectual property of society'.[35] Steven Dubin, affirming the power of politically motivated art, underlines how it can either inspire admiration or provoke condescension and critique. Acknowledging the many artists who routinely push boundaries of 'decorum, order and propriety' whether artistically, morally, or sexually, he notes how artists work from the periphery, daring deviance and asking questions others are not voicing.[36] Thus, artists and their work with artefactual agency invite engagement from those who might otherwise stay silent.

(ii) The Spear

Another example epitomising this catalytic symbolic power and artefactual agency is *The Spear* by Brett Murray from his 2012 exhibit *Hail to the Chief II* (see Figure 5.8). Based on a 1967 iconic poster of Russian leader Vladimir Lenin, *The Spear* mocks its subject, depicting then South African President Jacob Zuma with his genitalia exposed in Lenin's place. *The Spear* is one of a series of Murray's works satirically commenting on the greed, corruption, abuse of power, lack of morals, and bad governance of the ruling elite in South Africa.[37] Murray intentionally inverted South African liberation heroes into what he terms 'tenderpreneurs' (officials who use their power to secure lucrative government contracts). Illustrating aesthetic negotiation, *The Spear* generated intense media focus and impact around the country, triggering heated debates about the legacy of colonial and apartheid injustices, the politics of reconciliation, the status of traditional African cultural beliefs, and the freedom of expression.[38]

The controversy sparked by *The Spear* points to the capacity of aesthetic negotiation to reach deep beyond the content of an artwork to complex dynamics at play in transitional societies. Murray's work provided the president and his followers with a convenient opening when they used *The Spear* to deflect severe criticism and allegations of corruption that surrounded Zuma at the time. Feelings of blind fury generated by *The Spear* churned into a poisonous brew of racism and xenophobia.

[35] Powell (n 26).

[36] Steven C Dubin, *Arresting Images: Impolitic Art and Uncivil Actions* (Routledge 1992) 2.

[37] Steven C Dubin, *Spearheading Debate: Culture Wars & Uneasy Truces* (Jacana 2012) 177. The works in the show included sculptures, etchings, and silkscreens combining motifs of the ANC logo and insignia, with iconic symbols from freedom struggle posters integrated with Soviet propaganda.

[38] Murray's depiction of Zuma as Lenin calls up the Soviet state's promises of a better life for its citizens, and layered over this, the penis symbol refers both to patriarchy and the implied threat of sexual abuse. Murray's representation of Zuma was seen as a demeaning satire by a white political artist of a black leadership figure, perpetuating a racial caricature.

Figure 5.8 Brett Murray's *The Spear* (Image courtesy of Brett Murray)
Source: Brett Murray, *The Spear* (2010, acrylic on canvas, on exhibition at Goodman Gallery, Johannesburg, May 2012).

Harnessing this brew, the politically opportunistic ANC collectively united against a common enemy—something which had not occurred since it had come to power in 1994. Dubin reported that Murray felt 'emasculated', 'voiceless', and 'profoundly humiliated' when *The Spear* was labelled as racist;[39] he was upset that his intention had been misinterpreted. The defacing of this work by an angry visitor to the Goodman Gallery inflamed the public debate between the constitutional right to freedom of speech and racist insult. This brought into dialogue what Dubin calls

[39] Dubin, *Spearheading Debate* (n 37) 182.

'culture wars and uneasy truces'. Artefactual agency, as this example illustrates, is not determined by its creator but evolves in the complex cut and thrust of aesthetic negotiation.

When an art object's political and social artefactual agency sparks debate and protests, it becomes a leverage point from which understandings and dialogue can be deepened. For this to happen, the contestation around the object must be framed as an opening rather than a winner-takes-all contest of framing. When emotions run high and hostility and outrage are present, leadership is needed to mark and move into possible openings for engagement. As *The Spear* illustrates, when leaders eschew these openings and instead marshall controversies for their own ends, aesthetic litigation may ensue and the potential for democratic engagement inherent in aesthetic negotiation is lost. Bawa's admonition to 'use our constitutional democratic framework to mobilise the energy of the tension to make decisive strides toward socio-economic justice' remains a future possibility.[40]

(iii) The Blue Dress

Symbolic artefactual agency is also evident in our final example of Judith Mason's well-known work in the Constitutional Court. Albie Sachs, a founding constitutional judge whose vision was pivotal in the building's symbolic design and the prominence of art within it, calls *The Blue Dress* (see Figure 5.9) by Judith Mason one of the most well-known and admired artworks in the Court's collection. Also known as *The Man Who Sang and the Woman Who Kept Silent*, the work affirms individual human rights, dignity, and the Court's commitment to encouraging public engagement and deepening understandings of South African history.[41]

The work is a triptych commemorating the deaths of Phila Ndwandwe and Harold Sefola. As described by the Constitutional Court catalogue: 'Their killers confessed the murders during the Truth and Reconciliation Trials, admitting to their victims' bravery. Security police kept Ndwandwe naked for weeks during interrogation before knocking her unconscious and shooting her.'[42] To honour Ndwandwe, Mason assembled a dress out of blue plastic bags with this painted inscription:

> We only know your story because a sniggering man remembered how brave you were. Memorials to your courage are everywhere; they blow about in the streets and drift on the tide and cling to thorn-bushes. This dress is made from some of them.[43]

[40] Bawa (n 34) 10.

[41] Bronwyn Law-Viljoen (ed), *Art and Justice: The Art of the Constitutional Court of South Africa* (David Krut Books 2008) 123–25.

[42] 'The Constitutional Court Art Collection' <https://www.constitutionhill.org.za/pages/constitutional-court-art-collection> accessed 3 October 2022.

[43] Law-Viljoen (n 41) 123. Mason was asked to re-make the work as the plastic had started to disintegrate. There are currently three versions of the dress encased in Perspex boxes.

Figure 5.9 Judith Mason's *The Man Who Sang and the Woman Who Kept Silent*, photo-collage of artwork from the Constitutional Court of Art Collection, Braamfontein, South Africa (Image courtesy of the Constitutional Court Trust).
Source: Judith Mason, *The Man Who Sang and the Woman Who Kept Silent* (1998, oil on board, mixed media, and oil on board, Constitutional Court Art Collection) <https://ccac.concourttrust.org.za>.

Mason's work sparked ongoing, multi-dimensional aesthetic negotiation as it elicits strong emotions. In 2017, a public debate emerged around the 'absence of truth' in this work. Douglas Ainslie, a clerk to one of the Constitutional Justices, alleged flaws in how Judith Mason aesthetically interpreted the story told by Antjie Krog from the TRC hearings. Ainslie wrote: 'To start, I must point out that the artwork is obviously about two individuals, as it may have been a woman who "kept silent" but it was a man who sang ... All of that aside, perhaps the biggest difficulty with the whole matter for me is this. We know Krog is a story teller. We know she has, honestly and openly so, struggled with what the "truth" is during her time reporting on the TRC.'[44] Ainslie continues this line of thought with a question: 'Does the piece, as an artwork, necessarily need to rest on the truth of the underlying story?' 'My straightforward impression is "yes"', he responds.[45]

While Ainslie's intervention might be seen as a part of aesthetic negotiation, it actually fits better with Sierra León's frame of aesthetic litigation. Ainslie's blunt position that a work's value is lost if it is not literally true is combative, competitive, and binary. It may be that his legal training primed him to privilege truth over storytelling. Litigation, after all, is a contest to establish an accepted account of events and is not designed to take symbolic values into account.[46] It is also dangerous because it escalates conflict from the realm of aesthetic negotiation to

[44] Douglas Ainslie, 'Art, the TRC and the "Truth": Unstitching the "Blue Dress"' (2017) Constitutional Court of South Africa Working Paper.
[45] ibid.
[46] J Mason, 'Unstitching the Blue Dress: A Response' (2017) Counstitutional Court Art Colleciton Working Paper <https://ccac.concourttrust.org.za/uploads/files/2014/10/Unstitching-the-Blue-Dress-by-Judith-Mason.pdf> accessed 3 October 2022.

aesthetic litigation, foreclosing the prospect of synergistic dialogue. As Mason explained in her response: '[I] use the dress in a synecdochic way to celebrate Phila herself ... I set her in a landscape with its sense of space and entrapment depicted by using layers of honeycomb grids, a device I had been experimenting with some time. It simply represents the matrix in which the subject finds itself. It is not a border fence. I do not work literally, I work allusively.'[47] Mason was deeply wounded by the critique and refused to change her piece, writing 'I was delighted when Albie asked me for the work and I did not think to amend any of my images for a space which is used by people who are not necessarily versed in the language of contemporary art.'[48]

Acknowledging the possibilities and the perils of artefactual agency and aesthetic negotiation, Mason quotes opening remarks by Chief Justice Arthur Chaskalson at her retrospective exhibition: 'A work of art, once completed, takes on a life of its own. It has been created for others to see. What they see may not be what the artist intended ... At best an artist starts a conversation and has no control over how it develops, but imagery needs to be read aright in order for the conversation to develop at all.'[49]

While her point is accurate and viewers will always have multiple responses to an artwork, it is important to be vigilant about the uses to which art is bent. Any work can serve multiple agendas and its artefactual agency can be hijacked in various ways. Ainslie's self-serving motivation to 'prove' flaws in the original story undermines and misses the value of the symbolic and transformational power of an artwork. His quest to correct the rational facts of the story was misplaced, commandeering the possibility of aesthetic negotiation into aesthetic litigation with only one right answer in mind. Albie Sachs' comments are instructive in this regard:

> Rationality is sometimes seen as inimical to art, and passion as hostile to Justice. Our building shows how art and human rights overlap and reinforce each other. At the core of the Bill of Rights and of the artistic endeavour represented in the Court is respect for human dignity. It is this that unites art and justice.[50]

4. Conclusion: Art and Transitional Justice

As is clear from the foregoing, art and justice will not always be happily coupled and art will always be subject to interpretation. Aesthetic negotiation asks of everyone openness to ambiguities, genuine curiosity about the work and about others, and

[47] ibid.
[48] ibid.
[49] Mason (n 46).
[50] Albie Sachs, 'Art and Freedom' in Law-Viljoen (n 41) 23.

respectful engagement with both. When aesthetic negotiation slides into aesthetic litigation, experiences like those of Brett Murray are the result. Controversy around Murray's work, *The Spear*, descended into death threats and resulted in Murray's silence for two years. These threats had a more general impact on self-censorship for Murray and, very likely, other artists who were careful about political satire in their work. Judith Mason was so distressed by Ainslie's remarks that she offered to remove her work if it no longer served its function to inspire. Mason longed for aesthetic negotiation: multivalent, transformative conversations that the work had spawned and could continue to elicit if viewed respectfully both for its symbolic power and its capacity to evoke deep feeling. By resorting to litigation tactics that sought to 'prove' her wrong, Ainslee opened a debate about the wrong questions. People began to ask whether the work was historically factual and missed its aesthetic, emotional, and sensory effects. This very public attempt to discredit Mason's art about the TRC testimonies was devastating to her. Sadly, she died unexpectedly of heart failure less than a year later.

Though Judith is gone, *The Blue Dress* continues to anchor and communicate the raw emotion that attended the TRC hearings. Strong feelings about injustice are vitally important in the re-imagining needed to build a democratic future. When invoked in the spirit of aesthetic negotiation, they can be a part of the energy that becomes a reservoir for its construction. A written reflection from a Canadian law student who visited the Constitutional Court is illustrative:

> I still can't stop thinking about the Blue Dress. That image, and the words drawn across it, evoked more emotion and thoughtful connection with a moment in history and what that meant than anything I could have read in the TRC transcripts or history books. In my job, I can read case after case after case of child abuse or sexual assault, but... stopping and being encouraged to actually think about these images and spaces made me feel and think.[51]

Social transformation requires both material and distributive justice as a part of reconciliation. Respectful and generative aesthetic negotiation, drawing energy from potent artworks may be our best avenue to navigate the perilous journey of addressing the legacy of past historical injustice in both Colombia and South Africa.

[51] Email from Cait Fleck (UBC law student) to Professor Michelle LeBaron.

6

Aesthetic Litigation as a Mechanism for Building the Truth in the Colombian Truth Commission

Yolanda Sierra León

1. Introduction

One of the vital objectives of the Final Peace Agreement for the Termination of the Conflict and the Construction of a Stable and Lasting Peace (the peace agreement), ratified on 24 November 2016 between the Colombian government and the FARC-EP, is to achieve 'a peace that lasts beyond the ceasefire', so that the 'aftermath of violence' does not easily turn into a 'prelude to violence'.[1] This means, on the one hand, that every mechanism, instrument, organ, programme, and plan designed for this purpose should facilitate a transition towards social healing and mutual understanding. This is a process that must not simply involve the absence of confrontation, but rather must also entail the possibility of addressing disagreements through non-violent means: that is, through dialogue, through the recognition of (rather than through the submission to) the other, through the respect for life, and, ultimately, through the promotion of the long-term goal of a peaceful co-existence in Colombian society.

This transitional process not only seeks a ceasefire, ending hostilities and addressing the damages of the war—such as personal injuries, harm to the physical and mental integrity of the victims, or environmental or cultural damage—but must also identify and record the means through which violence manifested in society during the armed conflict. This becomes clearer when we acknowledge that there are forms of violence that precede and accompany concrete violations. These behaviours are entrenched in society, are part of its culture, occur daily, and have the power to open doors to the materialisation of human rights violations.

In this work, the aforementioned phenomenon is given the name of 'structural violence'.[2] This form of violence is silent, under the surface, and emerges with great

[1] Johan Galtung, *Violencia, guerra y su impacto: Sobre los efectos visibles e invisibles de la violencia* (*Foro para filosofía intercultural* 5, Polylog 2004).
[2] ibid.

Yolanda Sierra León, *Aesthetic Litigation as a Mechanism for Building the Truth in the Colombian Truth Commission*
In: *Transitional Justice, Distributive Justice, and Transformative Constitutionalism.* Edited by: David Bilchitz and Raisa Cachalia, with Magdalena Inés Correa Henao and Nathalia Bautista Pizarro, Oxford University Press. © Yolanda Sierra León 2023. DOI: 10.1093/oso/9780192887627.003.0006

force, particularly during armed conflict. This cultural and structural violence ultimately leads to direct violence,[3] because it acts as a legitimising factor which, in turn, reinforces itself, and even justifies political and economic changes that profoundly affect historically disadvantaged minorities, marginalised social sectors, populations neglected by the state, and stigmatised people in general.

In this regard, this chapter seeks to demonstrate that aesthetic and artistic processes occur in communities affected by the war, which aim precisely at recognising this particular violence. Consequently, these must be taken into consideration by the organs of the Comprehensive System of Truth, Justice, Reparation and Non-Repetition of the Peace Agreements, especially the Commission for the Clarification of Truth, Coexistence and Non-Repetition (hereinafter CEV). These cultural or artistic processes correspond to what in other works I have called 'aesthetic litigation',[4] which encompasses those artistic or cultural practices that, based on cultural heritage, denounce victimising acts and demand justice. In these manifestations, we can identify the rights of the victims. Their practice is also able to create an appropriate atmosphere to end the cycle of violence, especially of the structural kind, since they draw attention to the daily events that enable violence, such as social injustices, sexism, racism, and other degrading acts against human dignity. Consequently, the CEV, as an extrajudicial organ of the Comprehensive System of Truth, Justice, Reparation and Non-Repetition, can utilise the practices of aesthetic litigation since, as has been stated, its primary function is to expose the causes of the conflict and to promote activities that seek to eradicate its roots.

Hence, in order to articulate this function of the CEV and the practical feature of aesthetic litigation within the contexts of transition, this study will centre around the experience of the group *Hip-Hop Agrario* in the city of Medellín. To achieve this, the next section will present the meaning of the concept of aesthetic litigation. Thereafter, the functions of the CEV in the Colombian peace process will be explained and, finally, this chapter will examine whether the artistic production of *Hip-Hop Agrario* can positively contribute to the fulfilment of the CEV's objectives.

2. Aesthetic Litigation

Aesthetic litigation [*litigio estético*] is a phenomenon observed in several populations in Colombia who have been impacted by the cycles of violence of the armed

[3] ibid.

[4] Yolanda Sierra León, 'Relaciones entre el arte y los derechos humanos' (2014) 32 Derecho del Estado 77–100; see also Yolanda Sierra León (ed), *Reparación Simbólica: Jurisprudencia, cantos y tejidos* (Universidad Externado de Colombia 2018); Yolanda Siera León, *Teoría general de la reparación simbólica* (Universidad Externado de Colombia, Ejército Nacional de Colombia 2021).

conflict.[5] In these types of communities, people usually start processes of artistic or aesthetic expression aimed at denouncing violent facts, as well as finding a way to re-dignify and re-signify ordinary life and to recover their identity. In other words, they seek to 'banish the idea of violence as fatal'.[6] This, in part, explains the existence of plays, paintings, songs, weavings, or more generally, gestures, performances—oral, manual, or bodily expressions—and other material practices determined by culture in these communities. In this sense, aesthetic litigation is defined as the use of tangible or intangible cultural heritage, declared or undeclared by the state, as a mechanism to denounce (or demand from society or the state) facts related to (or needs derived from) massive human rights violations perpetrated by different armed actors, who brutally altered the daily order of individual and collective life.[7]

It is important to clarify that *cultural heritage* is used here to refer to the expression of the collective and creative identity of peoples that translates into 'cultural traits and practices that humans as social beings build, transmit and consolidate in their environment'.[8] Likewise, the term *aesthetic* refers to a form of knowledge or perception of the world through the senses and it is not used as a synonym of art.[9] In contrast, aesthetics acquires its meaning here if it is understood as a human form, independent of a disciplinary field, that deals with the study and the production of works of art.[10]

On the other hand, the concept of 'litigation'[11] refers to the way in which aesthetic or artistic expressions constitute an alternative means utilised by these communities to demand or claim justice, as they lack real access to ordinary judicial means or such means are, in practice, ineffective such as, for example, when these mechanisms do not recognise the occurrence of victimising acts. In contrast, the fact that a song, a play, or a weaving (for instance) serve as a way of denouncing human rights violations can be explained through the features that accompany this phenomenon, as has been observed in different studies.

First, aesthetic litigation occurs in marginal communities where 'marginal' means distant from the core or centre. The condition of marginality arises due to historical, geographical, cultural, and ideological reasons. This also leads to a lack

[5] This concept has been addressed by the author on several previous occasions. See Yolanda Sierra León, 'Relaciones entre el arte y los derechos humanos' (n 4); see also Yolanda Siera León, *Teoría general de la reparación simbólica* (n 4) 241 ff.

[6] Diana Taylor, *El archivo y el repertorio. La memoria cultural performática en las Américas* (Universidad Alberto Hurtado 2003) 190–211.

[7] ibid 25.

[8] Lourdes Arizpe, 'Los debates internacionales en torno al Patrimonio Cultural Inmaterial' (2006) 13(38) Cuicuilco 24.

[9] Yolanda Sierra León, 'Reparación Simbólica, Litigio estético y Litigio Artístico: Reflexiones en torno al arte, la cultura, y la justicia restaurativa en Colombia' (2014) 85 Serie virtual 'Documentos de Trabajo', Departamento de Derecho Constitucional, Universidad Externado de Colombia 7f.

[10] ibid, 7 f.

[11] From the Latin verb *litigare* (litigate, dispute, quarrel) derived from *litis* (contention, complaint, controversy) and *agere* (move, advance, promote), to advance a controversy, a claim or a complaint.

of presence of the state in the territories, which hinders the effective enjoyment and protection of fundamental rights. Since these populations are excluded from the central institutions, they seek to compensate for these deficits by resorting to their native traditions and cultural idiosyncrasies, in order to assert their wishes and aspirations.[12] In this sense, we can also observe that manifestations of aesthetic litigation are not promoted to reach some ideological, or political end. They are rather actions that rise from a communitarian and territorial interest. It is possible that over time they can eventually conform to a specific creed, political affinity, or religious organisation. Nevertheless, this is not their starting point. Consequently, it is common for individual parts of these communities to adopt their own visions, beliefs, or political expressions.[13]

Likewise, aesthetic litigation involves the natural or spontaneous incorporation of cultural traditions. It is important to highlight that these are not cultural or artistic activities with a technical content implemented by the state. Rather, they correspond to aesthetic processes narrated, directed, proposed, and developed by the community itself that shares a cultural reality and *ethos*. In their performative representations of reality, that is, the constitution of 'vehicles of memory',[14] they create a dialogue between the traumatic past and the reconstructed present. The expressions of aesthetic litigation are, hence, exercises of memory, truth, political, social, and cultural resistance, in respect of their condition of marginality, suffering, and mourning.

Moreover, we can also observe that aesthetic litigation tends to have an impact not only within the community that engages with it, but also at the national level, thus accomplishing the conveyance of their message even to the perpetrators of the victimising acts that are being denounced.[15] In this way, given their cultural expansion, it contributes to the construction of memory, not only at a local level, but also at a national level. This can be seen in the emblematic cases of the *Tejidos de Mampuján* [Mampuján weavings] and the songs of *Las Pavas*, cultural manifestations that have been awarded the Colombian National Prize of Peace. In this sense, it can be said that aesthetic litigation promotes national reconciliation.[16]

Another essential feature of aesthetic litigation is the incorporation of facts about violations of rights in the contents of their cultural heritage or in their artistic and cultural practices. Consequently, there is a record created of rights violations. Through this means, artistic or aesthetical expressions end up becoming a form of

[12] In this sense, see Felix Reátegui Carrillo, *Las víctimas recuerdan. Notas sobre la práctica social de la memoria* (Centro Internacional para la Justicia Transicional 2009) 38.

[13] Yolanda Sierra León, *Reparación Simbólica, Litigio estético y Litigio Artístico* (n 9) 9 f.

[14] Grupo de Memoria Histórica, *Memorias en tiempo de guerra. Repertorio de iniciativas* (Centro Nacional de Memoria Histórica 2009) 22; Catalina Carrizosa, 'El trabajo de la memoria como vehículo de empoderamiento político: la experiencia del Salón del Nunca Más' (2011) 25(42) Boletín de Antropología Universidad de Antioquia 36, 40 ff.

[15] Reátegui Carrillo (n 12) 36.

[16] ibid 38.

litigating or demanding justice for these rights which have been violated within a context in which, given the condition of marginality of the community, there is no real access to ordinary judicial means. Among several cases of aesthetic litigation in Colombia, we can observe these kinds of denouncements in the proposal of *Teatro por la Paz de Tumaco* [Theater for the Peace of Tumaco], which seeks to sensitise, denounce, and reconstruct the historical memory of their region. We can also highlight *Las Musas de Pogue*, a group of women of Chocó who intone their chants every year on 2 May to evoke the Bojayá Massacre.[17]

Lastly, the power of social transformation has also been recognised as an essential feature of aesthetic litigation. It allows that people not directly affected by the human rights violations receive these messages and, over time, engage with the movement initiated by the community. That, in turn, it is hoped can lead to a change in social behaviour in relation to the very causes that gave rise to the human rights violations.

3. The Colombian Commission for the Clarification of Truth, Coexistence and Non-Repetition (CEV)

A. Generalities of the CEV

Aesthetic litigation could be considered as an effective mechanism to fulfil the objectives of the CEV, especially as its task is to identify the structural violence that nurtures the Colombian armed conflict. The CEV is part of the Comprehensive System of Truth, Justice, Reparation and Non-Repetition, established in Chapter 5 of the peace agreement, created with the objective of achieving or facilitating the greatest possible satisfaction of the rights of the victims; accountability for what happened; legal security to its participants; co-existence, reconciliation, and non-repetition; and the transition from the armed conflict into peace.[18] In this sense, it provides that the Comprehensive System of Truth, Justice, Reparation and Non-Repetition must comply with the following fundamental aims: establishing the truth, serving justice, obtaining reparations for the victims, and guaranteeing non-repetition of the cycles of violence. To achieve this, several implementation mechanisms with constitutional and legal rank were established including the Special Jurisdiction for Peace as a judicial organ of the system, and the Search Unit for Missing Persons and the CEV as extrajudicial organs, alongside a set of reparation measures and non-repetition guarantees.[19]

[17] Comunidad de Pogue, *Pogue: un pueblo, una familia, un río. Historias contadas por la comunidad de Pogue* (Centro Nacional de Memoria Histórica 2015).
[18] Final Peace Agreement, 5.1.
[19] C-694/2015, Corte Constitucional (Judge Alberto Rojas Ríos).

Additionally, the right to the truth can be vindicated through criminal liability proceedings at the Special Jurisdiction for Peace or through extrajudicial remedies, such as the CEV, since truth commissions can more deeply contemplate abuses or wider dimensions of the armed conflict.[20] Thus, the CEV was born as a transitory, independent, and impartial institution that enjoys territorial and extrajudicial application, and has the objective of 'encouraging the participation of different sectors and actors ensuring that the information provided is not used to assign responsibility within judicial scenarios'.[21] It was officially installed on 8 May 2018.[22] It had a term of three years, in addition to a six-month preparation period, to create focused teams, define channels of communication, establish relations with the other organs of the system and the state, comprehend its mandate, as well as collect, systematise, and understand the experiences generated within the regions, while applying a territorial, ethnic, and gender-based approach.[23] Its final report was published on 28 June 2022.[24]

B. Essential Components for the Operation of the CEV

The meaning of determining the truth, and its implementation by the CEV, as established in the peace agreement, is something that must be assessed taking into account its essential components and objectives. In this sense, truth commissions have historically been conceived as non-coercive and non-judicial institutions that aim to achieve historical justice, focusing on the stories and statements of victims and survivors, to determine human rights abuses and violations of international humanitarian law in respect of a specific period. They do so from a holistic, global, and non-fragmentary point of view, comprising multiple variables such as the characteristics of each territory, its culture, ethnic groups, gender, economic, and socio-political conditions.[25] Although the experiences of truth commissions are all different, in the case of the Colombian CEV, three common aspects can be identified: a mandate, a methodology, and a report.

[20] C-017/2018, Corte Constitucional (Judge Diana Fajardo Rivera) [62].

[21] ibid [44]; the CEV is regulated by the following legal instruments: the peace agreement, the Legislative Act 01 of 2017 that grants it constitutional rank, and Decree 588 of 5 April 2017, issued by the government.

[22] 'Arranca formalmente la Comisión de la Verdad' (*Verdad Abierta* 2018) <https://verdadabierta.com/arranca-formalmente-la-comision-la-verdad/> accessed 31 January 2021.

[23] According to Decree 588 of 2017, art 1; see also Verdad Abierta (n 22).

[24] 'Hay futuro, si hay verdad', Comisión de la Verdad <https://www.comisiondelaverdad.co/hay-futuro-si-hay-verdad> accessed 31 July 2022.

[25] ibid paras 57–60.

(i) The mandate of the CEV

The mandate is the frame of reference or delimitation of the investigative work of the commission. It includes the conditions of time, means, and place of the broad, diverse, and multiform violations, which will be addressed within a context of armed violence.[26] In this regard, the Colombian CEV is regulated pursuant to Legislative Act 01 of 2017 and Decree 588 of 2017. Article 11 of Decree 588 establishes a series of clarification and recognition tasks, leaving unclear whether the mandate is limited to the thirteen subsections of the article, or whether in the development of the methodology and the investigation other tasks can be conducted. However, the mandate is directly related to the CEV's main objective: unravelling the causes, consequences, and impacts of the armed conflict, and understanding the circumstances, processes, and mechanisms that perpetuated it as well as the responses of the communities.

The thirteen subsections of article 11 of Decree 588 can be grouped into three categories, related to the CEV mandate: clarification, recognition, and co-existence. Clarification consists of understanding and explaining the armed conflict, its causes, impacts, and consequences, as well as all the factors that enabled or contributed to its perpetuation. It takes into account each population, ethnic group, according to gender, age, or any element that allows a differential approach to the consequences of the conflict (subsections numbered 1 and 3–11).

The recognition mandate (subsections numbered 2 and 12) involves three different levels. First, there is the recognition of victims as civil and political subjects of rights. Second, there is the recognition of the truth and responsibility of the perpetrators of the armed conflict, regarding the compensation of the victims and the historical understanding of what happened. Finally, there is the recognition by society of the dimensions of violence and indignity, and the avoidance of historical denials, justifications, or repetition of these circumstances or of new violations.

Lastly, the co-existence mandate refers to the creation of environments of real co-existence in the territories, where alternative mechanisms of peaceful resolution of conflicts and differences can be implemented, with values such as democracy, dialogue, respect, and tolerance, which allow the fulfilment of the three noted types of acknowledgements and the non-repetition of violence (numeral 13).

(ii) Methodology of the CEV

Truth commissions operate according to a methodology related to how they must proceed to fulfil their mandate, functions, and assigned objectives. This is the second component mentioned and provides the navigational route to the reconstruction of the truth. Thus, the CEV must define 'the investigation techniques, the types of evidence admitted, the forms of recollection and management of the

[26] ibid para 65.

information, the standards for the evaluation of the elements and the attention to witnesses and victims'.[27] Likewise, the CEV is autonomous in the adoption of its own methodology.[28] As part of its exercise of this power, during the first semester of 2017, the Working Group on the Artistic and Cultural Dimension of the Commission was created. This group aims to study the role of art and culture in the process of reception, systematisation, and dissemination of the truth.[29]

(iii) Final report

The CEV also had to draft a final report considering 'different contexts, reflecting the investigations around all the components of the mandate and containing the conclusions and recommendations of their work, including guarantees of non-repetition'.[30] This document must be made public, widely disseminated and socialised, including through 'the development of cultural and educational initiatives, such as, for example, the promotion of exhibitions and the recommendation of its inclusion in the educational curriculum'.[31] On 28 June 2022 the final report was officially presented to the national and international community.[32] Currently, the Truth Commission is dedicated to fulfilling a socialisation agenda in the territories.

Related to this, commissioner Alejandro Valencia has stated that there is an interest within the CEV in drafting a final report with not only the typical characteristics, namely, a written document with academic and investigative rigour, but which also takes into account a differential approach, that includes other forms of narration, such as oral and visual. This opens up new possibilities for spreading the truth in ways where art and culture would play an important role.

C. Aesthetic Litigation and the Objectives of the CEV

The essential objectives of the CEV have been tailored taking into account the importance of maintaining appropriate communication with different sectors of the Colombian population. In this sense, three fundamental aspects have been recognised, which can be addressed from the point of view of aesthetic litigation.[33] At this point it is essential to understand that, in accordance with the spirit of the peace agreement, the dialogue to clarify, recognise, co-exist, and

[27] ibid para 96 f.

[28] According to Decree 588 of 2017, art 14 (Presidencia de la República, 5 April 2017).

[29] For this reason, on 16 August 2018, at Externado University, a seminar was held where different experts from different disciplinary fields were invited to discuss and share experiences in this regard. It is expected that the future methodology of the CEV, will take into account all these cultural, artistic, and alternative processes in relation to the right to the truth and its dissemination.

[30] According to Decree 588 of 2017 (n 21) art 13.5.

[31] According to Decree 588 of 2017 (n 21).

[32] 'Hay futuro, si hay verdad', Comisión de la Verdad (n 24).

[33] According to Decree 588 of 2017 (n 21) art 2.

guarantee non-repetition, must be open, without class distinction, and involve the participation of the state, society, and the different actors involved in the armed conflict.

In this sense, it is important to understand that each objective of the CEV requires interaction and synergy with society and with the people in charge or who are believed to have contributed in some way to the origin and perpetuation of the conflict. Therefore, it cannot be a closed or erudite space for the commissioners and the victims, who already know their stories, as that methodology would not enable the indispensable reparation, the non-repetition, or the co-existence that are its central goals. In this regard, the practices that occur within the framework of aesthetic litigation could fulfil the objectives of the CEV. Such practices would allow for the expression and dissemination of diverse artistic and cultural experiences created from within the regions by communities of victims, who have indirectly contributed to pinpointing the objectives of the CEV in situations of armed conflict or in the daily structural cultural violence. This makes them valuable to the fulfilment of the mission of this organ. The next section will analyse the experience of *Hip-Hop Agrario*, in order to understand several possibilities of building or rebuilding the truth in the CEV.

4. *Hip-Hop Agrario*: A Manifestation of Aesthetic Litigation

> '*... They left my friends missing and dead. And everyone asks why it is necessary to forget? We answer: remember, even if they take away the primary.*'
>
> Memories of the future (InSURgentes, 2016–2017), *Hip-Hop Agrario*
> (Lyrics reproduced with the permission of Agroarte Colombia)

A. *Hip-Hop Agrario* and the Violence in the Thirteenth Commune of Medellín

Hip-Hop Agrario (in English: *Agrarian Hip-Hop*) is a Hip-Hop group from the city of Medellín (Colombia), a branch of a collective group or—as its members recognise—*family* called *Agroarte Colombia*.[34] *Agroarte* was born as a philosophy and a social project in 2002, in response to a series of military operations that took place in the Thirteenth Commune in Medellín, especially during 2002–2003.[35]

[34] The norms underlying this group are explored from a philosophical perspective in Bautista Pizarro, Chapter 3 in this book.

[35] Centro Nacional de Memoria Histórica, *Medellín: Memorias de una guerra urbana* (Centro Nacional de Memoria Histórica 2017) 197.

The dimensions, modalities, and repertoires of violence were inestimable, not only in terms of the numbers of victims, but also in its scale, disproportionality, and degradation.

The forms of victimisation originated mainly due to the dynamics of territorial control within the Thirteenth Commune, and resulted in forced disappearances, intra-urban displacements, the selective assassinations of neighbourhood leaders, massacres, sexual violence, threats, torture, and dispossession of property.[36] This context of violence escalated further with the conflicts between armed groups that sought to maintain territorial control in the Commune, such as militias, guerrilla groups, and paramilitaries and, especially, state military intervention.[37] Alongside this, there were a multitude of crimes committed against civilian and political resistance, which originated specifically to counter the control of illegal armed groups and state military intervention in the Thirteenth Commune.[38] Among these criminal acts, there have been reports of murders, threats, exile of trade unionists, the silencing, persecution, and intimidation of relatives of victims of forced disappearance, as well as the murder of teachers and eight students from Antioquia University. There have been murders, persecution, harassment, and abduction of human rights activists, social leaders, and other members of non-governmental organisations (NGOs).[39]

The complex dynamics of the armed conflict caused this wide range of attacks. In the case of the Thirteenth Commune, there was an ongoing situation, perpetuated over the last three decades, with different cycles and degrees of impact,[40] and translated into what has been called the *urbanisation of war*.[41]

There were many armed actors involved in these urban confrontations: the 'Revolutionary Armed Forces of Colombia (FARC-EP), the National Liberation Army (ELN), the United Self-Defence Forces of Colombia (AUC) (a paramilitary group (specifically, the Cacique Nutibara Bloc (BCN)'[42]) and the state forces led by the 'National Army, the National Police, the defunct Administrative Department of Security (DAS), the Colombian Air Force (FAC), the Technical Investigation Corps (CTI) and the Office of the Attorney-General'.[43]

This state of affairs triggered all the aforementioned violations, with the participation, accompaniment, and acquiescence of the Colombian government (during the presidency of Álvaro Uribe Vélez), through the so-called 'Democratic Security'

[36] ibid 201.
[37] ibid 59 ff, 72 ff.
[38] ibid 72 ff, 104 ff.
[39] ibid 203–04.
[40] *Yarce y otras v Colombia* [2016] (Excepción preliminar, Fondo, Reparaciones y Costas) [Inter-Am C] Serie C 325 (22 November 2016) [77].
[41] Grupo de Memoria Histórica, *Desplazamiento forzado en la comuna 13: La huella invisible de la guerra* (Aguilar, Altea, Taurus, Alfaguara 2011) 73.
[42] *Yarce y otras v Colombia* (n 40) [77].
[43] ibid [78].

policy, and within the framework of the 'social recovery plan'.[44] This meant setting up the Thirteenth Commune as 'the guinea pig', to show 'results in the application of the strategy. It focused on the fight against terrorism associated with guerrilla groups in Medellín, the city that played an important role in his election as president and occurred in a climate of political polarisation and rejection of the guerrillas.'[45]

The military operations *Mariscal* and *Orión* are perhaps the most important, due to the disproportionate attack by the forces of the state in an urban area, their impact, and the number of victims registered. The investigations of the National Centre of Historical Memory (CNMH) and the Centre for Popular Research and Education and Justice and Peace have managed to record in Table 6.1 the following military operations executed in the Third and Thirteenth Communes of Medellín, in 2002 and 2003.[46]

Additionally, other reports have recorded the following military operations: *Operación Furia* (21 February 2002), *Operación Fuego* (21 February 2002); *Operación Martillo* (4 May 2002); *Operación Júpiter* (17 June 2002); *Operación Jalisco* (24 June 2002); *Operación Jinete* (6 July 2002); *Operación Saturno* (4 September 2002).[47]

Bearing in mind this particular context of violence and armed conflict, the inhabitants of the Third and Thirteenth Communes decided to confront this situation, not in a passive or neutral way, nor in a violent way, but rather through art and culture as a form of resistance.[48] These artistic activities represent 'creative adaptation, negotiation and resistance'.[49] In this scenario of cultural and artistic resistance, *Agroarte* was born, as a family that brings together women, men, boys, and girls. It appeared first in the Thirteenth Commune, but later extended to other communes such as the Third Commune.[50]

Agroarte functions as a dynamic process, where people come and go, but a particular philosophy remains in the territory and is transmitted to generate empowerment, welfare, satisfaction, reconfiguration, and reconstruction of a community and its dynamics. This process was conducted by means of urban agriculture and by resorting to Hip-Hop culture, common to the people of the community. A member of the movement, explains:

44 ibid [77].
45 Grupo de Memoria Histórica, *Desplazamiento forzado en la comuna 13* (n 41) 73.
46 Some of the data regarding the place and the harmful effects of some of the operations have not been specified in the mentioned Centro Nacional de Memoria Histórica and Grupo de Memoria Histórica studies (n 35; n 41).
47 'Se hace memoria pero falta justicia a 13 años de la Operación Orión' (*Verdad Abierta*, 19 October 2015) <https://verdadabierta.com/se-hace-memoria-pero-falta-justicia-a-13-anos-de-la-operacion-orion/> accessed 22 September 2023.
48 Centro Nacional de Memoria Histórica (n 35) 204 ff, 215 ff.
49 ibid 205.
50 Interview with a music producer, *Agroarte* (Medellín, Colombia, 26 August 2017).

Table 6.1 Military operations registered in the 3rd and 13th Communes of Medellín. Prepared by the Historical Memory Research Group and Center for Research and Popular Education and Justice and Peace, 2003

Operation	Date	Neighbourhoods involved	Results
Primavera	February 1st–3rd, 2002	Belencito Corazón; Veinte de Julio; El Salado	18 illegally detained, accused of being suspected militants.
Otoño I	February 24th, 2002	Belencito; Corazón; Juan XXII	42 arbitrary detentions.
Contrafuego	February 29th, 2002	La Quiebra; La Divisa; Blanquizal	63 raids, 31 arrests and 5 civilians killed, presented as combatants KIA (the so called 'falsos positivos').
Otoño II	March 7th–8th, 2002	La Divisa	-
Marfil	March 15th, 2002	-	-
Águila	April 17th, 2002	El Saldo; 20 de Julio	-
Horizonte II	May 2002	San Antonio de Prado	-
Mariscal	May 21st, 2002	20 de Julio; El Salado; Independencias I, II and III; Nuevos Conquistadores	9 civilians killed (four of them minors), 37 injured and 55 people arbitrarily detained.
Potestad	June 15th, 2002	El Corazón; 20 de Julio	1 civilian killed
Antorcha	August 20th, 2002	Independencias; El Salado; 20 de Julio; El Corazón	37 injured civilians.
Saturno	September 14th, 2002	Las Independencias, Vallejuelos, Olaya Herrera, Blanquizal	-
Orión	From October 16th–November 2002	Belencito, Corazón, 20 de Julio, El Salado, Nuevos Conquistadores, Las independencias II	-
La Estrella VI	January 2003	3rd Commune: La Honda, El Cerro y Alto de la Cruz.	Illegal and arbitrary detentions.

Source: Grupo de Memoria Histórica, *Desplazamiento forzado en la comuna 13: La huella invisible de la guerra* (Aguilar, Altea, Taurus, Alfaguara 2011) 76.

> We understood that Hip-Hop is the street. Under the streets, there is land. The soil contains our history, our struggles and our memory. We also understood that the territory was not only built by the state; the territory was built by our old women, our old people, with grandmothers, grandparents, indigenous people. Then we began to generate internal processes within the territory. We started next to the *Escombrera*[51] sowing with mothers and making Hip-Hop with boys.[52]

Agroarte is rooted in forces from the territory of the community. Its work, therefore, focuses on different branches such as the recovery of identity, and rooting and belonging to a place; in the narration of the stories and memories lived in the community; in attending to the individual pain of each survivor, and in the healing processes of the soul and the body. In this sense, *Agroarte* highlights the following, according to one of its leaders:

> It is about recovering the common place, appropriating our territory, strengthening the voice of community empowerment, through planting and a family. This is the cycle of the process, and that's where we find memory. How? Thinking about the history of the pain of each one and its relationship with the conflict. This is where the process is born, the city, the country and the world.[53]

In relation to Hip-Hop (see Figure 6.1), this cultural movement was already part of the communities and the territory, and consequently was well received among the youth. It was a form of resistance by its expression of denunciation and was very useful in preserving the memory of violent events and overcoming them:[54]

> Young people made Hip-Hop the tool to tell their stories, to say 'no more' to violence. In this sense, the performance of the musical festival summoned by the *Hip-Hop Network La Élite* in the 13th Commune (2002) with the slogan 'In the 13th, violence does not overcome us', which preceded the 'Revolution without dead' festival (2004), was regarded as a journey for peace, memory and non-violence.[55]

Hip-Hop Agrario is a strategy of *Agroarte*, where young people, adults, and children tell their life stories, their stories about the conflict, and denounce the crimes of the state. At the same time, this is creative work and they also project themselves as artists, leaders, and survivors with the desire for de-stigmatisation, social justice,

51 A landfill of debris and garbage on the slopes of the Thirteenth Commune, which is believed to be hundreds of corpses of victims of military operations, especially *Orión*. It is considered one of the largest communal graves in Colombia.

52 Interview with Wilmar Botina, philosopher and leader, *Agroarte* (Medellín, Colombia, 26 August 2017).

53 ibid.

54 cf Grupo de Memoria Histórica, *Desplazamiento forzado en la comuna 13* (n 41) 215 ff.

55 ibid 205 f.

Figure 6.1 *Hip-Hop Agrario* performing at Externado University (Photography by Carolina Corredor, Universidad Externado de Colombia, Bogotá, Colombia, 16 August 2018)

and co-existence within their territories. Why was music chosen? According to Luis Fernando Álvarez, leader of the group, better known as AKA:

> For us Latinos, words create the world and thoughts; therefore, well-told and constructed words can generate a path to light. And if those words are built in the middle of the action, it becomes reality. Then people want to change the world, with their voice and others. It is not only the voice, but also turning into action, and action must become a voice; a double synergy. People connect and believe it, because it has passed through the body and turned it into words, and into action. People from the micro-world make micro changes; many voices are coming together, and a bigger dream is being built.[56]

B. Aesthetic Litigation: A Reading from Rap

'Insurgents! For a people that forget their own stories; Insurgents! There are many graves; forgetting in a country without memories; Insurgents!

[56] Interview with plastic artist and leader, Luis Fernando Àlvarez, *Agroarte* (Medellín, Colombia, 26 August 2017).

> *For a historically murderous government; Insurgents! Because although dead we are still alive.*'[57]
>
> InSURgentes, 2016–2017, *Hip-Hop Agrario*

Considering the essential characteristics of aesthetic litigation, this chapter will now determine how artistic productions such as *Hip-Hop Agrario* could aid in the achievement of the fundamental objectives of the CEV, and especially, in accordance with its mandates of clarification, recognition, and co-existence. This will be explained by selecting rap songs from different *Hip-Hop Agrario* records,[58] showing the elements of aesthetic litigation and the objectives of the CEV that relate to them.

(i) Describing the condition of marginality and the clarification mandate of the CEV

Hip-Hop Agrario is a group developed in a context that has been marginalised by society and the state, and its actions express communitarian interests, meaning, giving voice to those who cannot speak or have not been heard. In this sense, this music group does not adhere to the interests of any specific political party or similar associations. The marginality and its non-ideological feature defines it, and hence, its way of acting.

This can be observed when analysing some selected songs of *Hip-Hop Agrario*, which comprise testimonies concerning this condition of marginality and of a particular context of violence. Their songs usually talk about the neighbourhood, socio-economic problems, their forms of struggle and resistance. They suggest a series of victimising events or criminal occurrences, that merit investigation, review, and public reckoning in the search for justice or comprehension of the complexities, dynamics, and sequels to the conflict. In the case of the selected songs, they not only demonstrate practices derived from armed violence in the Communes, but also the daily violence derived from marginality, abandonment, and state subjection.

We find this phenomenon in the following songs: Disappeared [*Desaparecidos*] (2012); Who Tells the Story [*Quién cuenta la historia*] (2012); Thought Police [*Policía del pensamiento*] (2012); Again Rap [De *nuevo rap*] (2012); The Pain Routine [*La rutina de dolor*] (2012); I Miss You Father [*Me haces falta padre*] (2013); They Are Drums [*Son bombos*] (2014); Security [*Seguridad*] (2015); The Rubble [*La*

[57] '*¡Insurgentes!* para un pueblo que olvida sus propias historias; *¡insurgentes!* son fosas muchas, olvido de un país sin memorias; *¡insurgentes!* para un gobierno históricamente asesino; *¡insurgentes!* porque aún muertos, seguimos vivos' (InSURgentes, 2017).

[58] *Hip-Hop Agrario* has a catalogue of seven albums and several singles, from which ninety songs were analysed and twenty-five songs selected, as being most relevant for the subject matter of this chapter.

escombrera] (2015); Objections of Conscience [*Objeciones de consciencia*] (2015); Poetry of Land [*Poesía de tierra*] (2016–2017); Grammatical Bodies [*Cuerpos gramaticales*] (2016–2017); Toy Soldiers [*Soldados de juguete*] (2016–2017). In 'Again Rap' [*De nuevo rap*] we can appreciate the referred syncretism:

> Survivor of 6 operations: Otoño, Fuego, Mariscal, Antorcha, Orión. I greet the former president of the Convivir, always paramilitary, creator of massacres; his unjust argument: to safeguard order.
>
> Twenty years of absence, no social investment, the military surround the target, AUC, war plus war, the poor carry out the massacre, exile, the Commune is in front, the struggle is lost, the air and strength are exhausted, but the memory encourages me; do not stop, together those moments commemorate the departure, the offense grows, people are not attacked, the poor are respected and the offense is never forgotten.

Likewise, in 'Toy Soldiers':

> Obey, if you do not want to be weighed down, a paper toy that does not appear on that map. The rules are for everyone and you have to comply with them, without evading them, you leave the perimeter, the splinters kill you. Toy and puppet handled by the state, the law of the strongest has had you subjugated.
>
> ...
>
> Questions? There are no answers to death. Drawer and for the hole! Another story to the account.
>
> Barbados, whiskey, money, luca,[59] tombo,[60] the area is in dispute,
>
> The vaccine[61] pays for corrupt silence, checks, office, washing, mourning.
>
> Do you understand? They are toy soldiers, they left sequels in their bodies that do not lie. Underclaimed war buried their lives, the road was narrow in the suicidal city.

Thus, the artistic works of *Hip-Hop Agrario* allow for the identification and comprehension of the causes and particular forms of violence in the territory of the Thirteenth Commune, which reveals a deep condition of marginality and oppression in relation to the government, the public forces, and illegal armed groups. In this way, the work of this group constitutes a valuable contribution to the CEV as it helps to clarify the causes of violence, particularly, its structural kind.

59 Money.
60 Policeman.
61 Protection money.

(ii) Hip-Hop as part of culture and the recognition mandate of the CEV

On the other hand, the study of the production of *Hip-Hop Agrario* shows an incorporation and expansion of their cultural environment into their musical works, features that are present in the cases of aesthetic litigation observed in Colombia. All *Hip-Hop Agrario* songs are framed within the cultural tradition of the Thirteenth Commune, where Hip-Hop is present and has a fundamental role in the task of transforming reality and the perception of the neighbourhoods. In this way, the musical outputs have transformative and expansive capabilities. We can conclude that this enables the consolidation of processes of recognition of victims and of the liability of perpetrators, as well as the process of memory-building—which are central CEV mandates.

The process of recognition pursuant to the CEV mandate also relates to the restoration of the dignity of victims. When victims participate in artistic and cultural activities, they start a process of dignity restoration, since these scenarios allow them to recognise themselves once again as part of a citizen project while, at the same time, realizing their own personal projects. Likewise, through artistic and cultural practices, the stigmas and prejudices that facilitated violations of human rights can be eliminated, and the opportunity to change peoples' statuses from that of victims to creators (artist, singer, leader) presents itself, which allows for a transition from vulnerability to empowerment. Gerad Guzmán, a seventeen-year-old rapper of the Eighth Commune, reaffirms this perception:

> I think that many of us who have been displaced and have gone through those difficult times, can now tell the story, narrating it in a lyrical way; we can tell the story to others, to know how everything happened through music, art and everything that is done in the neighbourhood and all the projects made to address issues of displacement and violence. When you express yourself, you take a burden off and feel freer, as the wind, and also take it to the people so that they understand that something happens and we are still standing.[62]

In this regard, the songs that give account of this association are: What is Art? [*Qué es el arte?*] (2012); Again Rap [*De nuevo rap*] (2012); Dreams [*Sueños*] (2013); Seeds [*Semillas*] (2013); They Are Drums [*Son bombos*] (2014); Agroarte (2015); Behind [*Detrás de*] (2015); Insurgentes (2016); Memories of the Future [*Memorias del futuro*] (2016–2017); Poetry of Land [*Poesía de tierra*] (2016–2017); Hip-Hop Agrario (2016–2017); Grammatical Bodies [*Cuerpos gramaticales*] (2016–2017); Toy Soldiers [*Soldados de juguete*] (2016–2017); Hoppa Law [*Ley Hoppa*] (2016–2017); My Neighbourhood [*Mi Barrio*] (2018).

The following is stated, for instance, in *Poetry of Land*:

[62] Interview with a rapper, Gerad Guzmán, *Agroarte* (Medellín, Colombia, 26 August 2017).

> We received an inheritance and cannot be silenced; If silence bends us, our refuge is rap. We exist for the neighbourhood, we exist to sing, to not bend and never give up.
>
> ...
>
> It's me, it's us, we are seeds of memory of a rap that germinates; it's me, it's us, roots that close wounds are the light of our lives; it's me, it's us, we follow our path, we rap our destiny; It's me, it's us, looking for the truth that is denied to us in La Escombrera.
>
> Dignity is: to look for our dead, even if we do not find them.

Likewise, in regards to the recognition of the liability of the perpetrators of human rights violations, pursuant to the CEV mandates, the song Grammatical Bodies states:

> I, your murderer, the one they taught to not see, to not believe in tomorrow; who will give you a resounding shot and mess up your bed ... the place where nobody will find you, your mother and your family anguished, never in the future will find you.
>
> I will be the pawn of the owners of the land, pleasure of the elites ... the only shot that will confuse life and will lead you to death, with the silence of a war, in the oblivion of people, the same that chooses its oppressors, assassins who fire high-calibre weapons, from which bullets come out that make the ears buzz.

(iii) Social transformation and the co-existence mandate of the CEV

The last element of aesthetic litigation I shall address is its capacity to be a mechanism for social transformation for communities. By managing to involve indifferent or insensitive people, and actively contribute to modifying social behaviours that had supported human rights violations, we can affirm that it is compatible with the ends of justice, both ordinary and transitional. Concerning the mandates of the CEV, we can observe that, from this perspective, aesthetic and artistic activities could be useful in meeting the objective of co-existence. Indeed, the capability of social transformation of aesthetic litigation enables access to those uncomfortable truths, to the grey areas, to the historical complexity, and manages to blur the line between winners and losers.

The aforementioned is present in several songs of *Hip-Hop Agrario*, which link this ingredient of aesthetic litigation and the co-existence mandate of the CEV. The songs that account for this link are: Dreams [*Sueños*] (2013); Seeds [*Semillas*] (2013); *Agroarte* (2015); Behind [*Detrás de*] (2015); I Do Not Copy [*No Copio*] (2015); Grammatical Bodies [*Cuerpos gramaticales*] (2016–2017); My Neighbourhood [*Mi barrio*] (2018); No More of the Same [*No más de lo mismo*] (2018).

'I Do Not Copy' says:

> A life costs a lot and represents a lot of struggle. Now they kill a brother and after they kill him, the dead man is blamed. Understand that a life is not bought with money, don't be foolish because a being who is a dreamer, does not put a price on his dream. Understand once and for all that I will never tire of telling you that death, as I see it, must be natural. What is life must be respected, is the message that is given. When you listen to this rap, do not think about what this rapper needs to kill, that I did it with love for humanity.
>
> I do not fear death, I respect life, we do not copy from war, we are people without chains; I do not fear death, no, I respect life, yes, we do not copy from war, no, we are people without chains.

Furthermore, 'No More of the Same' recalls the death of a young man killed a year ago, during the commemoration of operation *Orión*, and aims to remember that living in territories begins with respecting life, and in the daily cohabitation in the communes:

> No more death, no more justice with bullets and a machete, we do not want thoughts that destroy the present ... May the world not confuse you and crush your heart, do not condemn the grave, nor rot in prison.
>
> We need ideas to confront the state, please no more war, see the past, the crossfire, how much damage it has caused to the people who struggle in the middle of an everyday life.

5. Conclusion

This chapter has focused on the necessity of identifying the various forms of violence in society (specifically structural violence) and its relation to the armed conflict as an essential part of the process of peacebuilding in Colombia. The behaviours that accompany victimising acts are part of the daily life of these communities and nurture human rights violations. Thus, the end of the conflict requires a thorough analysis of this phenomenon. In this way, we can understand the aims of the Colombian CEV in determining and eradicating structural violence. This labour of clarification also entails the fulfilment of a recognition mandate and the creation of spaces for contact between the members of Colombian society in order to structure a peaceful co-existence.

Communitarian aesthetic and artistic initiatives have been shown precisely to fulfil these three purposes. This is demonstrated in the case of aesthetic litigation. *Hip-Hop Agrario* joins these groups of cases and constitutes an example of the cultural richness of Colombia, which contributes through a method, content, and a mechanism that support the fulfilment of the objectives of the Colombian CEV. *Hip-Hop Agrario* songs can elucidate the causes and impact of street violence in the Thirteenth Commune of Medellín. Likewise, Hip-Hop is shown as a cultural movement of the city, that can transform the perception of reality, unmasking the causes of violence. This is also a process of personal transformation of those who form part of the artistic movement, by re-establishing their dignity, violated by the cycles of violence, through this act of recognition. Additionally, their production allows for the recognition of the liability of perpetrators responsible for human rights violations. It also contributes to the creation of an *ethos* and environment capable of resulting in peaceful co-existence. Its work could also be considered within the socialisation activities of the CEV's final report, which refers in several of its passages to the military operations episode carried out in the Thirteenth Commune of Medellín in 2002. It could also play a role in activities of memory-building and the creation of a culture of peace, according to the recommendations of the Commission.[63]

Finally, it is important to highlight the fact that the artistic works of the communities affected by the armed conflict in Colombia also show that poverty is one of the structural causes of violence. This type of denunciation is constantly replicated in the listening scenarios of the Colombian transitional justice system, as can be seen in the CEV's final report. Other factors of structural violence, such as racism and gender discrimination, are necessarily linked here.[64] Thus, the reality of the Colombian conflict has necessarily extended the scope of transitional justice to include important features of distributive justice.

[63] 'Hay futuro, si hay verdad', Comisión de la Verdad (n 24).
[64] ibid Hallazgos y recomendaciones (Findings and Recommendations).

7

Joint Reflection: How Do the Arts Function in Symbolic Reparations?

A Comparative Reflection Between Colombia and South Africa

Kim Berman, Michelle LeBaron, and Yolanda Sierra León

1. Introduction

In this joint reflection, we contrast research on artists resisting military operations in Colombia with reflections on the roles of the arts and artists in South Africa. Our exchange makes clear that art is a potent vehicle for engaging a wide spectrum of people. It can vividly highlight abuses and open roads to healing. Yet, the roles played by art and artists in post-conflict contexts vary, as we illustrate in our chapters in this book. Sierra León uses the term 'aesthetic litigation' to describe the disruptive effect of art; Berman and LeBaron suggest 'aesthetic negotiation' and 'artefactual agency' to describe the roles of art in South Africa. This chapter is the result of in-person and virtual discussions that draw on case studies to contrast the roles of arts in transitional and distributive justice contexts in Colombia and South Africa.

Our work suggests that the arts play pivotal roles in transitional justice in both contexts. By fostering democratic engagement and critical reflection, they mobilise the public to address human rights abuses and authoritarian excesses. As arts are dynamic and can attract multiple meanings, they are vehicles for addressing what cannot be named and for imagining more just ways forward. From Medellín, Colombia to South Africa's universities, we explain how the symbolic impact of arts is greater than the sum of its parts.

In her recent monograph, Eliza Garnsey argues that an account of transitional justice without aesthetic dimensions—especially art—is insufficient. Art, Garnsey maintains, plays a vital role in animating and activating individual narratives into collective awareness. Only as these narratives circulate can they inform new political futures. Thus artistic production becomes a radical form of political participation in times of political transition.

Our work aligns with Garnsey's four ideas about why art is central to transitional justice and vice versa.[1] First, arts mobilise the circulation of political sentiment,

[1] Eliza Garnsey, *The Justice of Visual Art: Creative State-Building in Times of Political Transition* (CUP 2019) 11–12.

Kim Berman, Michelle LeBaron, and Yolanda Sierra León, *Joint Reflection: How Do the Arts Function in Symbolic Reparations?* In: *Transitional Justice, Distributive Justice, and Transformative Constitutionalism.* Edited by: David Bilchitz and Raisa Cachalia, with Magdalena Inés Correa Henao and Nathalia Bautista Pizarro, Oxford University Press. © Kim Berman, Michelle LeBaron, and Yolanda Sierra León 2023. DOI: 10.1093/oso/9780192887627.003.0007

amplifying 'a past worth remembering'.[2] Second, arts mediate political agency as stories are told and retold in artistic forms, and previously unheard voices become perceptible in the public sphere. Third, arts foster political encounters that, fourth, open new collective spaces where politics can be re-envisioned. Garnsey elaborates that transitional justice contexts are processes that rely on '*feelings* of justice'.[3] Artworks elicit feelings, filling out what she calls a range of 'affective topologies'.[4] As viewers partake in the affective landscape, narratives take on significance in political sentiments and trajectories.

2. Artistic Intervention in South Africa and Colombia

Ongoing violence and disruption are common in transitional justice contexts as institutions are reformed and social coherence is sought. In both South Africa and Colombia, artists challenged past and ongoing violence, highlighting aggression by corrupt regimes against vulnerable populations. Sierra León, in her chapter, focuses on *Hip-Hop Agrario*, a musical group formed in response to military operations executed in the thirteenth commune of Medellín, Colombia in 2002. Its goal was to bring attention to crimes against the civilian population that had not been effectively redressed by the courts or even recognised widely in Colombian society. *Hip-Hop Agrario*'s work countered long-term cycles of violence and urban war, providing young people with a forum to tell their stories and bring to light human rights violations. They projected themselves as artists, leaders, and survivors who sought de-stigmatisation, social justice, and co-existence within their territories.[5] Sierra León describes *Hip-Hop Agrario* as involving aesthetic litigation, invoking a public focus on the truth.

South Africa, too, experienced violence, with policies of legally-enshrined racial discrimination and violence escalating over many decades. Even after more than twenty-five years of democracy, many questions remain about the failure of post-apartheid governments to deliver socio-economic and structural reform. Discontent and violence are widespread. As a central aspect of South African

[2] Carrol Clarkson, 'Drawing the Line: Justice and the Art of Reconciliation' in François du Bois and Antje du Bois-Pedain (eds), *Justice and Reconciliation in Post-Apartheid South Africa* (CUP 2008) 267, 278.

[3] Eugene McNamee, 'Fields of Opportunity: Cultural Invention and "The New Northern Ireland"' in Peter D Rush and Olivera Simić (eds), *The Arts of Transitional Justice: Culture, Activism, and Memory after Atrocity* (Springer 2014) 1, 22.

[4] Garnsey (n 1) 12.

[5] See Yolanda Sierra León, 'Reparación Simbólica, Litigio estético y Litigio Artístico: Reflexiones en torno al arte, la cultura, y la justicia restaurativa en Colombia (2014) 85 Serie de Documentos de Trabajo, Departamento de Derecho Constitucional, Universidad Externado de Colombia 18; Yolanda Sierra León, 'Arte y Justicias Alternativas: justicia restaurativa, transicional y simbólica' (2015) 86 Serie Documentos de Trabajo del Departamento de Derecho Constitucional, Universidad Externado de Colombia 17ff.

culture, art has been important in addressing the legacies of apartheid. One example from Berman and LeBaron's work is South African artist Willie Bester's 2000 sculpture of Sarah Baartman. In their chapter, they discuss how this sculpture became the focus of a process of aesthetic negotiation at the University of Cape Town (UCT).

Bester, a mixed-race artist, intended to draw attention to suffering and racism with his work. He was disappointed when, during the student protests of 2015 and 2016, his unclothed sculpture was wrapped in cloth by members of the Black Academic Caucus (BAC) Womxn's Collective who were offended by his depiction of Baartman. The sculpture remained robed until 2018 when the senior university librarian uncovered her, explaining that censorship was offensive to library professionals and to academic freedom. Members of the BAC Womxn's Collective responded: '[t]aking the robes off so unceremoniously is to shame all of us, reminding us once again, how black women's bodies easily become the repository for violent histories'.[6]

In both examples, arts became vehicles for expressing divergent views, revealing and amplifying voices that had been suppressed. In the following section, we compare and contrast the terms aesthetic negotiation and aesthetic litigation in relation to these and other examples.

3. Aesthetic Negotiation and Aesthetic Litigation

All three authors see the arts as potent and significant in transitional justice; they consistently 'punch above their weight' in social impact. Arts' power can be traced, in part, to aesthetic effects which reach people on sensed, somatic levels that make impact more likely and more visceral. Sierra León uses the term 'aesthetic litigation' to point to arts' role in challenging social landscapes of inequalities, structural violence, and human rights violations in the long transition to peace in Colombia; Berman and LeBaron refer to 'aesthetic negotiation'. We discuss the differences in the two national contexts that relate to the contrasting terminology in Section 4 of this reflection.

In Sierra León's chapter, she discusses how art draws attention to marginalised communities in their quest to claim justice and foster dialogue between the traumatic past and its reconstructed present. She suggests that art is an expressive and potent way to surface memory, truth, and resistance that can ultimately transform society. Sierra León also comments on aesthetic and artistic communitarian actions alongside the work of truth and reconciliation in Colombia, particularly that

[6] BAC Womxn's Collective, 'The Place of Sarah Baartman at UCT' (*University of Capetown*, 20 March 2018) <https://www.news.uct.ac.za/article/-2018-03-20-the-place-of-sara-baartman-at-uct> accessed 3 October 2022.

of the Colombian Commission for the Clarification of Truth, Coexistence and Non-Repetition (CEV). Aesthetic litigation (*litigio estético*), then, situates art as a forum-seeking action in which public light is shone on past wrongs. Its aim is not to yield a specific outcome but to 'put the case' for justice to the public, fostering increased awareness and dialogue.

Sierra León defines aesthetic litigation as 'the use of tangible or intangible cultural heritage ... as a mechanism to denounce or demand from the society or the state ... facts related to massive human rights violations'.[7] Her emphasis is on the way aesthetic or artistic expressions constitute alternative ways to claim justice for those who lack other means to pursue it. Litigation is an apt term given the confrontational nature of the demands: just as courts are adversarial, the artists and citizens involved in Sierra León's case examples seek visibility, voice, and attention, in adversarial ways, both from the state and the wider public in pursuit of transitional justice. When courts or other social conflict-addressing mechanisms cannot or will not address victimising acts, aesthetic litigation seeks acknowledgement and reparation.

Berman and LeBaron employ the term 'aesthetic negotiation' to examine the roles of the arts in symbolic reparations in South Africa. Negotiation is a ubiquitous process in which two or more people communicate towards an outcome. Transitional and distributive justice contexts call for on-the-ground negotiations to reknit torn relations. Parties must find ways to reorder their relations with each other, acknowledging past injustices and finding ways forward for which there are no clear maps. Given that courts and official state organs have often perpetrated injustice, parties may distrust litigated processes. Thus, Berman and LeBaron use the term 'aesthetic negotiation' to best describe the arts' roles in South African transitional justice. Many negotiations involve asymmetrical power relations and distrust, and involve parties with histories of oppression and mutual antagonism. Even in the midst of asymmetries, negotiation can yield benefits, as became clear in the process between Nelson Mandela (and the African National Congress) and FW de Klerk (and the National Party which controlled the South African state until 1993).

Differences between these scholars' preferred terms are rooted in the etymologies of negotiation and litigation. The word 'negotiation' originates from the Latin terms *nec* (not) and *otīum* (leisure), referring to business people who, unlike patricians, had no leisure time to arrange their affairs and thus were industrious in addressing their differences. Over time, the term included diplomatic as well as business interactions and later broadened to encompass dialogues where interests are communicated with the goal of reaching agreements. The term 'litigation' refers

[7] Yolanda Sierra León, 'Reparación simbólica, litigio estético y litigio artístico: reflexiones en torno al arte, la cultura, y la justicia restaurativa en Colombia' in Yolanda Sierra León (ed), *Reparación Simbólica: Jurisprudencia, cantos y tejidos* (Universidad Externado de Colombia 2018) 25ff.

to formal court proceedings and associated legal outcomes. Framing Colombian artists' work as aesthetic litigation points towards the forum they lack in their pursuit of voice and justice. Still, litigation as a frame imports a series of associations that ultimately are less resonant with the arts than negotiation, in the view of Berman and LeBaron. They maintain that while artists in transitional justice contexts long for formal recognition, it is as part of communities rather than as players in legal processes that they and their work have potency.

The unmarked metaphor most often mapped onto litigation is war: this metaphor with its 'winner-takes-all' associations is arguably incongruent with a vision of reconciliation or the need to uncover truth or right historical wrongs. Courts, after all, are hierarchical, offer limited remedies, and are not well-suited to crafting nuanced, symbolically powerful outcomes that accommodate multiple interests or acknowledge multiple narratives. Well-constructed negotiation processes yield a wider spectrum of outcomes towards reconciliation than litigation. At the same time, when groups of victims are unacknowledged and require greater distributive justice, they may resort to a litigation-like process because of a negotiation vacuum. While only a tiny fraction of past wrongs ever become part of formal litigation processes, adversarial engagement of the sort described by Sierra León may help foster ongoing negotiations.

All three scholars agree that the arts play meditative, reciprocal roles in opening possibilities towards change. The arts focus on felt, sensed experiences, and on relationships. In appealing to multiple modes of expression and diverse groups, artists reach across boundaries to uncover ways forward. Just as procedural fairness is important for people to accept outcomes, so aesthetic engagement draws attention to the *processes* of *making* and *responding* to art rather than to any specific outcome. Multiple paths to reconciliation and reparation are useful given, as Julián Andrés Pimiento Echeverri and Irit Milkes argue, democracies in transitional justice are full of paradoxes.[8] In these paradoxical contexts, citizen participation and victim compensation are vital—this is emphasised in the 2016 Colombian Final Agreement of November (CFA) to counter conditions that spawned cycles of violence.[9]

4. Comparing South African and Colombian Transitional Justice Processes

Contributors to this book have vigorously debated the relative efficacy of engaging injustice through participatory democracy, the arts, or the courts. In their joint chapter, Berman and LeBaron highlighted the transformative role of the

[8] Julián Andrés Pimiento Echeverri and Irit Milkes, Chapter 21 in this book.
[9] ibid.

arts to build capacities for active democratic participation and critical reflection. Aesthetic negotiation accords with the contributions from Raisa Cachalia and David Bilchitz, including Cachalia's emphasis on the importance of 'an ethos of respect, mutuality, and harmony' in South African government–citizen relations.[10] At the same time, many have criticised the formal South African Truth and Reconciliation Commission (TRC) process because it neglected the collective wrongs of apartheid, allowing the architects of apartheid impunity instead of requiring them to actively work to improve victims' lives.

While the arts are potent ways of addressing and repairing tears in society born out of contested histories, they cannot compensate for inadequate processes. In Colombia, crimes against humanity and other serious crimes gave rise to judgments on liability, imposing both retributive and restorative sanctions, depending on the degree of cooperation of the perpetrators with the law. When the South African TRC did not hold perpetrators accountable, and symbolic reparations were paid by the state rather than by perpetrators, many felt justice was not done. Thaddeus Metz contends that Colombia's approach was preferable to South Africa's because it is more oriented towards benefiting victims and sanctioning offenders.[11]

5. The Potency of the Arts in Symbolic Reparations: Artefactual Agency

As the arts enable crossing boundaries and discovering commonalities, they expand curiosity and presence beyond language and they give voice to what is often unheard. They resurface what has been covered over and bring us into aesthetic, often deeply felt, engagement with each other. Sierra León deems dialogue between the traumatic past and the reconstructed present fundamental to 'transforming reality and the perception of the neighbourhoods and the opportunity to change from victim status to creator status (artist, singer, leader), [and] to move from vulnerability to empowerment'.[12] The arts contribute to co-existence by revealing 'uncomfortable truths' and 'historical complexit[ies]', helping to 'blur the line between winners and losers'.[13]

Berman and LeBaron propose the term artefactual agency to draw attention to art's capacity to mobilise and to its dynamism and complexity. Artefacts are not inert, neutral, or passive: art processes and objects stimulate co-creation and foster relational, social justice-oriented dialogues. Artefactual agency links material objects to mobilisation and action. Johnson and Noorman argue that

[10] See Raisa Cachalia, Chapter 20 in this book; David Bilchitz, Chapter 11 in this book.
[11] See Thaddeus Metz, Chapter 2 in this book.
[12] See Yolanda Sierra León, Chapter 6 in this book.
[13] ibid.

artefactual agency accents the role of objects in constituting the material and relational world(s).[14]

Since artistic products have agency, they can be resisted or attacked just as human actions can. Thus artefacts of artistic processes spawn ongoing engagement, as those who encounter them contest meanings by protesting, defending, critiquing, or adopting that agency.

How can the artefactual agency of artworks be activated as a strategy for repair, healing, and social justice, given their contested meanings? Berman and LeBaron argue that healthy democracies must be spacious enough for aesthetic negotiation to shape and be shaped by ideals of social justice, and that artistic works and processes themselves can become focal points for the communal cultivation of moral imagination. Examples from UCT are related for illustrative purposes.

Artefactual agency and aesthetic negotiation complement each other in drawing attention to injustice and including citizens in shaping social and political transformation. In 2015, the symbolic potency of art in South African transitional justice led to the toppling of statues (most famously that of Cecil John Rhodes at UCT) and the burning of artworks on that university's campus. These aesthetic negotiations escalated into violence, sparking outrage. When the students seeking a 'free' and 'de-colonised' education turned to violence, the University's administration precluded further aesthetic negotiation by divesting from and removing the artworks. Also at UCT, conflict around South African artist Willie Bester's sculpture of Sarah Baartman, referenced earlier, illustrates aesthetic negotiation that did not escalate to violence.

Following Colombian human rights violations, Sierra León argues that the arts and artistic gestures have been useful mechanisms to foster dialogue. These gestures promote more equitable social relations and democratic reconstruction. In both the Colombian and South African contexts, aesthetic works served to catalyse alliances, uplift diverse voices, and mobilise change. Thus Berman and LeBaron's aesthetic negotiation and Sierra León's aesthetic and artistic litigation may be complementary in goal and effect.

Berman and LeBaron elaborate three dimensions in aesthetic negotiation that can be imagined as three concentric circles. At the centre is the symbolic domain, referring to what is most meaningful and shared amongst all parties. Human dignity and universal respect are examples of symbolic meanings. In the second concentric circle is relationship: aesthetic negotiation necessarily involves mutuality and relationship. In the outermost concentric circle are the material aspects that need to be changed. When aesthetic negotiation is effective, it is centred on shared

[14] Deborah G Jounson and Merel Noorman, 'Artefactual Agency and Artefactual Moral Agency' in Peter Kroes and Peter-Paul Verbeek (eds), *The Moral Status of Technical Artefacts* (Springer 2014) <https://link.springer.com/chapter/10.1007/978-94-007-7914-3_9> accessed 11 September 2023.

symbolic meanings and mobilised by relationships, yielding positive material outcomes.[15]

Artefactual agency further links the material realm with mobilisation and action. While art is a potent force that can foster collaborative processes, artefactual agency reminds us that visual and performed art can have contentious meanings. Actions, like the UCT administration's decision to sell or hide visual art, have not resolved deeper issues of whose work should be displayed and how.[16] Similarly, *Hip-Hip Agrario* and *Agroarte*'s actions in Colombia are an example of victims struggling, facing an invisible, silent, and ethereal 'other'. Thus they attempt to litigate using their art to draw attention to their plight, to mobilise negotiations, and to create a platform for later dialogue.

6. Conclusion

There are no clear maps for navigating transitional and distributive justice. In their respective chapters and the discussion in this reflection, Berman, LeBaron, and Sierra León examined the roles of the arts, aesthetics, and artefactual agency in transitional justice processes. They agree that achieving durable peace and social justice necessarily involves a full spectrum of social actors and actions. Disagreements will abound given the absence of clear ways forward and the urgency of addressing social ills arising from war or apartheid. How can symbolic reparation be made in ways that are satisfying, and that honour the right to multiple truths and human dignity? All three scholars agree that the arts are essential to answering this question. In both South Africa and Colombia, engagement with public arts has helped salve unrightable wrongs and surface the intersecting dynamics of transitional and distributive justice.

15 Kim Berman and Michelle LeBaron, Chapter 5 in this book.
16 ibid.

THEME 3

HISTORY, MUSEUMS, AND TRANSITIONAL JUSTICE

8

Journey to a New Space

The Apartheid Museum's Truth and Reconciliation Exhibition within the Context of Restorative and Transitional Justice

Adriénne van den Heever and Emilia Potenza

1. Introduction

Reconciliation cannot be confined to a single event. It is an ongoing process that shifts with time. South Africa still bears the wounds of apartheid and the struggle against it. If these are to heal fully, and if South Africa is to develop into a truly non-racial society, the past must be grappled with and understood. Without that, no full reconciliation can occur. This is the reason for the Apartheid Museum. As Christopher Till, the Director of the Apartheid Museum has poignantly explained:

> Those of us who lived through the bleak and brutal years of apartheid will always carry its shadow in our lives.... But memory is partial, and fleeting, even when it is personal. And those who did not live through the period need ways to understand the reality of racial domination and its consequences. And so it was clear, in the years immediately after the end of apartheid, that it would be important to develop a museum which could tell the story of apartheid in all its complexity.[1]

The Apartheid Museum is located on a seven-hectare stretch of former mining land on the southwestern edge of Johannesburg city.[2] Since opening its doors to the public in 2001, the Museum has become one of South Africa's most frequented—receiving an average of 200,000 visitors per annum. At the core of the Museum's narrative is the rise of the apartheid system of legalised segregation and its meteoric fall.

[1] *Apartheid Museum: Souvenir Guide* (Apartheid Museum 2010) 3.

[2] The site was originally part of the mineral-rich, and highly profitable gold mine, Crown Mines founded in 1909.

Adriénne van den Heever and Emilia Potenza, *Journey to a New Space* In: *Transitional Justice, Distributive Justice, and Transformative Constitutionalism.* Edited by: David Bilchitz and Raisa Cachalia, with Magdalena Inés Correa Henao and Nathalia Bautista Pizarro, Oxford University Press. © Adriénne van den Heever and Emilia Potenza 2023.
DOI: 10.1093/oso/9780192887627.003.0008

2. Revisiting the Darkness: The Apartheid Museum

The history of the Apartheid Museum, in some senses, is as significant as the subject matter it portrays. In 1996, South Africa's first democratically elected government reversed apartheid legislation that had outlawed gambling of almost any kind. With the passing of the National Gambling Act, the National Gambling Board was established to regulate the sector and coordinate the issuing of limited casino licences.[3] Akani Egoli, the consortium responsible for Gold Reef City, an amusement park themed on Johannesburg's gold mining history,[4] put in a bid for a casino licence. The social responsibility component of their bid detailed a commitment to build a museum on land adjacent to the theme park. The bid was successful and subsequently, the Gold Reef City Casino and Apartheid Museum were constructed.[5] Solely funded by the consortium, the Museum's construction costs were approximately R80 million. Since 2011, the precinct has been managed by Tsogo Sun. The Apartheid Museum is registered as a section 21 public benefit company (incorporated not for profit) and is independent of the Gold Reef City casino complex. It has an independent board of trustees chaired by Dr John Kani. To sustain its growth, the Museum relies on revenue from ticket sales, donations, and sponsorships.

> A journey through the Apartheid Museum takes you into the heart of the darkness of evil, and out again into the light.[6]

The Museum plays an important role in presenting a perspective of twentieth-century South Africa. The curated environment offers both a literal and psychological space where the essence of historical events can be recounted and examined in an accessible manner to a wide audience—60 per cent of visitors are school children, 20 per cent are South African adults, and the remaining 20 per cent are international visitors. Due to the emotional and graphic content which is exhibited, the Museum is not deemed suitable for children under the age of eleven.

The design of the Apartheid Museum was conceived by a consortium of leading South African architectural firms.[7] Covering an area of approximately 6,000 square metres, the stark and imposing structure lies half-buried in a rehabilitated

[3] SP Rule, T Da Silva, and C Sibanyoni, *The Social Impact of Gambling in South Africa: An Initial Assessment for the National Gambling Board* (HSRC Press 2000) 8 <https://www.ngb.org.za/SiteResources/documents/5_HSRC_Social_Impact.pdf> accessed 3 October 2022.

[4] R Ciraj and W Leslie, 'South Africa: A World in one Country. Moments in International Tourist Encounters with Wildlife, the Primitive and the Modem' (1996) 36(143) Cahiers d'études africaines 335, 343.

[5] https://www.apartheidmuseum.org/about-the-museum accessed 3 October 2022.

[6] *Apartheid Museum* (n 1) 70.

[7] Sidney Abramowitch Architect Architects: GAPP Architects & Urban Designers, Mashabane Rose Architects, Britz Roodt Project Association and Linda Mvusi Architecture & Design.

Figure 8.1 The Reflection Pond at the entrance to the Apartheid Museum. The quote by Nelson Mandela reads: 'To be free is not merely to cast off one's chains, but to live in a way that respects and enhances the freedom of others' (Photography courtesy of the Apartheid Museum)

Indigenous Highveld landscape which is shaped in such a manner that the neighbouring theme park and visitor parking lot are concealed from view. Austere building materials—off-shutter concrete, rock-filled gabions, red face brick, and rusted mild steel, were selected to pay homage to the harsh industries that created and define Johannesburg (see Figure 8.1). These materials reappear throughout the exhibition halls, creating an impersonal setting for the harrowing narrative.

Symbolically, the semi-subterranean structure of the Museum evokes the oppressiveness of the apartheid system,[8] while the seven towering concrete pillars at the entrance provide a counterpoint celebrating the core values of a post-apartheid society—democracy, diversity, equality, freedom, reconciliation, respect, and responsibility.

On arrival, visitors are randomly issued with a 'white' or 'non-white' race classification card. This determines which entrance must be used. It is a seemingly simple action, but a highly evocative one, that initiates an emotional response with many visitors. The indiscriminate classification of museum-goers is reminiscent of segregationist apartheid legislation[9]—the myriad of rules and regulations that controlled day-to-day life by enforcing the creation, and regulation, of separate social environments and amenities for different racial groups. The tone for the remaining journey through the Apartheid Museum is set.

[8] M Human, 'Encore Performing Arts Centre: An Investigation into the Contribution of Performing Arts Education to Urban Renewal' (MArch Prof dissertation, University of Pretoria 2003) ch 3 2 http://hdl.handle.net/2263/29632 accessed 3 October 2022.

[9] The Reservation of Separate Amenities Act No 49 of 1953 and it various amendments. 'The Act enforced segregation of all public facilities, including buildings, and transport, in order to limit contact between the different races in South Africa. The Act also stated that the facilities for different races did not need to be equal. In practice then, the best facilities were reserved for whites while those for other races were inferior.' <https://www.sahistory.org.za/dated-event/south-african-parliament-repeals-separate-amenities-act-1953> accessed 3 October 2022.

Visitors follow 'a looped journey through space and time along a linear path which travels both indoors and outdoors, beginning and ending at the same point'.[10] Inside the Museum there are approximately 5,000 square metres of dedicated exhibition space organised along a central 'spine'. From this spine, twenty exhibition spaces branch off, each narrating a period of the construction and brutalising effects of state-sanctioned racial segregation, and ultimately exposing how the apartheid system was overturned.

3. The Research Lens

From September 2018 to May 2019, research was conducted in the Apartheid Museum to explore whether the Museum's Truth and Reconciliation Commission (TRC) exhibit, which specifically focuses on one of the most consequential judicial processes undertaken in South Africa's democratic history, serves as a proactive tool in furthering the principles of restorative and transitional justice.

Quantitative and qualitative research methodologies were used to gain insights into how visitors engage with and respond to the exhibition. A quantitative investigation was conducted using a paper-based visitor survey with a random sample of visitors. Qualitative research followed a more pluralistic approach—informal interviews with Museum and independent tour guides, visitor observation, and discussions with TRC exhibition curators and advisors.

A. Unifying and Reconciling a Broken Nation: The Historical Context Framing the TRC Exhibition

For a fledgling democracy, a period of healing and bridging of the divisions instilled by apartheid was necessary. South Africa's interim government[11] would need to institutionalise processes where its fractured society could start to confront the past and find ways to heal. The new Constitution of the Republic of South Africa would provide the framework. As Dullah Omar, Minister of Justice (1994–1999) explained:

> There is a commitment to break from the past, to heal the wounds of the past, to forgive but not to forget and to build a future based on respect for human

[10] T Deckler, A Graupner, and H Rasmuss, *Contemporary South African Architecture in a Landscape of Transition* (Double Storey Publishers, U.S.A. 2008) 39.

[11] From 27 April 1994–3 February 1997, South Africa was governed by the Government of National Unity, a proviso set in the Interim Constitution of the Republic of South Africa, 1993.

> rights ... Human rights [are] not a gift handed down as a favour by government or state to loyal citizens. It is the right of each and every citizen.[12]

A consultative process between the state and civil society, which included human rights lawyers, the religious community, and victims, culminated in the Promotion of National Unity and Reconciliation Act 34 of 1995. The Act called for the establishment of the TRC. Archbishop Emeritus Desmond Tutu, an Anglican theologian and outspoken critic of apartheid, was appointed to chair the Commission alongside seventeen commissioners.

The TRC's work was divided between three committees. The 'Human Rights Violations Committee' investigated and bore witness to the nature, causes, and extent of violations committed in political conflicts between 1 March 1960 and 10 May 1994. The 'Reparation and Rehabilitation Committee' was charged with restoring victims' dignity with a view to restitution. The 'Amnesty Committee' granted amnesty for politically motivated human rights abuses, provided the perpetrators confessed to their crimes. Past injustices were to be addressed on the basis that there was a need for further understanding but not for vengeance, a need for reparation but not for retaliation.

Formal hearings commenced on 15 April 1996. The structure of the TRC allowed victims, perpetrators, and witnesses the opportunity to provide testimony about the clandestine and depraved acts committed by both the apartheid government and its agents (see Figure 8.2). It also addressed gross human rights violations perpetrated by the liberation movements. Hearings were broadcast live on the radio throughout the proceedings. Television broadcasts were restricted to selected hearings. The public nature of the TRC created a platform where all South Africans could engage with and confront the past. There was no place for future denial. The final 3,500-page report was handed to President Mandela on 28 October 1998. As Nelson Mandela remarked:

> The Commission was not expected to conjure up instant reconciliation.... The TRC has given us an aid to help reconcile and build our nation.[13]

Though South Africa's TRC became a widely adopted model for restorative and transitional justice internationally, there are divergent views on its successes and failures. A key limitation was that only a relatively small number of people—2,000—were able to appear before the TRC. Another weakness, acknowledged by

[12] D Omar, 'Justice in Transition' <https://www.justice.gov.za/trc/legal/justice.html> accessed 3 October 2022.

[13] South African Press Association, 'Truth Report Handed to Mandela' (29 October 1998) <https://www.justice.gov.za/trc/media/1998/9810/s981029r.html> accessed 3 October 2022.

Figure 8.2 A TRC Hearing (Photography by George Hallett and courtesy of the Apartheid Museum)

Tutu, was the insufficient focus on the effects of the policies and the economic inequalities perpetuated by apartheid. As Archbishop Desmond Tutu explained:

> The failure to examine the effect and impact of apartheid's policies resulted in the need for the perpetrators, or the 'trigger-pullers', to bear the collective shame of the nation and let those who benefitted from apartheid escape responsibility.[14]

B. Righting History: The Role of the Museum

Museums are not neutral places. Historically they have been places of cultural contestation, controversy, and injustice. The exertion of politics and power determined how a collection came into being, and decided which stories would be told and how. In a post-colonial world, museums have to address these challenges and inherent biases to enjoy legitimacy.

Contemporary museums, like the Apartheid Museum, which have had a democratic genesis, hold a unique position. Without the burden of the inherited

[14] D Tutu, 'Truth and Reconciliation Commission, South Africa' *Encyclopaedia Britannica* (2010) <https://www.britannica.com/topic/Truth-and-Reconciliation-Commission-South-Africa> accessed 3 October 2022.

challenges posed by colonial remnants, the contemporary museum can embrace cultural democracy with far more ease. These museums can become both a platform and an agent for divergent perspectives to be told and examined.

The Apartheid Museum is a custodian of contemporary history. It has a dual function—repository of history, and place of learning. The immediacy of apartheid, however, can be challenging. When is the right time to showcase difficult histories? While timing is a rhetorical conundrum, the responsibility to recount the past, despite its difficulty, is not. The TRC exhibition is a pertinent example.

Nomfundo Walaza, a clinical psychologist and trauma counsellor, made the following observations in a 2010 Institute for Justice and Reconciliation workshop that focused on how to equip teachers—and by default, the museum—to teach the TRC:

> We are carrying a lot of scars as a nation. This was never going to be simple. We are not dealing with theory; we are dealing with something that happened here, to us, to our parents, to our teachers. These stories can add to the baggage the learners already carry. Many of our learners are traumatised by their lives. They must be helped to process this material, otherwise we will traumatise them even more. It can create great anger and even the desire among some to do something about it. At the same time, we cannot afford not to teach our learners about this time in the history of our country.[15]

The principles of transitional and restorative justice have a synergy with the values and responsibilities of the Apartheid Museum. Both seek to redress past injustices by fostering dialogue, mediating different perspectives, and providing a space for the voices of those who were historically marginalised.

The challenge for the Museum is the audience. As the primary Museum visitors are schoolchildren, who did not experience the atrocities of apartheid first hand, the harrowing nature of the content needs to be recounted strategically and without spectacle. For victims and perpetrators engaged in either a transitional or restorative justice procedure, this is not obligatory. The Museum's commitment to education, critical examination of the past, and its large, young audience, ostensibly, takes the principles of transitional justice a step further.

[15] Institute for Justice and Reconciliation (IJR), *Teaching Sensitive Material in the Classroom: An Additional Resource to Teaching the Truth and Reconciliation Commission* (2012) 6 <http://www.ijr.org.za/home/wp-content/uploads/2017/05/An-additional-resource-guide-to-teaching-the-TRC.pdf> accessed 3 October 2022.

Figure 8.3 Installation view of Rossouw Van der Walt's sculpture 'Ways and Means' (Photography courtesy of the Apartheid Museum)

C. Twenty Years Later

To mark the twentieth anniversary of the TRC, the Apartheid Museum commissioned South African sculptor, Roussow van der Walt, to create an artwork to reference a deeply disturbing moment witnessed during one of the 1997 TRC hearings. Jeffrey Benzien, a former member of the Security Branch,[16] who had applied for amnesty for a host of human rights violations, was giving testimony. Benzien chillingly demonstrated the infamous 'wet bag'[17] method of torture, a technique that he frequently used to extract confessions from political detainees.

Entitled *Ways and Means*, Van der Walt's life-sized tableau would become part of a future exhibition dedicated to the TRC (see Figure 8.3). Cast in resin impregnated with white marble dust, the resultant lack of colour evokes memory and the notion of bleached recollections. The title refers to the plethora of torture techniques and inhumane methods that the Security Branch of the South African Police employed. The identity of neither the perpetrator nor the victim is revealed—a reminder that

[16] The Security Branch, also known as the Special Branch, was a section of the South African Police which was granted the powers to track down, detain, and torture suspected activists and opponents of apartheid.

[17] A torture method where a victim would be handcuffed with their hands behind their back and forced to lie prostrate on the ground. The perpetrator would then straddle the victim, and pull a wet bag over their head. The victim is repeatedly brought the brink of asphyxiation while being interrogated.

Benzien was only one of many perpetrators, who committed apartheid-related transgressions.

4. Reflection: Curating the TRC Exhibition

A protracted period of concept development followed before the current exhibition would open to the public in 2018. Conceptually, the notion of diametric opposition underpins the exhibition—the awkward interactions which emerged when victims forgave perpetrators, fraught examinations between commissioners who sought the truth, perpetrators who claimed they could not remember, victims who claimed they could not forget, and the complex mediation process faced by TRC interpreters who simultaneously translated the accounts of both perpetrators and victims.

The exhibition is comprised of three main elements: artworks, contextual text panels, and film installations (see Figures 8.3–8.6). In a partially obscured, alcove-like space, Van der Walt's dimly lit sculpture pays quiet homage to the many lives that were either irreparably damaged through torture, or fatally cut short. To view the work clearly, visitors need to focus through a perforated metal screen. The act of observation becomes suggestive of prying eyes secretly watching a lurid confession.

Visitors then move into an adjacent space where a film installation, projected on to three large screens with one soundtrack, plays on a loop. The film is a curated dialogue between victim and perpetrator. Produced in 2015/2016, the thirty-eight-minute film, entitled *Telling the Truth?*, provides a sense of the epic nature of the TRC (see Figure 8.4). Though the film installation has no real beginning, middle, or end, it provides a powerful sense of the conversation and confrontation required for South Africa's past to be illuminated.

Telling the Truth? is a synthesis of aspects of eight indelible hearings, most of which were amnesty hearings:[18]

- The submission of Singqokwana Ernest Malgas, a member of the ANC who and been incarcerated on Robben Island for fourteen years. His testimony provided a shocking account of the torture sustained at the hands of the security police during frequent detentions over twelve years.
- The amnesty hearing of Craig Williamson for the death of Ruth First, a leading intellectual of the ANC and South African Communist Party, and the wife of Joe Slovo. In 1963, First was detained and kept in solitary confinement for 117 days. After her release, she went into exile. In 1982, First sustained fatal

[18] 'Truth Commission Special Report' television series online archive <http://sabctrc.saha.org.za> accessed 3 October 2022.

Figure 8.4 A still from 'Telling the Truth?', on screen Tony Yengeni questioning Jeffrey Benzien about the torture Benzien inflicted on him (Photography courtesy of the Apartheid Museum)

injuries when a letter bomb exploded in her office in Maputo, Mozambique. Williamson who, at the time of First's death, was a member of the security police's foreign intelligence branch, claimed he was just following orders. Amnesty was granted.

- Jeffrey Benzien's amnesty hearing for the interrogation and torture of opponents of the apartheid state. During the proceedings, Tony Yengeni, a former MK Commander and one of Benzien's victims, asked him to demonstrate his preferred torture technique—the wet bag method. Amnesty was granted.
- Testimony from Eugene de Kock, about the involvement of high-ranking political figures who, during the TRC, did not testify or denied all knowledge of the atrocities that were being committed. Nicknamed 'Prime Evil', de Kock was a colonel in the South African Police (SAP). An assassin and torturer, de Kock served as the commanding officer of the SAP's secret counterinsurgency unit, C1. The headquarters of the unit were on a remote farm, Vlakplaas, outside Pretoria. C1 functioned as a paramilitary hit squad that captured political opponents of the apartheid government and either tried to convert them into *askaris*[19] or executed them. Vlakplaas was usually the site where these executions took place. De Kock was not granted amnesty and in 1996, he was tried

[19] A member of one of the liberation organisations who changed sides either through force or voluntarily to join the SAP.

Figure 8.5 A detail of Jo Ratcliffe's 'Vlakplaas, 2 June 1999 (drive by shooting)' (Photography courtesy of Jo Ratcliffe and courtesy of Stevenson, Cape Town, Johannesburg and Amsterdam)

and convicted on eighty-nine charges and sentenced to 212 years in prison. After serving nearly twenty years of his sentence, he was released on parole in 2015.

- The inquiry into the activities of Mandela United Football Club (MUFC)—a front established by Winnie Madikizela-Mandela to mobilise township youths to resist apartheid—and the death of fourteen-year-old Stompie Moeketsi Seipei. Seipei was a young United Democratic Front activist, who was kidnapped in late 1988, together with three other boys. They were all badly beaten. Madikizela-Mandela's bodyguards, who ran the MUFC, were responsible. Days after the kidnapping, Seipei was stabbed to death and his body was dumped. The 'coach' Jerry Richardson was convicted of the murder. During the TRC, Richardson confirmed that he was a police informer, and also claimed that Madikizela-Mandela had ordered the killing. Madikizela-Mandela pleaded innocence.
- Gideon Nieuwoudt's testimony relating to the abduction, poisoning, and murder of student activist, Siphiwo Mthimkhulu in 1982. Nicknamed 'Notorious', Nieuwoudt was implicated in the deaths of several anti-apartheid activists, including Steve Biko. He was granted amnesty for the death of Mthimkhulu and denied amnesty for his involvement in Biko's demise. While awaiting the outcome of his amnesty application for the murders of the 'Motherwell Four', he died of cancer.
- The 1993 St James Church Massacre hearing. Eleven people died and scores of church-goers were wounded when four gunmen, members of the Azanian People's Liberation Army (APLA),[20] opened fire and threw hand grenades into the congregation during a service. Survivors and relatives of the deceased testified at the Commission. APLA perpetrators were granted amnesty.
- Nason Ndwandwe's inquiry into the disappearance of his daughter Phila Portia Ndwandwe. The TRC revealed that in 1988, Ndwandwe, an MK commander, had been abducted in Swaziland by South African policemen. They had attempted to turn her into an *askari* through torture. Ndwandwe refused and was subsequently stripped naked, shot in the head, and buried in a shallow grave. TRC investigators exhumed the secret grave. Her remains were subsequently laid to rest in a dignified ceremony.

[20] APLA was the military wing of the Pan Africanist Congress.

Figure 8.6 A view of the final section of the TRC Exhibition (Photography courtesy of the Apartheid Museum).

This artwork, entitled *A Tale of Two Cradocks* (1994) (see Figure 8.6), has a concertina-like structure and tells two stories about Cradock, a small town in the Eastern Cape province. The stories exist side by side, but you can only engage with and see one side of the story properly at any one time. Again the notion of diametric opposition is evident. The one story is told through a deconstructed apartheid-era Cradock visitor guide booklet. The small Karoo is depicted as outwardly charming. Amenities are described—but they are only available for the white community. The adjoining black township, Lingelihle, is not mentioned once.

Lingelihle was the home of Matthew and Nyameka Goniwe. Matthew was a respected teacher and charismatic leader who was targeted by the apartheid government. The Goniwe story is told through montages that combine a transcription of an interview between the artist and Nyameka Goniwe, archival photographs, documents, and news clippings. On 27 June 1985, Goniwe and his three comrades, Fort Calata, Sparrow Mkhonto, and Sicelo Mhlauli, were intercepted at a police roadblock. They were abducted, assaulted, and then killed. Their burnt remains were found days later. They became known as the 'Cradock Four'. In one of the artwork's panels, there is a photograph from the police files that shows two policemen leaning over the bodies. A telefax (in Afrikaans), ordering the 'permanent removal' of Goniwe, is superimposed.

In 1999 the TRC denied amnesty to the six security policemen (one of whom was Gideon Nieuwoudt, cited earlier in the context of the amnesty hearing for the murder of Siphiwo Mthimkhulu) who were involved in the killings of the Cradock Four. Though the TRC recommended that they should be prosecuted in a court of law, this never came to pass.

In the final TRC report, several recommendations were made to assist and ensure that South Africa's journey into a new space could continue. These included:

- Calls for the prosecution of those who had failed to engage in the amnesty process, or had been refused amnesty;
- Compensation for victims in the form of individual, community, and symbolic reparations;
- Support for healing and rehabilitation;
- Institutional and policy reforms focusing on the security forces, the legal system, health and media sectors; and
- Public access to the TRC records.

These recommendations have largely been ignored by the government. Yet, nation-building and the promotion of a national identity constructed around the notion of unity in diversity have continued to be high on its list of priorities. Unfortunately, these have been reduced to government rhetoric.

The transformation and healing of any society that has experienced deep-seated trauma is an ongoing process. South Africa is no exception. Transformation is heavily reliant on reconciliation and healing, but what reconciliation is, and what healing entails remains contested. For some it is about forgiving and forgetting, whilst for others it is about financial compensation and the redistribution of wealth.

The processes that the TRC set in motion were unfortunately abruptly truncated, and the dialogue, by and large, has been reduced to a whisper. This has resulted in the formation of grassroots advocacy organisations, such as the Khulumani Support Group (KSG), the Institute for Healing of Memories (IHOM), and the Ahmed Timol Trust. These organisations are dedicated to building an inclusive and just society where the dignity of those affected by apartheid is restored. The KSG focuses on lobbying and litigation to hold the government accountable for promised compensation. The IHOM have a more restorative approach, where prevention, healing, and empowerment are facilitated through dialogue and workshops. The Ahmed Timol Trust is doing important work advocating for the prosecution of perpetrators of gross human rights violations during the apartheid era.

5. The Voice of the Visitor: Insights Gleaned from the Research Process

The quantitative research process comprised of a paper-based survey conducted with a random sample (see Figure 8.7). 195 surveys were completed comprising South African schoolchildren (SASC), South African adults (SAA), and international visitors (IV). Expressed as a percentage, the survey sample is SASC: 51.3 per cent, SAA: 31.3 per cent, and IV: 16.9 per cent.

While there was no specific question asking if participants were attending school, the question, 'What is your age group?' allowed for a reasonable deduction. Participants who selected 'Under 18', would constitute the SASC sample, while those who selected 'Between 19–25', would fall into the SAA category. However, the physical headcount of participant Grade 10, 11, and 12 schoolchildren was significantly higher than the number of 'Under 18' responses. Of the fifty-five 'Between 19–25' participants, surprisingly fifty were still attending school. Consequently, the actual survey breakdown is SASC: 76.9 per cent, SAA: 6.2 per cent, and IV: 16.9 per cent. To counterbalance the high SASC sample, informal, oral interviews were conducted with an SAA audience in the 'Between 26–45', 'Between 46–65', and 'Older than 65' age brackets.

Where survey responses are quoted, liberty has been taken to correct spelling and if required, grammar has been amended to allow for readability.

The gender breakdown was as follows: 44.6 per cent male and 55.9 per cent female. The 0.5 per cent discrepancy was due to one individual who indicated gender

Figure 8.7 South African schoolchildren completing the survey in the Constitution Hall of the Apartheid Museum (Photography courtesy of the Apartheid Museum)

fluidity. Not all surveys were completed in full. Reasons for this included time constraints, visitor apathy, emotional and/or physical exhaustion. When analysing the data, in instances where participants did not respond, calculations were adjusted accordingly if necessary.

Participants in the IV sample were random and came from the following countries, listed by percentage: United States 42.2 per cent, Brazil 12.0 per cent, United Kingdom 93 per cent, Italy 9.2 per cent, France 9.2 per cent, Bahamas 6.1 per cent, India 3.0 per cent, Ivory Coast 3.0 per cent, Netherlands 3.0 per cent, and Switzerland 3.0 per cent.

Bridging language barriers with visitors has been a challenge for the Apartheid Museum since its inception. South Africa has eleven official languages, and only 9.6 per cent of South Africans have English[21] as their home language. Nevertheless, English is the language used to present information throughout the Museum. In instances where African vernacular occurs, such as in a film, an English translation is provided through subtitling.

When asked whether English was the participant's home language, 54.5 per cent of the IV sample responded, 'Yes'. However, for every individual that agreed to partake in the survey, at least two declined due to a language barrier. 82 per cent of the SASC and SAA sample groups indicated that English was not their first language, 10 per cent less than the national average. Future surveys would need to interrogate this further. It is assumed that there is a level of proficiency in English, although the analysis of how written responses were answered suggests that comprehension and grammar skills are lacking, especially within the SASC sample.

The survey was designed in two parts. Part One was meant to be answered before entering the TRC exhibition, and Part Two afterwards. In some instances, this was not possible due to time constraints, high ambient noise levels, space limitations, and the need to avoid creating congestion within the Museum. This did not negatively impact the survey.

In Part One of the survey, questions were designed to:

a) establish rudimentary prior knowledge of the TRC;
b) ascertain whether visitors had prior awareness of the Museum's dedicated TRC exhibition; and
c) determine expectations.

In requesting participation in the survey, the TRC, and the Apartheid Museum's TRC exhibition were introduced to visitors. Responses to the questions, 'Are you familiar with South Africa's Truth and Reconciliation (TRC) process?' and, 'Are

[21] P Lehohla, 'Census 2011 Census in Brief' *Statistics South Africa* (2015) Report No 03-01-41 24 <http://www.statssa.gov.za/census/census_2011/census_products/Census_2011_Census_in_brief.pdf> accessed 3 October 2022.

you aware that the Apartheid Museum has a dedicated exhibition which explores the TRC?' were therefore skewed, especially within the SASC sample.

Verbal interaction with SASC beforehand and results from questions in Part Two (which will be elaborated on below) suggest that prior knowledge and familiarity with the TRC process is limited.

The SASC sample is commonly known as the 'Born-Frees', the generation of South Africans born after 1994, who do not have a lived experience of apartheid. While this contributes to the lack of familiarity, it also points to the absence of an inter-generational conversation regarding South Africa's past. Furthermore, challenging prejudice and discrimination by examining how human rights violations have been addressed in South Africa's history, is part of the Further Education and Training band (FET—Grade 10, 11 & 12) curriculum for Life Orientation[22]—a compulsory school subject. The TRC itself is a component of the Grade 12 History curriculum,[23] an elective subject in the FET band.

In Part Two of the survey, participants were asked to describe their experience of the TRC exhibition. Responses included:

- Emotional, brutal, sad, it is something that must be shown
- Powerful, could only watch for a little while
- Eye-opening, educational
- Too distant for our experience as foreigners
- It was a well-deserved exhibition as I was able to learn about what really happened during apartheid and know about the revolutionary leaders
- It cleared up a few misconceptions, really warmed me
- It was nerve-wracking
- It was deep and required a lot of understanding
- Chilled, cold
- Very haunting
- Well, it filled me with anger and vengeance
- What is amnesty? Firstly, lol . . . and I did not like it necessarily because I feel like the blacks didn't feel justified
- It was very informative and opened my eyes to a number of things
- I expected more critical information and critical analysis thereof
- That forgiveness and reconciliation may lead to a better life
- It is an exhibition that always moves me and makes me reflect

[22] Department of Basic Education, *Curriculum and Assessment Policy Statement Grades 10–12: Life Orientation* (2011) 21.

[23] Department of Basic Education, *Curriculum and Assessment Policy Statement Grades 10–12: History* (2011) 30.

- Hard to see how human beings do not learn anything from history and that everywhere, anytime, the human is the worst being. Hope we can leave a better world for our children.
- Very sobering and emotional, an eye-opener to all the torture innocent people had to go through during the apartheid era
- It was difficult to hear first-person accounts of the torture and abuse experienced during apartheid.
- Poignant, honest, visceral
- Loved that they were teaching us. I just got disgusted by how unfair the process was

Participants were then asked to indicate how they felt after engaging with the exhibition. A selection of responses was provided. These were: sad, happy, indifferent, angry, inspired, confused, guilty, and other. Participants could select, or provide more than one option. The responses are detailed in the following comparative column chart (see Figure 8.8).

Participants who selected 'Other', indicated responses that included:

- Bad feelings about racism
- Conflicted
- Depressed
- Disappointed
- Emotional
- Frustrated
- Grateful that such violence did not bring more violence
- Helpless—not the first time these things have happened and not the last
- Makes me aware that we are free. Thank you

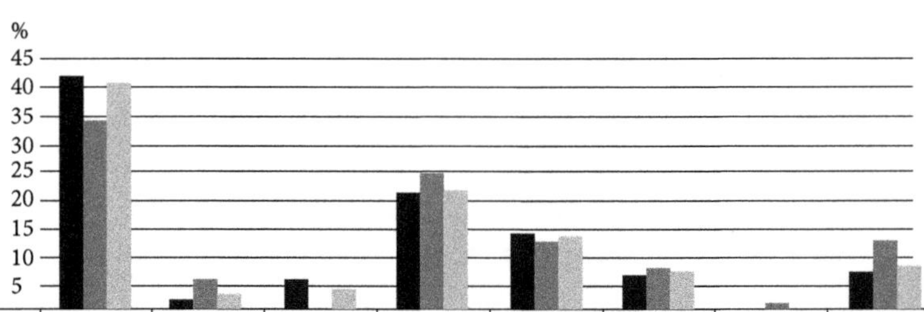

EMOTIONAL RESPONSES	Sad	Happy	Indifferent	Angry	Inspired	Confused	Guilty	Other
South African	42,4	2,2	5,6	21,2	14,1	7,1	0,4	7,1
International	34,4	6,3	0,0	25,0	12,5	7,8	1,6	12,5
Combined	40,8	3,0	4,5	21,9	13,8	7,2	0,6	8,1

Figure 8.8 Comparative chart reflecting the emotional responses of participants (Courtesy of the Apartheid Museum)

- Traumatised
- Upset

A number of participants selected 'indifference'. While it could be a reflection of contemporary culture, the result is concerning—especially in a country where the legacy of apartheid is still evident and where the democratic values enshrined in the constitution actively need to be upheld by ongoing engagement and active citizenship.

The next three survey questions were designed to assess which aspects of the exhibition visitors engage with most and to determine whether changes to the exhibition may be required. It is interesting to note that the written responses to these questions do not align with observed visitor behaviour.

Concerning the question, 'Did you engage with the sculptural installation depicting the Wet Bag torture method?' 47.7 per cent indicated they did; 39.5 per cent indicated that they did not; and the remaining 12.8 per cent did not answer the question. The possible reasons for the high number of participants who indicated that they did not engage with the sculpture, or did not answer the question could be:

a) the visceral nature of the work
b) limited viewing space—the sculpture is obscured when large numbers of people enter the auditorium
c) time constraints.

When asked if the associated text panels were read, 73.3 per cent of participants confirmed that they had read them, 19 per cent indicated that they either had read some in part, or not at all, and 7.7 per cent did not provide a response. Observation of visitor behaviour can confirm that the responses primarily reflect the reading of the introductory text panel. Supportive and more detailed information regarding the TRC process in the adjacent space was largely skimmed. This is problematic, especially considering that one of the main expectations revealed, was the need to attain more information and to establish clarity on the workings of the TRC. These two selected responses: '[i]t does not make it clear about what happened after the TRC' and 'I got the emotions and social impact but not the formal process behind it' provide evidence of the problem.

When asked, 'Did you watch the whole film?', 55.9 per cent of participants indicated that they had, 37.9 per cent indicated that they had not, and 6.2 per cent did not answer the question. Due to the way that the film was conceived, with no clear beginning, middle, or end, it is unclear whether visitors watched the full thirty-eight minutes. This is also confirmed by the conflicting results of SASC survey results and observed behaviour. Should subsequent surveys of the exhibition be conducted, the question should be rephrased to ask how much time a participant spent watching the film, or structured in a way where the respondent can indicate which hearing(s) were viewed.

When assessing whether engagement with the exhibition assisted in understanding the role that the TRC played in South Africa's transition to democracy, 79 per cent of responses were in the affirmative. It is difficult to assess whether or not this knowledge was gleaned only through an engagement with the TRC exhibition.

There is a disparity between the Yes-No and written responses to the question: 'Has this exhibition successfully conveyed the intentions of the TRC?' 76.4 per cent of the responses indicated 'Yes' and 13.8 per cent indicated 'No'. The written comments and explanations indicate that a basic understanding of the concept of amnesty is either absent or limited. Responses included: 'Because those who killed were amnesty-rewarded', 'Those who killed more than ten people don't get amnesty reward', and 'White people treated black people badly and they refused to amnist' (sic).

Furthermore, responses that paraphrase or repeat the question suggest a lack of comprehension of the question itself: 'It talks about the truth and the reconciliation which occurred' and 'Because it has the film and photos to convince our mind'. This raises questions about the functional literacy of South African respondents.

The following explanations point to some of the challenges which face South Africa—the perpetuation of a polarised society, inter-generational trauma, and voluntary amnesia:

- To give white people a confession stand so there is less guilt.
- It shows the perpetrators and confessions in what they did to Africans and victims.
- It is reminding us of apartheid when we should forget about it.

After engaging with, and experiencing brutal and unsettling content, many visitors express the need for debriefing. The following question was asked to establish how great that need is: 'Do you need to talk to someone or do something in particular to make sense of your experience?'

While one in three participants reflected that they needed to talk with someone, 60.5 per cent of the written responses indicated that the need related to accessing more information or participating in dialogue around the TRC. Debriefing, such as counselling, to deal with feelings of distress was also requested.

When assessing active citizenship, 77.9 per cent of the sample indicated that they felt inspired and committed to rectifying past injustices. When asked to describe what sort of change/contribution they envisaged, examples included increasing awareness, assisting justice programmes, curbing xenophobia, providing employment, and stemming the scourge of racism, inequality, and sexism.

Though the following types of responses were only expressed by 7.8 per cent, they do suggest that there is a need for mediation:

- Make them feel what our forefathers felt.
- I would like to change the thoughts of black children about hating whites.
- What has happened stays in the past.
- It will hurt young and innocent people.
- It will bring war.

The final question was designed to ascertain whether the actual visitor experience aligned with initial expectations: 72.3 per cent indicated their expectations were met, 14.9 per cent indicated that they were not, and the question was not answered by 12.8 per cent.

To supplement the survey process and to offset the high SASC sample, informal interviews targeting SAA over the age of twenty-six were conducted. Should future research be conducted, this segment of the sample requires concentrated attention. Focus groups are suggested.

Noteworthy points raised by a group of independent tour guides (ITG) included:

- There is a perception that the TRC exhibition perpetuates the polarisation of South African society—the perpetrator is white; the victim is black.
- Historical events are chronologically arranged within the Museum and the TRC is the penultimate exhibition. So it becomes the parting message. The final exhibition hall, 'Celebrating our Constitution', unfortunately, does not hold sufficient gravitas and the parting message is confusing and diluted.
- Time constraints were frequently raised. The duration of the TRC film is problematic, and omitting the TRC from the South African narrative is equally so. An abridged version of the TRC exhibition which provides an overview was suggested to mitigate this challenge.

To help foster a society with depth and understanding, the importance of history and critical dialogue was stressed. There was a grave concern that when the past is ignored, history could either repeat itself, or the superficial 'Kardashianisation' of our society could take place. The need for contemplation and reflection was also raised. A question, albeit a rhetorical one, was asked—do South Africans truly value what people sacrificed to achieve freedom? A suggestion was made that could contribute to the broader transitional and restorative justice dialogue: that perpetrators like De Kock could become ambassadors of the reconciliation process.

6. Concluding the Journey

The findings of this research confirm that many visitors do not initially understand the process behind South Africa's transition to democracy, nor the role that the TRC played. However, after engaging with the apartheid narrative systematically

Figure 8.9 The seven towering concrete pillars at the main entrance to the Apartheid Museum highlight the core values of South Africa's post-apartheid society—democracy, diversity, equality, freedom, reconciliation, respect, and responsibility (Photography courtesy of the Apartheid Museum)

and chronologically within the curated environment, the multi-layered experience of what segregation and oppression entailed allows for a greater understanding of apartheid and its demise. The design of the Apartheid Museum successfully allows the overarching apartheid narrative to unfold slowly (see Figure 8.9). This incremental approach provides visitors with the necessary socio-political framework to aid interpretation of the disturbing content portrayed in the TRC exhibition.

While visiting the Apartheid Museum is high on the tourist agenda, the Museum is also a critical educational resource for South Africans, in particular teachers and schoolchildren. The Museum offers educational programming, supplements the curriculum, and supports the development of historical consciousness inside and outside the classroom. Without being overly didactic, the Museum creates a platform where large numbers of people from diverse backgrounds can engage with challenging content about a painful past. Deepening their understanding of the country's painful past is an important feature of the broader goals of transitional justice in South Africa.

Fatigue and information overload were highlighted in several SASC responses. Possible remedies to address this include encouraging schools to conduct repeat visits and for the Museum to supplement its educational programme[24] with

[24] The Museum's educational programming includes two publications, *Understanding Apartheid*, one for teachers, and the other for learners. *Understanding Apartheid* is structured around the requirements

additional theme-specific programmes. For example, as the TRC is only studied in the Grade 12 History curriculum, a tour and educational programme that is TRC-specific would provide learners with more time, and opportunity to engage in some of the more in-depth discussions and debates surrounding the issues and complexities raised by the exhibit and the broader restorative and transitional justice discourse.

The data collected during this research also indicates that visitors have an understanding of the importance of dialogue and debate as a means of fostering reconciliation and social cohesion—fundamental mechanisms of the reconciliation process. Further insights were gleaned from the emotional responses recorded.

Owing to the inherent subjectivity, attempting to analyse emotional responses has potential pitfalls. It is impossible to ascribe absolutes; emotions vary from person to person, and from one situation to the next. These challenges aside, the responses collected in the survey provide indicators that can contribute to the broader reconciliation and historical trauma discourse. They can also benefit the Apartheid Museum when future educational programming and exhibition development takes place.

While the lack of commitment to implementing the recommendations of the TRC Report is a factor contributing to the truncation of South Africa's reconciliation dialogue, insufficient consideration has given to the inter-generational damage caused by apartheid to current and future generations. South Africa's reconciliatory threads wear thin and will snap if the government and civil society fail to address socio-economic marginalisation and injustice, and pervasive racism:

> Our world is troubled in many ways today and peace is threatened so often because people do not understand their neighbours. Conflict resolution and reconciliation are essential elements for the attainment of sustainable peace and unity.... As custodians of the cultural soul of the nation, museums must have the capacity to broker peace, unity and understanding in times of conflict and disorder and they must speak out when there is fear and danger.[25]

Finally, the Museum needs to offer visitors the opportunity to debrief. This could be offered by tour guides with the assistance and support of a Museum counsellor, or an organisation focused on healing historical trauma. This would help to mediate both the TRC exhibition and the Museum experience as a whole by providing

of the current Senior and FET phase curricula. Also, learners in Grades 6–9 receive and work through grade-specific workbooks and *Timeliners*, a series of educational comics, when they visit the Museum. Educational resources are available on the Museum's website and can be downloaded free of charge.

[25] E Arinze, 'The Role of the Museum in Society' (1999) <https://pdfcoffee.com/the-role-of-a-museum-pdf-free.html> accessed 28 September 2022.

visitors with an opportunity to constructively process some of the more negative and uncomfortable responses.

While not strictly within the remit of the Museum's core activities, debriefing processes could bolster the positive contribution the Museum has made, and continues to make, to society. By fostering an environment where the past and present merge in meaningful dialogue, different perspectives can be bridged, and solutions created for a more equitable and just future.

9

Exploring Visitor Expectations and Experiences of Conflict and Transitional Justice Exhibitions in Bogotá, Colombia

Nancy Rocío Rueda Esteban

1. Introduction

Colombia has experienced more than fifty years of conflict and violence committed by armed groups. There have been multiple peace treaties with guerrilla groups, and throughout the country, many communities have tried to find peace through different processes. The conflict in Colombia cannot be reduced to a single, straightforward narrative of events between only two actors—victims and perpetrators. Rather, it should be understood as a complex set of narratives involving multifaceted objectives and interests from a variety of players.

This chapter, and the empirical research upon which it is based, reflects on visitor expectations and experiences of museum exhibitions in their coverage of the Colombian armed conflict and the subsequent peace processes that have followed. The empirical research that was conducted for the purposes of this chapter took place in two museums: the Museo Nacional de Colombia in Bogotá (MN) and the Centre of Memory, Peace and Reconciliation of Bogotá (CMPR). The latter museum was created in 2012, with the permanent exhibition opening in 2018 entitled '*Recordar: Volver a pasar por el corazón*' (Remember: follow your heart) about the conflict in Colombia.[1] In this context, it bears emphasis that there is no museum that is singularly dedicated to recounting the diverse narratives of Colombia's violent past. In fact, even with the recent peace and transitional justice processes involving the Revolutionary Armed Forces of Colombia—People's Army (FARC-EP)—there is a notable failure to reflect fully and meaningfully on this complex web of violent events in Colombia. The exhibitions that do exist have been narrowly focused on regional and territorial accounts of historical events and the processes of memory and fail, ultimately, to provide a holistic picture of the country's conflict-ridden past.

[1] 'Paz y Reconciliación' *Centro de Memoria* (nd) <http://centromemoria.gov.co/informacion-general/> accessed 3 October 2022.

Nancy Rocío Rueda Esteban, *Exploring Visitor Expectations and Experiences of Conflict and Transitional Justice Exhibitions in Bogotá, Colombia* In: *Transitional Justice, Distributive Justice, and Transformative Constitutionalism.* Edited by: David Bilchitz and Raisa Cachalia, with Magdalena Inés Correa Henao and Nathalia Bautista Pizarro, Oxford University Press.
 DOI: 10.1093/oso/9780192887627.003.0009

In the end, it seems that the absence of an exhibition that is specifically dedicated to relating the multifaceted narratives of the enduring conflict in Colombia, and to explaining properly the peace processes that have followed, is a challenge from a transitional justice perspective. This is because one of the goals of a peace project must be to facilitate a deeper process of social healing and understanding in the wake of a violent past by seeking out a fuller understanding of past events and experiences of violence. Museums—if used in ways that give spatial expression to diverse narratives of violence and injustice—can play a meaningful and important role in advancing societal healing as part of a broader project of transitional justice in countries emerging from conflict.

2. Conflict in Colombia and the Beginning of the Transitional Justice Process

The perspectives on the history of conflict and violence in Colombia have been diverse. Some academics argue that the different periods of conflict that began in the nineteenth century have worked as continuous chains, resulting in successive periods of further violence in the twentieth and twenty-first centuries.[2] There are, however, those who disagree with this account arguing that these were isolated historical events that are not interrelated. In fact, it seems that violence and conflict in Colombia appeared long before the appearance of outlawed revolutionary groups. During the nineteenth century, civil wars were characterised as partisan conflicts between two dominant political parties: liberal and conservative. These partisan battles continued throughout the twentieth century, with moments of calm, followed by further periods of conflict. These wars had great economic, social, and political consequences for Colombia as a country.[3] According to Sánchez, Díaz, and Formisano, one of the long-term consequences of this struggle was the creation of 'rural self-defence groups that advocated for land ownership and protection of life' (*Autodefensas Campesinas*).[4] Some groups had communist beliefs, while others followed more liberal principles; but both challenged the conservative government and the political ideals that were dominant at that time. Over time, grassroots resistance led to the formation of guerrilla groups in different areas of Colombia. In 1958, the National Front (*Frente Nacional*)—whereby governmental power was divided equally (for four years each) between conservatives and liberals—ended the bipartisan violence. The alternating rule of the liberal and conservative parties was a way of controlling popular and political differences. However, while some

[2] F Sánchez, A Díaz, and M Formisano, *Conflicto, violencia y actividad criminal en Colombia: un análisis espacial* (Universidad de los Andes 2003).
[3] ibid.
[4] ibid 5.

political parties were included in the agreement with outlawed communist guerrilla groups, others were left out.[5] One such group was the Revolutionary Armed Forces of Colombia (FARC), which established itself as a communist guerrilla movement at the First Guerrilla Conference in 1965.[6] In 1982, they added 'EP' (*Ejército del Pueblo*) meaning 'Popular Army' to their name forming what is known today as 'FARC-EP'. In 2003 Sánchez, Díaz, and Formisano explained that this guerrilla group, from its origins, went from being composed of ten fronts in five regions of the country in 1980 to more than thirty-five fronts by the end of 1987, thus exerting influence in almost all areas. By 2000, the FARC-EP had approximately sixty-six fronts throughout the country.[7] Their success has been the result of the systematic failures of the different peace processes; successful financing based on extortion, kidnapping, and their alliance with drug cartels; as well as legal and illegal bonanzas, such as oil, cocoa, poppies, coal, and bananas.[8] All these factors have influenced the expansion and strengthening of the FARC-EP.[9] Its growth in the number of supporters and fronts over forty years was unprecedented, making it one of the most prominent guerrilla groups in the history of Colombia.

However, FARC-EP was not the only guerrilla group that formed and flourished in the twentieth century. The National Liberation Army (ELN) was established before the FARC-EP, in 1962. This group started with only sixteen men. By 2000, they had reached a staggering number of 4,500 combatants.[10] Their expansion was largely due to extortion and the exploitation of oil, gold, and coal.[11] By the end of 2000, the FARC-EP and the ELN were the largest and strongest guerrilla groups in Colombia due both to their numbers and also their scale of action.[12]

A third group emerged by the end of 1980 which provided private security to debilitate and control the guerrilla armies.[13] These self-defence groups (paramilitaries) were created as a purely reactive phenomenon and worked with alliances between both traditional and conservative regional powers. They acquired an important presence on the periphery and in small municipalities, where institutions were scarce and the influence of the state was weak. Local communities had ongoing issues with the government due to the high levels of conflict, instability, and the lack of safety.[14] Known as the United Self-Defence Forces of Colombia

5 ibid.
6 D Tawse-Smith, 'Conflicto armado colombiano' (2008) 19 Desafíos 269.
7 Sánchez, Díaz, and Formisano (n 2).
8 Tawse-Smith (n 6).
9 H Gómez Buendía, 'La Violencia Contemporánea en Colombia, un Punto de Vista Liberal' (Fondo Editorial Cerec 1991) cited in Sánchez, Díaz, and Formisano (n 2) 12.
10 Sánchez, Díaz, and Formisano (n 2).
11 Tawse-Smith (n 6).
12 Sánchez, Díaz, and Formisano (n 2).
13 Tawse-Smith (n 6).
14 ibid.

(*Autodefensas Unidas de Colombia* or AUC), they became a significant player in the armed conflict, committing acts of violence in various parts of the country.[15]

Other outlawed groups also formed guerrilla armies, including the EPL (Popular Liberation Army); M-19 (April 19 Movement); PRT (Revolutionary Workers' Party), MAQL (Quintín Lame Armed Movement); CRS (Socialist Renewal Current); MIR-Patria Libre (Revolutionary Integration Movement or '*Patria Libre*'), but none achieved the scale of political, social, and economic influence that was achieved by the FARC-EP, ELN, or AUC. All of these outlawed armies followed different ideals and gained strength over time. According to Tawse-Smith, the 'diversity of illegal armed organisations has been characterised by their different social origins, political-ideological projects, organisational structures, war tactics, regional roots, types of relationship with the population, among others'.[16]

It is because of the range, division, and autonomy of these different illegal armed groups that peace processes have also been diverse and developed specifically to respond to particular events and groups, and not to all of them at the same time. A stable and lasting peace has been unattainable because, while a negotiation process is taking place with one guerrilla group, the conflict with another continues in a different area. Also, the close relationship between these groups and drug trafficking adds a further layer of complexity to this already difficult situation.[17] Colombia's armed conflict has resulted in forced displacement and countless deaths. It has also left in its wake many victims of homicides, forced disappearances, sexual violence, social intolerance, extortive kidnappings, massacres, and arbitrary detentions.[18]

There have been several peace processes (including, eg, treaties, amnesties, and pardons) in Colombia over the prolonged years of the conflict.[19] To elaborate on this, during the military government of General Rojas Pinilla in 1953, a truce was reached, and amnesty was given to those who left the conflict.[20] This ended the partisan violence in Colombia.[21] Since then, political solutions to other conflicts in the form of peace agreements have been achieved during different presidencies.[22] In 1988, President Virgilio Barco began a peace process with the M-19 that culminated in an agreement in 1990. This resulted in the surrender of weapons and an agreement that allowed M-19 to become a political organisation.[23] During

[15] Sánchez, Díaz, and Formisano (n 2).

[16] Tawse-Smith (n 6) 280.

[17] ibid. See also R Uprimny and MP Saffon, 'Usos y abusos de la justicia transicional en Colombia' (2008) 4 Anuario de derechos humanos 165.

[18] Uprimny and Saffon (n 17) 169.

[19] M Osorio, 'Acuerdos y amnistías en la historia reciente de Colombia' *EL Espectador* (2016) <https://www.elespectador.com/noticias/paz/acuerdos-y-amnistias-historia-reciente-de-colombia-articulo-656856> accessed 3 October 2022.

[20] Sánchez, Díaz, and Formisano (n 2).

[21] Osorio (n 19).

[22] Tawse-Smith (n 6).

[23] 'Virgilio Barco, el presidente "del proceso de paz más exitoso"' *El Tiempo* (2016) <https://www.eltiempo.com/archivo/documento/CMS-16703433> accessed 3 October 2022.

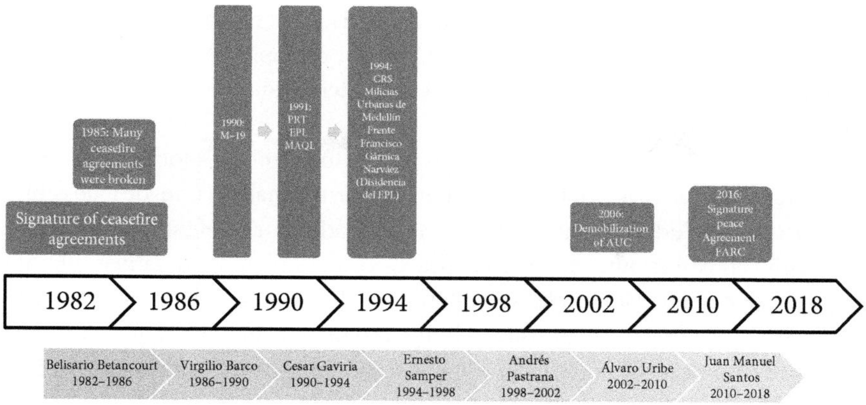

Figure 9.1 Peace process and agreements in Colombia 1982–2016 (Author's own creation based on literature review)

President Cesar Gaviria's government (1990–1994), a peace process with PRT, EPL, MAQL, CRS, and several other militias in the city of Medellín was achieved.[24]

At the end of 2002, with Álvaro Uribe Vélez as president, the peace process with the AUC began, and in 2006 the demobilisation of its members took place.[25] Then in 2012 during the presidency of Juan Manuel Santos, the peace process with the FARC-EP, which had started on 24 November 2016, ended with the signing of the Final Peace Agreement.[26] The 2016 agreement made provision for agrarian reform; participation in politics; the combatting of illicit drug activity; reparations for victims; and a special jurisdiction for peace as a final step in bringing an end to the decades of war and conflict in Colombia[27] (see Figure 9.1).

3. Tourism: A New Opportunity for Colombia

The 2016 Peace Agreement, which brought an official end to decades of conflict in Colombia, has given rise to a further development: tourism. The role of tourism (or 'cultural tourism') is particularly important for the purpose of this chapter and in thinking more deeply about the positive role that memory can play in post-conflict societies. In particular, encouraging tourists (nationals and internationals) to visit

[24] Osorio (n 19).

[25] 'Firman acuerdo de paz con los paramilitares entre 2002 y 2008' *El Tiempo* (2010) <https://www.eltiempo.com/archivo/documento/CMS-8601880> accessed 3 October 2022.

[26] M Gómez, 'Así está Colombia, un año después de las Farc' *El Tiempo* (2017) <https://www.eltiempo.com/politica/proceso-de-paz/efectos-en-colombia-tras-un-ano-de-la-firma-del-acuerdo-de-paz-con-las-farc-152740> accessed 3 October 2022.

[27] Osorio (n 19).

places that memorialise history and its diverse narratives can have a positive impact on the transitional justice project through, for example, encouraging a more meaningful and inclusive process of societal understanding and healing in the aftermath of conflict.

So then, what has accounted for the growth in tourism in Colombia? For one thing, the change of image, both nationally and internationally, has made it possible for tourists to include Colombia as a travel destination for the first time in many years. This can be attributed to the 2016 peace process and other initiatives such as the promotion of tourism locally and internationally; strategic planning; training; and tax benefits.[28] All this has resulted in the exponential growth of international tourism in the last seven years: in 2012 alone the number of arrivals was 3,491,762. Then, in 2014 and 2016 the numbers increased to 4,779,188 and 5,092,052 respectively.[29] It is now possible to visit several destinations recognised for their unique cultural and natural richness, that 'during the more than five decades of war had been difficult, if not impossible, to visit'.[30] Newspapers such as *The New York Times* have pointed out that 'the road to peace has motivated many travellers to discover the many magical corners loaded with culture and history, and landscapes full of biodiversity'.[31] Several social, economic, and political strategies were required to open these once restricted places to general public visits and tourism. An attempt has also been made to rebuild the social fabric destroyed by the war, which has been propelled by the development of a sustainable tourism framework where support for families interested in tourism development, tourism projects, and technical assistance has been developed.[32]

Tourists have many reasons to visit Colombia, with interests varying from enjoyment of the country's natural wonders (such as bird watching), participation in extreme sports, visiting Colombia's magnificent beaches, and engaging in a process of cultural and historical learning, amongst others. According to Rodríguez, Colombia has approximately 2,134 cultural resources.[33] There are also 318 museums registered in the Information System of Colombian Museums (SIMCO).

[28] Revista Semana, '¿Cómo está ayudando el posconflicto al turismo en Colombia?' *Semana* (2018) <https://www.semana.com/contenidos-editoriales/colombia-me-encantas-/articulo/como-esta-ayudando-el-posconflicto-al-turismo-en-colombia/577405> accessed 3 October 2022.

[29] 'Informe de turismo extranjero en Colombia' *Procolombia* (2018) http://www.procolombia.co/publicaciones/informe-de-turismo-extranjero-en-colombia accessed 3 October 2022.

[30] E Zach, 'In Southwest Colombia, Treasures Are Forbidden No More' *New York Times* (2018) <https://www.nytimes.com/2018/07/09/travel/colombia-southwest-san-agustin-purace.html?action=click&module=RelatedLinks&pgtype=Article> accessed 3 October 2022.

[31] C Rodríguez, 'Turismo y posconflicto: las cifras no mienten' *Portafolio* (2018) <http://blogs.portafolio.co/pensamiento-emprendedor/2018/04/12/turismo-en-el-posconflicto/> accessed 3 October 2022.

[32] Procolombia (n 29).

[33] Rodríguez (n 31).

This has made Colombia a potential destination for cultural tourism, where museums play a very important role.[34]

Various museums across the country have curated small, isolated exhibitions about the conflict in Colombia. There are also a number of social organisations that are working toward the reconstruction of memory in the country. These organisations have initiated the recording of many acts of violence that have taken place across the country. Individual communities have also taken part in the process of building a collective memory of conflicts that have affected them. There are three notable community-driven exhibitions in this regard—'the Embroidery Women of Bojayá' who, after the massacre that ended the lives of 117 civilians, began a practice to express their fears[35] through doing embroidery depictions of their memories. Then there are 'the Weavery Women of Mampuján', who have expressed the suffering caused by forced displacement and violent murders through patchwork art;[36] and 'the Matriarchs of Trujillo' who, after a social cleansing that killed approximately 245 people, tell the story of the massacre through the construction of a 'park-monument'.[37] In this way, creative depictions of memory can advance the goals of transitional justice. While confronting historical violence can be painful for victims, doing so can advance long-term peace through fostering a deeper process of healing and catharsis within communities.

Law 1448 of 2011 states that measures of care, assistance, and integral reparation are to be given to victims of the internal armed conflict. The Centre of Historical

[34] Ministerio de Cultura Informe de Gestión (2016–2017) <http://www.mincultura.gov.co/sitios/ministerio/Informeestion-VFinal.pdf> accessed 3 October 2022.

[35] F Martínez, 'Las prácticas artísticas en la construcción de memoria sobre la violencia y el conflicto. Colombia' (2013) 9 Eleuthera 39; Grupo de Memoria Histórica de la Comisión Nacional de reparación y reconciliación, *Bojayá, la guerra sin límites. Colombia* (2010) <http://www.centrodememoriahistorica.gov.co/descargas/informes2010/informe_bojaya.pd> accessed 3 October 2022; A Neira, 'Agonía sin fin: 12 años de la masacre de Bojayá' *Semana* (2014) <https://www.semana.com/nacion/articulo/masacre-de-bojaya-12-anos-despues/385639-3> accessed 3 October 2022.

[36] S Rodríguez, 'Tejidos de Paz desde Mampuján' *Arcadia* (2016) <https://www.revistaarcadia.com/arte/articulo/tejedoras-de-mampujan-en-exposicion/54330> accessed 3 October 2022; G Castrillón, 'Las tejedoras de Mampuján: la fuerza femenina del perdón' *El Espectador* (2015) <https://www.elespectador.com/cromos/hoy-historias-cronicas/las-tejedoras-de-mampujan-la-fuerza-femenina-del-perdon-16675> accessed 3 October 2022; W-Radio, 'Las tejedoras de Mampuján estarán en Bogotá' *W-Radio* (2018) <http://www.wradio.com.co/noticias/sociedad/las-tejedoras-de-mampujan-estaran-en-bogota/20180313/nota/3723358.aspx> accessed 3 October 2022.

[37] Comisión Nacional de Reparación y Reconciliación-Área de Memoria Histórica, *Trujillo, una tragedia que no cesa Primer informe de memoria histórica de la Comisión Nacional de Reparación y Reconciliación* (2008) http://www.centrodememoriahistorica.gov.co/descargas/informes2008/informe_trujillo.pd accessed 3 October 2022; Y Luna, *Repertorios de duelo de mujeres rurales sobrevivientes de cuatro masacres en Colombia* (tesis de grado) (Universidad del Valle, Santiago de Cali, Colombia 2016) <http://bibliotecadigital.univalle.edu.co/bitstream/10893/9906/1/0534289-S-2016-2.pdf> accessed 3 October 2022; 'Estado pidió perdón por la masacre de Trujillo' *El Espectador* (2016) <https://www.elespectador.com/noticias/judicial/estado-pidio-perdon-masacre-de-trujillo-articulo-628779> accessed 3 October 2022; 'Parque Monumento a las víctimas de Trujillo' *Centro de Memoria Histórica* (nd) <http://www.centrodememoriahistorica.gov.co/multimedias/MemoriasExpresivasRecientes/Memoria_H/valledelcauca/parquemonumento/index.html> accessed 3 October 2022; Museo de memoria histórico de Colombia (nd) <http://museodememoria.gov.co/arte-y-cultura/historia-de-la-masacre/> accessed 3 October 2022.

Memory was designated to design, create, and manage a Museum of Memory to strengthen the collective memory of the recent period of violence in Colombia's history (Law 1448 of 2011, art 148).[38] To start this process, workshops involving victims, organisations, academics, research centres, and the media have been held to collect insights and make recommendations. They have also installed multiple temporary exhibitions to begin the process of memorialising the past and in so doing, to create the conditions for long-term healing as a necessary part of transitional justice. With these inputs, the building plans are complete and construction of a Museum dedicated to telling the diverse stories of the conflict years is scheduled to begin soon.[39]

Bogotá's Centre of Memory, Peace and Reconciliation of the District opened in 2002, with a mission:

> [t]o contribute to the construction of peace by encouraging the participation of different population groups of Bogotá; promoting and strengthening the processes of memory that make visible the different experiences related to the armed conflict; and to create spaces for meeting and reconciliation thereby leading to the transformation of consciousness and the promotion of human rights.[40]

The activities of this museum are focused on the reconstruction of memory through participative activities, but they also create exhibitions embodying artistic expression to allow dialogue and the construction of collective memory to take place.[41] Nonetheless, it was not until 2018 that a permanent exhibition was opened called '*Recordar: Volver a pasar por el corazón*' (Remember: follow your heart) about the conflict in Colombia. The aim of this exhibition is:

> to make visible the impact of the armed conflict in Bogota and to rely on citizen initiatives for peace to transform the consciousness of the war and its consequences for the city. Ultimately, it is about promoting a process of reconciliation through recognition of the victims in the capital and the peace actions that have been carried out there.[42]

The exhibition has seven sections/themes: the incalculable weight of forced displacement; the objects of memory; polyphonies of fear; faces that transform the

[38] Ley 448 de 2011, 'Por la cual se dictan medidas de atención, asistencia y reparación integral a las víctimas del conflicto armado interno y se dictan otras disposiciones' 148.

[39] Museo de Memoria Histórica de Colombia Proyecto (nd) <http://museodememoria.gov.co/proyecto/voces-para-transformar-a-colombia/> accessed 3 October 2022.

[40] Centro de Memoria, Paz y Reconciliación (nd) <http://centromemoria.gov.co/informacion-general/> accessed 3 October 2022.

[41] ibid.

[42] Centro de Memoria, Paz y Reconciliación (2019) EXPOSICIÓN PERMANENTE 'RECORDAR: volver a pasar por el corazón' Sentidos y propósitos, 2.

city; peace in movement; views of the war in the city; and peace in play.[43] It is designed to promote understanding of what happened in the capital city specifically:

> Remembering these stories allows us to understand the dynamics of a war that forever marked the lives of the inhabitants of Bogotá. Remembering is not a word that explains the past, but a verb that gives meaning to the present. Remembering is an opportunity to feel in solidarity with what others lived through in those dark times and an invitation to go through the heart again.[44]

On the other hand, the Museo Nacional de Colombia is an administrative unit of the Ministry of Culture, whose mission is to safeguard national cultural heritage by relating the history of the country so that all citizens are reflected and ultimately included in the broader narrative.[45] It accepts that '[m]emory is not unique'[46] and citizens' memories are created through different experiences. The MN also offers a place for dialogue.[47] It has seventeen rooms where the pre-Hispanic, colonial, and republican histories are explained. Regarding the history of conflict and transitional justice, the Museum has to date designed only a single poster[48] exhibition called '[p]resent, past and future of peace in Colombia' that provides a brief overview of the story of the conflicts and peace treaties from 1902 until 2016 and the recent signing of the peace process with the FARC. These posters (fourteen in total) have been distributed to many municipalities in the country and can be found on the Museum's web page.[49] In the end, what is clearly missing from the Museum is a dedicated space or exhibition that meaningfully explains the recent conflict and which provides an informative account of the current transitional justice process that is underway.

4. The Empirical Study

A. Methodology

The qualitative methods adopted to research the social phenomena in this chapter proceeds from the principle that 'the social world is constructed with meanings

[43] ibid.
[44] ibid 1.
[45] Ministerio de Cultura (n 34).
[46] Museo Nacional (n.d.) Exposiciones <http://www.museonacional.gov.co/exposiciones/permanentes/Paginas/default.aspx> accessed 3 October 2022.
[47] ibid.
[48] Posters with a set of images and texts around a certain subject.
[49] Museo Nacional (n.d.) Iconografías—Presente, pasado y futuro de la paz en Colombia. <http://www.museonacional.gov.co/exposiciones/carteles/paz/Paginas/Paz%20en%20Colombia.aspx >accessed 3 October 2022.

and symbols, which implies the search for this construction and its importance'.[50] Quantitative methods have also been applied to collect and analyse quantifiable data and to establish relationships between variables[51] in order to determine what visitors think and feel in response to museum exhibitions. To collect this information, surveys were used. The surveys had multiple-choice questions and were applied in two phases and in two different museums: the Museo Nacional de Colombia in Bogotá, and the Centre of Memory, Peace and Reconciliation (CMPR) of Bogotá. This provided an opportunity to gauge general opinions and identify trends.[52] It is important to note that the research was limited to the capital city, Bogotá, and was not undertaken in other parts of the country.

The first phase took place in the MN. The survey involved fifty-four people and the questions were about their interest in a possible exhibition about the Colombian conflict and the transitional justice process, and how they would feel about visiting a museum dedicated to this purpose. It also explored their understanding of what transitional justice is. Surveys were completed on Thursday, 29 November and Sunday, 2 December 2018. The survey comprised three parts: the first part included socio-demographic information (city, age, gender, and the reason for visiting the Museum); the second part asked about their familiarity and general knowledge of the transitional justice process in Colombia pertaining to the 2016 Peace Agreement; and the third part focused on the feelings and interests of participants in visiting an exhibition about transitional justice and the Colombian conflict, as well as questions pertaining to when it would be appropriate to start talking about Colombia's violent past.

The second phase took place at the CMPR, which opened its permanent exhibition about the historical conflict in Colombia in December 2018—even though it has yet to include an exhibition about transitional justice specifically. The survey comprised twenty-three people both before they entered the exhibition and after they left. These surveys, also conducted in three parts, were administered on Friday 15 March, Saturday 16 March, and Thursday 22 March 2019.

The surveys were completed in Spanish. Responses in brackets were translated by the author and liberty has been taken to make these accessible in English. In cases where visitors were not fluent in Spanish, the person conducting the interview translated the questions into English or French and the responses were noted.

[50] MC Cordero, 'Historias de vida: Una metodología de investigación cualitativa' (2012) 5(1) Revista Griot 50, 51.

[51] N Bautista, *Proceso de la Investigación Cualitativa. Epistemología, Metodología y Aplicaciones* (Editorial El Manual Moderno 2011); R Hernandez Sampieri and others, *Metodología de la investigación* (McGraw Hill México 1998).

[52] H Cerda, *Los Elementos de la Investigación* (3rd edn, El Buho 2013).

B. What People Think and Feel: Expectations and Experiences

In total, fifty-four surveys were completed at the MN. 65 per cent of the participants were Colombians and 35 per cent international tourists. Of the national visitors, 48 per cent were locals (from Bogotá) and 17 per cent were tourists (2 per cent Medellín, 7 per cent Rionegro, 4 per cent Barranquilla, and 4 per cent Pereira). Further, of the participants 24 per cent were between 19 and 25 years of age; 44 per cent between 26 and 45; and 22 per cent between 46 and 64. Only 7 per cent were older than 65. In the CMPR, 23 surveys were conducted whereby 74 per cent were Colombian nationals and 26 per cent international tourists. Of the national visitors, 61 per cent were from Bogotá and 13 per cent were from neighbouring cities. Further, of the participants 26 per cent were between 19 and 25 years of age; 26 per cent between 26 and 45; 22 per cent between 46 and 64; and 26 per cent were older than 65.

In building an understanding of why people visit these places, in the MN, 76 per cent of the participants stated that they were tourists; 8 per cent stated they were visiting because the exhibition was a temporary one; 8 per cent said that they were visiting for academic reasons; and 17 per cent because of other reasons. In respect of the CMPR, 22 per cent of the participants that visited the Centre were tourists; 4 per cent because it was a temporary exhibition; and 83 per cent for different reasons.

Regarding their general knowledge about the transitional justice process in Colombia (see Figure 9.2), in the MN, 52 per cent said they were familiar with the process, of which 44 per cent were nationals. And 48 per cent of the total participants were not familiar with the process at all, of which 11 per cent were nationals.

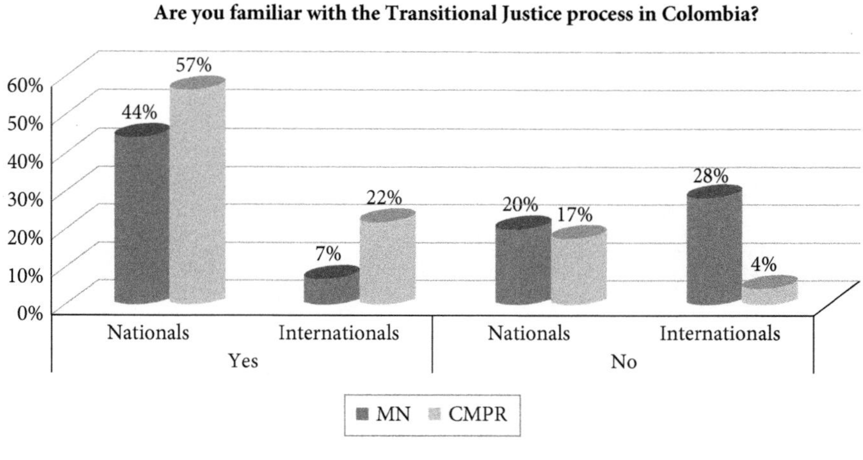

Figure 9.2 Answers to the question: 'Are you familiar with the transitional justice process in Colombia?' (Author's own creation based on surveys)

In the CMPR, 78 per cent said they were familiar with the process, of which 57 per cent were nationals; and 22 per cent stated that they were not familiar with this process at all, of which, 17 per cent were nationals.

On the same point, 53 per cent of the participants in the MN stated that they understood what transitional justice means (see Figure 9.3), with 46 per cent of this group being Colombian nationals. Then, 47 per cent stated that they did not understand the process at all. From the CMPR, 74 per cent affirmed that they understood the process—52 per cent of which were Colombian nationals. Only 26 per cent stated that they did not understand the process at all. This shows that the Colombians are generally the ones who believe they understand the transitional justice process, although there remains a significant percentage of people (both nationals and internationals) who do not understand the process at all.

Nonetheless, from the surveys in the MN, only seventeen (53 per cent) of the twenty-eight participants that said they understood the process and explained briefly what they thought transitional justice is; and in the CMPR only thirteen (74 per cent) of the seventeen explained their answers (four answers did not explain the meaning of transitional justice at all). Some examples of answers that were given were that the process involved:

- government giving guarantees of non-repetition to the victims and the people involved in the peace process;
- temporal modifications to the law due to the peace process;
- a process of reincorporation into society;

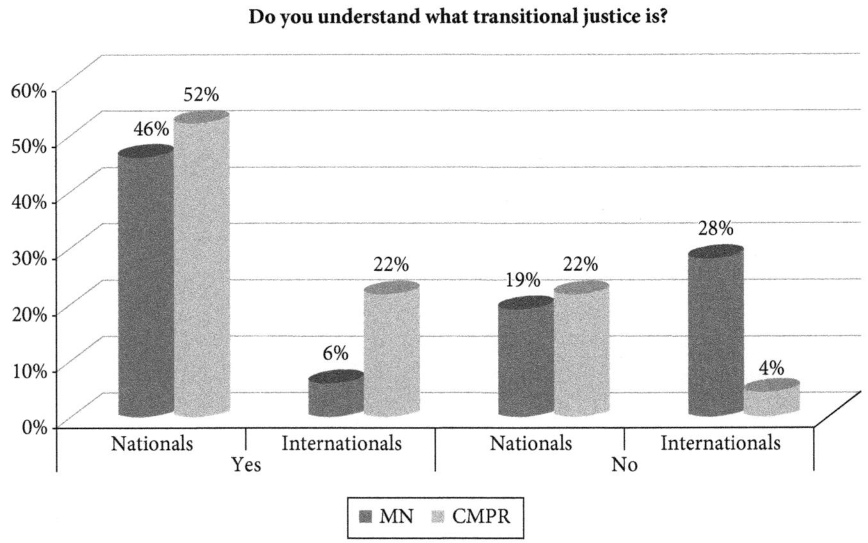

Figure 9.3 Answers to the question: 'Do you understand what transitional justice is?' (Author's own creation based on surveys)

- a peace process with the FARC;
- a process for ex-combatants only;
- a change regarding the armed conflict process;
- a transition from conflict to peace;
- becoming an example to the world;
- giving forgiveness in exchange for confessions;
- legal changes for a period of time;
- pertaining to the compromises that were agreed in the table of negotiation;
- compliance with the agreement signed on 24 November 2016;
- concerned with justice and a legal transition to peace, truth, and reparation;
- reparations for victims of the conflict;
- everything done in the process of advancing justice and peace;
- justice after the war;
- support for victims;
- justice that occurs at critical moments, a non-criminal kind of justice.

These responses show that people connect transitional justice to the legal processes after the conflict; to a lesser extent to reparations for the victims and forgiveness for offenders. Nonetheless, the overall understanding of the process is not deep and does not extend to the complexities of the process as a whole. Concerning the possibility of visiting an exhibition about transitional justice (see Figure 9.4), 87 per

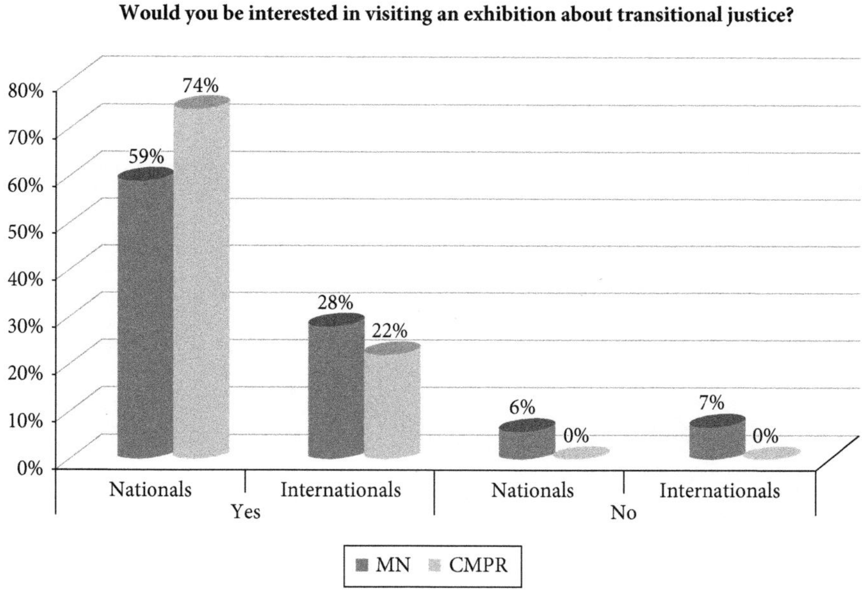

Figure 9.4 Answer to the question: 'Would you be interested in visiting an exhibition about transitional justice?' (Author's own creation based on surveys)

cent of the participants in the MN answered that they would be interested, of which 59 per cent were Colombians; and 13 per cent said they would not. At the CMPR, 96 per cent answered they would be interested and only one person declined to answer the question.

Consequently, 93 per cent of the participants responded that they would be interested in visiting an exhibition about the recent conflict in Colombia (see Figure 9.5). Of this percentage, 61 per cent are nationals. Only 7 per cent said they would not be interested at all. When asked in the CMPR why they would be interested in visiting an exhibition about the conflict in Colombia, some answers were general such as relating to, for example, a wider interest in visiting museums or general curiosity about the past; but some were more specific and spoke to a desire to:

- understand the conflict as part of the broader history of Colombia;
- know what happened factually in the conflict;
- live like other people live;
- understand the violence;
- help to learn from its mistakes; or
- confront the past as victims.

When asked about their expectations of the exhibition before entering, they said that they expected to:

- know the history of the conflict;
- understand the corrupt and unjust events of the conflict;

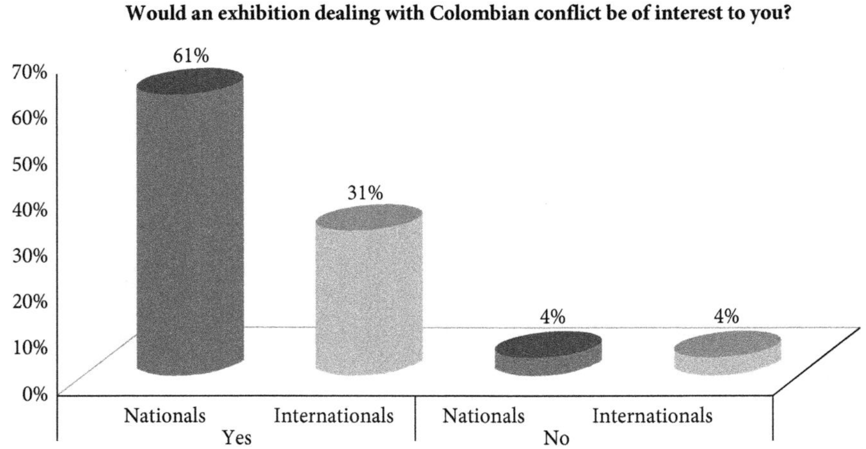

Figure 9.5 Answer to the question: 'Would an exhibition dealing with the Colombian conflict be of interest to you?' (Author's own creation based on surveys)

- see even the harsh things that happened such as photographic evidence of murders and destruction;
- be given information about the victims of the conflict;
- see real and impartial exhibitions;
- engage with testimonials from those affected by the conflict;
- increase their awareness of the violence, and in so doing, help make some positive contribution to the process of moving forward;
- see an exhibition that was truthful.

Some visitors did not have expectations at all. Then, when the participants were asked about their expected feelings after visiting an exhibition about the Colombian conflict and transitional justice, the answers were varied. In the MN, 30 per cent said they would feel sad; 20 per cent happy; 2 per cent indifferent; 33 per cent inspired; 9 per cent confused; 6 per cent guilty; 22 per cent uncomfortable; 11 per cent interested; 2 per cent compromised; 2 per cent motivated; 2 per cent optimistic; 2 per cent intrigued; 2 per cent powerless; and 2 per cent informed. In the CMPR, 30 per cent said sad; 4 per cent indifferent; 22 per cent angry; 4 per cent inspired; 13 per cent confused; 9 per cent uncomfortable; 4 per cent powerless; 17 per cent curious; 4 per cent interested; 4 per cent tired; 17 per cent with expectations; 9 per cent pain and suffering; and 4 per cent finding themselves.

These feelings, compared with the feelings expressed *after* visiting the exhibition about the conflict, are very similar, although, after the visit they were more negative: 42 per cent said sad; 8 per cent uncomfortable; 8 per cent confused; 5 per cent angry; 3 per cent happy; 3 per cent guilty; 3 per cent peace and forgiveness; 3 per cent bad energy; 3 per cent there is still a lot to learn; 3 per cent satisfaction of knowing that these things can be done; 3 per cent frustration; 3 per cent astonishment; 3 per cent anger directed at the state; 5 per cent anguish, 3 per cent less hope; 3 per cent hope; and 3 per cent nostalgia. Regarding their experiences after the visit to the exhibition, 96 per cent of the participants in the CMPR stated that it helped them to develop a better understanding of the conflict in Colombia, and when asked to describe their experience, their answers varied:

- good;
- very sad and shocking but informative;
- very good, I did not know many of these things;
- good but it leaves me very sad;
- remembering and seeing people you know;
- interesting, there is a lot of information and it complements what I know;
- very good, somewhat exaggerated;
- want to come back later to analyse more things;
- unhappy, overwhelmed, sad;
- sad, a lot of cruelty, everything involves the state;

- very well-organised, very informative;
- very interesting, it produces fear;
- shocking;
- complete information;
- nostalgia, I live in a conflict zone;
- very sad, all the facts;
- very complete exhibition;
- I liked very much the peace treaties and memories provided.

In fact, 61 per cent of the participants answered that they needed some kind of activity to make sense of their visit; 22 per cent said they did not; and 7 per cent did not answer. Those who felt the need for more engagement explained that they needed to clarify some of their doubts; to help understand what had happened; to gain more context; or to speak with someone about what they had seen.

And the final question was: 'When do you think it would be appropriate to talk about Colombia's past and visit an exhibition about the Colombian conflict and the transitional justice process?' To this question, 74 per cent of participants in MN answered now; 7 per cent answered between two and four years; 7 per cent answered between five and seven years; 2 per cent between seven and ten years; 9 per cent ten years or more; and 2 per cent before ten years. In the CMPR, 96 per cent of participants said that now would be appropriate; and 4 per cent between seven and ten years. This means that most people think it would be appropriate and necessary to start the process of learning and engaging with the country's difficult past 'now'.

5. Conclusion

The conflict in Colombia can be traced back more than fifty years, during which time people have suffered, died, and been displaced because of the violence and ongoing conflict in the areas in which they were living. The process of healing is only in its early stages. Nonetheless, there are still many people who do not have a real working knowledge and understanding of the reasons for the conflict or what actually happened during those terrible years. They also tend to have a limited understanding of transitional justice and its underlying purposes and what it means for Colombia in particular. This chapter shows that, the establishment of a museum—dedicated to the twin purposes of memorialising the Colombian conflict and deepening an understanding of the consequent peace processes—could play an important educative role in the transitional justice context and, in so doing, facilitate a deeper process of societal healing for posterity.

When analysing the two examples: the Museo Nacional and the Centre of Memory, Peace and Reconciliation of the District, some of the answers were distant and vastly different. This could be due to differences in the types of visitors (one being a museum that traces the national history of the country from pre-Hispanic times to more recent Colombian history; and the other, an exhibition dedicated to the story of the conflict in the country, but which does not engage with transitional justice and the peace process specifically). Therefore, the expectations in visiting one, rather than the other are, perhaps understandably, different. It seems that a future study dedicated to understanding why responses differ according to context would be worthwhile as this would further studies into specific aspects that were not fully investigated in this study (such as, visitor experiences of an exhibition on the peace process specifically and how best to respond to visitor emotions after visiting a museum on Colombia's conflict).

In general, survey answers indicated that many participants are interested in Colombia's recent violence and the subject of transitional justice specifically. In the CMPR, when participants were asked why they are interested, many answered that they wanted to understand the history of the conflict and what happened to avoid making the same mistakes again.

About the expectations of an exhibition on the conflict and the feelings it would provoke, they expected 'to know' or 'understand' what really happened; they expected objectivity, impartiality, truth; but there were also people who expected to see the dark and more harrowing side of the conflict. It should be noted that it is not possible to present an exhibition about the conflict without showing disturbing images. Regarding feelings that they expected to experience in this regard, these could be divided into the positive and the negative feelings. On the negative side, feelings included sadness, confusion, guilt, discomfort, powerlessness, tiredness, pain, and anger. On the positive side, feelings included happiness as well as feeling inspired, committed, interested, motivated, and optimistic.

After the visit to the CMPR, the feelings that were experienced were mostly negative: sadness, discomfort, confusion, anger, guilt, bad energy, frustration, anguish, hopelessness, and nostalgia. Positive feelings included those of happiness, hopefulness, forgiveness, peace, and general satisfaction of knowing what had happened. When they elaborated on their experiences, some acknowledged there were a lot of things that they did not know, that it was informative and interesting; nonetheless, many, if not most, felt sadness, shock, and nostalgia. In addition, it is also important to note that there were visitors who required someone to help them make sense of their experience through a process of debriefing.

In drawing these themes together, it is clear that this subject awakens diverse feelings and emotions; some are positive, others are negative, some are comfortable, while others are uncomfortable. Nevertheless, it is clear that participants considered the experience of visiting a museum on the past conflict and present peace process to be an important first step in the process of social healing through learning about what happened during the conflict years and about the importance of the transitional justice process to moving the country forward. The majority of participants considered that 'now' would be an appropriate time to start talking about this subject, even if doing so would be a sad or shocking experience for them. This shows that people believe in the importance of memory in transitioning from conflict towards a more peaceful future.

10

Joint Reflection: Journey to a New Space

A Comparative Analysis of Museum Exhibitions Within the Context of Restorative and Transitional Justice

Nancy Rocío Rueda Esteban, Emilia Potenza, and Adriénne van den Heever

1
how do we learn from what we talk
and from what we hear
how do we learn
that when an eye is poked out
what remains is a hole
that this assaulted space
will never be the same again
that the hole that remains is like a womb
it throbs and throbs with memory . . .

2
the eye,
with its hasty footsteps moves and moves
yet when it rests, like a river which heaves with breath
but spreads and spreads in motionlessness
we read what the eye writes
like
eyes can break like a branch loaded with fruit

3
since there is no such thing as choice
like
the eyes see what they see
let the hole throb
scars are moments where we have been
like
one with one foot must move must still move

Shadows In Motion: Bra-Zeke Mphahlele, Mongane Wally Serote[1]
(Courtesy of Mongane Wally Serote)

[1] <https://charterforcompassion.org/south-africa> accessed 3 October 2022.

Nancy Rocío Rueda Esteban, Emilia Potenza, and Adriénne van den Heever, *Joint Reflection: Journey to a New Space*
In: *Transitional Justice, Distributive Justice, and Transformative Constitutionalism.* Edited by: David Bilchitz and Raisa Cachalia, with Magdalena Inés Correa Henao and Nathalia Bautista Pizarro, Oxford University Press. © Nancy Rocío Rueda Esteban, Emilia Potenza, and Adriénne van den Heever 2023. DOI: 10.1093/oso/9780192887627.003.0010

1. Introduction

The recall, understanding, and interpretation of traumatic events and subsequent restorative and transitional justice processes in countries after periods of conflict and violence are not immediate. There is often a long period of reflection and consolidation before these complex processes can be interpreted and presented outside of the judicial context. This comparison reflects on the role of museums in dealing with, and understanding how, museum visitors engage with and experience exhibitions that concern traumatic pasts and associated transitional justice processes. The focus is on two primary aspects: the expectations, and the experience and reaction of a museum visitor who has engaged with specific exhibitions in South Africa and Colombia that focus on historic conflict and the associated transitional justice processes.

Initial research questions posed included: Can a museum exhibition, which focuses on a traumatic history that has been addressed by a subsequent transitional justice process, serve as a proactive tool to educate, and reaffirm what the aims and principles of transitional justice are? Do museum visitors understand the process of transitional justice?

The transitional justice processes that have occurred in Colombia and South Africa span two very different timeframes. In Colombia, it has only been two years since the government signed a peace deal with the Fuerzas Armadas Revolucionarias de Colombia (FARC)[2] and twenty-one years since the Truth and Reconciliation Commission (TRC) proceedings were concluded in South Africa.[3] Could Colombia draw from the experience of South Africa?

The Apartheid Museum which is seen as a beacon of hope that has shown the world how South Africa has and is coming to terms with its oppressive past, and how it is working towards a united future for all its citizens,[4] provided the platform for the Museum's TRC exhibit, the focus. The Museum is well-established and is located within a contextually relevant environment. The context in Colombia is notably different, and an equivalent counterpoint exhibition does not exist. Currently, only small, isolated exhibitions have emerged across the country that reflect on aspects of the conflict, the peace process, and the construction of memory. Despite this, the Museo Nacional de Colombia (MN) and the Centro de Memoria, Paz y Reconciliación (CMPR) recently curated conflict-related exhibitions, provided adequate points for reflection and comparison.

The Museo Nacional de Colombia is intended to provide a meeting place where the citizens of Colombia and the world can come together to celebrate, recognise,

[2] The agreement was signed on 24 November 2016.

[3] The final TRC report was presented to the South African government on 28 October 1998.

[4] Apartheid Museum (nd) The Apartheid Museum's Genesis <https://www.apartheidmuseum.org/about-museum> accessed 3 October 2022.

and reflect upon Colombia's heritage, to converse on the present, and plan for the future.[5] The Centro de Memoria, Paz y Reconciliación's mission is to contribute to the construction of peace through the participation of Bogotá's different population groups. The Centre aims to promote and strengthen memory through various processes that acknowledge the varied experiences people have had during the country's armed conflict while providing and creating spaces for reconciliation and promoting human rights.[6]

In this reflection, a brief literature review has been provided. This review highlights the role that museums play in interpreting traumatic pasts, the importance of constructing memory, and the need to recall and create narratives that reflect on historic conflicts. A comparison of the expectations and experiences of visitors reviewed in the previous chapters is also provided.

2. The Context Explored through a Literature Review

The construction of memories and the creation of narratives concerning past conflicts, wars, or violence are important aspects of the healing and reconciliation process. Anything that offers ways of comprehending, or providing means of connecting with that past[7] are important tools to aid this process. The creation of historical narratives is challenging. It relies on the present context, the past event, and how the relationship between the two is managed. As no two societies, or individuals, remember and recall the past in precisely the same way, the process is delicate and needs to be considered carefully.

Memory is not only useful to understand the past, but it also relates to the present.[8] The present and the past have a direct relation: the events of the past will influence the experience of the present, and the future will influence what, and how, people recall the past.[9] Father Sean O'Leary, an advocate for peace and justice, succinctly explains this: 'You have to link what happened in the past to what is happening in the present. If you sow the seeds of hatred, division, and violence, you reap a harvest of hatred, division, and violence.'[10]

[5] Museo Nacional de Colombia (2018). Quiénes somos – Misión <http://www.museonacional.gov.co/Paginas/default.aspx> accessed 3 October 2022.

[6] Centro de Memoria, Paz y Reconciliación (nd) <http://centromemoria.gov.co/informacion-general/> accessed 3 October 2022.

[7] A Rice, 'A Home for Ourselves in the World: Caryl Phillips on Slave Forts and Manillas as African Atlantic Sites of Memory' (2012) 9 Atlantic Studies 363, 371.

[8] L Weissberg, 'Learning Culture' in D Ben-Amos and L Weissberg (eds), *Cultural Memory and the Construction of Identity* (Wayne State University Press 1999).

[9] ibid.

[10] Foundation for Human Rights, *Making Rights Real: Celebrating 10 years of the Foundation for Human Rights 1996–2006* (Foundation for Human Rights 2006) 17.

3. Speak the Truth in a Million Voices. It is the Silence that Kills (Saint Catherine of Sienna)

With specific reference to contemporary war, historian Natalia Starostina stresses the importance of creating narratives of what happened during periods of conflict and violence.[11] While the conflict experienced in Colombia and oppression exerted by the system of apartheid in South Africa cannot strictly be considered 'warfare', the trauma and indelible scars left are akin to it. Starostina stresses that as victims of wars often feel overwhelmed by their tragedy, talking about their experience is often evaded, and silence becomes a way of remembering.[12] On a personal level, opting for silence can be a way of coping and reconstituting the self.

However, for a society attempting to heal in a post-conflict, post-struggle period, silence is problematic as it contributes to social amnesia. George Santayana's aphorism that those who cannot remember the past are condemned to repeat it, needs to be heeded.[13] Following this idea, historian Theresa Edlmann (2017) argues that by telling personal stories and sharing individual and collective memories, a process of peacebuilding is initiated that enables positive changes in society. Edlmann maintains that when people tell their stories, and when others who might previously have been their enemies hear these stories, there is an acknowledgement of the burden that all sides carry.[14] She argues that the narrative process has the potential to facilitate shifts from previously acrimonious and exclusionary modes of remembering to more collective ways that have lower levels of antagonism and violence.[15]

The narrative process also provides victims with a sense of agency. In periods of conflict and oppression, perpetrators attempt to compel the oppressed to deny their own experiences. South African academic and author, Njabulo Ndebele, argues that the passage of time that brings forth freedom provides legitimacy and authority to those whose voices were previously silenced.[16] He argues that this experience can be one of the essential conditions for the emergence of a new consciousness—the rewriting of history based on validating the mass experience. While Njabulo particularly refers to the South African context, where the voices of the majority were silenced during apartheid, the same is true for Colombia.

[11] Attributed to Saint Catherine of Siena.

[12] N Starostina, *Between Memory and Mythology: The Construction of Memory of Modern Wars* (2014) xli.

[13] G Santayana, 'Introduction and Reason in Common Sense' in G Santayana, *The Life of Reason* (1908) 172 <https://www.iupui.edu/~santedit/sant/wp-content/uploads/2019/01/Common-Sense-ebook.pdf> accessed 3 October 2022.

[14] T Edlmann, 'A Reflection on Narrative Based Historical Memory Work in Peacebuilding Processes' (2017) 15 Intervention 230, 231.

[15] ibid.

[16] N Ndebele, 'Memory, Metaphor and the Triumph of the Narrative' in S Nutall and C Coetzee (eds), *Negotiating the Past: The Making of Memory in South Africa* (OUP 1998).

The museum sector has an important civic and educational role in the recording and interpretation of history. The curated environment provides both a literal and psychological space where the essence of historical events can be recounted and presented in an accessible manner to a wide audience. Museums create and shape knowledge and identity[17] while providing platforms for visitors and communities to exchange and debate ideas.[18]

Julia Rose, the former director of West Baton Rouge Museum in Louisiana, USA maintains that as 'historical events bring out the very worst human qualities, and the very best',[19] museums have an obligation to show different perspectives. Responsible institutions must find sensitive ways to engage with, and encourage visitors to learn about the past and reflect on contemporary society. This allows for a deeper understanding, where emotional and intellectual responses can merge.

Rose argues that while history museums have the potential to reach broad and diverse audiences, the portrayal of violent and oppressive histories are difficult to interpret.[20] Museum interpretations can provide visitors with opportunities to learn about themselves and about the people they want to be, but the same exhibits can be shocking, confusing, and daunting. She proposes a 'Commemorative Museum Pedagogy'. This approach anticipates visitor resistance and so proposes gradually and sensitively engaging with content, even if it is difficult.[21] There are five phases in this pedagogy: reception, resistance, repetition, reflection, and reconsideration. These phases develop in 'unpredictable sequences over varying lengths of time, depending on the individual learner's personal connections and responses to the difficult knowledge'.[22]

An alternative approach is the 'Pedagogy of Remembrance'. Its genesis is associated with the development of post-Second World War German pedagogical thought on the role of museums and memorial sites and how historical didactics connects with socio-civic education. This approach suggests that exhibitions, which explore violent and oppressive histories, should promote active involvement with the past. The goal of this approach is to uphold the memory of victims on the one hand, while forming an attitude and social behaviour that is desirable within a democracy, on the other.[23]

[17] E Hooper-Greenhill, *Museums and Education: Purpose, Pedagogy, Performance* (Routledge 2007).

[18] K Kaitavuori and others, *It's all Mediating: Outlining and Incorporating the Roles of Curating and Education in the Exhibition Context* (Cambridge Scholars Publishing 2013).

[19] J Rose, 'Commemorative Museum Pedagogy' in B Trofanenko and A Segall (eds), *Beyond Pedagogy: Reconsidering the Public Purpose of Museums* (Sense 2014) 115.

[20] ibid 115.

[21] ibid 126.

[22] ibid.

[23] T Kranz, 'The Pedagogy of Remembrance as a Form of Museum Education the Person and the Challenges' (2014) 4(2) Journal of Theology, Education, Canon Law and Social Studies Inspired by Pope John Paul II 4 257–58.

These theoretical contexts provide important points of reflection on the curation of the Apartheid Museum's TRC exhibition and the emergence of transitional justice exhibitions in Colombia.

A. Between Two and Twenty-one: From a Peace Agreement Signature in Colombia to the Handover of South Africa's TRC Report

The differences between Colombia and South Africa's histories are evident; nevertheless, both countries have experienced pasts characterised by trauma. Indelible wounds have been left on the social fabric of both countries. This damage cannot be healed overnight. The healing process, in both Colombia and South Africa, is long and arduous. The objective of the preceding research was not to analyse the conflict, nor was it to critique the transitional justice processes. The focus was to gain an understanding of what museum visitors expect, know, understand, and experience when they are faced with content that explores the restorative and transitional judicial processes which have been instituted to deal with past atrocities.

The process of conducting visitor surveys has provided the means to compare and contrast the two countries. Surveys were designed to provide several areas of overlap: familiarity, expectation, experience, emotional response, understanding, debriefing, and active citizenship.

(i) Familiarity with transitional justice

Participants were asked about their familiarity with the transitional justice process that both countries have, and are experiencing. The term 'transitional justice' is not colloquially used in South Africa, so the question was phrased to establish familiarity with the TRC.

National and international responses have been combined in both countries to determine the results illustrated in Figure 10.1.

Awareness in the Colombian sample was significantly higher. The possible reason for this could be the recent nature of the conflict. Also, the survey sample in Colombia consisted of individuals aged eighteen and over, all of whom had a level of understanding and acknowledgement of the country's recent judicial and political changes.

By comparison, lack of awareness or ignorance of the transitional justice process was notably higher within the South African sample. Possible contributing factors include the high number of born-free[24] respondents, who have no living memory

[24] The generation of South Africans born between 1994 and 2000.

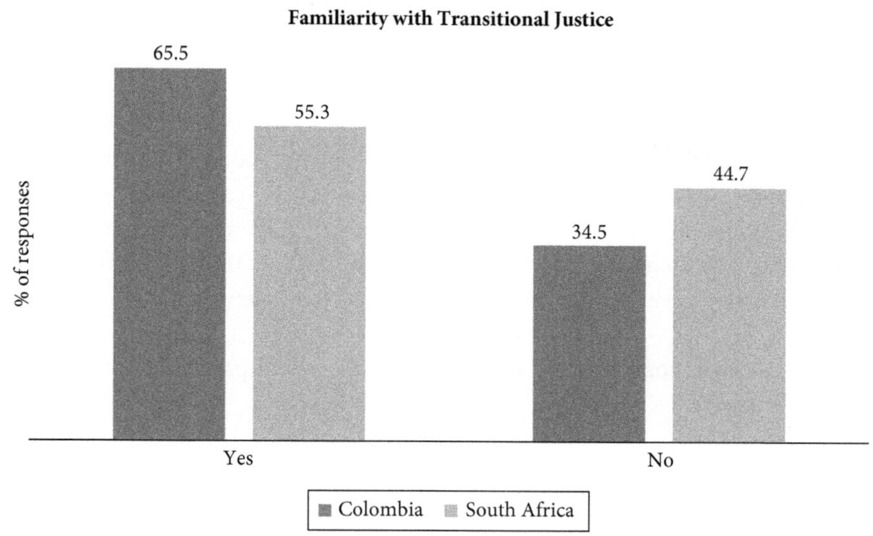

Figure 10.1 Familiarity with transitional justice (Author's own creation based on surveys)

or knowledge of apartheid and the transition to democracy, and international respondents unacquainted with the complexities of South African history.

The concerning number of South African respondents over the age of eighteen, who are still attending school, also points to one of the more significant consequences of apartheid—the legacy of inequality within the education system which remains deep-rooted. In spite of educational reform after 1994, historical disadvantages are still pervasive within South Africa's education system. This reflects the long-term socio-economic impact of apartheid and how it continues to affect the distribution of economic resources in society—that is a legacy that transitional processes and museums too might reflect better both in their pedagogy and content (ie considering the socio-economic impacts of the past and not only the grand narratives of political events).

(ii) Expectations of museum visitors

The commonality of this response talks to our shared humanity, and the responsibility of museum institutions. It also is suggestive of the trust that people place in these institutions. At a Public Lecture on 'Museums, Peace, Democracy and Governance in the 21st Century' held in 1999, the late Emmanuel N Arinze, who at the time was president of the Commonwealth Association of Museums, succinctly expounded this responsibility:

> In our modern society, it has become necessary and indeed urgent for museums to redefine their missions, their goals, their functions and their strategies to reflect the expectations of a changing world. Today, museums must become agents of change and development: they must mirror events in society and become instruments of progress by calling attention to actions and events that will encourage development in the society. They must become institutions that can foster peace, they must be seen as promoting the ideals of democracy and transparency in governance in their communities, and they must become part of the bigger communities that they serve and reach out to every group in the society.[25]

In the Colombian context, two significant expectations of participants were expressed as follows:

- exhibition content that is honest and impartial to allow Colombian society to better understand the political and social factors that caused the conflict and how it evolved over the years;
- first-hand accounts from those who were part of the militia, and those who suffered during the conflict period (to support the notion of honesty).

Outlier responses from the South African sample can be attributed to the physical layout of the Apartheid Museum and the interwoven nature of the TRC with the broader apartheid story. These responses expressed an expectation for the TRC exhibition to be a neat synopsis of the apartheid narrative. This perspective suggests that some respondents have the initial perception that the TRC is the proverbial full stop that concludes the apartheid period.

In both countries, respondents unanimously expected that the respective exhibitions would be impartial and provide insight, truth, and disclosure.

(iii) Emotional responses: feelings, understanding, and debriefing

Survey participants in Colombia were asked to indicate how they expected to feel before, and after, engaging with conflict-related exhibitions. South African responses were collected only after visitors had concluded their visit.

In both contexts, a selection of optional responses was provided. These were: sad, happy, indifferent, angry, inspired, confused, guilty, and other. Participants in Colombia could also select 'uncomfortable'. In both countries, participants could select, or provide more than one option.

The post-visit comparative results showing visitors emotional responses is illustrated in Figure 10.2.

[25] E Arinze, 'The Role of the Museum in Society' (Museums, Peace, Democracy and Governance in the 21st Century, Public Lecture, 17 May 1999).

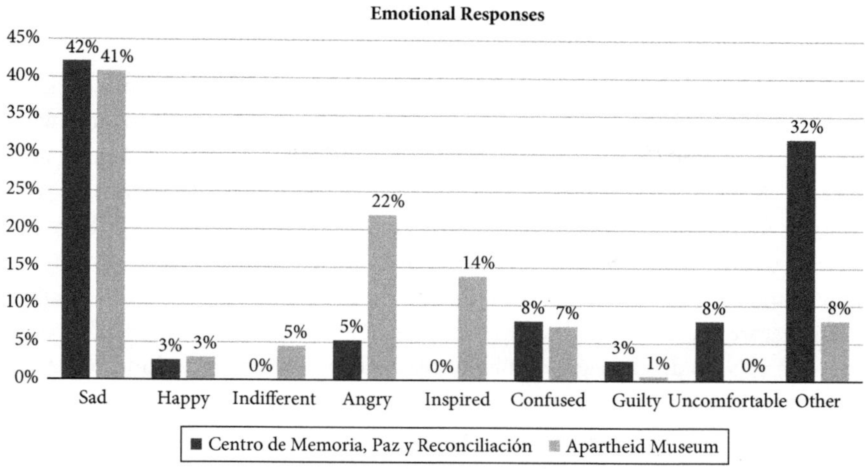

Figure 10.2 Post-visit emotional responses (Author's own creation based on surveys)

The findings align with the pedagogical theory proposed by Rose (2014).[26] Visitors experience a certain amount of resistance before and after engaging with exhibitions that contain traumatic content. They anticipate that the experience will not raise positive feelings.

In Colombia, when comparing what people expected to feel before visiting the respective exhibitions with what they felt afterward, the most common response was sad. This was followed by inspired, angry, uncomfortable, and confused. Other notable feelings expressed by participants included: powerless, suffering, frustration, anguish, depression, disappointment, trauma, and upset.

Positive feelings were also experienced in both contexts, which ultimately is one of the aims of exhibition development—to create awareness and empower audiences to contribute positively to the future. The emotions experienced included such words as: optimistic, motivated, awareness of one's freedom, forgiveness, peace, hopeful, and grateful. In the TRC exhibition, 77 per cent of participants answered that they felt inspired and committed to actively rectifying past injustices and committed themselves to taking personal actions such as increasing awareness, assisting justice programmes, curbing xenophobia, providing employment, and stemming the scourge of racism, inequality, and sexism.

Current and future museum curators and educational programmers need to be attentive to two specific reactions that were recorded—vengeance and indifference. In the Colombian context, indifference was reflected in two survey responses, one by an international visitor to the MN, and the other by a national at the CMPR.

[26] Rose (n 19) 115.

Indifference in the South African context was experienced only by nationals. There is scope to interrogate these types of responses in future research.

The aforementioned emotional responses, coupled with the context of a difficult past, should motivate both current and future museums to provide visitors with emotional support. Consistent with the Commemorative Museum Pedagogy, and the role of museums as places of construction and diffusion of memories, as well as places for education, visitors might need help to understand what they have experienced, or someone to talk to about their thoughts and feelings to assist their understanding of the history learned in the exhibition. The need for debriefing of this nature was also expressed in the surveys where people answered that they needed help with debriefing for different reasons: to provide counselling, to clarify understanding, or to provide additional information.

After their visit, the majority of participants stated that the exhibition helped to explain the conflict in Colombia CMPR (96 per cent) and the role of the TRC in post-apartheid South Africa (76 per cent). However, it should be noted that this may not necessarily be the direct result of the exhibition or their engagement with it.

(iv) Active citizenship

Concerning active citizenship, there is a remarkable synergy between both countries. In Colombia, an average of eight out of ten respondents indicated that they believe it is appropriate and necessary to start an immediate learning process that actively acknowledges the country's difficult past. In South Africa, seven out of ten respondents indicated their commitment to making a positive contribution to the future.

4. Conclusions

For museum curators and researchers, finding ways to explain transitional justice to a wide audience, often unfamiliar with the context, remains a challenge.

The Apartheid Museum can offer positive lessons for museum curators faced with the task of developing conflict-related exhibitions in Colombia. While the circumstances and detail of apartheid and Colombian-conflict are vastly different, the complexity, long duration, and merger of the social, economic, and political in both conflicts are common to both.

Stand-alone exhibitions devoid of the broader context can be challenging for visitor engagement. The physical design and the findings of the research in the Apartheid Museum show that visitors benefit from content that adopts a scaffolded approach.

The multiplicity and diversity of museum visitors presents a challenge for museum curators. Generational differences, inter-generational trauma, nationality, age, language, and prior knowledge of the historical context are elements that have to be considered. This is particularly so when the subject matter entails contested pasts and presents such as those pertaining to transitional justice processes.

This research has also confirmed the importance of relevant and focused education programming for younger museum audiences. Despite this being an established part of the school curriculum, South Africa's post-apartheid generations are often unfamiliar with both the apartheid narrative and the TRC. As a result, the significance and impact of the transitional justice process for a society healing from past injustice is muted.

Furthermore, as this demographic are the custodians of the country's future, the importance of developing their historical consciousness needs to remain high on the collective agenda, both in the formal education sector and within the museum environment. This needs to be coupled with skills that empower active citizenship in order to forge an inclusive future for all.

In Colombia, where the transitional justice process is underway, the research process reveals that, though Colombian society should have an awareness of the transitional justice process, many do not. Furthermore, the complexity of the long-term conflict in the country compounds the challenge. The high percentage of Colombian responses that indicated that 'now is the time' for a conflict-related exhibition to be developed should be considered by the museum sector.

In both countries, debriefing should also be explored further. In Colombia this could be part of how the narrative is developed for future exhibitions, or as a separate, yet integrated service or educational programme offered by the museum or institution.

The role of historical museums goes beyond presenting and explaining significant moments in history; they have an important contribution to make in facilitating an understanding of historical events and processes. Moreover, in societies with difficult pasts, they can promote acceptance of what happened, highlight critical lessons to be learnt, and encourage active participation in building a better future.

PART II

SOCIO-ECONOMIC RIGHTS AND THE RELATIONSHIP BETWEEN TRANSITIONAL AND DISTRIBUTIVE JUSTICE

THEME 4

THE ROLE OF HISTORY IN SOCIO-ECONOMIC RIGHTS JURISPRUDENCE: LINKING TRANSITIONAL AND DISTRIBUTIVE JUSTICE

11

Does History Make a Difference?

The Role of History in the Interpretation of Socio-Economic Rights in South Africa

David Bilchitz

1. Introduction: Historical Injustice and Socio-Economic Rights

Since the Second World War, socio-economic rights have been recognised in international law. These rights were enshrined in the Universal Declaration on Human Rights (UDHR). Article 25, for instance, seeks to protect the right of everyone to 'a standard of living adequate for the health and well-being of himself and his family, including food, clothing, housing and medical care and necessary social services'.[1] The International Covenant on Economic, Social and Cultural Rights (ICESCR) is itself dedicated to the protection of these rights.[2] Such international recognition testifies to the fact that socio-economic rights are seen as universal entitlements all individuals can claim. The ICESCR roots the justification for these entitlements in the 'inherent dignity of the human person'.[3]

This international recognition has increasingly led socio-economic rights to be included in many constitutions, particularly those drafted in the 1990s in Latin America, Africa, and Eastern Europe. These constitutions recognise the universal importance of these rights for those within their territories. Yet, the inclusion of socio-economic rights also occurred against the backdrop of particular histories which were characterised by serious injustices. The wrongs of the past often involved segments of the population being severely deprived of socio-economic rights and their inclusion in modern constitutions was an attempt to provide some form of historical redress.

The historical context in which these rights were included in constitutions raises important issues. First, it provides an independent argument for socio-economic rights as a form of correction for past injustice. Mahomed J famously distinguished

[1] See <http://www.un.org/en/universal-declaration-human-rights/> accessed 3 October 2022.
[2] See <https://www.ohchr.org/en/professionalinterest/pages/cescr.aspx> accessed 3 October 2022.
[3] ibid.

David Bilchitz, *Does History Make a Difference?* In: *Transitional Justice, Distributive Justice, and Transformative Constitutionalism.* Edited by: David Bilchitz and Raisa Cachalia, with Magdalena Inés Correa Henao and Nathalia Bautista Pizarro, Oxford University Press. © David Bilchitz 2023. DOI: 10.1093/oso/9780192887627.003.0011

between constitutions that simply seek to preserve the status quo and constitutions that are transformative, which seek to provide the blueprint for a project of societal reconstruction.[4] Hailbronner argues that many features of the German Constitution and subsequent jurisprudence—such as the strong commitment to human dignity—represent a clear rejection of the past Nazi order and a commitment to reconstruct society on a different basis, namely, respect for individual rights.[5] The constitutions—such as those in South Africa and Colombia—which include socio-economic rights, can be seen to offer a similar commitment: that a central component of the historical injustice that preceded the constitution was the deliberate consignment of individuals or groups to economic hardship and that such a state of affairs must change fundamentally under the new order to correct these wrongs.

A second important dimension to the historical context concerns its relationship to the universal dimension of socio-economic rights.[6] At an international level and, in many constitutions, it is recognised that these entitlements are not able to be realised immediately. The obligation instead is one of 'progressive realisation', which requires states to take measurable steps to effect improvements in the realisation of these rights.[7] An assumption underlying these rights is, therefore, that there is a gap between the ideal enshrined in the constitution and the existing reality which needs to be bridged. I have in past work argued that this bridging dimension is central to fundamental rights more generally.[8] Yet, if this divide is to be breached, in situations of past historical injustice, it requires us to engage with additional dimensions. There is a need to understand properly and address the relationship between the causes of the injustice and the actual socio-economic deprivation. That may involve also engaging with underlying status inequalities in the society.[9] The failure fundamentally to engage with the historical conditions of deprivation may well jeopardise long-term success in achieving socio-economic rights.

[4] See *S v Makwanyane* [1995] ZACC 3; 1995 (3) SA 391 (CC) [261] and, defining transformative constitutionalism, see also K Klare, 'Legal Culture and Transformative Constitutionalism' (1998) 14 South African Journal on Human Rights 146, 150.

[5] M Hailbronner, 'Transformative Constitutionalism: Not Only in the Global South' (2017) 65 American Journal of Comparative Law 527, 541–46.

[6] C Mbazira, *Litigation Socio-Economic Rights in South Africa: A Choice Between Corrective and Distributive Justice* (Pretoria University Law Press 2009) 103–04 also draws attention both to the corrective and distributive dimensions of socio-economic rights, arguing the Constitution and courts prefer a distributive justice lens.

[7] Committee on Economic, Social and Cultural Rights 'General Comment 3: The Nature of State Parties' Obligations' (E/1991/23, 14 December 1990) para 9.

[8] D Bilchitz, 'Fundamental Rights as Bridging Concepts: Straddling the Boundary Between Ideal Justice and an Imperfect Reality' (2017) 40 Human Rights Quarterly 119.

[9] S Liebenberg and B Goldblatt, 'The Interrelationship between Equality and Socio-Economic Rights under South Africa's Transformative Constitution' (2007) 23 South African Journal on Human Rights 335, 338–41.

Thus, the context of historical justice is of importance not only in providing an independent justification for socio-economic rights but also the necessary detail as to how the content of these rights is to be constructed and the path to implementation developed. It is these broad issues that I consider and explore in this chapter. The focus of the discussion will be on South Africa, whose Constitution has set itself clearly the task of addressing a legacy of historical injustice brought about by colonialism and the system of apartheid.[10] The focus will be on attempting to ascertain the manner in which this context of historical injustice has affected the approach courts have adopted to giving effect to socio-economic rights.

In the second section of this chapter, I focus on providing a background for the rest of the piece and begin with a very brief, high-level account of historical injustice in South Africa and its connections with economic deprivation, particularly, of Black people. I then consider, briefly again, the specific historical context that provides the background to the recognition of the right to housing in the South African Constitution that will be the focus of this chapter. The choice is motivated by its being a key socio-economic right which has attracted several important judicial decisions. The right also implicates complex questions of both access to land and the provision of resources, issues that have been tied up with historical injustices in South Africa. That does not mean it is more fundamental in any way than the other socio-economic rights but the need to focus is justified by the desire to achieve greater depth and specificity in the analysis than simply providing a cursory overview of the jurisprudence on multiple rights. The focus does of course limit the generality of the findings in this chapter, although I contend that similar trends are evident in the jurisprudence on other rights.[11]

The third section and heart of this chapter will focus on the jurisprudence of the South African Constitutional Court in relation to the right to housing. In analysing the jurisprudence, I engage in detail with a few seminal judgments: the focus is thus on a qualitative analysis rather than seeking wide-ranging coverage of all the cases that address this right. In doing so, I consider four key issues. First, do judges expressly recognise the historical context in which the interpretation of the right takes place? ('mention'); secondly, does the historical context clearly play a role in determining the content attributed to the rights in the Constitution? ('interpretation'); thirdly, does the historical context clearly affect the processes that the Court thinks are necessary to address a socio-economic deprivation? ('process');

[10] This is what Sandra Liebenberg refers to as the 'backward-looking aspect' of the South African Constitution in S Liebenberg, *Socio-Economic Rights: Adjudication under a Transformative Constitution* (Juta 2010) 25.

[11] For instance, many of the themes such as the refuge into proceduralism are evident in some of the early jurisprudence on the right to education in such cases as *Head of Department: Mpumalanga Department of Education v Hoërskool Ermelo* [2009] ZACC 32; 2010 (2) SA 415 (CC) and *MEC for Education in Gauteng Province v Governing Body of Rivonia Primary School* [2013] ZACC 34; 2013 (6) SA 582 (CC).

and finally, does the historical context expressly influence the order or judicial outcome? ('remedy').

The chapter concludes with a summary of the findings that emerge from this analysis concerning the impact of historical context on the jurisprudence of the Constitutional Court in relation to the right to housing. In so doing, it charts, in a specific area and jurisdiction, the important connection that exists between transitional justice and achieving a measure of distributive justice through the realisation of socio-economic rights.[12]

2. The Historical Context: Socio-Economic Rights as Transformative

A. Economic Deprivation and South African History: A Brief Background

As long as human society has existed, there has been competition over resources.[13] Yet, the current situation in South Africa of vast inequality between the wealthy and the poor—with most of the poor being Black people—can be traced back to deliberate policies of the governing authorities over time. Whilst there was conflict as European settlers moved into the interior of South Africa, it was the discovery of diamonds in 1867 and gold in 1884, that fundamentally changed the economic landscape. These developments led to a huge demand for labour: to ensure such supply, colonial administrations imposed coercive measures, such as a hut and poll tax on Africans. To pay these, many Black men were forced to leave their homes and enter the mines.[14] African men were transformed from being self-sufficient to living in meagre, prison-like conditions around the mines.[15]

These dynamics were only intensified by the policy of apartheid implemented after 1948 that sought to maintain Black people as an economic under-class and a source of cheap labour for the advancement of White capitalist economic

[12] On this connection, see I Muvingi, 'Sitting on Powder Kegs: Socioeconomic Rights in Transitional Societies' (2009) 3 International Journal of Transitional Justice 163–82; A Cahill-Ripley, 'Foregrounding Socio-Economic Rights in Transitional Justice: Realising Justice for Violations of Economic and Social Rights' (2014) 32 Netherlands Quarterly on Human Rights 181–213; and E Schmid and A Nolan, '"Do No Harm"? Exploring the Scope of Economic and Social Rights in Transitional Justice' (2014) 8 International Journal of Transitional Justice 362–82.

[13] This historical section draws on segments of my chapter 'The Performance of Socio-Economic Rights in the South African Constitution' in T Roux and R Dixon (eds), *Constitutional Triumphs, Constitutional Disappointments* (CUP 2017) 45–87.

[14] See M Nkosi, *Mining Deep: The Origins of the Labour Structure in South Africa* (David Philip 2011) 79–80.

[15] J Davenport, *Digging Deep: A History of Mining in South Africa* 1852– 2002 (Jonathan Ball 2013) 114–15.

interests.[16] One of the main architects of apartheid, Hendrik Verwoerd, had expressly indicated the racist view that Black people did not need further education as their destiny was to be physical labourers.[17] The apartheid government deliberately instituted a policy of providing inferior education to Black people (known as Bantu education), prevented most Black people from going to university, and confined Black people who were not needed for cheap manual labour to areas that were economically under-developed through a permit system that prevented free movement across South Africa. The effects of these policies (and others) was to create a situation where the vast majority of Black people had a limited education and were living in conditions of poverty. Since the focus of this chapter is on the right to housing, I now turn to a brief history for understanding the current context.

B. A Brief History of the Right to Have Access to Adequate Housing

As people moved from rural areas to urban areas (or surrounding mines), clearly issues of housing became a major challenge.[18] The apartheid government developed a pass system whereby it controlled the movement of Black people into urban areas, known as influx control. Since Black people were only meant to be there in limited numbers, no planning or provision was made to house them. Thus, in the Cape Peninsula area (including the city of Cape Town) from 1962, there was a freeze placed on the provision of family housing for African people.[19] Despite this, African people continued to move to urban areas due to colonial dispossession and a rigidly enforced racial distribution of land which had disrupted the rural economy and rendered African farming precarious.[20] This led to the growth of informal settlements around urban areas in South Africa.

As the Constitutional Court details in the *Grootboom* case, the 'cycle of the apartheid era, therefore, was one of untenable restrictions on the movement of African people into urban areas, the inexorable tide of the rural poor to the cities, inadequate housing, resultant overcrowding, mushrooming squatter settlements, constant harassment by officials and intermittent forced removals'.[21] This led to

[16] See H Wolpe, 'Capitalism and Cheap Labour-Power in South Africa: From Segregation to Apartheid' (1972) 1 Economy and Society 425 ff.

[17] See D Harrison, *The White Tribe of Africa: South Africa in Perspective* (Macmillan South Africa 1981) 190–97 for a discussion of these views, its impact on policy, and long-term effects. During a debate in Senate about the Bantu Education Act of 1953, Verwoerd made these racist remarks.

[18] For a collection on urbanisation and housing history, see D Smith (ed), *The Apartheid City and Beyond: Urbanisation and Social Change in South Africa* (Witwatersrand University Press 1992).

[19] This history is recounted in *Government of the Republic of South Africa v Grootboom* [2000] ZACC 19; 2001 (1) SA 46 (CC) ('*Grootboom*') [6]. For purposes of this brief historical account, I draw on the background provided by the judges.

[20] ibid.

[21] ibid.

two key violations of rights: first, there was the ability to evict individuals rather easily through legislation such as the Prevention of Illegal Squatting Act 52 of 1951 (PISA). If occupation of property was found to be unlawful, individuals could be evicted and they were subject to criminal prosecution. Secondly, there was a failure to plan and provide housing for Black people which led to a massive housing shortage. There was, for instance, a shortage of more than 100,000 housing units in the Cape Metropolitan area upon the advent of democracy in 1994.[22]

It is in this light that section 26 of the Constitution needs to be seen. It provides that:

> (1) Everyone has the right to have access to adequate housing.
> (2) The state must take reasonable legislative and other measures, within its available resources, to achieve the progressive realisation of this right.
> (3) No one may be evicted from their home, or have their home demolished, without an order of court made after considering all the relevant circumstances. No legislation may permit arbitrary evictions.

The right to housing is aimed both at correcting the historical injustices of the past whilst recognising a universal entitlement for all. It creates negative obligations not to interfere with an individual's housing and only to do so in a manner where the court has considered all relevant considerations and is 'non-arbitrary'. It also, in the first two sub-sections, envisages a range of positive obligations on the state actively to expand access to housing. These obligations are qualified by the notions that the government has a duty to adopt 'reasonable' measures, that it must do so only within its 'available resources', and that the right is to be achieved through a process of 'progressive realisation'. The manner in which past injustices intertwines with the Constitutional Court's interpretation of these rights will now be analysed.

3. Historical Injustice and the Interpretation of Socio-Economic Rights in the South African Constitution

In considering the interaction between history and constitutional interpretation, as mentioned, I will engage with a number of key judgments and examine the following issues outlined in the introduction of this chapter: a) mention; b) interpretation; c) process; and d) remedy. This chapter's length constraints prevent it from being exhaustive in relation to all the jurisprudence of the Constitutional Court, even in relation to the right that is being considered. Instead, it adopts a qualitative approach: it engages in some detail with certain key judgments in which the Court

[22] ibid.

considers the relationship between historical injustice and socio-economic rights. The goal is ultimately to try and ascertain what difference a consideration of history makes to the jurisprudence of the Constitutional Court in this area.

A. The Right to Housing: Negative Obligations

I first consider two cases that address the situation where individuals illegally occupy the land of other persons. Such illegal occupation often results from the desperation of people having nowhere to live that is their own. The issue here concerns both the intersection of the right to property with the right to housing and, in particular, negative obligations not to harm people in their existing possession of housing.

(i) PE Municipality

This is one of the ground-breaking judgments issued by the Constitutional Court on housing.[23] The judgment dealt with a proposed eviction of sixty-eight people (amongst whom were twenty-three children) who had occupied privately-owned land within the jurisdiction of this municipality. The people had been occupying this land for between two and eight years. The land was undeveloped but had been occupied without the consent of the municipality. A number of residents of the area where the land was situated had signed a petition to have these people evicted. The Constitutional Court had to decide on whether to allow the eviction to proceed. In doing so, it used the opportunity to outline a new framework of principles to govern evictions.

Notable is the deep engagement with historical context that occurs in this judgment. The Constitutional Court begins by referencing the history of legislation relating to evictions—PISA both allowed for the eviction of unlawful occupiers as well as for their conviction on criminal charges.[24] The Court acknowledged how this legislation entrenched racial segregation whereby Black people were compelled to live in particular areas—largely rural—and dispossessed them of much of their land.[25] Black people were only regarded as temporary workers in urban areas and as a result, they lived in overcrowded, poor areas whereas White people lived in relatively well-off suburbs.

The Court recognised this historical context as the background to the inclusion of section 26(3) in the Constitution, which specifically attempts to address evictions. To give effect to this section, the Prevention of Illegal Eviction from and

[23] *Port Elizabeth Municipality v Various Occupiers* [2004] ZACC 7; 2005 (1) SA 217 (CC) ('*PE Municipality*').

[24] ibid [8]. See also Section 2B of this chapter.

[25] ibid [9].

Unlawful Occupation of Land Act of 1998 (PIE) was passed. The Court expressly states that '[i]ts provisions have to be interpreted against this background'.[26] The Court describes how PIE essentially sought to address the legacy of PISA: it decriminalised illegal occupation, sought to provide procedural and substantive protections to individuals facing eviction, and to treat individuals in such circumstances with respect.[27]

The goal was thus to introduce humanity into the process through a constitutional matrix that the Court outlined. It recognised that property rights had to be understood in light of the need for 'the orderly opening-up or restoration of secure property rights for those denied access to or deprived of them in the past'.[28] The property right in section 25 had also to be understood in light of the grossly unequal distribution of land in South Africa.[29] Moreover, section 26(3) sought to address the circumstances in which eviction could take place, and specifically required judicial control over any evictions process. The question posed by the Court was how judicial officers were to make decisions in that regard.

Justice Sachs, writing for a unanimous court, held that, in light of this history, title would no longer take precedence over every other competing interest. Instead, there is a need for judges 'to balance out and reconcile opposed claims in as just a manner as possible taking account of all the interests involved and the specific factors relevant in each particular case'.[30] The historical context required taking account of another set of crucial interests, namely, those of the occupiers who have no land and home. The courts had to balance all competing interests and attempt to do justice in the concrete circumstances of each case.

The Court then outlines a multi-factoral test flowing from PIE that attempts to structure this process of balancing to determine when eviction orders should be granted. These factors include: whether the occupation was a result of an emergency or the desire to acquire housing quicker than others similarly situated; the period of occupation on the land; and the availability of suitable alternative accommodation. Interestingly, in expanding on the criteria relating to the circumstances of the occupation, the Court states that it would have less sympathy for those who 'deliberately invade land with a view to disrupting the organised housing programme and placing themselves at the front of the queue'.[31] Here we see the Court demonstrating a concern that the South African transition in relation to property rights must occur in an orderly manner and not through anarchy.

The Court also emphasises that the difficulty of balancing competing interests and mitigating historical injustices requires innovative solutions. One possibility

[26] ibid [11].
[27] ibid [12].
[28] ibid [15].
[29] ibid [16].
[30] ibid [23].
[31] ibid [26].

is to require the parties themselves to engage and reach solutions: 'Wherever possible, respectful face-to-face engagement or mediation through a third party should replace arms-length combat by intransigent opponents'.[32] The Court thus requires that landowners should see the individuals occupying their land as bearers of rights and occupiers should also see themselves as moral agents. Mediation can, in a sense, transform the relations between the parties and provide solutions that adversarial judicial processes cannot. The Court also refers to the way in which mediation can help heal past relations: where communities were divided and hostile, it can encourage 'respectful good neighbourliness for the future'.[33] This doctrine of mediation—known as 'meaningful engagement'—was developed into an official requirement for evictions in the *Olivia Road* case.[34] In the latter case, the Court also indicated that it would ensure that any agreement that results from mediation be consistent with the constitutional requirement of reasonableness.[35]

In deciding what to do in the concrete case of *PE Municipality*, the Court saw the plight of the occupiers as giving expression to the 'hard realities of urbanisation and homelessness in South Africa'.[36] It stated that the obligation of the municipality was to understand the complex socio-economic problem that led to unlawful occupation in the country.[37] Given the relatively long time that people had been occupying the land, the fact that they were not 'queue-jumpers', the lack of the need for the land by others, and the failure to investigate proper alternatives or to engage with the people, the Court decided to refuse to grant an eviction order.

The approach of the Court in *PE Municipality* is thus infused with an understanding of the historical context in which unlawful occupation exists in South Africa. This context in turn affects the way in which the Court interprets the rights at issue. It sees this interpretation as requiring an individualised, context-sensitive approach that balances out various considerations. The approach also helps shift the prior legal position to recognise that title is not determinative and the interests of those who are landless must be considered seriously. The history too affects the process by which the Court believes these matters should be addressed: it sees mediation as offering numerous benefits and helping to heal the divisions of the past. Where evictions are needed, a court-supervised process is also required. The Court is also concerned to maintain social peace and prevent large-scale land invasions which would harm the rule of law. Finally, the historical backdrop leading to the plight of the unlawful occupiers plays a role in the final order given by the Court as well.

[32] ibid [39].
[33] ibid [43].
[34] *Occupiers of 51 Olivia Road, Berea Township and 197 Main Street Johannesburg v City of Johannesburg* [2008] ZACC 1; 2008 (3) SA 208 (CC).
[35] ibid [18], and [28]–[30].
[36] *PE Municipality* (n 23) [49].
[37] ibid [56].

A historically informed approach to constitutional adjudication thus has a number of important consequences here: it requires that people not be made worse off; it requires a change in the way in which individuals are considered and addressed; it attempts to shift the power relations between individuals and the state; it guides the judicial function; and, finally, it entails the development of particular consensual-driven processes.

(ii) Blue Moonlight

This case[38] concerned the rights of eighty-six individuals who were in unlawful occupation of an old and run-down commercial property in the Johannesburg inner city. The private company that owned the property intended to re-develop it and thus sought to evict the individuals who resided there. The case concerned both the obligations of the private owner and whether the Johannesburg municipality—in the eventuality that an eviction was allowed—had an obligation to provide temporary accommodation to the occupiers.

In framing the case, the Court references the fact that '[s]eventeen years into our democracy, a dignified existence for all in South Africa has not yet been achieved. The quest for a roof over one's head often lies at the heart of our constitutional, legal, political and economic discourse on how to bring about social justice within a stable constitutional democracy.'[39] It thus recognises that part of the goal of South African democracy is to move beyond a past where people lacked adequate housing and to achieve a 'dignified existence' for all individuals.

The Court goes on, in its reasoning, to reference the need to consider the 'social and historical context of property and related rights'.[40] That context gives rise to a need to balance complex competing interests. The right to property itself, according to the Court, involves a balance between existing property rights and the public interest.[41] The apartheid system, the Court recognises, led property to be taken arbitrarily from Black people and helped create terribly unequal social conditions.[42] The right to housing serves to counter-balance the property right but also 'highlights the transformative vision of the Constitution'.[43] The Court recognises that the PIE Act seeks to address this past whilst protecting property and references the relevant factors identified in *PE Municipality* for deciding upon evictions.

Its recognition of the historical context, however, leads to an important development beyond the *PE Municipality* case. The Court claims that, where private

[38] *City of Johannesburg Metropolitan Municipality v Blue Moonlight Properties 39 (Pty) Ltd* [2011] ZACC 33; 2012 (2) SA 104 (CC) ('*Blue Moonlight*').

[39] ibid [2].

[40] ibid [34].

[41] In ibid, it quotes the seminal judgment in *First National Bank of South Africa Limited t/a Wesbank v Commissioner for the South African Revenue Services; First National Bank of South Africa Limited t/a Wesbank v Minister of Finance* [2002] ZACC 5; 2002 (4) SA 768 (CC).

[42] *Blue Moonlight* (n 38) [35].

[43] ibid.

landowners know about the presence of occupiers for a long period, they can reasonably be expected to allow these people to remain on their property for a temporary period of time. The Court does not require private landowners to provide land for the homeless indefinitely but states that 'in certain circumstances an owner may have to be somewhat patient, and accept that the right to occupation may be temporarily restricted ... [a]n owner's right to use and enjoy property at common law can be limited in the process of the justice and equity enquiry mandated by PIE'.[44]

In this paragraph, the Court highlights a number of important issues. The confiscation of land from Black people and the apartheid system has created a situation in which the legitimacy of existing property rights and distributions cannot simply be assumed. The Court does not assert a right of people simply to occupy land—with the possible anarchic consequences this would cause and, once again, it expressly rejects 'queue-jumping'.[45] At the same time, the Court recognises that people who have already been living in a place for a significant amount of time cannot simply be evicted, even by private landowners. Since the past privileged certain groups of landowners, it is just to place certain burdens of corrective justice upon them. Common law individual rights may thus have to be restricted in advancing a fairer distribution of land and landowners have a limited positive obligation to allow existing unlawful occupations to continue. The past thus has a direct effect on how we view existing property relations and the consequent obligations that emerge.

Given the holding of the Court that a private owner did not have to provide housing indefinitely, the question then became under what circumstances an eviction order could be granted. The second part of this balanced framework was the Court's finding that an eviction order would be just and equitable if it were linked to the provision of temporary accommodation. Such an obligation, the Court held, fell upon the local municipality. The Court then ordered that an eviction could only take place four months after the judgment within which period the city had to offer the people temporary accommodation.

Blue Moonlight follows on from *PE Municipality* and, once again, highlights the role of historical injustice in the reasoning of the Court. Interestingly, it does not absolutely prevent an eviction but, once again, provides support for principles that attempt to balance the interests of competing parties. The historical situation also affects the substantive legal position, weakening common law rights and justifying a positive obligation on private parties. Whilst the Court refuses to turn away from how historical injustice has advantaged certain private individuals over others, it recognises, ultimately, that the public sphere is responsible for long-term provisioning to correct past injustice: the city's obligations are constructed in this light.

[44] ibid [40].
[45] Ibid [93]–[94].

We can thus see the influence of historical reasoning on the concrete rights jurisprudence of the Court in these two seminal cases. Its main influence is to encourage balancing; to reject self-help non-legal approaches to addressing past injustice; to impose stronger obligations in certain instances; to adopt procedural solutions that encourage compromise and long-term alleviations of hurt and hardship; and to generate remedial solutions that avoid consigning people to the continued desperation of homelessness.

B. The Provision of Housing: Positive Obligations

We have thus far considered the use of historical arguments in protecting an individual's existing access to housing and the negative obligation to avoid rendering them worse off and, potentially, homeless. Does an awareness of history also affect the Court's approach in cases concerning positive obligations: in other words, the duty actively to advance and fulfil fundamental rights? I turn now to consider two judgments: the first relates to the state's positive obligations and the second relates to those of private parties.

(i) Grootboom

This famous case concerned a group of people who landed up on a sports-field with only plastic sheeting to cover them in the driving rain of the Western Cape.[46] They had nowhere else to go and, through a lawyer, claimed that the state had a duty to provide them with adequate housing in accordance with section 26 of the Constitution. The case called for an interpretation of this right and the development of an approach to positive obligations in relation to housing.

The Court, interestingly, frames the case in a forward-looking manner, focusing on the aspirations of the new constitutional order to improve the quality of life of all and attaining social justice. The Court does not initially focus on the past but rather identifies the present 'intolerable conditions under which many of our people are still living'.[47] The Court appears concerned about the possibility that the plight of individuals may affect the constitutional order as it could lead people to take the law into their own hands.[48] A continuing concern for a law-based, orderly approach is also expressed at the end of the judgment where it is stated that 'land invasion is inimical to the systematic provision of adequate housing on a planned basis'.[49]

46 *Grootboom* (n 19).
47 ibid [2].
48 ibid.
49 ibid [92].

After looking forward and describing present conditions, the Court recognises that the current housing crisis emerges from the past apartheid system which determined that Black people were not meant to come into the Western Cape. No adequate provision of housing was made for them since 1962, despite the fact that thousands of Black people moved into these urban areas in search of jobs. That urbanisation took place also against a backdrop of rural inequities with 'colonial dispossession and a rigidly enforced racial distribution of land'.[50] These factors led to the growth of informal settlements and the current housing shortage which the Court quantified as being around 100,000 units in 1994.[51]

Apart from this general contextual background to the case, in interpreting the socio-economic rights in the Constitution, the Court also moves between past, present, and future. Granting socio-economic rights, it holds, is 'key to the advancement of race and gender equality and the evolution of a society in which men and women are equally able to achieve their full potential'.[52] Such future-orientated statements are supplemented by a recognition that these rights must be interpreted in their social and historical context.[53]

It can be strongly argued that history does affect the ultimate 'reasonableness' approach the Court adopts towards socio-economic rights. In rejecting the 'minimum core approach' developed by the UN Committee on Economic, Social and Cultural Rights, the Court expresses the worry that determining such a threshold may lead to rigidity where there is a need for flexibility, particularly where there are large variations in people's circumstances arising from 'the economic and social history and circumstances of a country'.[54] Instead of determining a relatively fixed standard of provision, the Court adopted an approach that requires the government to adopt a programme that meets the standard of 'reasonableness'. The Court states that '[i]n determining whether a set of measures is reasonable, it will be necessary to consider housing problems in their social, economic and historical context and to consider the capacity of institutions responsible for implementing the programme. The programme must be balanced and flexible and make appropriate provision for attention to housing crises and to short, medium and long term needs.'[55] It could thus be strongly argued that one of the motivating factors for the Court to adopt its rather vague and expansive standard of reasonableness was its flexibility and adaptability for addressing varied sets of historical circumstances.

Having outlined this test, the Court evaluated the government's programme and found that it fell short of the reasonableness standard in failing to make provision for those currently in desperate need. The Court, in its summary of this

50 ibid [6].
51 ibid.
52 ibid [23].
53 ibid [25].
54 ibid [32].
55 ibid [43].

case, recognised that 'it is an extremely difficult task for the state to meet these obligations in the conditions that prevail in the country. This is recognised by the Constitution which expressly provides that the state is not obliged to go beyond available resources or to realise the rights immediately.'[56] Existing conditions thus shift the obligations to the government. They do not require the government to meet individuals' needs on 'demand' nor can individuals take the law into their own hands and simply move onto properties when they wish.[57] Instead, the government must adopt a well-designed programme that achieves adequate housing for individuals in a reasonable manner.

We can thus discern three important features in which historical reasoning influences the Court in this judgment. First, in relation to content, it encourages the Court to adopt an approach which is more flexible and ambiguous over one that is rigid and detailed. Secondly, the Court also rejects an approach which allows individuals to claim any specific resources. Instead, it adopts a 'programmatic approach' which requires the government to adopt a *programme* that is reasonable. This obligates the government to develop a systematic plan to ensure the realisation of these rights over time. Linked to this programmatic dimension, thirdly, is the importance for the Court of planning and its disapproval of disorderly ways of addressing past injustice. As part of a commitment to transformative constitutionalism, socio-economic rights require law-governed change[58] and, as such, are inimical, the Court holds, to individuals taking the law into their own hands.

(ii) Daniels

This case[59] emerges from the history of South Africa where Black people were systematically dispossessed of their land and forced to live on the farms of White people with minimal security of tenure. With the advent of constitutional democracy, South Africa passed various laws—including the Extension of Security of Tenure Act 62 of 1997 (ESTA)—which sought to enhance these people's security of tenure. Ms Daniels was a domestic worker who inhabited a dwelling on the land of a farmer. She wished to make improvements to her property which were necessary—according to both parties—to render it habitable. Yet, the landowner refused to allow her to do so. The case concerned the question whether ESTA—viewed through a constitutional prism—entitled her to make these changes. Whilst the case is framed in terms of tenure security (and thus the property right in the South African Constitution), it also fundamentally concerns housing and, consequently, is considered here.

[56] ibid [94].
[57] ibid [92].
[58] Klare (n 4) 150 sees this as one of the defining features of transformative constitutionalism.
[59] *Daniels v Scribante* [2017] ZACC 13; 2017 (4) SA 371 (CC) ('*Daniels*').

The historical context is strongly present in the reasoning of the majority and two other concurring judgments. The majority situates the case in light of the past history which 'succeeded in pushing Africans off their land and into white farms, mines and other industries'.[60] The Court recognised that, 'in some instances this is not just history':[61] there is a strong continuity between the past—of forcing Black people onto the land of White people as labourers—and existing tenure insecurity with occupiers under ESTA being 'a vulnerable group susceptible to untold mistreatment'.[62] This history provided the backdrop for understanding the purpose of section 25(6) of the Constitution and ESTA, which gives effect to it: namely, to afford 'occupiers the dignity that eluded most of them throughout the colonial and apartheid regimes'.[63] History, here, clearly influences interpretation since the majority construes the legislation to involve a right to 'reside' on property in ways which conduce to human dignity. This means that the conditions for inhabiting such a property must be tolerable and, if improvements are necessary to ensure decent conditions, then these may be effected.

However, the Court goes even further after considering a provision in ESTA that a landowner may, upon eviction of an occupier, have to pay for the improvements made by that occupier.[64] The argument by the landowner was that this provision would amount indirectly to imposing a positive obligation upon the owners of property to provide habitable housing to the occupiers.[65] Past holdings of the Court, he argued, precluded imposing positive obligations to ensure the fulfilment of constitutional rights on private parties.

The majority of the Court developed its prior jurisprudence, finding that the Constitution could, in appropriate circumstances, allow for the imposition of positive obligations on a private actor for the fulfilment of a constitutional right. Whether such an obligation exists, it held, will depend on a number of factors. These include: the nature of the right, the history behind the right, what the right seeks to achieve, the best manner in which it can be achieved, the potential invasion by private parties, and whether letting off private persons would negate the essential content of the right.[66] The majority judgment specifically includes a historical dimension in determining the existence and nature of these obligations.

In this case, the Court finds that the right to tenure security clearly imposes direct obligations on landowners in the context where vulnerable occupiers like

60 ibid [2] and [17].
61 ibid [22].
62 ibid.
63 ibid [23].
64 ESTA, s 23.
65 This was phrased in terms of section 25(6) of the Constitution which provides a right to secure legal tenure and/or comparable redress.
66 *Daniels* (n 59) [39].

Ms Daniels live on their land. These include, in particular, the obligation upon landowners to allow occupiers to make improvements to their dwellings even if this would mean compensation should eventually be paid to those occupiers.

Despite these far-reaching holdings, the Court nevertheless recognised that the rights of the landowner to property remained of importance and there was, therefore, a need to strike a balance between the various rights at stake. That could be achieved by recognising that the occupiers could not simply disregard the owner completely and, themselves, have obligations to engage meaningfully with the landowner concerning the improvements. Doing so, could itself lead to a resolution of any dispute. If it does not, the courts could be approached to address any conflict. In this way, the Court utilises a procedural solution to balance the rights between the conflicting parties. Individuals are encouraged to address conflicts between them by themselves and only where that fails to approach the courts. The Court though re-affirms the principle that '[t]he occupier cannot resort to self-help'.[67]

This majority judgment demonstrates clearly how an engagement with history can fundamentally affect the interpretation of a right and its content—in this case, enabling occupiers to make improvements to their dwellings pursuant to their rights to tenure security and dignity. Past injustice also transforms the obligations of private actors: landowners can no longer simply claim their existing property rights allow them to do as they wish. Instead, they must be mindful of the dependency that other individuals have upon them and, in conformity with constitutional values, enable those who live on their premises to live with dignity. The Court, once again, develops a broad multi-factoral test to determine when it is legitimate to impose such obligations and their extent. Again, one important consideration relates to the history of the occupation which might give rise to such obligations.

Two of the minority judgments also expressly engage with history and its implications for the Court's jurisprudence in this area. Cameron J issues an important note of caution on the use of history by judges.[68] He notes that judges are not historians and should be cautious in their historical pronouncements.[69] Yet, at the same time, he acknowledges the need for judges to draw on history in addressing present injustices.[70]

Froneman J writes a moving judgment in which he considers the implications of the history of land dispossession and tenure insecurity for some of the wider

[67] ibid [65].

[68] See also the caution expressed by De Vos in P De Vos, 'A Bridge Too Far—History as Context in the Interpretation of the South African Constitution' (2001) 17 South African Journal on Human Rights 1 about using a fixed 'grand narrative' approach to history that cannot capture fully the complexity of the past and its impact on constitutional interpretation.

[69] *Daniels* (n 59) [149].

[70] ibid [154].

issues flowing from Ms Daniels' case. One of the key aspects he notes is the importance of acknowledging the injustices of the past and the denial of dignity to Black people.[71] He writes of the history which led to a focus on addressing the problems of 'poor Whites' while expressly consigning Black people to inferior and inhuman conditions of living. He claims that today people often avoid engaging with the historical injustices that took place and that amnesia, wilful or otherwise, leads to a situation where they can deny someone like Ms Daniels the ability to make basic improvements to her dwelling. The judge writes '[t]here is no reason to continue countenancing the continuation of inhuman and undignified living on farms any more. It cannot be tolerated in light of the constitutional mandate to heal the divisions of the past.'[72] The judge utilises this understanding of history to support the notion that property rights as recognised in South Africa cannot be absolute.

Moreover, such protection cannot be justified in the name of 'efficiency' alone. The judge states that 'it does not follow that, where people were actively excluded from even some initial distribution, the basic assumptions for economic efficiency have been met'.[73] Thus Froneman J links past and present: a recognition of historical injustice shifts the nature of the protection that property rights offer and requires constructing them in light of the imperative to ensure every individual can live in conditions of dignity.

The *Daniels* judgment is truly fascinating and represents a deep engagement by the Constitutional Court with the South African historical context and its implications for socio-economic distributions. Clearly, Froneman's argument is relatively radical and could require a wholesale rethinking of existing distributions. The majority judgment is more narrowly focused through its holding that correcting past injustice essentially requires ensuring individuals can live in dignified conditions in the present. The context of unequal property relations and the naked exercises of power by landowners, the Court held, had to be addressed through a series of measures. First, the law had to evolve to provide protection for the occupiers living on the property of landowners. Secondly, individual landowners had obligations that went beyond simply leaving the occupiers alone and had to enable them to make renovations (with the possible result that the landowner may in time have to pay for those improvements). Finally, there was a need in light of these complex historical relations for human face-to-face dialogue and engagement to try and address matters in a decent, consensual manner, failing which the courts would step in.

[71] ibid [110].
[72] ibid [132].
[73] ibid [142].

4. Concluding Observations: The Impact of History on Socio-Economic Rights Jurisprudence

A close engagement with a few seminal cases on the right to have access to adequate housing has revealed that the explicit recognition of historical injustice has had significant impacts on the interpretation of this socio-economic right in South Africa. This concluding section seeks to distil what has emerged. The focus has largely been on attempting to capture qualitatively what these effects have been in relation to the four dimensions examined in this chapter: mention, interpretation, process, and remedy. A further question not addressed in this chapter concerns whether in fact the implications drawn by the Court result in a normatively desirable approach to addressing past injustice.

It is not necessary to struggle to find references to history in the Court's jurisprudence on the right to have access to adequate housing—they are quite clearly present. Whilst the Court is concerned with people's present living conditions, it expressly recognises they emerged from a past characterised by deep division and inequality. This historical context is not just acknowledged but clearly affects the substantive dimensions of the Court's decisions. The Court grapples with how to address the divisions generated by past injustice in the context of disputes between current competing interests. What clearly emerges is the focus on procedural mechanisms and structures of reasoning to address these historical injustices, the core dimensions of which I now attempt to capture.

The Court first recognises that individuals must follow law-governed processes in resolving disputes. It often expresses concern and disapproval of 'self-help' and 'queue-jumping': anarchic processes are clearly not the way to proceed, in its view.[74] Instead, fundamental to South African transformative constitutionalism is an affirmation that historical injustices and related disputes are to be resolved in a lawful manner.[75] In this way, the Court gives expression to one of the broad goals of transitional justice—to create viable and stable systems of law and governance through which social and historical conflicts are resolved.

The second core dimension of the Court's approach is a strong strand which places the responsibility of resolving disputes on the parties themselves. Whether it be a landlord and labour tenant (such as in *Daniels*), or a municipality and unlawful occupiers (such as in *PE Municipality* and *Blue Moonlight*), the preference of the Court is for individuals and institutions to engage in good faith and achieve their own resolution to complex disputes. Ultimately, the Court places an obligation on parties to a dispute to do so and, at times, has indicated it will refuse to

[74] For a detailed critical analysis of the notion of queue-jumping, see Katharine Young, 'Rights and Queues: On Distributive Contests in the Modern State' (2016) 55 Columbia Journal of Transnational Law 65–137.

[75] Klare (n 4) 150.

intervene if they have not initially attempted to engage meaningfully. It could be argued that the negotiated manner in which South Africa resolved its historical conflict has influenced the Court's approach. In a sense, it appears to reject the notion that the passing of the Constitution was a once-off historical affair but rather recognises transitional justice as a process requiring continuing negotiation by individuals and institutions on the concrete implications of the constitutional settlement.[76] This approach is not confined to the right to housing but also influenced Justices Froneman and Skweyiya, for instance, expressly to acknowledge in a case concerning the right to education that 'participation and engagement are central to our constitutional project, a reflection of our "negotiated revolution"'.[77] This approach is also aimed very much at restoring relationships that have been ruptured between people:[78] in the process of negotiation and engagement, ultimately, it is to be hoped that people will come to recognise each other's humanity and reach out to one another across historical divisions. This focus on relationships is consistent with the Court's emphasis on embodying the African value of *ubuntu*—which seeks to develop harmonious relationships—in the relations between the state and the individual.[79]

If the parties themselves cannot resolve their disputes, the Court recognises in these judgments that history must affect the approach it adopts towards its own interpretation of constitutional rights. It always acknowledges the interests on both sides of the dispute and does not seek to create a clear normative hierarchy between them. The third dimension of the Court's approach is that, in attempting to address the concrete disputes, it aims to do justice in the particular circumstances. Doing so perhaps, in its view, helps to diffuse conflict by limiting its interventions to particular contexts and not permanently prioritising one set of interests over another.

One particularly controversial aspect of the Court's approach here appears to be a refusal to affirm concrete standards that apply beyond particular cases. The Court wants—both in relation to evictions and positive obligations in relation to the right to housing—to tailor its responses to specific circumstances without laying down general principles. Instead of a clear-cut obligation to address the needs of those without shelter, the Court instead evaluates the reasonableness of government programmes on a case-by-case basis. This approach allows the Court maximum flexibility to address concrete situations and also limits its potential to clash directly

[76] For the notion of continuing negotiation in the aesthetic realm, see Berman and LeBaron, Chapter 5 in this book.

[77] See *Head of Department, Department of Education, Free State Province v Welkom High School; Head of Department, Department of Education, Free State Province v Harmony High School* [2013] ZACC 25; 2014 (2) SA 228 (CC) [139].

[78] On the importance of a relational approach to transitional justice, see Metz, Chapter 2 and Bautista Pizarro, Chapter 3 in this book.

[79] See, particularly, *Joseph v City of Johannesburg* [2009] ZACC 30; 2010 (4) SA 55 (CC) fn 39 and D Bilchitz, 'Citizenship and Community: Exploring the Right to Receive Basic Municipal Services' (2011) 3 Constitutional Court Review 45–78.

with the approach adopted by other branches of government. Doing so, as critics point out, comes at the cost of clearly articulated entitlements which set the normative framework for the state's obligations in this area.[80] Recently, a minority of the Court in a regressive judgment has gone further in a holding that seems to water down the notion that the right to have access to housing is an individual right at all. It held that the 'failure to provide a house cannot cause an injury or damage to an individual in need of a house'.[81] The vagueness of the Court's approach also lacks the ability to provide guidance both to individuals and institutions of what may legitimately be claimed. Without clear entitlements, it becomes less evident to individuals in what way socio-economic rights provide them with real redress for past injustices. As such, it may be contested whether the Court's approach is effective in addressing historical injustice (an issue which has not really been the focus of academic attention).

A fourth feature of the jurisprudence of the Court is its recognition that the past requires private parties to bear obligations to address present and past injustice. All societal relationships were seriously affected by the apartheid system and the Court recognises that it is not simply the government that has duties to address the legacy of the past: every individual and institution must do so too.[82] The Court has gradually placed more extensive obligations on private parties: from a duty temporarily to tolerate illegal occupation to positive obligations potentially to pay for improvements to individual dwellings where that is necessary to ensure their housing is decent. The Court recognises that the reconstruction of the South African political community cannot simply leave individuals alone but requires them to be actively involved in redressing the harmful legacy of the past. At times, it places substantive, positive obligations on them; at other times, it places a duty on them to enter into a process to try in good faith to ameliorate the legacy of past injustice.

The Court also, in a fifth facet, recognises the need in resolutions of conflict to acknowledge the past and to require other parties—whether state or non-state parties—to do the same. Acknowledging the past, can lead to a shift in attitudes and enhance compassion; it can also change entrenched approaches in the law itself. Throughout the Court's jurisprudence, there is a sixth facet which involves a deep sensitivity to those who are badly off as a result of past injustice. The Court thus attempts to give stronger weight to the interests of those who are vulnerable

[80] The focus of criticisms has generally been on the limits of 'reasonableness' to provide rights with meaning, content, and a basis for their enforcement: see, for instance, D Bilchitz, *Poverty and Fundamental Rights* (OUP 2007) 176 and Liebenberg (n 10) 176–79.

[81] *Thubakgale v Ekurhuleni Metropolitan Municipality* [2021] ZACC 45 ('*Thubakgale*') [150].

[82] Arguably, this point is recognised by section 8(2) of the Constitution which contemplates the extension of obligations flowing from fundamental rights to non-state parties. See M Madlanga, 'The Human Rights Duties of Companies and Other Private Actors in South Africa' (2018) 29 Stellenbosch Law Review 367–68.

in its decision-making processes and to ensure, in its orders, that their plight is addressed.[83]

The analysis in this chapter has thus demonstrated a number of clear influences that an analysis of historical context has had on the jurisprudence of the Constitutional Court in relation to the right to housing as a key socio-economic right. Addressing past wrongs—questions at the heart of transitional justice—are shown to be strongly interconnected with the approach adopted to achieving a measure of distributive justice. It is not clear that a number of these choices are inevitable. Indeed, an engagement with a comparative context can help illuminate which dimensions are contingent and what choices have been made. That, in turn, can facilitate a deeper understanding of which approaches are better in advancing both historical and distributive justice.

[83] The recent judgment of *Thubakgale* (n 81) is an unfortunate exception, effectively upholding the terrible disregard the authorities showed for the rights of vulnerable individuals.

12

Historical Injustice and Socio-Economic Rights in Colombian Constitutional Jurisprudence

The Case of Victims of Forced Displacement

Magdalena Inés Correa Henao

1. Introduction

In 1991 Colombia included various socio-economic rights in the Constitution. Whilst this document prioritises the justiciability of civil and political rights, subsequent court jurisprudence has also rendered socio-economic rights justiciable. The Court has in this regard been willing to engage in far-reaching interventions to ensure these rights are extended to individuals and, sometimes, even groups and communities. The inclusion of such a rich constitutional guarantee of a minimum level of material equality, did not take place in a historical vacuum: various forms of past injustice have led to serious socio-economic exclusion in Colombia. At the time of drafting the 1991 Constitution (and twenty-four years later in the recent 2016 Peace Agreement), it has been recognised that addressing this legacy of exclusion is of great importance to ensuring peace in Colombia going forward.

This chapter focuses on a particular facet of the post-1991 developments surrounding socio-economic rights, namely the case law of the Colombian Constitutional Court (hereinafter CCC) on victims of forced displacement. The analysis places emphasis on judgments in which the petitioners are farmers, rural women, and members of Indigenous and Afro-Colombian communities, given the differential impact the domestic conflict has had on the lives of these people whose existence has an indissoluble connection with their territory.[1]

[1] For victims, the meaning of the place from which they have been forced to abandon involves strong relations with the concepts of land, territory and territoriality (identity). See J A Tamayo Castro, 'El territorio como categoría en el estudio del proceso de políticas públicas. La política pública de desplazamiento forzado (Medellín)' (September 2013) *Presentación en el VII Congreso Latinoamericano de Ciencia Política, organizado por la Asociación Latinoamericana de Ciencia Política (ALACIP), Bogota* <https://alacip.org/cong13/380-castro-7c.pdf> accessed 3 October 2022; D Ruiz Serna, 'El territorio como víctima. Ontología política y las leyes de víctimas para comunidades indígenas y negras en

Magdalena Inés Correa Henao, *Historical Injustice and Socio-Economic Rights in Colombian Constitutional Jurisprudence*
In: *Transitional Justice, Distributive Justice, and Transformative Constitutionalism.* Edited by: David Bilchitz and Raisa Cachalia, with Magdalena Inés Correa Henao and Nathalia Bautista Pizarro, Oxford University Press. © Magdalena Inés Correa Henao 2023. DOI: 10.1093/oso/9780192887627.003.0012

It seeks to identify the extent to which historical injustice has been taken into account when interpreting the social and economic rights of these victims and when developing procedural safeguards and remedies. This is due to the fact that the violations of the said rights are not only as a result of their infringement within a context of armed conflict, but is also about the historical disregard and marginalisation by political powers of rural populations from development and material citizenship.

In investigating this question, I proceed as follows: Section 2 explains briefly the historical injustices relevant to Colombia's constitutional history as well as its current consequences. Section 3 examines the structural orders of the CCC on victims of forced displacement. In particular it focuses on the famous ruling T-025 of 2004 and some of its follow-up decisions[2] relating to farmers, rural women, and members of ethnic communities as specific groups amongst the victims. Section 4 examines some individual cases where the Court analyses the violation of the right to housing, as claimed by these victims. The chapter concludes that in its interpretation of the socio-economic rights of the victims of forced displacement and its implementation of remedies to address the violation of these rights specifically, the Court has gone far beyond what has been done previously for other socio-economic rights' holders. Nevertheless, the Court does not expressly use 'past injustice' as a significant justification for its decisions. Instead, it references the existing inadequate 'state of unconstitutional affairs'—a kind of a 'present injustice'—as the basis for addressing victim injustice.

Thus, the study elucidates the meaning of transformative constitutionalism in the jurisprudence of the CCC, which is manifested in the recognition of specific and reinforced rights' positions and guarantees of socio-economic rights when their holders are victims of the armed conflict. This has imposed significant burdens on the state and even on private, third parties. At the same time, it highlights the Court's willingness to advance distributive justice through developing criteria to address the violation of the socio-economic rights of farmers, rural women, and those from Indigenous and Afro-Colombian communities.

The lack of historical perspective is notable and, in some sense unfortunate, as taking account of past injustices could help improve the quality of the Court's justification for its intervention and the persuasiveness of its protection of socio-economic rights as well as the efficiency of its orders. Although the Court has sought to achieve measures of transformative constitutionalism and distributive justice, its important work would be strengthened through situating its remedies and procedures more explicitly in the context of historical injustices.

Colombia' (2017) 53(2) Revista Colombiana de Antropología Instituto Colombiano de Antropología e Historia –ICANH 85–113 <https://www.redalyc.org/jatsRepo/1050/105052402005/html/index.html> 3 October 2022.

[2] Concerning the meaning of the follow up decisions, see n 77.

Finally, it bears noting that the case law analysed here is not part of the decisions with which the CCC has participated in the transitional justice processes undertaken during the last twenty years.[3] On this basis, it would integrate what in Colombia has been called 'transitional justice without transition',[4] since it occurs as a constitutional response to the massive violations of fundamental rights of the forcibly displaced population. This is regardless of the uncertainties during the negotiations with the armed groups or precisely as a reaction to the fragmented, weak, and incomplete peace process. In this way, the suggested groundbreaking jurisprudence on socio-economic rights could be understood as part of an ongoing transitional justice process that attempts to correct past wrongs and in so doing, consolidate a stable and lasting peace in Colombia for posterity.

2. The Relationship between Historical Injustice and Current Injustice

Historical injustice matters in Colombia, and in Colombian constitutional law, for several reasons. In this section, I highlight some of the key ingredients of Colombia's historical and political framework and assess why they led to socio-economic exclusion and widespread inequality among the rural population. Second, I consider whether the 1991 Constitution was enacted at least partially as an attempt to correct these past wrongdoings. Third, I provide some current statistics on the precarious living conditions of farmers, rural women, Indigenous peoples, and Afro-Colombians, in order to describe the impact of past injustice, the domestic conflict, and the breach of the constitutional mandates borne by the state.

A. Background of Past Injustice

Historical injustice in Colombia dates back, at least, to the very beginning of the encounter between Spain and the Indigenous peoples. The occupation and domination by the Spanish Crown from the sixteenth century was based upon the power of the sword and the cross. After the dispossession of their lands, the Indigenous population was forced to work on plantations and in gold mines, the latter being

[3] See, eg, the rich jurisprudence about 'Justice and Peace Law' (Ley de Justicia y Paz, 2005) <https://www.corteconstitucional.gov.co/relatoria/LEY%20DE%20JUSTICIA%20Y%20PAZ.php>, the 'Marco Jurídico para la Paz' (2012) <https://www.corteconstitucional.gov.co/relatoria/MARCO%20JURIDICO%20PARA%20LA%20PAZ.php>, and the implementation of the 2016 Peace Agreement <https://www.corteconstitucional.gov.co/relatoria/Procedimiento%20Legislativo%20Especial%20para%20la%20Paz%20(Fast%20Track).php> all accessed 3 October 2022.

[4] R Uprimny and others, *¿Justicia transicional sin transición? Reflexiones sobre verdad, justicia y reparación para Colombia* (Dejusticia 2006) 14 <https://www.dejusticia.org/wp-content/uploads/2017/04/fi_name_recurso_201.pdf> accessed 3 October 2022.

the main economic activity during this period.[5] The harsh treatment, as well as the spread of old-world diseases, led to the extermination of several Indigenous communities.[6] Thereafter, the labour force was supplanted with slaves brought from Africa.[7] Subsequently, difficult living conditions for Indigenous and Afro-descendent communities worsened with the expansion of the colonial economy during the seventeenth and eighteenth centuries.

This situation did not change drastically following independence. Led by emblematic Creole white military elites at the beginning of the nineteenth century (1810), the foundation of the republic (1819–1821) involved many restrictions on political rights, which hindered full democratic inclusion. Additionally, colonial institutions remained entrenched, thus deepening inequality rather than fostering liberal ideals.

In the nineteenth century, seven national constitutions were enacted to address a situation of continuous civil war, resulting from fragile political institutions.[8] Whether conservative or liberal, it is important to note that the two political parties that fought for power always sought to preserve, as grundnorms of the Colombian state, the rule of law and democratic political and representative principles, as well as a clear liberal economic orientation.[9]

The last of these constitutions, enacted in 1886, became the basic law of Colombia and remained so until 1991. Despite multiple amendments it retained its spirit: a confessional regime, a strong presidential system, and a centralised state.[10] These three structural cornerstones that provided the foundation for the Colombian state and maintained it for more than 100 years served as the basis for the historical denial of ethno-cultural diversity, for social segmentation, and the lack of adequate public institutions or socio-economic development in most of the rural areas of the national territory.

During the first half of the twentieth century, political violence took on an unusual force, which provided the motivation, in the late 1950s, for a political pact between the liberal and conservative parties called the National Front (*Frente Nacional*).[11] This pact entailed alternating power between the parties for the

[5] Á Tirado, *Introducción a la historia económica de Colombia* (first published 1974, La Carreta 1978) 105–12.

[6] D Bushnell, *Colombia, una Nación a pesar de sí misma. Desde los tiempos precolombinos hasta nuestros días* (Planeta 1994) 33.

[7] Tirado (n 5) 105–12.

[8] R Pardo, *Historia de las guerras* (Ediciones B-Colombia 2008) 454–60.

[9] ATrujillo, 'El constitucionalismo en el siglo XIX' in A Trujillo, L Javier Moreno, and C Mario Molina (eds), *Historia Constitucional de Colombia, Tomo I. Siglo XIX* (Academia Colombiana de Jurisprudencia 2012) 25.

[10] C Restrepo Piedrahita, *Constituyentes y constitucionalistas del siglo XIX* (Universidad Externado de Colombia 2009) 118.

[11] The military government of Rojas Pinilla (1953–1958) 'used by the elites of the traditional parties to overcome the ungovernability of the country expressed in the political violence of the 1940s and 1950s', was followed by 'the National Front' (*Frente Nacional*), 'a bipartisan coalition whose system of government was first approved by plebiscite and would last through four presidential terms'. Liberals and Conservatives between 1958 and 1974 'would alternate in the presidency while equally sharing cabinet posts and other appointive offices'. See N Idrobo, 'Mayoral Appointments During the National Front in

following four presidential periods. This pact is widely acknowledged as being a key political moment in the consolidation of the republic,[12] but it also weakened democracy and constitutionalism.[13]

Moreover, the conflicts that existed were not only political but also economic. The policies adopted by the state accentuated social inequality, especially in rural areas. They preserved models based upon extractive industries and monocultures, with low levels of industrialisation and poor infrastructure. This implied the granting of concessions to foreign companies and the creation of large monopolies run by national companies.[14]

In 1936 and during the second half of the twentieth century, liberal governments enacted constitutional amendments,[15] new laws,[16] and the ratification of human rights treaties[17] to guarantee a few social and economic rights. Nevertheless, these norms were not effective due to the lack of political will to implement them.[18] The economy grew and developed, but its benefits were concentrated in the largest cities and in the hands of a few.[19] For instance, much land was held in large estates, formed legally[20] or illegally[21] by specific elites, which consolidated a situation of unequal land distribution.[22]

Colombia: A Duration Analysis' (2015) <https://repositorio.uniandes.edu.co/bitstream/handle/1992/12938/u713408.pdf?sequence=1> accessed 3 October 2022; CA Ayala Diago, 'Frente Nacional: acuerdo bipartidista y alternación en el poder' *Credencial Historia No. 119, Banco de la República* (Noviembre 1999) <https://www.banrepcultural.org/biblioteca-virtual/credencial-historia/numero-119/frente-nacional-acuerdo-bipartidista> accessed 3 October 2022; A Acevedo, 'El Frente Nacional: Legitimidad institucional y continuismo bipartidista en Colombia (1958–1974)' (2015) 36(1) Económicas CUC 49–78 <doi: http://dx.doi.org/10.17981/econcuc.36.1.2015.22> accessed 3 October 2022.

[12] M De la Rosa and G Mejía, *Historia concisa de Colombia (1810–2013)* (Ministerio de Cultura, Universidad del Rosario, Universidad Javeriana 2014) 86–91.

[13] M Quinche, *Derecho Constitucional Colombiano* (Universidad del Rosario 2009) 34.

[14] Tirado (n 5) 216.

[15] The most important was the Constitutional Amendment 1/1936 that provided specific socio-economic duties for the state, such as labour rights, the social function of property, and the right to social assistance (arts 10, 16, 17). See Acto Legislativo 1/1936 http://www.suin-juriscol.gov.co/viewDocument.asp?id=1824914 accessed 3 October 2022.

[16] For instance, Law 200/1936 regulated the social function of property and Law-decree No 2663/1950 (Labor Code) further developed labour rights. See <https://www.adr.gov.co/wp-content/uploads/2021/08/L17_Ley_200_de_1936.pdf https://www.suin-juriscol.gov.co/viewDocument.asp?id=1874133> accessed 3 October 2022.

[17] Law 74/1968 that approved the ICESCR <https://www.suin-juriscol.gov.co/viewDocument.asp?ruta=Leyes/1622486> accessed 3 October 2022.

[18] In relation to the history of land distribution, see CCC ruling C-644/2012; Marco Palacios, *Entre la legitimidad y la violencia. Colombia 1875–1994* (Norma 1995).

[19] De la Rosa and Mejía (n 12) 126–41.

[20] See Á Albán, 'Reforma y contrarreforma agraria en Colombia' (2011) 13 (24) Revista Economía Institucional <http://www.scielo.org.co/pdf/rei/v13n24/v13n24a11.pdf?origin=publication_detail> accessed 3 October 2022.

[21] See M Palacios, '¿De quién es la tierra? Propiedad, politización y protesta campesina en la década de 1930' (2011) 1(47) Revista Historia Crítica Universidad de los Andes <http://www.scielo.org.co/scielo.php?script=sci_arttext&pid=S0121-16172012000200013> accessed 3 October 2022.

[22] In this regard, the CCC has noted in T-601/2016 [36]–[39] that 'conditions of marginalisation and exclusion … do not only arise from slavery', but also from policies developed afterwards,

In the 1960s and the 1970s, popular, peasant, and left-wing guerrilla groups were created to demand social inclusion. In the 1980s, far-right paramilitary groups that had formed defended the interests of landowner elites.[23] In addition, starting in the 1970s, drug-trafficking began to impact on the economy, the use of land, and the armed conflict. Drug-related crimes perpetuated the internal armed conflict by becoming the main financial source for all armed actors[24] which, in turn, enabled them to increase their control of large areas of territory and its population.

The war against drug-trafficking was prioritised in the public agenda of successive governments in the 1980s. This involved the allocation of considerable public funds, the reinforcement of the armed forces, and measures to eradicate illegal plantations. These measures severely affected agriculture, lands, and the rights of the rural population including farmers and ethno-cultural communities.[25]

B. 1991 Constitution: A Constitution to Address Historical Injustice?

Bounded by the complexity of Colombia's history, the start of the 1990s gave rise to the necessity of reforming the 1886 Constitution. A popular initiative[26] led to the establishment of a Constituent Assembly,[27] which led to a major and defining constitutional change: the 1991 Colombian Constitution.

which explains why Afro-descendent communities still face 'institutional and structural barriers and discrimination'.

[23] Grupo de Memoria Histórica, '¡Basta Ya! Colombia: Memorias de guerra y dignidad' *Informe general Grupo de Memoria Histórica* (2016) 111–43 <https://centrodememoriahistorica.gov.co/descargas/informes2013/bastaYa/basta-ya-colombia-memorias-de-guerra-y-dignidad-2016.pdf> accessed 3 October 2022.

[24] ibid 143–47.

[25] A complete explanation of the contribution of the history and the insurgencies, paramilitaries, and drug-trafficking on the domestic conflict, see Comisión de la Verdad, *Hay futuro si hay verdad: Informe Final de la Comisión para el Esclarecimiento de la Verdad, la Convivencia y la No Repetición. Tomo II. Hallazgos y recomendaciones* (Primera edición, Comisión de la Verdad 2022) 212–462 <https://www.comisiondelaverdad.co/hay-futuro-si-hay-verdad> accessed 3 October 2022.

[26] After the assassination of four presidential candidates and, as a response to the general crisis, at the end of the 1980s university students began a movement clamouring for constitutional reforms to expand the mechanisms of political participation and reviewing the political system, the state's intervention in the economy, and territorial decentralisation. The initiative resulted in a request to include a 'séptima papeleta' (seventh ballot) in the elections of Congress in March 1990, so that the citizens could vote whether or not to approve the convening of a national constituent assembly for such purposes. Although it lacked direct legal effect, a favourable vote of 89 per cent was obtained. The 'séptima papeleta' became the direct antecedent of the Constituent Assembly of 1991. See C Torres (ed), *La Séptima Papeleta: la revolución de los estudiantes publicado en Séptima Papeleta: historia contada por algunos de sus protagonistas* (Universidad del Rosario, Bogotá, Colombia 2010) <http:// https://editorial.urosario.edu.co/pageflip/.../laseptima-papeleta-historia-contada.pdf> accessed 3 October 2022.

[27] President Gaviria Trujillo was elected in May 1990. Once in office he issued Legislative-Decree 1926/1990 establishing the Constituent Assembly and defining the rules for the election of the

During the process of its framing, the official records (*travaux preparatoires*) show that the drafters frequently allude to a historical legacy of inequality, discrimination, dispossession, abandonment, deprivation, and poverty, which endured until the formation of the Constituent Assembly. These allusions constituted the justification for the new paradigm of the state[28] and the guarantee of civil and political[29]—and especially social, economic, and cultural[30]—rights to be adopted. There were also a few explicit references to historical injustice within these initiatives to give special protection to some groups in the population: farmers,[31] women,[32] Indigenous people, and Afro-descendants.[33]

constituents and the subject of the constitutional reform to be carried out. This decree was declared constitutional by the Colombian Supreme Court of Justice in ruling 138, October 9/1990, Rad. 2214 (351-E).

[28] A Galán, 'La satisfacción de las necesidades básicas para todos como fin esencial del Estado' Proyecto de Reforma Constitucional No 126b [Comisión Tercera 1991-03-08] 98; <https://babel.banrepcultural.org/digital/collection/p17054coll28/id/377> accessed 20 September 2023; C Lemos and others, 'Régimen económico y finalidad social del estado' Ponencia [Comisión Quinta 1991-04-10] 5–6. <https://www.cervantesvirtual.com/obra/regimen-economico-y-finalidad-social-del-estado-895734/> accessed 20 September 2023.

[29] M T Garcés, 'Ampliación de la democracia' Proyecto de Reforma Constitucional no. 13 [Comisión Cuarta 1991-02-19] 8–10 <https://www.cervantesvirtual.com/obra/ampliacion-de-la-democracia-895098/> accessed 20 September 2023; H Serpa and others, 'Derechos, libertades y deberes fundamentales' Proyecto de Reforma Constitucional No 84 [Comisión Primera, Comisión Segunda, Comisión Quinta 1991-03-08] 7–10 <https://www.bibliotecadigitaldebogota.gov.co/resources/2086674/> accessed 20 September 2023.

[30] G Guerrero, 'Derechos sociales' Proyecto de Reforma Constitucional No 3 [Comisión Quinta 1991-02-13] 3–7 <https://babel.banrepcultural.org/digital/collection/p17054coll28/id/421> accessed 20 September 2023.

[31] H Serpa, 'Sector agropecuario' Proyecto de Reforma Constitucional no 92 [Comisión Primera 1991-03-08] 3–5 <https://babel.banrepcultural.org/digital/collection/p17054coll28/id/450> accessed 20 September 2023. A Garzón and others, 'Derechos agrarios'. Ponencia para la ampliación del sector agrario y dignificación del trabajo campesino [Comisión Quinta 1991-05-29] 1–2 <https://www.cervantesvirtual.com/obra/derechos-agrarios-894858/> accessed 20 September 2023; Gaceta constitucional No 101, 'Plan de alivio social al campesino' [Junio 18/1991] 14–15 <https://babel.banrepcultural.org/digital/collection/p17054coll26/id/3703/> accessed 20 September 2023; Gaceta constitucional No 108 'Propuesta para Sustitución y Rebaja de Egresos de Funcionamiento del Estado' [Junio 26/1991].<https://www.bibliotecadigitaldebogota.gov.co/resources/2095428/> accessed 20 September 2023.

[32] I Marulanda and others, 'Derechos de la familia, el niño, el joven, la mujer y la tercera edad' Ponencia [Comisión Quinta] 24–29 <https://www.cervantesvirtual.com/obra/derechos-de-la-familia-el-nino-el-joven-la-mujer-la-tercera-edad-y-minusvalidos-894594/> accessed 20 September 2023; H Serpa and others, 'Los derechos de la mujer' Proyecto de Reforma Constitucional No 90 [Comisiones Primera, Segunda, Quinta 1991-03-08] 2–6 <https://www.cervantesvirtual.com/obra/los-derechos-de-la-mujer-896634/> accessed 20 September 2023.

[33] F Rojas, 'Los derechos de los grupos étnicos' Ponencia [Comisión Primera 1991-04-30] 3–45; L Muelas, 'Propuesta indígena de reforma constitucional' Proyecto de Reforma Constitucional No 83 [Comisión Segunda 1991-03-08] 1–9 <https://babel.banrepcultural.org/digital/collection/p17054coll28/id/317> accessed 20 September 2023; Orlando Fals Borda and others, 'Pueblos indígenas y grupos étnicos' Ponencia [Comisión Segunda 1991-04-05] 4–8, 13–17 <https://data.cervantesvirtual.com/manifestation/895503> accessed 20 September 2023; Gaceta constitucional No 29 'Proyecto de Acto Reformatorio de la Constitución Política de Colombia No. 119' [F Rojas] 3, 6, 11–14 <https://babel.banrepcultural.org/digital/collection/p17054coll26/id/3710> accessed 20 September 2023; Gaceta constitucional No 40 'Pueblo Indígenas y grupos Étnicos' [abril 8/1991] 2–8 <https://www.bibliotecadigitaldebogota.gov.co/resources/2095431/> accessed 20 September 2023.

This historical background elucidates two main purposes of the 1991 charter: (i) to overcome the internal armed conflict and achieve peace,[34] since one of the motives justifying the constitutional change was to face the causes and consequences of the armed conflict;[35] and (ii) to serve as a permanent basic norm to provide the contours—and attempt to ensure the realisation—of fundamental rights and key institutions of the state. The transformative project of the Constitution has to be understood against the background of a state model that did not work substantially and had increased inequality, exclusion, and poverty. Nevertheless, this history of violence and public malfunctioning that the Constitution sought to address was not mentioned expressly in its text. In contrast, the new Constitution enshrines formal and material equality as a principle and orders the state to protect the most vulnerable members of society (arts 13 and 334), along with an extensive catalogue of civil and political rights (arts 11–41), socio-economic rights (arts 42–77), and collective rights (arts 78–82).

Furthermore, these mandates are reinforced by three crucial ingredients: (i) the tasks of defending and protecting constitutional rights would be borne by newly created institutions (eg the Constitutional Court and Ombudsman's Office); (ii) strong enabling provisions allowing access to courts to claim the protection of constitutional rights (ie the historical public action of unconstitutionality[36] and the new protective actions: a tutela for fundamental rights,[37] and class actions—popular and 'de grupo'—for collective rights[38]); (iii) increasing the status of international treaties relating to fundamental rights in the constitutional system through what is termed 'the block of constitutionality'. This notion has a double meaning: *stricto sensu*, which involve ratified international treaties and agreements that 'recognise human rights and prohibit their limitation in states of emergency' (art 93 para 1) which operate as 'a set of norms with constitutional rank';[39] and in

[34] For that reason, Teitel, among some others, has regarded the 1991 Constitution as a transitional constitution. See R Teitel, *Justicia transicional* (Universidad Externado de Colombia 2017) 477.

[35] See Transitory arts 12 and 13 of the Constitution; H Vargas, 'El papel de los jueces en los tiempos de transición: acceso a la justicia en las zonas afectadas por los grupos armados organizados' in F Padrón and M Correa (eds), *El Estado constitucional en jaque 3; Estado constitucional en periodos de transición* (Universidad Externado de Colombia 2018)176.

[36] On this action, see J Roa Roa, *Control de constitucionalidad deliberativo. El ciudadano ante la justicia constitucional, la acción pública de inconstitucionalidad y la legitimidad democrática del control judicial al legislador* (Universidad Externado de Colombia 2019) 656.

[37] Enacted by art 86 of the 1991 Constitution and regulated by Decree 2591/91, the 'tutela' is the judicial action by which any person can request a speedy decision (within ten days) by a judge to protect his or her fundamental rights. Tutela action appeals are decided by the tutela judge's superior in the court hierarchy, and all cases end up in the docket of the CCC, who can discretionally review any case. See R Uprimny, 'Should Courts Enforce Social Rights? The Experience of the Colombian Constitutional Court' *Bogotá, Dejusticia* (2006) 5 <https://www.dejusticia.org/wp-content/uploads/2017/04/fi_name_recurso_67.pdf> accessed 3 October 2022.

[38] Art 88 Const, Law 472/1998.

[39] M Góngora-Mera, 'The Block of Constitutionality as the Doctrinal Pivot of a *ius commune*' in A von Bogdandy and others (eds), *Transformative Constitutionalism in Latin America: The Emergence of a New Ius Commune* (OUP 2017) 248.

the *lato sensu*, involving 'the remaining ratified treaties on human rights' (art 93 para 2), which serve as 'a parameter of constitutionality'[40] to interpret constitutional rights and duties.

For the purposes of this study, it is important to highlight the following provisions concerning socio-economic *rights*:

- The right to decent housing, which requires the state to establish conditions for the guarantee of that right and to promote 'plans of public housing, long-term funding systems and associative forms for the execution of these programs' (art 51). It was initially regarded as a progressive right, but the CCC has defined a fundamental content that must be guaranteed to all, based on its usage of international law (through the *stricto* and *lato sensu* block of constitutionality notions),[41] and considering the deplorable housing conditions under which multiple population groups live.[42]
- The rights of specific groups of the population that have endured historical discrimination and structural exclusion. A brief summary of their rights are as follows:
  - Rights of farmers (i) to 'the gradual access of agricultural workers to land property' and (ii) to social, finance, and technical services, 'with the purpose of improving their income and quality of life' (arts 64–66).[43] These rights represent, according to the CCC, constitutional guarantees to include and recognise 'a population that has been historically invisible'[44] or 'traditionally condemned to poverty and social marginalisation'.[45]
  - Rights of women (i) who 'have equal rights and opportunities' as men; (ii) who 'cannot be subjected to any type of discrimination'; (iii) who, during pregnancy and after childbirth, have 'the benefit of special assistance protection as an onus of the State' and to 'food subsidies', if mothers find themselves 'unemployed or abandoned'; (iv) who are entitled to special support if they head households; and (v) who have special protection for their labour rights (arts 43, 53). Further entitlements have been developed

[40] ibid.

[41] It refers, among others, to the Universal Declaration of Human Rights (art 25); International Covenant on Economic, Social and Cultural Rights (ICESCR) (art 11); the American Declaration of Rights and Duties of Man (art XI), and the 'Protocol of San Salvador' (art 26), as well as to *General Comments No. 4* (1991) and *No. 7* (1997), on the right to housing, by the United Nations Committee on Economic, Social and Cultural Rights (CESCR).

[42] See P Robledo, 'El derecho a una vivienda digna en el marco de las competencias municipales de ordenación del territorio' (2010) Revista Derecho del Estado 207.

[43] The article 64 was recently modified by Acto Legislativo 1/2023.

[44] CCC ruling C-006 of 2002.

[45] CCC ruling C-623 of 2015.

through international human rights law (IHRL) and the increasingly progressive case law of the CCC.[46]

- Rights of ethno-cultural communities, Indigenous and Afro-descendent, based upon the principle of constitutional pluralism (arts 1, 7, 8) and reinforced by institutional guarantees (arts 63, 246). These include fundamental rights (i) to preserve their autonomy and cultural identity; (ii) to collective property in the territories where they have historically lived; and (ii) to prior consultation whenever the state intends to adopt decisions and policies that affect these territories (arts 330 and Transitory art 55, and mainly ILO Convention No169).

In summary, although historical injustice is not explicitly addressed in the Constitution, it was certainly not ignored. It is visible in several of the social state of law constitutional provisions that can only be explained as mandates to address a historical backdrop of exclusions and deprivations for much of the Colombian population, in particular the specific groups identified in this chapter.[47]

I now consider whether such an implicit recognition of historical injustice in the Constitution has led to a transformation in the living conditions of the main groups that have suffered. In doing so, it is necessary to consider the relationship between this historical injustice and the continuation of armed conflict after 1991.

C. Injustice After 1991: Solely Attributable to the Domestic Conflict?

During the last twenty-five years, statistics concerning access to socio-economic rights have improved in absolute terms, particularly in urban populations. However, in relative terms, the position of groups affected by historical injustices—such as farmers, rural women, and ethnic groups—has not improved and, in many ways, has worsened.[48]

[46] CCC rulings C-754 of 2015; C-117 of 2018. For a more detailed discussion of the jurisprudence relating to the rights of farmers, see D I Güiza Gómez and others, *La constitución del campesinado: luchas por reconocimiento y redistribución en el campo jurídico* (Dejusticia 2022) 168–217 <https://www.dejusticia.org/wpcontent/uploads/2023/02/Constitucion-del-campesinado_web.pdf> accessed 20 September 2023.

[47] The CCC has observed that the Constituent Assembly was aware that, in Colombia, discrimination was 'rooted in historical injustice' which 'invisibilised segregation and unequal, inhuman and opprobrious treatment' (CCC, ruling T-601 of 2016 [30]–[31]). The shift from a monocultural paradigm to a multicultural and pluralist one reflects this reality through rights, guarantees, and obligations being designed to compensate and address 'structural discrimination' as well as to preserve the physical, cultural, and spiritual subsistence of Afro-descendent communities ([33], [40], [45]–[47]).

[48] The 2011 Human Development Report noted that, concerning land distribution, Colombian Gini coefficient was 0,87. See United Nations Programme for Development (UNPD), *Informe Nacional de Desarrollo Humano 2011. Colombia rural. Razones para la esperanza*. Resumen Ejecutivo. 28–30 <https://www.undp.org/es/colombia/publications/informe-nacional-de-desarrollo-humano-2011> accessed 20 September 2023.

At first glance, this outcome seems to have been caused by the intensification of the domestic conflict after 1991, since the main interests at stake were rural lands and territories of ethnic communities.[49] Accordingly, in 2015, the National Centre of Historical Memory (CNMH) reported that 87 per cent of the 6.5 million victims of forced displacement were moved out of the countryside. Of these, women comprised more than half the group and 40 per cent were Indigenous or Afro-Colombian.[50] It is also noted that around '8.3 million hectares have been stripped or abandoned by force'.[51] Nonetheless, further studies have found that, before being displaced, victims of forced displacement lived in unequal conditions, which were even worse than those of the poor urban population.

Indeed, in 2011, the UN Programme for Development (UNPD) reported that, in addition to the actions of armed groups, the high vulnerability of farmers, women, Indigenous and Afro- descendants was caused by inadequate political representation, their lack of public recognition as differentiated social groups, the concentration of the land's ownership and the rural economic model adopted in the country over several years.[52] Those conclusions have been confirmed in the recent final report of the Truth Commission (June 2022), created by the peace agreement with the FARC guerrilla (2016).[53]

The 2014 census of the Colombian rural population revealed that 45.7 per cent of farmers were poor,[54] whereas the national percentage of individuals living in poverty was 21.9 per cent.[55] In 2020, public statistics of the multidimensional poverty index (MPI) in Colombia estimated the percentage of people in MP in capital cities to be 12.5 per cent and in the populated and dispersed rural centres, 37.1 per cent. This means that MP in rural areas is not twice but three times bigger than in capital cities.[56]

[49] ibid Human Development Report 56–57. See also JA Ocampo, *Misión para la transformación del campo* (DNP 2014) 4; CNMH, *Una nación desplazada. Informe nacional del desplazamiento forzado en Colombia* (Imprenta Nacional de Colombia 2015) 225.

[50] Currently, the number of registered victims is 8,288,516 <https://www.unidadvictimas.gov.co/es/registro-unico-de-victimas-ruv/37394> accessed 3 October 2022, meaning 17.17 per cent of Colombians (48,258,494 inhabitants, after the 2018 National Census) have been forcedly displaced <https://www.dane.gov.co/index.php/estadisticas-por-tema/demografia-y-poblacion/censo-nacional-de-poblacion-y-vivenda-2018/cuantos-somos> accessed 3 October 2022.

[51] CNMH (n 49) 16.

[52] UNPD (n 48) 65.

[53] For instance, it underlines after studies and statistics that meanwhile Gini of land distribution in Europe is 0.57; in Africa 0.56; in Asia 0.55; and in Latin America 0.79, in Colombia is 0.92. See Comisión (n 25), 650, and multidimensional poverty of the rural population was in 2020 37.1%, while in the capitals of the main cities was 12.5%. See Comisión (n 25) 650, 597.

[54] DANE, *Tercer Censo Nacional Agropecuario: Hay campo para todos. Tomo II Resultados* (2016) 827 <https://www.dane.gov.co/files/images/foros/foro-de-entrega-de-resultados-y-cierre-3-censo-nacio nal-agropecuario/CNATomo2-Resultados.pdf> accessed 3 October 2022.

[55] DANE, 'Pobreza Monetaria y multidimensional en Colombia' (2014) *Boletín Técnico* <https://www.dane.gov.co/files/investigaciones/condiciones_vida/pobreza/bol_pobreza_14_.pdf≥ accessed 3 October 2022.

[56] DANE, Pobreza multidimensional 2020 <https://www.dane.gov.co/index.php/estadisticas-por-tema/pobreza-y-condiciones-de-vida/pobreza-multidimensional/pobreza-multidimensional-2020> accessed 3 October 2022.

Living conditions of rural women have improved in absolute terms; nevertheless their situation is still worse in comparison to urban women and to rural men.[57] This latter point is reflected in the substantial disparity in the Poverty Gap Index between female and male heads of household.[58] Regarding ethnic groups, the MPI suggests that 69.5 per cent of the Indigenous population and 58.2 per cent of the Afro-descendent communities are living in poverty, again, a much higher proportion than the national average.[59]

In relation to the focus of this chapter, studies related to land rights of victims of forced displacement reveal that approximately 40 per cent to 50 per cent of rural property is occupied informally.[60] That means that those farmers, who are victims of forced displacement, have no legal title to the land of which they have been deprived. Existing legal land title procedures represent insurmountable obstacles for most rural farmers.[61] Furthermore, rural women face additional barriers relating to access to land grants, credits,[62] and technical assistance.[63]

A similar situation explains the lack of progress when ethnic communities try to obtain the formal recognition of collective property rights to their land and territory, even after many years of applying—the data shows 500 Indigenous petitions[64] and 270 Afro-descendent requests.[65] Concerning the limited access to decent housing, 17.1 per cent of rural houses have no electricity;[66] 94 per cent have no sewage; 57.2 per cent have no access to water; and 15.7 per cent do not have access to any of those services.[67] In relation to ethnic communities, 46.2 per cent have no

[57] CINEP, *Mujeres Rurales en Colombia* (2017) <https://www.academia.edu/es/35241245/Informe_Mujeres_rurales_en_Colombia> accessed 3 October 2022.

[58] M Bailara and S Parada, *El empleo de las mujeres rurales. Lo que dicen las cifras* (CEPAL 2009) 63. In this context, Ocampo notes that Colombian rural women and their families are mired in a trap of poverty, which is very difficult to overcome. See Ocampo (n 49) 65–66.

[59] DANE (n 54) 854.

[60] N Neva, *Bases conceptuales procesos de regularización de la propiedad rural y acceso a tierras* (Unidad de Planificación Rural Agropecuaria 2014) 18 <https://upra.gov.co/documents/10184/11165/Bases_conceptuales_procesos_regula_propie_rural.pdf/c6f34b46-9887-4b87-8f33-aa9d7c8d953a> accessed 3 October 2022.

[61] Peña and Zuleta have found that, alongside the domestic conflict, the intervention of regulatory institutions has been another cause of land dispossession and concentration, since 'massive land property transactions, coercive or not, do not and cannot take place in an institutional vacuum'. See R del Pilar Peña and S Zuleta, 'El derecho al despojo en Colombia: Un análisis de la regulación de la adjudicación de baldíos desde abajo' (2018) Análisis Político 3, 4; R Peña and others, 'Legal Dispossession and Civil War in Colombia' (2017) Journal of Agrarian Change 759.

[62] Consejo Nacional de Política Económica y Social, *Documento Conpes social 161: Equidad de género para las mujeres* (DNP 2013) 19 <http://www.equidadmujer.gov.co/ejes/Documents/Conpes-Social-161-de-2013-Equidad-de-Genero.pdf> accessed 8 July 2022.

[63] DANE (n 54) 601 and 611.

[64] CIDH, *Informe Anual de DDHH* (2010) 404 <http://www.cidh.oas.org/pdf%20files/ANUAL2010.pdf> accessed 22 January 2021.

[65] Observatorio de Territorios Étnicos y Campesinos, Universidad Javeriana, Semana Sostenible' *Revista Semana* (Bogotá, 13 Abril 2019) <https://www.semana.com/impacto/articulo/titulacion-colectiva-de-tierras-una-deuda-del-estado-colombiano/43904> accessed 3 October 2022.

[66] DANE (n 54) 691.

[67] ibid.

electricity, 80 per cent have no access to water mains, and 94.8 per cent have no sewage.[68]

From the current data, we can infer that forced displacement was not the only factor that put victims 'in conditions of vulnerability, exclusion and marginality'.[69] There is a harmful relationship between victimisation and land concentration, informal title, inequality, and socio-economic rights' deprivation[70] (land, property, education, access to water, sanitation, and labour opportunities).[71] The armed conflict can be said to have exacerbated and, in fact, exploited these existing inequalities.[72]

As the final report of the Truth Commission observed, the 1991 Constitution has not fundamentally been able to achieve peace and to redress the historical injustices, since the models of democracy and security and the economic policies adopted by the political authorities to develop its mandates, have both breached and disregarded the rights and needs of farmers, rural women, and Indigenous and Afro-Colombians—the population most deeply affected by the internal conflict.[73]

D. Historical Injustice: Does It Matter?

The historical injustice characterised by social exclusion and deprivation remains present in the lives of farmers, rural women, and rural ethnic communities more generally. This is despite the fact that the 1991 Constitution implicitly sought to addresses this past, changing the paradigm of the state and reinforcing socio-economic rights and the rights of the most vulnerable population groups. Their living conditions have dropped as a result of the violence of the domestic conflict and because of the breach of constitutional mandates of social and distributive justice.

It is understandable then why the Peace Agreement of 2016, in its substantive provisions, contemplates not only a transitional justice system that addresses the rights of victims, but social and democratic measures and policies specifically directed at the rural population, women, and ethnic groups. These measures have expressly sought to address the historical causes and reasons for the internal conflict.[74]

[68] ibid 730.

[69] CCC ruling T-596 of 2011.

[70] See L Jorge Garay and F Vargas, *Memoria y reparación: Elementos para una justicia transicional províctima* (Universidad Externado de Colombia 2012); D Fajardo, *Las guerras de la agricultura colombiana 1980–2010* (ILSA 2014).

[71] Ocampo (n 49) 6–9.

[72] A comprehensive list of human rights violations of the victims of the domestic conflict appears in Comisión (n 25) 133–211.

[73] Comisión (n 25) 46, 107, 387, 428, 465, 490, 507, 522, 542–43, 551.

[74] See 'Final Agreement to end the armed conflict and build a stable and lasting peace' (24 November 2016) 3, 10, 34, 132, 136, 139, 140, 144–47, 194 <https://www.peaceagreements.org/viewmasterdocument/1845> accessed 3 October 2022. Unfortunately, aside from the CCC considering the peace

Likewise, it is reasonable that the final report of the Truth Commission of June 2022, after analysing the historical context of inequality, institutional design, and violence that have determined the 'Great War' (or the survival and exacerbation of the Colombian domestic conflict after 1991)[75], concludes that stable and lasting peace in Colombia imposes, among other measures, the need: (i) to 'recognise not only the "interrelations between economic and social development, with the forms of use and occupation of the territory", but also the cultural and political-institutional patterns that have been at the base of territorial conflicts'; and (ii) to 'break the urban bias to be built from the perspectives, needs and agendas of those populations, sectors and territories historically stigmatised and impoverished'.

In addition, it states that it is essential to implement a model of territorial planning in which are recognised: (iii) 'the great inequalities that have historically characterised the Colombian territorial configuration and its relationship with the persistence of the armed conflict'; (iv) that 'the rights to property and use of land in peace and on equal terms of a significant portion of rural dwellers, have been systematically denied or violated'. Such a model has to accept as an important truth that the rural population (as victims of the domestic conflict) has historically been prevented from (v) 'participating decisively in public affairs, including those that affect them most'; from (vi) 'enjoying public goods and services fundamental to human well-being'; and from (vii) having the opportunity to 'produce and derive profit in the wealth' of the country and to develop a 'sustainable economic activity'.[76] Thus, historical injustice does matter.

I now examine the question whether the CCC, in its developing jurisprudence, has recognised expressly historical injustice as an element of its reasoning when addressing the plight of forced displacement victims. Specifically, I seek to identify the relevance that past injustice has had on judicial reasoning in these cases, as well as the remedies granted and whether they actually address not only the direct rights' violations but also transform their conditions of vulnerability.

agreement to be a political framework for implementation of the transition to peace (CCC, ruling C-630 of 2017), the measures adopted, and the resources allocated until now, seem to have forgotten, once again, the history behind this agreement. See Echavarría Álvarez, Josefina and others, *Seis años de implementación del Acuerdo Final: retos y oportunidades en el nuevo ciclo político* (Matriz de Acuerdos de Paz/Instituto Kroc de Estudios Internacionales de Paz/Escuela Keough de Asuntos Globales 2023) 18–21, 23–24, 48–54 <https://curate.nd.edu/downloads/und:jw827943q15> accessed 20 September 2023.

[75] Comisión (n 25) 110. See also CCC SU-020 of 2022.

[76] ibid 654–56.

3. Structural Cases for Victims of Forced Displacement and Historical Injustice

In this section, I present the case law that has sought structurally to address the plight of victims of forced displacement. In doing so, I will first study the Court's reasoning in the leading case T-025 of 2004. Second, I will focus on the follow-up decisions[77] adopted concerning rural women and ethnic communities.[78] I conclude by identifying the differences between those cases in relation to their engagement with past injustice.

A. Ruling T-025 of 2004

This ruling is undoubtedly the landmark decision in Colombia on forced displacement. The Court decided to combine more than 100 cases in which more than 1,150 victims claimed the violation of their fundamental rights. Instead of simply deciding the individual cases at hand, it also sought to address the violation of the rights of the entire displaced population, thus making it a structural decision. As a consequence, it ordered general measures to improve public policies targeted at this population and implemented a special mechanism to monitor the fulfilment of its orders (follow-up decisions).

Due to the conditions of extreme vulnerability that victims endured as well as the continuous failure of the state to provide them with timely and effective protection, the Court makes a list of the violated rights in the Constitution as well as those in the United Nations Guiding Principles of Forced Internal Displacement (1998).[79] It also remarked that this situation had been occurring in a massive, prolonged, and repeated manner, and was not attributable to a single authority. Instead, it stated that this situation reflected a structural problem that affects the entire set of protective policies designed by the state: (i) insufficient resources allocated to policy funding; and (ii) a limited institutional capability to implement the policies. For these reasons, the CCC declared what it termed an 'unconstitutional state of affairs'.[80]

[77] The follow-up decisions come from one of the most relevant measures adopted in T-025: the Court's power to monitor the compliance of authorities with its orders, through a special chamber. Those decisions, which refer to both policies benefitting the public and specific victim groups, have often not only verified the fulfilment of T-025 orders, but also set new criteria and policies to be implemented.

[78] Tutela rulings and follow-up decisions are adopted by a chamber of the CCC. However, I will always refer to 'the Court' since those decisions are made through the exercise of its jurisdiction.

[79] Thus, it includes civil and political rights, the right to special protection right of certain groups, the right to equality and to peace, as well as the rights to health, work, adequate food, education, and decent housing. T-025 of 2004, 5.2.

[80] ibid 2.2; 6.3; 7.

Concerning the socio-economic rights of victims of forced displacement, ruling T-025 of 2004 points out that authorities have (i) a negative duty to avoid 'advancing, promoting or executing ostensibly regressive policies, programs and measures in the area of economic, social and cultural rights';[81] and (ii) a positive duty to adopt measures to guarantee these rights.[82] Thereafter, it defines (iii) the minimum level of satisfaction of constitutional rights of displaced persons, pursuant to international and constitutional obligations of the state.[83]

To address these violations, the CCC prescribes two type of orders: (i) 'simple orders', aimed at responding to the specific requests of petitioners; and (ii) 'complex executive orders, related to the unconstitutional state of affairs, aimed at guaranteeing the rights of the entire displaced population'.[84] These latter orders are complex because they involve several public entities in charge of assisting victims and because authorities have the duty to undertake measures to address the aforementioned structural problems,[85] in a manner that takes the differential treatment owed to victims who are particularly vulnerable and thus in need of special protection.[86]

B. Follow-Up Decisions Related Specifically to Rural Women, Indigenous and Afro-Colombian Communities

From the numerous follow-up decisions, I have chosen the leading ones where the CCC focuses on the specific categories of the rural population displaced and dispossessed by the conflict considered in this study:[87] women and Indigenous or Afro-Colombian peoples.

A-092 of 2008 is the first follow-up decision that analyses the impact of the policies and measures designed and implemented by the authorities regarding female victims of forced displacement.[88]

After the CCC studied the information sent by the government and by social organisations, it observed that what public authorities had done to address the plight of female victims of forced displacement 'has been manifestly insufficient'.[89] Thus, it confirmed that the 'unconstitutional state of affairs' has not been overcome regarding the design, procedures, and outcomes of the adopted policies and

[81] ibid 8.1.
[82] ibid.
[83] ibid 9.
[84] ibid 10.
[85] ibid.
[86] ibid 5; 8.1.
[87] The Court has also adopted specific decisions related to other categories of victims, such as children and adolescents (A-251 of 2008), and disabled people and the elderly (A-006 of 2009).
[88] See also follow-up decisions A-237 of 2008, A-098 of 2013, A-009 of 2015, A-443 of 2015, and A-737 of 2017, on issues relating to female victims of forced displacement.
[89] A-092 of 2008, II.2.

measures. To address this situation, it established new obligations relating to thirteen public programmes:[90] (i) identifying the 'basic problems that the programs in question must address'; (ii) emphasising the differential approach[91] to be undertaken, as a constitutional criterion to guide policy design and execution; (iii) fixing 'minimum elements of rationality'; and (iv) observing a minimum level of satisfaction of socio-economic rights of female victims.[92]

A year later, in separate follow-up decisions the Court analysed the policies undertaken specifically towards ethnic groups who were victims of forced displacement: these were A-004 of 2009 on Indigenous peoples and A-005/2009 on Afro-Colombians communities. Both decisions concluded that the government had not fulfilled the T-025/2004 mandates and that the state of unconstitutional affairs has not been overcome in relation to these groups. Consequently, the Court ordered authorities: (i) to adopt special programmes, plans, and measures to assist these groups of victims, with a differential approach[93] and effectiveness; (ii) to guarantee their fundamental individual and collective rights; and (iii) to protect their leaders and authorities, ethnic territories, and the cultural and social bonds of the communities.

Furthermore, in A-004 of 2009, it stated that measures must *inter alia*: (i) be previously approved via prior consultation; (ii) prevent and address the disproportionate impact that forced displacement causes to Indigenous communities; (iii) guarantee a safe return to their territories in conditions of dignity if the communities voluntarily decided to return there; and (iv) support special cases where members, families, and communities cannot return due to current threats of armed groups in their territory.[94] Likewise, in A-005 of 2009, analysing social and economic rights, the CCC ordered that public measures must contain amongst other matters: (i) a 'strategy to combat discrimination against the displaced the Afro-Colombian population'; (ii) a guarantee of effective access to any goods and services available to the displaced population; (iii) a 'plan to provide and/or improve housing solutions' for this population; and (iv) an economic plan to generate

[90] One example would be the Programme for the Prevention of Sexual Violence.

[91] In Inter-American Human Rights law and Latin American Constitutional law, the ethnic, genre, human rights approaches ('*enfoques diferenciales*') is a mandate, mostly borne by the state, to guarantee minorities' rights in the determination of public policy, following a methodology that focuses on discrimination, invisibility, as well as on the identities, capabilities, positionality, and limitations of minorities. See United Nations, Office of the High Commissioner for Human Rights Colombia (2020) <https://documents-dds-ny.un.org/doc/UNDOC/GEN/G20/110/95/PDF/G2011095.pdf?OpenElement> accessed 3 October 2022.

[92] A-092 of 2008 V.B.

[93] In Auto 266 of 2017, the Court justified a differential approach due to the specific risks posed by forced displacement to the physical and cultural existence of Indigenous and Afro-Colombian as minority groups. It also acknowledges 'the causes behind these risky situations, which have to do ... with the persecutions and forms of discrimination that, from the past, have existed against ethnic communities and, which within the framework of the armed conflict, operate as the cause of their displacement' (see A-266 of 2017 [8.2]).

[94] A-004 of 2009, 'Measures to be adopted'.

income, taking into account the knowledge and ethno-development experiences of Afro-Colombian people.[95]

C. Present and Past Injustice in Structural Case Law

There is no doubt about the fact that the structural case law reflects a serious judicial engagement by the CCC with the meaning and purpose of fundamental rights law in general, but mostly with the rights of the most vulnerable people. Moreover, ruling T-025 of 2004 and the studied follow-up decisions have interpreted judicial powers relating to the socio-economic rights of the victims of forced displacement as enforceable to the full extent of what is possible. This is shown by the complexity of the remedies and procedures prescribed, including prescribing policies to be designed and implemented by the public administration, including identifying a minimum content to be attributed to the relevant constitutional rights that must be given effect to.

However, in the judicial reasoning, historical injustice has not been considered to the extent that one might have expected. Indeed, ruling T-025 of 2004, the leading case, does not mention historical injustice or the past prior to the forced displacement. Concretely, it does not recognise the disregard of the countryside by political institutions or the exclusion of the rural population from development and material citizenship as a cause of the conflict and the violation of human rights suffered by these communities. Instead, it emphasises 'present injustice' when it interprets socio-economic rights, stating that the constitutional paradigm of the state imposes (i) the positive duty to 'correct visible social inequalities'; (ii) the negative duty to avoid regressive policies and measures that openly lead to 'injustice, exclusion and marginalisation';[96] and (iii) the positive duty to apply the 'clause of eradication of present injustices'.[97] The focus is thus on remedying present, unacceptable living conditions and advancing distributive justice, without an engagement with the historical conditions that led to the current situation.[98]

In contrast, in the follow-up decisions A-092 of 2008, A-004 of 2009, and A-005 of 2009, historical discrimination or historical injustice[99] forms part of the

[95] A-005 of 2009 [182].

[96] T-025 of 2004 [8.1].

[97] ibid.

[98] In the recent ruling SU-288 of 2022, in the context of confirming the prohibition of acquisitive prescription on vacant land belonging to the nation in the absence of domain title, the Court did not refer specifically to the situation of the victims of forced displacement. It did, however, formulate its arguments with reference to the historical lack of protection afforded by the state to the farmers, and Indigenous and Afro-Colombian populations who had sought to legalise their possession of rural land.

[99] It should be noted that these allusions are not exclusive to this case law, being common in rulings where the Court analyses the rights and guarantees of women and Indigenous or Afro-Colombian population in general, as subjects of constitutional special protection. Regarding women see, eg, SU-096 of 2018, C-586 of 2016 and ethnic groups, see, eg, T-691 of 2012, T-098 of 2014, T-601 of 2016, T-572 of 2017, C-017 of 2018, T-063 of 2019, C-480 of 2019.

reasoning. In those decisions, the Court recognises the differential and disproportionate impact the conflict has had on women and ethnic communities due to their historical vulnerability.

Decision A-092 of 2008 refers, at the outset of the case, to the existence of historical conditions of discrimination against women, in order to expound upon the specific risks and extraordinary burdens that violence imposes on them due to their gender.[100] Historical discrimination is also mentioned when discussing the causes of female subjection to domestic or labour exploitation,[101] and when considering women's position of disadvantage and asymmetry vis-à-vis the recognition of their property rights.[102]

In both decisions about Indigenous and Afro-Colombian victims of forced displacement, the Court alludes to the historical injustice as having led to a traditional culture of discrimination which lies behind the social and economic exclusion of such minorities. In A-004 of 2009, this can clearly be inferred when the Court underlines the special impact of the domestic conflict on Indigenous peoples that—based on a series of territorial and socio-economic processes, legal uncertainty, and material outcomes—has been exacerbated or intensified by the war.[103] In A-005 of 2009, the argument is made explicit when the Court insists that, 'given the situation of historical marginality and segregation' they have faced, Afro-Colombian people 'shall enjoy a special protection borne by the State'.[104]

The CCC thus appears to be concerned with historical injustice when considering the causes of victimisation of particular groups—such as women and ethnic communities—and as a basis to explain their present conditions of exclusion and vulnerability. Nonetheless, historical injustice does not feature within the arguments to determine the remedies required since those follow-up decisions are only designed to apply the general framework set by T-025 of 2004 to these groups. In that framework, it is actually 'present injustice' that really counts in light of the principles, international obligations, and policies pertaining to forced displacement.

As such, the past injustices and discrimination are not drawn on as a basis to address the situation at hand but rather as an explanation and ground for identifying certain groups as particularly vulnerable. Accordingly, the reference to past injustice could be interpreted as being simply a rhetorical argument recognising how current inequalities of these groups—which are exacerbated by their forced displacement—are based upon patriarchal and prejudicial cultures. These statements are thus, in the main, not central to the outcomes or remedies but are invoked for emotive effect.

100 A-092 of 2008 II.1.
101 ibid IV.B.1.7.
102 ibid III.1.8.
103 A-004 of 2009 [2].
104 A-005 of 2009 [19].

The next section of this chapter considers the question whether the approach to past injustice and the prevalence of 'present injustice' so far found in the CCC leading case, will be the interpretative line to be generally applied in individual tutela cases relating to the socio-economic rights of the victims of forced displacement. The section concentrates the analysis on the case law of the right to decent housing.

4. The Right to Decent Housing of Victims of Forced Displacement

Forced displacement generates multiple infringements of fundamental rights. One of the most visible of these is the violation of the right to decent housing. Victims are not only forced to leave the homes and territories to which they have long been attached, but must now live in their new places of relocation, often with inadequate accommodation.[105] The tutela rulings studied in this section do not address the 'state of unconstitutional affairs', but rather pertain to individual petitions to guarantee the right to decent housing of victims of forced displacement. First, I consider two rulings about evictions against farmers; and second, I consider three cases in which safeguarding of this social right entails an alternative understanding of the principle of equality before the law.

The purposes of examining these cases is to examine the judicial reasoning relating to, on the one hand, interpreting the right to housing of the victims, and, on the other hand, to the procedures and remedies proposed to resolve the complaint. The focus of the analysis is on the role that historical injustice plays in the reasoning and specifically, on whether the focus is solely on present injustice.

A. The Right to Decent Housing of Victims of Forced Displacement: Evictions and Public Obligations

Rulings T-239 of 2013 and T-523 of 2014, among many others,[106] deal with the tutelas filed against the execution of eviction orders by local authorities for violating the right to decent housing of the occupiers, most of them victims of forced displacement. In both cases, the Court utilises arguments about the situation of vulnerability and deprivation of victims of forced displacement, that may not be disregarded by the state and imposes heightened obligations on private

[105] T-025 of 2004 [5.2].

[106] The Court has heard a significant number of cases with similar facts. The judgments analysed here have been chosen because they reflect the most relevant aspects of constitutional jurisprudence on the right to decent housing of the displaced population in the face of eviction orders from private property. For a complete list of the decisions taken on this matter, see CCC SU-016 of 2021.

owners. The victims' right to housing is considered fundamental and its constitutional understanding and protection differs from the one generally followed in the Court's jurisprudence.[107]

The most important case is ruling T-239 of 2013, since the CCC clearly develops the principle of differential treatment, distinguishing allocations and procedures among petitioners and land occupiers who are victims of forced displacement and those who are not.

In favour of the occupiers who were from historically poor families but not victims of forced displacement, the ruling ordered local authorities: (i) to inform them about existing programmes (eg subsidies) to access housing and (ii) to adopt affirmative actions and preferential treatment—taking account of their conditions of special vulnerability—to materialise the effective enjoyment of the right. However, the Court provided neither a determination of how the first order would have to be complied with nor a concrete guarantee of special protection in respect of the second. In this manner, evictions could still be enforced against the occupiers. The right to housing of these kinds of land occupiers appears to be weaker, and more progressive in nature rather than a core obligation.

For occupiers who were victims of forced displacement, however, ruling T-239 of 2013 establishes three strong orders for local and/or national authorities: (i) to stop evictions as a transitory solution to protect their right to housing;[108] (ii) to include victims in housing plans or to ensure the fulfilment of their right to decent housing at a minimum level, within the following three to six months;[109] and (iii) to define and execute serious and continuous socio-economic stabilisation programmes 'until the conditions, which gave rise to the violation of their fundamental rights, disappear'.[110]

In relation to the victims of forced displacement, the CCC affirmed the right to housing as a strong fundamental right. It not only imposed particular, positive obligations upon public authorities, but it also, significantly, prevented evictions as a provisional guarantee of these victims' right to housing, which, in turn, has strong implications for the owners of the occupied lands.[111] Even more far-reaching is the

[107] See CCC A-008 of 2009, A-209 of 2011, and A-373 of 2016.
[108] T-239 of 2013 decision 5.
[109] ibid decision 4.
[110] ibid decision 6.
[111] See the recently issued ruling, SU-016 of 2021, where the Court consolidated the constitutional jurisprudence on tutela measures in the context of evictions of subjects of special constitutional protection, confirming partially the remedies arising from ruling T-239 of 2013. Indeed, to the victims of forced displacement, it determined that the suspension of eviction orders applies for as long as is necessary for the authorities to offer urgent, temporary shelter to affected persons. This will apply only to victims who do not have the resources or institutional support to enforce the right to housing. Nevertheless, the Court underlines that both measures will have a maximum term of seven months each. To other subjects of special constitutional protection (those not affected by forced displacement), the Court reiterated that in the short-term the focus should be on the guarantees of due process and information pertaining to care programmes. However, in the medium to long term, the emphasis should be on the protection of the right to housing, consisting mainly of inclusion in housing programmes.

judicial constitutional guarantee, derived from ruling T-239 of 2013, that declared that the statements and orders of the judgment will have legal effect not only for the victim petitioners but for all the victims of forced displacement who are in the same situation.[112]

Concerning the duties upon private parties, it is to be noted that the CCC does not provide arguments in that case to justify the burdens imposed on the owners of occupied lands vis-à-vis the occupying victims of forced displacement. This lack of argumentation is addressed in ruling T-523 of 2014. In this judgment, the Court observed that, due to the strong impact of forced displacement on the right to housing, it is constitutional that there be a 'possible interruption of the right to property of private owners by a *de facto* occupation, as an exceptional protection to be granted'.[113] It also found that the interests of private owners might be provisionally limited by virtue of a principle of solidarity[114] and that the specific restriction on the right to property in this case, is not an excessive burden on the owners, 'since the authorities are called to seek, within a reasonable time, suitable solutions'[115] to fulfil the occupying victims' (of forced displacement) right to housing.

B. The Right to Housing of Victims of Forced Displacement: Farmers, Indigenous Families, Rural Women, and Equality before the Law

In order to broaden the analytical perspective of the constitutional jurisprudence on the right of victims of forced displacement to decent housing, it is useful finally to examine three decisions relating to tutelas filed by a peasant, an Indigenous family, and a female householder. These were aimed at protecting that social right in the face of situations other than eviction but share a number of similarities.

In ruling T-596 of 2011, the plaintiff was a sixty-six-year-old farmer with limited education and children under his care. After being forcibly displaced, he acquired a house in poor condition and, to ensure its habitability, he started construction on top of the structure. He had not, however, requested the required permit and, hence, local authorities imposed a large fine on him. The Court declared this to be a violation of his right to housing. Although the fine against the petitioner was legal, it breached the obligation of the state in relation to a victim of forced displacement who deserves special protection.[116] The Court established two substantive

[112] This is called '*inter comunis effects*'. A remarkable feature of this ruling is that it is applicable regardless of whether or not the victims were parties to the constitutional trial. The same measure was adopted in ruling SU-016 of 2021 [161] and decision 1.

[113] T-523 of 2014, s 3.5.

[114] This is similar to the South-African Constitutional Court's decision, *City of Johannesburg Metropolitan Municipality v Blue Moonlight Properties 39 Ltd* [2011] ZACC 33; 2012 (2) SA 104 (CC).

[115] T-523 of 2014, s 3.5.

[116] T-596 of 2011 [7.4].

obligations on the government: (i) a negative obligation not to apply public regulations without considering the unequal conditions faced by the petitioner; and (ii) positive obligations to adopt a differential approach, and to consider alternative solutions to enable the plaintiff to comply with property law and to enable him to gain access to programmes for the displaced population.[117] Lastly, the Court clarified that if the petitioner is reluctant to accept the alternatives proposed by the administration and continues to engage in illegal behaviour, he must be subjected to penalties, since public authorities are required to ensure compliance with urban planning rules.[118]

In ruling T-952 of 2010, an Indigenous family began to build a house on land they received from their community. When the authorities found out, they ordered the suspension of construction arising from a lack of a permit required by law and the fact that the proposed construction would take place in a zone in which construction was forbidden due to the high risk of a natural disaster. The Court concluded here that the administrative order to suspend the construction did not violate the right to housing, since the concept of habitability—identified in international human rights law—is an essential component of the right to decent housing and includes 'the prevention of structural risks and the guarantee of physical safety of the occupants'.[119] Authorities only sought to prevent risks to the family, 'clearly preserving the right to life of members of the Indigenous community'.[120] As a result, it established a moratorium on law enforcement, to allow the Indigenous family and their community 'to act pursuant to the regulations'.[121] The Court also rejected an argument based on Indigenous autonomy[122] since 'not even maximising the autonomy principle could outweigh the state's obligation to prevent building a house in risky areas'.[123] Finally, the Court decided that the suspension order must be accompanied by remedies to support and advise the Indigenous family and the community about gaining access to the housing programmes adopted in favour of victims of forced displacement.[124]

Both rulings reveal that being a victim of forced displacement is sufficient reason to alter the general principle of formal equality before the law in order to guarantee their right to housing. Nevertheless, these judicial orders do not mean that victims

[117] ibid [7.8].
[118] ibid [7.7].
[119] See CESCR (n 41) [8].
[120] T-952 of 2010 [5.5].
[121] ibid.
[122] This is a constitutional principle interpreted by the case law, derived from the criterion that 'the greater the conservation of cultural identity is, the greater the autonomy they are entitled to'. See T-903 of 2009; C-463 of 2014; T-063 of 2019.
[123] T-952 (n 120) [5.5].
[124] Hence, the Court in this case ordered local authorities to coordinate with Indigenous authorities and to hire experts to weigh the real risks of natural disasters in the land assigned to the Indigenous family. Once the study was conducted, both authorities had to agree to the location of a 'suitable and safe place for the construction of the home assigned to the family'.

are above the law, but rather that their subjection to the law must be carried out by the authorities in a reasonable manner that takes account of their vulnerability.

The third case is ruling T-479 of 2011, in which the Court dealt with a female head of a household, who had not received a housing subsidy for which she was eligible, before lodging the case. The CCC accepted the argument of the authorities that there had to be equality in the treatment of the subsidy petitioners, since the beneficiaries were all Colombians and not only the victims of forced displacement. However, it declared an infringement of her right to housing due to the inadequate disbursement procedure for subsidies.[125] The Court also observed that, despite the subsidy being granted once the public budget was assigned, its inefficient disbursement was caused by 'the slow handing process of housing subsidies'.[126] Therefore, it ordered authorities 'to set a reasonable time for the disbursement' thereof, as a guarantee to preserve the right to housing of the woman and her family.[127]

The contrast between the remedies adopted in judgments T-596 of 2011 and T-952 of 2010 and those embraced in ruling T-479 of 2011 reveals a surprising finding. Despite the first two having opposite results, both consider the application of the law in unequal conditions, due to the situation of the farmer and the Indigenous family who were both victims of forced displacement. However, in the third case, the degree of vulnerability of being a female victim did not really affect the Court's reasoning as it offered a remedy that would be due to any citizen after such serious omissions by the authorities.

C. Right to Decent Housing of Victims of Forced Displacement: Present and Past Injustice

Having scrutinised the substantive content of these Tutela judgments, what can be observed in relation to the role of historical injustice in these decisions?

From my analysis, the focus of the CCC in rulings T-239 of 2013, T-523 of 2014, and T-596 of 2011 was on the duties of authorities to repair the 'present injustices' caused by forced displacement.[128] This is especially visible in T-239 of 2013. In this case, the Court clearly treats the claims to the right to housing of forcibly displaced victims differently to that of other vulnerable people who were not displaced.

Whilst the CCC was not clear about justifying such a differential treatment, it is evident that it was the 'present injustice' caused by forced displacement and its consequences on the right to housing of victims that determined the Court's approach. A similar inference can be drawn about the duties imposed on private

[125] See T-479 of 2011 [3.3]; A-008 of 2 of 2009; ICESCR art 11.1; CESCR (n 41).
[126] T-479 of 2011 [4.6].
[127] ibid [4.7].
[128] T-239 of 2013 [4]; T-523 of 2014 [3.5]; T-596 of 2011 [4] and [6.2].

parties which were only applicable in cases concerning illegal occupants who were victims of forced displacement.

Rulings T-952 of 2010 and T-479 of 2011, in which the plaintiffs belonged to the specific groups of rural victims, do, however, highlight some instances where the Court mentions briefly past injustice. For instance, it recognises that the 1991 Constituent Assembly, 'aware of the historical injustices suffered by traditionally segregated social groups ... decided to adopt the political form of the social state under the rule of law',[129] where 'equality before the law and the prohibition of discrimination ... are accompanied by the obligation to adopt positive measures to overcome traditional exclusion patterns, defeat historical injustices and protect those in a vulnerable situation or a condition of manifest weakness'.[130] It also stated, in the latter case very broadly, that the state cannot disregard the situation of manifest vulnerability of female victims of forced displacement, which was aggravated by their precarious socio-economic conditions, gender marginalisation, discrimination, and the lack of opportunities for employment and access to housing.[131]

These passing statements, however, do not appear to have been at the centre of the Court's reasoning: the focus, ultimately, was on the current condition of the petitioners as victims of forced displacement. As was found in the discussion of the 'structural' case law, the Court's approach, in interpreting the right to housing and establishing procedures and remedies to address its violation, is rooted in a response to present injustice caused by the domestic conflict, rather than historical injustices.

5. Conclusion

This chapter began by outlining the historical injustices of Colombian history, which had a particular impact on the rural population comprised of groups such as farmers, rural women, and Indigenous and Afro-Colombian communities and individuals. The Constitution, however, does not contain any express reference to this past, but, implicitly, could be seen to address it through establishing a set of principles, rights, and guarantees that seek to ensure at least a minimum level substantive equality, with a focus especially on improving the position of the most vulnerable groups of the population. Sadly, the historical disadvantages experienced in Colombia have been exacerbated by the internal armed conflict that continued since the passing of the Constitution and turned many in the rural population

[129] T-952 (n 120) [4].
[130] ibid.
[131] T-479 of 2011 [3.4].

into victims of forced displacement (I refer to this as 'present injustice'). In this context, the chapter has reviewed the case law of the CCC—both structural and individual—on the victims of forced displacement and their socio-economic rights and considered the extent to which past injustice has affected the substantive reasoning and remedies provided by the Court.

The study has highlighted the far-reaching measures taken by the CCC in recognising the victims as subjects of special constitutional protection—in light of their extreme vulnerability and the unequal impact of displacement on each of the groups that have suffered from it. The Court has also implemented groundbreaking judicial remedies and put in place procedures to address the infringement of victims' rights and to ensure their efficacy. It has, however, found that what substantially guides the Court's reasoning is 'present injustice' or the injustices derived from the forced displacement (arising from the internal armed conflict post-1991) and its consequences. Historical injustice or the injustices existing before forced displacement are largely absent from the express reasoning and, where it is mentioned, does not appear to have a major effect on the outcome of the cases. This is particularly true when it analyses the situation of the victims in general, who do not belong to a specific group of victims. In one of the important tutela rulings discussed, it was also evident that 'present injustice' was the basis for differential treatment of victims of forced displacement from those were historically poor—often as a result of past injustice—but not displaced. Present injustice also explains why the victims' right to housing imposes obligations on the state and on private owners of the occupied lands. It is the urgent protection of the fundamental rights of the victims that has thus justified limiting the rights of third parties.

As detailed, the CCC does allude to historical injustice in the follow-up decisions about the socio-economic rights of women, and Indigenous and Afro-Colombian victims of forced displacement, and in the tutela rulings filed by persons belonging to some of these groups of victims. It is one of the reasons utilised to explain both the particular impact of forced displacement on these groups and the differential treatment that victims deserve. This past of deprivation and social exclusion prior to being victimised by the domestic conflict is not, however, utilised as a basis to define the fundamental meaning of the victims' socio-economic rights and the means to address their non-compliance. Past historical injustice, thus, does play a role in the case law of the CCC relating to these groups, but, largely, as a rhetorical argument with the purpose of highlighting patterns of injustice in Colombian society (patriarchy and traditional prejudices). It appears to have no visible, normative effect on the Court's protection of the rights of women, or Indigenous and Afro-Colombian victims of forced displacement.

Considering the indisputable existence of past historical injustice endured by the rural population and its impact on the causes of displacement, it is difficult to understand its lack of real consideration by the CCC. It can only be inferred that the magnitude of the current injustices arising from the recent domestic conflict to their victims is so serious that it in a sense became the sole focus of judicial attention in addressing violations of their socio-economic rights. Otherwise, it must be noted that, the jurisprudence usually refers to forms of corrective and distributive justice that relate to ameliorating the present dire circumstances of victims. Corrective justice here refers to an 'integral restitution (*restitutio in integrum*)'—which consists in returning the victims to the situation they were in prior to the displacement, taking diverse measures to guarantee breached rights or to compensate for the damages suffered.[132] Distributive justice involves establishing a minimum level of socio-economic well-being to which all victims are entitled.[133]

In my view, past injustice is a missing element of the Court's jurisprudence, among others, for the following reasons. First, without a proper understanding and engagement with past historical justice, it is not possible accurately to evaluate what situation victims should be returned to or meaningfully to address the systematic violation of their rights (which is what the Court seems to aim at). Secondly, although access to social benefits can help compensate victims for critical deprivations, past injustice takes the matter further by engaging not only with present conditions because of the conflict but the underlying causes thus helping to identify the substantive measures that could be introduced to guarantee the non-repetition of violent acts. Thirdly, a recognition of the past historical structural injustice suffered by farmers, women, and ethnic communities in rural areas, would also provide a better justification for the differential treatment and special protection to be accorded to all vulnerable groups including, but not limited to, victims of forced displacement. Fourth, a real transformative justice focused on ameliorating the capacity of victims to exercise their rights and liberties, starts with correction for past wrongs.[134]

Through including, whenever relevant, a deeper understanding of complex historical injustices that explains many of the current patterns of poverty and inequality in Colombia today, the case law on socio-economic rights would reinforce

[132] After C-370 of 2006 [4.5.9]; following Interamerican Human Rights Court, case *Moiwana community v Suriname* [June 15/2005] [178].

[133] Meaning 'based on the duty to ensure the effectiveness of socio-economic rights ... as well as the mandate of substantial equality ... granting specific benefits or special treatment to disadvantaged or traditionally discriminated groups of the population'. C-912 of 2013 [25]–[28].

[134] Where reparation must return victims to the situation prior to the violation, 'as long as this situation guarantees their fundamental rights'; otherwise, the state has the obligation to transform 'the structural causes that gave rise to victimisation' C-715 of 2 of 2012 [8.2.3.2].

the justification, accuracy, efficacy, and balance of the orders and remedies and its limited but ultimate contribution to transformative constitutionalism.[135] Moreover, since the 2016 Peace Agreement and the final report of the Truth Commission of June 2022 emphasises that engagement with the past is a necessary component of peacebuilding, it is hoped that the CCC will adopt a greater historical consciousness in its future approach to adjudication.

[135] A constitutionalism in which the transformation is based on constitutional and international human rights mandates and obligations, but substantially developed by constitutional and human rights judges (see A von Bogdandy and others, 'Ius Constitutionale Commune en América Latina: A Regional Approach to Transformative Constitutionalism' in A von Bogdandy and others (eds), *Transformative Constitutionalism in Latin America: The Emergence of a New Ius Commune* (OUP 2017)) and still much lesser by political authorities and democratic procedures.

13

Joint Reflection: The Difference History Makes

Comparative Reflections on Socio-Economic Rights and Historical Consciousness in South Africa and Colombia

David Bilchitz and Magdalena Inés Correa Henao

1. Introduction: Divergent Approaches to the Role of History in Constitutional Court Jurisprudence

Both the South African Constitutional Court and the Colombian Constitutional Court are widely regarded as having made significant contributions towards entrenching the justiciability of socio-economic rights. Whilst having very different legal systems, they, nevertheless, both committed themselves to a new constitution that was supreme in the 1990s. Both Constitutional Courts have the power to strike down acts of parliament or conduct of the president for unconstitutionality. Both courts are also faced with contexts in which there is large-scale inequality—both having amongst the highest Gini coefficients in the world[1]—and heartbreaking levels of absolute poverty.

In Colombia, socio-economic rights are enshrined in Title II, Chapter 2 which was not clearly designed to become justiciable by individuals. Nevertheless, over the years, court doctrine has led these rights, under certain relatively relaxed conditions, to become immediately enforceable by individuals who bring a tutela, at least in relation to a minimum threshold of need.[2] The Constitutional Court has

[1] Despite the difference in the origins thereof, there is no doubt about the existence of significant economic and social inequality. Data of the World Bank indicates that the latest available Gini index in South Africa in 2014 was 0.63, and, in Colombia in 2020 was 0.542 <https://data.worldbank.org/indicator/SI.POV.GINI?view=map> accessed 3 October 2022.

[2] According to the statistics of the Constitutional Court, during its thirty years, some of the most common social and economic rights that have been demanded (and guaranteed) include the right to social assistance (SU-1150/2000, T-888/2013), the right to health (T-395/1998, T-016/2007, T-206/2013,) and the right to education (T-202/2000, T-458/2013). See <https://www.corteconstitucional.gov.co/lacorte/estadisticas.php> accessed 3 October.

David Bilchitz and Magdalena Inés Correa Henao, *Joint Reflection: The Difference History Makes* In: *Transitional Justice, Distributive Justice, and Transformative Constitutionalism.* Edited by: David Bilchitz and Raisa Cachalia, with Magdalena Inés Correa Henao and Nathalia Bautista Pizarro, Oxford University Press.
DOI: 10.1093/oso/9780192887627.003.0013

also aggregated individual tutela actions together, allowing it to address more systemic forms of disadvantage in terms of the doctrine of 'unconstitutional state of affairs'.[3] In South Africa, socio-economic rights are not separated into a different chapter but form an essential part of the bill of rights. Whilst being clearly justiciable, court doctrine has rendered it relatively difficult for individuals to gain access to these rights. It has essentially required individuals to challenge an entire government programme for a lack of reasonableness to be eligible for a remedy, thus rendering litigation based on these rights much more difficult.[4]

Our analysis in the two preceding chapters has also uncovered another key set of differences in the degree to which history is mentioned, and used in the interpretation and remedial approaches of these courts in their jurisprudence on the right to housing.[5] The South African Constitutional Court almost invariably refers to the history of the apartheid system and, at times, the prior colonial segregationist regimes and the deliberate inequalities these regimes sought to create. Such an explicit reference is not, however, simply for show: the Court appears (as Bilchitz has sought to show in his chapter) to have shifted the interpretations it provides of certain rights, and, at times, to adopt certain remedies on the basis of this history. The Court has preferred an approach that is largely procedural and often attempts to ensure the parties themselves resolve the difficulties which brought them to court. Enabling correction of skewed economic distributions is part of the overall mission of the Court itself.

The Colombian Constitutional Court, on the other hand, often provides descriptions of the concrete, impecunious circumstances of the litigants, but rarely engages with the historical causes of these circumstances. When it does so, it focuses on the past injustices suffered by specific groups such as women, Indigenous, and Afro-Colombians and its mention thereof appears to be largely rhetorical. It is moved particularly, as Correa seeks to show, by 'present injustice' and existing vulnerability, and, to this effect, will offer individualised remedies to address rights violations with specific and heightened protections offered to vulnerable groups. The Colombian Constitutional Court is clearly sensitive to existing unequal distributions, but its focus is largely on improving the circumstances of individuals, rather than correcting for past injustice. What then are the reasons for these differences in the approach to past historical injustice? The purpose of this comparative reflection is to attempt to answer this question.

[3] See, eg, the cases on displaced population (T-025/2004, A. 385/10, A. 647/17, A. 737/17), and prisons (T-153/98, T-388/13).

[4] See S Wilson and J Dugard, 'Constitutional Jurisprudence: The First and Second Waves' in M Langford and others (eds), *Socio-Economic Rights in South Africa* (CUP 2013) 44–45.

[5] This study is limited by our focus on the right to housing alone. An interesting project would be to test these findings in the context of other parts of the jurisprudence. Our hunch, based on our knowledge of other elements of the socio-economic rights jurisprudence, is that similar findings will emerge.

2. Explanations for the Divergent Approaches to Historical Injustice

A. A Different History Behind the Constitutions

The first explanation we venture relates to a difference in the historical circumstances of Colombia and South Africa. In South Africa, there were (as with all countries) multiple forms of historical injustice against a range of groups. Yet, there was one major historical wrong against which the Constitution of South Africa reacts—that is the attempt to entrench a system of racial segregation and White superiority known as apartheid.[6] This can be analogised to the Constitution of Germany in the aftermath of the Second World War—the major historical wrong against which it was established was the system of Nazism which rendered it legitimate to discriminate against Jews, Roma, and gay people and, ultimately, justified the genocide against these groups.[7] While the international community reacted to the Nazi atrocities and set up the international human rights system, however, much of the White population of South Africa voted for a party that entrenched the legalised segregation of, and discrimination against, Black people. The history of conflict between European settlers and communities of Africans who were already living in the territory now covered by South Africa clearly predates the formal enactment of apartheid. Yet, the struggle to end the extensive entrenchment of a specific system of apartheid with all its demeaning features and its implications for the socio-economic well-being of Black South Africans can be said to be the primary struggle that dominated the 1980s in South Africa and led to the negotiated transition to a new constitutional order. There was consequently one historical dimension whose effect on South Africa was so great that it required a major process of transformative constitutionalism to undo.[8]

Colombia too has a colonial history that followed the conquest by Spain in the 1500s. Despite having achieved independence relatively early in 1819 and having a state formally under the rule of law with democratic institutions, Colombia has struggled to consolidate the nation and maintain inner peace with several armed conflicts breaking out.

Indeed, the history of Colombia as a state, can be divided into two long periods of 'civil wars'. The first of these relates to a long chain of civil wars during the nineteenth century until the 1950s, which were fought for political, ideological,

[6] This is referred to as the 'grand narrative' by P De Vos, 'A Bridge Too Far—History as Context in the Interpretation of the South African Constitution' (2001) 17 South African Journal on Human Rights 1 who cautions against too univocal a notion of history.

[7] M Hailbronner, 'Transformative Constitutionalism: Not Only in the Global South' (2017) 65 American Journal of Comparative Law, 527, 541–42.

[8] Karl Klare coined this term in 'Legal Culture and Transformative Constitutionalism' (1998) 14 South African Journal on Human Rights 150.

economic, regional, and religious reasons. The '*Frente Nacional*' in 1958 was meant to end this violence with a power-sharing arrangement between Liberals and Conservatives for sixteen years. The arrangement did not work: political exclusion of groups outside these two political blocs, during the sixties and seventies, pushed individuals to join armed groups (the strongest being FARC-EL, ELN, EPL, and M-19). The political arrangements also had economic effects which fuelled the armed conflict with rural peoples being dispossessed of land or excluded from opportunities.[9] In the 1980s, paramilitary groups grew into self-defence armies to combat the guerrilla groups and guarantee landowners security and their properties.[10] In the same period, the illegal drug trade exploded and both far-left and far-right armed groups often exploited conflict with the government to make money through the sale of drugs.[11]

From the historical, structural point of view as well as the fundamental political and socio-economic disparities and lack of political will of elites, there is a clear link between these two periods of Colombian history. That was meant to change in the 1980s with the commencement of various peace processes which culminated in the passing of a new constitution for Colombia in 1991. A former armed group—the M-19—was transformed into a political movement. In 2002, the government initiated a peace process with the AUC, the formal organisation of the paramilitary groups, concluding the complete demobilisation thereof in 2006; and in 2012, it was the turn of the peace process instituted with the FARC which culminated in the signing of a peace agreement in 2016. For its implementation, transitory and transitional amendments have been incorporated into the Constitution of 1991. Finally, negotiations with the ELN were initiated in 2016 but they broke down after the armed group carried out a bomb attack at the beginning of 2019. Nowadays, the expansion of this guerrilla movement, together with the dissidents of the FARC, the heirs of the paramilitarism, and the multiple new criminal organisations, has led to the spread of fragmented violence across Colombia.[12] According to the Ombudsman's Office, between 2016 and 2022, 1,113 social leaders and human rights defenders have been murdered.[13]

[9] See AL Pérez, 'Tradiciones de resistencia y lucha: un análisis sobre el surgimiento y la permanencia de las guerrillas en Colombia' (2010) 70 Análisis Político 63–80.

[10] See JC Dugas, 'Paramilitaries and the Economic Origins of Armed Conflict in Colombia' (2012) 41 Latin American Research Review 205–13; W Tate, 'Paramilitaries in Colombia' (2001) VIII The Brown Journal of World Affairs 163–75.

[11] A Moreira, M Forero, and AM Parada, 'Conflicto en Colombia: antecedentes históricos y actores' (2015) in *Dossier proceso de paz en Colombia*<https://www.cidob.org/publicaciones/documentacion/dossiers/dossier_proceso_de_paz_en_colombia/dossier_proceso_de_paz_en_colombia> accessed 3 October 2022.

[12] JC Garzón Vergara, 'Las 10 dinámicas que marcarán la violencia organizada en 2021' *La Silla vacía* (30 January 2021) <https://lasillavacia.com/silla-llena/red-de-la-paz/las-10-dinamicas-marcaran-la-violencia-organizada-2021-77594> accessed 3 October 2022.

[13] Defensoría del pueblo, Comunicado 22 (23 January 2023) <https://defensoria.gov.co/-/el-2022-marc%C3%B3-un-lamentable-r%C3%A9cord-de-homicidios-a-l%C3%ADderes-sociales-y-personas-defensoras-de-derechos-humanos>> accessed 25 September 2023.

This brief history of Colombia[14] thus displays a more complex picture of Colombian constitutionalism since 1991, than is evident in the case of South Africa. The 1991 Constitution was a peace agreement that did not end all hostilities and, in a sense, it initiated a continuing process that has not yet reached completion. Clearly, the armed conflicts have been the cause of many of the historical injustices in Colombia. Yet, the origins of those conflicts have often not been examined and engaged in much detail in legal judgments (nor perhaps in public discourse more generally). Furthermore, no attempt was made in Colombia to implement a repugnant ideological system such as Nazism or apartheid. Colombia thus lacked a simple, ideological evil to which the Constitution was a reaction. There was instead a more complex array of factors which formed the background to its adoption. As a result, Uprimny and García have remarked that the 1991 Colombian Constitution became a legal document which was 'forward looking' and 'tends to project a model of the society to be built'.[15] The lack of a readily identifiable, grand narrative thus partially explains why courts in Colombia may find it more difficult to reference a clear, and relatively uncontested, historical narrative in their decisions.

B. A Difference in Goals: Social Transformation Versus Victim-Centred Reasoning

The differences in history also perhaps explain other social differences that exist and the approaches of the courts in this regard. In South Africa, all Black people were victims of the racist apartheid laws: almost all Black people in South Africa during apartheid received lower-quality education and a very limited number were able to go to university. In urban areas, Black people were consigned to poorly-serviced and overcrowded townships. These are just some of the examples of deliberate policies that consigned Black people to an economic underclass. As such, to correct these policies, there was the need to address the serious poverty of all Black South African people—the majority of the population—and not just a particular segment thereof. There were indeed individuals who suffered more than others and were the subject of particularly grave human rights violations which were dealt with through the Truth and Reconciliation Commission (TRC). Nevertheless, they were not the only victims. Indeed, one of the criticisms of the TRC was its focus only on these grave violations rather than the systemic negative effects of apartheid.[16]

[14] For a deeper understanding, see JA Robinson, 'La miseria en Colombia' (2016) 76 Revista Desarrollo y Sociedad, primer semestre 9–90.

[15] R Uprimny and M García Villegas, 'Corte Constitucional y emancipación social' in B de Sousa Santos and M García Villegas (eds), *Emancipación social y violencia en Colombia* (Norma 2004) 470.

[16] E Stanley, 'Evaluating the Truth and Reconciliation Commission' (2001) 39 The Journal of Modern African Studies 525, 530.

Consequently, in the socio-economic sphere, apartheid had generally privileged the White population over the Black population and, thereby, created serious harms to the relations between these two groups (and other racial minorities).[17] To address these historical wrongs of the past, the Constitutional Court essentially takes the view that it is not possible to adopt a wholly individualised approach. It does so in the context of transitional justice[18] but, also, arguably, in relation to its approach to socio-economic rights. As we saw in Bilchitz's chapter, its approach does not simply allow for a claim to succeed on the basis of an individual lacking a certain entitlement. Rather, the overall government programme needs to be challenged as being unreasonable. That allows for a consideration of the wider distributive effects of any decision. Moreover, as was seen in the analysis, the Court refuses simply to entrench existing private relations between persons and also prefers consensual remedies that are negotiated, perhaps thereby seeking to help heal the societal divisions that were created under apartheid.

In Colombia, matters are both similar and different. The harms of the armed conflicts in Colombia are not evenly distributed amongst the population and not all Colombians can be said to have suffered equally. Individuals in the large urban centres such as the capital Bogotá have suffered from an occasional terror attack and a reduction in personal safety. Yet, they have, in the main, been relatively unaffected. Rural populations in particular areas of the country have been much more significantly impacted upon. Indeed, millions have been displaced from their homes and there are specific groups which have suffered the worst effects. Farmers, Indigenous, and Afro-Colombian peoples, specifically, have been seriously affected and the conflict has also had particularly harmful effects on rural women and children. It is not surprising then that the Colombian Constitutional Court has adopted an approach that is focused particularly on the victims of the armed conflict. The Constitution, through the tutela action, enables an approach that is much more individualised in nature and allows particular people to claim remedies for their socio-economic deprivations. Recognising the limitations of this approach, the Constitutional Court has sought to group claims together, at times, to address the systemic problems that arise. The famous T-025 of 2004 case focused, for instance, on the victims of forced displacement as an entire population and the obligations on the government to improve their position. Correa's chapter highlights how the Court has extended the effects of the ruling to prevent the eviction of all victims of forced displacement from properties they were occupying.[19]

[17] Strictly speaking, there were complex tiers of privilege with White people being the most privileged, Indian South Africans also having some privileges, Coloured persons being lower down in the hierarchy, and Black people at the bottom.

[18] See *Azanian Peoples Organisation v The President of the Republic of South Africa* [1996] ZACC 16; 1996 (4) SA 672 (CC) ('*AZAPO*') [44]–[47].

[19] CCC ruling T-239 of 2013.

The disproportionate impact of the armed conflict on specific persons explains the reasoning and particular vulnerability of victims of forced displacement.

Having said that, Colombia is also a society that over the years of armed conflict has become extremely divided, with attitudes having hardened. There is often a failure to empathise between groups, thus demonstrating the need for a process of societal reconstruction. The Colombian Constitutional Court appears to recognise the need to address the socio-economic disparities in that process but its limited reference to historical injustice suggests an approach that is very much forward-looking rather than backward-looking. Ultimately, the Court is concerned to remedy the particular vulnerabilities of individuals in the present through establishing obligations upon the state. Improving individual living conditions appears to be its preferred route to societal healing. Whilst it has not adopted an absolutist view of property, it has not, until recently,[20] developed strong obligations on private (or public) actors to adopt processes of mediation when their rights clash, as the South African Constitutional Court has done. Its focus is on remedies to address the situation of victims without considering the full historical context. In contrast, the South African Constitutional Court recognises the need to engage with history directly: without doing so, it appears to be of the view that the mischiefs of the past and their effects on the relationships between individuals—and existing power disparities—cannot adequately be addressed.

C. A Different Attitude to the Value of History

That view of history leads us to another possible explanation for the differences between the courts which could be diverging perspectives on the *value* of history in addressing past injustice. We have noted above the major differences in the historical contexts between the two constitutions and jurisdictions. Nevertheless, there is a debate to be had about the role of history in informing the interpretation of rights in the present—this is a matter that can be examined against the backdrop of this comparison.

The South African Constitutional Court clearly is of the view that an express engagement with history is of importance in interpreting rights. In seeking to show how its approach responds to past injustice, the Court essentially seeks to heal some of the wounds of the past. Historical consciousness, it is hoped, can perhaps also help to avoid a repetition of some of the injustices of the past. At the same time, such an approach, arguably, keeps alive the memory of past injustice and could, to an extent, exacerbate tensions and divisions in a society that remains severely scarred by those very injustices. It also, arguably, roots the current interpretation

[20] See ruling T-523 of 2014 in Colombia which arguably was influenced by the South African doctrine of meaningful engagement.

of at least some socio-economic rights in a philosophy that seeks correction for past injustices rather than achieving a just distribution for all in the present and the future. Ideally, both need to be achieved but, there can be trade-offs between them. For instance, an approach that seeks to correct past socio-economic injustices would justifiably focus on improving the conditions of Black people who were the worst affected by the apartheid system. However, such an approach inevitably requires utilising and re-asserting the racial categorisations of the past. In turn, that can entrench those categories in society, inhibiting the ability to move towards a society that rejects such a system of racial organisation. This has been one of the criticisms of the Court's jurisprudence on affirmative action.[21]

The Constitutional Court itself has also recognised this tension in an important judgment on the rights of women. In the *Hugo* case, the Court had to deal with the charge of unfair discrimination against the president who had issued a pardon only for female prisoners who had children under the age of twelve. The majority found the discrimination in this case was not unfair: part of its reasoning involved recognising the relevance of the historical and current reality that 'mothers, as a matter of fact, bear more responsibilities for child-rearing in our society than do fathers'.[22] Justice Kriegler, in a strongly worded dissenting judgment, argued that this generalisation about women as the primary-caregivers of children 'is a root cause of women's inequality in society … [i]t is a relic and a feature of patriarchy which the Constitution so vehemently condemns'.[23] As such, he was concerned about the effect of perpetuating these historical stereotypes and 'perceptions foundational to patriarchal attitudes that limit the access of women to the workplace and other sources of opportunity'.[24]

In addition, the Court was also faced with the difficult question whether victims of gross human rights violations by the apartheid government should have been awarded the right to claim civil damages from the state.[25] In its judgment, the Court acknowledged the extensive nature of the class of victims in South Africa (all Black, Coloured, and Indian peoples).[26] However, the Court reasoned that recognising large claims to compensation from specific victims of serious human rights violations could hamper the society's ability to address the wider legacy of apartheid. Whilst recognising the history, the Court here adopts a more forward-looking approach focused on the achievement of wider distributive justice for a broad class of South Africans rather than on the correction of specific injustices that could undermine the broader economic reconstruction of the society.[27]

[21] M Brassey, 'The More Things Change … Multiracialism in Contemporary South Africa' (2019) 9 Constitutional Court Review 443, 468–69.
[22] *The President of the Republic of South Africa v Hugo* [1997] ZACC 4; 1997 (4) SA 1 (CC) [37].
[23] ibid [80].
[24] ibid [83].
[25] *AZAPO* (n 18) [39]–[48].
[26] ibid [43].
[27] ibid [44]–[46].

The Colombian Court, as we saw in Correa's chapter, really focuses on the present conditions of individuals as well as those with particular vulnerabilities. Its engagement with the history that led to the present situation is very limited; and its focus is upon addressing current severe economic desperation. Historical consciousness is much less present in the work of the Court: on the positive side, this allows the Court to focus on the universal content of these entitlements and what, ultimately, they are designed to guarantee to all Colombians. Its approach allows it to avoid being mired in controversies surrounding the origins and nature of the armed conflicts which have caused much of the misery in Colombia. The downside of this approach is precisely the fact that it lacks historicity: that, in itself, can lead to a failure to identify adequately the causes of current economic injustice. It may, on occasion, lead to a failure to recognise the economic harms that have perpetuated an unjust status quo, thus limiting the analysis to the effects of forced displacement and armed conflict without an adequate understanding of the deeper structural underlying causes of the current situation—without which it becomes more difficult to address.

Lastly, one of the major difficulties with this approach is that it takes a snapshot of the present but without any sense of the unjust human relations that brought it about. That, in turn, may lead to a failure to identify, acknowledge, and recognise some of the sources of conflict in the society and so make healing these divisions more difficult. For instance, a large number of urban Colombians who are relatively removed from the armed conflicts voted against the peace agreement between the government of Colombia and the FARC rebels largely based on the limited punishments included therein. Rural Colombians closest to the conflict who wished it to end as soon as possible voted in favour.[28] Urban Colombians, in some sense, failed to understand their own historical role in the conflict and adopted a more distanced perspective based on abstract punishment. A closer attention to history and the origins of the conflict could lead every Colombian to understand better their connection to the very issues that lead to economic desperation in the present. Indeed, a recognition of historical injustice is central to giving effect institutionally to transitional justice—whether by the courts through judgments relating to socio-economic rights or the political branches. The peace agreement does now contain specific facets that require dealing with the past and, as Correa notes, it is to be hoped that the Colombian Court will adopt a greater historical consciousness in its adjudication going forward.

[28] See Y Basset, 'Claves del rechazo del plebiscito para la paz en Colombia' (2018) 52 Estudios Políticos 241–65.

D. A Difference of Legal Culture and Judicial Role

South Africa and Colombia also have very different legal cultures with the former being a common law jurisdiction and the latter a civil law jurisdiction. South Africa, famously, has had a rather formal and proceduralist dimension to its legal culture. This was noted in the famous article by Karl Klare who argued that transformative constitutionalism requires a shift from a conservative, formalistic legal culture to one that was more explicit and transparent about the political dimensions of judicial decision-making.[29] Theunis Roux has challenged that view, arguing that transformative adjudication does not require the wholesale embrace of legal realism but could be accomplished by utilising Ronald Dworkin's interpretive approach and avoiding a complete elision of the law/politics divide.[30] Both theorists seem to agree about the need for more substance in legal reasoning.[31] Arguably, the historical consciousness evident in the Court's reasoning is utilised as an attempt to create an objective reference point that guides its interpretation of rights without requiring it to stray too much into the contested sphere of politics.[32]

That, however, is not adequate in itself to develop the substantive content of rights and many legal theorists have criticised the Court for its vague reasoning.[33] A similar critique has been made in the sphere of socio-economic rights where theorists express their disappointment with the failure of the Court to engage in any detail with the substantive content of these rights and the refuge its seeks in the ambiguous notion of 'reasonableness review'.[34] The approach to the right to housing described in Bilchitz's chapter can be said to reflect its jurisprudential approach: the Court has outlined rather vague substantive principles and preferred procedural mechanisms such as meaningful engagement for resolving conflicts. The Court has also addressed very few cases in comparison to Colombia. The reason for this appears to lie in the general inaccessibility of the courts to poorer individuals and the fact that there is no equivalent to the tutela action in South Africa.[35] The reasonableness approach of the Court renders it relatively difficult for individuals to construct a successful case as they need to challenge an entire

[29] Klare (n 8) 170–71.

[30] T Roux, 'Transformative Constitutionalism and the Best Interpretation of the South African Constitution: Distinction Without a Difference?' (2009) Stellenbosch Law Review 269.

[31] In T Roux, *The Politics of Principle* (2013), he demonstrates the usefulness of seeking refuge in the comfort of legal formalism, at times, to render decisions with major political implications and still build the Constitutional Court's institutional legitimacy.

[32] See De Vos (n 6) who challenges the Court's 'grand narrative' approach to history.

[33] See, for instance, A Cockrell, 'Rainbow Jurisprudence' (1996) 12 South African Journal on Human Rights 1; and S Woolman, 'The Amazing Vanishing Bill of Rights' (2007) 124 South African Law Journal 762.

[34] See D Bilchitz, *Poverty and Fundamental Rights* (2007) ch 5 and S Liebenberg, *Socio-Economic Rights: Adjudication under a Transformative Constitution* (Juta 2010) 173–86.

[35] On the lack of access to justice in South Africa and how to address it, see D Bilchitz, 'Socio-economic Rights and Expanding Access to Justice in South Africa: What Can Be Done?' in P Dann, M Riegner, and M Bönnemann (eds), *The Global South and Comparative Constitutional Law* (OUP 2020).

government programme rather than focus on their individual plight alone. For this reason, the Constitutional Court has seen a relatively small number of cases on socio-economic rights and only adjudicates complex, systemic issues that reach it. Its jurisprudence suggests a more cautious and restrained understanding of its role in the society.

In Colombia, there is also an inherited formalism from the European traditions of civil law and judgments tend to be written in a rather formulaic manner. The Constitutional Court has, however, interpreted its mandate in a substantive manner: namely, to ensure justice is served to those who are most vulnerable. The tutela action in article 86 of the Constitution places an express mandate on judges and tribunals in this regard and this has led to justice being highly accessible to individuals.[36] The action itself places the focus on rendering justice to specific individuals and so addressing concrete conditions. That has resulted in the Court having to engage with thousands of cases per year.[37] That individualised focus has, in some sense, led the Court to address the recurring problems it sees in individual cases through a wider, more systemic approach which has developed into the doctrine of the 'unconstitutional state of affairs'. The very development of that doctrine suggests a willingness of the Court to engage with the substantive injustices in Colombian society and to seek their resolution without forgetting the circumstances of individuals. The Court has also sought to outline and develop a clearer idea of the minimum standards that must be met by the government in relation to socio-economic rights.

Moreover, the Court has, importantly, not reasoned in an overtly political way: it has maintained strongly the law/politics distinction.[38] Yet, it has been willing, at times, to hold public hearings with politicians and economists to draw in wider expertise and perform a relatively political function of hearing diverse societal groups and voices in the formation of its judgments.[39] Its assumption of that role has also been necessitated by the crisis of other democratic institutions

[36] In this regard, between 1992 and August 2023, the judges have decided a total of 9,552,540 tutelas. See Estadísticas Corte Constitucional <https://www.corteconstitucional.gov.co/lacorte/estadisticas.php> accessed 25 September 2023.

[37] Indeed, between 1992 and August 2023, the Constitutional Court has reviewed 20,709 of them. See ibid.

[38] There are, however, some scholars and many politicians who consider that the Court has taken too activist a role, effectively becoming a form of legislator. See, eg, NJ Restrepo, 'La judicialización de la política: El papel de la corte constitucional en Colombia' (2014) 6 Forum: Revista Departamento de Ciencia Política 37–50.

[39] To mention some examples: CCC, ruling C-252 of 2019 which related to the constitutional analysis of the investment agreement between Colombia and France. There was a public hearing on 13 December 2018, with the participation of academics, as well as the private sector, public institutions, and non-profit organisations; CCC, ruling SU 214/2016 which dealt with same-sex couples' cases relating to legalising their bond. A public hearing on 21 May 2015 took place with the participation of registral authorities and experts for and against the civil marriage of same-sex couples; CCC, C-700/1999 dealt with the law which adjusted the system for calculating the value of the Constant Purchasing Power Unit, UPAC used for housing credits. A public hearing on 27 July 1999 took place with the participation of autonomous institutions, ministries, representatives, financial corporations, and citizens.

in the society. The Colombian Court has been prepared to step in when the other branches have shirked their responsibilities to the most vulnerable and failed to show the leadership necessary in addressing crises relating to housing, health care, and forced displacement. The Court's willingness to do individual justice as well as to stand above the political fray on grounds of defending justice both for the present and the future has granted it a high degree of legitimacy.[40] Consequently, in comparison to the South African Constitutional Court, we can see the Colombian Court assuming the mantle of leadership and playing a more active, substantive, and forward-looking role in the political community of the country.

3. Conclusion: Remedying Historical Injustice and Distributive Justice for All

We have placed a very specific lens on the socio-economic rights jurisprudence in South Africa and Colombia. It is a lens that raises questions about the relationship between corrective and distributive justice; it also demonstrates the past historical injustices that both societies have experienced and its effect on current distributions. Nevertheless, it uncovers a fairly strong and interesting difference in the approach of the South African and Colombian Constitutional Courts towards referencing the historical backdrop to current socio-economic injustices.

This comparative reflection has engaged with some of the factors that may explain that difference. Those factors are of interest in deepening our understanding of both societies, sharpening the differences between them and identifying the respects in which they are similar and can learn from one another. There are clearly important imperatives in both societies to address past injustice and to ensure that every individual has the resources necessary to live a decent life in the present. Connecting the two requires judgement and insight.

Our analysis has engaged both the normative and descriptive—yet, we have not sought, ultimately, to make specific prescriptions but rather to understand the benefits and disadvantages of the different approaches. We hope that such a comparison helps to illuminate an important aspect of the two courts' jurisprudence and, in so doing, contributes to a wider discussion of the role history should play in strengthening democratic constitutionalism and distributive justice both in South Africa and Colombia.

40 See R Uprimny Yepes and M Villegas García, 'Justicia y Democracia' in M Garcia Villegas and MA Ceballos Bedoya (eds), *Democracia, justicia y Sociedad: Diez años de investigación en Dejusticia* (Centro de Estudios de Derecho, Justicia y Sociedad, Dejusticia 2016) 60–83; CA Rodríguez, M García Villegas, and R Uprimny, 'Justice and Society in Colombia: A Sociolegal Analysis of Colombian Courts' in LM Friedman and R Pérez-Perdomo (eds), *Legal Culture in the Age of Globalization* (Stanford University Press 2003).

THEME 5

COLLECTIVE MECHANISMS FOR THE ADVANCEMENT OF SOCIO-ECONOMIC RIGHTS

14

Class Actions and the Scarce Resource of the Law

Meghan Finn[*]

1. Introduction

Section 38(c) of South Africa's Constitution provides that 'anyone acting as a member of, or in the interest of, a group or class of persons' has 'the right to approach a competent court, alleging that a right in the Bill of Rights has been infringed or threatened, and the court may grant appropriate relief, including a declaration of rights'. Class action litigation enables one person, or a group of persons, to bring an action in the interests of a class of persons who all have the same, or similar, causes of action.

For this reason, class actions are an especially apt form of litigation in a society where both the government and private corporations exercise extensive power which can be wielded in ways that cause similar harm to large groups of people. Class action suits can be an important tool in enforcing rights against large corporations and holding them accountable. This is in part because of the extensive economic and legal resources that such entities can deploy in litigation brought against them, which may otherwise scupper litigation brought on an individual, rather than aggregate, basis.[1] All too frequently, those who have suffered loss cannot pursue their claims individually, not least because doing so is enormously expensive, and because sometimes each individual claim is not large enough to warrant litigation on its own. The class action device remedies this: individual interests can be protected by aggregating claims, and by pursuing these claims through the representative(s) acting on behalf of the class. Class actions thus can provide effective access to justice to small claimants in cases of mass injury.[2]

[*] This chapter reflects the law as it was in late 2022.

[1] S Abdool Karim and P Kruger, 'Unsavoury: How Effective Are Class Actions in the Protection and Vindication of the Right to Access to Food in South Africa' (2021) 37 South African Journal on Human Rights 59, 69–70; J Brickhill, 'A River of Disease: Silicosis and the Future of Class Actions in South Africa' (2021) 37 South African Journal on Human Rights 31.

[2] *Trustees for the time being of Children's Resource Centre Trust v Pioneer Food (Pty) Ltd* [2012] ZASCA 182; 2013 (2) SA 213 (SCA) ('*Children's Resource Centre*') [19].

Meghan Finn, *Class Actions and the Scarce Resource of the Law* In: *Transitional Justice, Distributive Justice, and Transformative Constitutionalism.* Edited by: David Bilchitz and Raisa Cachalia, with Magdalena Inés Correa Henao and Nathalia Bautista Pizarro, Oxford University Press. © Meghan Finn 2023. DOI: 10.1093/oso/9780192887627.003.0014

This is significant in South Africa's legal context for at least two reasons: first, class actions can further distributive justice as they constitute an additional tool for shifting the pattern of distribution of social goods (including, as some commentators have observed, access to courts). Second, class actions can be important in the context of transitional justice, and the imperative of addressing historic wrongs. The wrongs of South Africa's colonial and apartheid past were not purely individual. Instead, many were collective and so require collective redress.

In Section 2 of this chapter, I discuss the evolution of rules of standing in South African law, tracing how the Constitution enables litigation through class action. I then provide an overview of class action suits thus far, noting that in South Africa's legal system, although class action litigation is in its 'adolescence',[3] recent years have seen a proliferation of this litigation. In Section 3, drawing especially on Moshikaro's insights,[4] I argue that class action litigation serves important distributive justice ends. This is in part because class actions enable access to courts, thereby ensuring a more equitable distribution of legal representation. In this way, class action suits in themselves are constitutive of an element of distributive justice, with the courts themselves as the good that is distributed. In Section 4, I demonstrate that class actions can be used instrumentally to serve distributive justice goals, in that they provide a procedural mechanism that enables the vindication of a bundle of socio-economic rights. Finally and against the backdrop of transitional justice, Section 5 canvasses how class actions can and have been used to address historic wrongs, drawing on the recent silicosis litigation in *Nkala v Harmony Gold Mining Co Ltd*.[5]

2. An Overview of Class Actions in South Africa

A. Constitution, Standing, and Procedure

During colonial and apartheid legal regimes, South African courts approached the question of standing restrictively.[6] As a general rule, any claimant who could not establish a direct personal interest in the case would lack *locus standi* to bring litigation.[7] This was underpinned by an individualised conception of standing,[8] and

[3] T Broodryk, 'Review: Class Action Litigation in South Africa' (2018) 223 Tydskrif vir die Suid-Afrikaanse Reg 223.

[4] K Moshikaro, 'Against the Interests of Justice: Ignoring the Role for Distributive Justice when Regulating Court Process' (2015) 7 Constitutional Court Review 291.

[5] [2016] ZAGPJHC 97; 2016 (5) SA 240 (GJ) ('*Nkala*').

[6] C Loots, 'Standing, Ripeness and Mootness' in S Woolman and others (eds), *Constitutional Law of South Africa* (2nd edn, Juta 2013) 7-2.

[7] *Patz v Greene & Co* 1907 TS 427, 433–35; *Cabinet for the Transitional Government for the Territory of South West Africa v Eins* 1988 (3) SA 369 (A) 389I. See, however, *Wood v Ondagwa Tribal Authority* 1975 (2) SA 294 (A) as a pre-constitutional exception to the ordinary approach, and T Ngcukaitobi, 'The Evolution of Standing Rules in South Africa and their Significance to Promoting Social Justice' (2002) 18 South African Journal on Human Rights 4.

[8] Ngcukaitobi (n 7).

effectively restricted access to courts and avoided judicial determinations of public importance.[9]

South Africa's Interim and 1996 Constitution fundamentally altered this. The Constitutional Court has repeatedly held that courts must adopt a 'broad' and 'generous' approach to standing.[10] As Chaskalson P noted in an early judgment of the Constitutional Court:

> I can see no good reason for adopting a narrow approach to the issue of standing in constitutional cases. On the contrary, it is my view that we should rather adopt a broad approach to standing. This would be consistent with the mandate given to this Court to uphold the Constitution and would serve to ensure that constitutional rights enjoy the full measure of the protection to which they are entitled.[11]

Expansive standing is normatively valuable, then, particularly 'in our country where we have a large number of people who have had scant educational opportunities and who may not be aware of their rights'.[12] Echoing this, section 38 of the Constitution provides:

> Anyone listed in this section has the right to approach a competent court, alleging that a right in the Bill of Rights has been infringed or threatened, and the court may grant appropriate relief, including a declaration of rights. The persons who may approach a court are—
> (a) anyone acting in their own interest;
> (b) anyone acting on behalf of another person who cannot act in their own name;
> (c) anyone acting as a member of, or in the interest of, a group or class of persons;
> (d) anyone acting in the public interest; and
> (e) an association acting in the interest of its members.

Section 38(c) of the Constitution thus expressly allows for the possibility of class action litigation. However, while South Africa's Constitution envisages such actions, there is no distinct legislative procedural framework governing class actions.[13] This is notwithstanding an early recommendation from the South African Law Commission that both legislation and court rules be enacted.[14] As Phooko

[9] C Loots, 'Keeping *Locus Standi* in Chains' (1987) South African Journal on Human Rights 66.

[10] See, eg, *Ferreira v Levin NO; Vryenhoek v Powell NO* [1995] ZACC 13; 1996 (1) SA 984 (CC) ('*Ferreira v Levin*') [165] (Chaskalson P for the majority) and [229] (O'Regan J concurring); *Giant Concerts CC v Rinaldo Investments (Pty) Ltd* [2012] ZACC 28; 2013 (3) BCLR 251 (CC) [39].

[11] *Ferreira v Levin* (n 10) [165].

[12] *Kruger v President of the Republic of South Africa* [2008] ZACC 17; 2009 (1) SA 417 (CC) [23].

[13] M Phooko, 'The Development of Class Actions In South Africa: Where Are We through Case Law?' (2021) 37 South African Journal on Human Rights 7.

[14] South African Law Commission, *The Recognition of a Class Action in South African Law* Working Paper 57 (1995).

notes, this legislative lacuna is unfortunate as litigants would benefit from accessible and clear regulation of class actions.[15]

The development of class actions has therefore been exclusively judicial in character. In addition to section 38(c), section 173 of the Constitution provides that courts have 'the inherent power to protect and regulate their own process, and to develop the common law, taking into account the interests of justice'. Drawing on these inherent powers (as well as the remedial discretion conferred by section 172(1)(b) of the Constitution to make any order that is 'just and equitable'), courts have fashioned a procedure for class action litigation in a series of groundbreaking judgments.[16]

B. How Class Actions Operate in South Africa

Put crisply, a class action enables one person or a group of persons to bring an action in the interests of a class of persons who all have the same, or similar, causes of actions.[17] Initially, class actions developed in South Africa on the basis of Bill of Rights violations.

The judgment of the Supreme Court of Appeal in *Ngxuza*[18] was pivotal in recognising the availability of class actions to assert constitutional rights. The government of the Eastern Cape terminated the social grants of a large number of beneficiaries without notice, without reasons and without affording the beneficiaries any rights to be heard. Building on Froneman J's judgment *a quo*, Cameron JA's judgment in the Supreme Court of Appeal resoundingly found that class actions are crucial mechanisms in constitutional litigation:

> [I]t is precisely because so many in our country are in a poor position to seek legal redress, and because the technicalities of legal procedure, including joinder, may unduly complicate the attainment of justice that both the interim Constitution and the Constitution created the express entitlement that 'anyone' asserting a right in the Bill of Rights could litigate 'as a member of, or in the interests of, a group or class of persons'.[19]

However, because section 38(c) of the Constitution establishes class action standing for an infringement or threat to constitutional rights, for a period it was unclear whether class actions could also be employed to assert common law rights.[20] The

[15] Phooko (n 13).

[16] *Permanent Secretary, Department of Welfare, Eastern Cape v Ngxuza* [2001] ZASCA 85; 2001 (4) SA 1184 (SCA) ('*Ngxuza*'); *Children's Resource Centre* (n 2); *Mukaddam v Pioneer Foods (Pty) Ltd* [2013] ZACC 23; 2013 (5) SA 89 (CC) ('*Mukkadam*'); *Nkala* (n 5).

[17] *Children's Resource Centre* (n 2) [16].

[18] *Ngxuza* (n 16).

[19] ibid [6].

[20] Phooko (n 13) 9.

position was clarified by the Supreme Court of Appeal and the Constitutional Court respectively in *Children's Resource Centre* and *Mukaddam*, which 'represent a watershed moment in relation to South African civil redress'.[21] Bread producers in the Western Cape were guilty of anti-competitive conduct, which drove up the pricing of bread—a staple for South Africans. This had deleterious effects on the right to access to food,[22] and most severely impacted low-income households. A range of non-governmental organisations (NGOs), the largest trade union federation in the country, and five individuals instituted a class action against the bread producers. Wallis JA for the Supreme Court of Appeal developed the common law to find that class actions are available outside the realm of constitutional litigation, and 'are equally useful in the context of mass personal injury cases of consumer litigation'.[23]

(i) Certification

Procedurally, the Supreme Court of Appeal found that the class representatives needed to obtain a court's certification that the matter could be litigated by way of a class action. In effect, certification is a threshold enquiry, requiring a court 'to sanction the use of the class action mechanism before parties and courts become embroiled in matters not suited to be litigated on a class basis'.[24] The second stage of the class action is the assessment of the merits, and whether the defendant ought to be held liable.

In *Children's Resource Centre*, the Supreme Court of Appeal established a number of factors that a court is required to consider when determining whether to certify. These are:[25]

(1) the existence of an identifiable class to be determined by objective criteria;
(2) a cause of action raising a triable issue (that is, a *prima facie* case);
(3) commonality, in that the right to relief depends upon the determination of issues of fact, or law, or both, common to all members of the class;
(4) that the relief sought, or damages claimed, are ascertainable and can be determined;
(5) that any damages can be allocated appropriately to the members of the class;
(6) that the proposed representative of the class is suitable; and
(7) whether a class action is the most appropriate means of determining the claim.

[21] M Du Plessis, 'Class Action Litigation in South Africa' in M Du Plessis and others (eds), *Class Action Litigation in South Africa* (Juta 2017) 6.
[22] Abdool Karim and Kruger (n 1).
[23] *Children's Resource Centre* (n 2) [21].
[24] G Jephson and O Mngomezulu, 'Constitutional Litigation Procedure' in J Brickhill (ed), *Public Interest Litigation in South Africa* (Juta 2018) 142.
[25] *Children's Resource Centre* (n 2) [26].

A year after *Children's Resource Centre*, the Constitutional Court determined whether distributors (rather than consumers) of bread could certify a class action, relating to the same price-fixing conduct of bread producers. Jafta J's majority judgment differed from the Supreme Court of Appeal, in that he found that the factors set out by Wallis JA must not be treated as necessary conditions for certification. Instead, an all-things-considered, overarching enquiry into the 'interests of justice' is to be determinative. As I explain in Section 3B, the approach ultimately endorsed by the Constitutional Court has been stringently criticised.

In *Mukkadam*, the Constitutional Court was split on whether certification of the class is required in every instance or whether, instead, certification is dependent both on the nature of the claim and on the nature of the defendant. The South African Constitution envisages that rights can bind the state as well as private persons, in certain instances. The majority found that class actions on the basis of Bill of Rights claims against the *state* do not require certification, leaving it open whether Bill of Rights claims against *private persons* do. This is puzzling—there is no clear reason to make the applicable process turn on the nature of the duty-bearer. Mhlantla AJ's dissent in the Constitutional Court is to be preferred—she would have found that certification ought to apply in all circumstances (no matter the identity of the defendant), not least because this protects the interests of members of the class whose rights would otherwise be extinguished by a class action. As others have pointed out, this approach is both principled and practical.[26]

At first blush, the requirement of certification may seem to complicate and delay the determination of the dispute, and so impede access to justice. Jephson notes that prior certification limits the right of access to courts, but that the limitation is reasonable and justifiable on the basis that it balances the right with the imperatives of judicial economy and of preventing misuse of the procedure.[27] Brickhill argues that although certification adds a layer of proceedings to class actions, it ultimately (if counterintuitively) promotes access to justice because it avoids preliminary skirmishes, and provides active participation of class members, including in allowing for members to opt into or out of the litigation.[28]

Following certification, the class can proceed on either an opt-in or an opt-out basis. An opt-in class action is a class action in terms of which claimants can choose, on an individual basis, whether to join the class.[29] Unless claimants expressly opt

[26] N Ally and A Konstant, 'Difficulties in Regulating Class Action Litigation: Is There a Need to Articulate the Rules?' (2014) De Rebus 35. See, however, *Council for the Advancement of the South African Constitution v Ingonyama Trust* [2021] ZAKZPHC 42; 2022 (1) SA 251 (KZP) [70]–[71].

[27] G Jephson, 'Does Prior Certification Advance Access to Justice?' (2021) 37 South African Journal on Human Rights 83.

[28] Brickhill, 'A River of Disease' (n 1).

[29] *Mukaddam* (n 16) [23].

in, they are not bound by the outcome of the litigation. Conversely, opt-out class actions automatically include potential claimants within the ambit of the class, allowing for the possibility that individual claimants may choose not to be members. Our courts have recognised the possibility of a class action being conducted in dual opt-out/opt-in stages.[30]

As a procedural device, then, a class action enables a party to initiate a claim against a wrongdoer as a representative on behalf of a larger group of people whose rights have also, or similarly, been infringed by the wrongdoer, without having to join all the members of the group. A court must be satisfied that a class action is the appropriate procedure to determine the matter. Once it is, the court can allow the litigation to proceed on that basis, and the court's decision on the merits does not only benefit, but also binds all the members of the class.[31] While other jurisdictions require that the representative bringing the suit is herself a member of the class, South African law does not include this as a necessary requirement.[32]

(ii) Judicial oversight

Generally, certified class actions in South Africa tend not to proceed past the first stage of certification to trial (the second stage of litigation).[33] Instead, the action is typically settled out of court. In practice, this means that class actions have been certified, but once this initial procedural hurdle is passed no class action has gone beyond this step. Settlements have the invaluable benefit of resolving the dispute and affording relief or compensation to plaintiffs without having to pursue lengthy (and expensive) trial processes to completion. However, settlements may give rise to other concerns.[34] Settlement negotiations can raise potential tensions between representatives (who may have a seat at the negotiating table) and broader members of the class. Further, when a matter is settled out of court its precedential effect is limited, for a court has not had the opportunity to determine the test case or to develop the law for future cases. For this reason, there can be a tension assisting clients, and pursuing broader strategic objectives.[35] Courts exercise discretion over whether a class is to be certified, and act as a controlling mechanism in this regard. More generally, it can be anticipated that the courts will have to take on an active

[30] *Nkala* (n 5).

[31] R Mulheron, *The Class Action in Common Law Systems: A Comparative Perspective* (Hart Publishing 2004) 3; *Children's Resource Centre* (n 2) [16].

[32] See, eg, *Minister of Health and Welfare v Woodcarb (Pty) Ltd* 1996 (3) SA 155 (N).

[33] However, see discussion by T Broodryk, 'An Empirical Analysis of Class Actions in South Africa' (2020) 24 Law, Democracy and Development 54. At the time of writing, a trial date has not yet been set for the listeriosis class action (discussed in n 46), which may proceed past certification although it is possible that the matter will be settled in advance of any trial.

[34] O Fiss, 'Against Settlement' (1984) 93 Yale Law Journal 1073.

[35] J Brickhill and M Finn, 'Ethics and Politics of Public Interest Litigation' in J Brickhill (ed), *Public Interest Litigation in South Africa* (Juta 2018).

role in managing class action processes beyond certification;[36] or, as in the class action recently brought to vindicate consumer claims against credit-providers accused of fraud, by way of appointing a judicial manager.

Indeed, courts can also opt to exercise ongoing judicial oversight over class action settlements. The largest class action instituted in South Africa's constitutional history (and indeed, one of the most complex multi-defendant and multi-class cases internationally)[37] is the silicosis claim brought by affected mineworkers in *Nkala v Harmony Gold Mining Co Ltd*.[38] In *Nkala* after the class was certified,[39] but before the matter proceeded to trial stage, the parties entered into settlement negotiations. The High Court had previously found any settlement agreement that came about as a result of these negotiations would need to be approved by the Court. This was partially on the basis that the Contingency Fees Act 66 of 1997 applied: in terms of that legislation, lawyers representing litigants can conclude agreements with their clients to litigate at their own risk, but then be paid up to 25 per cent of any amount awarded to the client. Such agreements are subject to the court's scrutiny, and must be disclosed. Of course, it will not always be the case that legal representation in class action occurs on a contingency fee basis. In addition, even in the absence of a contingency fee agreement a court may opt to exercise supervisory jurisdiction over any settlement agreement on the basis that '[t]he effect of a settlement of the claims of individual litigants may have the effect of thwarting precedent-setting litigation'.[40]

In the context of class actions, the prospect of settlement can affect not just whether precedent is established generally but, more worryingly, can give rise to a tension between the individual class representatives and the broader class (because there may be significant differences in opinions as to whether settlement should take place, and in some instances insufficient transparency as to who benefits from the settlement agreement). To mitigate this worry, the High Court in *Nkala* held that any settlement agreement after certification had been granted must also be approved by the certifying court to ensure that the settlement is 'fair, reasonable, adequate and that it protects the interests of the class'.[41] The High Court subsequently approved of the procedure to govern the settlement that had been reached by class representatives and certain of the defendant mining companies (with a return date for the final step of making the settlement agreement an order of court).[42]

[36] In *Stellenbosch University Law Clinic v Lifestyle Direct Group International (Pty) Ltd* [2021] ZAWCHC 133; 2022 (2) SA 237 (WCC), the High Court appointed a special master/judicial manager to oversee the class action.

[37] Brickhill, 'A River of Disease' (n 1) 31.

[38] *Nkala* (n 5).

[39] T Broodryk, 'Inappropriately Assessing Appropriateness of Class Proceedings: *Nkala v Harmony Gold Mining Company Ltd*' (2021) 37 South African Journal on Human Rights 21 takes a critical approach to the court's reasoning on certification, arguing that although the court was ultimately correct to certify the action, its failure to consider the appropriateness of the proceedings is unfortunate.

[40] Brickhill and Finn (n 35) 118.

[41] *Nkala* (n 16) [39].

[42] *Ex Parte Nkala* [2018] ZAGPJHC 657.

In July 2019, the High Court approved the historic R5 billion settlement agreement, noting that the applicable test is whether the settlement is 'fair, reasonable, adequate and that it protects the interests of the class'.[43] A trust was set up to make payments to the members of the settlement class, and the mining companies were also ordered to pay the substantial fees of the law firms who represented the class members. Following the approval of the settlement agreement, class members were again afforded an opportunity to opt out of the agreement.[44]

C. Recent Developments in Class Action Litigation

In recent years, there has been a proliferation of class action suits being launched as well as emerging scholarship on class actions.[45] Significant litigation includes the class action suit brought on behalf of those who lost family members or were sickened by a listeria outbreak;[46] a class action launched for compensation on the basis that unconscionable contractual agreements defrauded thousands of consumers;[47] and the class action brought by shareholders affected by the Steinhoff financial fraud saga (which was unsuccessful, as the High Court refused certification).[48]

Class action litigation can also be used to assert equality- and anti-discrimination-based claims. Christoffels-Du Plessis argues that the Promotion of Equality and Prevention of Unfair Discrimination Act 4 of 2000 enables a class of persons to approach the Equality Court, as was the case in litigation in the early 2000s by a group of small-scale fishers and non-governmental organisers against the Minister of Environmental Affairs and Tourism, on the basis that the failure to allocate artisanal fishing rights undermined the right to equality.[49] More recently a suit launched in the Equality Court by thousands of clients contending that they have been subject to unfair discrimination, principally on the grounds of race, by a number of banks.[50] Going forward and consistent with precedent in

[43] *Ex Parte Nkala* [2019] ZAGPJHC 260 [17].

[44] See Brickhill, 'A River of Disease' (n 1) for a detailed discussion of the litigation, settlement, and its ramifications for class actions (and other litigation in the public interest) in South Africa more generally.

[45] Broodryk (n 33) 54; J Handmaker, 'Introduction to Special Issue: Class Action Litigation in South Africa' (2021) 37 South African Journal on Human Rights 1 and the series of articles published in a special issue of the *South African Journal on Human Rights*, discussed at various points in this chapter.

[46] *Tiger Brands Limited v Pillay* [2020] ZAGPJHC 160.

[47] *Stellenbosch University Law Clinic* (n 36).

[48] Order of the High Court in the matter between *Monthla Welhemina Ngobeni v Tiger Brands Limited* Case no: 2018/12835—no judgment was handed down.

[49] *George v Minister of Environmental Affairs and Tourism v George* 2005 (6) SA 297 (EqC); A Christoffels-Du Plessis, '"Fishers' Rights Are Human Rights": *George v Minister of Environmental Affairs and Tourism* 2005 (6) SA 297' (2021) 37 South African Journal on Human Rights 126.

[50] *De Bruyn v Steinhoff International Holdings NV* [2020] ZAGPJHC 145; 2022 (1) SA 442 (GJ). Although the certification of the class action in South Africa was refused, as a result of multi-jurisdictional litigation the company has subsequently agreed to payouts to shareholders internationally in a settlement offer of over $1.5 billion: (Reuters 15 February 2022) <https://www.reuters.com/

other jurisdictions, one possible frontier for development is class action litigation brought to address the manifold devastations of climate change, although Schuster cautions that more straightforward action brought in the public interest may be more apposite (and less procedurally complex) for strategic climate change litigation.[51] I now turn to consider the distributive dimensions of class action litigation.

3. Class Action and Distributive Justice: Access to Courts

Achieving distributive justice entails questioning and reconfiguring the patterns and structures—politically, socially, and economically—that determine the distribution of benefits and burdens in societies. This is a particularly important task for South Africa's democratic dispensation, which continues to be characterised by gaping inequalities that are the legacies of colonial, apartheid, and patriarchal oppression.

A. Reconfiguring the Distribution of Access to Courts

The first and most apparent way in which class actions serve distributive justice is by reconfiguring the distribution of access to courts. Access to justice is one societal good that is inequitably distributed in South Africa: whether a potential litigant is able to pursue a claim is highly contingent on financial and social capital. Cameron JA observed in *Ngxuza*, the watershed judgment on Bill of Rights class action:

> The law is a scarce resource in South Africa. This case shows that justice is even harder to come by. It concerns the ways in which the poorest in our country are to be permitted access to both ... The procedure has particular utility where a large group of plaintiffs each has a small claim that may be difficult or impossible to pursue individually.[52]

Class actions, then, enable litigants who would be unable or unlikely to obtain legal redress (for a variety of reasons that can range from poverty to geographical remoteness to the limiting fact that individual claims may be small to the exorbitant costs of litigation) to assert their rights.[53] Geographic determinants of access to

article/steinhoff-intln-settlement/south-africas-steinhoff-starts-payouts-in-1-62-billion-settlement-idUSKBN2KK20L> accessed 3 October 2022.

[51] E Schuster, 'Class Actions in a Changing Climate' (2021) 37 South African Journal on Human Rights 102.

[52] *Ngxuza* (n 16) [1].

[53] ibid [11]–[12]:

courts cannot be overstated. Accessing any form of legal representation is extraordinarily difficult in rural and remote areas.[54] Class actions ameliorate some of these difficulties in very obvious ways—certification can occur without individual members of the class having to be identified, and opt-out class actions allow for benefits to be widely spread without imposing the burden on litigants to seek out legal representation directly.

As Brickhill and Bleazard note, this has the additional benefit of 'promot[ing] judicial economy, maximising the use of the court's limited resources'.[55] Class actions therefore are a partial attempt to achieve a pro-poor procedure.[56] Moshikaro cogently argues that class actions instantiate distributive justice in a fundamental manner: by allowing access to the limited resource that is the justice system.[57] Class actions enable claimants who would otherwise not be able to litigate—because of the exorbitant costs of doing so, and because of insufficient access to legal representation—to seek justice.

This is vividly characterised in one of the earliest class action judgments in South Africa, *Ngxuza*. As was mentioned, welfare authorities in the Eastern Cape cancelled tens of thousands of social grants, without providing reasons or the beneficiaries with any opportunity to be heard. This had devastating effects for the beneficiaries, many of whom were reliant on grants as their sole form of income and only means for staving off the harshest impacts of extreme poverty. Froneman J, in the High Court, found that this clearly infringed the right to administrative action in section 33 of the Constitution, and that a class action brought in terms of section 38(c) was available. On appeal, a unanimous judgment of the Supreme Court of Appeal by Cameron JA castigated the governmental entities for seeking to avoid accountability by raising a slew of procedural and technical points in opposition. Instead, the beneficiaries' rights to institute class action proceedings was 'unassailable',[58] not least because class actions—unlike unwieldly procedures such as joinder—better facilitate legal redress.[59]

> [T]he situation seemed pattern-made for class proceedings. The class the applicants represent is drawn from the very poorest within our society—those in need of statutory social assistance. They also have the least chance of vindicating their rights through the legal process. Their individual claims are small: the value of the social assistance they receive—a few hundred rands every month—would secure them hardly a single hour's consultation at current rates with most urban lawyers. They are scattered throughout the Eastern Cape Province, many of them in small towns and remote rural areas.

[54] *Nkala* (n 5) [103]–[104].

[55] J Brickhill and J Bleazard, 'Chapter 4: Bill of Rights Class Actions' in Du Plessis (n 13) 61.

[56] For a criticism of the Constitutional Court's procedures in this regard, see J Dugard, 'Court of First Instance? Towards a Pro-Poor Jurisdiction for the South African Constitutional Court' (2006) 22 South African Journal on Human Rights 261.

[57] Moshikaro (n 4).

[58] *Ngxuza* (n 16) [14]–[15].

[59] ibid [4].

B. Distributive Justice and Duties of the Courts

That class action litigation can have these profound political and distributional effects places important legal and moral demands on the courts. For this reason, commentators have criticised the Constitutional Court for failing to provide clear procedural guidelines for certification.[60] Without this clarity, future litigants are left uncertain as to how to proceed when certifying a class action. In *Mukaddam*, the Constitutional Court backpedalled from the position established by the Supreme Court of Appeal in *Children's Resource Centre* which had established clear factors, necessary to be established in order for a court to certify a class action. The Constitutional Court disagreed, instead resorting to an all-things-considered value judgment with the 'interests of justice' as the ultimate test. Ally and Konstant, too, point out that relying on this malleable standard has drawbacks: 'it is a principle that is inherently nebulous',[61] and criticise the Constitutional Court's approach in *Mukkadam* for having rendered the factors set out by the Supreme Court of Appeal opaque.

In an area of litigation that can already be complex and uncertain, the Constitutional Court's stance does potential claimants no favours. Relying simply on a broad, value-laden enquiry into 'the interests of justice' undermines the rule of law's imperative of predictability and certainty. It leaves claimants, seeking to use the mechanism of a class action to vindicate their rights, to the whims of a particular judge. Moreover, the worry that a clearer test would prevent a class from being certified is easily answered: the test need not be overly rigid or impose restrictive factors, as *Children's Resource Centre* itself demonstrates.

While it is welcome that courts have developed procedural rules to fulfil access to justice and facilitate claimants' ability to vindicate their distributive entitlements, this does not mean an unprincipled, open-ended approach is warranted. Under the guise of instituting an open-ended, value-laden enquiry, the Constitutional Court has in fact made it more difficult for prospective claimants to anticipate how to formulate their case in advance of litigation—and this inhibits, rather than advances, access to justice.

C. Access to Courts and Participatory Democracy

Access to courts is valuable not simply in enabling litigants to assert their claims but also because it expands political enfranchisement. Rooney compellingly argues that expanded class action has the potential of achieving another constitutional

[60] Moshikaro (n 4); Ally and Konstant (n 26); Phooko (n 13).
[61] Ally and Konstant (n 26).

objective: promoting participatory democracy.[62] First, it facilitates engagement on a range of concerns that affect individuals who, by virtue of socio-economic disempowerment, may not otherwise have their concerns represented through democratic processes. Second, it compels accountable governmental decision-making. Third, because of the broader approach to standing, the class-action mechanism simplifies rules and legal processes that would otherwise impede 'meaningful participation by those whose rights are affected'.[63]

D. Navigating the Power Imbalance Between Lawyer and Litigant

However, Rooney issues an important caution, which is that the 'juridical power imbalance between lawyer and client'[64] can be acute in the context of class actions, particularly because only a few members of the class will be represented in the certification stage (as opposed to later in the class action proceedings). This has the potential to cut against the promise of participatory democracy, which focuses

> not just on the inclusion of the grievances of socio-economically disempowered groups within governmental decision-making, but on the vindication of the dignity and agency of the members of that group by enabling them to have an active participation in that decision-making.[65]

The power imbalance between lawyer and litigant (driven by information asymmetry as well as, in South Africa, profound socio-economic status differentials) can be a significant dimension of litigating class actions, and raises potential ethical quandaries for legal representatives who are charged with furthering their clients' cases while giving effect to their autonomy and—in the best case—litigating in a manner that promotes, rather than undermines, participatory democracy.

For the legal representative, the ethical dimensions of litigation on this scale are manifold, and not simply limited to the relationship between lawyer and client. In this respect, a sobering aspect of the litigation for *Nkala* must be mentioned. While *Nkala* demonstrates the potential for class action litigation to be used to address historic injustice that would otherwise be extraordinarily difficult to litigate on a piecemeal, incremental basis, the way in which the litigation was run came under heavy criticism[66] (and catalysed changes in the rules regulating advocates).

[62] J Rooney, 'Class Actions and Public Interest Standing in South Africa: Practical and Participatory Perspectives' (2017) 33(3) South African Journal on Human Rights 406.
[63] ibid 421, quoting S Liebenberg, 'Participatory Approaches to Socio-Economic Rights Adjudication' (2014) 32 (4) Nordic Journal on Human Rights 312, 313.
[64] Rooney (n 62) 422.
[65] ibid 420.
[66] Brickhill, 'A River of Disease' (n 1) 50–51.

This was predominantly on the basis that the advocates who were briefed on the matter were overwhelmingly white, perpetuating dramatically skewed and unjust briefing patterns in the profession (which favour white and male advocates), and re-inscribing power imbalances.[67] This, in turn, undermines some of the aims of transitional justice in addressing historic patterns of disadvantage.

A final point on the ethics of class action litigation is this: because class actions are often litigated on a contingency fee basis, with representing lawyers claiming up to 25 per cent of damages ultimately awarded to plaintiffs, there are distributive justice concerns that are pertinent not just in respect of accessing the courts, but also in how the tangible orders of courts are distributed, and who they enrich.[68] South Africa has not yet had to confront this on an institutional scale. However, other jurisdictions where class action litigation is more developed have had to wrestle with this difficulty. Class action litigation should not be pursued simply as a means to line lawyers' pockets, and legislative and judicial mechanisms to avoid this must be actively employed.

4. Class Action and Distributive Justice: Access to Resources

The second way in which class action mechanisms can vindicate distributive justice is in the outcomes that they can secure. Class actions need not necessarily be instituted to alter patterns of the distribution of goods. However, one of the advantages of class action litigation is that, because claims can be pursued in an aggregative fashion, smaller claims that would otherwise not be possible to litigate can now be determined. This, in turn, can have important distributional effects, particularly in vindicating socio-economic rights claims.[69]

The South African Constitution recognises justiciable socio-economic rights, and imposes positive obligations on the state to realise these rights. The realisation of these rights in turn is meant to go some way in addressing the radically unequal distribution of resources, and to achieving substantive equality.[70] Substantive equality is pertinent here for articulating abstract distributive justice concerns 'that arise from a multiplicity of social and economic causes'.[71] It is also relevant

[67] Brickhill and Finn (n 35) 108.

[68] On the risks of contingency fees in class action contexts, see M Wallis, 'Ordinary Justice for Ordinary People: The Eighth Victoria and Griffiths Memorial Lecture' (2011) 127(3) South African Law Journal 369. Brickhill, 'A River of Disease' (n 1) also critically comments on a range of ethical issues relating to lawyer fees in the context of the silicosis class action.

[69] Abdool Karim and Kruger (n 1) argue this point in the context of the right to food, noting that the price fixing of bread, as well as the listeriosis suits, feature the role of class actions to realise this right in various forms.

[70] P Langa, 'Transformative Constitutionalism' (2006) 3 Stellenbosch Law Review 351, 352–53; Catherine Albertyn and Beth Goldblatt, 'Equality' in Woolman (n 6).

[71] C Albertyn, 'Substantive Equality and Transformation in South Africa' (2007) 23 South African Journal on Human Rights 253.

because material deprivations continue to run along tracks of historic inequality, often mapping onto colonial apartheid's pernicious racial and spatial geography.[72]

Mbazira argues that South Africa's context demands that socio-economic rights be enforced in order to satisfy distributive justice imperatives. He contends that socio-economic remedies should not be deployed 'maximally for the benefit of selected victims who are able to litigate'.[73] In this respect and unlike the ordinary procedures for litigation, class action procedures can expand the ambit of who is able to litigate.

As such, class action litigation can be a crucial mechanism for advancing distributive justice. This has been evident not only in the use of class actions to assert justiciable socio-economic rights, recognised in the Constitution (as in *Ngxuza*) but also to assert other substantive rights which are not directly sourced in the Constitution. *Ngxuza*, which I discussed earlier, is a very clear instance of the procedure being used to enforce justiciable socio-economic rights. There, the right to access social security was paired with the right to administrative justice, which enabled accountability for the unlawful exercise of public power, while ensuring that the substantive right to access social assistance was realised.

The same can be said of the bread price-fixing saga, discussed earlier. Bread producers were found guilty of price-fixing in the form of a cartel, which is proscribed by the Competition Act 89 of 1998. The effect of this conduct was to drive up the price of bread—a staple consumer good. The adverse impact of increases in the price of consumer basics is mostly keenly felt by impoverished households, who, as a result, have to divert a greater proportion of their spending on food staples. The bread producers' unlawful conduct, then, squarely involved distributive justice and socio-economic concerns:[74] it impacted on the distribution of resources, reinforcing extant inequality.

Another significant instance of class action litigation used in this manner is the *Linkside* litigation brought in the Easter Cape.[75] The litigation arose when the Eastern Cape Department of Education failed to appoint teachers to substantive posts that it had itself identified as being important to fill. The system of providing for teacher posts at a provincial level is set up to account for a range of factors, including the relative poverty of schools and the need to allocate teachers equitably so that the gaping inequality of schooling is ameliorated. Accordingly, this breach of obligations by the Eastern Cape Department had clear impacts on the right to education and children's rights, with learners' well-being being imperilled. As a

[72] See, eg, M Pieterse, 'Geography, Marginalisation and the Performance of the Right to Have Access to Health Care Services in Johannesburg' (2016) 20 Law, Democracy and Development 1; T Coggin, 'Redressing Spatial Apartheid: The Law of Nuisance and the Transformative Role of Social Utility and the Right to the City' (2016) 133(2) South African Law Journal 434.

[73] C Mbazira, *Litigating Socio-Economic Rights in South Africa: A Choice between Corrective and Distributive Justice* (PULP 2009) 10.

[74] Abdool Karim and Kruger (n 1).

[75] *Linkside v Minister for Basic Education* [2015] ZAECGHC 36.

result, school governing bodies stepped into the breach to appoint teachers and pay them out of funds diverted from other items that the schools had budgeted for. This in turn had some adverse effects, as many no-fee and low-fee schools were either unable to retain or appoint the necessary number of teachers, or suffered from not being able to allocate funds to school infrastructure and other projects. The Legal Resources Centre (a public interest law organisation) launched litigation, first to compel the Eastern Cape Department to comply with its obligations and second, as class action litigation brought on behalf of the school governing bodies. The Eastern Cape High Court certified the class, with ninety schools opting in to the class action. The Court ordered a creative remedy, including that reimbursement to the school governing bodies be administered by an independent claims-administrator, and that the Department has continuing obligations to publish bulletins and advertisements, so that vacant teaching posts are published. Ultimately, however, only the schools which had facilities to keep accounting records could easily prove that funds had been diverted to pay teachers—with the result that schools which were unable to keep those records—that is, the most disadvantaged schools—were unable to benefit.[76]

However, the Department continues to act incompetently—or, at times, intransigently—as non-compliance with the post-provisioning system is still rife. Subsequently, further litigation was brought on behalf of the teachers who were compensated at a far lower rate for their services, in an attempt to vindicate their interests as well as principles of accountability.[77]

In sum, then, class actions can be used as vehicles to secure a variety of socio-economic rights—and so, to vindicate distributive justice. In some ways, they are well-suited to this: as Rooney points out, class actions are typically run on behalf of large groups of socio-economically disadvantaged, geographically remote persons.[78] However, as we have seen repeatedly in recent years, securing relief in court often does not necessarily translate into changed distributional outcomes, not least because of widespread governmental non-compliance with court orders.[79]

5. Class Action and Addressing Historic Wrongs

Finally, in addition to serving distributive justice, in the context of South Africa's political transition class actions can be used as a mechanism for addressing historic wrongs.

[76] Rooney (n 61) 415.
[77] *Grootboom v MEC: Department of Education, Eastern Province* [2019] ZAECGHC 1.
[78] Rooney (n 61) 412.
[79] H Taylor, 'Forcing the Court's Remedial Hand: Non-Compliance as a Catalyst for Remedial Innovation' (2019) 9 Constitutional Court Review 247.

No class action was brought in the immediate years of South Africa's democratic transition. In 2002, Khulumani Support Group, an organisation that represents 100,000 victims of apartheid and their families, initiated litigation in the United States under that country's Alien Tort Statute. The litigation sought reparations against a host of multinational corporate entities, for having provided goods and services to (and broadly done business with) the apartheid regime. However, this litigation was not styled as a class action, and ultimately was scuppered by the United States Supreme Court's finding in *Kiobel*[80] that the Alien Tort Statute does not apply extraterritorially.

However, this is not to say that class actions do not allow for the possibility of providing redress for historic wrongs. *Nkala* is an exemplar of this. Mineworkers were exposed to high levels of harmful silica dust, which is the exclusive cause of silicosis, an irreversible and incurable lung disease. While silica dust does not cause tuberculosis, there is a proven association between exposure to excessive silica dust and the risk of contraction of tuberculosis. During apartheid, pernicious conditions in the mines were given the imprimatur of legality: for example, occupational health and safety standards were applied to white employees, but not to black ones. Infection thus mapped onto stark race and class divisions, and onto the migratory labour system that sustained the gold mining industry. And, because many of the mineworkers who became ill were then looked after by female family members, there was an additional gendered dimension of caring at play too.[81] Put crisply, then, the mass contraction of silicosis and tuberculosis by mineworkers, and the devastating effects borne by those workers and their families, was itself a direct consequence of the colonial and then apartheid legal regimes, and the large corporate entities that were able to exploit the social conditions that these regimes created.

In an action brought against the major gold mining companies, the applicants approached the High Court to certify two classes. The first was a silicosis class (comprised of current and former underground mineworkers who had contracted silicosis, and the dependents of those who had died of silicosis, where the mineworkers had worked after March 1965 in one or more of the gold mines). The second was a tuberculosis class (applicable for the same period, but requiring that the mineworkers had contracted or died of tuberculosis and had worked for at least two years in a specified gold mine).

Mojapelo DJP certified the class, with the action to proceed in two stages. The first stage would see issues common to both classes determined (with members granted an opportunity to opt out of the class action), while the second would address issues specific to individual members of the classes (and in this stage, class

80 *Kiobel v Royal Dutch Petroleum Co.*, 569 US 108 (2013).

81 B Goldblatt and S Rai, 'Recognising the Full Costs of Care? Compensation for Families in South Africa's Silicosis Class Action' (2017) 27 Social & Legal Studies 671.

members were required to opt in). The Court noted the significance of being able to litigate via class actions:

> Class action is the only option open to the mineworkers and their dependants. It is the only way they would be able to realise their constitutional right to access to court, bearing in mind that they are poor, lack the sophistication to litigate individually, have no access to legal representatives, and are continually battling the effects of two extremely debilitating diseases.[82]

Litigating the claim as a class action was hugely advantageous. One reason for this is that because of the bifurcated nature of class action litigation—with certification occurring as an anterior step—some of the defences that would otherwise be raised in an individual's case are held over for determination in the main claim. The defence that a claim for a historic wrong will have prescribed is one of the key weapons in a defendant's arsenal. South Africa's laws of prescription impose a statute of limitation of three years to pursue any debt (which is construed relatively broadly to include justiciable harms). This quite obviously attenuates the ability to hold actors accountable for wrongs that have happened in the more distant past, and so denudes claimants of the possibility of claiming compensation or redress for historical wrongs.

When an action is litigated as part of a class, however, that itself may bring pressure to bear on a defendant to settle, rather than to take formalistic or procedural points. This was how *Nkala* ultimately played out: while the mining companies indicated that they would raise prescription as a defence should the class action proceed past certification, ultimately, the settlement that was brokered saw claimants being compensated, notwithstanding that their claims notionally may have prescribed. This is not to say that class actions necessarily preclude the defence of prescription; instead, only that the extensive publicity and mass mobilisation that can accompany class action litigation in turn incentivises defendants to settle, or at least to avoid raising defences that may be legally available, but are morally questionable.

As Du Plessis observes, with the advent of class action litigation:

> [W]e are likely to see a significant increase in what previously was glaringly omitted from the South African legal landscape, namely collective redress in private damages claims… [T]his is a good thing, and perhaps more so in South Africa than in many other jurisdictions, particularly given the ravages of our past and the need for courts to act as vehicles for transformative social change.[83]

[82] *Nkala* (n 5) [100].
[83] Du Plessis (n 21) 13.

6. Conclusion

This chapter has considered class actions as a tool for securing collective relief, in the context of a society that is still defined by gaping inequality, which extends to marked inequality in the ability to access courts through litigation. Class action litigation in South Africa, expressly provided for in section 38(c) of the Constitution, is burgeoning. I discussed the evolution of rules of standing in South African law, and the emerging mechanisms of class action suits. I argued that developments in class action procedures advance the state's distributive justice mandates in two significant ways. First, class actions enable access to courts in a context where litigation is costly and opaque, and justice difficult to come by. In this way, class actions make possible a more equitable distribution of legal representation, and so themselves are constitutive of an element of distributive justice, with access to the courts itself as the good that is distributed. Secondly, class actions can be used instrumentally to serve distributive justice goals, in that they provide a procedural mechanism that enables the vindication of socio-economic rights. Additionally, class actions do not only serve distributive justice ends. In a transitional society marred by historic injustice stretching back to colonialism and entrenched by apartheid, I argued that class actions can serve as a mechanism—albeit partial, and imperfect—for redressing historic wrongs.

15

Forced Displacement and Social Change

Light and Shadows in the Implementation of the Judgment T-025 of 2004

Andrés Mauricio Gutiérrez Beltrán

In light of the available figures, it is not excessive to characterise Colombia as a displaced nation[1]

Gonzalo Sánchez
Director of the National Centre for Historical Memory

1. Introduction

Along with the South African Constitutional Court and the Supreme Court of India, the Colombian Constitutional Court is regarded by academics as one of the most powerful activist courts in the Global South.[2] Therefore, the Court is a perfect subject for assessing the effects (and effectiveness) of judicial activism. The Court is recognised worldwide for several reasons: it has developed an influential body of jurisprudence on the protection of social rights; it has (sometimes controversially) endorsed the rights of minority groups, such as the LGBTQ community, as well as people of Indigenous or African descent; it has successfully prevented the over-concentration of power in the Executive branch; it has limited the Legislature's power to effect constitutional amendments, thereby preserving the essence of the

[1] M Hernández Sabogal and others, *Una nación desplazada: Informe nacional del desplazamiento forzado en Colombia* (Centro Nacional de Memoria Histórica 2015) 16.

[2] D Landau, 'Political Institutions and Judicial Role in Comparative Constitutional Law' Harvard International Law Journal (2010) 51(2) 319–77; C Rodríguez Garavito and D Rodríguez Franco, *Radical Deprivation on Trial. The Impact of Judicial Activism on Socioeconomic Rights in the Global South* (CUP 2015); D Bonilla Maldonado (ed), *Constitutionalism of the Global South: The Activist Tribunals of India, South Africa, and Colombia* (CUP 2013).

Andrés Mauricio Gutiérrez Beltrán, *Forced Displacement and Social Change* In: *Transitional Justice, Distributive Justice, and Transformative Constitutionalism.* Edited by: David Bilchitz and Raisa Cachalia, with Magdalena Inés Correa Henao and Nathalia Bautista Pizarro, Oxford University Press. © Andrés Mauricio Gutiérrez Beltrán 2023.
DOI: 10.1093/oso/9780192887627.003.0015

1991 Constitution; and it seems to have provoked deeper changes in Colombia's legal culture more broadly.

These factors explain the important role played by the Court in the protection of democracy in Colombia, and justifies the burgeoning interest it has stimulated in comparative constitutional law. The Court's use of unorthodox strategies to advance the protection of human rights is the main reason behind the deep influence it has had in the field. The doctrine of 'unconstitutional state of affairs' is a good example of its resourcefulness in this regard. The Court adopted this doctrine with the purpose of ending the widespread and systematic violations of human rights in the country. Instead of limiting its order to the restoration of the individual rights of the victims in particular court proceedings, the Court went further by ordering the creation, amendment, and implementation of public policies. In this way, thousands, if not, millions of people who did not take part in the court process could conceivably benefit from its decision.

In this chapter, I will refer to judgments of this kind as 'structural judgments', regardless of whether the Court maintains ongoing jurisdiction to ensure actual compliance with these decisions. Structural judgments seek to concretise the ideal of distributive justice in environments of extreme marginalisation and poverty. They are not aimed solely at returning victims to the living conditions in which they were prior to their rights having been violated. On the contrary, structural judgments seek to transform the living situation of affected persons in a substantive sense. The Constitutional Court recognised that the application of *restitutio in integrum*—that is, the restoration to an original condition, the guiding principle behind tort law— could be extended to the violation of infringed fundamental rights. In fact, according to the Court, actively aiming for a return to pre-displacement conditions would perpetuate the precariousness, exclusion, and poverty which enabled the widespread and systematic violations of the victims' rights in the first place. In other words, structural judgments have an explicit transformative role to play and are thus closely related to the notion of 'transformative constitutionalism'.[3]

Considering that this judgment was handed down during the armed conflict in Colombia, it may also be said to exemplify a form of transitional justice. While the Court's decision was handed down more than a decade before the peace agreement with FARC-EP was signed in 2016, Judgment T-025 of 2004 ought nevertheless be seen as part an extended period of social and political reform that in fact began with the Political Constitution of 1991. Put differently, despite the Colombian armed conflict having started in the mid-1940s, Judgment T-025 was

[3] P Langa, 'Transformative Constitutionalism' (2006) 17 Stellenbosch Law Review 351; K Klare, 'Legal Culture and Transformative Constitutionalism' (1998) 14(1) South African Journal on Human Rights 146–88; M Pieterse, 'What Do We Mean When We Talk About Transformative Constitutionalism?'(2005) 20(1) SA Publiekreg = SA Public Law 155–66; T Roux, 'Transformative Constitutionalism and the Best Interpretation of the South African Constitution: Distinction Without a Difference?' (2009) 20(2) Stellenbosch Law Review 258–85.

in fact issued by virtue of the changes provoked in the legal culture brought on by the 1991 Constitution. Certainly, a decision of this kind would never have been possible prior to the passing of the new Constitution. Therefore, this chapter analyses the successes and failures in the implementation of this decision, as a product of the new form of constitutionalism that began in 1991.

Furthermore, these decisions seek to guarantee victims' rights, especially social rights. They do not pursue the restoration of the victims' prior situation or position. Structural judgments try to satisfy, amongst others, the rights to food, housing, and health care. This has—or should have—an equalising effect on the community. In this way the Court is able to influence the allocation of benefits and burdens across all members of the society and thus advance greater distributive justice in society.

Similarly, in the specific case of Colombia, structural judgments can also advance the goals of transitional justice. While the causes of the armed conflict are varied, there is no doubt that deep social inequalities have fed the conflict. The failure of the state to secure social welfare in the territory and the lack of public policies aimed at securing social rights, among other causes, has contributed to the rise of illegal groups and to the ongoing violence in the country. In the context of the new landscape created by the 2016 Peace Agreement, structural orders aimed at promoting social changes can be seen as necessary for securing lasting peace. Addressing social issues in this way can serve as a conflict-mitigation tool and in so doing contribute positively to the broader transitional justice project.

T-025 of 2004 is arguably the most famous structural judgment that has been handed down by the Court. For some scholars, 'it is the most explicit and systematic judicial attempt in Latin America to implement a structural decision'.[4] This judgment addresses the desperate situation of millions of people who were forced to flee their homes due to the armed conflict in Colombia. By 2004, the number of internally displaced people (IDP) had already reached 3.6 million. Nowadays, despite the peace agreement signed between the government and FARC-EP, this number has risen to 8.2 million people. These IDPs face gross violations of their basic rights to food, adequate housing, education, and health services, among others. In 2004 their situation was depicted by the Court as follows:

> 92% of the displaced population has unsatisfied basic needs and 80% is in a situation of indigence. 63.5% of the displaced population live in inadequate housing, and 49% do not have access to public services. Regarding food consumption, it is concluded that the 'calorie gap' of the displaced households is 57%; in other words, they only consume 43% of the calories recommended by the WFP [World Food Program]. Moreover, it was found that 23% of children under six years of age have a food intake below the minimum standard.... With respect to access

[4] Rodríguez Garavito and Rodríguez Franco (n 2) 34.

> to education, this Court established that 25% of boys and girls between 6 and 9 years old do not attend school, while this proportion for youngsters between 10 and 25 years old is 54%. Finally, concerning the right to health: the mortality rate of the general displaced population is 6 times higher than the national average.[5]

Although the Court stated that this dire situation was not provoked solely by the public authorities, in its view it was undeniable that the latter had contributed to it by its negligent behaviour. According to the Court, forced displacement is a consequence of the 'armed conflict and—more importantly—a result of the actions of illegal armed groups'.[6] However, the government should be held accountable for failing to put in place public policies capable of meeting the needs of displaced people. Although there were some relevant programmes in operation at the time of the ruling, and though the Congress had passed a statute regulating this issue, the Court ruled that these policy attempts 'had not counteracted the serious deterioration in the conditions of vulnerability of the displaced people; [had] not led to the protection of their constitutional rights; and had not provoked the overcoming of the causes that allowed these violations in the first place'.[7]

The Court concluded that the existing policies had two major failures. First, the organs in charge of designing and implementing them had poor institutional capacity from the perspective of fulfilment their duties. This means that they did not possess the human, budgetary, and logistical resources needed to satisfy the rights of internally displaced people. This situation was the result of poor institutional planning, in which duties had been assigned without being allocated the resources needed to conduct the foreseen activities properly. The second failure highlighted by the Court was the chronic lack of funds dedicated to implementation of these policies. In the Court's view, this was 'the central cause of the failures in the implementation of the policies of attention to the displaced population'.[8]

By ordering the rectification of these shortcomings, the Court attempted to address one of the largest humanitarian crises in modern history. Until the signing of the peace agreement, the Colombian conflict was the longest-running internal armed conflict in Latin America. The seriousness of this situation is stressed by the fact that up until now, 'Colombia continued to report the highest number of internally displaced people [in the world], with 8.3 million at the end of 2020'.[9] These circumstances explain why judicial intervention in this area has propelled towards

[5] All quotes have been translated from their original language (Spanish) by the author.
[6] Judgment T-025 of 2004 [6].
[7] ibid.
[8] ibid [6.3.2].
[9] United Nations High Commissioner for Refugees, Global Trends: Forced Displacement in 2020 <https://www.unhcr.org/60b638e37/unhcr-global-trends-2020> accessed 14 September 2022.

judicial activism[10] and why it has been the most contested area in the history of the Court.

The passing of T-025 of 2004 was just the beginning—rather than the end—of this process, as the Court also decided to maintain jurisdiction in order to ensure compliance with its orders. Throughout its monitoring process, the Court handed down more than 300 decisions assessing the actions taken by public authorities (hereafter 'autos') and requiring them to comply with the orders imposed. Additionally, the Court held public hearings where highest-level senior officials, such as the directors of ministries and of national agencies, were held to account for the actions taken by their departments. The extraordinary increase of the budget devoted to IDPs is another reason for the widespread interest in this process.

2. Evaluating the Effectiveness of Structural Judgments

The sociology of law has warned that one of the most important challenges in assessing the effectiveness of judicial decisions is found in what has been called the 'gap problem'.[11] This refers to a methodological error in which we evaluate the effectiveness of judgments according to different objectives than those that the courts themselves have established in their decisions.

Judgment T-025 of 2004 is a prime example of this difficulty: does the effectiveness of the ruling depend on whether the displaced *fully* enjoy their fundamental rights, or conversely, is it sufficient for the public authorities to demonstrate that they have made all the public policy adjustments requested by the Court? In the first case, emphasis would be placed on the situation of the victims, since the evaluation of the effectiveness of the ruling would depend on actual, concrete changes experienced directly by the victims. In the second case, the assessment would

[10] While I recognise the potential ambiguity behind the term *judicial activism*, I conclude that there is agreement in the scholarship on two of its basic characteristics. The first is subjective: judicial activism is related to a certain attitude, which could well be described as heterodox, which certain judges and courts enjoy in the performance of their duties. This subjectivity represents the foundation of the phenomenon. The second characteristic, which is objective in nature, refers to the (objective) consequences produced by judicial decisions made based on the aforementioned subjective attitude. The existence of even slight subjectivity in rulings thus implicate judges and courts in areas that would otherwise be reserved for representative authorities. In light of these two characteristics, there is no doubt that Judgment T-025 of 2004 is a classic example of judicial activism. The way in which the Colombian Constitutional Court intended to bring about social change by way of this subjective power explains the interest aroused by this ruling in comparative law. On the concept of judicial activism, see, among others, KD Kmiec, 'The Origin and Current Meanings of Judicial Activism'(2004) 92 California Law Review 1441; KM Holland (ed), *Judicial Activism in Comparative Perspective* (Springer 1991); PN Bhagwati, 'Judicial Activism and Public Interest Litigation' (1984) 23 Columbia Journal of Transnational Law 561; C Green, 'An Intellectual History of Judicial Activism' (2008) 58 Emory Law Journal 1195.

[11] D Nelken, 'The Gap Problem in the Sociology of Law: A Theoretical Review' (1981) 35(1) Windsor Yearbook of Access to Justice 35–61; A Sarat, 'Legal Effectiveness and Social Studies of Law: On the Unfortunate Persistance of a Research Tradition' (1985) 9(1) Legal Studies Forum 34–69.

only take into account the actions carried out by the public authorities. The consequences of adopting one or other criteria are considerable: if we adopt a victim-centric perspective, it might not be enough for the state to prove that it had acted with diligence and determination for the ruling to be considered effective. The state would also have to prove that its actions have had a positive and transformative impact on the lives of the displaced. If however we adopt a policy-centric perspective, the evaluation would be less rigorous, as the state would only have to prove that it had carried out the actions set forth in the ruling for the latter to be proven effective. The actual modification of the living conditions of the displaced would not be relevant criteria for evaluating the effectiveness of the judicial decision.

Avoiding the 'gap problem' thus requires a clear understanding and strict definition of the ruling's objectives. This is where neo-realism and constructivism, two schools in the scholarship on the sociology of law, disagree. In general terms, neo-realism carries out its assessments based on two central questions: have the actions set forth in the judicial decisions been carried out by the public authorities? And, has the general purpose pursued by the rulings—that is, overcoming the serious violations of the fundamental rights of the displaced—been achieved? Despite the broadness of the last question, the neo-realism evaluation framework is relatively limited: it only addresses the state's actions resulting from the judgments to determine their effectiveness. In fact, it is necessary to go further by considering *all* changes attributable to the judgments, whether or not these changes were foreseen by the courts.

An interesting example of a change that constructivists would take into account, and that neo-realists would overlook, is a change in public opinion towards a particular issue. According to constructivism, for example, it would not be possible to assess the effectiveness of historical decisions in South African jurisprudence, such as *Grootboom*[12] or *TAC*,[13] without looking at the changes in thinking and public opinion of the affected society. In other words, in addition to evaluating the degree of compliance with rulings on the part of authorities, it would also be necessary to examine how these rulings may have affected public opinion towards racism and people carrying the HIV virus in South Africa.

Another example of constructivism's particular interpretation of the effectiveness of judgments is found in the value attached to judicial defeats. As these may be used to portray the injustice of a system or the discrimination suffered by a particular social group, the approval of these decisions can be, in the long run, a positive event. Therefore, decisions contrary to a certain objective of social transformation, such as the US judgments of *Plessy v Ferguson*[14] or *Dred Scott v*

[12] *Government of the Republic of South Africa v Grootboom* [2000] ZACC 19; 2001 (1) SA 36 (CC) ('*Grootboom*').

[13] *Minister of Health v Treatment Action Campaign (No 2)* [2002] ZACC 15; 2002 (5) SA 721 (CC) ('*TAC*').

[14] 163 US 537.

Sandford[15] (both of which were part of the larger goal of eliminating white supremacy) should not necessarily be interpreted as judicial failures.

In my opinion, both perspectives incur errors that discourage their strict adoption. Neo-realism's main flaw lies in its methodological naivety. Its supporters hope that judicial rulings alone will be enough to drive social transformations that require the support of other public powers and, additionally, the approval of an important sector of society. They appear to be unaware that effective compliance with these rulings constitutes an arduous undertaking, which cannot be achieved solely through judicial rulings. Such transformations require profound cultural modifications, important budget investments, and many other actions that are beyond the direct powers of the courts. They should be reminded of Hamilton's sharp characterisation of the Judiciary: the courts as a whole would be the least powerful branch, since they 'lack the sword and the purse'.[16] It is not surprising, then, that the evaluations made by neo-realism of transformative judgments, such as Judgment T-025 of 2004, tend to yield negative results.

Constructivism incurs a diametrically opposite error: when taking into account all the repercussions—direct and indirect—that judgments produce, we lose sight of the fact that people's living conditions should be, in my opinion, the starting basis of any assessment. Because of this, it is possible that judgments that have actually failed in their intention to promote social change may be evaluated positively from this perspective, as constructivism attributes the same value to *all* the consequences that a sentence produces. For this reason, the preservation of a situation that was intended to be modified, may be offset by the achievement of other positive results, such as the modification of public opinion (for the better), the issuance of new (positive) legal norms, or an increase in the budget allocated to relevant matters. In other words, constructivism's main flaw is that it does not place people—the victims who require social changes to re-establish their rights—at the centre of their investigation into the effectiveness of judicial decisions.

These shortcomings highlight the need to adopt an intermediate position. Elsewhere, I have called this intermediate model a 'complex perspective with an emphasis on the victim'.[17] According to this perspective, it is necessary to consider the totality of the consequences that judicial decisions produce while assigning a relative value to each of them. Here, the most important criterion is the transformative effect that decisions have on people's real living conditions. This perspective thus considers all the variables that neo-realism ignores, including all indirect results that appear (eg the changes in institutional discourse and public opinion or

15 60 US 393.

16 A Hamilton, 'Federalist No.78' in C Rossiter (ed), *The Federalist Papers* (New American Library 1961).

17 Andrés Mauricio Gutiérrez Beltrán, *El Amparo Estructural de los Derechos* (Centro de Estudios Políticos y Constitucionales 2016).

greater journalistic coverage of the issues) but assigns them a lower value than the real changes experienced directly by the victims.

According to this perspective, the study of the effectiveness of the *Grootboom* ruling should emphasise the concrete changes experienced by people in extreme poverty who suffered the violation of their right to adequate housing. Although changes in public policy, increases in the budget, and bureaucratic burdens must also be recorded, the overall assessment of the effectiveness of the ruling should not depend solely on these criteria. The primary variable in evaluating a ruling's effectiveness should be found in the real, and not merely discursive, transformations that have occurred. In this example, this would be in the lives of the extremely poor South Africans who are lacking in access to adequate housing. Herein lies the emphasis on the victim, which is at the heart of the model that I defend.

3. Assessing the Effects Produced by T-025

In order to examine the results achieved so far, it is necessary to consider the first set of goals set by the court in its initial judgment. Not doing so carries the risk of falling into the 'gap problem'. According to the orders set forth in T-025, there were two main goals to be achieved, namely addressing failures associated with 'the insufficient budget devoted to the effective enforcement of those rights and [to improve] the institutional capacity required to implement the corresponding constitutional and legal mandates'.[18] For that purpose, the Court ordered the entities that make up the National Council of Comprehensive Attention to the Displaced[19] to take steps to resolve these two failures according to very precise deadlines. The second order was aimed at assuring the effective enjoyment of a minimum core of social rights. To achieve this goal, the Court ordered the Council to complete, within a period of six months, 'the actions required to guarantee to every single displaced person the effective protection of the minimum core of social rights, as described in section 9 of th[e] judgment'.[20]

In order to simplify this case study, the term 'public policy objective' will be used to refer to the correction of those failures derived from the lack of institutional capacity by the state, and from the lack of budget allocation. The expression 'minimum assistance objective' will be used to refer to the effective enjoyment of the nine basic rights that the Court demanded be protected in its ruling.

It is important to highlight the relevance of the latter, given that a significant number of scholars have centred their attention almost exclusively on the public

[18] Judgment T-025 of 2004, resolutive part, order 1.

[19] Body responsible for the design and implementation of this policy and for the allocation of the budget to specific programmes.

[20] Judgment T-025 of 2004, resolutive part, order 5.

policy objective. Even though this goal is of great importance, the emphasis on this consideration has given rise to a view that this was the Court's only objective. The Court itself has contributed to this myth by focusing the vast majority of its subsequent decisions on this aspect, which has also been emphasised in its public hearings on this issue.

According to T-025 however, the authorities were (and remain) obliged to guarantee continuous improvement in the material conditions of the displaced population. This explicit obligation underlines the reality that public policy alone is not enough to guarantee its full and timely implementation. It is necessary that these reforms bring forth a real change in the living conditions of the victims. This is the idea behind the 'complex victim-centred perspective' that this chapter adopts.

A. Internal Displacement under the Constructivist Perspective

According to constructivism, the dialectic activism displayed by the Court is an optimal model of judicial activism that translates efficiently into the achievement of social change.[21] This strategy combines the following three elements: (i) strong tracking of the actions taken by public authorities; (ii) the passing of moderate remedies that retain a discretionary margin in favour of the authorities; and (iii) strong rights that may be endorsed by the Judiciary.

Constructivism not only focuses on the enforcement of the orders issued by the Court, but also considers the indirect and symbolic effects that these orders provoke. Even though these effects are not established in the ruling, they appear during the follow-up process. The first indirect effect identified by those who adopt this viewpoint is the restructuring of the framing of internal displacement.[22] This concept refers to the change in perspective that occurred in both citizens and public authorities with respect to forced displacement. Constructivist scholars argue that, before the Court started tracking internal displacement, the latter was simply seen as a collateral and unavoidable effect of the internal conflict. As such, the displacement, despite its magnitude, did not bring about any of the expected outcomes that such a serious situation should have produced. Constructivists continue to argue that due to this judicial intervention and the increased visibility it brought to the matter, internal displacement has stopped being considered a mere sequel of war and started to be regarded as a serious human rights issue requiring state action.

The second indirect effect that—according to constructivism—has provoked this structural judgment is the so-called 'participatory effect'. This effect manifests

[21] C Rodríguez Gavarito and D Rodríguez Franco, *Cortes y cambio social: cómo la Corte Constitucional transformó el desplazamiento forzado in Colombia* (Dejusticia 2010); Rodríguez Garavito and Rodríguez Franco (n 2).

[22] Rodríguez Gavarito and Rodríguez Franco (n 2) 165–82.

itself through the active participation of several members of civil society in the follow-up process. Even though the Court required the authorities to guarantee the involvement of IDP-representing organisations,[23] it did not issue any order to incentivise the participation of the unaffiliated society in this process. Despite that, several members of society have participated in the process seeking to scrutinise the actions taken by the state and to propose public policy improvements. This opportunity has been seized by non-governmental organisations (NGOs), academics, the Catholic Church, and by international actors such as the United Nations High Commissioner for Refugees (UNHCR). Furthermore, the Court's intervention has inspired the creation of institutions specifically designed to implement this structural judgment, such as the *Comisión de Seguimiento a la Política Pública de Desplazamiento Forzado* [Monitoring Committee of the Public Policy on Internal Displacement],[24] established in August 2005, and of the Follow-Up Commission, Auto No 092 of 2008.[25]

For years, the achievement of this feat was marred by the failure to fulfil the initial objective that the Court had set. Despite the fact that the judgment unexpectedly triggered the participation of a significant group of institutions, the victims of forced displacement themselves did not take an active part in the monitoring process. Because of this, the process became elitist rather than inclusive. Fortunately, the situation has since undergone a drastic change, which has been expressly recognised by the Constitutional Court. In Auto No 373 of 2016, the Court declared the 'unconstitutional state of affairs' as resolved, at least in terms of 'the public policy component [of the process, as relevant to the victims' direct participation], seeing as the IDPs have gained access to participation methods which, despite continued challenges, are progressively and steadily coming to represent an effective enjoyment of the right [of participation]'.

The remaining four consequences that, according to the constructivist view, have been produced by the Court are related to the targets of public policy and minimum assistance. The public policy objective has led to two key results which indicate an improvement in policy relating to IDPs. The first consequence 'the unblocking effect' refers to overcoming institutional constraints limiting the agency of the Administration: 'The [Colombian Constitutional Court] used socio-economic rights as *destabilising rights*, as pressure points to break the institutional

23 Judgment T-025 of 2004 [10.1.2].

24 This committee has produced several reports that have been considered by the Court when assessing the actions taken by government. Additionally, the committee—along with the Universidad Nacional de Colombia— has conducted three major surveys on the social situation faced by the IDPs.

25 In the Auto No 092 de 2008, the Court declared that sexual violence against women is a practice 'that is common, widespread, systematic and invisible to the public eye in the context of the Colombian civil conflict'. In this context, a group of eleven feminist organisations—supported by UNHCR and UN Women—established this follow-up Commission for tracking the decision. The Commission has produced several reports about the enforcement of the orders issued in this auto and has participated actively in the public hearings where the actions taken by government have been assessed.

inertia and to provoke the action of the executive power'.[26] According to this argument, the frequent passing of judicial orders aimed at correcting the flaws in public policy has bolstered the capability of the authorities. Concretely, this 'unblocking effect' led to the reactivation of the organisation in charge of coordinating this policy (the National Council of Comprehensive Attention to the Displaced) and to the subsequent substantial budget allocated to solving the problem.

The second consequence of the ruling is financial. The increase in the budget devoted to the policy's financing has been considered one of the judicial intervention's most significant achievements. In accordance with the figures presented by the DNP (the government's primary think tank) and the Ministry of Finance, the policy's budget has increased more than sevenfold since 2004.[27]

The third consequence of the ruling according to constructivists, is 'the design of a national long term policy for the IDPs, and also the establishment of the mechanisms required to implement, finance and supervise these programs'.[28] In other words, the ruling did not lead to a simple improvement of the pre-existing policy, but instead led to the 'formulation of a *new* public policy',[29] its principal focus being a human rights-based approach. This new policy has caused a radical transformation in the way the state proceeds, which can be corroborated by examples such as the issuing of Decree 250 of 2005 'under which the National Plan for the Comprehensive Attention to the Internally Displaced Population due to Violence, and other dispositions, are issued'. It is worth mentioning that this decree was approved a year after the ruling.

The fourth consequence refers to the aforementioned minimum assistance objective. Even though constructivists acknowledge that the surveys conducted by the Monitoring Committee and the Universidad Nacional de Colombia—which are the main institutions relied on by the Court to evaluate the situation of the displaced population—do not really reflect positive results, they argue that 'multiple causalities and limitations of the available data ... block the establishment of a definitive effect on socio-economic conditions'.[30] According to their comments, the main methodological difficulty experienced was the lack of information regarding the conditions under which the internally displaced were living before the issuing of the ruling. They argue that, without this information, it is difficult to evaluate with certainty the progress made in this regard. Nevertheless, constructivists claim

[26] Rodríguez Gavarito and Rodríguez Franco (n 2) 44 (emphasis added).

[27] In 2003, the year prior to Judgment T-025, the government had allocated a mere 1.3 trillion pesos to care for the displaced population (less than 0.1 per cent of the 2003 GDP). This contrasts starkly with the most recent published figures: by 2019, 12.3 trillion pesos (1.1 per cent of GDP) had been allocated to the issue. *Informe presupuestal de la política pública dirigida a la población víctima del desplazamiento forzado 2018–2019*, Departamento Nacional de Planeación (1 March 2019) <https://colaboracion.dnp.gov.co/CDT/Poltica%20de%20Vctimas/InformeAuto219.pdf> accessed 8 May 2020.

[28] Rodríguez Gavarito and Rodríguez Franco (n2) 45.

[29] ibid 107 (emphasis added).

[30] Rodríguez Gavarito and Rodríguez Franco (n 2) 208.

that significant achievements in terms of education and health care have been achieved. They highlight that this progress has given rise to a 'partial lifting' of the T-025's declaration of an unconstitutional state of affairs.[31] This has meant that the government is no longer required to report on actions taken to achieve the measured results, as it has officially fulfilled at least part of its obligations in matters of healthcare. The government was however required to continue reporting on the actions taken in the field of health care relevant to Afro-descendant and Indigenous communities, as the level of progress made in this sector was not sufficient to warrant a lifting of the unconstitutional state of affairs. Despite the lukewarm results, constructivists acknowledge that the overall situation remains one 'of deep precariousness, and one of continuous violations of the human rights of the displaced people'.[32]

Thus, according to the constructivist perspective, the positive developments brought about by the Court's judgment, though neither complete nor perfect, show that the dialectic activism adopted by the Court constitutes a successful example of judicial intervention. From this perspective, the Court has not only succeeded in changing the behavior and the attitude of the authorities about internal displacement—as confirmed by the 'restructuring of the framing', 'unblocking', and the 'public policy' effects—but has also brought the state of affairs to light within civil society, thereby provoking unexpected and widespread civil involvement in the matter (the 'participatory effect').

B. Analysis from a Complex Victim-Centred Perspective

The analysis from the complex victim-centred perspective—proposed in this chapter—recognises the difficulty of provoking social changes through the Judiciary alone.[33] This viewpoint values the achievement of parallel cultural transformations, such as the symbolic and indirect effects, as previously defined. These parallel developments have a real and undeniable impact on the implementation process of structural judgments. Nevertheless, the main characteristic of the proposed approach relies on the particular attention it gives to changes in the living conditions of victims. By anchoring itself in this way, this perspective aims to avoid constructivists' tendency to attribute excessive importance to matters that have little impact in the achievement of real and tangible social change.

As the symbolic effects produced by T-025 have already been discussed, the following sections review the implementation of 'public policy' and the 'minimum

[31] This decision was made by the Court in Auto No 219 of 2011.
[32] Rodríguez Gavarito and Rodríguez Franco (n 2) 204.
[33] Regarding the extent of this method of analysis, see A Gutiérrez Beltrán, *El amparo estructural de los derechos* (Centro de Estudios Políticos y Constitucionales 2018).

assistance' objectives. In order to examine public policy objectives, the thematic division as proposed by the Court will be used. The topics analysed thus include (i) the recovery of institutional capacity, and (ii) the improvement of budgetary efforts. The study of the minimum assistance objective, will provide an overall assessment of the Court's attempts to advance the effective enjoyment of the nine rights that, from 22 July 2004 onwards, the authorities were required to guarantee for the internally displaced population.

(i) Public policy objective: recovering institutional capacity

Given the exponential increase in the budget devoted to this policy as well as the aforementioned 'unblocking effect', important results in the enhancement of the institutional capacity of the organisations in charge of implementing the public policy should have been expected. However, the Court has concluded that the progress achieved in this regard remains quite limited. According to the Follow-Up Decision 008 of 2009 (Auto No 008 of 2009), the Court declared that 'inadequate institutional capacity continues to play a central role in the persistence of the unconstitutional state of affairs'.[34] This was stated by the Court after noting that the government did not have an official study that would have allowed it to establish the scope of this public policy weakness. Consequently, it was not clear what the latter's impact had been on the provision of care to the displaced population, nor what concrete actions would have to be taken in order to rectify the situation. After realising that the government had not adopted a plan directed to overcome this deficiency, the Court ordered the National Council of Comprehensive Attention to the Displaced to design and implement a programme that would solve the persistent gaps in performance in an efficient manner.

Two years later, in Auto No 219 of 2011, the Court stated that 'results in overcoming the insufficiency of institutional capacity remain[ed] very low'.[35] Even though 89 per cent of government entities, excluding the National Council of Comprehensive Attention to the Displaced, had approved particular programmes to help build their capacity, the Court warned that there had still not been any substantial advancement in this area. The Court's concern stemmed from the fact that, by 2011, the institutional capacity-building plan, which was yet to be implemented in 30 June 2009—was still in its preliminary phase.

In the Court's opinion, this persistent non-compliance was evidence that for 'the entities that are part of the National Council ... this is a marginalised activity, one that is not institutionalised, nor articulated with the rest of the activities that are done to guarantee the effective enjoyment of the right of the internally displaced population. [It is clear that it was only] realised with the purpose of merely presenting a report to the Court'.[36] The severity of this finding is highlighted by the

[34] Auto No 008 de 2009, para III.3.
[35] Auto No 219 of 2011 [32].
[36] ibid [36].

measures that were adopted to alter the situation. Aside from demanding the effective implementation of the institutional capacity recovery programme, the Court pressed the supervisory bodies to provide information on the judicial, disciplinary, and fiscal processes that had been initiated in light of the order's non-compliance. The latter decision proves that the dialectic approach had not been as efficient as the Court envisioned, which then forced the Court to adopt a less flexible approach. In other words, the breach of the obligations that had been imposed on the authorities ultimately forced the Court to abandon the position of dialogue that it had originally adopted in Judgment T-025. Instead, it adopted a stricter attitude and restricted the discretionary powers of the government, an area of authority which the Court had earlier tried to preserve.

Auto No 266 of 2017 is the most recent evaluation of the policy's current situation specifically regarding communities of African and Indigenous descent. This decision once more highlighted that, thirteen years after the declaration of an 'unconstitutional state of affairs', the lack of institutional capacity of the authorities continued to be one of the main failures of this policy:

> The context of violence within the territories of the afro descendant and indigenous communities continues to encourage multiple and continuing cases of forced displacement and restrictions on mobility. On the other hand, *the lack of institutional capacity to reverse those damaging effects persists, causing exclusion and neglect of the plight of these people in urban spaces.* This is in addition to the low compliance of the orders issued and to the persistence of institutional blocking and unconstitutional practices. In consequence, this special Chamber will proceed to declare that the state of unconstitutional affairs that surrounds the rights of the afro descendants and indigenous communities persists.[37]

The assessment carried out by the Court shows that, despite the numerous warnings made during the follow-up process, the authorities' lack of institutional capacity was not adequately resolved. The persistent lack of compliance—the latter a fundamental requirement on which the totality of public policy relies—is a clear example of the limited attention paid by the Executive branch to the enforcement of the ruling. This being said, the Court has not, however, resorted to any further mechanisms to pressure the state into adopting certain necessary measures.

(ii) Public policy objective: improvement of the budgetary effort

The exceptional increase of the budget allocated to this issue is clear proof of the transformations that resulted from the Court's intervention. The judgment sparked an immediate positive change that increased over time. In fact, the 2004

[37] Auto No 266 of 2017 [7] (emphasis added).

budget already represented an increase of over 300 per cent when compared to the previous year's budget. Since then, the Executive and the Legislative bodies have intensified this effort, thus considerably increasing the resources that the National System of Comprehensive Care to the Internally Displaced Population has had at its disposal. Since the judgment, the state has allocated over 9 billion pesos—roughly 2,812 million euros—to finance the policy. These efforts have not gone unnoticed by the Court, which, in 2016, declared that it

> appreciate[d] that since the passing of Statute 1448 of 2011, there has been a significant increase in the budget allocated to the assistance, attention and comprehensive reparation to the victims of forced displacement. The latter is understood on the basis of the historical behavior of the resources allocated for this purpose from 2000 up until the past year, which follows an upward trend as described by the following: over the years 2000 to 2015, the resources have increased from 0.4% of the GNP to 4.39%.[38]

From a constructivist perspective, and even from a neo-realist viewpoint, this achievement is an undeniable triumph which demonstrates that the Court has been able to promote a radical shift in the authorities' behaviour. Nevertheless, this conclusion also has to take account of the changes produced in the material conditions of the IDPs. Despite its undeniable importance, the budgetary increase can only be considered an intermediate goal. More pertinent would be for this increase to translate into an effective improvement in the social and material rights of the IDPs. If such improvements were not achieved, it could be concluded that, at best, the state's efforts have not been efficiently implemented by the authorities; at worst, the budget has been channelled into alternative streams, such as inefficiency or corruption.

Taking this into account, it is difficult to share the optimistic conclusions proposed by constructivists on this matter. As will be explored later in respect of minimum assistance, the budget increases have not produced significant changes in the living conditions of the displaced population. On the contrary, according to Auto No 219 of 2011, 'despite the budgetary efforts and the correction of some wrongdoings ... there is not any evidence of significant changes in the majority of indicators that reflect the effective enjoyment of rights from the internally displaced population'.[39] In fact, up until the signing of the peace agreement, the conditions

[38] Auto No 373 of 2016.

[39] Already in 2009, once the bodies in charge of this policy had been awarded the budget which, according to government figures, should have been adequate to assist the IDPs, the Court stated that 'it suffices to notice that, despite the fact that the Government has declared the resources sufficient to ensure the practical enjoyment of the IDPs' rights, the level of coverage of almost all components remains far from an acceptable level, thus confirming the grave gaps in institutional capacity'. Auto No 008 of 2009 [41.III.3].

of IDPs had deteriorated. It is altogether surprising and unfortunate that such an increase in investment—by all accounts an extraordinary effort from the state, regardless of outcome—has not translated into tangible improvements in the socio-economic conditions of the IDPs.

A clear example of this paradox can be found in the Monitoring Committee's court-commissioned report. This report was based on a third national survey, conducted in 2010. Among other findings, the Committee warned that, at the time of data gathering, '66% of the internally displaced population had not yet received any type of assistance'.[40] This does not however imply that a third of the displaced population had received *all* the social services envisaged by the state, which would have represented a rather laudable result. Actually, this implies that a third of the target population had received *at least one* of the many services guaranteed by the state. In fact, 'in 2010, only 0.5% of the households part of the Unique Registry of the Displaced Population had received every component included in the immediate assistance [plan]'.[41] It is therefore difficult to reconcile the increase in the budget with the limited achievements for the conditions of displaced persons.

On the other hand, the civil and public organisations that had been participating in the follow-up process have also expressed their concerns over the severe failures of the policy:

> The supervisory bodies (the Commission of Follow-Up and Monitoring of Law 1448 of 2011 (CSyM in Spanish) and the Monitoring Committee to the Public policy on Forced Displacement (CSPPDF in Spanish)) raised some inquiries over: i) The coherence and sufficiency of the budget allocated up to that moment (and those projected for the implementation of the victims' law up to the year 2021) in relation to the reality of forced displacement, as anticipated based on the registry's current list of victims; ii) The fact that the allocated and projected budgets are heavily dependent on the contribution of resources belonging to the General Participation System (SGP in Spanish); iii) The unmet budget requirement of approximately $33.6 billion pesos, needed to guarantee the victims' necessary indemnification as well as the implementation of the housing activities, as outlined as part of the planned reparation's implementation indicators.[42]

In sum, the increase in budgetary allocation has not yet led, as per the latest documents available, to significant achievements in the two matters the Court most wanted to influence. The institutional capacity of the authorities in charge of public

[40] Comisión de Seguimiento a la Política Pública sobre Desplazamiento Forzado, *Tercer informe de verificación sobre el cumplimiento de derechos de la población en situación de desplazamiento* (Bogotá, December 2010) 65 <https://mesadesplazamientoydiscapacidad.files.wordpress.com/2011/01/iii-informe-de-verificacic3b3n-cs-2010.pdf> accessed 26 September 2023.

[41] ibid 65.

[42] Auto No 373 of 2016 [1.6].

policy had not improved, and there has not yet been a significant, measurable impact in the living conditions of the internally displaced population.[43] In other words, as seen from a complex victim-centred perspective, the developments observed thus far have failed to lead to substantial transformation in the victims' conditions. It is thus evident that the authorities have lacked both transparency and efficiency in the allocation of the increased resources, denying IDPs their promised improvements in living conditions.

(iii) Evolution of the Minimum Assistance Objective

One of the reasons that led the Court to order the reformulation of the whole policy in 2004 was the absence of a specialised instrument that could effectively measure the practical enjoyment of human rights. The absence of this instrument made it impossible to determine with objectivity the real situation of the population, as well as to evaluate the extent of the policy's impact on their conditions. Since then, around 300 indicators have been developed to help map the compliance levels on the provision of twenty-two rights.[44] The design of these indicators was carried out by members of the government, as well as members of the supervisory bodies and of the organisations that were a part of the follow-up process. The creation of those indicators is, without a doubt, one of the most significant achievements that the Court's intervention has enabled.

Unfortunately, the results of the latest evaluation of the policy are not particularly encouraging. Despite the differences between the evaluation generated by the government and those produced by other participants in the follow-up process—which have produced their own independent evaluations on the basis of the official indicators—all evaluations conclude that the IDPs, in general terms, continue to live in extremely precarious conditions.

According to a report published by the Monitoring Committee, in 2010, only 10.5 per cent of IDP households lived in decent housing conditions; 45 per cent lived in overcrowded conditions, and barely 55 per cent had access to public services. Regarding their right to adequate food, the report concluded that '65.2% of the registered displaced population and 65.9% of the unregistered displaced population suffered some symptoms associated with a lack of adequate food intake'.[45]

[43] According to the reports produced by the Monitoring Committee and the supervisory bodies, the failures in invested resources are due to the following three problems: problems executing the budget, failures in the pertinence and the nature of the expenses incurred, and a lack of transparency in those investments. On top of the aforementioned, it is necessary to add that the government has not complied with the demands made by the Court to disclose in their reports the distinction between the resources designated for the attention to the victims from those employed for the proper administration of the system.

[44] The performance indicators are described in Autos No 109 of 2007, 233 of 2007, 116 of 2008, and 155A of 2012.

[45] Auto No 219 of 2011 [290].

structural flaws that were denounced by the Court in 2004 and subsequently still persist. The available figures prove that the reforms carried out have not been able to generate substantial changes in the alarming social and economic conditions in which the internally displaced population finds itself.

Structural judicial interventions of this kind may cause symbolic effects that could have a meaningful, social impact on the vulnerable populations' lives. Yet they are not enough to achieve the material changes they seek to bring about in the target populations; at least not by themselves. It is therefore necessary that both the Court and the general population remain aware of the judicial system's limitations when promoting social change. Judicial interventions such as T-025 must be complemented with actions of other kinds—for instance those associated with political and social mobilisation—in order to achieve the desired results. Only through the joint participation of different political and social movements will it be possible to achieve ambitious objectives such as those listed in T-025. If these goals are to be achieved, it will be necessary to involve all political actors that contribute to this issue, as well as to ensure a more participatory role by the victims who, in the end, represent the prime beneficiaries of the judgment.

Given that the objective of this chapter is to study the effectiveness of the Court's intervention, the participation of other government branches has not been considered or analysed here. Admittedly, other analyses of comparative law, such as of the desegregation of the American educational system, seem to show that the participation of representative authorities can lead to positive changes in this area. After *Brown v Board of Education*,[47] for example, the changes that had been demanded by the Warren Court only appeared once the Executive and Legislative powers also gave their support to that Court's actions. This could mean that, in addition to the strategic litigation that is carried out before the courts, the groups interested in these transformations should also aim to have an impact on representative authorities as a means of promoting more effective change. This hypothesis will, however, have to be tested in future research.

[47] 347 US 483 (1954).

16

Joint Reflection: Litigating for a Collective

Structural Judgments and Class Actions in Colombia and South Africa

Meghan Finn and Andrés Mauricio Gutiérrez Beltrán

1. Introduction

What are the procedural and remedial mechanisms that are available to litigants to seek relief? And how can these tools be utilised in ways that aggregate claims and secure broad-ranging change—beyond simply justice for individual litigants?

In our preceding pieces, we both grappled with this question in Colombian and South African contexts. Our pieces proceed from divergent vantage points: while Gutiérrez Beltrán focuses on the collective effects of a single judgment of Colombia's highest court, Finn looks at the development of class action litigation more broadly in South Africa. However, both pieces are centrally concerned with the potential for particular forms of litigation to provide access to justice for claims on a structural or collective level. Both pieces also emphasise the importance of securing distributive justice in the form of real changes in lived conditions, and the court's role in doing so.

In his chapter, Gutiérrez Beltrán explores the advances and failures of the pivotal judgment of the Colombian Constitutional Court, Judgment T-025 of 2004. The Court declared that the situation of forcibly displaced people who had fled their homes as a result of the armed conflict constituted an 'unconstitutional state of affairs'. The Court ordered the government to formulate public policy, which was a novel remedy. In theory, this order could result in thousands—and, on some estimates, millions—of people benefitting from the decision. In this way, T-025 of 2004 is perhaps the most famous 'structural judgment'[1] that has been handed down in Colombia. This is because the judgment attempts to secure systemic change, and

[1] We note that the term 'structural judgment' in Colombia must be distinguished from 'structural interdict' as is used in a South African context. A structural order by a Colombian court would require the government to put in place broad—often policy-laden—solutions, rather than provide specific orders for individual claims. In South Africa, a structural (or supervisory) interdict involves an order where the court continues to exercise jurisdiction so as to ensure compliance with its order.

Meghan Finn and Andrés Mauricio Gutiérrez Beltrán, *Joint Reflection: Litigating for a Collective* In: *Transitional Justice, Distributive Justice, and Transformative Constitutionalism.* Edited by: David Bilchitz and Raisa Cachalia, with Magdalena Inés Correa Henao and Nathalia Bautista Pizarro, Oxford University Press. © Meghan Finn and Andrés Mauricio Gutiérrez Beltrán 2023. DOI: 10.1093/oso/9780192887627.003.0016

to do so not only for the litigants immediately before the Court but for all those affected by the unconstitutional state of affairs. However, as Gutiérrez Beltrán points out, in order to assess the effectiveness of the judgment, the 'gap problem' must be confronted—that is, the methodological error in which the effectiveness of judgments is evaluated according to different objectives, other than those articulated by the courts. This in turn gives rise to profound questions about the ability of courts to achieve widescale social change.

In her chapter, Finn discusses the burgeoning area of class action litigation in South Africa. Finn argues that class actions enable access to courts and can serve as a mechanism to further distributive justice goals in the South African context. She also suggests that class actions can be a partial tool for addressing historic wrongs, particularly in the context of transitional justice.

In this joint reflection we focus on four themes that manifest in both pieces. First, we discuss the role of the courts and judicial activism in crafting novel processes and remedies. Second, we contrast the procedures available for litigation for collective ends in Colombia and South Africa. Next, we consider the participatory dimensions of both structural judgments and class actions, which potentially allow for rights that might not otherwise be represented through democratic processes to be vindicated. This in turn gives rise to a number of paradoxes. Finally, we turn to the symbolic effects of the forms of collective action, as well as the limits of law—and particularly, of litigation—in securing meaningful social change.

2. The Role of Courts and People in Realising the Constitution

According to tradition, constitutions are legal norms addressed to the legislature. This idea is a consequence of the common understanding from the nineteenth century. At that time, constitutions were conceived solely as instruments to achieve the limitation of power and to secure the protection of individual freedom.[2] It explains why the Declaration of the Rights of Man and of the Citizen stated that '[a]ny society in which the guarantee of rights is not assured, nor the separation of powers determined, has no Constitution'. Therefore, principally the legislature was tasked with fulfilling the commitments entrenched in the Constitution.[3] No other public branch had the democratic legitimacy or the special qualification required to accomplish this relevant task.

However, the role played by constitutions in contemporary societies has changed. These norms are not seen today as much as mere limits, but as political

[2] S Ratner, 'Corporations and Human Rights: A Theory of Legal Responsibility' (2001) 111 Yale Law Journal 443.

[3] A Harel and A Shinar, 'Between Judicial and Legislative Supremacy' (2012) 10 International Journal of Constitutional Law 950.

programmes committed to the fulfilment of goals related to social change and effective enjoyment of human rights. Naturally, constitutions are still barriers to abuse of power, so they remain the central piece of the system created to ensure compliance with the rule of law. Nevertheless, transformations over the last two centuries have drastically shifted the ideas of *constitution* and *constitutionalism*, and so too, changed the role played by the judiciary.

This is the background against which our investigations are carried out. The constitutions of Colombia and South Africa are emblematic examples of what scholars have called 'transformative constitutions'.[4] The main feature of these constitutions is the purpose of transforming societies as well as the aim of overcoming dramatic episodes of injustice in recent history. In South Africa, the passing of the 1996 Constitution was the first legal step taken by the South African community to build a future of reconciliation, after apartheid. In the Colombian case, the approval of the 1991 Constitution was meant to cause and depict the end of the armed conflict. Although the peace agreement with FARC-EP only occurred almost three decades later, there is little doubt that the changes provoked by the Constitution were an important cause of the signing of this agreement. On top of that, in these two countries it was apparent that both apartheid and civil war existed in—and were made possible by—a society marred by poverty and social exclusion. For that reason, social transformation is the real *raison d'être* of these constitutions.

As a result, the question about who has the responsibility for fulfilling a constitution's programme becomes particularly hard. It is clear that the judiciary and the constitutional courts have an important duty in this regard. However, as the Colombian and South African constitutions commit to the ideal of representative democracy, it is uncertain how broad the mandate given to the courts actually is. Shall they maintain in all cases a deferential attitude towards the legislature? When the latter proves inactive or unwilling, should the courts intervene in public policies in order to guarantee the protection of rights? Do these constitutions propose a model of *judicial behaviour* that needs to be observed by the courts?

With varying degrees of success, these two Constitutional Courts have adopted a proactive attitude in the fulfilment of the promises entrenched in the respective constitutions of these countries. In Colombia, structural judgments are an example of a novel approach to remedy and procedure. In T-025 of 2004, the Court continued to exercise oversight, and to require concrete policy changes. While traditionally this role would have fallen on the Executive and Legislative branches, the Court drew on its remedial resourcefulness to address what had become a constitutional crisis. Similarly, class actions in South Africa have required litigants to

[4] K Klare, 'Legal Culture and Transformative Constitutionalism' (1998) 14(1) South African Journal on Human Rights 146; D Bonilla Maldonado (ed), *Constitutionalism of the Global South: The Activist Tribunals of India, South Africa, and Colombia* (CUP 2013); P Langa, 'Transformative Constitutionalism' (2006) 17 Stellenbosch Law Review 351; M Pieterse, 'What Do We Mean When We Talk About Transformative Constitutionalism?' (2005) 20 (1) SA Public Law 155.

draw on expanded procedural mechanisms made possible under the Constitution, including the broad approach to standing. And, as in T-025 of 2004, in the class action context South African courts have shown a willingness to extend their jurisdiction by continuing to exercise supervisory powers.

Litigants themselves are vital players—and in turn, affect how judges decide cases and how jurisprudence evolves ultimately.[5] Accordingly, judicial actions are important not only because they enable the functioning of the judiciary but because they allow the intervention of people in the fulfilment of constitutional mandates. Class actions, in South Africa, and *acción de tutela*, in Colombia, prove the relevance of this contribution and explain that the process of constitution accomplishment is not always top-down.

The Courts' proactive attitudes in both jurisdictions also explains why the developing case law has stimulated a remarkable interest at a comparative level. The contribution they have made is the design of new strategies aimed at securing the effective realisation of social rights as well as the real implementation of the constitutional clauses that seek the elimination of exclusion in these societies.

3. Collective Litigation in Comparison

Both Colombia and South Africa feature constitutional dispensations that have been mandated to navigate difficult socio-political transitions. For this reason, it is fruitful to compare their respective procedural mechanisms for collective litigation.

Articles 88 and 89 of the Political Constitution of Colombia, 1991, envisages both group and popular actions. These allow for the protection of collective interests and rights, enabling a group of people to claim for damages that are common. Law 472 of 1998 further developed popular actions and class (or group) actions. A class action is defined in Colombian law as a group of at least twenty persons, who have suffered loss arising from the same cause of action.[6] Unlike South Africa, then, Colombia prescribes a numerical threshold for class action litigation.

While popular actions are typically used to *prevent* future harms (often by way of an injunction), group actions, brought by a 'plural number of individuals' are generally *corrective*, seeking compensation for the infliction of harm on a group of clearly identified individuals.[7] As a result of this distinction, 'it is apparent that

[5] M Galanter, 'Why the Haves Come Out Ahead: Speculations on the Limits of Legal Change' (1974) 9 Law & Society Review 95.

[6] Ruling of 11 May 2001 by Supreme Court of Justice Carlos Ignacio Jaramillo J.

[7] M Gómez, 'Will the Birds Stay South? The Rise of Class Actions and Other Forms of Group Litigation Across Latin America' (2012) 43 University of Miami Inter-American Law Review 481 <https://repository.law.miami.edu/umialr/vol43/iss3/4/> accessed 20 September 2023.

[class actions] tend to protect individual rights', rather than collective or public rights.[8] Put differently, in Colombia class actions function as an aggregation of individual harms, rather than a vindication of group rights.

Class actions in Colombia are not litigated on the basis of constitutional rights violations and instead are more circumscribed in their scope, and typically delictual in nature. Conversely, South African law draws a distinction between litigation instituted as a class (as section 38(c) of the Constitution envisages) and litigation instituted in the public interest (as section 38(d) provides for). Both are permitted, and both procedural forms allow for collective litigation, including the vindication of constitutional rights.

Unlike in South Africa, which generally puts in place a certification threshold enquiry, in Colombia, the formal requirements for instituting a popular or group action are minimal, though support from either the Ombudsman or Public Prosecutor's office must be obtained.

In the landmark T-025 of 2004 judgment, the mechanism of a class action was not employed: instead, the Colombian Constitutional Court aggregated the constitutional complaints (tutelas) of 1,150 displaced families.[9] Nevertheless, it is illuminating to consider the role that 'structural judgments' play in Colombia, with T-025 of 2004 having significantly extended protection to those who were not parties (as they had not been joined to the proceedings). Such extended protection required ensuring that the prospective beneficiaries of the judgment—a group of internal displaced people—were identified and represented. To do so, the Colombian Constitutional Court invoked its remedial powers.

Action to secure collective relief has thus exerted significant influence on both jurisdictions.

4. Perspectives on Participation

A. Participatory Dimensions

In both of our preceding chapters, we touched on various forms of litigation that could be invoked to promote participatory—as opposed to simply representative—democracy. As Roux points out:

[8] T Jamarillo, 'Chapter 3: Colombia' in *Class Actions Law Review* (3rd edn, Law Business Research Ltd, London 2019) 44 <chrome-extension://efaidnbmnnnibpcajpcglclefindmkaj/https://www.matheson.com/docs/default-source/practice-area-attachments/the-class-actions-law-review---edition-3.pdf?sfvrsn=c90e85f8_1> accessed 20 September 2023.

[9] C Rodríguez-Garavito, 'Beyond the Courtroom: The Impact of Judicial Activism on Socioeconomic Rights in Latin America' (2011) 89 Texas Law Review 1669, 1670.

> [P]articipatory democracy is essentially about the question whether, and if so, how, citizens should be given the right to participate in the making of decisions that affect them, notwithstanding the fact that the basic form of political organization in the modern nation state is, and is likely to remain, representative democracy.[10]

In South African jurisprudence, participatory governance has been contrasted with apartheid's exclusion of the majority 'from meaningful participation in virtually every sphere of life'.[11] Cachalia notes elsewhere in this collection that 'the principle of participatory governance is deeply embedded in the very fabric of South Africa's conception of democracy'.[12]

Similarly, in Colombia citizen participation has been understood as a mechanism for greater democratisation,[13] with the Colombian Constitutional Court affirming the important role that citizens can play in public administration.[14]

Participatory democracy is valued for both intrinsic and instrumental reasons: intrinsically, because it bolsters and deepens democracy as a valuable end in itself, and instrumentally because broadening who participates in democratic decision-making leads to better, more context-sensitive outcomes.

Finn draws on earlier work by Rooney to make the point that, in the South African context, class action litigation can promote participatory democracy.[15] This is principally because such litigation enables individuals, who would otherwise not necessarily have their concerns represented through democratic processes, to vindicate their rights and compel accountable governmental decision-making.

Gutiérrez Beltrán notes that T-025 of 2004 had potentially participatory effects, as diverse representatives of Colombian society actively took part in the follow-up process. Participatory dimensions are particularly acute in instances where, as a result of socio-economic disadvantage and geographical remoteness, litigation would be inaccessible and unaffordable.

[10] T Roux, 'Democracy' in S Woolman (ed), *Constitutional Law of South Africa* (Juta 2013) 10–14; drawing on C Pateman, *Participation and Democratic Theory* (CUP 1970) 5.

[11] *Doctors for Life International v Speaker of the National Assembly* [2006] ZACC 11; 2006 (6) SA 416 (CC) [5].

[12] See Cachalia, Chapter 20 in this book.

[13] D Recondo, 'Local Participatory Democracy in Latin America—Lessons from Mexico and Colombia' (2005) *New Frontiers of Social Policy: Development in a Globalizing World* <http://siteresources.worldbank.org/INTRANETSOCIALDEVELOPMENT/Resources/Recondo.rev.pdf> accessed 14 May 2019.

[14] Law 152 of 1994, Law 434 of 1998, Law 1448 of 2011. See Open Democracy 'Postconflict in Colombia' (2016) <https://www.opendemocracy.net/en/democraciaabierta/postconflict-in-colombia-15-citizen-participat/#_ftnref2> accessed 14 May 2019.

[15] J Rooney, 'Class Actions and Public Interest Standing in South Africa: Practical and Participatory Perspectives' (2017) 33(3) South African Journal on Human Rights 406.

B. Participatory Paradoxes

While structural judgments in Colombia and class action litigation in South Africa can be vehicles for advancing participatory democracy, they are not always so—or at least, even as they further particular dimensions of participatory democracy they can also give rise to other dilemmas.

As others have pointed out, this is in part because of a central paradox: at its best, participatory democracy has the effects of promoting more active citizens, and ameliorating socio-economic inequality. However, these two effects are also 'prerequisites'[16] for the possibility of participatory democracy in the first place. Although structural judgments and class actions as forms of litigation can broaden the scope for participation in democratic structures and outcomes, at the same time these participatory dimensions can be thwarted by the absence of the very conditions that are needed for participation to be meaningful, and by the general inaccessibility and unaffordability of litigious processes.

Gutiérrez Beltrán cautions that the apparently participatory effect of the structural judgment has had some unforeseen and unfortunate consequences. Principally, the judgment has not achieved the broad involvement of victims of forced displacement—participation was principally driven by civil movements, rather than at the level of individual involvement. This is notwithstanding that governmental compliance with the Court's ambitious order is only possible through the joint participation of the various social and political forces that are implicated.

Finn also notes that class actions enable the pursuit of claims that may otherwise not be litigated, and so allows for the ventilation of issues and vindication of rights. At the same time however, because a class action is often lawyer-driven, this carries the risk that the litigants themselves are distanced from the litigation that is pursued on their behalf. As Rooney notes, there is significant imbalance of juridical power between class members and the lawyers who act to litigate their claims. This is driven by socio-economic inequalities, and the extent to which litigious processes are inaccessible, expensive, and opaque. Unless this is carefully navigated, this can undermine the potential for class action litigation to promote democratic participation.

This is not an inevitable consequence—particularly in the area of public interest litigation—whereby organisations and lawyers have long had to wrestle thoughtfully with the tension that can arise between clients' interests and a cause. But these paradoxes do give cause for pause, especially as the forms of litigation burgeon in both jurisdictions.

[16] Roux (n 10) 10–15, citing CB Macpherson, *The Life and Times of Liberal Democracy* (OUP 1977) 99–100.

5. Symbolic Effects and the Limits of Litigation

Empirical assessment of the effectiveness of judicial decisions has proven very hard. In principle, this should be fairly simple, entailing a mere comparison between a judicial remedy and the changes that occurred afterwards within the legal and factual context of a case. However, none of the three elements involved in this is easy to establish: First, it is relatively common that judicial remedies are not completely precise, which may give rise to debate about the real scope of the judicial decision. Second, it is not clear that compliance with judicial orders depends exclusively on the defendant's behaviour. Third, the causal link between the actions taken to comply with the order and the changes that eventually emerge may be unclear. In such cases there is no certainty about the real causes that produce the social changes that develop after a judgment.

In the field of Sociology of Law, these difficulties are referred to as the 'gap problem'.[17] They represent the main challenge to the development of studies on judicial activism and, in general, to determine the real influence of courts in effecting social change. In spite of the efforts being made to establish objective criteria to evaluate this issue, significant progress is yet to be achieved. This is why we consider it important to stress the necessity of a complex, victim-centred perspective that recognises the difficulty of achieving social change through the judiciary alone. In our view, although the significance of other effects—such as the symbolic and indirect effects[18]— is undeniable, ultimately the effectiveness of the judgments that seek social transformation have to be established by considering the changes provoked in the living conditions of victims. Taking a different point of view may lead to the mistake of assessing inefficient judicial decisions as if they were successful in their purpose of accomplishing social rights.[19]

As shown in our respective chapters, this perspective points out the limits of litigation. In this regard, the cases of Colombia and South Africa show that the effective realisation of the constitution's programme needs more than judicial—and popular, as we explained earlier—commitment. It is true that courts may provoke important changes that otherwise would take very long. Examples of this kind of impact include securing the rights of minorities who have previously been seen as lower-class citizens, and the empowerment of these communities. However, it is necessary that these symbolic and indirect effects materialise in tangible and positive transformations for the victims. To achieve this, it is essential to obtain the

[17] D Nelken, 'The Gap Problem in the Sociology of Law: A Theoretical Review' (1981) 35(1) Windsor Yearbook of Access to Justice 35–61; A Sarat, 'Legal Effectiveness and Social Studies of Law: On the Unfortunate Persistence of a Research Tradition' (1985) 9(1) Legal Studies Forum 34–69.

[18] C Rodríguez Garavito and D Rodríguez Franco, *Juicio a la exclusión: El impacto de los tribunales sobre los derechos sociales en el Sur Global* (Siglo XXI editores 2015); M García Villegas, *La eficacia simbólica del derecho: Sociología política del campo jurídico en América Latina* (2nd edn, Debate 2014).

[19] A Gutiérrez Beltrán, *El amparo estructural de los derechos* (Centro de Estudios Políticos y Constitucionales 2018).

support of the political branches of government. Political mobilisation is arguably the best means to get this support and—in our opinion—the best complement for judicial action.[20]

6. Conclusion

In this joint reflection, we have paused to take stock of the valuable comparative lessons that can be drawn out across our earlier pieces. Class action litigation allows for individual claims to be aggregated and pursued, often in instances where an individual would be unable to litigate on her own. As a structural judgment, T-025 of 2004 attempts to secure broad change that is targeted at a policy level, rather than at the level of an individual litigant. Both chapters therefore consider mechanisms for litigating for collective relief.

After contrasting the procedural mechanisms available in the jurisdictions, we discussed three themes that emerged: first, the role that courts play in the context of structural judgments and class actions in Colombia and South Africa respectively; second, how both forms of litigation can promote participatory democracy; and third, the symbolic—rather than always substantive—impacts of this litigation.

Both the Colombian Constitutional Court's judgment in T-025 of 2004 and the development of class actions in South Africa instantiate remedial and procedural resourcefulness. As Gutiérrez Beltrán notes, T-025 of 2004 as a structural judgment was an exercise of constitutional imagination. Similarly, class actions in South Africa would never have been possible without a sea change in the approach to standing under the Constitution. Going forward greater innovation—or at the very least, the imaginative application—of procedural rules is required. Further, both Colombia's structural judgments and South African class action cases have required courts to take on very active roles, including by exercising ongoing jurisdiction regarding the supervision of orders and putting in place mechanisms for case management.

Both our chapters considered the effects of the legal mechanisms in question on participatory democracy. Finn noted that for class actions in South Africa, although the form of litigation can operate as a way of allowing claimants to access justice where this would otherwise not be possible, the litigation is also frequently lawyer-driven which raises its own set of issues. Gutiérrez Beltrán canvassed that T-025 of 2004 ostensibly involved citizens but with a paradoxical consequence, with the role of the victim left uncertain and lived conditions unchanged.

This in turn links to the symbolic effects that such litigation can have. In Colombia, arguably the greatest impact of T-025 of 2004 has been symbolic,

[20] In a South African context, see S Budlender and others, *Public Interest Litigation and Social Change in South Africa: Strategies, Tactics and Lessons* (The Atlantic Philanthropies 2014).

shifting how the arms of government understand forced displacement, and the obligations that are owed to its victims. And in theory, both structural judgments and class action litigation can provoke real social change. However, in many respects courts are not constructed as engines of broad structural change. As a result, in both jurisdictions, litigation has frequently proven to be insufficient for social reform.

Colombia and South Africa's constitutions represent an opportunity to break with the past and—at least in principle—envisage the possibility of more just societies. At the same time, the constitutional promise of widescale social change has fallen dramatically short in both countries, with litigation often proving to be an imperfect, incomplete tool for tackling systematic injustice. Going forward, our hope is that the comparative lessons that we can draw from our two jurisdictions will hone the tools that are available to shape our constitutional societies.

PART III

THE ROLE OF NOVEL LEGAL STRUCTURES IN REALISING TRANSITIONAL AND DISTRIBUTIVE JUSTICE

THEME 6

INDIGENOUS PEOPLES AND TRANSITIONAL JUSTICE

17

Twenty-Five Years of Democracy

The Consequences of South Africa's Post-Apartheid Constitution and Political Economy for Traditional Peoples

Sindiso Mnisi Weeks

1. Introduction

South Africa is well known for having emerged from centuries of colonialism followed by decades of apartheid; narrowly avoiding civil war, it successfully entered into democracy in April 1994. The vision fought for by millions of South Africans, supported by allies abroad, was for freedom accompanied by full citizenship, equal rights, and democratic access for all—regardless of race, culture, gender, or any other identity characteristic. While cultural diversity would be respected, none would be forcibly subjected to a separate system of law based thereon. All would have equal protection and rights under the new, unified system of law, with the progressive Constitution being supreme. This negotiated agreement followed centuries of discrimination against Khoi-San and 'Bantu' people in South Africa under the Dutch and then British colonial regimes, which had been followed by decades under the Nationalist Party's system of oppression (euphemistically termed 'separate development' or 'apartheid').

It has now been over a quarter of a century since the Interim Constitution of South Africa, 1993, was adopted as the first legal formalisation of South Africa's transition from apartheid to democracy. This marker of the end of the oppressive and segregationist regimes of colonialism and apartheid—which social contract would form the backbone of South Africa's transitional and restorative justice processes to come—was followed by the Final Constitution of 1996 shortly thereafter. The aim of this chapter is to provide a socio-legal analysis of the situation of traditional peoples in post-apartheid South Africa subsequent to this transition from a tumultuous past to the democratic present. The question is asked whether the final transition to a constitutional democracy in 1996 resulted in greater land rights

Sindiso Mnisi Weeks, *Twenty-Five Years of Democracy* In: *Transitional Justice, Distributive Justice, and Transformative Constitutionalism*. Edited by: David Bilchitz and Raisa Cachalia, with Magdalena Inés Correa Henao and Nathalia Bautista Pizarro, Oxford University Press.
DOI: 10.1093/oso/9780192887627.003.0017

access and security for these marginalised groups. Put differently, the question is whether the transitional justice arrangements in the Constitution, while professed to be deeply transformative, have indeed yielded restorative justice on the ground.

The chapter begins in Section 2 by defining the application of the term 'traditional peoples' in South Africa and providing a brief summary of their history until South Africa's official entry into its modern democratic era. This discussion is set against the backdrop of the constitutional negotiation process, which brought about the legal recognition of their rights for the first time. The section also engages with the way in which Parliament and the Constitutional Court have thus far interpreted the legal status of traditional peoples and their governing laws. In Section 3, the process, meaning, and consequences of the negotiated transition to democracy for traditional peoples in South Africa is canvassed. In this regard, the most important aspects of the transition from apartheid to democracy are emphasised, such as the recognition in the Final Constitution of the status of customary law,[1] rights to property,[2] political participation,[3] and access to justice[4] as well as the potential tensions between Khoi-San and traditional African communities.[5] This section goes on to discuss the ways in which the cumulative impact of the socio-economic and politico-legal realities in post-apartheid South Africa have yielded limited land rights protection for traditional peoples and, consequently, not altered the conditions of material and social precarity that affected these groups. The chapter argues that the main reason for this failed impact of the democratic transition is the disproportionate powers given to traditional leaders.

2. Who Are Traditional Peoples in South Africa?

The South African Constitution, 1996, describes African communities that would previously have been referred to as 'tribal' using the language of their living under 'customary law' and being subject to 'traditional authority' and 'traditional leadership'.[6] Subsequent legislation regulating these communities has used the language

[1] Constitution of the Republic of South Africa (hereafter 'Constitution'), ss 39(2) and 211(3).

[2] Constitution, s 25.

[3] Constitution, s 195(e). See also *Doctors for Life International v Speaker of the National Assembly* [2006] ZACC 11; 2006 (6) SA 416 (CC).

[4] Constitution, s 34.

[5] F Nkhwashu, 'UPDATE: Khoisan Rejects Proposed Traditional and Khoisan Leadership Bill' *Rekord East* (20 June 2019) <https://rekordeast.co.za/210444/khoisan-rejects-proposed-traditional-leader-bill/> accessed 6 July 2020; J Gerber, 'Ramaphosa Signs Contentious Traditional and Khoi San Leadership Bill into Law' *News24* <https://www.news24.com/news24/southafrica/news/ramaphosa-signs-contentious-traditional-and-khoi-san-leadership-bill-into-law-20191129> accessed 6 July 2020.

[6] Constitution, s 211:

(1) The institution, status and role of traditional leadership, according to customary law, are recognised, subject to the Constitution.
(2) A traditional authority that observes a system of customary law may function subject to any applicable legislation and customs, which includes amendments to, or repeal of, that legislation or those customs.

of 'traditional communities'.[7] In this chapter I retain use of this language of 'traditional' to refer loosely to these rural African communities who are descendants of 'Bantu' people. However, rather than using the contested nomenclature and definitions of the government, 'traditional communities', I refer to 'traditional peoples',[8] thus leveraging the international language of 'peoples' as self-determined.[9] This allows me to discuss further, as I do in the following paragraphs, the ways in which the terminology and categorisation used by the government is contested and debatable.

The Khoi-San peoples with whom traditional peoples of South Africa might be contrasted are the composite of nomadic Khoikhoi pastoralists and San hunter-gatherers who were found in South Africa and southern Namibia by Dutch and German colonisers after thousands of years in the area. Colonisers historically referred to them by the terms, 'Bushmen' and 'Hottentots'.[10] The Bantu peoples of South Africa are but a subset of the hundreds of ethnic groups in sub-Saharan Africa (residing right up to Central Africa and the Great Lakes region)[11] who speak the 440 to 680 Bantu languages in existence.[12] The word, 'bantu', literally means 'people'.

Under apartheid, the overwhelming majority of Black people were legally allowed to possess and occupy land situated in reserves that made up only 6 per cent of South Africa (this number was later increased to 13 per cent of the territory to be held for Black people under the South African Development Trust). These categories of persons were denied citizenship in the rest of the country. In these reserves and black spots, the 'natives' were considered mere 'subjects' of 'despotic chiefs'.[13]

s 212(1): 'National legislation may provide for a role for traditional leadership as an institution at local level on matters affecting local communities.'

[7] See, eg, the Traditional Leadership and Governance Framework Act 41 of 2003 (TLGFA 2003), and Traditional and Khoi-San Leadership Act 3 of 2019 (TKLA 2019), which has been signed into law but has yet to come into operation.

[8] African Charter of Human and Peoples' Rights (Banjul Charter), OAU Doc CAB/LEG/67/3/Rev.5 (1981) (African Charter 1981). Also see R Kiwanuka, 'The Meaning of "People" in the African Charter on Human and Peoples' Rights' (1988) 82 American Journal of International Law 80.

[9] African Charter 1981. See also W Wicomb and H Smith, 'Customary Communities as Peoples and Their Customary Tenure as Culture: What We Can Do with the Endorois Decision' (2011) 11 African Human Rights Law Journal 422.

[10] M Brenzinger, 'The Twelve Modern Khoisan Languages' in S Ermisch and R Voßen (eds), *Khoisan Languages and Linguistics: Proceedings of the 3rd International Symposium* (Köppe 2010); A Barnard, *Hunters and Herders of Southern Africa: A Comparative Ethnography of the Khoisan Peoples* (CUP 1992); I Schapera, *The Khoisan Peoples of South Africa: Bushmen and Hottentots* (Routledge 1930).

[11] SA Tishkoff and others, 'The Genetic Structure and History of Africans and African Americans' (2009) 324 Science 1035; C Schlebusch and M Jakobsson, 'Tales of Human Migration, Admixture, and Selection in Africa' (2018) 19 Annual Review of Genomics and Human Genetics 405.

[12] M Guthrie, *Comparative Bantu: An Introduction to the Comparative Linguistics and Prehistory of the Bantu Languages*, vols 1–4 (Gregg International 1967); JF Maho, 'The Bantu Line-Up: Comparative Overview of Three Bantu Classifications' (Unpublished manuscript, Göteborg University 2002).

[13] M Mamdani, *Citizen and Subject: Contemporary Africa and the Legacy of Late Colonialism* (PUP 1996).

From Law 4 of 1887, to the Land Act of 1913, to the Native Administration Act 38 of 1927, to the Bantu Authorities Act 68 of 1951; the list goes on, the colonial, union, and apartheid governments in South Africa tried to answer what Mahmood Mamdani, in *Citizen and Subject*,[14] calls 'the native question': how could a minority population take charge of and control the majority population? The way that this state problem-solving manifested, as Mamdani details, is through 'indirect rule', which he terms 'de-centralised despotism'—that is, the attempt to use, shape and distort indigenous and traditional systems of law and governance to advance state objectives.[15]

According to the 2019 estimates, Black South Africans make up 80.7 per cent of the population, while White South Africans constitute 7.9 per cent, Coloured South Africans 8.8 per cent, and Asian South Africans 2.6 per cent.[16] Some Khoi-San people, having lost their traditional languages to the imposition and dominance of Afrikaans[17] during apartheid, might be characterised as Coloured. Black South Africans (those who would typically be classified as Bantu) can be subdivided into several major ethnic groups presented in order of size: AmaZulu, AmaXhosa, BaSotho (South Sotho), BaPedi (North Sotho), BaTswana, VhaVenda (VhaNgona), VaTsonga (Shangaan), EmaSwati (Swazi), and AmaNdebele.[18] Much like the Bantu people of South Africa, the remaining South Africans referred to as Khoi-San are culturally and linguistically diverse.[19] Given the artificiality of colonial borders imposed in Africa, several of these Bantu and Khoi-San groups are transnational—extending from South Africa into Lesotho, Botswana, Zimbabwe, Mozambique, Swaziland, and Namibia.

In recognition of this diversity and the essential place of language in ethnicity, the South African Constitution recognises eleven official languages that align with the nine Bantu groups that have been named (which can be loosely divided into Nguni, Sotho-Tswana, and TshiVenda-Xitsonga languages) plus the two dominant European languages in South Africa, English and Afrikaans.[20] No Khoi-San languages are recognised as official languages; however, section 6(5)(a)(ii) of the Constitution recognises their status, and the many other languages spoken by South Africans, as deserving of government protection, promotion, and development. Sections 30 and 31 further protect linguistic and cultural rights.[21]

[14] ibid.
[15] ibid.
[16] Statistics South Africa, 'Mid-Year Population Estimates, 2019' (Statistics South Africa 2019) <http://www.statssa.gov.za/?page_id=1854> accessed 6 July 2020.
[17] Afrikaans is the linguistic descendent of Dutch and was imposed by the Dutch settler population once it took over governance of South Africa from the British in 1948.
[18] See Constitution, s 6(1).
[19] Brenzinger (n 10); Barnard (n 10).
[20] Constitution, s 6(1).
[21] Constitution, s 30:

> Language and culture.
> Everyone has the right to use the language and to participate in the cultural life of their choice, but no one exercising these rights may do so in a manner inconsistent with any provision of the Bill of Rights.

In this chapter, I focus on the various traditional peoples in South Africa. In reality, the colonial-apartheid government drew little explicit distinction between 'Bantu' and Khoi-San people in its policies. For instance, the Native Administration Act 38 of 1927 was designed to regulate all communities who were organised as 'tribes'.[22] Some Khoi-San people would be regulated as Coloureds (descendants of mixed race heritage), especially when not organised as 'tribal' groups. Today, under international law, the distinction is drawn between 'indigenous' and 'tribal peoples'.[23] As South Africa's 'first peoples', the Khoi-San would arguably fall under the former category.

Within South Africa, there is precedent for nominally considering 'Bantu' people 'indigenous'. For instance, the early Constitutional Court cases referred to what have since been labelled 'customary communities' (or, in the African Commission and Inter-American Commission on Human Rights, 'tribal communities')[24] as 'indigenous'. Specifically, the court in the *Alexkor*[25] case, concerning the traditional lands of the people of Richtersveld, Northern Cape (the Nama, who are the largest surviving clan of the traditional nomadic/transhumance herders known as the Khoikhoi, who once occupied the entire south-western part of Africa), generically referred to their customary normative arrangements as 'indigenous law'.[26] Then-Chief Justice Sandile Ngcobo did the same with reference to all customary law in the case challenging the Communal Land Rights Act 11 of 2004: *Tongoane*.[27]

s 31:

Cultural, religious and linguistic communities.

(1) Persons belonging to a cultural, religious or linguistic community may not be denied the right, with other members of that community—
  (a) to enjoy their culture, practise their religion and use their language; and
  (b) to form, join and maintain cultural, religious and linguistic associations and other organs of civil society.

(2) The rights in subsection (1) may not be exercised in a manner inconsistent with any provision of the Bill of Rights.

[22] s 1 says, 'The Governor-General shall be the supreme chief of all Natives'; s 2(7) adds that he 'may recognise or appoint any person as a chief or headman in charge of a tribe or of a location'; and s 5(1)(a) then says he 'may define the boundaries of any area of any tribe or of a location' whenever he sees fit.

[23] ILO, 'Convention concerning indigenous and tribal peoples in independent countries' (1989): C169; UN General Assembly, 'United Nations Declaration on the Rights of Indigenous Peoples' (13 September 2007) <https://www.un.org/development/desa/indigenouspeoples/wp-content/uploads/sites/19/2018/11/UNDRIP_E_web.pdf> accessed 18 September 2023.

[24] See *Moiwana Village v Suriname*, Judgment of 15 June 2005. Series C No 124 [85] and [134]–[135]. See further Inter-American Commission on Human Rights (IACHmR), Report No 9/06 *The Twelve Saramaka Clans (Los) v Suriname* (2 March 2006); Inter-American Court of Human Rights (IACtHR), *Case of the Saramaka People v Suriname* (Judgment of 28 November 2007) [80]–[84].

[25] *Alexkor Ltd and Another v the Richtersveld Community* [2003] ZACC 18; 2004 (5) SA 460 (CC) ('*Alexkor*').

[26] ibid [7].

[27] *Tongoane v National Minister for Agriculture and Land Affairs* [2010] ZACC 10; 2010 (6) SA 214 (CC) ('*Tongoane*') [20].

Otherwise, the Constitutional Court has mostly dropped the language of 'indigenous law' in favour of 'customary law' and, more specifically, 'living customary law', which it contrasts with the 'official customary law' that was enacted by the state and authored in academic texts.[28] Recent legislation, the Traditional and Khoi-San Leadership Act 3 of 2019 (TKLA 2019),[29] which replaced the Traditional Leadership and Governance Framework Act of 2003 (TLGFA 2003),[30] distinguishes between traditional and Khoi-San groups while it superimposes the colonially-imagined forms of regulation for traditional peoples onto the governance arrangements for Khoi-San peoples.

It is clear from the discussion so far that it is not that easy to distinguish regulatory impacts on traditional versus Indigenous people in South Africa. However, aspiring to the greatest precision possible, I will limit the discussion in the remainder of this chapter to traditional peoples. Hence, the next section will describe how and why the regulatory response under the Constitution has ultimately not helped with advancing the land rights security and self-determination of traditional peoples.

3. What Have the Implications of the Transition to Democracy Been for Traditional Peoples in South Africa?

The negotiations leading to the end of apartheid were not without conflict.[31] They are worth mentioning here, especially, because process (and participation) is often deeply tied to resultant content in reaching agreements that end conflict. When the time came to negotiate a transition to democracy in South Africa, traditional leaders were invited to be observers to the initial 'talks about talks'.[32] As Mandela explained their invitation: 'Just as such leaders were present at the formation of the ANC [African National Congress], they should be present at the watershed events that herald the dawn of a new, democratic South Africa'.[33] With traditional leaders' revered place ensured at the Convention for a Democratic South Africa (CODESA) I and II negotiation table, their greatest victory was securing

[28] *Alexkor* (n 25) fn 51; *Bhe v Magistrate, Khayelitsha; Shibi v Sithole* [2004] ZACC 18; 2005 (1) SA 580 (CC) ('*Bhe*') [87]; *Shilubana v Nwamitwa* [2008] ZACC 9; 2009 (2) SA 66 (CC) ('*Shilubana*') [46]; *Gumede v President of the Republic of South Africa* [2008] ZACC 23; 2009 (3) SA 152 (CC) [11] and [29] all acknowledge the 'customary law' referred to in the Constitution as that which is lived and developed through practice by the people who observe it. This is otherwise termed 'living customary law'.

[29] TKLA 2019.

[30] TLGFA 2003.

[31] H Klug, 'Challenging Constitutionalism in Post-Apartheid South Africa' (2016) 2 Constitutional Studies 41.

[32] B Oomen, *Chiefs in South Africa: Law, Power and Culture in the Post-Apartheid Era* (James Currey Ltd 2005) 45.

[33] Nelson Mandela, 'Participation of Traditional Leaders at Codesa' <http://www.anc.org.za/ancdocs/pr/1991/pr1217.html> ANC, 1991, as cited in Oomen, *Chiefs in South Africa* (n 32) 45.

constitutional recognition, first in the Interim Constitution,[34] which ultimately led to their office being named in the Final Constitution.[35]

A. Customary Law in the Bill of Rights

The 1993 Constitution granted South Africans of all races citizenship of the country, which Black people had not had under apartheid. As the Preamble made the point, 'there is a need to create a new order in which all South Africans will be entitled to a common South African citizenship in a sovereign and democratic constitutional state in which there is equality between men and women and people of all races so that all citizens shall be able to enjoy and exercise their fundamental rights and freedoms'.[36] In the transitional justice arrangements articulated in the Interim Constitution, and the Final Constitution of 1996 thereafter, traditional communities also were secured recognition of their cultures and normative orders.[37] Under the Constitution, which was established as the supreme law of South

[34] Interim Constitution, ss 181–184, and Constitutional Principle XIII. Also see *Certification of the Constitution of the Republic of South Africa, 1996* [1996] ZACC 26; 1996 (4) SA 744 (CC), in which the Constitutional Court had to consider whether the relevant sections in the New Text (the Final Constitution) complied with those in the Interim Constitution.

The Court summarised the traditional leader objections in para 189 as follows:

> The objectors complained that NT 211 and 212 fail to protect the 'institution, status and role' of traditional leadership, as required by CP XIII. They argued that these words encompass the powers and functions that traditional authorities have long exercised; such powers and functions must not only be acknowledged, but 'protected'; and their substance has to be determined not by national legislation but 'according to indigenous law'. They argued that the use of the word 'role' in addition to the words 'institution' and 'status' suggests that a constitutionally entrenched function is called for.... The implication is that the provisions of CP XIII must contemplate a role for traditional leadership in government, otherwise the proviso would be redundant. They argued that the purpose underlying a guaranteed and active role for traditional leaders in government is to ensure an appropriate place in the constitutional structure for elements of traditional forms of government that have deep historical roots in the country and that continue to have direct relevance for millions of people, particularly many living in rural areas, where the perceived reality of government is the traditional authority rather than the modern state [footnotes omitted].

The Court found, however, as it stated in para 197, that:

> the NT complies with CP XIII by giving express guarantees of the continued existence of traditional leadership and the survival of an evolving customary law. The institution, status and role of traditional leadership are thereby protected. They are protected by means of entrenchment in the NT and any attempt at interference would be subject to constitutional scrutiny. The CA cannot be constitutionally faulted for leaving the complicated, varied and ever-developing specifics of how such leadership should function in the wider democratic society, and how customary law should develop and be interpreted, to future social evolution, legislative deliberation and judicial interpretation.

It is the latter three categories of debate that are discussed in the remainder of this chapter.

[35] Constitution, ss 211(1) and 212(1) (as quoted in n 6).

[36] Also see Constitution, s 20: 'Every citizen shall have the right to enter, remain in and leave the Republic, and no citizen shall without justification be deprived of his or her citizenship.'

[37] See Constitution, s 31: 'Every person shall have the right to use the language and to participate in the cultural life of his or her choice'; s 181(2): 'Indigenous law shall be subject to regulation by law'; and

Africa, all law must be consistent with the Constitution and the Bill of Rights.[38] Flowing therefrom is the understanding that all 'legal' solutions must be consistent with the Constitution's principles. The Constitution recognises customary law as distinct from common law. However, difficulties invariably arise in identifying and describing customary law; after all, 'customary law' (like 'culture') is not defined in the Constitution. At times, this challenge with defining it has resulted in civil law being superimposed on customary law and its adherents.[39]

Still, the Constitution places the courts (and legislature) under the obligation to respect and accommodate customary law in the South African legal system. Section 211(3) provides that '[t]he courts must apply customary law when that law is applicable, subject to the Constitution and any legislation that specifically deals with customary law'. Sections 30 and 31 of the Bill of Rights entrench the individual and group rights to culture, respectively. In subsections 39(2) and (3) customary law is subjected, along with common law, to development by the courts in accordance with 'the spirit, purport and objects of the Bill of Rights'.

This explicit constitutional recognition, however, does not place customary law beyond contention. Subsection 7(2) provides that '[t]he state must respect, protect, promote and fulfil the rights in the Bill of Rights'. And, then, subsection 8(1) states that '[t]he Bill of Rights applies to all law, and binds the legislature, the executive, the judiciary and all organs of state'. In sections 30 and 31, the right to culture is subject to the qualification that it may not be exercised 'in a manner inconsistent with any provision of the Bill of Rights'. Since this condition rarely accompanies rights in the Bill of Rights, the words obviously cannot be ignored, and these qualifications may be read as claw-back provisions. Thus, while no rights in the Constitution are absolute but subject to being balanced against other rights when infringement is alleged, the impression created by the text of the Constitution is that the right to culture is not to be treated like all other rights and is always subordinate to them.

The Congress of Traditional Leaders of South Africa (CONTRALESA) repeatedly makes this argument that customary law is subordinated to the Constitution.[40] It was the argument this traditional leader lobby group presented at the initial negotiations around the Constitution. Yet, at that point, women's rights groups won (in part) by succeeding in having customary law subjected to the Bill of Rights—especially the right to equality on the basis of gender, among other things.[41] Yet

CP XIII(1): 'Indigenous law, like common law, shall be recognised and applied by the courts, subject to the fundamental rights contained in the Constitution and to legislation dealing specifically therewith.'

[38] Preamble and Constitution, ss 1I, 7(2), 8(1), and 211(3).

[39] In *Bhe* 2004 (n 28), the Court developed customary law by applying the Intestate Succession Act 81 of 1987. See discussion in S MnisiWeeks, 'Customary Succession and the Development of Customary Law: The Bhe Legacy' in M Bishop and A Price (eds), *A Transformative Justice: Essays in Honour of Pius Langa* (Juta 2015).

[40] JL Comaroff and J Comaroff, *Ethnicity, Inc* (University of Chicago Press 2009).

[41] F Kaganas and C Murray, 'The Contest Between Culture and Gender Equality under South Africa's Interim Constitution' (1994) 21(4) Journal of Law and Society 409.

CONTRALESA has not given up its campaign against the terms of transitional justice settled upon in the constitutional drafting process and continues to advocate for the Constitution to be changed to reflect the sovereignty of traditional leaders and allegedly, with that, the autonomy of customary law and its communities.[42] On this point, several scholars have argued that traditional leaders' allegations are incorrect and, in fact, self-serving.[43] Empirical evidence detailed in the following two sections supports this scholarly claim.

B. *Land: A Primary Site of Contestation*

A prime site for this debate in South Africa today is land. Section 25(6) of the Constitution prescribes that '[a] person or community whose tenure of land is legally insecure as a result of past racially discriminatory laws or practices is entitled, to the extent provided by an Act of Parliament, either to tenure which is legally secure or to comparable redress.' Furthermore, aimed at restorative justice, section 25(7) provides that '[a] person or community dispossessed of property after 19 June 1913 as a result of past racially discriminatory laws or practices is entitled, to the extent provided by an Act of Parliament, either to restitution of that property or to equitable redress.'[44] As affirmed by the Constitutional Court judgment in *Alexkor*,[45] traditional communities' land can be so categorised.[46] Furthermore, the Constitution makes it an obligation that 'Parliament must enact the legislation referred to in subsection (6)'.[47] This provision is complemented by the government's obligation, per section 25(5), to 'take reasonable legislative and other measures, within its available resources, to foster conditions which enable citizens to gain access to land on an equitable basis'. Yet the government has not made sufficient advances in furthering redistributive justice in this sense.

[42] Comaroff and Comaroff, *Ethnicity, Inc* (n 40).

[43] V Bronstein, 'Reconceptualizing the Customary Law Debate in South Africa' (1998) 14 South African Journal on Human Rights 388; S MnisiWeeks, 'Regulating Vernacular Dispute Resolution Forums: Controversy Concerning the Process, Substance and Implications of South Africa's Traditional Courts Bill' (2002) 12 Oxford University Commonwealth Law Journal 133; S MnisiWeeks, 'Securing Women's Property Inheritance in the Context of Plurality: Negotiations of Law and Authority in Mbuzini Customary Courts and Beyond' (2011) Acta Juridica; Comaroff and Comaroff 140, *Ethnicity, Inc* (n 40); L Ntsebeza, *Democracy Compromised: Chiefs and the Politics of Land in South Africa* (HSRC Press 2006); B Oomen, *Tradition on the Move: Chiefs, Democracy and Change in Rural South Africa* in M Maurick and M Cornelis (eds), *NIZA-Cahiers*, vol 6 (Netherlands Institute for Southern Africa 2000) 10–29 and 62–69.

[44] The date given is when the Natives Land Act 27 of 1913 came into operation.

[45] *Alexkor* (n 25) [36]–[37].

[46] Ibid [50]–[64]. In para 103, the Court 'declared that ... the first plaintiff [the Richtersveld Community] is entitled in terms of section 2(1) of the Restitution of Land Rights Act 22 of 1994 to restitution of the right to ownership of the subject land (including its minerals and precious stones) and to the exclusive beneficial use and occupation thereof'.

[47] Constitution, s 25(9).

The sections of the property clause that I have named, which are most directly relevant to traditional peoples in South Africa, necessitate taking a look at the distribution statistics demonstrating the tremendous implications apartheid had and continues to have for land justice. It is often claimed that, in 1994, 87 per cent of South Africa's 122,081,300 hectare land mass was owned by White people, with only 13 per cent in Black ownership.[48] However, this was the apartheid government's goal, which it had not managed to achieve by the time apartheid ended. Thus, in reality, the land was broken up into 67 per cent under White commercial agricultural ownership; 15 per cent constituting 'Black' communal areas (then known as 'Bantustans' or 'Homelands') which were mostly under state ownership; 10 per cent other state land (such as state offices and conservation areas); and a remaining 8 per cent that included metropolitan and other urban areas.[49] The latest numbers from 2017 show that, according to the World Bank, '[a]lthough 80 percent of land claims had been settled by 2016, the amount of land transferred is still small. The target of transferring 30 percent of arable land to Black landholders by 2014 was not achieved, and there is limited information on the current level of transfer.'[50]

As the 2018 World Bank report accurately captures, tenure security in South Africa continues to be governed by the Interim Protection of Informal Land Rights Act 31 of 1996 (IPILRA 1996), which was supposed to be stop-gap legislation when it was passed twenty two years ago but has had to be renewed annually since.[51] IPILRA is aimed at securing 'the rights of people occupying land without formal documentary rights, such as rights to household plots, fields, grazing land, or other shared resources'.[52] However, its effectiveness is limited by the absence of a robust land administration system to support it. As a consequence, at present the formal administrative processes necessary to identify and record rights, or resolve arising disputes, are lacking. This is despite the fact that the Department of Land Affairs (as it was named at the time of IPILRA's passing) has internal policies that aim to

[48] Cherryl Walker Institute for Poverty, Land and Agrarian Studies (PLAAS) *Fact Check No. 1: Land Reform* <http://repository.uwc.ac.za/xmlui/bitstream/handle/10566/4455/fc_1_distribution_land_south_africa_overview_2013.pdf?sequence=1&isAllowed=y> accessed 17 May 2019 ('PLAAS 2013').

[49] ibid.

[50] World Bank Group, *An Incomplete Transition: Overcoming the Legacy of Exclusion in South Africa. Systematic Country Diagnostic* (World Bank 2018) 12, 43–44 <https://openknowledge.worldbank.org/handle/10986/29793> accessed 4 June 2019. That said, some have concluded that, in total, 17,439 million hectares of White-owned land have been transferred since 1994, under the 'willing buyer, willing seller' policy. This is 21 per cent of the 82,759 million hectares of South African farmland that is in freehold. Of this, 11 million hectares have been transferred via restitution and redistribution programmes, with an additional 4,027 million hectares being due to state procurement. The remainder is accounted for by private land purchases. See W Sihlobo and T Kapuya, 'SPECIAL REPORT: The truth about land ownership in South Africa' *Rand Daily Mail* (Johannesburg, 23 July 2018) <https://www.businesslive.co.za/rdm/politics/2018-07-23-special-report-the-truth-about-land-ownership-in-south-africa/> accessed 4 June 2019.

[51] World Bank (n 50) 44.

[52] ibid.

clarify the process for systematically documenting rights, and thus preventing disputes, under the Act. These policies are not implemented.

The World Bank aptly observes that '[a]n important provision of the act is to ensure proper community consultation in cases where external investors wish to access communal land'.[53] The fact that the Department of Rural Development and Land Reform has mostly failed to observe these protections (due to a lack of political will, a shortage of trained personnel, and the absence of comprehensive legislation) has led to some external investors violating them, especially in the realm of exploitation of mineral resources by the extractive industry. The World Bank also describes the 'best' case scenario where some potential investors decline to invest due to uncertainty on how to negotiate leases on communal land or that they can trust that the arrangements will be respected.

It has been over a quarter of a century since South Africa gained its independence and yet legislation to strengthen tenure security, and related institutions, in the former homelands is yet to be implemented. The Communal Land Rights Act was duly struck down by the Constitutional Court in 2010.[54] The Communal Land Tenure Bill[55] that is pending presently is likely to meet the same fate as its predecessor. As the World Bank correctly summarises, '[a]t the heart of the long-standing stalemate regarding tenure reform in communal areas is the significant power given to traditional leaders'.[56]

C. Traditional Leaders Stand in the Way

'They want to sell us.' Those are the haunting words of an elderly woman in the forty-eight-minute narrative documentary, *This Land* (2017), about the struggle of Black, rural people for protection of their rights and accountability on communal land in rural KwaZulu-Natal. Her words and expression, well-worn hands covering her face, capture the painful controversy of the democratic government's undemocratic approach to land reform in rural South Africa. Who are 'they' who want to sell poor, rural people like this woman? In short, traditional leaders in cahoots with the government.

[53] ibid.

[54] *Tongoane* (n 27). Had the Act been implemented, it would have severely undermined the tenure rights of millions of Black, rural South Africans, as shown in A Claassens and S Mnisi, 'Rural Women Redefining Land Rights in the Context of Living Customary Law' (2009) 25 South African Journal on Human Rights 491 and S MnisiWeeks and A Claassens, 'Tensions Between Vernacular Values that Prioritise Basic Needs and State Versions of Customary Law that Contradict Them' (2011) 22 Stellenbosch Law Review 823.

[55] Department of Rural Development and Land Reform, Government Gazette No 40965 Vol 625 (7 July 2017).

[56] World Bank (n 50) 44.

This old woman was describing the reality that Former President Kgalema Motlanthe later acknowledged after hearing hundreds of rural people across South Africa give testimony on their experiences of land confiscations, insecurity, and destitution, especially in mineral-rich areas such as the Platinum Belt in the northern provinces and land under the jurisdiction of the Ingonyama Trust Board (ITB) in KwaZulu-Natal. These testimonies culminated in the 'Report of the High Level Panel on the Assessment of Key Legislation and the Acceleration of Fundamental Change',[57] which was released in October 2017.

Speaking at a land summit in May 2018, Motlanthe said of the ITB, 'People who have lived there for generations must pay the Ingonyama Trust Board R1,000 rent which escalates yearly by 10%'.[58] Specifically, the ITB approaches and advertises to poor, rural people under its jurisdiction that they have insecure tenure in the form of apartheid-era 'Permission to Occupy' (PTO) certificates or no documented right to occupy the land they have inhabited, in many instances, for generations. It tells them that, they can 'upgrade' their land rights by entering into long-term leases with the ITB so that they can have proof of residence to register to vote, open bank accounts, register cellular phones, or obtain rural allowances from employers.

These are people who typically have either (i) PTO certificates, which are apartheid-era documentation that is upgradeable to ownership in terms of the Upgrading of Land Tenure Rights Act 112 of 1991; or (ii) informal land rights established by long-term occupation that are likely to be considered customary ownership and thus entitle the people to compensation under IPILRA. The ITB, having gotten these people unknowingly to trade in their rights that are more akin to ownership for the status of tenants, then extorts these people, escalating annual rental fees.

The ITB allegedly continues to issue this solicitation via its Facebook and Twitter accounts and advertisements despite the fact that, in March 2018, the Chair of the Portfolio Committee on Rural Development and Land Reform directed the ITB to stop this practice, and a senior official of the Department confirmed that the Trust's income-generating scheme is unauthorised, and violates both the Constitution and the Public Finance Management Act 1 of 1999. Motlanthe shared this example as a member of President Cyril Ramaphosa's task team which was meant to 'clear existing confusion' on the African National Congress's (ANC) position on 'the land question'.[59] At the time, Motlanthe was quoted as concluding:

[57] *Report of the High Level Panel on the Assessment of Key Legislation and the Acceleration of Fundamental Change* (Parliament of South Africa, October 2017), <https://www.parliament.gov.za/storage/app/media/Pages/2017/october/High_Level_Panel/HLP_Report/HLP_report.pdf> accessed on 4 June 2019.

[58] H Nhlabathi, 'Motlanthe: Traditional leaders must not control ANC' *The Witness* (Durban, 21 May 2018) <https://www.pressreader.com/south-africa/the-witness/20180521/281681140535742> accessed 4 June 2019.

[59] T Madia, 'Traditional leaders act like village tin-pot dictators – Motlanthe' *News24* (Boksburg, 19 May 2018) <https://www.news24.com/SouthAfrica/News/traditional-leaders-act-like-village-tin-pot-dictators-motlanthe-20180519> accessed 4 June 2019.

> Some traditional leaders support the ANC, but the majority of them are acting like village tin-pot dictators to the people there. The people had high hopes the ANC would liberate them from these confines of the homeland systems, but clearly we are the ones who are saying the land must go to traditional leaders and not the people.[60]

Unsurprisingly, the comment attracted a lot of criticism of the former president, particularly from traditional leaders[61] and other insiders and traditional leader allies such as Mangosuthu Buthelezi.[62] But is what Motlanthe said really unwarranted? The core debate is about who owns the land—whether (i) the traditional leaders and/or kings; or (ii) the people who have lived on the land, burying their ancestors, grazing their cattle, fetching grass, wood, and water there.

The essential challenge is one of reconciling a global and local political economy that centres on individual and exclusive forms of ownership with the customary system of nested, overlapping, and relative rights co-existing at multiple levels of social organisation from the strongest family level rights to the weakest community level rights. As the Court in *Alexkor* correctly observed, in considering 'the nature of the indigenous law [land] rights exercised by the Richtersveld Community', 'to understand them properly these rights must be considered on their own terms and not through the prism of the common law'.[63] The government has failed at cultivating this understanding, instead embracing the arguments of traditional leaders that they are entitled to control and benefit from the land as effective owners. Eschewing any efforts at restorative and redistributive transitional justice in former homeland areas, the ITB has proceeded on the argument that the Zulu King owns the land and rents it to the people on it. The King has therefore interpreted the High Level Panel report produced under Motlanthe's chairmanship as an attack on Zulu land and sovereignty, and has mobilised *amabutho* (warriors) to do whatever is necessary to protect them, including threatening secession.

In May 2018, Deputy President David Mabuza was reported as saying in response to questions in the National Assembly that insecure tenure sometimes emanates from the 'false view' that 'land under traditional leadership is owned

60 ibid.

61 Staff Reporter, 'Zulus won't sit and watch while major decisions are made about their land—Zwelithini' *City Press* (Johannesburg, 1 July 2018) <https://city-press.news24.com/News/zulus-will-not-sit-and-watch-while-major-decisions-are-made-about-their-land-zwelithini-20180701>accessed 4 June 2019. See also B Friedman, 'Contralesa deeply insulted by Motlanthe's "tinpot dictator" comment' 702 (Johannesburg, 22 May 2018) <http://www.702.co.za/articles/304572/contralesa-deeply-insulted-by-motlanthe-s-tinpot-dictator-comment> accessed 4 June 2019.

62 News24 Wire, 'Motlanthe's "village tin-pot dictators" comment a long-unstated position of the ANC—Buthelezi' *Polity* (Johannesburg, 28 June 2018) <http://www.polity.org.za/article/motlanthes-village-tin-pot-dictators-comment-a-long-unstated-position-of-the-anc-buthelezi-2018-06-28> accessed 4 June 2019.

63 *Alexkor* (n 25) [55].

by traditional leaders'.[64] He continued, '[i]n terms of custom it is the people who own the land; traditional leaders are only custodians of the people's land'.[65] Unfortunately, this language of 'custodianship' does not settle the issue. It is slippery language that the ANC has used for decades to justify allowing traditional leaders control of customary land on behalf of 'their people' (who are regarded and treated as their subjects). Barbara Oomen describes post-1994 South Africa as a 'Patchwork Democracy' and writes, '[a]lthough the South African Department of Native Affairs was renamed Traditional Affairs after the transition to democracy, many things stayed the same'.[66] This department has since been renamed again the Department of Cooperative Governance and Traditional Affairs, but the reality described by Oomen has deepened even further. As John and Jean Comaroff argue, the democratically-elected government of South Africa adopted instruments of coercion when it took over from the apartheid government. This is part of the global trend that the Comaroffs refer to as the 'fetishism of the law', whereby the legal sphere 'is objectified, ascribed a life-force of its own, and attributed the capacity to configure a world of relations in its own image'.[67]

The upshot is that the legislation passed on governance and land tenure since the ANC took over in 1994 has actually been built on the frameworks and foundations of the apartheid legislation that preceded it. It has thus perpetuated the fictitious structures that the oppressive regimes of South Africa's segregationist past created and branded 'tribal' in the Native Administration Act 38 of 1927 and Bantu Authorities Act 68 of 1951. The rhetoric surrounding these legislative actions would have the public believe that the government is protecting and continuing traditional peoples' culture and traditions and, thereby, advancing transitional justice. However, a close examination of the evidence shows that this is not the case.

D. 'Citizens' with No Consultation and No Choice

There is a key concept in African communities: 'Inkosi iyinkosi ngabantu', or 'Kgosi ke kgosi ka batho'. It translates as '[a] chief/king is a chief/king by, through, and because of the people'. This saying is a permutation of the principle of 'Ubuntu' or 'Botho', which literally states that 'umuntu ungumuntu ngabantu', or 'motho ke motho ka batho'. That is, 'a *person* is a *person* by, through, and because of (other) people'. In essence, traditional leaders (like all of us) are made by those whom they

[64] J Khumalo, 'Traditional leaders are only custodians of the land – David Mabuza' *City Press* (Johannesburg, 29 May 2018) <https://city-press.news24.com/News/traditional-leaders-are-only-custodians-of-the-land-david-mabuza-20180529>accessed 4 June 2019.

[65] ibid.

[66] Oomen, *Chiefs in South Africa* (n 32) 37.

[67] JL Comaroff and J Comaroff, 'Reflections on the Anthropology of Law, Governance and Sovereignty' in F von Benda-Beckmann, K von Benda-Beckmann, and J Eckert (eds), *Rules of Law and Laws of Ruling: On the Governance of Law* (Ashgate 2009) 33.

serve—no matter whether their title is hereditary. Despite the fact that for most South Africans these statements are part of popular discourse, not once does the TLGFA provide for recognition of 'traditional' structures to be dependent upon consultation with the people who are to be governed by them. It is therefore no surprise that government does not honour requirements for holders of informal land rights on rural land to be consulted; after all, its legislative pronouncements do not essentially deem such consultation to be part of rural people's rights under traditional forms of government.

It is also worth noting that seventeen years after the TLGFA was initially passed, the elections of 40 per cent of traditional council members that it provides for have yet to be seriously carried out in most of the country.[68] According to the legislation, the other 60 per cent of traditional councillors are to be appointed by the traditional leader whose own recognition is not at all contingent upon acceptance and recognition by his/her people.[69] By the government's own admission,[70] elections have been held for few traditional councils and there are contests and disputes with respect to the overwhelming majority of traditional communities and the institutions of traditional leadership recognised over them.

In the meantime, having entered into effect on 1 April 2021, the TKLA has indeed fully revived and more deeply entrenched separate territorial enclaves in which poor, Black people are stripped of their citizenship rights (such as the right to speak for themselves). Under the TKLA's arrangements, rural people are instead forced to be governed as subjects by imposed authorities that the government names 'traditional' as it gives these authorities un-traditional and un-democratic 'roles, functions and power' wholly to speak on 'their people's' behalf as so-called 'custodians of our culture' and 'custodians of our land'.[71]

In this context, the insistence of the Portfolio Committee (PC) on Justice and Correctional Services (on the recommendation of traditional leaders), in its deliberations on the Traditional Courts Bill [B1-2017], that allowing people to opt out of the jurisdiction of traditional courts would undermine these courts' power is a dangerous re-enactment of apartheid principles. Doing away with the right of people to opt out, as the PC directed the Department of Justice to do, is a fundamental rejection of the customary law principle that 'Kgosi ke kgosi ka batho'. The question implicit in debates on traditional governance is whether ordinary rural people are, in the words of Mamdani, 'citizens or subjects'.[72]

[68] TLGFA 2003, ss 3(2) and 28(4).

[69] ibid.

[70] 'Ministry Cooperative Governance and Traditional Affairs Republic of South Africa: National Assembly Questions For Written Reply—Question Number: 3378, Date Of Publication: 4 September 2015' <https://pmg.org.za/files/RNW3378-151019.docx> accessed 4 June 2019.

[71] Comaroff and Comaroff, *Ethnicity, Inc* (n 40) 6.

[72] Mamdani (n 13).

In the world's most unequal country, poverty remains highly racialised with 93 per cent of the total 30 million (55.5 per cent) of South Africans declared poor being Black. Put differently, following a pattern that is consistent with apartheid's design, 64.2 per cent of 'African/Black'; 41.3 per cent of 'Coloured'; and 5.9 per cent of 'Indian/Asian' South Africans live in poverty while a mere 1 per cent of White people live under the poverty line.[73] Moreover, poverty is most severe in the deeply rural former 'homeland' areas systematically disadvantaged by the apartheid government's policies.[74]

This reality is consonant with the division between 'citizen' and 'subject' that was entrenched by the colonial and apartheid governments, which has been perpetuated and even deepened by maintaining these repressive governments' imagination of traditional communities as being subject to near-despotic leaders. This is preserved by legislation such as the TLGFA and TKLA, when they provide in section 28 and section 63 respectively (on 'transitional arrangements') that '[a]ny traditional leader who was appointed as such in terms of applicable provincial legislation and was still recognised as a traditional leader immediately before the commencement of this Act, is deemed to have been recognised as such in terms of section 9 or 11, subject to a decision of the Commission in terms of section 26'.[75] The TLGFA then goes on to state that 'any tribe' that, immediately before the commencement of this Act, had been established and was still recognised as such is deemed to be a traditional community contemplated in section 2',[76] which the TKLA then perpetuates in section 63. Finally, 'any tribal authority that, immediately before the commencement of this Act, had been established and was still recognised as such, is deemed to be a traditional council' under the TLGFA[77] as well as the TKLA's section 63(4). These 'transitional arrangements' do not comport with the constitutionally set goals of transitional justice for people living in the former Bantustans of South Africa because they fail to redistribute power over the resources people rely upon for subsistence.

E. Poor Democracy Makes Vulnerable People Poorer

The two problems of endemic poverty and impoverished democracy for traditional communities are not unrelated. As demonstrated by the example of the ITB, traditional leaders' and institutions' relatively unchecked power over poor, rural people results in deepening poverty for people who are the most marginalised. A striking illustration of this reality can also be found in the extent of abuse that takes place by

[73] Statistics South Africa (n 16).
[74] ibid.
[75] TLGFA 2003, s 28(1).
[76] ibid s 28(3).
[77] ibid s 28(4).

means of traditional leaders' ongoing imposition of 'tribal levies' that were rejected by residents of the former homelands as a form of double taxation insofar as rural residents pay taxes to the government and are then required to pay these levies in addition. Constituting the majority of people living in rural areas, and many of them unemployed and largely dependent on social grants, women feel the burden most severely. This is because they end up paying a meaningful share of these subsistence grants to support traditional institutions that are already financed by the government and traditional leaders who earn a substantial salary as public office bearers.[78]

To be clear, sections 226 to 230A of the Constitution reserve revenue-raising to national, provincial, and local government and subject the power 'to impose taxes, levies, duties and surcharges' to strict procedures—especially for levels of government below the national sphere. Yet section 4(2) of the TLGFA, by subtly implying that traditional councils might be able to receive gifts and levies so long as they keep proper records, suggests that traditional councils have legitimate scope for levying taxes.[79] It therefore appears that such levying powers of traditional institutions as are implied by the TLGFA are not constitutionally justified. Should readers be tempted to assume that these levies are voluntary contributions based on elective membership of traditional communities, I would remind them that laws such as the TLGFA do not make membership of traditional communities and subjection to traditional leaders contingent on consultation of community members. Traditional communities continue to be defined by apartheid boundaries; traditional leaders remain mostly people placed in position by the apartheid government.

Moreover, Aninka Claassens[80] demonstrates just how punitive traditional leaders and councils often are in compelling payment of levies for traditional leaders' marriages or teenagers having children outside of marriage, for example, as well as enforcing payment of these fees. Punishments include refusing to give people letters of residence that are necessary for rural people to secure identity documents, open bank accounts, or apply for child support grants and pensions. In particularly cruel cases, rural residents have been prevented from burying deceased loved ones until they settle the debt of years in outstanding levies.

[78] Independent Commission for the Remuneration of Public Office-bearers Act 92 of 1997.

[79] This implication is carried over and even rendered explicit in some of the provincial framework acts that are promulgated under the TLGFA: North West Traditional Leadership And Governance Act 2 of 2005, Traditional Leadership and Governance Act 4 of 2005 (Eastern Cape), KwaZulu-Natal Traditional Leadership and Governance Act 5 of 2005, Limpopo Traditional Leadership and Institutions Act 6 of 2005, Free State Leadership and Governance Act 8 of 2005, Mpumalanga Traditional Leadership And Governance Act 3 of 2006, Northern Cape Traditional Leadership and Governance and Houses of Traditional Leaders Act 2 of 2007.

[80] A Claassens, 'Resurgence Of Tribal Levies: Double Taxation for the Rural Poor' (2011) 35 South African Crime Quarterly 11.

One place where this intimate connection between impoverished democracy in traditional communities and endemic poverty is rife is in the mineral-rich areas of South Africa where accumulating evidence shows that traditional leaders are leveraging their political power for personal economic gain, and members of government, accounting firms, law firms, and consultants are profiting along with them. This has now been shown in a number of different disputes involving Kgosi Nyalala Pilane of Bakgatla Ba Kgafela in the North West Province, including in the Constitutional Court case of *Pilane*[81] and the Maluleke Commission on the corruption of this senior traditional leader.[82] This community's experience is not unique as shown by the findings of the Commission of Inquiry into the Traditional Leadership Disputes in respect of Bapo I and II Community Disputes,[83] which found similar levels of corruption and abuse of power in the relevant traditional institution.

As land rights activist, Mbhekiseni Mavuso of Makhasaneni in Kwazulu-Natal, is quoted as saying in the documentary *This Land*, sharing the similar suffering of his community: 'We have seen that the chiefs are selling land to business people, mining companies, giving land to foreigners to build malls. We know that sometimes our land rights are not properly written in the law. But we know that traditionally we have a land right'. The key point conveyed here by Mavuso is that rural people's rights exist—whether under customary law or state law.

As it happens, the Constitutional Court has clearly recognised the land rights of rural people under custom as protected in law under our Constitution. For instance, in *Tongoane*,[84] the Court recognised that the government was displacing something when it passed the Communal Land Rights Act. The Court observed:

> But, the field that CLARA now seeks to cover is not unoccupied. There is at present a system of law that regulates the use, occupation and administration of communal land. This system also regulates the powers and functions of traditional leaders in relation to communal land. It is this system which CLARA will repeal, replace or amend. The communities contended that the land which they

[81] *Pilane v Pilane* [2013] ZACC 3; 2013 (4) BCLR 431 (CC) ('*Pilane*').

[82] Z Booi, 'Dispossession without compensation the legacy for poor rural communities' *Daily Maverick* (Cape Town, 11 June 2018) <https://www.dailymaverick.co.za/article/2018-06-11-dispossession-without-compensation-the-legacy-for-poor-rural-communities/> accessed 5 June 2019. Also see K Bloom and S Wales-Smith, 'Stealing the Crust: How the Bakgatla Ba Kgafela Were Robbed of Their Inheritance' *Daily Maverick* (Cape Town, 1 February 2018) <https://www.dailymaverick.co.za/article/2018-02-01-stealing-the-crust-how-the-baktatla-ba-kgafela-were-robbed-of-their-inheritance/#.WnmPzqiWY2x> accessed 6 June 2019; A Reporter, 'NW chief knew about Bakgatla Ba Kgafela company's financial problems' *IOL News* (Rustenburg, 14 June 2018) <https://www.iol.co.za/news/south-africa/north-west/nw-chief-knew-about-bakgatla-ba-kgafela-companys-financial-problems-15478739> accessed 6 June 2019; T Seleke, 'Done And Dusted: The Bakgatla Ba Kgafela Commission' *Sunday Standard* (Johannesburg, 27 Aug 2018) <http://www.sundaystandard.info/done-and-dusted-bakgatla-ba-kgafela-commission> accessed 6 June 2019.

[83] Provincial Gazettes (North West) No 7838 of 26 December 2017.

[84] *Tongoane* (n 27).

> presently occupy is administered by them in accordance with the rules of indigenous law that have evolved over time. This is true of all land to which the provisions of CLARA apply, they contended. Indeed all the parties approached the matter on the footing that the land which the four applicant communities occupy *is* regulated by indigenous law.[85]

This finding is consistent with the repeatedly affirmed precedent of the Court that was stated as follows in *Shilubana*:[86]

> The import of this section [211], in the words of Langa DCJ in *Bhe*, is that customary law 'is protected by and subject to the Constitution in its own right.' Customary law, like any other law, must accord with the Constitution. Like any other law, customary law has a status that requires respect. As this Court held in *Alexkor v Richtersveld Community*, customary law must be recognised as 'an integral part of our law' and 'an independent source of norms within the legal system.' It is a body of law by which millions of South Africans regulate their lives and must be treated accordingly.[87]

Nevertheless, the democratically-elected government continues to undermine the customarily- and constitutionally-protected land rights of rural people in the name of protecting the power, position, and privilege of traditional leaders. This has thwarted the goals of the restorative and redistributive transitional justice envisioned in the country's democratic Constitution.

4. Conclusion

Nelson Mandela and many traditionalists in the ANC were, and are arguably, sentimentally attached to a more democratic traditional leadership that has been significantly disrupted and distorted through the process and political economy of colonialism and apartheid, and continues to be so through the elite alliance between the traditional leader lobby and the ANC. In this context, traditional leaders are said to speak on behalf of and in the interests of 'their people' (treated as subjects) but the truth is that—in the contemporary socio-economic and political context—most speak for their own interests and are not accountable to their people.[88]

85 ibid [79].
86 *Shilubana* (n 28).
87 ibid [43] (references omitted).
88 Comaroff and Comaroff, *Ethnicity, Inc* (n 40) 6.

As struggle heroes, Albert Luthuli, Nelson Mandela, and Govan Mbeki wrote over sixty years ago, as a result of the deep impact of the political economy and disruptions of traditional institutions caused by colonialism and apartheid, traditional authorities derive their power and supposed legitimacy from the government rather than from their people.[89] Furthermore, they primarily look out for the interests of their own position, role and status, and their economic interests, not those of the overwhelmingly poor people living in their jurisdictions. This is particularly true of those traditional authorities ensconced in government and the formalised traditional leader lobby.[90]

In other words, the observations and critiques levelled against traditional leadership under apartheid, by Mandela and his peers, that the so-called tribal institutions put in place by the apartheid government are not 'in any sense of the term' traditional, remain pertinent today. Moreover, they were designed not to be traditional but instruments of the government for managing and dispossessing the Black masses of their land. As summarised by Chief Justice Ngcobo in the *Tongoane* case implicating the TLGFA: 'Under apartheid, these steps were a necessary prelude to the assignment of African people to ethnically-based homelands.... According to this plan, there would be no African people in South Africa, as all would assume citizenship of one or other of the newly created homelands'.[91] We can therefore conclude that the rural governance structures that the ANC is perpetuating are indeed an apartheid construct, and lie at the heart of the apartheid government's efforts to subjugate and oppress Black people. It is therefore not surprising that they have resulted in undermining any gains made by traditional peoples in South Africa's transition from apartheid to democracy, thus preventing both transitional and restorative justice from being realised.

The African Commission on Human Rights, in the *Endorois* case,[92] affirmed the findings of the Inter-American Commission and Court of Human Rights with respect to the land rights protections available to 'indigenous and tribal communities' under international law. Specifically, it noted that they 'require special measures that guarantee full exercise of their rights, particularly with regard to their enjoyment of "property rights" in order to safeguard their physical and cultural survival'.[93] As clearly conveyed by Former President Motlanthe[94]

[89] Nelson Mandela, Verwoerd's Grim Plot, No 36, May 1959; A Luthuli, *Let My People Go* (Fontana Books 1962); G Mbeki, *The Peasants' Revolt* (Penguin Books 1964).

[90] Comaroff and Comaroff, *Ethnicity, Inc* (n 40) 6.

[91] *Tongoane* (n 27) [25].

[92] 276/2003—Centre for Minority Rights Development (Kenya) and Minority Rights Group International on behalf of Endorois Welfare Council v Kenya, 46th Ordinary Session, 11–25 November 2009, African Commission on Human and Peoples' Rights.

[93] ibid.

[94] Nhlabathi (n 58) and Madia (n 59).

when announcing the findings of the High Level Panel Report,[95] the ANC-led democratic South African government has failed to provide this kind of protection to its traditional communities and betrayed the trust given to it by ordinary rural people in the process of transitioning from apartheid to constitutional democracy.

[95] High Level Panel, 'Report of the High Level Panel on the Assessment of Key Legislation and the Acceleration of Fundamental Change' (*Parliament of South Africa*, October 2017) <https://www.parliament.gov.za/storage/app/media/Pages/2017/october/High_Level_Panel/HLP_Report/HLP_report.pdf> accessed 25 September 2023.

18

Evaluating the Impact of the Peace Agreement on the Indigenous Peoples of Colombia

Land Rights and Compensation

Diana Carolina Rivera-Drago and Filipo Ernesto Burgos Guzman

1. Introduction

The Final Agreement for the Termination of the Conflict and the Construction of a Stable and Lasting Peace,[1] signed in Havana in 2016 ('peace agreement') resulted from a long-running war between the state and the guerrilla group of the Revolutionary Armed Forces of Colombia (FARC).[2] The agreement signified the official start of a transitional justice process in Colombia that would finally bring an end to decades of violence, economic injustice and political instability in the country. The period since the adoption of the peace agreement and its coming into effect has been met with an array of reactions and often polarised political opinions. For example, there has at times been heated conflict between the state and those in positions of power, on the one hand, and civil society and the Colombian population more generally,[3] on the other. This is notwithstanding the fact that the peace process and the peace agreement specifically has enjoyed the support of the United Nations (UN) and the international community more broadly.[4]

[1] Oficina del Alto Comisionado para la Paz Presidencia de la República, *Biblioteca del Proceso de Paz Tomos 1* (Alto Comisionado para la Paz 2018).

[2] For information on the history and characteristics of the FARC, see E Pizarro, *Las FARC de la Autodefensa a la Combinación de Todas las Formas de Lucha* (Universidad Nacional 1991); C Arango, *FARC 20 Años de Marquetalia a la Uribe* (Aurora 1984); LF Trejos, *Un Actor no Estatal* (Universidad del Norte 2015); R Karl, *La Paz Olvidada* (Lerner 2018) 261–309; Ferán González, *Poder y Violencia en Colombia* (Universidad Javeriana 2014) 249–364.

[3] L Gamboa, 'Latin America's Shifting Politics: The Peace Process and Colombia's Elections' (2018) 29 Journal of Democracy 54; JP Hayes, 'Peace is on the Ballot: Polarization and the Colombian Peace Process' (2017) 3 University of Saskatchewan Undergraduate Research Journal 1; C Tognato, 'Superar la Polarización' (*La Silla Vacía*, 3 February 2016) <http://www.lasillavacia.com/elblogueo/blog/superar-la-polarizacion-52942> accessed 20 February 2018.

[4] 'In Bogotá, United Nations deputy rights chief says "peace is the only option" for Colombia' (*United Nations News*, 21 April 2015) <http://www.news.un.org/en/story/2015/04/496672-bogota-un-dep

Diana Carolina Rivera-Drago and Filipo Ernesto Burgos Guzman, *Evaluating the Impact of the Peace Agreement on the Indigenous Peoples of Colombia* In: *Transitional Justice, Distributive Justice, and Transformative Constitutionalism*. Edited by: David Bilchitz and Raisa Cachalia, with Magdalena Inés Correa Henao and Nathalia Bautista Pizarro, Oxford University Press. © Diana Carolina Rivera-Drago and Filipo Ernesto Burgos Guzman 2023.
DOI: 10.1093/oso/9780192887627.003.0018

This transition—long awaited by some and criticised by others—is clearly a necessary ingredient to the process of bringing lasting peace to Colombia but, as is to be expected, the process has faced challenges. For example, there continues to be unhappiness with the negotiated terms of the agreement as well as seemingly intractable difficulties relating to its implementation in various respects. A further challenge, with which this chapter is concerned, is the plight of the long-neglected Indigenous peoples of Colombia who have also been direct victims of the Colombian armed conflict. In particular, the damaging impact of decades of armed conflict on the personal and community security of these peoples as well as the widespread dispossession of land that they have suffered, has frequently been overlooked. Further, due to the armed confrontations between the guerrillas and the state, these peoples were often forced to vacate their territories, posing a threat to the survival of their cultural and ancestral practices.[5]

It is important to bear in mind that the peace agreement of 2016 was incorporated as a fundamental chapter of the Colombian Political Constitution of 1991, under which the country is currently governed. Prior to the 1991 Constitution coming into force, Colombian Indigenous communities were unrecognised and unrepresented in the country. In fact, they experienced high levels of discrimination and marginalisation in society. With the 1991 Constitution, these communities finally obtained constitutional recognition. The struggle for the vindication of their rights is, however, ongoing. The signing of the Havana peace agreement represents an important step in the history of this struggle. For this reason, this chapter is not limited to the events surrounding the signing of the peace agreement, but is located in the broader struggle of the Indigenous peoples for distributive justice that began with the Political Constitution of 1991 and which has gained impetus and special significance under the more recent peace agreement.

In this context, the purpose of this chapter is to analyse the provisions of the transitional justice system contained in the peace agreement that impact directly on the Indigenous peoples of Colombia and to explore the extent to which they address the plight of these marginalised groups, particularly in relation to the restoration of land and the recognition of compensation for harm occasioned by the armed conflict. In short, the aim of this chapter is to illustrate that, despite the high hopes of the peace agreement (as incorporated into the 1991 Political Constitution), the long-running difficulties associated with advancing economic justice and restoring the land and dignity to these marginalised peoples is likely to endure. These two issues—land restitution and economic reparation—speak to the

uty-rights-chief-says-peace-only-option-colombia> accessed 20 February 2018; R Segura, 'Colombia Further Polarized by President's Action on Transitional Justice Law' (*Global Observatory*, 11 April 2019) <http://www.theglobalobservatory.org/2019/04/colombia-polarized-president-action-transitional-justice-law/> accessed 20 February 2018.

[5] *Mayagna (Sumo) Awas Tingni v Nicaragua* [2001] IACHR Series C No 79; *Yakye Axa v Paraguay* [2005] IACHR Series C No 125; *Sawhoyamaxa v Paraguay* [2006] Series C No 146.

need for distributive and restorative justice, both of which are crucial for the success of the transitional justice project as a whole.

To this end, this chapter is divided into three parts. In Section 2, we begin by describing the Indigenous communities of Colombia and explore the extent to which these communities have been given legal recognition in recent years, with a particular focus on land rights and access to justice systems. Some of the challenges pertaining to discrimination will also be explored in this context. Then, in Section 3 the particular provisions of the peace agreement insofar as they are applicable to the Indigenous peoples will be examined, especially those relating to meaningful land redistribution (3A) and economic compensation (3B), being issues which are directly related to distributive justice.[6] We also evaluate each of these provisions in light of the question whether they are likely to address the plight of the Indigenous peoples of Colombia. Finally, in Section 4, we provide concluding reflections on some of the practical consequences of the peace agreement for these groups. We also explore a possible way forward and provide a theoretical reflection on how the issues affecting Indigenous communities in Colombia could be linked with the transitional justice process implemented by the peace agreement, from the perspective of the territorial and compensation questions underpinning distributive and restorative justice.

2. Who are the Indigenous Peoples of Colombia and How Are They Legally Protected?

Before describing 'who' the Indigenous peoples of Colombia are, it is necessary to explain the reason why the particular terminology of 'Indigenous peoples' has been chosen. The Royal Academy of the Spanish Language Dictionary establishes that 'indigenous' means 'originating from the country in question'.[7] Furthermore, Article 1(b) of the International Labor Organisation (ILO)'s Indigenous and Tribal Peoples Convention No 169 of 1989 explains that the term applies to peoples in independent countries, considered indigenous due to the fact that they are 'descendants from populations that used to live in the country or in a geographical region to which the country belonged at the time of the conquest, colonisation or establishment of the current state borders and who, irrespective of their legal status, preserve some or all of their own social, economic, cultural and political institutions'.

[6] The final agreement contents six different chapters: 1. Integral Rural Reform; 2. Politic Participation; 3. Conflict Termination; 4. Drugs Problem Solutions; 5. Agreement for the Conflict Victims; and 6. Implementation, Verification and Endorsement in which there is an Ethnic Chapter focused on the implementation of the Agreement for the Ethnic Peoples in the Country. This chapter will analyse mainly the effects of the first (Integral Rural Reform), the fifth (Agreement for the Conflict Victims), and the sixth (Ethnic) chapters.

[7] Real Academia Española: *Diccionario de la lengua española*, 23rd edn [version 23.3 online] <https://dle.rae.es> accessed 21 April 2020.

In Colombia, all those who are regarded as Indigenous peoples comply with the aforementioned definition and with the characteristics that will be described.

International treaties and Colombian law provide the criteria for identifying Indigenous peoples in this country. Principally, they are groups of the population that, since the Spanish conquest and colonisation, have conserved and practised their own culture and traditions; shared a historical relationship with the land and the other members of the group; and have been governed by their own customs and authorities, surviving all the atrocities to which they have been subjected throughout history.[8] In the country nowadays, there are about eighty-four Indigenous groups or Indigenous communities with a total population of 1,378,884, which represents 3.3 per cent of the total national population.[9] Among all these peoples, it is important to highlight that they are not homogenous: there is wide diversity in the linguistic, governmental forms and cultural practices of these groups. They range from nomadic men (such as the Nukak Maku tribe in the Amazon region of Colombia who do not speak Spanish and live in complete isolation) to the Indigenous people in the city (such as the Muisca community who are quite adapted to the city and speak Spanish as well as their own Chibcha language). Other tribes, to name a few, who do not live in the city are the Iku, Knkuamos, Misak, and Huitotos peoples.[10]

Having clarified the definition and characteristics of Colombia's Indigenous peoples, it is important to remember that, in general, it is well known that the recognition of the rights of these groups is a fairly new phenomenon, having only found their way into various international instruments and domestic laws of different countries in which these peoples reside in recent years. However, as early

[8] International Labour Organisation, Indigenous and Tribal Populations Convention (No 107), 1957, art 1 states:

> Members of tribal or semi tribal populations in independent countries, whose social and economic conditions correspond at a stage less advanced than that reached by the other sectors of the national community and that are governed totally or partially by their own customs or traditions or by special legislation; b) members of tribal or semi tribal populations in independent countries, considered Indigenous by the fact that they are descendants from populations that lived in the country, or in a geographic region to which the country belongs, at the time of the conquest or colonisation and that, whatever their legal status, they live more in accordance with the social, economic and cultural institutions of that time than with the institutions of the nation to which they belong.

In the same way, the Colombian Decree 2164 of 1995 reads:

> Group or groups of families of Amerindian descent, who are aware of their identity and share values, traits, uses or customs of their culture, as well as forms of government, management, social control or regulatory systems that distinguish it from other communities, whether or not they have title deeds, or that cannot legally certify them, or that their Reservations (resguardos) were dissolved, divided or declared vacant.

[9] Official Governmental Census, 2005 <https://www.dane.gov.co/index.php/estadisticas-por-tema/demografia-y poblacion/grupos-etnicos> accessed 3 September 2018.

[10] F Burgos, 'El Derecho de la Libre Determinación de los Pueblos y los Indígenas en la Ciudad a la Luz de la Jurisprudencia Colombiana' in F Padrón and M Correa (eds), *¿El Estado Constitucional en Jaque?* (Universidad Externado de Colombia 2019).

as 1537 Pope Paul III in the Sublimis Deus declared the Indigenous people of the Americas as rational beings with souls and argued that ideas to the contrary were inspired by Satan. He went on to condemn, in strong terms, the subjugation of these peoples under the system of slavery. The Pope asserted that Indigenous groups should be entitled to the rights to liberty and property, and thus called for their evangelisation and emancipation.[11] However, Sublimis Deus Bull's principles were largely ignored by the colonisers and, in fact, despite the Bull's protestations, it was more than a century before any recognition of the rights of Indigenous peoples was recognised in legal instruments. In Colombia specifically, Indigenous peoples have been victims of high levels of discrimination. In fact, they were not even regarded as human beings, but mere animals or soulless beings[12] until the twentieth century when, due to mounting pressure from the international community and by following examples from other countries (such as Australia, the United States, and parts of Africa), the Colombian government began to introduce legal and social changes to respond to the plight of these peoples.

Prior to 1991, Colombia was governed by the 1886 Political Constitution, which did not confer any kind of legal protection on Indigenous tribes.[13] The enactment of the 1991 Constitution heralded an enormous change for the country—a shift that had mainly been brought about by the student movement and the influence of ideological pluralism.[14] One of the principal effects of this change was, for the first time, to grant legal recognition to Indigenous people, who after being considered wild and largely invisible, finally achieved a level of constitutional protection.[15] Thus, since the 1991 Political Constitution (which incorporates the final agreement), Indigenous peoples' rights have been recognised and respected in ways that acknowledge their particular vulnerability. This can be seen in the protection of their cultural diversity (art 8); official recognition of their language rights, particularly the right to teach Indigenous languages in the schools of these communities (art 10); safeguarding their right to land (art 63); entrenching their right to be educated in accordance with their cultural principles (art 68); and protection of their cultural and archaeological heritage (art 72). In short, they have the right to live in their territories and organise their societies in accordance with their customs and traditions. In addition, the principle of 'self-identification of Indigenous peoples' as a fundamental criterion for determining a sense of belonging to a particular group has been a significant gain.[16]

[11] Paulo III, Bula Sublimis Deus (first published 2 June 1537) <http://webs.advance.com.ar/pfernando/DocsIglLA/Paulo3_sublimis.html> accessed 6 March 2019.

[12] An example can be found in the Colombian Act 69 of 1890, provisioned 'the manner in which the savages must be governed in order to reduce them to the civilised living'.

[13] In the Colombian Constitution of 1886 there is no reference to the Indigenous peoples, and consequently no rights were conferred on these peoples.

[14] J Pérez, *Derecho Constitucional colombiano* (Temis 2004) 201–24.

[15] Colombian Constitution 1991, Chapter XI.

[16] Declaration on the Rights of Indigenous Peoples 2007, art 33: 'Indigenous peoples have the right to determine their own identity or belonging according to their customs and traditions'.

With regard to indigenous lands, the Colombian legal system recognises the property rights over all the lands that Indigenous peoples own with good title, as well as over all the lands that they have ancestrally occupied.[17] To protect the indigenous territories, the Constitution, in addition to giving them property rights, recognises that these territories are inalienable and imprescriptible (art 63). It is understood that the Indigenous peoples' relationship with territory can be expressed in different ways, depending on the group concerned and the specific circumstances in which it is found. This may include: traditional use or continuous presence in the area, either through spiritual or ceremonial ties; settlements or sporadic crops; hunting, fishing, or seasonal or nomadic gathering; use of natural resources linked to their customs; and any other characteristic elements of their culture.[18] One of the fundamental aspects, from the Indigenous peoples' perspective, is the recognition of the extraordinary significance that land and territories have for them. In this respect, differentiating each aspect of their public and private life is a complicated matter since for them every part of their ideology and philosophy is necessary for the proper functioning of the world.[19] For example, economics and politics cannot work without religion and spirituality. Moreover, for the development of a spiritual life, it is necessary for spiritual practices to be performed in designated places that have historical significance. These peoples' relationship with the land could be compared to a relationship with a mother who must be respected and loved and whose loss implies not only immense pain, but may also threatens their very existence. It is for this reason, among others, that the territorial claim and the recognition of their property rights over their ancestrally occupied territories, is fundamental to achieving distributive justice for them.

Nowadays, there is recognition of a right to property. This right—whether collective or individual—shall be recognised in favour of the members of the populations in question on the lands traditionally occupied by them.[20] What is more, it is widely recognised that the traditional possession of land by Indigenous people is equivalent to the title of full legal ownership. For this reason, Indigenous people are endowed with the right to demand official recognition of their property, its registration, and delimitation.[21] Moreover, the Colombian Constitution establishes that indigenous territories are part of a decentralised, territorial administrative system (local government), thus recognising their autonomy to manage their own interests and the possibility of governing themselves by their own practices and

[17] According to Colombian secondary legislation, in particular Decree 2664 of 1994, elaborating on Act 160 of 1994, the indigenous territories are not limited to areas that are titled or possessed on a regular basis by communities, but include those that are not possessed, that constitute the traditional scope of their social, economic, or cultural activities.

[18] *Sawhoyamaxa* (n 5).

[19] *Mayagna*, *Yakye Axa*, *Sawhoyamaxa* (n 5).

[20] International Labor Organisation, Indigenous and Tribal Peoples Convention, 1989 (No 169) arts 11 ff.

[21] See (n 6); *Sawhoyamaxa* (n 5) [14].

customs. That said, as it will be explained further on, while the peace agreement—bolstering the rights recognised since 1991—has provided a glimmer of hope, full recognition of Indigenous land rights in Colombia is still a long way off.

Also significant is article 246 of the Colombian Constitution, which has created a special jurisdiction for Indigenous people that is independent from the official Colombian legal system. Thus, each community has the right to create and apply its own rules and courts, and their authorities have judicial powers with just one limitation: respect for human rights and the principles of the national Constitution. This chapter thus entrenches the right of Indigenous peoples to apply their own rules, laws, and customs and to be judged by their own authorities. To make this right effective, a Special Indigenous Jurisdiction was established together with guiding criteria[22] to facilitate the resolution of conflict according to the unique customs of different Indigenous groups. This is a very important achievement that was first introduced in 1991 and strengthened by the peace agreement. It stands in contrast to the previous position under the Colombian civil law legal system where custom was treated as a subsidiary legal source.[23]

The Constitutional Court, seeking to justify the constitutional recognition of the Special Indigenous Jurisdiction, established that in order to make it operative, the autonomy of the Indigenous communities should be maximised and their restrictions should be minimised. Thus, they are not subject to the whole 1991 Constitution nor to the entire law. On this basis, the Court reasoned that greater protection for their customs requires greater autonomy; fundamental constitutional rights mandate the co-existence of all individuals in society; and the imperative legal norms of public order of the Republic take precedence over the customs of Indigenous communities (provided that they directly protect a constitutional value superior to the principle of ethnic and cultural diversity). Furthermore, the customs of an Indigenous community take precedence over dispositive legal norms.[24] Consequently, in order to determine where and to whom the Indigenous law is applied, today there is case law from the Colombian Constitutional Court that affirms the principle that there is greater autonomy in respect of matters purely internal to the community, for example in respect of its territory and issues affecting its members. The question is thus the extent to which a community can be differentiated from the majority population in ascertaining the applicable rules.[25]

[22] The Colombian Constitutional Court has established that it is possible to resolve a conflict in the Special Indigenous Jurisdiction if all the interested parties in the conflict are part of the same Indigenous group and if the situation or conflict has occurred in their own territory.

[23] Colombian Constitution, article 246. Colombian Constitutional Court, 9 April 1996, decision: C-139 of 1996, Judge Carlos Gaviria Díaz.

[24] Colombian Constitutional Court, 30 May 1994, decision: T-254 1994, Judge Eduardo Cifuentes Muñoz. The Indigenous groups' autonomy is greater when it comes to the purely internal relations of the community (in its territory and among its members), inasmuch as a community can be differentiated from the majority population.

[25] Colombian Constitutional Court, 10 July 2003, decision: T-552-03, Judge Rodrigo Escobar Gil; 26 July 2013, decision: T-496-13, Judge Luis Guillermo Guerrero; 8 September 2011, decision: T-669-11,

The aforementioned rights and provisions related to the special jurisdiction are already recognised and effective in practice. However, there remain significant challenges arising from the new judicial mechanism provided for in the peace agreement. In the context of the termination of the armed conflict, one of the most important conditions for the Treaty's signature was the implementation of a 'Special Peace Jurisdiction' (a system of transitional justice) to hear cases pertaining to crimes perpetrated during that period.[26] Thus, and from that moment on, the question as to which forum has jurisdiction over a particular issue is no longer limited to whether to subject a dispute to the Special Indigenous Jurisdiction or the civil law courts. It is now, in addition, necessary to consider the applicability of this new transitional model to all the cases relating to Indigenous peoples and the armed conflict.

It can be said then that the Colombian legal framework as a whole welcomes, values, and respects diverse ethnic groups and their territories, including the customary law of each community. Through these constitutional provisions, Indigenous tribes in Colombia have been granted administrative, economic, political, and legal autonomy, which is a significant achievement.[27] However, despite these legally entrenched rights, the fact that Indigenous peoples in Colombia have been subjected to policies of cultural assimilation and violence for 150 years, has impeded the practical realisation of their rights and the practical manifestation of distributive justice.[28] It seems that this reality endures today—notwithstanding the high hopes of the peace agreement.[29] This can be seen in the limitations of the agreement in meaningfully diverting land back into the hands of Indigenous groups and in the failure to exact economic reparations for harms suffered.

3. Land and Justice: Evaluating the Provisions of the Colombian Peace Agreement from the Perspective of Indigenous Peoples

The existing legal framework attempts to remedy the effects of decades of violence for Indigenous peoples through themes such as identity, territory, and indigenous justice. The Colombian armed conflict has had a terrible and enduring impact on the enjoyment of the rights recognised in the Constitution for these peoples.

Judge Humberto Antonio Sierra Porto; 22 August 2013, decision T-548-13, Judge María Victoria Calle; 20 February 2015, C-081-15, Judge Luis Guillermo Guerrero; among many others.

[26] Final Peace Agreement, Chapter 3.

[27] Colombian secondary legislation contented in Decrees 1953 of 2014, 4633 of 2011, and 4635 of 2011.

[28] O Ruiz, 'The Right to Cultural Identity of Indigenous Peoples and National Minorities: A Look from the Inter-American System' (2006) 5 Revista Sur 43, 69.

[29] ibid.

During the years of conflict there was a clash of various geographic, military, and economic interests which in turn gave rise to, among other things, armed confrontations between various groups; the militarisation of areas occupied by communities, including the building of military bases; forced displacements; violent land dispossessions; selective assassinations and aerial spraying of illicit crops.[30] As a result, many Indigenous peoples were forcibly dispossessed of their territories; most of the selective assassinations and other crimes went unpunished; and the application of Indigenous systems of justice were rendered inoperative in this context.[31] Moreover, these communities began to lose their autonomy and control over these territories and were thus forced to fulfil the directives of the armed groups and to 'coexist' with strangers who had different ways of living and different values to them.[32]

Upon the signing of the final peace agreement on 24 November 2016, the armed conflict between the FARC and the state of Colombia formally ended.[33] It is important to highlight the fact that the agreement was not exclusively directed at the Colombian Indigenous communities. Instead, it was directed at the population in general and at the victims of the conflict in particular. Nonetheless, it has important repercussions for Indigenous groups. This is particularly in light of the fact that these groups were clearly victims of the conflict,[34] with the result that virtually all of the provisions in the agreement have a direct effect on them.[35] Included, however, in the last part of the agreement is a chapter dedicated to Indigenous peoples ('Ethnic Chapter') and which seeks to integrate and harmonise the proposed solutions for the end of the conflict with the rights of Indigenous groups.[36]

Nevertheless, it is crucial to explain at this point that, although the agreement attempted to address the plight of the Colombian Indigenous population directly,

[30] In this sense, see Colombian Constitutional Court, 26 January 2009, decision: Auto 004 2009 Judge Manuel José Cepeda Espinosa and Colombian Constitutional Court, 26 January 2009, decision: Auto 005 2009, Judge Manuel José Cepeda Espinosa, which mention the impact of the armed conflict and drug trafficking on the ethnic communities.

[31] While all the issues that the final agreement contains are important for Indigenous communities, in this chapter we focus on the territorial issue.

[32] Colombian Constitutional Court, 26 January 2009, decisión Auto 004-09, Judge Manuel José Cepeda Espinosa.

[33] Redacción El Tiempo, 'Hoy se firma el final de 52 años de guerra' *El Tiempo* (Bogotá, 26 September 2016) <https://www.eltiempo.com/politica/proceso-de-paz/firma-de-la-paz-en-colombia-2016-31456> accessed 10 March 2019.

[34] P Jaramillo, *Etnicidad y Victimización* (Universidad De los Andes 2014).

[35] Rural reform and distribution of territory, eradication of illicit crops including those plants for ancestral use, implementation of transitional justice and entry to it if one has been involved in the conflict, either as victim or perpetrator, among others.

[36] It would exceed the objectives of this chapter to describe in depth the content of the Final Agreement for the Termination of the Conflict and the Construction of a Stable and Lasting Peace. However, it is worth describing its make-up and the chapters that comprise it. Chapter one is entitled 'Towards a new Colombian field: an integral rural reform'; chapter two, 'Political participation: A democratic opening to build peace; chapter three, 'The end of the conflict'; chapter four, 'A solution to the problem of illicit drugs'; chapter five, 'An agreement on the victims of the conflict'; and chapter six, 'Implementation, verification and endorsement'.

it did not sufficiently achieve this goal, as has been the case historically. Once again, the real interests of these communities have not been adequately responded to, particularly in respect of the meaningful redistribution of land ('the territorial question') and in respect of economic reparation for the sustained injustices experienced by these communities during the armed conflict, but more generally on account of colonisation ('the compensation question'). We will elaborate on each of these aspects in the ensuing discussion in subsections A and B below.

A. The Territorial Question

From a territorial point of view, during the period of Spanish colonialism the Indigenous peoples of Colombia lost the vast majority of their territories, which became part of the Crown's lands. Since that time there has been constant tension over the issue of land. This was notwithstanding the introduction of legal guarantees for the protection of the rights of Indigenous peoples in the 1991 Constitution. One of the reasons for this is the fact that Colombia is a landowner country (a legacy of Spanish colonialism) and the majority of land that was once indigenous is currently privately owned or owned by the state.

For this reason, one of the themes of greatest importance for the Indigenous communities in the final peace agreement was precisely the territorial one. Chapter 6 of the final agreement, which contains the implementation, verification, and public endorsement measures, includes an 'Ethnic Chapter'. This was included out of a recognition of the importance of the contribution of Indigenous groups to the construction of peace and to the progress of the country. This is evidenced specifically by article 6.2.2 of the aforementioned chapter, which records that in interpreting and implementing the final agreement, ethnic and cultural considerations should be taken into account and that in no circumstances would it be permissible to implement the peace agreement in a way that would contravene the rights of the Indigenous communities. The approach contained in this Ethnic Chapter further defines how the other chapters in the agreement should be implemented insofar as Indigenous communities are concerned. For example, article 6.2.3 affirms the importance of taking into account national and internationally recognised principles of law for Indigenous groups including self-determination, autonomy, and self-government. It also recognises the significance of participation and consultation for these groups. In this regard, the agreement recognises that the prior consultation mechanism[37] should be respected to the effect that all decisions affecting the Indigenous population must be subject to consultation with these groups. Also relevant are considerations of socio-economic and cultural identity,

[37] The mechanism for prior consultation has been defined and developed internationally under Convention 169 of the International Labor Organisation (ILO).

and social integrity and land rights, which extend to recognition of ancestral territorial practices of these groups.

In respect of territorial rights specifically, as it was previously mentioned, one of the most serious matters in Colombia has been land and its distribution. For this reason, one of the conditions for signing the agreement to end the conflict was the implementation of what is titled 'Comprehensive Rural Reform', which came into effect under Decree 902 of 2017. The aim of this decree is to promote democratic access to land and to further the goals of equality and rural development through land redistribution in favour of (primarily) peasants and to a lesser extent, Indigenous peoples. In this way, the final agreement in Chapter 1 dedicates an entire chapter to rural reform, and even goes so far as to create a 'Land Fund'. This fund comprises 3 million hectares of unexploited, donated, expropriated, and vacant land that would be available for distribution. The aim of doing so is to develop programmes that would focus on the transformation of the Colombian countryside through, among other things, housing, and other productive projects; the provision of technical agricultural support; commercialisation; and equal access to the means of production. In this respect, the 'Ethnic Chapter' of the agreement aims to ensure that through the implementation of rural reform, the current legal conditions surrounding collective ownership and the mechanisms for the protection and legal security of the occupied and ancestrally owned territories would be guaranteed. This would extend to maintaining the integrity of indigenous territories, including their cultural and spiritual aspects.

Furthermore, the 'Ethnic Chapter' affirms in article 6.2.3 (a) that the state is committed to ensuring that Indigenous communities benefit by giving them access to land and to assigning property to them specifically.[38] This has the purpose of constituting, creating, restructuring, extending, and demarcating the area concerned and reinstituting their Indigenous Reserves (*resguardos*).[39] Moreover, it has clarified that in the case of indigenous communities, their ancestral relationships

[38] <https://www.peaceagreements.org/viewmasterdocument/1845> accessed 10 May 2019. Final Agreement, 6.2 'Ethnic Chapter', 6.2.3 Safeguards and Guarantees (a) in Relation to Comprehensive Rural Reform:

> Ethnic peoples will be included as beneficiaries of the different measures agreed for access to land without impairment of the rights already acquired. The allocation of plots of land and land titling procedures will be performed with a view to the constitution, creation, expansion, entitlement, demarcation, restitution and resolution of disputes over land use and tenure.

[39] According to Decree 2164 of 1995, the Indigenous Reservation (*resguardo*) is a legal and socio-political institution of a special nature. It is made up of one or more Indigenous communities, which, with a collective property title, enjoys the guarantees of private property, owns its territory, and is governed by the management of this and its internal life by an autonomous organisation protected by the indigenous jurisdiction and its own normative system. This legal figure is recognised by the Colombian legal system and is denominated the indigenous territorial organisation, par excellence. However, the communities consider that the territories that have been given to them under an Indigenous Reservation (*resguardo*) title do not always correspond to those that they consider to be their property because they were ancestrally owned or inherited.

with the territory will not be interfered with[40] at the point of selecting the land that will form part of the 'Land Fund'. Finally, in the same article, it is stated that any territorial measure or its implementation in areas having an indigenous presence must fulfil all the necessary legal requirements, including adherence to the relevant prior consultation processes.[41] On this point, the general opinion of the Indigenous communities was that the aforementioned provisions were problematic for two principal reasons. The first is that through the Land Fund, the state is still entitled to dispose of land that has ancestral and thus spiritual significance for Indigenous groups. The second is that rural reform in the form of fair territorial distribution is insufficient in and of itself to affect real change for the Indigenous population; what is needed is a more meaningful commitment to the reconstruction of land and recovery of traditional territories (*resguardos*) in favour of these groups.[42]

On a more positive note, it is important to highlight that rural reform, through the prior consultation process, has made it possible for Indigenous communities to have written confirmation, through Decree 902, that their rights in respect of territorial matters will be safeguarded. Furthermore, the territorial Land Fund affirms that there will be a farmers sub-account and an indigenous sub-account through which the restructuring of the *resguardos* will be prioritised. The continuity of allocation of resources has thus been assured and the territorial rights of Indigenous communities thereby guaranteed. The access of the communities to production projects was also considered and it was agreed that there would be a territorial register that would contain the details of all those individuals whose land rights had not been formally registered.[43] These are all positive developments that will surely make a meaningful difference in addressing the plight of these vulnerable groups and advancing distributive justice more broadly.

[40] One of the objectives pursued under rural reform is the redistribution of the unproductive land, which is concentrated in the hands of major landowners to deliver it to the farmers who will be able to exploit it. The 'Ethnic Chapter' makes clear that in the case of the Indigenous groups, their territories will remain intact even if they are unproductive, for they have ancestral value and are for this reason culturally distinct.

[41] https://www.peaceagreements.org/viewmasterdocument/1845: Final Agreement, 6.2 'Ethnic Chapter', 6.2.3 Safeguards and Guarantees '[t]he principal and non-subsidiary nature of free and informed prior consultation and the right to cultural objection as a guarantee of non-recurrence will be respected, whenever appropriate. Consequently, the phase of implementation of the agreements, as far as ethnic peoples are concerned, should be carried out in guaranteeing the right to prior free and informed consultation respecting constitutional and international standards', accessed 10 May 2019.

[42] Organización Nacional Indígena de Colombia, *Informe General: Estrategia de Consulta Previa en el Marco del Fast Trak, con el fin de aunar esfuerzos para garantizar el derecho a la consulta previa, libre e informada para la implementación del acuerdo final para la terminación del conflicto y la construcción de una paz estable y duradera* (Organización Nacional Indígena de Colombia 2017).

[43] Text to n 42. This information was obtained thanks to the participation of author Diana Carolina Rivera in the prior consultation process under Decree 902 of 2017 and in the debates and discussions that took place among Indigenous communities, before it was approved.

As mentioned, for the Colombian Constitutional Court, one factor that has made Indigenous communities particularly vulnerable to the armed conflict is their land situation, since neither the formal titling of land nor the formation of *resguardos* guarantees them material possession. Their culture is severely affected since the loss of control over the territory impacts further on identity formation and ancestral connection, as well as internal systems of autonomy and government.[44]

For these reasons, as this chapter has sought to emphasise, Indigenous communities generally view the commitments enshrined in the agreement with scepticism and believe that the enacted measures, since as far back the 1991 Constitution, have not been adequate in ensuring the full and meaningful protection of their territorial rights. This is because they believe that their entitlements extend to all of the territories that were lost to them since colonial times, not just a portion thereof. What is more, they are of the view that this new situation could further result in the reinstatement of previous dispossession in certain circumstances.[45] Given the former, it is highly unlikely that much of the ancestrally-owned land that is being defined or registered under a state-owned title will remain within the Land Fund. This is a reasonable fear because, except for the claims that they have raised, in most of the cases there is no legal proof of those territorial rights. Moreover, there is a risk that the land which already forms part of the *resguardos* may be confiscated because they are shared with the farming community which has an interest in exploiting them. For these reasons the communities believe that the creation of a law that defines indigenous territorial rights in a clear and complete manner is necessary before further implementation of the agreement can take place.[46]

The vital point is that the implementation of rural reform in terms of the peace agreement is not without its challenges. This is especially given the fact that overcoming the legacy of centuries of dispossession and injustice since colonial times was never the purpose of the peace agreement. Its core purpose was to end the armed conflict, rather than to address the aforementioned historical claims of Indigenous people directly.[47] Another issue is that the reforms substantially privilege the interests of the farming community at the expense of the Indigenous peoples' territorial claims.

[44] Colombian Constitutional Court, Auto 004 2009 (n 30).

[45] In Colombia, during the Conquest and the Colony, the Indigenous groups were dispossessed of their land and forced to live in the previously mentioned Indigenous Reservations (*resguardos*). In this respect, the historical struggle of the communities has been the struggle to recover their land and thus to be able to expand the reservations and restore the spiritual balance arising from the loss of their territory.

[46] Text to n 42.

[47] <https://www.peaceagreements.org/viewmasterdocument/1845> Final Agreement, 'Chapter I Comprehensive Rural Reform', art 1.1.3 Beneficiary Persons.

B. The Compensation Question

The next issue of importance for Indigenous communities within the final agreement concerns the conflict between the special indigenous jurisdiction and the transitional justice system established by the agreement in Chapter 5, being the 'Special Jurisdiction for Peace'. This is particularly in respect of reparations (principally in the form of economic compensation) for the injustices caused by the armed conflict. As a result of the violence and the terror driven by the FARC,[48] the freedom of Indigenous peoples was severely curtailed. A significant number of people were killed and parts of their territory and ancestral habitat became a centre of illicit operations, extortion, homicide, kidnapping, and forced disappearances.[49] The presence of the guerrilla groups, paramilitaries, and even the Army, turned the Colombian countryside into a battlefield in which its Indigenous peoples were caught in the crossfire.

From the outset, Indigenous groups declared themselves as standing on neutral ground in the face of the armed conflict and, therefore, preferred not to get involved in the fighting by siding with one or other party in this war-torn context. Throughout this period, these Indigenous communities sought to maintain a peaceful stance and to prevent the country's public order situation from affecting the continued practice of their customs and traditions. However, despite this neutrality and commitment to peace,[50] these groups were victimised as a result of not having supported one or other group.[51] In response, it was hoped that the peace dispensation would bring economic redress for the violence and injustices that were inflicted upon the Indigenous groups during the conflict years.[52] To date, within the new transitional justice framework, there have been no decisions issued that order compensation and comprehensive reparation to any of the Indigenous peoples who were victims of the armed conflict. It must be borne in mind, however, that the macro judicial processes[53] taking place at the Special Jurisdiction of Peace

[48] In this case, we refer exclusively to the conflict with the FARC, although it should not be forgotten that the Indigenous peoples have also been victims of other armed actors, such as the National Liberation Army (ELN) and the United Self-Defense Forces of Colombia (AUC).

[49] Colombian Constitutional Court, Auto 004 2009 (n 30).

[50] Organización Nacional Indígena de Colombia, Mandato Político General de los Pueblos Indígenas arts 86–88, Bogotá, 2013: 'By making use of that moral stance, we manifest our outright rejection about the way that the historical, social, economic, political and cultural conflicts of society and peoples are intended to be resolved through armed confrontation in our territories and, by involving us in a situation of high risk and vulnerability to our way of living and of looking at the world.'

[51] eg the Arhuaca Indigenous community continues to fight for justice arising from lack of state action for the murder of three prominent spiritual leaders more than twenty years ago at the hands of the National Army.

[52] Organización Nacional Indígena de Colombia, *Moemorias: Primer Encuentro de la Organización Nacional Indígena—ONIC con el Sistema Integral de Verdad, Justicia, Reparación y No Repetición* (Organización Nacional Indígena de Colombia 2018).

[53] The Special Jurisdiction of Peace does not judge particular cases but focuses on systematic crimes and serious violations of rights in a broad context. Nowadays there are seven macro processes: kidnapping, 'false positives', Unión Patriótica's genocide, forced recruitment, and the territorial situation of

require lengthy periods of time to reach final results. In this regard it is important to mention that there are already three ongoing processes, in which significant advances have been achieved in terms of intercultural dialogue, connecting the cases to the victims in the territory, determination of damages, and restorative justice practices through meticulous dialogical construction of the truth. These are specifically cases 02,[54] 04,[55] and 05[56] of the Special Jurisdiction of Peace, which are detailed on the official website of the tribunal.[57]

Indigenous peoples hope that, finally, the work of this Jurisdiction will make it possible for them to be compensated for the damage caused by the conflict, taking into account that, although the FARC guerillas originally appeared to be a group willing to fight for the interests of the Indigenous peoples, before long their true

three regions in the country in which the aim is to compensate ethnic communities as victims of the armed conflict.

[54] The Special Jurisdiction for Peace opened Case 02 on 10 July 2018. This case prioritises serious human rights violations and serious infractions of international humanitarian law, that mainly affect Indigenous peoples, Black communities, Afro-Colombians, peasants, women, and LGBTQI people in the municipalities of Tumaco, Ricaurte, and Barbacoas in the region of Nariño. In this case, approximately 3,000 victimising acts have been studied. They are grouped into twelve sets of damages allegedly committed by members of the extinct FARC-EP and members of the public forces in the noted municipalities between 1990 and 2016. 78 per cent of these lands legally belong to Indigenous and Afro-descendant peoples.

Available <https://www.jep.gov.co/especiales1/macrocasos/02.html> accessed 11 July 2022.

[55] For its part, the Special Jurisdiction for Peace opened Case 04 on 11 September 2018. This case prioritises the territorial situation based upon the events of the conflict that occurred in the Urabá region between 1986 and 2016. To date there are 43,385 acts of victimisation, of which 255 are against individuals while the rest make up part of 117 subjects collectively discriminated against as follows: twenty Community Councils, three Black community organisations, one union, three peasant organisations, nineteen communities having Black ethnicity, and seventy-one Indigenous communities included in sixty-nine ancestral territories and four people groups: Embera (Dobida, Eyabida, Katio), Wounaan, Sinú, and Guna Dule. In this case, progress has been made in reaching agreement on the articulation and coordination route between the Special Jurisdiction for Peace and the ethnic authorities of the four Indigenous groups. As a result, there is currently an inter-jurisdictional coordination arrangement between the Special Jurisdiction for Peace and the Special Indigenous Jurisdiction for Antioquia and Chocó. Likewise, there is an inter-cultural dialogue route and coordination with the Special Jurisdiction for Peace with the ethnic-territorial authorities of the Black and Afro-Colombian people of Urabá, Bajo Atrato, and Darién <https://www.jep.gov.co/especiales1/macrocasos/04.html> accessed 12 July 2022.

[56] This is the last of the three territorial cases that the Special Jurisdiction for Peace has opened. It began on 16 November 2018, due the fact that in the area conformed by the south of Valle del Cauca and the north of Cauca, the armed conflict left 7,582 dead. In 2001, in municipalities such as Santander de Quilichao and Corinto, the rate of homicides was 100 deaths per 100 thousand inhabitants. Macro Case 05 is very important for the Special Jurisdiction for Peace because it is an area in which especially vulnerable peoples (Indigenous, Afro-descendants, and peasants) have historically lived, and whose human rights were systematically violated by the armed actors in the period studied by the Jurisdiction. This macro case is one of the benchmarks at the national level as it presents concrete achievements of inter-cultural dialogue and inter-jurisdictional coordination between the Special Jurisdiction for Peace and the Special Indigenous Jurisdiction. In this macro case, 129 collective entities have been recognised as victims, that bring together forty-five Indigenous peoples, sixty-seven community councils, and eight victim organisations that join together more than 180,000 victims. In addition, the ancestral and collective territory of Çxhab Wala Kiwe, and seventy individuals, five of them belonging to the LGBTQI population have also been recognised <https://www.jep.gov.co/especiales1/macrocasos/05.html> accessed 12 July 2022.

[57] <https://www.jep.gov.co/Paginas/Inicio.aspx> accessed 12 July 2022.

motives became clear as they began to perpetrate violent acts against Indigenous communities and even began to recruit their children, convincing them that they would have a better life within the FARC only to murder them or allow them to die at the hands of the Army later.[58] The guerillas settled in the Indigenous settlements and demanded food and shelter, with any community resistance being countered with heavy handedness and violence.

There are not enough words to describe all the damage that was inflicted upon the Indigenous communities of Colombia during the harshest years of the conflict. When asked about this specific period of time, both young and old agree that it was one of the most difficult times in the history of the country. Every day, there were deaths within these communities, either in rural areas or in the vicinity of cities and municipalities. The memory of well-known paramilitary leaders and guerrillas remains vivid in the minds and hearts of the victims. Under Auto 004 of 2009, the Constitutional Court affirmed the cruelty and injustices suffered by the Indigenous peoples in the context of a conflict in which they wanted no part. The Court was also critical of the state and society for continuing to talk about multiculturalism and respect for ethnic diversity whilst at the same time failing to respond to the plight of these vulnerable groups.

Given the foregoing, it is clear that the Indigenous communities of the country have a real and substantial interest in the conflict coming to a permanent end. This is why the signing of the peace agreement gave them strong hope that they would finally be compensated for all the harm and suffering that they endured during the conflict and ultimately, that truth and justice would be realised.

Indeed, as noted, Chapter 5 of the agreement makes special and direct reference to the victims of the conflict. It indicates that the principle of victim compensation is at the centre of the peace process and for this reason it was necessary to establish the 'Integral System of Truth, Justice, Reparation and Non-Repetition'. The hope was that this system would contribute to the fight against impunity by combining mechanisms for the investigation and punishment of serious human rights violations and as well as making provision for compensation for the harm caused to people, groups, and territories, as a whole. It also provides for complementary extrajudicial mechanisms that were intended to contribute to the attainment of truth by assisting in the search for loved ones who had gone missing.[59]

As an example of the application of the ethnic approach, a special agreement between the Indigenous communities of Colombia and the Special Jurisdiction

[58] GA Rodrígez, *La consulta previa, un derecho fundamental de los pueblos indígenas y grupos étnicos de Colombia* (Grupo Semillas 2008) 36–37.

[59] The Integral System comprises the Commission for the Clarification of Truth, Unity and Non-Repetition; the Special Unit for the Search of those People who have disappeared during the Armed Conflict; the Special Jurisdiction for Peace; integral reparation measures for the construction of peace; and the Guarantees of No Repetition.

for Peace[60] was signed on 5 June 2019 to provide for the coordination, inter-jurisdictional articulation, and inter-cultural dialogue between the Special Indigenous Jurisdiction and the Special Jurisdiction for Peace. One of the most important principles in this regard is reparation for harms suffered. Under this principle, reparation implies the re-establishment of the balance and harmony of the peoples, their culture, their territories, and their spirituality which were historically violated. It is supposed to integrate a set of transformative measures aimed at strengthening the self-determination of peoples and eliminating the patterns of discrimination. The Special Jurisdiction for Peace is required to recognise individual and group injustices from a territorial and cultural perspective.[61]

From this, it is fair to conclude that the peace agreement has achieved some recognition for the plight of Indigenous peoples in the *formal* sense, which can be seen in the advances shown in the aforementioned macro cases 02, 04, and 05. This is especially clear from the provisions of the aforementioned 'Ethnic Chapter' of the agreement, which establishes some general guidelines directed specifically at Indigenous groups. It does so through the design of the 'Integral System of Truth, Justice, Reparation and No Repetition'; respect for the dispute-resolution powers of 'traditional authorities'[62] in specific territories; incorporation of ethnic and cultural perspectives into the design of the different judicial and extrajudicial mechanisms agreed upon; and the establishment of a special coordination programme for the reincorporation of those disengaged Indigenous peoples with representative organisations, among other things. These are significant gains. However, at the level of implementation much work still needs to be done.

In accordance with the ambitions of Chapter 5 of the agreement, both the FARC and the national government committed themselves to recognising their responsibility towards the victims of the conflict—including the Indigenous peoples—and to restoring their rights, allowing their participation in the attainment of truth, and, ultimately, compensating them for the harms and injustices that they endured.[63] However, as mentioned before, the implementation of this aspect of the agreement has experienced significant challenges; starting with the fact that it has not yet been

[60] A number of Judicial Panels for justice were established, including a Judicial Panel for Amnesty and Pardon and a Tribunal for Peace, to administer justice and investigate, clarify, prosecute, and punish serious human rights violations and serious infringements of international humanitarian law. The special jurisdiction for peace forms part of the comprehensive system for truth, justice, reparation, and non-repetition and, since it is exclusively and temporarily devoted to conduct directly and indirectly related to the armed conflict, does not replace ordinary jurisdiction, and is defined in Chapter 5.1 (b) of the peace agreement.

[61] Jurisdicción Especial para la Paz, Protocolo para la coordinación, articulación interjurisdiccional y diálogo intercultural entre la jurisdicción especial indígena y la jurisdicción especial para la paz (Bogotá, 24 July 2019) <https://www.jep.gov.co/DocumentosJEPWP/protocolo.pdf> accessed 23 March 2021.

[62] Each Indigenous community has its own governmental authorities, referred to as 'traditional authorities', who are responsible for maintaining their political structure.

[63] Final Agreement for the Termination of the Conflict and the Construction of a Stable and Lasting Peace (n 36).

possible for the system to begin to function fully. This is because its basic principles are being re-evaluated by the current government;[64] many of the officials in charge of these new bodies have not been able to fulfil their roles and responsibilities[65] and some of the members of the FARC have continued committing crimes in defiance of the peace process.[66] This situation, in many cases, has prevented reparation and compensation from happening in a material way, and in others, it has led to the problematic lengthening of resolution time frames. Accordingly, based on what has transpired up until now, it seems unlikely that economic redress will ever be realised in favour of Indigenous groups. This is made abundantly clear from the fact that, five years after the signing of the agreement, there has not been a single case where compensation was awarded to an Indigenous group. At present, the 'Special Justice for Peace' continues to investigate and collect information about what transpired from the perspective of victims from Indigenous communities but real, tangible economic redress remains elusive from a distributive justice perspective.[67]

Furthermore, in respect of the prior consultation mechanism in the context of Chapter 5 of the agreement, this was carried out before the 'Indigenous Authorities' were able to understand the requirements and procedures for implementing the system. This brought about more disagreement than consensus and resulted in the communities simply conceding most of the points due to a lack of understanding of the meaning of the provisions in the agreement.

The upshot is that no concrete results for the benefit of Indigenous peoples have been realised: they are still awaiting compensation for the injustices that they have suffered as well as the attainment of truth in relation to the many homicides and disappearances of their loved ones who were victims of the armed conflict.

4. Concluding Reflections

This chapter has sought to highlight the plight of the Indigenous population in Colombia, who have suffered a protracted and enduring history of maginalisation

[64] LC Pinto, 'Presidencia de la República presenta al Congreso objeciones a Ley Estatutaria de la JEP' *Senado de la República* (Bogotá, 11 March 2019) <http://www.senado.gov.co/actualidad/item/28744-presidencia-de-la-republica-presenta-al-congreso-objeciones-a-ley-estatutaria-de-la-jep> accessed 10 May 2019.

[65] Redacción Judicial, 'Procuraduría suspendió por 5 meses a Néstor Raúl Correa, exsecretario de la JEP' *El Espectador* (Bogotá, 6 May 2019) <https://www.elespectador.com/noticias/judicial/procuraduria-suspendio-por-5-meses-nestor-raul-correa-exsecretario-de-la-jep-articulo-854079> accessed 15 May 2019.

[66] Justicia, 'Capturan por narcotráfico a Jesús Santrich, por petición de EE. UU.' *El Tiempo* (Bogotá, 9 April 2018) <https://www.eltiempo.com/justicia/investigacion/capturan-a-jesus-santrich-lider-de-la-farc-203104> accessed 15 May 2019.

[67] See n 54; Jurisdicción Especial para la Paz, *Diversidad Étnica y Cultural: Pluralismo Jurídico y Consulta Previa* (Jurisdicción Especial para la Paz 2019) <https://www.jep.gov.co/DocumentosJEPWP/protocolo.pdf> accessed 11 May 2020.

and discrimination, dating back to colonial times. The armed conflict, through which the entire country has been victimised, has affected the Indigenous peoples of Colombia in a very specific way: it displaced these communities from their home territories, coerced their involvement in the ensuing violence, violated their cultural traditions, and caused thousands of deaths and disappearances.

Although the earlier Political Constitution of 1991 brought about significant changes in the recognition of the rights and cultural values of these peoples, in practice there has been no change or redress. This remains true under the 2016 peace agreement. As this chapter has sought to show, both the territorial and compensation issues raise significant questions about the extent to which the Colombian peace process has been able to advance distributive and restorative justice. Our conclusion is that, given the limited tangible gains for Indigenous peoples in respect of land restitution and financial compensation, Colombia's transitional justice process is far from complete. In moving forward, it is necessary for those driving the peace process to pay more careful attention to the ways in which these implied forms of justice—that the Indigenous communities value most—can be more meaningfully realised within the broader transitional justice process that is currently underway.

19

Joint Reflection: The South African and Colombian 'Peace Agreements'

Restoration of Rights or Continuing Difficulties for Indigenous Peoples?

Sindiso Mnisi Weeks and Diana Carolina Rivera-Drago

1. Introduction

This comparative reflection is based on the experiences of South Africa and Colombia following the entry into force of the respective peace agreements of each country; namely, South Africa's 1996 Constitution and the 2016 'Final Agreement for the Termination of the Conflict and the Construction of a Stable and Lasting Peace' in Colombia, which has since been integrated into the Political Constitution of 1991. It analyses both the expectations of greater land access as a manifestation of distributive justice, as well as the limited effectiveness of the transitional justice systems for the traditional peoples of South Africa and the Indigenous peoples of Colombia. This will lay the basis for a deeper discussion of what each country could learn from the other to better advance the goals of their respective transitions to peace, and how in both of them the Indigenous and traditional peoples have contributed to the constriction of peace and the implementation of transitional justice. To this end, this reflection is divided into two parts and a conclusion. The first section describes some important similarities and differences between the two countries in respect of their histories and processes. The second section explores the expectations in respect of greater land access and then turns to an assessment of the effectiveness of the transitional justice system as it relates to traditional peoples and Indigenous groups. In so doing, it explores specifically the possible reasons why these expectations were not fulfilled in both countries. The final section concludes with reflections on the different lessons that South Africa and Colombia could learn from each other's experiences, postulates possible ways forward for both countries to better advance the goals of their transitions by fostering deeper respect and acknowledgment for these vulnerable peoples, and explains how Indigenous movements have contributed to the construction of peace and justice both in South Africa and in Colombia.

Sindiso Mnisi Weeks and Diana Carolina Rivera-Dragos, *Joint Reflection: The South African and Colombian 'Peace Agreements'* In: *Transitional Justice, Distributive Justice, and Transformative Constitutionalism.* Edited by: David Bilchitz and Raisa Cachalia, with Magdalena Inés Correa Henao and Nathalia Bautista Pizarro, Oxford University Press. © Sindiso Mnisi Weeks and Diana Carolina Rivera-Dragos 2023. DOI: 10.1093/oso/9780192887627.003.0019

2. Different Contexts with Similar Problems

Although South Africa and Colombia are geographically distant countries, they have more similarities than one would think. We start from a common historical fact: the post-conflict claims to the recognition of rights of the 'Indigenous' and 'traditional' people in the two countries arise from their having been colonised by foreigners. The settlers in Africa as in America, under the theory of 'terra nullius', understood the land to be vacant or unoccupied and thus became self-declared owners of everything and subjected all people and things on the claimed land to their own law.[1] Despite the scourge of violence in Colombia and the discrimination against Indigenous peoples, there is no doubt that what occurred to traditional peoples in South Africa had much greater numerical scope and impact. For instance, while in Colombia the Indigenous population does not exceed 4 per cent of the total population, in South Africa, the Black population surpasses 80 per cent with 17 million people (29 per cent of South Africans) living under traditional leadership in rural areas and up to double that number maintaining some relationship with these 'homelands', albeit as labour migrants to cities.[2] Put differently, the phenomenon of discrimination and violation of rights was not confined to a minority but affected the majority of the population. Furthermore, in South Africa, colonisation lasted well into the twentieth century and was then succeeded by apartheid—a segregationist policy of 'separate development' imposed by Afrikaner nationalists through laws. By contrast, Colombia became independent more than a century prior, in 1810. Of course, one should not lose sight of the fact that, in Colombia, the recognition of pluralism and the rights of Indigenous peoples still occurred late: it was not until the 1991 Constitution that these advances could be evidenced and the country began to recognise its multi-ethnic and multicultural character.

The two countries underwent significant constitutional change in the 1990s, but the vision and scope of each must be understood in the respective contexts of these countries. In South Africa, until 1990–1994, there prevailed a regime where a white minority systematically excluded the Black majority from citizenship and power in terms of law as it attempted entirely to expel them to separate 'homelands' (Bantustans) that would be governed by 'despotic chiefs'. In Colombia, Indigenous people have always been considered minorities that are characterised by historical

[1] M Mamdani, *Citizen and Subject: Contemporary Africa and the Legacy of Late Colonialism* (PUP 1996) and CA Uribe, *Geografía humana de Colombia nordeste indígena Tomo II* (Instituto Colombiano de Cultura Hispánica 1992).

[2] A Claassens, 'Recent Changes in Women's Land Rights and Contested Customary Law in South Africa' (2013) 13 Journal of Agrarian Change 71; D Budlender and others, *Women, Land and Customary Law* (Community Agency for Social Enquiry (CASE) 2011) <https://idl-bnc-idrc.dspacedirect.org/handle/10625/47347> accessed 12 June 2020. CASE reports that, in 2010, only 33 per cent of fathers across three traditional survey sites were resident homestead members and 57 per cent of children aged nineteen and under were living with their mothers.

continuity with the original inhabitants. Between 1821 (Colombia's formal independence) and 1991, the state intended to culturally assimilate the Indigenous groups into the majority, with some differentiated rights being granted.[3]

Today, in the two constitutional texts drafted in the 1990s (the 1996 South African Constitution and the 1991 Colombian Constitution), beyond the individual rights, collective rights are recognised. However, they reflect different histories, needs, demands, and entitlements. In Colombia, the Constitution seeks to recognise the legal, territorial, and political autonomy of Indigenous people as a long-standing minority.[4] In the South African case, only after the current Constitution, was the majority of the society recognised as possessing the fullness of its rights, particularly citizenship. Until then, the situation of the majority population in South Africa might be compared to that of Indigenous Colombian people at the end of colonialism when the Spaniards considered them 'poor' and 'miserable minors', which served as a justification for restricting the rights of these peoples.[5]

The two countries today are characterised by the express recognition of the ethnic and cultural diversity of each nation. The difficulty, however, is that eradicating the ravages of centuries of injustice does not simply happen by decree. Moreover, both countries' constitutions, being based on the idea of a liberal state that assumes that the nation bears a single cultural identity, have had to confront complex questions concerning how best to balance the need for unity with the importance of ethnic and cultural diversity and legal pluralism.

Finally, the consequences and value of the post-conflict agreements reached in South Africa and Colombia are ambivalent. On the one hand, there is no doubt that the ushering in of democracy in South Africa and the cessation of hostilities in Colombia have been to the benefit of all members of the population. Yet, on the other hand, in neither country have traditional and Indigenous peoples benefitted as much from these changes, as was hoped, specifically in terms of restoration of land and transitional justice.

3. Great Expectations, Weak Outcomes

It would be very complex to compare two historical processes that occurred in countries with such different contexts and circumstances. Yet, evidently, both in Colombia and South Africa, the historical context for the traditional and Indigenous peoples has had similar characteristics in terms of the discrimination and deprivation of their ancestral territories and violence of varying degrees.

[3] Act 69 of 1890 entitled, 'The manner in which the savages must be governed in order to reduce them to civilised living'.

[4] Colombian Constitution 1991, Chapter XI.

[5] Mamdani, *Citizen and Subject* (n 1).

Moreover, the related struggle for the recovery of the land as well as their autonomy and the survival of their cultures is shared in both places. In both cases, it is precisely this struggle and resistance that led the Indigenous and traditional communities to develop very high expectations for the outcomes of the post-conflict agreements, particularly in respect of the advancement of distributive and transitional justice. In both cases, however, these high hopes that the respective transitions would result in significant benefits, mainly with respect to land and justice issues, have generally not materialised. That said, in Colombia, it is too early to judge the outcome of the peace agreement processes, given that the Special Jurisdiction of Peace has only just taken its first steps.

The purpose of this section is therefore to analyse two aspects. On the one hand, those relating to the existing expectations regarding the benefits of the post-conflict agreements for the traditional and Indigenous peoples of both countries in terms of restoration of land (A). On the other hand, those relating to the failings of the respective transitional justice systems established in the transitional documents in terms of effective results for pre-colonial inhabitants (B).

Considering the aforementioned, the South African post-conflict agreements were consolidated into a political constitution with all the demands and recognition that this implies. The Constitution of 1993 therefore attributed South African citizenship to traditional populations and, largely through its passing, apartheid finally came to its formal end. The negotiations that produced the Interim (then, in 1996, Final) Constitution followed decades of resistance (both peaceful and armed) from a range of actors, primarily led by the African National Congress (ANC). The transition to democracy under the new Constitution would affect everyone and has had tremendous consequences for traditional peoples who were not previously considered citizens of South Africa.

Nonetheless, the extent to which the democratic transition has changed the institutional arrangements governing traditional peoples, and thus altered the material situation for traditional communities, has been extremely limited. Worse still, the gains have proven to be vulnerable to systematic erosion. Today, the South African legislature has sought to recognise Khoi-San peoples in the compromised manner similar to traditional peoples under the Traditional and Khoi-San Leadership Act 3 of 2019, which same legislation claws back some of the hard-won rights of traditional communities.

By contrast, in Colombia, the peace agreement resulted from a long-established war between the state and the guerrilla group (FARC). Further, as can be inferred, the document that contains it is not a political constitution but a document that forms part of the existing Constitution, in which the two parties agreed on the outcome of the preceding talks and negotiations. This agreement had a major impact on the country because through it the ceasefire and the end of the war became official. As a result, its consequences have been positive for the entire Colombian population and, especially for the peace and security of the rural population, including the Indigenous peoples.

A. Slow and Uncertain: Land Restitution as Yet Unrealised

Marginalised and impoverished by the exclusionary and oppressive systems in both countries, therefore, Indigenous and traditional peoples in both Colombia and South Africa had hoped for the return of the land of which they had been historically dispossessed. In principle, in both countries, it was expected that after signing the agreements that formally ended the long-term conflict, any piece of land traditionally owned and any land not yet granted title deeds would be awarded to them. However, it was not to be.

One of the most important expectations derived from the Colombian 'Peace Agreement' was the possibility of accessing some of the lands that traditionally belonged to Indigenous peoples through the dedicated sub-account of the Lands Fund that the peace agreement creates.[6] A serious matter in Colombia has been land and its distribution, for this reason one of the guerrilla conditions to sign the end of the conflict was the implementation of 'Comprehensive Rural Reform' as an intrinsic feature of the agreement. The aim of this rural reform was to promote democratic access to the land and to further the goals of equality and rural development through redistribution against concentration of land, in favour principally of peasants and, to a minor extent, Indigenous peoples. In this way, the final agreement proposed a complete chapter (Chapter 1) referred to the 'Comprehensive Rural Reform', which has to take place, with the creation of a 'Land Fund' (composed of 3 million hectares from unexploited, donated, expropriated, and vacant land), and, at the same time, the 'Chapter on Ethnic Perspectives' of the agreement aimed to ensure that, through the implementation of this rural reform, the current legal conditions surrounding collective ownership and the mechanisms for the protection and legal security of the occupied and ancestrally owned territories would be guaranteed, whilst at the same time taking care of the integrity of indigenous territories, including their cultural and spiritual aspects.[7]

[6] Final Peace Agreement, Chapter 1 Towards a New Colombian Countryside, Comprehensive Rural Reform. 1.1. Access and Use. Non-productive land. Land titling. Agricultural frontier and protection of reserve areas:

> 1.1.1. Comprehensive Rural Reform Land Fund: With a view to achieving the democratisation of access to land, to the benefit of small-scale farmer communities and especially rural women without land or with insufficient land and the rural communities most affected by poverty, neglect and the conflict, regularising property ownership rights and as a result reversing concentration and promoting fair distribution of land, the National Government is to create a Land Fund for the free distribution of land. The Land Fund (Fondo de Tierras), which will be permanent in nature, will have 3 million hectares of land available during its first 12 years of existence ...

[7] Final Peace Agreement, 6.2 Chapter on Ethnic Perspectives, 6.2.3. Safeguards and guarantees:

> a. In relation to Comprehensive Rural Reform The implementation of the CRR Chapter will guarantee the application of an ethnic and cultural perspective, the current legal conditions

In the case of Colombia, it was expected that the territories of those who were displaced by the armed conflict would be restored and, in general, fair redistribution of the territories that had been expropriated from the time of the respective colonisation would be made possible. This is seen by Indigenous peoples as going hand in hand with the real recognition of their culture and their normative orders. Specifically, Colombia has a continental area of 114,174,800 km^2,[8] of which 30 per cent (36 million) are titled under indigenous territories.[9] However, in many of them, there are peasant reservations, exploration and exploitation projects for extraction of natural and mineral resources, urban and rural settlements, and damage to graves caused by the internal conflict, among other phenomena that impede the use and real enjoyment of the collectively-owned land. There are also many Indigenous people residing in the city who have been completely dispossessed of their territories and many others who believe that the land awarded to them in the Indigenous Reserves (*resguardos*) does not even represent half of what is actually theirs.[10]

As previously described, the reality in South Africa is not dissimilar. Until 1994, 67 per cent of land was under white commercial agricultural ownership, 15 per cent constituted Black 'Bantustans' (or 'Homelands') that were predominantly under state ownership, and another 10 per cent was land for state use and a remaining 8 per cent metropolitan and other urban areas.[11] The goal was set that, by 2014, at least 30 per cent of the productive land would have to be transferred back to historically dispossessed peoples but this has not yet been met.[12] That said, while

of collective ownership, and the mechanisms for the legal protection and security of land and territories occupied or owned ancestrally and/or Final Agreement 24.11.2016 219 traditionally. The holistic nature of territoriality and its cultural and spiritual dimensions, and the heightened protection for peoples at risk of extinction and their safeguard plans, will also be observed. Access to land including the Land Fund. Ethnic peoples will be included as beneficiaries of the different measures agreed for access to land without impairment of the rights already acquired. The allocation of plots of land and land titling procedures will be performed with a view to the constitution, creation, expansion, entitlement, demarcation, restitution and resolution of disputes over land use and tenure. It shall be understood for the case of ethnic peoples that the ecological function of property and their own ancestral forms of relationship with the territory take precedence over the notion of non-exploitation. The ethnic peoples and communities will participate with their representative organisations in creating mechanisms to resolve disputes about land tenure and use, and about strengthening of food production, when the disputes concerned compromise their rights.

8 Agustín Codazzi Geographical Institute, available: <https://www.igac.gov.co/es/search/node/superficie%20de%20colombia> accessed 26 June 2020.

9 Official Governmental Census, 2005 <http://www.dane.gov.co/index.php/transparencia/138-espanol/103-grupos-etnicos> accessed 7 September 2023.

10 Colombian Constitutional Court, 26 January 2009, decision: Auto 004 2009 Judge Manuel José Cepeda Espinosa.

11 C Walker, Institute for Poverty, Land and Agrarian Studies (PLAAS) *Fact Check No. 1: Land Reform* <http://repository.uwc.ac.za/xmlui/bitstream/handle/10566/4455/fc_1_distribution_land_south_africa_overview_2013.pdf?sequence=1&isAllowed=y> accessed 17 May 2019 ('PLAAS 2013').

12 World Bank Group, *An Incomplete Transition: Overcoming the Legacy of Exclusion in South Africa. Systematic Country Diagnostic* (World Bank 2018) 12, 43–44 <https://openknowledge.worldbank.org/handle/10986/29793> accessed 4 June 2019.

reliable data on the transfer of land so far achieved is limited, by some estimates, roughly 21 per cent of (white-owned) farmland that is in freehold had been transferred between 1994 and 2018—with roughly 1/8 of that transfer achieved through the government's restitution and redistribution programmes and the lion's share done through private land purchases.[13] Furthermore, as in Colombia, extractive industry presents an enduring threat to rural people who are being further dispossessed and displaced, their graves desecrated, and their lands and waters polluted by corporations who wish to exploit the mineral-rich lands and collude with traditional leaders for profit.[14] To date, the government has failed to protect rural people against this terrible threat.

What is therefore clear from the distributive justice perspective, at least from the point of view of the Indigenous peoples in Colombia and traditional peoples in South Africa, is that the commitments made by their governments are not sufficient to protect their territorial rights or achieve greater protection in this regard. There is even widespread fear that their interests may be harmed and that the situation in the post-conflict context could in fact be worse than it was previously, thereby negatively impacting advancement of the goal of greater transitional justice. Hence, in both countries there are discussions of re-negotiation and replacement of the precepts relating to land in their transition documents. In Colombia, this is for two principal reasons. On the one hand, because in the constitution of the aforementioned Land Fund, even if not entitled to lands that are ancestrally indigenous, the state could dispose of them. This creates a reasonable fear because, in most of the cases, the Indigenous groups have no evidence of their property rights except for the claims that they have made. On the other hand, if the goal of the reform was fair territorial distribution, in the concerns of the Indigenous peoples, it was necessary to promote the restructuring and recovery of their traditional territories (*resguardos*)[15] they lost since colonial times, more so than the chance of participation in the benefits of the Fund.[16]

[13] W Sihlobo and T Kapuya, 'SPECIAL REPORT: The truth about land ownership in South Africa' *Rand Daily Mail* (Johannesburg, 23 July 2018) <https://www.businesslive.co.za/rdm/politics/2018-07-23-special-report-the-truth-about-land-ownership-in-south-africa/> accessed 4 June 2019.

[14] A Claassens and Boitumelo Matlala, 'Platinum, Poverty and Princes in Post-Apartheid South Africa: New Laws, Old Repertoires' (2014) 4 New South African Review 116; S Mnwana, 'Mining, Accountability and the Law in the Bakgatla-Ba-Kgafela Traditional Authority Area' (2014) 49 South African Crime Quarterly 21; A Manson and B Mbenga, *Land, Chiefs, Mining: South Africa's North West Province Since 1840* (NYU Press 2014).

[15] In Colombia, during the Conquest and the Colony, the Indigenous groups were dispossessed of their land and forced to live in the previously mentioned Indigenous Reservations (*resguardos*). In this respect, the historical struggle of the communities has been the struggle to recover their land and thus to be able to expand the reservations and restore the spiritual balance afflicted by the loss of their territory.

[16] Organización Nacional Indígena de Colombia, *Informe General: Estrategia de Consulta Previa en el Marco del Fast Trak, con el fin de aunar esfuerzos para garantizar el derecho a la consulta previa, libre e informada para la implementación del acuerdo final para la terminación del conflicto y la construcción de una paz estable y duradera* (ONIC 2017).

B. Transitional Justice Challenges: Inadequate Economic and Social Redress for Violence

In terms of transitional justice, except in a few cases, Colombia has addressed its violent past by means of judicial process. Amidst notable violence, South Africa conducted its transitional negotiations in the first and second multi-party Convention for a Democratic South Africa (CODESA), which took place during 1990–1993, as well as a democratically-elected Constitutional Assembly formed on 5 February 1991.[17] Thereafter, South African transitional justice claims relating to 'gross human rights violations'; such as abductions, killings, and torture were almost entirely handled through the Truth and Reconciliation Commission (TRC), which operated during December 1995–October 1998 (when its report came out) and which granted amnesty to many perpetrators of terrible crimes.[18] The spectacle of the TRC, as a performative space, has been extensively analysed.[19] Having received and reviewed reams of amnesty applications and written testimony, the TRC Commissioners travelled around the entire country to hear the heart-wrenching stories of victims of violence under apartheid and choreograph performances of repentance and reconciliation in strategically selected communities in locations chosen, at least in part, for their symbolism.

For its part, following the signing of the peace agreement in Colombia, several discussions have taken place and it has not been easy to determine the way forward in terms of the application of the transitional justice system for the Indigenous peoples established by this agreement. The Permanent Committee for Concertation (Mesa Permanente de Consertación)[20] has met with the Colombian government several times in order to determine the way to harmonise the operation of the 'Special Indigenous Jurisdiction'[21] and the 'Special Jurisdiction for Peace' established in Chapter 5 of the agreement, related specifically to reparation and compensation for the damages caused by the armed conflict, through obtaining justice, gaining knowledge of the truth, and being awarded appropriate compensation, in those cases in which there is a conflict of competencies. For example, there are many cases of Indigenous people who belonged to the ranks of the guerrillas and who,

[17] H Klug, 'Challenging Constitutionalism in Post-Apartheid South Africa' (2016) 2 Constitutional Studies 41.

[18] Act 34 1995 Promotion of National Unity and Reconciliation.

[19] RA Wilson, *The Politics of Truth and Reconciliation in South Africa: Legitimizing the Post-Apartheid State* (CUP 2001); CM Cole, *Performing South Africa's Truth Commission: Stages of Transition* (Indiana UP 2010).

[20] The Permanent Committee for Concertation (Mesa Permanente de Concertación) is a representative body of the Colombian Indigenous communities, formed by one or more representatives from each community, whose main function is to discuss and concert with the state all the administrative and legislative decisions that may affect them, to evaluate the implementation of the state's indigenous policy, and to monitor compliance with the agreements reached.

[21] In the Colombian Constitution, under art 246, a special jurisdiction for Indigenous people has been created, which is independent from the Colombian official legal system. Thus, each community has the right to create and apply its own rules and courts, and their authorities have judicial powers with just one limitation: respect for human rights and the principles of the national Constitution.

after the signing of the agreement, should be judged by the Special Jurisdiction for Peace, but their communities require them to be judged under their own customary law. This would obviously imply a violation of the *non bis in idem* principle (no legal action can be instituted twice for the same cause) and has led to complex discussions that have not yet been resolved. The same situation applies to the Indigenous victims of the armed conflict, since at the point of commencing the process of repairing damages there has been no clarity as to the jurisdiction to which to resort or the procedure to be used. This often means that victim's compensation and the right to truth, justice, and reparation remain up in the air.

It is worth noting that traditional peoples in South Africa and Indigenous peoples in Colombia have not obtained any kind of symbolic and economic compensation for the terrible damage that violence caused them. In Colombia, recognition and reparations for these damages have not been possible yet and should be addressed in future. Given the investment of Indigenous communities in the end of the conflict, they had strong hope that, with the signing of the peace agreement, the long-awaited opportunity to obtain compensation for all the harms suffered would be realised, justice would be exercised, and the truth would be known. However, three years after the signing of the agreement, in terms of justice and compensation, there has not been a single case resolved as pertains to the rights of Indigenous peoples. Transitional (and distributive) justice have thus not materialised in a visible way, and no mechanism has been implemented to make effective the level of recognition they expected.[22]

With the TRC in South Africa, the goal was the pursuit of unification of the 'rainbow nation', predominantly through the creation of a shared narrative. That national goal was privileged over localised and individualised material needs, thus the TRC recommended that the 19,000 apartheid victims it identified should receive R30,000 payments for their pain and suffering. By 2018, roughly 16,800 had been paid their measly sums.[23] Of course, the TRC's attempts at creating a hegemonic view of South Africa's transition as one that centralised truth and reconciliation, did not leave all South Africans satisfied. There is a rich body of research reflecting the ways in which the concepts of justice operationalised by the TRC did not match the conceptions embedded in ordinary South African society. Some scholars have discussed how the TRC sought to craft a master narrative that centred political organisations over individuals and worked hard to affirm the message that wrong was done on both sides of the struggle between the apartheid state and its supporters, on one hand, and the opponents of apartheid, on the other.[24] More

[22] Jurisdicción Especial para la Paz, *Diversidad Étnica y Cultural: Pluralismo Jurídico y Consulta Previa* (Jurisdicción Especial para la Paz 2019) <https://www.jep.gov.co/DocumentosJEPWP/protocolo.pdf> accessed 11 May 2020.

[23] C Makhaye and N Mkhize, 'Thousands of Apartheid-Era Victims Still Waiting for Compensation' *Business Day (online)* (14 December 2018) <https://www.businesslive.co.za/bd/national/2018-12-14-thousands-of-apartheid-era-victims-still-waiting-for-compensation/> accessed 3 July 2020.

[24] D Posel and G Simpson (eds), *Commissioning the Past: Understanding South Africa's Truth and Reconciliation Commission* (Wits UP 2002); N Rush Smith, *Contradictions of Democracy: Vigilantism and Rights in Post-Apartheid South Africa* (OUP 2019).

pertinently, Mahmood Mamdani wrote that the TRC focused on individual perpetrators and victims of physical violence over collective beneficiaries and victims of the more widespread economic and social harm.[25] In keeping with this critique, it is striking that South Africa remains a deeply unequal country where 55.5 per cent of the general population were reported to be poor in 2018, of which 93 per cent were Black, with the most poor being located in traditional areas in the former homelands.[26]

3. Conclusion: Looking Forward and Learning

It is undeniable that in both Colombia and South Africa a major step forward has been taken in as much as the states have signed agreements and committed to peace with important consequences for their Indigenous and traditional populations. Yet, as we have shown, this is not the only story to be told about these countries' transitions—especially with respect to the impact on Indigenous and traditional communities.

Both countries have yet to see full realisation of the promise offered by their post-conflict agreements. The gains made still need to be consolidated and the negotiated points require enforcement, including the need for necessary and just legislation to be put in place. Consequently, it is too soon to reach final conclusions. Nevertheless, it must be affirmed that in both cases the first and most important step has already been taken. What remains is for the implementation of the highest ideals of the post-conflict agreements to be realised in favour of the rights of Indigenous and traditional peoples in each country, especially regarding land and justice for past wrongs.

In terms of shared lessons, we observe that both Colombia and South Africa's historical and transitional experiences reinforce a familiar lesson: post-conflict agreements are the product of circumstance and also negotiation.[27] Thus, the historical narrative, circumstantial context, political actors, and priorities that lead to and surround the negotiation of post-conflict agreements deeply impact the content and quality of the agreements reached.

Indigenous and traditional peoples often have limited power and voice in these processes. In fact, they are often used as tropes or rhetorical devices in advancing the interests of various groups and stakeholders who are manoeuvring for position and advancement of personal and political objectives in the process of negotiating

[25] M Mamdani, 'Amnesty or Impunity? A Preliminary Critique of the Report of the Truth and Reconciliation Commission of South Africa (TRC)' (2002) 32 Diacritics 33.

[26] Statistics South Africa, 'General Household Survey, 2018' <http://www.statssa.gov.za/?page_id=1854> accessed 11 June 2020.

[27] H Klug, *Constituting Democracy: Law, Globalism, and South Africa's Political Reconstruction* (CUP 2000); H Klug, *The Constitution of South Africa: A Contextual Analysis* (Bloomsbury Publishing 2010); CE Umaña, *La justicia al encuentro de la paz en contextos de transición: reflexiones actuales para desafíos colombianos* (Universidad Externado de Colombia 2018).

agreements. This may include the exploitation by their own leaders who sometimes conflate their personal interests and those of their communities for personal gain. Paying attention to these forms of vulnerability and attempting to shore up the power and effective participation of ordinary Indigenous and traditional peoples is therefore all the more important.

A similarly critical factor to pay attention to is the increasingly well-documented neo-colonialist exploitation of Indigenous and traditional peoples by corporations hungry for land and its sub-surface assets—especially those in extractive industries. Indigenous peoples in Colombia and traditional peoples in South Africa are clearly similarly vulnerable to this practice. Enforcing principles of rigorous consultation to ensure free, prior, informed, and continuous consent of ordinary members of communities (rather than just their leaders or governments) becomes particularly important in this context.[28]

Yet another important consideration that both countries would benefit from taking into account is the threat and tyranny associated with physical violence. Fortunately, both Colombia and South Africa have recognised the need to attend to land redistribution (and, more broadly, socio-economic transformation) in their countries—at least, rhetorically. As both countries grapple with how to realise the promises made in their post-conflict agreements, it is fitting for them to keep in mind the enduring threat posed by physical violence and its way of understandably attracting an exorbitant amount of attention and energy.

Yet they should both also try to balance that awareness with an appreciation of the need not to place an excessive focus on violence at the expense of attending to interrelated socio-economic concerns. After all, it is important to address the full diversity of needs and priorities—especially those that are structural, systemic, social, and economic.[29] Of course, violence is often deeply related to a wide range of structural and socio-economic elements. Moreover, enabling Indigenous and traditional peoples to participate equitably and effectively in determining their own futures through the relevant negotiation processes is often very dependent on their material, social, and economic security—personally and structurally.[30]

As South Africans debate the possibility of constitutional amendments to strengthen the efficacy of the property clause, perhaps Colombia is an example to look to in order to see what possibilities, challenges, and limitations are presented by such efforts. As this reflection has argued, Colombia's peace agreement was a missed opportunity to strengthen elements of its Constitution affecting Indigenous peoples and their interests. South Africans would therefore do well to think more carefully about the implications, for example, of basing a future amendment of the

[28] W Wicomb and H Smith, 'Customary Communities as Peoples and Their Customary Tenure as Culture: What We Can Do with the Endorois Decision' (2011) 11 African Human Rights Law Journal 422.

[29] S MnisiWeeks, *Access to Justice and Human Security: Cultural Contradictions in Rural South Africa* (Routledge 2018).

[30] J Galtung, 'Violence, Peace, and Peace Research' (1969) 6 Journal of Peace Research 167.

property clause solely on expropriation with or without compensation and without considering wider structural and economic issues such as how better to secure the property rights of rural people from abuse and exploitation by their own traditional leaders operating in elite alliances.[31]

Likewise, as Colombia looks ahead to resolving questions of what greater clarity of regulation is necessary to give Indigenous communities more sure recognition, it could benefit from consideration of the South African experience. As representatives of Indigenous communities maintain their struggle for the complete recognition of their autonomy and the sovereignty of customary law irrespective of the Constitution and state law, Colombia should be wary of what this could lead to. South Africa's experience may serve to remind Colombians that checks and balances are always appropriate and necessary. This is especially so when it comes to recognising customary forms of law that have been severely impacted and compromised by the political economy of colonialism and other oppressive regimes. They also often entrench subjugation of persons on grounds of gender and sexual orientation, for instance, which are matters that should not be subordinated to the recognition of the rights of Indigenous and traditional peoples.

Ultimately, both countries need to think, together and apart, in more sophisticated ways about how to address the related problems of endemic poverty and impoverished democracy, especially for Indigenous and traditional peoples, who are typically the most marginalised in each country.

Ultimately, it is important to observe that in both Colombia and South Africa, the Indigenous and traditional peoples' movements have made a special contribution to the implementation and effectiveness of the transitional justice models flowing from their peace agreements. They have also demonstrated an ability to advance distributive justice through greater recognition of territorial, property, or land rights, and compensation for harm done.

As regards the Colombian case, some examples of this contribution can be found in the incorporation of an Ethnic Chapter in the 2016 Peace Agreement, the objective of which is to harmonise the solutions created to end the conflict with the rights of Indigenous peoples;[32] the creation of an Ethnic Commission for Peace and

[31] The heated debate over whether to amend section 25 of the Constitution, which provides for the right to property, has centred rather narrowly on whether land expropriation by the government can take place without any compensation being paid to the purchaser (or must always be concluded on the basis of the 'willing buyer, willing seller' principles). The particular needs, vulnerabilities, and interests of rural communities living under customary law has not featured in the debate. See, eg, T Roux, 'The Politics Behind South Africa's Property Clause Amendment' *The Conversation (Africa)* (17 February 2020) <https://theconversation.com/the-politics-behind-south-africas-property-clause-amendment-131575> accessed 7 May 2021. For more discussion see S MnisiWeeks, 'The Politics of Reforming Traditional Land in South Africa' *Africa is a Country* (18 December 2018) <https://africasacountry.com/2018/12/a-faustian-bargain-the-politics-of-reforming-traditional-land-in-south-africa> accessed 7 May 2021.

[32] <https://www.peaceagreements.org/viewmasterdocument/1845> accessed 14 July 2022. Final Agreement, 6.2 'Ethnic Chapter', 6.2.3 Safeguards and Guarantees (a) in Relation to Comprehensive Rural Reform:

> Ethnic peoples will be included as beneficiaries of the different measures agreed for access to land without impairment of the rights already acquired. The allocation of plots of land and

Defense of Territorial Rights within the Special Jurisdiction for Peace (comprising authorities of Indigenous and Afro-descendant peoples) with the objective of safeguarding territorial and collective rights of ethnic populations in negotiating and implementing the peace agreement;[33] the joint operation as between the Indigenous Jurisdiction and the Special Jurisdiction for Peace in those cases in which members of the Indigenous peoples are involved as victims or perpetrators; and a novel and very important aspect, accrediting some territories as 'victims'. In this regard, within the framework of the Special Jurisdiction for Peace, it has been recognised that the territory is a 'living entity', which has sustained identity and harmony and that suffers harm when it is violated or desecrated by internal armed conflict.[34]

In South Africa, some of the most innovative cases that have substantially moved the law forward on the conceptualisation of relationally grounded land rights,[35] gender,[36] and what is law more generally, as well as who makes it,[37] have turned on the struggles of traditional peoples[38] to advance democracy by compelling an oft-reluctant government to thoughtfully and robustly integrate ordinary people's vernacular conceptions and normative convictions and values with the Constitution's restorative, redistributive, and transitional justice aspirations.[39] In this way, traditional peoples have pressed the case that Indigenous and traditional peoples' struggles for full citizenship under South Africa's neo-apartheid arrangements[40] today are in fact the struggles of *all* of South Africa to leave behind apartheid and become a fully-fledged constitutional democracy.

land titling procedures will be performed with a view to the constitution, creation, expansion, entitlement, demarcation, restitution and resolution of disputes over land use and tenure.

[33] For more information <http://convergenciacnoa.org/wp-content/uploads/2017/07/ComisionEtnicaPaz.pdf> accessed 14 July 2022.

[34] B Izquierdo and L Viaene, 'Descolonizar la justicia transicional desde los territorios indígenas' *Afrontar el pasado, construir juntos el futuro* No 34 – June 2018 <https://www.icip.cat/perlapau/es/articulo/descolonizar-la-justicia-transicional-desde-los-territorios-indigenas/> accessed 14 July 2022.

[35] *Maledu v Itereleng Bakgatla Mineral Resources (Pty) Limited* [2018] ZACC 41; 2019 (2) SA 1 (CC); *Council for the Advancement of the South African Constitution v The Ingonyama Trust* [2021] ZAKZPHC 42; 2022 (1) SA 251 (KZP).

[36] *Bhe v Khayelitsha Magistrate* [2004] ZACC 17; 2005 (1) SA 580 (CC); *Gumede (born Shange) v President of the Republic of South Africa* [2008] ZACC 23; 2009 (3) SA 152 (CC).

[37] *Alexkor Ltd and Another v Richtersveld Community* [2003] ZACC 18; 2004 (5) SA 460 (CC); *Shilubana v Nwamitwa* 2008] ZACC 9; 2009 (2) SA 66 (CC); *Mayelane v Ngwenyama* [2013] ZACC 14; 2013 (4) SA 415 (CC); *Ramuhovhi v President of the Republic of South Africa* ZACC 41; 2018 (2) SA 1 (CC).

[38] K O'Regan, 'Tradition and Modernity: Adjudicating a Constitutional Paradox Customary Law' (2013) 6 Constitutional Court Review 105; S Sibanda and TB Mosaka, 'Bhe v Magistrate, Khayelitsha: A Cultural Conundrum, Fanonian Alienation and An Elusive Constitutional Oneness Part III: Reflections on Themes in Justice Langa's Judgments' (2015) 2015 Acta Juridica 256; G Budlender, 'Afterword Searching for the Constitutional Living Customary Law' (2021) 47 Journal of Southern African Studies 327.

[39] DM Davis and K Klare, 'Transformative Constitutionalism and the Common and Customary Law' (2010) 26 South African Journal on Human Rights 403; S MnisiWeeks and A Claassens, 'Tensions between Vernacular Values that Prioritise Basic Needs and State Versions of Customary Law that Contradict Them—We Love These Fields that Feed Us, But Not at the Expense of a Person Law and Poverty Special Edition' (2011) 22 Stellenbosch Law Review 823.

[40] T Madlingozi, 'Social Justice in a Time of Neo-Apartheid Constitutionalism: Critiquing the Anti-Black Economy of Recognition, Incorporation and Distribution' (2017) 28 Stellenbosch Law Review 123.

THEME 7

PROCEDURAL JUSTICE, THE LAW, AND TRANSITIONAL JUSTICE

20

Exploring the Relationship Between Violent Protest and Procedural Injustice in South Africa's Democratic Transition

Raisa Cachalia

1. Introduction

South Africa is undergoing a major social, economic, political, and legal transition, which began in 1994 with the abolition of apartheid and especially since the coming into effect of the democratic Constitution in 1996.[1] No transition is, however, linear or seamless. As South Africa perseveres with its journey to a more just political order,[2] one of the significant challenges to the consolidation of peace and democracy is the scale and frequency of violent protests on a national level.[3] Examples range from the burning and destruction of property at universities across the country arising from demands for state-sponsored higher education; protracted violent demonstrations over the inadequate provision of basic services; and heated protests over what is perceived to be a culture of poor governance, corruption, and an overall deterioration in the quality of decision-making at various levels government.[4] Although the causes of these protests, and many others, are complex and varied, studies have found that an increasing number of citizens feel that resorting to violence is the only means to ensure that the government will listen to them.[5] Popular laments such as '*You only listen when I'm*

[1] Constitution of the Republic of South Africa, 1996 (hereafter 'Constitution').

[2] RG Teitel, in *Transitional Justice* (OUP 2000) 5 locates the notion of 'transitional justice' within 'a shift in political orders'.

[3] Violent protests are generally defined as those which evidence damage to property and/or injury to persons. See, eg, P Alexander and others, 'Frequency and Turmoil: South Africa's Community Protests 2005–2017' (2018) 63 SA Crime Quarterly 27–42; South African Research Chair in Social Change Media Briefing 'Community protests 2004–2013: Some research findings' (2013).

[4] See, eg, E Fakir, 'Circling the Square of Protests: Democracy, Delivery and Discontent in Bekkersdal' Ruth First Lecture (2014); 'Service delivery protests increasing and most are violent' *TimesLive* (14 May 2018) <https://www.timeslive.co.za/news/south-africa/2018-05-14-service-delivery-protests-increasing-and-most-are-violent/≥; 'Service delivery protests in SA hit record high' *EWN* <https://ewn.co.za/2018/07/11/service-delivery-protests-in-sa-hit-record-high>, both accessed 3 October 2022.

[5] See L Lancaster and G Mulaudzi, 'Is Protest the only way to achieve change' (19 May 2017) *Institute for Security Studies*<https://issafrica.org/iss-today/is-protest-the-only-way-to-achieve-change>; J Burger, 'The reasons behind service delivery protests in South Africa' *Institute for Security Studies*

Raisa Cachalia, *Exploring the Relationship Between Violent Protest and Procedural Injustice in South Africa's Democratic Transition* In: *Transitional Justice, Distributive Justice, and Transformative Constitutionalism.* Edited by: David Bilchitz and Raisa Cachalia, with Magdalena Inés Correa Henao and Nathalia Bautista Pizarro, Oxford University Press.
DOI: 10.1093/oso/9780192887627.003.0020

violent'[6] or '*Burn to be heard*'[7] have thus become the political language surrounding societal discontent and raise deeper questions about the quality of South Africa's post-apartheid democracy.[8]

Against this backdrop and in the context of the twin themes of this book, I argue that these articulations of citizen dissatisfaction speak to questions of both distributive *and* transitional justice. In the former respect, resorting to violent protest action can be seen as a citizen demand for more equitable allocation of vital state goods and services (substantive justice) whereas in the latter respect, these actions are perhaps an expression of a desire for better quality democratic engagement between citizens and the state (procedural justice).

In this chapter, I focus on the procedural aspect and consider specifically the relationship between the high levels of violent protest action in South Africa and societal perceptions of procedural unfairness.[9] In so doing, I consider the positive role that procedural principles such as participatory governance, impartiality, and justified decision-making—as instantiated in particular institutional mechanisms—can play in dissuading people from resorting to violence as the modality for compelling government responsiveness. The essence of the argument is that public decision-making which takes sufficient cognisance of these principles both helps to create stability and a sense of legitimacy in political institutions, which can encourage more peaceful and constructive resolution of societal conflict. There are two reasons for this. The first is the 'outcomes' reason: officials who exercise their powers fairly, impartially, and in a manner that can be justified are more likely to make good quality decisions (those that are rational, informed, and taken in the public interest).[10] This promotes a culture of respect for government decisions—even those that are unfavourable—which can in turn assuage societal

<https://www.issafrica.org/iss-today/the-reasons-behind-service-delivery-protests-in-south-africa>; D Bilchitz and R Cachalia, 'Violent protests are a symptom of people being ignored' *Mail & Guardian Newspaper* (29 July 2009) <http://mg.co.za/article/2016-05-19-00-violent-protests-are-a-symptom-of-people-being-ignored-by-politicians>; Protest nation: government needs to listen better' (19 May 2016) *Daily Vox* https://www.thedailyvox.co.za/protest-nation-government-needs-listen-better/ all accessed 3 October 2022.

[6] L Lancaster and G Mulaudzi, 'You only listen when I'm violent' *Institute for Security Studies* (14 June 2016) <https://issafrica.org/iss-today/you-only-listen-when-im-violent> accessed 3 October 2022.

[7] J Duncan, 'Why student protests in South Africa have turned violent' (29 September 2016) *The Conversation* <https://theconversation.com/why-student-protests-in-south-africa-have-turned-violent-66288> accessed 3 October 2022.

[8] See M Paret, 'Violence and Democracy in South Africa's Community Protests' (2015) 42(143) Review of African Political Economy 107–23, concluding that 'disruptive protests become a more effective way for communities to express their grievances'(at 115) and that 'direct violence—destroying property, burning tyres, barricading roads—represents an alternative form of democratic participation that is significantly more effective than following the formal channels created by the democratic state' (at 120).

[9] However, given the intersecting reasons underpinning violent protest action, some attention must invariably be given to the issues surrounding citizen demands for greater substantive or distributive justice.

[10] It is important to note that better outcomes are also more likely to advance the goals of distributive justice.

tensions and inclinations towards violence.[11] The second is the 'process' reason: a more involved, better informed and respected citizenry is more likely to accept public decisions and, as a result, will be less likely to resort to violent self-help in order to be heard.

Section 2 will begin by exploring the 'procedural dimension' of South Africa's transition to constitutional democracy, which I locate in the broader substantive vision of making a 'decisive break'[12] from the unjust and authoritarian style of government under apartheid to a form of democratic government that values caring, inclusive, and mutually respectful societal relations. I argue that underlying this objective are the following procedural principles: (1) 'participatory governance', the creation of meaningful opportunities for citizen involvement in public discourses; (2) 'impartial governance', a commitment to a style of government that is non-partisan and which does not display 'naked preferences';[13] and (3) 'justified governance', the requirement that government must regularly explain and ultimately defend its actions to citizens. Each of these facets, I endeavour to show, emerges from the goals of South Africa's transition expressed in the constitutional text and given interpretive content by the courts.

Then, in Section 3, I explore the positive role that these procedural principles—with their origins in the goals of the country's transition—can play in mitigating resort to violent protest action as the preferred mode of expression on the part of citizens. I begin by examining the scale and frequency of, and underlying reasons for, the upward trend in violent protest action in South Africa. The objective here is not to present the relationship between violence and procedural injustice as an empirical truth but to make out a reasonable case for the link, which has some empirical basis. I then shift the discussion to developing a legal response to the situation. I begin by exploring the substantive reasons for valuing procedural justice from a conflict-mitigation perspective with reference to the 'outcomes' and 'process' justifications. I go on to argue that the principles of participation, impartiality, and justification are rooted in these two justifications and should be more energetically relied on to alleviate existing tensions in South Africa. In this regard it is crucial to divert citizens away from seeing violence as the only means of gaining political traction by, for example, maintaining effective institutional mechanisms for constructive democratic engagement based on the procedural principles identified in this chapter.

[11] See, eg, J Snipes, E Maguire, and D Tyler, 'The Effects of Procedural Justice on Civil Disobedience: Evidence from Protestors in Three Cities' (2019) 42(1) Crime and Justice 32–44; TR Tyler, 'Procedural Justice, Legitimacy, and the Effective Rule of Law' (2003) 30 Crime and Justice 283–357; S Liebenberg, 'Participatory Justice in Social Rights Adjudication' (2018) 18 Human Rights Law Review 1–27, 9.

[12] *S v Makwanyane* 1995 (2) SACR 1 (CC) ('*Makwanyane*') [262].

[13] C Sunstein, 'Naked Preferences and the Constitution' (1984) 84 Columbia Law Review 1689 relied on in *Prinsloo v Van der Linde* [1997] ZACC 5; 1997 (3) SA 1012 (CC) ('*Prinsloo*') [25].

2. The Procedural Dimension of South Africa's Transition to Constitutional Democracy

At the dawn of democracy in 1994, the socio-political and legal milieu changed dramatically: apartheid was formally abolished and, with the coming into effect of the Final Constitution in 1996, a new country was forged founded on the values of human dignity, equality, and freedom; non-racialism and non-sexism; supremacy of the Constitution and the rule of law; and a system of democratic government based on accountability, responsiveness, and openness.[14] Capturing the spirit of South Africa's transition, Mohammed J in *Makwanyane* explained that:

> The South African Constitution is different: It retains from the past only what is defensible and represents a decisive break from, and a ringing rejection of, that part of the past which is disgracefully racist, authoritarian, insular, and repressive and a vigorous identification of and commitment to a democratic, universalistic, caring and aspirationally egalitarian ethos, expressly articulated in the Constitution.[15]

Langa DP echoed these sentiments in *Hyundai* where he emphasised the inclusive and dignity-enhancing nature of South Africa's journey to constitutionalism:

> The Constitution is located in a history which involves a transition from a society based on division, injustice and exclusion from the democratic process to one which respects the dignity of all citizens, and includes all in the process of governance.[16]

More recently, in the *UDM* judgment, Mogoeng CJ remarked that 'the vision or spirit of transitioning from division, exclusion and neglect to a transformed, united and inclusive nation, led by accountable and responsive public office-bearers'[17] must inform an understanding of the constitutional project. Flowing from these iterations of the substantive goals of South Africa's democratic transition, I have identified at least three principles that speak to procedural democracy, each of which will be analysed in Sections 2A–2C of this chapter. The fact that South Africa's constitutional arrangements encompass both a substantive as well as a procedural dimension was affirmed in *Premier, Mpumalanga* where O'Regan J explained that 'a characteristic of our transition has been the common understanding

[14] Constitution, s 1.

[15] *Makwanyane* (n 12) [262].

[16] *Investigating Directorate: Serious Economic Offences v Hyundai Motor Distributors (Pty) Ltd In re: Hyundai Motor Distributors (Pty) Ltd v Smit NO* [2000] ZACC 12; 2001 (1) SA 545 (CC) [21].

[17] *United Democratic Movement v Speaker of the National Assembly* [2017] ZACC 21; 2017 (5) SA 300 (CC) ('*UDM*') [31].

that [both dimensions] need to be honoured'[18] and that the Constitution '*dictates not only the end*, which is the establishment of a non-racial, non-sexist democracy, but also *regulates the means, including the obligation to observe procedural fairness*'.[19]

A. Participatory Governance

This principle speaks to the desire to move from a culture of exclusion and indignity to one of dignified inclusion and is thus central to the objective of restoring the humanity of those who suffered systematic exclusion and degradation at the hands of the apartheid state. In *Doctors for Life*, Ngcobo J connected 'the historical importance'[20] of South Africa's participatory democracy to the country's 'shameful past', explaining that apartheid operated to exclude the black majority 'from meaningful participation in virtually every sphere of life; indeed from recognition as human beings with inherent dignity'.[21] Later, he went on to conclude that the 'emphasis on democratic participation' in the Constitution was in fact 'born in the struggle against injustices' of the past.[22] In *Welkom*, Froneman and Skweyiya JJ similarly affirmed that 'participation and engagement are central to the constitutional project, a reflection of South Africa's "negotiated revolution" '.[23]

Another way in which history has contributed to the participatory character of the democratic system is with reference to African notions of 'ubuntu' and the belief that 'one only becomes complete when others are appreciated, accommodated and respected'.[24] Part of the transition was thus a desire to restore the dignity of African notions of governance by recognising the importance of participation to the way traditional societies practiced democracy:

> The idea of allowing the public to participate in the conduct of public affairs is not a new concept. In this country, the traditional means of public participation is imbizo/lekgotla/bosberaad. This is a participatory consultation process that was, and still is, followed within the African communities ... This traditional method

[18] *Premier, Province of Mpumalanga v Executive Committee of the Association of Governing Bodies of State Aided Schools: Eastern Transvaal* [1998] ZACC 20; 1999 (2) SA 91 (CC) ('*Premier, Mpumalanga*') [1].

[19] ibid [7] (emphasis added).

[20] *Doctors for Life International v Speaker of the National Assembly* [2006] ZACC 11; 2006 (6) SA 416 (CC) ('*Doctors for Life*') [5].

[21] ibid.

[22] ibid [112].

[23] *Head of Department, Department of Education, Free State Province v Welkom High School; Head of Department, Department of Education, Free State Province v Harmony High School* [2013] ZACC 25; 2014 (2) SA 228 (CC) ('*Welkom*') [139].

[24] *City of Tshwane Metropolitan Municipality v Afriforum* [2016] ZACC 19; 2016 (6) SA 279 (CC) ('*Afriforum*') [11]. See further *Bhe v Khayelitsha Magistrate* [2004] ZACC 17; 2005 (1) SA 580 (CC) [45].

> of public participation ... is both a practical and symbolic part of our democratic processes. It is a form of participatory democracy.[25]

Against this historical backdrop, the participatory nature of South Africa's democracy is now evident from many of the express provisions of the Constitution such as the constitutional duty to facilitate citizen involvement in the law-making processes of various legislative bodies;[26] the duty of local government 'to encourage the involvement of communities and community organisations';[27] the right to procedural fairness in respect of administrative action;[28] the right to have disputes adjudicated in a fair public hearing before a court or other independent tribunal or forum;[29] and in the constitutional requirement that the public administration be responsive and provide opportunities for citizen participation in the policy-making initiatives of the administration.[30]

However, even beyond these express provisions, the Constitution has been interpreted to recognise a 'deep principle of participatory democracy in the South African Constitution'[31] that has, in fact, become 'a distinctive part of our national ethos'.[32] This has its roots in the historic *Doctors for Life* decision where the Court referred to this principle as a 'basic and fundamental' feature of South Africa's conception of democracy,[33] explaining that '[t]he democratic government that is contemplated is partly representative and partly participatory'.[34] The Court in this case and subsequent cases fashioned this 'deep principle' from the founding values of 'accountability, responsiveness and openness' as did Mureinik, one of South Africa's most influential scholars, when he explained that 'participation' together with the principle of 'justification' are essential to the advancement of the democratic goal of 'responsive government'.[35] The Court has also connected the principle of participation to the value of human dignity and the rule of law. Regarding

25 *Doctors for Life* (n 20) [101]. See further J Fowkes, *Building the Constitution: The Practice of Constitutional Interpretation in Post-Apartheid South Africa* (CUP 2016) 191–92.

26 Constitution, ss 59(1), 72(1), and 118(1)(a).

27 ibid s 152(1)(e). There are also extensive requirements pertaining to community participation in various statutes. See, eg, the Local Government: Municipal Systems Act 32 of 2000 (MSA), ss 4, 5, 16, and 17.

28 Constitution, s 33. See J Klaaren and G Penfold, 'Just Administrative Action' in S Woolman and M Bishop (eds), *Constitutional Law of South Africa* (2nd edn, Juta 2012) 63-1, 63-5.

29 Constitution, s 34.

30 ibid s 195(1)(e).

31 D Bilchitz and S Heleba, 'Public Participation and Reasonableness: Exploring the Case Law and Jurisprudential Philosophy of the South African Constitutional Court' in C Hugo and TMJ Möllers (eds), *Transnational Impacts on Law: Perspectives from South Africa and Germany* (Juta 2017) 381–416, 382.

32 See *Minister of Health v New Clicks South Africa (Pty) Ltd* [2005] ZACC 14; 2006 (2) SA 311 (CC) ('*New Clicks*') [625] (Sachs J); *Doctors for Life* (n 20) [227].

33 *Doctors for Life* (n 20) [115].

34 ibid. See Fowkes (n 25). Confirmed in later cases such as *Matatiele Municipality v President of the Republic of South Africa (2)* [2006] ZACC 12; 2007 (1) BCLR 47 (CC) [57] ('*Matatiele*'); *Masetlha v President of the Republic of South Africa* [2007] ZACC 20; 2008 (1) SA 566 (CC) ('*Masethla*') [181].

35 E Mureinik, 'Reconsidering Review: Participation and Accountability' (1993) Acta Juridica 35.

the former, in *New Clicks* Sachs J said that '[t]he right to speak and be listened to is part of the right to be a citizen in the full sense of the word. In a constitutional democracy dialogue and the right to have a voice on public affairs is constitutive of dignity.'[36] And in *Doctors for Life*, Ngcobo J explained how ongoing public participation 'enhances the *civic dignity* of those who participate by enabling their voices to be heard and taken account of'.[37] Regarding the relationship between participation and the rule of law, in *Albutt*,[38] the Court recognised the duty to extend procedural fairness to affected persons as an incident of rationality, which forms part of the rule of law[39] and in *Afriforum*, the Court confirmed that public participation in the renaming of streets is a requirement of the rule of law.[40]

The courts have also read the Constitution contextually, and as a whole, to require the government to foster public participation through the administrative principle of procedural fairness. For example, in *Joseph*[41] the Court found that the requirements of procedural fairness had to be observed when a municipality took a decision to disconnect electricity to tenants residing in an inner-city building. Interestingly, given the absence of a contractual nexus between the tenants and public service provider in question, the Court forged this procedural duty out of the 'the broader constitutional relationship'[42] between a public service provider and the members of the local community, taking into account a plethora of constitutional and legislative provisions.[43]

B. Impartial Governance

One of the central objectives of the transition has been to demonstrate a 'ringing rejection'[44] of the arbitrary, unequal, and nakedly preferential manner in which public power was exercised by the apartheid state. The rejection of a system of

[36] *New Clicks* (n 32) [627].
[37] *Doctors for Life* (n 20) [115] (emphasis added).
[38] *Albutt v Centre for the Study of Violence and Reconciliation* [2010] ZACC 44; 2010 (3) SA 293 (CC) ('*Albutt*').
[39] This was in order to give effect to the principle of victim involvement in a decision to pardon offenders for political crimes.
[40] *Afriforum* (n 24) [108].
[41] *Joseph v City of Johannesburg* [2009] ZACC 30; 2010 (4) SA 55 (CC).
[42] ibid [33].
[43] The Court relied on constitutional principles, such as those pertaining to 'democratic and accountable government' (s 152(1)) and the developmental duties of local government (s 153). It also relied on provisions in legislation, particularly s 9(1)(a)(iii) of the Housing Act 107 of 1998 (every municipality must ensure that 'services in respect of water, sanitation, electricity ... are provided in a manner which is economically efficient') and the MSA (n 27), in respect of the duty to give local communities equitable access to municipal services. See, in this regard, D Bilchitz, 'Citizenship and Community: Exploring the Right to Receive Basic Municipal Services in *Joseph*' (2010) 3(1) Constitutional Court Review 45.
[44] *Makwanyane* (n 12) [262].

'naked preference'[45] in favour of equality and equal protection thus gives expression to the principle of 'impartial governance'.

In varying forms, the Constitution has thus entrenched the principle of impartiality governing the exercise of public power. For example, the courts and Chapter 9 institutions have a general duty to exercise their powers 'fairly'[46] and 'without fear, favour or prejudice'.[47] Moreover, the public administration is duty-bound to adhere to democratic values and to provide services 'impartially, fairly, equitably and without bias'.[48] The Public Service Commission is specially singled out and constitutionally instructed to be 'independent', 'impartial', and to exercise its powers and perform its functions without fear, favour, or prejudice for the maintenance of effective and efficient public administration and to ensure a high standard of professional ethics in the public service.[49]

However, beyond these provisions a deeper constitutional principle of impartiality can be said to exist. This is located in two constitutive values: the rule of law[50] and the principle of equality. In respect of the former, the Court in *Prinsloo* connected the notion of 'naked preference'—which is in essence a manifestation of partiality—with the rule of law when it explained that the state may not 'regulate in an arbitrary manner or manifest naked preferences that serve no legitimate governmental purpose, *for that would be inconsistent with the rule of law and the fundamental premises of the constitutional state*'.[51] In respect of the principle of equality, the Preamble of the Constitution commits us to a system where 'every citizen is equally protected by the law' and s 9(1) entrenches a right to equal protection and benefit of the law. In giving content to this notion, the Court in *Prinsloo* explained that what the equal protection provision 'makes clear' is 'that no-one is above or beneath the law and that all persons are subject to law *impartially applied and administered*'.[52] What is also of significance is that these equality provisions clearly lie in the struggle against the discriminatory and segregationist policies of the apartheid state. In *Makwanyane* the Court explained that '[i]n reaction to our past ... the constitutional right to equality before the law [is] deeply foundational to the creation of the "new order" referred to in the preamble'.[53] And in *Brink*, the Court again highlighted the 'particular relevance' of South Africa's history to the role and place of equality in South Africa's constitutional order: 'The policy of apartheid ... systematically discriminated against black people in all aspects of

[45] Sunstein (n 13).
[46] Constitution, s 34.
[47] ibid s 165(2) and s 181(2).
[48] ibid s 195(1)(*d*).
[49] ibid s 196.
[50] See J Waldron, 'The Rule of Law and the Importance of Procedure' (6 October 2010) New York University School of Law, Public Law Research Paper No 10-73 <https://ssrn.com/abstract=1688491> or <http://dx.doi.org/10.2139/ssrn.1688491> accessed 14 September 2023.
[51] *Prinsloo* (n 13) [25] (emphasis added).
[52] ibid [22] (emphasis added).
[53] *Brink v Kitshoff NO* [1996] ZACC 9; 1996 (4) SA 197 (CC) [156].

social life ... The deep scars of this appalling programme are still visible in society. *It is in the light of that history and the enduring legacy that it bequeathed that the equality clause needs to be interpreted*.'[54]

C. Justified Governance

This principle has emerged from the transitional goal of breaking away from the heavy-handed, coercive, and authoritarian style of governance to one in which all government action is expected to be explained and ultimately defended to the citizenry. It can be traced back to Mureinik's celebrated account of the shift to constitutionalism as epitomising a 'bridge' from a 'culture of authority'[55] to one of justification where every exercise of public power would, going forward, need to explained and, ultimately, defended. He explained this notion as follows:

> [T]he leadership given by government rests on the cogency of the case offered in defence of its decision, not the fear inspired by the force at its command. The new order must be a community build on persuasion, not coercion.[56]

The courts have also located the principle of justification in the goals of South Africa's constitutional transition. In *Makwanyane*, for instance, Ackermann J referred to the 'new constitutional state' as being one of 'reason and justification when rights are sought to be curtailed'[57] explaining that '[w]e have moved from a past characterised by much which was arbitrary and unequal in the operation of the law to ... a constitutional state where state action must be such that it is capable of being analysed and *justified rationally*'.[58] In *Prinsloo*, the Court reiterated the fact that all government action must now 'relate to a *defensible vision* of the public good'.[59] This notion of 'justification' arises from a particular conception of democratic citizenship, which is grounded in the notion of reciprocity or a 'duty of civility' that members of a polity owe to one another. It resembles, in some respects, the liberal idea of 'public reason'[60] and the belief that legitimate public decisions are essentially those that can be rationalised and explained to those that are affected by them with reference to a set of publicly accepted values.

[54] ibid [40] (emphasis added).
[55] See E Mureinik, 'A Bridge to Where? Introducing the Interim Bill of Rights' (1994) 10 South African Journal on Human Rights 31, 32.
[56] ibid. Cited with approval in *Makwanyane* (n 12) [156].
[57] *Makwanyane* (n 12) [156].
[58] ibid (emphasis added).
[59] *Prinsloo* (n 13) [25] (emphasis added).
[60] This conception of social deliberation originates from the early work of the social contract theorists, such as Immanuel Kant (see, eg, his essay 'An answer to the question: "What is enlightenment?"' (1784) as developed in the work of, among others, John Rawls in *Political Liberalism* (1993) and later in J Rawls, 'The Idea of Public Reason Revisited' (1997) 64(3) University of Chicago Law Review 765.

The responsibility to justify and explain exercises of public power is given its clearest expression in the duty to give reasons in respect of administrative actions.[61] However this principle can also be said to arise from the value of human dignity and particularly the belief that citizens—as the bearers of intrinsic worth—must be shown respect through an explanation for policies adopted or decisions taken by the state.[62] It also emerges from the founding value of accountability, which has been interpreted to embody the spirit of justification.[63] In *UDM*, for example, Mogoeng CJ explained that:

> Since State power and resources are for our common good, checks and balances to ensure accountability enjoy pre-eminence in our governance system ... For this reason, *public office-bearers ... must regularly explain how they have lived up to the promises that inhere in the offices they occupy.*[64]

In drawing these themes together, one of the essential goals of the South African transition is to transform governance through a commitment to principles of inclusivity, mutual respect, and, ultimately, fairness—values that were conspicuously absent under the apartheid legal system. I have endeavoured to show that this commitment to a more humane and democratic style of governance has a clear procedural dimension or, put differently, that the principles of participation, justification, and impartiality are actually procedural manifestations of this broader vision. What is also apparent is that these principles have in some respects been given institutional manifestation. For example, the justification principle is most clearly instantiated in the administrative law duty to give reasons for how public power is exercised and the participatory governance principle has been given life in the constitutional duty to involve citizens in the legislative process and in the duty to extend procedural fairness for administrative action.

However, what the wave of violent protest action reveals is that these procedural goals of South Africa's transition have not been properly implemented. On the one hand, this is because the Executive has failed to take these principles seriously in executing its governance function, which has resulted in citizens losing faith in its willingness and institutional ability to respond to their needs. On the other hand, there has perhaps also been a failure on the part of citizens to take adequate advantage of the opportunities for democratic engagement that have been provided to them, which has further weakened the state's ability to govern responsively.

[61] Constitution, s 33(2) as given effect to the Promotion of Administrative Justice Act 3 of 2000 (PAJA), s 5(1).

[62] D Meyerson, 'The Moral Justification for the Right to Make Full Answer and Defence' 2015 Oxford Journal of Legal Studies 237, 249–50.

[63] Mureinik, 'Reconsidering Review' (n 35) 36.

[64] *UDM* (n 17) [7]–[8] (emphasis added).

3. Mitigating Violent Conflict through Procedural Justice

A. What Is Driving the High Levels of Violent Protest?

In South Africa at present a grim picture emerges of the government-citizen relationship.[65] As mentioned in the introduction, there is no shortage of examples of citizen demonstrations turning violent, often leaving damage, destruction and injury in their wake. In 2016, for instance, South Africans watched over twenty schools burn to the ground in the Vuwani area when a demarcation dispute turned violent.[66] In the same year, we saw the emergence of the student movements and have since witnessed libraries, vehicles, and artworks being torched by angry students. These protests have largely taken place under such banners as #FeesMustFall and #RhodesMustFall where students have asserted demands for free, decolonised tertiary education.[67]

While the statistical results of assorted bodies monitoring these developments have varied, it is reasonable to conclude that a high percentage of South African protest action has included elements of violence.[68] This is consistent with the findings of a study conducted by the Centre for Social Change (CSC) at the University of Johannesburg,[69] which attempts to present a consolidated picture of 'community protest'[70] action during the period 2005–2017. Broadly, the study concludes that during the relevant period, there was an upward trend in the frequency of protest action in the country with a tendency towards the action being 'disorderly', that is, disruptive and/or violent. Statistically, the CSC estimates the number of disorderly protests to be at around 43 per cent. The statistical outcomes of other monitoring bodies suggest that, in respect of municipal-related demands specifically, the levels of violent protest action are higher. For example, the Civic Protests Barometer

65 The focus of this chapter is on what has often been referred to as service delivery protests. Events such as the July 2021 riots in parts of South Africa fall beyond its scope, given indications that the trigger for this unrest was the imprisonment of South Africa's former President, Jacob Zuma. See in this regard, J Visagie, I Turok, and S Swartz, 'What lies behind social unrest in South Africa, and what might be done about it?' <https://theconversation.com/what-lies-behind-social-unrest-in-south-africa-and-what-might-be-done-about-it-166130> accessed 3 October 2022.

66 See Human Sciences Research Council Report '"We didn't ask for a municipality"—Unintended consequences of municipal boundary re-determination: Vuwani at a glance' (28 September 2017) <http://www.hsrc.ac.za/en/research-outputs/view/9137> accessed 3 October 2022.

67 J February, 'South Africa's politics of rage' (*Institute for Security* Studies, 19 September 2016) <https://issafrica.org/iss-today/south-africas-politics-of-rage> accessed 3 October 2022.

68 ibid 31. Quantifying the levels of violent protest in the country is fairly complicated due to the fact that different monitoring bodies have approached the problem in distinct ways: eg unlike the relatively blunt dichotomy adopted by the Civic Protests Barometer (conceptualising protests as either 'violent' or 'peaceful'), the CSC adopts a three-way categorisation of protests ('orderly', 'disruptive', and 'violent') and explains that while all violent protests are disorderly, not all disorderly protests are necessary violent, some are merely disruptive.

69 See Alexander (n 3).

70 ibid 28 where the CSC defines a 'community protest' as one in which 'collective demands are raised by a geographically defined and identified "community" that frames its demands in support and/or defence of that community'.

estimated that between 2013 and 2016, in the range of 90 per cent of civic protests were regarded as violent and that in the first seven months of 2016, the figure reached a remarkably high 95 per cent. Moreover, the Municipal IQ Monitor (focusing specifically on service delivery protests) estimated that between 2004 and 2016, about 75 per cent of these protests were violent, with a low of 67 per cent in 2011 and a high of 86 per cent in 2016. This number seems to have risen in 2018 with this body estimating that in the first half of 2018 in the range of 94 per cent of recorded protests turned violent.[71] Notably, the CSC's estimates for disorderly 'community protests' are lower, suggesting that around 69 per cent (2011) and 82 per cent (2016) of these protests were disorderly, but not necessarily violent.[72] Also noteworthy is the finding by the Institute for Security Studies' Public Violence and Protest Monitor that in respect of the 585 recorded cases of public protest (January 2013–April 2021)—over water and sanitation delivery failures specifically—378 (65 per cent) of these incidents turned violent.[73]

A survey of recent studies suggests that one of the key drivers of the violence is the poor quality of governance and widespread unhappiness with the manner in which ordinary people are treated by the government. For example, February refers to a commonly held belief among South Africans that 'destruction is the only way to make oneself heard'.[74] Similarly, Lancaster and Mulaudzi explain that '[f]or many communities, a grievance related to service delivery would not have emerged in the first place had they been consulted in a meaningful way by those tasked with providing the services'.[75] They remark further, that, '[w]hen a community feels a government department has failed to respond or meaningfully engage with their demands, this leads to an increased sense of disempowerment, frustration and ultimately anger. This can exacerbate existing trauma, stress and discontent.'[76]

Take the Bekkersdal area for example, which has experienced ongoing protest action since 2005. The initial protests were sparked by a demarcation dispute which developed into a broader expression of dissatisfaction over poor service provision, contemptuous leadership, corruption, and what has been described as an increasingly 'securocratic' approach by the state.[77] In examining the possible causes, Fakir suggests that the protests can in part be seen as a response to 'the limited opportunities for influencing decision making', thus revealing 'deficiencies in participatory decision-making'.[78] He also points to governance deficiencies such as the 'vicious

[71] Municipal IQ, '2018 service delivery protests spiral' (14 May 2018).

[72] See Alexander (n 3).

[73] C Gould, 'Lessons in preventing violent protest in South Africa—Good communication and respectful responses to local service delivery problems can prevent anger and violence' (*Institute for Security* Studies, 4 May 2021) <https://issafrica.org/iss-today/lessons-in-preventing-violent-protest-in-south-africa> accessed 3 October 2022.

[74] February (n 67).

[75] Lancaster and Malaudzi, 'You only listen when I'm violent' (n 6).

[76] ibid.

[77] Fakir (n 4) 5.

[78] ibid 16.

cycle of stonewalling, arrogance, obfuscation and manipulation' that has defined the Bekkersdal community's interactions with the state, a reality that he suggests can only be 'resolved through a less arrogant leadership more willing to engage the community seriously'.[79] In the end he concludes that '[i]f anything, the protests, are a demand for a better quality democracy with more robust representation and responsiveness, as well as, ethical government'.[80] Similarly, Friedman regards these sentiments as a citizen demand for 'public service, not [service] delivery'.[81] The despondency with the quality of governance is further evidenced in the outcomes of a 2016 SAIFAC survey which found that of the random representative sample of 608 adults in Gauteng, only 40 per cent felt that Parliament represents them, with less than half agreeing that their politicians were responsive to their needs. Alarmingly, more than 60 per cent of the sample perceived participation in, and access to, democratic institutions as a problem, with only 20 per cent or less agreeing that any form of participation was easy.[82]

From the picture presented here, we can conclude that the levels of violent protest action in South Africa are *high* and that one of the key elements driving this trend is a pervasive feeling of discontent with the manner in which governance is administered in the country.[83] As I have sought to argue, this increasing resort to violence seems to stem from both a desire for greater substantive justice in the distribution of state resources and services and also from a feeling of not being heard in the procedural sense,[84] the latter of which is the focus of this chapter.

[79] ibid 19–20.

[80] ibid.

[81] S Friedman, 'People are demanding public service not service delivery' *Business Day* (29 July 2009) <http:// www.bdlive.co.za/articles/2009/07/29/people-are-demanding-public-service-not-service-delivery> accessed 3 Octoer 2022.

[82] See SAIFAC survey entitled 'Constitutional legitimacy: A survey of the Gauteng adult population' (November 2015) <http://www.constitutionnet.org/files/annex_a_survey_of_the_gauteng_adult_population_1.pdf> accessed 3 October 2022.

[83] S Liebenberg, 'The Participatory Turn in South Africa's Social Rights Jurisprudence' in KG Young (ed), *The Future of Economic and Social Rights* (CUP 2019) 187–211. See also Paret (n 8) 116, stating that '[v]iolent tactics—most notably property destruction and social disruption—are thus a response to the failures of formal democracy'.

[84] A clear example of a procedural failure is in respect of the seeming unwillingness on the part of state bodies to respond to information requests made in terms of the Promotion of Access to Information Act, 2000 (PAIA). In this regard, a 2018 report by the Access to Information Network <https://cer.org.za/wp-content/uploads/2019/09/ATI-Network-Shadow-Report-2018.pdf> refers to a 'noticeable trend amongst most public bodies who were requested to provide information … *to show a lack of interest in attending to PAIA requests* and, even when they do, to not do so timeously' (at 4, emphasis added) accessed 3 October 2022. eg the report finds that of the number of requests to public bodies only 45 per cent of requestees received a response within the statutory prescribed time frame and that 35.4 per cent were deemed refusals in the sense that no response was given at all (at 3).

B. How Can Participation, Impartiality, and Justification Mitigate Violence?

I have thus far shown that the growing resort to violent forms of self-help—which is 'inimical to a society in which the rule of law prevails'[85]—exposes the high levels of strain that the government-citizen relationship is experiencing at present. It also suggests that the procedural dimension of the transition is not being given sufficient attention. It is in this context that I engage with the 'outcomes' and 'process' justifications for valuing procedural rights, both of which provide grounds for believing that procedurally just decisions enjoy greater legitimacy and ultimately public acceptance. Acceptance of (and not necessarily agreement with) public decisions is, in my view, necessary for dissuading citizens from resorting to violence as the preferred mode of expressing discontent. This approach has some empirical support in the work of Tyler where he explores citizen responses to legal authorities (particularly courts and the police) and concludes that there is an empirically supported connection between fair procedures and societal acceptance of decisions taken by legal authorities.[86] He points to '[c]onsiderable evidence' revealing that '*the key factor shaping public behavior* is the fairness of the processes legal authorities use when dealing with members of the public'.[87] Meyerson, relying on empirical research in the area of social psychology, similarly concludes that 'people care as much about processes as about outcomes';[88] that '[p]erceptions of procedural fairness or unfairness make an independent contribution to evaluations of experiences with legal authorities'; and that 'when decisions are made in ways that people regard as fair *this cushions the impact of negative outcomes*'.[89] Summers also suggests that one of the positive consequences of a commitment to process values is public confidence, respect for the rule of law, and acceptability of outcomes.[90] Most recently, Snipes and others explore the impact of procedural justice on the relationship between citizens and the police in public demonstrations in the United States. In addition to encouraging acceptance of outcomes,[91] the authors go further by considering specifically the connection between procedural injustice and violence explaining that procedurally unjust practices tend to increase both the likelihood of 'resistance and rebellion against legal authorities'[92] and can even lead to 'outrage and escalation by citizens during their encounters with police'.[93] The authors

85 *Chief Lesapo v North West Agricultural Bank* [1999] ZACC 16; 2000 (1) SA 409 (CC) [11].
86 Tyler (n 11).
87 ibid 283 (emphasis added).
88 Meyerson (n 62) 238.
89 ibid 255 (emphasis added).
90 R Summers, 'Evaluating and Improving Legal Process—A Plea for "Process Values"' (1974) 60(1) Cornell Law Review 1–52, 13.
91 Snipes, Maguire, and Tyler (n 11) 33.
92 ibid.
93 ibid.

conclude that 'procedural justice *has strong effects* on protesters' violence-related attitudes and behaviors'.[94]

In the remaining parts of this chapter, I consider how the particular procedural principles I have identified support both the 'outcomes' and 'process' justifications for valuing procedural justice and explore the ways in which these principles can be used to temper resort to violence on the part of citizens.

(i) Outcomes justification

This is a result-orientated approach, which is premised on the belief that officials who take meaningful cognisance of the demands of procedural justice are *more likely* to be accountable and reach good outcomes, including decisions that are rational, informed, and taken in the public interest. Doing so fosters a culture of respect and 'buy-in' for public decisions,[95] which can in turn restrain societal inclinations towards violent self-help. In other words, acceptance (not necessarily agreement) of public decisions is necessary for deterring resort to violence by citizens.

The relationship between good outcomes and societal acceptance of public decisions finds support in Rawls' 'imperfect procedural justice' model[96] and Meyerson's 'error reduction' account. Both scholars apply these notions to the criminal trial context concluding that the value of a trial fairly administered does not lie in the guarantee of a correct outcome,[97] rather, it lies in the *likelihood* of a good outcome by, for example, reducing the risk of an erroneous conviction. In particular, the fact that an accused person is presented with the opportunity to share their side of the story and judges are required to preside over matters impartially and later justify their judgments with reference to reasons is more likely to result in a correct outcome, than if these procedural safeguards were not in place.[98] How then do the principles of participation, impartiality, and justification support the outcomes justification by discouraging violent expressions of discontent?

For one thing, meaningful citizen involvement minimises arbitrariness in decisional outcomes. It does so by ensuring that decisions are taken on an informed basis, that is, rooted in the necessary facts and circumstances. Such decisions are more likely to be met with societal acceptance which, as I have argued, reduces the desire on the part of citizens to communicate using violence. In his dissenting judgment in *Masethla*, Ncgobo J referred to the 'inter-relationship between a failure to act fairly and arbitrariness' explaining that '[a]cting fairly provides the decision-maker with the opportunity to hear the side of the individual to be affected by the decision' thus enabling an informed decision to be taken 'after

[94] ibid 34 (emphasis added).
[95] Tyler (n 11) 286.
[96] J Rawls, *A Theory of Justice* (Harvard University Press 1971) 85–87.
[97] ibid 86; Meyerson (n 62) 240–41.
[98] See, further, Waldron (n 50) 12.

considering all relevant facts and circumstances', which he said is 'essential to rationality, the sworn enemy of arbitrariness'.[99] The information-gathering role of the participation principle was also recognised in the *Albutt* decision where the Court was concerned that the failure to hear the victims' version of events in the course of issuing pardons for political crimes could result in an erroneous outcome, namely the pardoning of a person who had not in fact committed a political crime.[100]

Turning to the principle of impartiality, some of the feedback from South African citizens in the context of violent protest action pertains to the common complaint that corruption and self-interested decision-making has resulted in bad decisional outputs, such as unlawfully-awarded procurement contracts.[101] Requiring that a decision-maker 'approach a matter with an open mind that is free of prejudgment or prejudice'[102] can improve the quality of public participation by ensuring that there is a '*willingness to consider all views* expressed by the public'[103] and in so doing, minimise the risk of arbitrariness in decisional outcomes. In short, a functionary is more likely to apply his or her mind to a matter in a fair and regular manner if non-partisan.[104] In this way, the principle of impartiality also performs a crucial accountability role by ensuring that entrusted power is exercised in the public interest, rather than for self-interested reasons.[105] In effect, an impartial decision is more likely to be of a better quality, which increases the likelihood of acceptance and lessens the need for violent opposition.

The final principle, 'justification' also reinforces both the rationality and accountability elements underpinning the 'outcomes' justification because public decisions are more likely to be rational where they have been defended with reference to reasons. And, a culture of justification of decisions can translate into a deeper culture of acceptance of public decision-making, which can lessen the desire of citizens to rely on violence to voice their concerns.

This positive relationship between reason-giving and rational outcomes finds support in a number of cases. In *Mphahlele*, regarding the duty of judges to provide reasons, the Constitutional Court explained that reason-giving performs the crucial function of explaining to the 'parties, and to the public at large ... why a case is decided as it is' and is thus a 'discipline which curbs arbitrary judicial decisions'.[106] Similar justifications have been said to apply in the context of the administrative law duty to give reasons.[107] Hoexter and Penfold explain that one of its

99 *Masethla* (n 34) [184].
100 *Albutt* (n 38) [70].
101 See Fakir (n 4).
102 M Groves, 'The Rule Against Bias' (2009) 39 Hong Kong Law Journal 485.
103 *Poverty Alleviation Network v President of the Republic of South Africa* [2010] ZACC 5; 2010 (6) BCLR (CC) ('*Poverty Alleviation*') [51].
104 *Janse van Rensburg v Minister of Trade and Industry* [2000] ZACC 18; 2001 (1) SA 29 (CC) [24].
105 L Baxter, *Administrative Law* (Juta 1984) 538–39.
106 *Mphahlele v First National Bank of South Africa Ltd* [1999] ZACC 1; 1999 (2) SA 667 (CC) ('*Mphahlele*') [12].
107 Constitution, s 33(2); PAJA, s 5.

key objectives is to ensure that administrators are able to explain, and ultimately defend, the basis of their decisions to those affected by them. This holds them accountable[108] and can safeguard against arbitrary decision-making.[109] In a similar vein in *JSC*,[110] concerning the refusal of the Judicial Service Commission[111] to provide reasons for the non-appointment of certain candidates for judicial office, Brand JA affirmed that '[i]t is difficult to think of a way to account for one's decisions other than to give reasons'[112] and further that 'it is rather cynical to say to an affected individual: you have a constitutional right to a rational decision but you are not entitled to know the reasons for that decision'.[113]

The crucial point is that soliciting the viewpoints of a broader range of people, by expanding the opportunities for involvement and exchange; promoting impartiality and even-handedness as well as a culture of reason-giving, can result in better decisional outcomes. Since fairer decisions are also more likely to result in just outcomes, citizens are more likely to accept these outcomes and, for this reason, feel less inclined to turn to violence to voice their unhappiness. Better outcomes are also more likely to be just in the substantive sense and, as a result, enhancing procedural justice could advance or complement the goals associated with distributive justice as well.

(ii) Process justification

The focus of the process justification is different: it looks at the positive effect that procedurally just decisions have on citizens, both in the 'dignitarian' and 'relational' senses. The dignitarian account is based on the Kantian notion of treating human beings not merely as 'means' but as 'ends' in themselves. On this approach, adhering to procedural principles gives expression to the rational aspect of a citizen's identity by showing respect for them as autonomous beings with inherent worth and the capacity to reason.[114] The 'relational' account is similar but is concerned more with the positive impact that procedural values can have on a citizen's feelings of self-respect in their relationships with state authorities, what Meyerson refers to as a kind of 'relational self-respect'.[115] In this regard, Meyerson relies on empirical research to find 'a causal connection between the experience of fair treatment and the enjoyment of self-respect' explaining that '[w]hen authorities treat

108 See *Mphahlele* (n 106) [8].

109 C Hoexter and G Penfold, *Administrative Law in South Africa* (3rd edn, Juta 2021) 629–30. See further *Transnet Ltd v Goodman Brothers (Pty) Ltd* 2001 (1) SA 853 (SCA) [5] citing with approval Baxter (n 105) 741 explaining that reasons 'assist decision-makers in rationalising their decisions'.

110 *Judicial Service Commission v Cape Bar Council* [2012] ZASCA 115; 2013 (1) SA 170 (SCA) ('*JSC*').

111 This is a constitutional body tasked with recommending persons for appointment to judicial office.

112 *JSC* (n 110) [44].

113 ibid.

114 Meyerson (n 62) 249–50; Waldron (n 50) 17.

115 Meyerson (n 62) 261.

individuals in ways they regard as fair, thereby conveying the message that they have standing as full members of society, this promotes feelings of self-worth'.[116] She singles out 'polite treatment, respect for rights and treatment that evidences trustworthiness'[117] as examples of the kinds of actions that contribute to the formation of a positive social identity. Similarly, Tyler concludes that people 'value the quality of their interpersonal treatment by the authorities', and care very much whether they are being 'treated with dignity and respect by authorities with whom they deal'.[118] From the perspective of the process justification, if citizens feel that their dignity (in the sense of their capacity to engage rationally in public discourses) as well as their self-respect (owing to a positive social identity) are appreciated, this can foster a culture of respect for decisions taken by the state. Respect and acceptance are, as I have argued, important for discouraging resort to violence. How then do the three principles I have identified in the first part of this chapter support the process justification by lessening the need for violence?

Meaningful citizen participation reinforces both the dignitarian and relational accounts underpinning the process justification by providing an opportunity for citizens to feel a sense of inclusion and self-worth as well as an opportunity to shape the public discourse.[119] In this way, a decision-maker signifies to citizens that 'their views matter' and are deserving of consideration and genuine engagement. It can thus be said to enhance 'the civic dignity of those who participate by enabling their voices to be heard and taken account of'[120] and is, in fact, 'necessary to preserve human dignity and self respect'.[121] These themes are also of value on an interpersonal level by giving expression to a particular quality of democratic relationship; namely one in which government and citizens, as members of a political community, are encouraged to interact and share views as a 'symbolic marker' of their inclusion.[122]

The consequence is that a feeling of being respected, meaningfully engaged with, and ultimately included fosters a sense of legitimacy and acceptance of the actions of the state and a deeper feeling of trust in the democratic system.[123] A positive social identity[124] can also have the desirable effect of discouraging the resort to violence in order to be heard. In this regard, the Court in *Afriforum*, concerning the emotionally charged issue of changing apartheid-era street names, explained that '[i]n principle and in anticipation of predictable tensions, everything reasonably

[116] ibid 258.
[117] ibid 256.
[118] Tyler (n 11) 298.
[119] Liebenberg, 'Participatory Justice in Social Rights Adjudication' (n 11) 5–6.
[120] *Doctors for Life* (n 20) [115].
[121] *Matatiele* (n 34) [66].
[122] Bilchitz and Heleba (n 31) quoting Meyerson (n 62).
[123] See *Doctors for Life* (n 20) [115]; *Joseph* (n 41) [46].
[124] *Doctors for Life* (n 20) [115].

possible must be done to alleviate strife or dampen all likely tensions' and that a proper public participation process naturally lends itself to this purpose.[125]

Turning to the principle of impartiality, a key element that emerged from Tyler's study is that '[p]eople think that decisions are being more fairly made when authorities are neutral and unbiased and make their decisions using objective indicators, not their personal views'.[126] In this way 'evidence of even-handedness and objectivity'[127] enhances societal perceptions of fairness. In fact, much of the discontent associated with the wave of violent protest action can be attributed to a belief that politicians are self-interested, often corrupt, and not acting in the best interests of the public.[128] In this context, it is helpful to draw on the rule against bias (*nemo iudex in sua causa*) from administrative law, particularly the distinction drawn between actual and perceived bias. As I have explained, the requirement against actual bias is important because it ensures that decision-makers have an open mind[129] and act in the public interest. However, perceptions of impartiality matter too, especially if we want to build relationships on the basis of mutuality and trust, rather than suspicion and distrust.[130] Public confidence is, in the end, fostered not only when justice is done but also when it is 'manifestly and undoubtedly seen to be done'.[131] In effect, positive public perceptions that officials are acting in the public interest and that they possess a genuine willingness to consider the views of citizens are essential to the process of building trust in, and acceptance of, public decision-making. This can, in turn, discourage violent expressions of discontent.[132]

Finally, I consider the value of the principle of justification. For one thing, a regular practice of explaining decisions to citizens signifies respect for their rational worth and is important for building a culture of constructive engagement between the state and citizens. In the context of the administrative law duty to give reasons, one of its crucial purposes is to be 'properly informative'[133] by helping an aggrieved person understand what the nature and impact of a particular decision is for them. Reasons must thus enable an aggrieved person to say, in effect '[e]ven though I may not agree with it, I now understand why the decision went against me'.[134] The point is that a commitment to this principle is empowering and can

[125] *Afriforum* (n 24) [51].
[126] Tyler (n 11) 298.
[127] ibid.
[128] Fakir (n 4).
[129] *Poverty Alleviation* (n 103) [60].
[130] See, eg, *Absa Bank Limited v Public Protector* [2018] ZAGPPHC 2; [2018] 2 All SA 1 (GP).
[131] Much quoted words of Hewart CJ in *R v Sussex Justices, Ex Parte McCarthy* ([1924] 1 KB 256; [1923] All ER Rep 233).
[132] *Merafong Demarcation Forum v President of the Republic of South Africa* [2008] ZACC 10; 2008 (5) SA 171 (CC) ('*Merafong*') [51].
[133] Hoexter and Penfold (n 109) 627.
[134] *Minister of Environmental Affairs and Tourism v Phambili Fisheries (Pty) Ltd; Minister of Environmental Affairs and Tourism v Bato Star Fishing* (Pty) Ltd 2003 (6) SA 407 (SCA) [40].

bolster people's senses of self-worth by giving them the tools to engage in rational criticism and provide guidance as to how to self-correct in the future.[135]

The dignity and relational-enhancing potential of reasons is especially helpful when thinking about the violence that accompanied the decision to abolish, by constitutional amendment, cross-border municipalities in South Africa through the alteration of provincial borders (the 'Constitutional Amendment'). In the context of the particular decision to move the Merafong City Local Municipality, a cross-border municipality, out of Gauteng into the North West province, it is perhaps helpful to explore whether reason-giving could have had a placatory effect on the violence that accompanied this decision.

Recalling what transpired, the community opposed the decision to be moved to the North West, insisting that the quality of services would be substantially worse than if it were to be governed by the more affluent Gauteng province. Following this announcement, a consultative processes took place between representatives of the Gauteng Provincial Legislature (GPL) and the community. However, during the process, the GPL's representative, acting on a negotiation mandate from National Council of Provinces (NCOP), decided to support the community's desire to remain in Gauteng. This could only, however, be made effective through a further amendment to the proposed Constitutional Amendment. However, during the subsequent NCOP deliberations, the GPL was told that it could only accept or reject the Constitutional Amendment as a whole and that it was not allowed to ask for the inclusion of the specific amendments that would allow the community to remain in Gauteng. The result was that the GPL felt compelled to accept the proposed amendment in its existing form with the consequence that the community was moved to the North West. Bishop, in his mixed empirical and legal account of the *Merafong* judgment, reflected on what happened after the GLP reneged on its earlier resolution to ensure the community remained in Gauteng: 'Merafong erupted. Residents turned to the streets ... and then blockaded them with rocks and burning tyres ... Firebombs and more rocks were thrown'[136] with the community calling for 'more face-to face consultation'.[137]

Although the majority of the Court accepted that the GPL had adequately discharged their constitutional obligation to facilitate public involvement in the process of adopting the relevant legislation, one of the lingering questions was whether the GPL ought to have returned to the community to explain what had transpired before the NCOP. The majority of the Court accepted that the GPL had behaved disrespectfully[138] and affirmed that reporting back to the community 'may well have been desirable' as a way of fostering a better understanding of why adhering

[135] *Goodman Brothers* (n 109) [5].

[136] See M Bishop, 'Vampire or Prince? The Listening Constitution and *Merafong Demarcation Forum & Others v President of the Republic of South Africa & Others*' (2009) 2 Constitutional Court Review 313, esp 314–15 where he documents in detail the violent responses to this decision.

[137] ibid.

[138] *Merafong* (n 132) [55], [58].

to the position taken in the negotiating mandate could not be sustained.[139] The majority did not, however, see the failure to 'report back' as being sufficient to warrant the striking down of the legislation. Sachs J, in this minority judgment, disagreed. He concluded that this 'lack of appropriate political respect'[140] was enough reason to strike down the legislation. Sachs J reasoned that in failing to return to the community and 'explain its abrupt about-turn ... diminished [its] civic dignity' and 'produced a total lack of legitimacy for the process and its outcome in the eyes of the people'.[141] All this culminated in what he referred to as a 'disastrous breakdown of relations between the community and government',[142] which 'tore at the heart' of what participatory democracy aims to achieve.

Irrespective of whether or not the failure to report back ought to have resulted in the invalidity of the legislation in question, what is especially interesting for present purposes—and which Sachs J's judgment highlights—is the negative impact that a decision can have on the quality of relations between government and citizen, and raises the pertinent question whether greater political respect on the part of the GPL could have diminished the community's decision to resort to violence. In his analysis of this aspect of the judgment, Fowkes suggests that it would have done little to re-engage the community about abandoning its initial position. If anything, he said that 'a return to the community to explain would have been seen as a frustrating exercise by the community'.[143] I disagree. In these circumstances—particularly given the heated opposition to the decision and the fact that the community was led to believe that its wishes would in fact be acceded to—justifying why the GLP position's had changed would have significantly enhanced the meaningfulness of the state's involvement in the process. As pointed out by Bishop, the purpose of an explanation here was not 'to extend the deliberation or change a decision already reached' but rather, 'to offer the last word in the process ... as a prophylactic measure to ensure that the participation itself was worthwhile'.[144]

4. Conclusion

In the early years of constitution drafting, Mureinik posed the following prescient question: 'Will we achieve democracy?' The answer, he contended, will depend upon the:

> *routine relationships between government and subject*—upon how officials treat the people they govern in daily dealings ... *It will depend deeply, in other words,*

139 ibid.
140 ibid [287].
141 ibid [292].
142 ibid [299].
143 Fowkes (n 25) 205, see earlier discussion 199–204.
144 ibid 341.

> *upon the everyday decision-making processes of government.* Whether we attain democracy will consequently depend upon administrative law: upon the legal forces which pull—or fail to pull—government decision-making towards democratic decision-making.[145]

Mureinik's emphasis on the importance of the decision-making *processes* of the state and the quality of treatment of the people it governs is particularly important when considering the transitional goal of moving away from the authoritarian, secretive, and unjust style of governance that epitomised the apartheid system. Central to the transition has thus been a concern with responding to this poor state of affairs by democratising governance through a greater emphasis on procedural justice.

This project, I have argued, has not properly been implemented which is evidenced by the alarming levels of violent protest action in South Africa at present. While much of this citizen discontent has to do with the failure of the post-apartheid government to advance the cause of distributive justice by delivering on its socio-economic promises, the focus of this chapter has been on an apparent feeling of procedural injustice in citizen interactions with the state. In developing a legal response to this situation, I have revisited the procedural goals of South Africa's transition and explored specifically the ways in which the principles of participation, impartiality, and justification could be used as a violence-mitigation tool in South Africa. I have argued that these principles are supported by the 'outcomes' and 'process' justifications for valuing procedural justice, both of which are premised on the view that fairer decision-making processes can translate into greater societal acceptance of public decision-making, which is important for diverting citizens away from violent strategies of communication.

Vitally, if one of the causes of violence is that citizens feel unheard and unacknowledged, then it is incumbent on public decision-makers, and where possible citizens, to reaffirm their commitment to those procedural principles in our law that can help deter their resorting to violent protest. As Bilchitz and Heleba argue, there is immense value in grounding the government-citizen relationship in 'an ethos of respect, mutuality and harmony',[146] not only for enhancing the quality of decisional outcomes and improving democratic relationships, but as a means of encouraging the resolution of societal conflict in constructive and non-violent ways. In the end, constantly affirming these high standards of fairness in the decision-making *processes* of the state can lay the foundations for peace to flourish. But, in compromising on those same standards, the state condones poor quality decision-making, which weakens democracy, the rule of law, and, crucially, a nation's hope for sustained, long-term peace.

[145] Mureinik, 'Reconsidering Review' (n 35) 35.
[146] Bilchitz and Heleba (n 31).

21

Beyond Democracy

Meaningful Public Participation as a New Approach to Public Decision-Making in the Context of Colombia's Transitional Justice Process

Julián Andrés Pimiento Echeverri and Irit Milkes

1. Introduction

Transitional justice should not only guarantee the peaceful termination of armed conflict, but its principal function should be to prevent the recurrence of conditions that generated the conflict in the first place and to create an environment in which peace becomes stable and enduring.[1] The process which culminated in the 'Final Agreement to End the Armed Conflict and Build a Stable and Lasting Peace' ('peace agreement' or 'agreement') laid the foundation for a profound transformation of the Colombian state.[2] In addition to providing the necessary conditions for a formal end to the conflict, the process also strived to change the social conditions that led to the armed conflict in the first place.

A fundamental goal of this necessary transformation is thus the creation of adequate conditions for guaranteeing citizen participation in public decisions, an objective which would signal greater democratisation and help guarantee that public decisions are truly in line with the real needs of the population. In this sense, citizen participation is a means of legitimising transitional justice processes

[1] See International Centre for Transitional Justice, *What is Transitional Justice?* (April 2018) <https://www.ictj.org/sites/default/files/ICTJ-Global-Transitional-Justice-2009-English.pdf.> accessed 3 October 2022, where it was explained that '[t]ransitional justice is a response to systematic or widespread violations of human rights. It seeks recognition for victims and promotion of possibilities for peace, reconciliation and democracy. *Transitional justice is not a special form of justice but justice adapted to societies transforming themselves after a period of pervasive human rights abuse.* In some cases, these transformations happen suddenly; in others, they may take place over many decades' (emphasis added). For this reason, it is also true 'that the transformation demonstrates the ability of the new regime to accept the collective past, make it is own and build a new political regime, hopefully, the most democratic possible, on foundations that represent the negation of the past regime'.

[2] See Juan Carlos Henao, 'Justice transitionnelle: le cas de la Colombie' (2018) Revue de Droit Public 1023.

Julián Andrés Pimiento Echeverri and Irit Milkes, *Beyond Democracy* In: *Transitional Justice, Distributive Justice, And Transformative Constitutionalism.* Edited by: David Bilchitz and Raisa Cachalia, with Magdalena Inés Correa Henao and Nathalia Bautista Pizarro, Oxford University Press.
DOI: 10.1093/oso/9780192887627.003.0021

and sustaining the decisions adopted in such contexts. This process of integrating citizens into democratic decision-making had already begun with the Political Constitution of 1991.[3] Thirty years after its promulgation, this essential idea is now found at the centre of the peace agreement. Citizen participation can also be found in the Constitutional Court's decisions outlining and defining the obligations contained in the peace agreement, which have influenced its implementation both internally and externally.

In this regard, and with the understanding of citizen participation as an expression of a transitional approach towards the peaceful implementation of public decisions, this chapter will be divided into four sections. Section 2 will discuss how the Colombian legal system has established citizen participation and its interpretation as a legal and constitutional mandate. In Section 3, we will discuss the manner in which the Peace Agreement established citizen participation as one of its fundamental pillars. Section 4 will attempt to highlight some of the difficulties involved in public participation, particularly where, as in the Colombian experience, it has worked at times against the building of peace. In response, in Section 5, we argue that the mere existence of a concrete model of participation is insufficient, on its own, to advance the goals of transitional justice. We argue further that what is needed is for participation to be 'meaningful' if participatory mechanisms are to be effective in advancing the process of building a stable and lasting peace in Colombia. For this reason, in the final section of this chapter, we propose certain elements which, in our view, should inform the 'meaningfulness' standard.

2. Democratic Guarantees and Public Participation as a Constitutional Mandate in Colombian Law

Public participation is an essential goal of the Colombian state, as is stated in the first article of the Political Constitution.[4] Articles 40[5] and 41[6] contain both a citizen's right and a value of citizenship. Furthermore, it is a collective right, whose protection must be guaranteed by the state in terms of articles 3,[7] 78, and 79.[8] There

[3] Constitution of the Republic of Colombia, 1991 (hereafter 'Constitution').

[4] Constitution, s 1: 'Colombia is a social state under the rule of law, organised in the form of a unitary republic, decentralised, with autonomy of its territorial units, democratic, participatory, and pluralistic, based on the respect of human dignity, the work and solidarity of the individuals who belong to it, and the prevalence of the general interest.'

[5] Constitution, s 40: 'Any citizen has the right to participate in the establishment, exercise, and control of political power.'

[6] Constitution, s 41: 'In all educational institutions, public or private, the study of the Constitution and civics will be mandatory. In this way, democratic practices for the teaching of principles and values of citizen participation will be promoted. The State will publicise the Constitution.'

[7] Constitution, s 3: '[t]he State will guarantee the participation of the organisations of consumers and users in the study of the provisions that concern them. In order to enjoy this right, the organisations must be representative and observe internal democratic procedures.'

[8] Constitution, s 79: 'Every individual has the right to enjoy a healthy environment. The law will guarantee the community's participation in the decisions that may affect them.'

is also an entire chapter devoted to the question of democratic mechanisms of participation (Chapter 1 of Title IV).

The Constitution of 1991 brought together two democratic models, representative democracy and participatory democracy,[9] as a sign of the consolidation of an inclusive society.[10] For the Constitutional Court, in its judgment in T-469/92, participatory democracy implies that citizens are not limited to voting once in a while, but rather that they are entitled to influence directly the decision-making process and actions of the government at different levels. The Court has also extended this model of participatory democracy to issues related to *inter alia* public spaces,[11] access to public documents,[12] and community action committees.[13]

The model of participatory democracy is of great importance in the interpretation of the political text as a whole. It has been considered to be one of the essential goals of the Colombian state (art 2). Thus, a series of specific mechanisms for citizen participation have been established (art 103), such as a right to vote, plebiscites or referendums, popular consultations, open town council meetings, and involvement in legislative initiatives. Concretely, in the analysis of the norms issued to implement the peace agreement, the Court affirmed that participatory democracy, as a value, is based on the participation of the citizenry as part of a collective destiny for Colombians as a whole. Participation, in this regard, gives expression to the relationship between the state and the citizens: different mechanisms allow the citizenry to participate in the design and operation of governmental institutions[14] and, for this reason, participation is one of the pillars on which the peace agreement is built.

[9] These are not opposing concepts, since 'when the Colombian Constitution embraces a participatory proposal, it should be understood the elements of political representation continue to have a place there.' See Carlos Echeverri Jiménez, 'La participación ciudadana en Colombia: reflexiones desde la perspectiva constitucional y la normatividad estatutaria' (2010) LXVII Estudios de Derecho 67.

[10] Jacques Chevalier, *L'État post-moderne*' (5th edn, Librairie générale de droit et jurisprudence 2017) 171, explains that the idea 'has deeply modified the meaning of the administrative relationship and the logic on which the administrative institution has been built or constructed. Once the traditional status of the subject is left behind, obliged to submit to each of the prescriptions of the public administration, whose content cannot be negotiated. Thus, the citizen is promoted to the "rank" of stakeholder and is granted a right of control over the functioning of the services. At the same time, the Public Administration, invited to open up to its users, is led to renounce certain essential features of the bureaucratic personality in order to become "democratic": better yet, it becomes a privileged place for the realization of the democratic demand.'

[11] Constitutional Court, C-265/02.

[12] Constitutional Court, C-221/16.

[13] Constitutional Court, C-126/16.

[14] Constitutional Court, C-379/16. Reiterated in Constitutional Court, C-019/18.

3. Democratic Guarantees and Public Participation in the Peace Agreement

A. Public Participation as a Model of Transitional Justice

There are many theoretical approaches to the concept of transitional justice. Perhaps the most classical definition used is that coined by Ruti Teitel when she explains that '[t]ransitional justice can be defined as the conception of justice associated with periods of political change, characterised by legal responses to confront the wrongdoings of repressive predecessor regimes'.[15] From this definition, one could argue that transitional justice is a form of justice that should break from the predominantly retributive nature that characterises the ordinary justice system. Thus, 'the concept of transitional justice brings together the notions of "transition" and "justice"'.[16] This, in turn, speaks to the process of transition that societies make towards a more legitimate form of government after a period of political turmoil.

However, this vision, which establishes the legitimacy of a new political regime as its central element, should be implemented through a broader understanding of the guarantees of non-recurrence and the creation of conditions to ensure a lasting peace that transcends the judicial sphere.[17] In this sense, transitional justice should also integrate a 'full range of processes and mechanisms associated with a society's attempts to come to terms with a legacy of large-scale past abuses, to ensure accountability, serve justice and achieve reconciliation'.[18] From this perspective, it is important to note that the transitional justice that we defend in this chapter pursues 'an ideal of accountability and fairness in the protection and vindication of rights and the prevention and punishment of wrongs'.[19] Therefore, the institutional reforms adopted by a state in transitional justice contexts should be aimed

[15] Ruti Teitel, 'Transitional Justice Genealogy' 2003 16(69) Harvard Humans Rights Journal 72–74. See also Ruti Teitel, *Transitional Justice* (OUP 2000).

[16] Drazan Dukic 'Transitional Justice and the International Criminal Court—In the "Interests of Justice"?' (2007) 89 International Review of the Red Cross 691 (May 2018) <https://www.icrc.org/eng/assets/files/other/irrc-867-dukic.pdf> accessed 3 October 2022. See also Alice Panepinto, 'Transitional Justice: International Criminal Law and Beyond' (2014) 3 Dalla Comunità internazionale, Archivo Penale <http://www.archiviopenale.it/2014-3--a-panepinto-transitional-justice-international-criminal-law-and-beyond/contenuti/4468> accessed 3 October 2022.

[17] Yesid Reyes, '¿Es injusta la Justicia Transicional? A manera de estudio preliminar' in Yesid Reyes (ed), *¿Es injusta la Justicia Transicional?* (Universidad Externado de Colombia 2018) 32.

[18] United Nations Security Council, *The rule of law and transitional justice in conflict and post-conflict situations: Report of the Secretary General* S/2004/616 (23 August 2004), which states that 'a given transitional justice process may include a combination of the following measures: successor trials (both criminal and non-criminal), truth commissions, lustrations (vetting), restorative measures (reparations, restitutions, etc.), constitutional and legal reform, reforming the security sector, opening and granting access to secret files, memorialisation, public apologies, state-building (and trust-building) activities, amnesties, and more, linked to the rule of law, democratisation and human rights'.

[19] Kai Ambos, *The Legal Framework of Transitional Justice* (2007) 7.

at obtaining 'justice in a transitional period, starting from state oppression or an armed conflict'.[20]

However, other transitional justice approaches teach that what should be demonstrated is 'the capacity of the new regime to assume its collective past, to make it its own and to build a new political regime'.[21] This broad idea of transitional justice 'has become increasingly common to define the transition regarding a comprehensive transformation in social and political life'.[22] As a result, transitional justice processes require political legitimacy,[23] while at the same time guaranteeing the social appropriation of the decisions adopted in such processes.[24]

To give more significance to participation in social and political processes, it is interesting to reflect on what Saffon and Tacha have pointed out previously.[25] The objective of citizen participation in the adoption or implementation of political measures or policies is to ensure that they are endowed with legitimacy. This is achieved by demonstrating that the decision-making process has taken into account the necessities, proposals, and viewpoints of the recipients or affected persons.[26] In this way, citizen participation in transitional justice processes provides a solid foundation for the effective implementation of a new regime.

These discussed approaches regarding the concept of transitional justice converge when identifying as a defining element, the need to 'prioritise reconciliation over retribution',[27] through mechanisms that permit a transition 'towards a prosperous democracy'.[28] Therefore, 'the main objectives of transitional justice measures are to attain peace and societal stability within a conflict-torn society through means of justice and truth'.[29]

[20] The Office of the Prosecutor of the International Criminal Court, *La Justicia Transicional en Colombia y el Papel de la Corte Penal Internacional*. Principal discourse of James Stewart, Deputy Prosecutor of the International Criminal Court. Bogotá DC, 13 May 2015. (May 2018) 5 <http://www.eltiempo.com/contenido/politica/justicia/ARCHIVO/ARCHIVO-15749076-0.pdf> accessed 3 October 2022.

[21] Fabrice Hourquebie and Xavier Philippe, 'La justice transitionnelle et le droit public: une introduction et quelques réflexions' (2018) Revue de Droit Public 4.

[22] Edyta B Pietrzak, 'Transitional Justice in Relationship to Public Sphere and Civil Society: Theoretical Approaches' (2018) 47(1) Polish Political Science Yearbook 58.

[23] Gutiérrez Ramírez states that 'the legal aspect of legitimacy in transitional justice implies the manifestation of a political will that is squeezed through the public powers as a consequence of the principle of representation or, directly through the nation in the logic of direct democracy'. See Luis Miguel Gutiérrez Ramírez, 'Au nom de quoi? Au nom de qui? Réflexions sur la légitimité de la justice transitionnelle' (2018) Revue de Droit Public 4.

[24] For a discussion on the construction of a reflexive legitimacy in which there exists a true social appropriation of the necessary mechanisms for interpreting the norms that arise from agreements, see ibid.

[25] See María Paula Saffon and Viviana Tacha, 'La participación en las medidas de justicia transicional. Un estudio comparado' (2018) Dejusticia 17.

[26] ibid 17.

[27] Panepinto (n 16) 7.

[28] Francisco Valderrama and Marvin Ortiz, 'Justicia transicional: noción de la justicia en la transición colombiana' (July–December 2017) 16 Opinión Jurídica 262.

[29] Anja Mihr, 'Transitional Justice and the Quality of Democracy' (2013) 7(2) International Journal of Conflict and Violence 299.

Following from this premise, it is argued that adequate social acceptance of decisions adopted within a transitional justice framework can constitute a mechanism that advances the non-repetition of armed conflict. In this way, 'the links between new civil society and transitional justice emerge from the cohesion of transitional justice with continuities of injustice'.[30] Starting from this premise, in which victims occupy the most disadvantaged role within an armed conflict, transitional justice stands as a mechanism par excellence to ensure that (i) victims know the truth and receive reparations; and (ii) the causes that give rise to armed conflict in the first place—like in the case of Colombia—are not repeated.[31]

It is worth mentioning that these purposes are also evident in the peace agreement:

> *The end of the conflict constitutes the best opportunity to guarantee the rights of the victims to truth, justice, reparations and non-repetition*, and in general to ensure the full realisation of the human rights of all.[32]

Citizen participation in the peace agreement is framed within a broad concept of transitional justice and can positively influence the transitional justice process in three ways:[33] First, it can facilitate community involvement, which can help guarantee that transitional measures are tailored to local needs; secondly, it can encourage support from citizens for the changes that are required; and, lastly, it can place a special focus on the problems of marginalisation and 'invisibilisation' suffered by the communities most affected by violence.[34]

Thus, public participation is a necessary part of the transitional justice process, particularly as an expression of the principle of the centrality of victims in such processes and as an essential guarantee of non-repetition of violence. Both principles constitute fundamental pillars of the Colombian peace agreement.

[30] Edyta B Pietrzak, 'Transitional Justice in Relationship to Public Sphere and Civil Society: Theoretical Approaches' (2018) 47(1) Polish Political Science Yearbook 63.

[31] ibid 263.

[32] Emphasis added.

[33] Saffon and Tacha refer to three objectives that participation attempts to achieve in order to legitimise transition mechanisms: the expression of viewpoints, the creation of impact, and the transformation of power relations. Saffon and Tacha (n 25) 17.

[34] USAID, *Community Participation in Transitional Justice: A Role for Participatory Research* (2014) 1 <https://www.usaid.gov/democracy/document/community-participation-transitional-justice-role-participatory-research> accessed 29 September 2023. In effect, the inclusion of public participation as a part of transitional justice mechanisms brings different benefits: 'First, feedback received from the public can assist the state in creating a transitional justice system that better responds to local needs.' Anna Triponel and Stephen Pearson, 'What Do You Think Should Happen? Public Participation in Transitional Justice' (2010) 29 Pace International Law Review 103 (May 2018) <http://digitalcommons.pace.edu/pilr/vol22/iss1/3> accessed 3 October 2022. It is worth discussing in detail, however, the new citizen modalities that can arise from the relationship between civil society and transitional justice. Regarding this point, although we do not share the same conclusions, see P Gready and S Robins, 'Rethinking Civil Society and Transitional Justice: Lessons from Social Movements and "New" Civil Society' (2017) 21(7) The International Journal of Human Rights 956–75.

B. The Citizen Participation Model in the Peace Agreement

Following from what we have argued regarding the broad focus of the transitional justice model adopted in Colombia, the peace agreement contains in its text a concrete focus on citizen participation, which guarantees the participation of distinct sectors that stand to be affected by the agreement's implementation.

The purpose of the peace agreement is expressed clearly in the following terms: 'to build a stable and lasting peace, with the participation of all Colombians'. In the same way, the agreement states that the territorial focus should 'attempt to implement the different measures in an integral and coordinated manner, with the active participation of citizens'.[35] Moreover, one of the central foci of the agreement is that:

> [c]itizen participation is the foundation of each agreement that constitutes the Final Agreement. Participation, in a general sense of society in building peace, and participation in the specific sense of planning, executing and monitoring the plans and programs in the territories, which is, additionally, a guarantee of transparency.[36]

The way in which the participation of victims is established in the agreement, as a guarantee for its peaceful implementation and as a guarantee of non-repetition, shows how all aspects of the transitional justice system are permeated with this citizen participation model. Thus, it is clear that the peace agreement considers participation as a fundamental value and as a guarantee for the non-recurrence of the conditions that led to the cycle of violence.

Concerning the actors whose participation is necessary, the peace agreement's citizen participation framework recognises various stakeholders: some are related to the agreement's implementation, while others are related to the institutional aspects, such as the *Jurisdicción Especial para la Paz* (JEP),[37] the *Comisión Especial para la Verdad* (CEV),[38] and the *Unidad de Búsqueda de Personas dadas por Desaparecidas* (UBPD).[39] In terms of the agreement, it has been pointed out that the participation of the different actors is crucial. In fact, it seeks to highlight the importance of their intervention with differential approaches,[40] allowing for intercultural dialogue with different communities and ethnicities.[41] The participation of different stakeholders cannot omit—at any time—the differential, gendered,

[35] Peace agreement, arts 1.1 and 1.2.
[36] Pease agreement, art 1, Concerning the list of principles on the Peace Agreement.
[37] Special Jurisdiction for Peace (JEP).
[38] Special Commission for the Truth (CEV).
[39] Missing Persons Search Group (UBPD).
[40] See Law 1922 of 2018, art 1c. This law adopts the procedure for the JEP (*Jurisdicción Especial para la Paz*).
[41] Peace agreement, art 1.1.8.

and territorial perspectives that are unique to each community. These criteria are intended to guarantee the participation of a diverse range of stakeholders whose intervention is necessary for the purposes of truth, justice, and reparation within the broader transitional justice framework.[42]

In other words, the agreement's different sections consider participation to be an essential element for implementation. This fact is apparent starting from the first section of the agreement, *Comprehensive Rural Reform*, which states that 'the planning, execution, and monitoring of plans and programmes, will be carried out through active community participation—from both men and women—which is, additionally, a guarantee of transparency coupled with accountability, citizen oversight and special monitoring of the competent bodies'. As a whole, *Comprehensive Rural Reform* focuses on guaranteeing the participation of distinct population groups, especially peasants and women.[43]

Section 2 of the peace agreement, *Political Participation: Democratic Opening to Build Peace*, not only contains all the aspects related to political participation, but also contemplates a new model of citizen participation in public decisions. Thus, a new focus of territorial development is consolidated, which is centred on citizen participation. This focus guarantees different mechanisms of public policy design that recognise the right on the part of citizens to participate in the different steps of the agreement's implementation. Concerning citizen participation in the political sphere, for instance, mechanisms were designed to contribute to citizen participation through community, institutional, and regional media operations. In addition to being a means to promote civic values, it aims to foster the recognition of ethnic, cultural, political, and social differences and to strengthen democracy.[44] In this sense, the peace agreement established participation as one of its guiding principles in the Integral System of Truth, Justice, Reparation, and Non-Repetition. For example, when discussing the CEV, the peace agreement established the importance of participation by explaining that:

> [t]he Commission will put in place a process of broad, pluralistic, and balanced participation in which different voices and visions will be heard. This process will start with the victims of the conflict, who have been related to the conflict in any way, both individuals and groups, and it will also include those who directly or indirectly participated in the conflict, as well as other relevant actors.[45]

[42] Peace agreement, art 5.1. Concerning the participation of victim injustice and reparation processes, see also Mijke de Waardt and Sanne Weber, '"Beyond Victims" Mere Presence: An Empirical Analysis Participation in Transitional Justice in Colombia' (2019) 11(1) Journal of Human Rights Practice 209–28 and Claire Garbett, 'The International Criminal Court and Restorative Justice: Victims, Participation and the Processes of Justice' (2017) 5 Restorative Justice 198–220.

[43] Peace agreement, art 4.1.3.5.

[44] Peace agreement, art 2.2.3.

[45] Peace agreement, arts 2 and 2.1.

Regarding the participation of each stakeholder, other mechanisms have been designed to materialise this democratic principle. Although these instruments are not strictly considered part of a judicial process, they can be analysed from an institutional approach. The Integral System for Truth, Justice, Reparation, and Non-Repetition of Victims has promoted the creation of opportunities for coordination and dialogue with victims and state organisations, the creation of spaces for information and education, as well as the design of procedures for monitoring and accountability from institutional bodies. These all provide examples of the importance of citizen participation in the implementation of the agreement.[46]

The emphasis on the importance of citizen participation throughout the peace agreement is an unprecedented step forward for Colombia's democracy. The decisions that will be taken to implement the agreement must take account of the views of various stakeholders. This is, however, subject to some instrumental and substantive limits, which we will explored in more detail later in this chapter. In effect, and for the sake of clarifying and developing the participatory model, it is important to analyse how the institutional design of the mechanisms recognise the necessity of citizen participation and the manner in which participation will be expressed concretely. Regarding the agreement's implementation, although the necessity of participation is clear, the manner in which such participation should be carried out is not.

C. Paradoxes of Democracy in Relation to Public Decision-Making

Citizen participation is a cross-cutting issue in the peace agreement. It must be accepted that there are different moments in which citizen participation will have a concrete impact. In previous sections of this chapter, we pointed out that the participation of different stakeholders is necessary for both the design and implementation of the agreement. Although citizen participation is a central issue in the peace agreement, particularly as a guarantee for peace in transitional justice contexts, participatory democracy remains full of paradoxes.

Consider the following example: from a political point of view, the Colombian government decided to approve the peace agreement through a plebiscite, in which the citizens were called to the polls to vote either 'yes' or 'no' to the peace agreement.[47] Taking into account the national government's interest, the Constitutional Court, in its analysis of the constitutionality of the plebiscite,[48] decided that, as a

[46] See Jurisdicción Especial para la Paz (JEP), 'Manual para la participación de las víctimas ante la JEP' (February 2021) <https://www.mapp-oea.org/wp-content/uploads/2020/11/Manual-para-la-Participacion-de-las-Victimas-ante-la-JEP-version-corta.pdf> accessed 3 October 2022.

[47] The plebiscite was established by Law 1806 of 2016.

[48] Constitutional Court, C-379/16.

result of utilising a plebiscite, the result would be binding. However, in the event that the peace agreement was rejected, then it would have to be renegotiated but without having to be submitted to a popular referendum. This is in fact what transpired. The result of the plebiscite was a rejection of the peace agreement, albeit by a small margin.[49] This reveals a paradox: decisions arising from a peace process do not necessarily have the support of the political majority. In effect, similar to many aspects related to fundamental rights, the decisions that the government must take in the name of 'peace' can be counter-majoritarian. In other words, submitting such decisions to the rules of democracy in all circumstances can block attempts to implement transitional justice more generally. In the last few years, a democracy crisis has emerged in response to decisions that have apparently been 'democratically' taken but which nevertheless seem to contravene certain social and cultural perspectives, such as equal marriage for all irrespective of sexual orientation.[50] As a result, it appears that participatory democracy may not be a guarantor of peace and human rights in all circumstances.

In the context of the peace agreement, participation thus undermined the aims of the peace agenda and a deep institutional crisis emerged as a result of the lack of political consensus. What followed was, in our view, a significant and necessary relativisation of the democratic principle in the framework of the referendum on the peace agreement. This relativisation can be seen in the Constitutional Court's jurisprudence and the government's position, which accepted that the citizenry only had a limited right to participation, one that did not encompass a right to impede the realisation of the agreement. Regarding this difficulty, the Constitutional Court stated:

> The referendum process through prior popular consultation acquires fundamental importance when citizen intervention is related to the manner in which a constitutional mandate is complied with, but it does not eliminate or suspend

49 The final result was 50.21 per cent voting 'no' and 49.78 per cent voting 'yes'.

50 Concerning this point, the conclusions of Ronald Dworkin are relevant. Dworkin explains the difficulties of allowing the majority to decide the rights of the minorities, as well as the difficulties inherent in employing a strictly majoritarian focus within a conception of democracy. He reminds us that '[i]ndividual rights of equality and freedom must be in place and protected from the majority as well' (see Ronald Dworkin, 'The Partnership Conception of Democracy' (1998) 86 California Law Review 458). '[W]e have to consider the suggestion—implicit in Dworkin's argument—that allowing the majority to decide upon the conditions under which majority decisions are to be accepted may be objectionable because it makes them judge in their own case' (see Ronald Dworkin, *Law and Disagreement* (OUP 1999). cf Mauro Arturo Rivera León, 'Jurisdicción Constitucional: Ecos del argumento contramayoritario' (2010) Revista Mexicana de Derecho Constitucional 223–60. The Colombian Constitutional Court has used this argument repeatedly, particularly in relation to equal marriage where it stated 'in a social rule of law, there is a set of fundamental rights, whose essential content forms a "Coto forbidden" for the majority, which is an aggregate of non-negotiable rights and privileges, among which exists the right of every person, in conditions of equality, to freely join with another and to form a family, in order to make a common life plan'. See also Constitutional Court, SU-214/16.

> such a mandate. For example, in contexts like those that caused the issuance of Legislative Act 1 of 2016 [which provided for popular pronouncement through a plebiscite], to the extent to which the Constitution is not reformed, the President of the Republic has the duty to guarantee public order, provide national defense and security, and celebrate peace agreements (Articles 22 and 189, numerals 3, 4, and following). In the same way, if a determined plan of the peace policy is submitted to a plebiscite, expressed in an agreement with armed groups, and the nation votes in the negative, the President of the Republic must respect this decision and abstain from implementing it as it is.

In Sentence C-379 of 2016, the Court explained that, for the aforesaid reason:

> the correlative consequence of an unfavourable vote or of the lack of a sufficient number of votes for the [ratification of the agreement], is the legal impossibility for the President to move forward with the implementation of this specific Agreement. But that pronouncement does not neutralise his constitutional obligation to achieve peace (Art. 22), and therefore, he should pursue other ways of carrying out this mandate.[51]

In essence, the Constitutional Court determined that the Colombian legal system establishes some alternatives to comply with the constitutional mandate to achieve a stable and lasting peace,[52] such as when a particular policy choice (ie the peace agreement) is not accepted by the citizens. One of the alternatives is to introduce changes to the text of the Final Agreement, with the aim of addressing the concerns and disagreements of the population. This is in accordance with the purpose of the plebiscite, which is a mechanism for hearing the opinion of citizens[53] and acting in accordance with it. However, it is not necessary for the changes made to be subject to a new direct mechanism of voting. The peace agreement is clear:

> If such modifications are the fruit of a process in which the results of a previous citizen consultation are respected, interpreted and developed in good faith, in a

[51] Constitutional Court, C-699/16.

[52] According to scholars, peacebuilding pertains (broadly) to 'external interventions that are designed to prevent the eruption or return of armed conflict' but these scholars nevertheless accept that there are 'critical differences among actors regarding its conceptualization and operationalization': Michael Barnett and others, 'Peacebuilding: What Is in a Name?' (2007) 13(1) Global Governance 37. In Colombia, it seems that the peacebuilding project, conceived of in this way, is under threat. See, in this regard, Constitutional Court, SU-020/22 where the Court concluded that the Colombian government had not complied with the measures related to the security of former combatants established in the peace agreement. In effect, the Court recognised that even some of the implemented mechanisms since the signing of the peace agreement have failed to guarantee no return to the armed conflict.

[53] Constitutional Court, C-150/15.

search for greater consensus, such modifications can reasonably be said to have the actual effect of citizen participation (Constitution, Arts. 1, 2, 22, 40, 83 and 103).[54]

It is obvious that there was a governmental interest in endowing the agreement with legitimacy through democratisation by means of a plebiscite, but the result ended up causing a legitimacy crisis. Nonetheless, the Constitutional Court gave convincing reasons for qualifying the democratic participation in these types of decisions, which required the adoption of counter-majoritarian measures in the interests of peace. This also applies to decisions taken that seek to achieve peace or fundamental rights in which there is no clear political consensus.

In the end, the problem seems to be that this democratic model is bound to the majority, despite the fact that the conflict affected the population in a differential manner. In fact, paradoxically, citizens in the regions most affected by the conflict generally voted in favour of the peace agreement.[55] Those least affected had the luxury of voting against the agreement and having those most affected suffer the consequences. In this regard, it is necessary to move past the simplistic idea of a formal, procedural, and majoritarian democracy, to a different form of citizen participation that guarantees the confluence of different interests reflected in these types of decisions.

4. A New Approach: 'Meaningful' Participation as a Constitutional Mandate

This new model of participation, which goes beyond democratisation, permeates the spirit of the peace agreement and can be found in each of the mechanisms created to implement it. We consider that this new model raises two points, which we intend to develop in this section: (i) on the one hand, to determine whether the participation and consultation mechanisms existing in the Colombian legal system and the jurisprudence of the Constitutional Court should be used in the implementation of the agreement; and (ii) on the other hand, to question whether the traditional mechanisms are sufficient or whether it is necessary to make some specific modifications to ensure a balance between participation and effectiveness.

54 Constitutional Court, C-699/16.

55 See Eduardo Álvarez Vanegas and others, 'Voting for Peace: Understanding the Victory of "No"' *Wilson Center and Fundación Ideas Para la Paz* (2016) <https://www.wilsoncenter.org/article/voting-for-peace-understanding-the-victory-no> accessed 29 September 2023.

A. Defining 'Meaningful' Participation in Colombian Law

Various descriptions have been used in the context of the right to participation of victims and stakeholders in processes aimed at seeking truth, justice, and reparation.[56] The term 'meaningful' as an adjective has provoked a range of views pertaining as to its interpretation.[57]

Saffon and Tacha have pointed out that citizen participation in a transitional justice framework has three objectives:[58] (1) to express points of view; (2) to create impact; and (3) to empower or to 'visibilise'.[59] These dimensions of participation ought not only promote the expression of determined viewpoints—which is relevant—but should also lead to impactful decisions and 'visibility' of the communities most affected by the armed conflict. In other words, public participation strengthens and renews the concept of democracy, through the recognition of minorities and encouraging debate among different sectors of society, to give legitimacy to the transition.[60] In the words of Mihr:

> [I]nter-linkage, multi-causality, or rather correlation between transitional justice and quality of democracy depends largely on the level of responsiveness and accountability of political elites, transparency, adherence to international human rights norms, and participation by citizens.[61]

This vision is encapsulated in the concept of legitimising transitional justice in the Colombian context. In effect:

> participation must start from the presumption of disparity, and not of parity, and its goal must be to generate real transformations in this disparity. Only if this

[56] We frame the concept of 'meaningful' participation in the Colombian context as developed by the jurisprudence of the Constitutional Court and the scope that has been given to it exclusively in the national context. Therefore, any other scope or interpretation of the concept of 'meaningful' participation was not taken into account for the purposes of this chapter.

[57] de Waardt and Weber (n 42) 215–19. On the relevance of the interaction of stakeholders and victims in the framework of a judicial process, see also Mara Schiff, 'Satisfying the Needs and Interests of Stakeholders' in Gerry Johnstone and Daniel W Van Ness (eds), *Handbook of Restorative Justice* (2011) 228–46.

[58] Saffon and Tacha (n 25) 17.

[59] Although they have a common origin and it is evident that citizen participation constitutes an expression of the democratic principle, we wanted to distinguish them because it is our view that this traditional vision of democracy is formal and dangerous in the context of a transitional process. It is formal because it understands the mechanism as a process through the act of calling the community to decide concerning a determined public decision. It is dangerous because, on the one hand, if it is given a lot of value, it could result in the consolidation of risks from a majoritarian democracy, which would imply ignoring minorities' rights—such as those of victims—which are essential.

[60] In this area, there are many possibilities for configuring the transitional process. As Mihr (n 29) 299 states, 'the country's political and bureaucratic institutions must guarantee a basic level of accountability, transparency, and free participation. When and how to apply these mechanisms depends on the context of the conflict and the post-conflict situation'.

[61] ibid 311.

> happens, can it be said that participation effectively contributed to the transformation of power relationships and is, therefore, a source of legitimacy for transitional justice measures.[62]

Concretely, the Colombian legal order demands, therefore, that this participation be meaningful. In this regard, this section will discuss the content of the *meaningfulness* standard, which will be followed by a determination of examples in which meaningful citizen participation could be used for the effective implementation of the peace agreement. While we argue that the participation of affected parties should be guaranteed in order to entrench the rights of citizens to be involved in the decisions that affect them, this should not negate the importance of attaining efficiency and effectiveness in the implementation of the peace agreement. Ultimately, a balance must be struck between these, at times, competing constitutional mandates and in achieving this balance, we thus endorse a conception of participation that is not merely formal, but which is also substantive and functional.[63]

From this perspective, it is first necessary to identify the variables that underpin a workable model of citizen participation to be used for advancing a lasting peace going forward. The goal should be to guarantee the peaceful application of public decisions that are produced within and outside of the agreement's scope because, in the end, the goal is to avoid a repetition of the conditions that led to the conflict in the first place. What does meaningful participation in the Colombian legal system and the peace process entail? The answer to this question is twofold. It is necessary first to define its objectives and second, its variables.

It is possible to build a *meaningful participation* standard with reference to its main features. In its jurisprudence, the Constitutional Court has stated that public participation has to be active *and* effective.[64] *Active participation* means that the goal is not simply to inform citizens about the decisions that are going to be made, but rather to allow interested parties to intervene and be heard in matters that affect them. *Effective participation* means that those expressed views should have an impact on the final decision, even if it does not mean that the views of communities or interested parties should prevail.[65]

Concretely, to guarantee meaningful participation that is both active and effective, in our view, public authorities should consider at least the following variables: (i) the nature of the public decision in question; (ii) the stakeholders who will be affected; and (iii) the appropriate mechanism of participation. We elaborate on

62 Saffon and Tacha (n 25) 24.

63 By this we mean that it is not enough for the legislator to refer to citizen participation in the legal text. The content of 'meaningful participation' refers to the set of external mechanisms and instruments that make it possible to really implement it.

64 Constitutional Court, T-376/12.

65 See SU-097/17 and SU-011/18 (Colombian Constitutional Court).

each of these in the ensuing discussion with reference to the jurisprudence of the Colombian Constitutional Court.

(i) The nature of public decision-making

This pertains to the identification of two aspects: (1) the nature of the decision; and (2) its generality or specificity. Regarding the former, public decisions can be taken by authorities from all three branches of government, but not all decisions need be subject to public participation.[66] When a public decision is set to affect a certain community in a *specific* (opposed to a general) way, the standard of meaningful participation should be applied. Nonetheless, it must be noted that judicial decisions are not subject to this principle because of other principles that are specifically applicable to the judicial branch of power, such as autonomy and independence. In respect of the latter consideration, the scope of the decision is important. This is because the more general a public decision is, the less likely there will be a need to undertake public participation unless a general decision—such as a law—is proven to have a major impact on a specific community. In such a case, that community must be consulted.[67]

Previously, it was determined that any decision that would have a positive[68] or negative[69] impact on the social, economic, environmental, or cultural conditions of a given community ought to be submitted to popular consultation. Therefore, to determine when to use the consultation mechanisms, it would be helpful if there was an assessment as to whether the decision would have a direct impact on the population in one of these ways. If it does, an appropriate mechanism ought to be designed by the public authorities to consult the affected population.[70]

(ii) Identification of stakeholders

Here the concern is about identifying, with a measure of specificity, the key stakeholders who ought to be included in the participatory process.[71] This will

[66] See Judy B Rosener, 'Citizen Participation: Can We Measure Its Effectiveness?' (1978) 38 Public Administration Review 457–63.

In effect, 'the objective of impact as receptivity should be understood as meaning that all the participants' interests and preferences will be heard and taken into account and that contradictions will be resolved in a democratic and grounded manner'. Saffon and Tacha (n 25) 17.

[67] For example, the Constitutional Court in Decision SU-123/18 concluded that the 'prior consultation cannot be merely a formal procedure; on the contrary, its implementation must involve a series of measures by the public authorities to identify the perspectives of the communities affected'. These mechanisms should be focused on the characteristics of the target population group to be consulted.

[68] An example of the positive impact of a direct effect or impact was studied in decision T-201 of 2017 in which it conducted a prior consultation for the implementation of food and nutrition programmes in Afro-descendant communities. See Constitutional Court, Decision T-201/2017.

[69] Among the cases of direct effect due to a negative impact, the prior consultation in the case of the 'Media Luna Dos' people can be mentioned, in which the expansion of the Cerrejón company's port was being discussed. See Constitutional Court, Decision T-704/2016.

[70] Constitutional Court, Decisions SU-123/18 and SU-383 of 2003.

[71] See Jemima García-Godos and Knut Andreas O Lid, 'Transitional Justice and Victims' Rights before the End of a Conflict: The Unusual Case of Colombia' (2010) 42(3) Journal of Latin American Studies 487–516.

encourage the broadest possible spectrum of participants[72] and viewpoints and in so doing enrich the participatory process more generally.[73]

However, the most difficult task in these cases is determining how to identify these stakeholders. In our view, this ought to be done with reference to (1) the community or communities impacted by the decision; and (2) in a way that ensures that those who do participate adequately reflect the voices of the community as a whole.[74] Concerning (1), there is a set of indicators that can help with that task: geographic considerations (communities located in the area in which a public decision is set to be enforced); material considerations (the anticipated impact of an activity on a community or communities); and subjective considerations (whether a decision specifically targets a community or communities in a particular way).[75] In the decision-making process, public authorities are obliged to identify both (1) and (2), in order to guarantee meaningful participation.

(iii) Participatory mechanisms

Here the concern is that public authorities have to identify two separate, but intertwined, issues: whether participation is a requirement for the execution of the measure, or whether there is simply the need to obtain the opinion of the community regarding the proposed measure. This determination depends on the impact of the measure on the community and the identity of the recipient. The more specially protected or vulnerable a certain community is in the Constitution (eg ethnic groups), the deeper the commitment to meaningful participation should be.[76] On the other hand, meaningful participation should be flexible, which means that

[72] In this regard, eg, Archon Fung points out that 'citizens can be the shock troops of democracy. Properly, deployed, their local knowledge, wisdom, commitment, authority, even rectitude can address wicked failures of legitimacy, justice, and effectiveness in representative and bureaucratic institutions.' Archon Fung, 'Varieties of Participation in Complex Governance' (2006) Public Administration Review 66–74. We agree with the author since the identification of each stakeholder in the decision-making process is essential to achieve true '*meaningful*' participation and take into account the diverse interests of the participants.

[73] For the author, the decision-making process is composed of multiple points. It is pointed out that 'Administrative rulemaking, often comprises moments in which interested individuals and stakeholders comment on proposals in public hearings and moments in which regulators (experts) make decisions on their own. Decision making in a complex urban development project, for example, often results from interactions among multiple arenas, such as planning agencies, stakeholder negotiations, neighborhood councils, and public hearings.' See ibid 67.

[74] The Colombian Constitutional Court in decision SU-011/18 pointed out that: 'Popular and prior consultation is a space for intercultural dialogue, aimed at overcoming the insufficient democratic representation of Indigenous and Afro-descendant peoples, caused by factors such as geographical location, precariousness, historical discrimination, and cultural diversity.'

[75] We consider that even if public authorities have broad powers to identify those who should be consulted, judges, through adjudication in constitutional actions, can intervene to redress a bad or partial identification of such stakeholders and oblige public authorities to guarantee meaningful participation to a specific community or to broaden the scope of the participation process.

[76] In the same way, the Constitutional Court in decision SU-383 of 2003, noted that 'prior consultation is a definitive step towards leaving behind the assimilationist or integrationist approach of the State's relationship with Indigenous peoples, towards one based on respect for difference and the maximization of the autonomy of ethnically differentiated communities and peoples'.

depending on the characteristics of those to be consulted, a methodology for participation should be put in place. Indeed, the guarantee of active and effective participation will depend on certain aspects. For instance, participation of Indigenous peoples in matters pertaining to the Amazonian forest will involve a different approach to that of a group of people who live in large capital cities. Those subjective aspects, according to the jurisprudence of the Constitutional Court, will affect the approach or 'the tools' required to achieve the aim of participation (eg the use of internet or social networks), and even the procedure through which active and effective participation is set to occur.[77]

Beyond the cases discussed, this methodological proposal can have a positive effect on the entire range of public decisions that require public participation. This proposal as to the substantive content of the participation principle can also be used in the peacebuilding context specifically to ensure that citizen involvement is active and effective and thus capable of advancing the aims of transitional justice in the Colombian context. It is, however, not enough to identify the nature of the decision, the stakeholders and the participation mechanisms to be used if the balancing of interests is not taken into account. It is to this context that we now turn.

B. Balancing Meaningful Public Participation and Constitutional and Legal Mandates in the Peace Process

In order to guarantee meaningful participation, a methodological approach to public decision-making is required.[78] This entails a consideration and weighing of the various interests that may coincide, or even, collide, and striking the best possible balance between protecting constitutional principles and rights and other issues discussed later in this chapter.

Therefore, a methodology must be proposed, which can apply to the implementation of the peace agreement's obligations, but which also transcends it. This is because such a methodology is required to have an impact on the full range of public decisions that require citizen participation. We believe the idea of participation is not an end in itself but a means or an instrument of pursuing other goals.[79] In this sense, *meaningful participation* is a vehicle by which the protection of other fundamental rights or purposes of public authorities may be pursued. Put differently, its implementation in the fulfilment of government purposes is not a goal in and of itself, but rather a means by which other objectives may be achieved.

[77] In this regard, see also Constitutional Court in decision SU-123 of 2018.

[78] Regarding all of these points, we proceed from the model adopted in the Constitutional Court Sentence SU-123 of 2018, related to prior consultation derived from the Convention 169 of the ILO, albeit with a few modifications.

[79] ibid 18.

It is clear that the guarantee of meaningful participation is an expression of constitutionally protected rights, as it is a manifestation of the principles binding the exercise of authority. However, a question arises: how does the law balance meaningful participation with other constitutionally protected principles, such as the efficiency of public action, or the advancement of other constitutionally protected interests (eg mining and environmental issues)?

This issue is of upmost importance in rejecting the idea that public participation is the answer to every question related to public decision-making.[80] In the following section, we outline the limits of public participation and the correlative obligations that authorities are required to enforce in order to ensure participation is compatible with efficient public decision-making.

(i) Meaningful participation cannot mean giving the community a right to veto a public decision

A veto right means that communities would be entitled to impose their views on public authorities, thus preventing decision-makers from balancing different interests that are also protected by the law. This is not acceptable. It should be noted that, depending on the specific constitutional protection of the individual or group to be consulted, the effects of participation can be more or less significant. In this scenario, the public authority takes into account the other interests which are also protected by law. Although at first sight, this would seem to detract from the usefulness of citizen participation, the balancing exercise could mitigate or reduce the negative effects that a particular decision could have on a minority group or those who did not participate.[81] This rigorous exercise during the public decision-making process will ensure that it can be effective and functional at the time of implementation.[82]

Such an example can be seen in the Constitutional Court's decision SU-123/18 where, regarding a popular consultation involving an Indigenous community living near a hydrocarbon exploitation project, the judge stated that consultation is a process of intercultural dialogue between equals (*inter partes*). This means that Indigenous peoples cannot block state decisions, nor does the government have the right to impose any decision on them without adequate consultation.

However, although it is a dialogue between equals, this does not mean that Indigenous peoples have the same power as the state. In general, where

[80] As two great Spanish administrative professors stated: 'participation is the great political and social entelechy of our time'; Schmitt-Glaeser has said there is a true 'Partizipationeuphorie, and additionally Chevalier had qualified it as an ideology of participation'. These quotes are referenced in Eduardo García de Enterría and Tomás-Ramón Fernández, *Curso de Derecho Administrativo* (Thomson Reuters 2007) 15 and 108.

[81] See Christoph Van Der Elst and Lientje Van Den Steen, 'Balancing the Interest of minority and Majority Shareholders: A Comparative Analysis of Squeeze-out and Sell-out Rights' (2009) European Company and Financial Law Review 4, 391.

[82] See Rosener (n 66) 457–63.

communities are disadvantaged due to discrimination to which they have been historically exposed, the state must take the necessary measures to strengthen the position of these communities. For example, to ensure the effective involvement of communities, it may be necessary to take account of their geographical location and language. However, this does not mean that the decision-maker must necessarily agree with stakeholder claims in this context.

(ii) Public participation must respect the constitutional and legal powers attributed to public authorities

Given there are constitutional and legal powers attributed to public authorities, not every decision can or should be made available for public participation.[83] Even if citizen participation is necessary, the final decision must reside with the authorities, who must explicitly express the way in which public concerns and opinions were taken into account in the final decision.[84] In this case, meaningful participation means that public authorities have an obligation to inform citizens of the considerations that informed decisions that were taken.[85]

Thus the public decision-making process should be transparent, especially in explaining why a certain decision is made and how the authority has balanced the interests at play, as well as the reasons for the final choice.[86] The benefits of this approach are simple: the community is consulted, but also all citizens can know how the decision was made and how effective their intervention was in the process.[87] The reasons can, of course, be subject to judicial review.

[83] 'Not every decision can and should be submitted to the citizenry for approval. Some decisions must be assumed by the public authority i.e., there are public decisions that due to their complexity, duration, scope and, intensity because they generate different kinds of "participation costs". It is well known that certain kinds of decisions necessitate the participation of highly trained "experts", while others do not. Certain policy decisions are long-term, cover large geographical areas, and affect the lives of thousands of people. Others require no specialized knowledge, are of limited duration, and primarily affect small groups of citizens. In assessing effectiveness, it is dangerous to assume that costs (in time, money, energy, and expertise) of participating are the same for all kinds of policy issues.' ibid 459.

[84] In Decision T-204/12, the Constitutional Court stated that the duty of the authorities to provide reasons for their decisions is a manifestation of the democratic principle that public authorities are accountable to the citizenry.

[85] 'The ability to do this will provide public administrators and citizens with knowledge of what "works" and what does not. Knowing what "works" and what does not should minimize the frustration felt by administrators who are confused about what is expected of them, and at the same time it will minimize the distrust felt by citizens who complain that public participation programs are a charade.' Rosener (n 66) 459–61.

[86] In effect, the objective of impact as receptivity should be understood as meaning that all the participants' interests and preferences will be heard and taken into account and that contradictions will be resolved in a democratic and grounded manner'. Saffon and Tacha (n 25) 17–21.

[87] See Irit Milkes, 'Buena administración y la motivación de los actos administrativos expedidos en ejercicio de facultades discrecionales' (2019) 21 Revista Digital de Derecho Administrativo 153–78 (March 2021) <https://revistas.uexternado.edu.co/index.php/Deradm/article/view/5703> accessed 3 October 2022.

As has traditionally been known, the duty to give reasons[88] helps some other valued goals to be achieved. Three advantages can be identified in the development of this duty, namely: (a) the fact that the authorities will be increasingly aware of making better and accurate decisions; and (b) 'public confidence' can be furthered through enjoying the respect afforded through providing an explanation. This means that the fact of giving reasons to citizens is a sign that the public authorities carry out a coherent, careful, and conscientious process of decision-making. In this way, the reasons given to citizens contribute to the building of public confidence in government institutions;[89](c) giving reasons is therefore as much a sign of respect for the dignity of the individual and the citizenry, as it is an attempt to persuade that person to respect the decision taken by the authorities. This is a change in the traditional role of the citizen, where it is intended that 'they personally talk about the decision rather than just *deal with it*'.[90] Since a fully transparent administrative decision-making process by the authorities will provide citizens with the tools to challenge the decision, the fact of understanding the reasoning process involved in taking a decision, allows the citizen to disagree with the reasons given by the public authority. In any case, it is important to note that all the decisions taken by public authorities may be subject to judicial review by the administrative judge, as an additional opportunity for the citizen to disagree with the decision made by the public authority in certain circumstances.

In conclusion, *meaningful participation* is undoubtedly a guarantee of transparency, fairer public decision-making, and respect of fundamental rights. However, it is necessary to exclude any result that would subvert constitutional and legal mandates.

5. Conclusion

As shown in this chapter, citizen participation helps to guarantee a dual purpose related to legitimacy: it aims to legitimise the peace agreement, despite the risks that are entailed, and it aims to guarantee the legitimacy of the decisions taken in its implementation. In this chapter, we have demonstrated that the peace agreement envisions a participatory model which permeates all of the decisions that are adopted in giving effect to it. Therefore, participation is one of the pillars of transitional justice, understood as a transition towards a new political model, which addresses the causes of conflict and guarantees their non-recurrence.

[88] See Jarrod Hepburn, 'The Duty to Give Reasons for Administrative Decisions in International Law' (2012) 61(3) The International and Comparative Law Quarterly 641–63.

[89] See P Paterson, 'Administrative Decision-Making and the Duty to Give Reasons: Can and Must Dissenters Explain Themselves?' Auckland University Law Review (March 2021) <http://www.austlii.edu.au/au/journals/AukULawRw/2006/2.pdf> accessed 3 October 2022.

[90] ibid 644.

We saw, however, the challenge that arises in that public participation can work against peace in some circumstances. This raised the question of what participation in fact entails. In our view, the agreement does not promote participation in the formal sense but instead proposes a model of *meaningful* participation, through which multiple values including diversity, efficiency, and effectiveness are taken into account. In other words, meaningful participation requires that all viewpoints are heard and that they have a real impact on decisional outcomes. However, it is necessary to balance the right to participate in decisions with other rights as well as the competencies attributed to administrative authorities.

In this regard, we have proposed a methodological model which aims to advance *meaningful* participation, influenced in broad terms by the Colombian Constitutional Court's jurisprudence. At the first level, the model provides for the formal and substantive aspects required for guaranteeing meaningful participation. At the second level, the model aims to guarantee that the scope of such participation does not rupture the institutional structure. For this reason, it establishes two guarantees: institutional or competency guarantees and guarantees for the full and comprehensive expression of legal and factual arguments about the decisions that are adopted.

Additionally, although the proposed model has been built from the experience of implementing popular consultation and other mechanisms, we have tried to illustrate how this participation mechanism takes into account the diverse interests of victims and communities. We have also endeavoured to show how its observance—in the transitional justice context—can help legitimate citizen participation by ensuring transparency at each level of the process of implementing the agreement. This will, in turn, empower citizens to challenge the way in which decisions are taken.

Finally, the proposed model is a sample of the long and rich experience in Colombia, which currently presupposes a harmonisation of the interests of all stakeholders in public decision-making processes. The recognition of diversity, as an essential element of any transitional justice process, will be one of the criteria that will guarantee that the participation mechanisms fulfil their core purpose of legitimising the transition to a more peaceful society.

22

Joint Reflection: Comparative Reflections on Transitional Justice and Political Inclusion in South Africa and Colombia

Raisa Cachalia and Irit Milkes

1. Introduction

In our preceding chapters, we examine the procedural dimension to transitional justice in the context of the goals of the transitional arrangements of our respective jurisdictions. Cachalia's chapter is located in South Africa's ongoing—nearly thirty-year—transition to constitutional democracy and within the framework of the country's 1996 Constitution.[1] Pimiento and Milkes's chapter is positioned in Colombia's lengthy transition from what was, in essence, a half century of civil war, and with a specific focus on the more recent 2016 Peace Agreement.

In this regard, both chapters highlight the fact that one of the objectives of the transitional justice project is to consolidate peace through the building of viable and stable democracies.[2] The chapters then, in different ways and contexts, grapple with the relationship between 'procedural justice'[3] and transitional justice; examining in particular whether procedural values have a role to play in promoting peace and stability in countries emerging from conflict. On the one hand, Cachalia's chapter reflects on the positive role that a trio of procedural values—namely, participatory governance, impartiality, and justification—can potentially play in tempering the high levels of violent protest action that have engulfed the country in recent years. These protests have resulted in significant political instability in South Africa and pose a threat to the country's sustained peace and democratic prosperity going forward. On the other hand, Pimiento and Milkes' chapter is more narrowly focused on a particular form of procedural justice, namely, citizen participation and they examine its role in the Colombian peace process that is currently underway, with particular reference to the events surrounding the 2016 plebiscite.

[1] Constitution of the Republic of South Africa, 1996 (hereafter 'Constitution').

[2] In this regard, see further A Mihr, 'Transitional Justice and the Quality of Democracy' (2013) 7(2) International Journal on Conflict and Violence 298–313.

[3] The authors use the term 'procedural justice' to refer to the full spectrum of procedural rights, which includes (but is not limited to) the principle of participatory governance.

Raisa Cachalia and Irit Milkes, *Joint Reflection: Comparative Reflections on Transitional Justice and Political Inclusion in South Africa and Colombia* In: *Transitional Justice, Distributive Justice, and Transformative Constitutionalism.* Edited by: David Bilchitz and Raisa Cachalia, with Magdalena Inés Correa Henao and Nathalia Bautista Pizarro, Oxford University Press. © Raisa Cachalia and Irit Milkes 2023. DOI: 10.1093/oso/9780192887627.003.0022

While the authors agree, in principle, that a commitment to more just procedures *can* impact positively on the process of transitioning societies to more stable, peaceful, and democratic futures, a tension clearly emerges: on a reading of the chapters alongside one another, it is clear that procedural values can both *support* and *undermine* peace within a transitional justice framework, depending on how they are conceived and ultimately applied. In this joint reflection we explore the nature of this tension by examining specifically the proper role that procedural values should play in transitioning South Africa and Colombia to more peaceful and democratically stable futures. We argue that the tension between the *supporting* and *undermining* potential of these values can be practically and constructively managed if emphasis is placed firmly on the *purpose* of involving citizens in the peacebuilding projects[4] of our respective countries and, relatedly, on the *quality* of citizen involvement in a given context. Each of these themes is considered and developed in Sections 2 and 3 of this chapter, with brief concluding remarks being made in Section 4.

2. The 'Purpose' of Citizen Involvement in Transitional Justice: Inclusion Not Consent

The role of procedural values—and, particularly, the participation principle—in the resolution of political questions is an enduring debate in political theory. Jeremy Waldron, one of the strongest proponents of a majoritarian conception of democracy, insists that the participation principle should be regarded as an end in itself and that the intended outcome of a participatory process should be to endorse the view of the majority; independently of whether the outcome of the process would ultimately be wrong or unjust.[5] For him a majoritarian resolution of political disputes should thus be adopted because the right to participate—what he refers to as the 'right of rights'[6]—is *fundamental* to democracy and to the dignity of citizens. In his view, any limitation on this specially important right would be unjustified if doing so would run counter to the views of the majority.

Aileen Kavanagh, one of many scholars who have given critical attention to Waldron's work on participatory democracy, has responded by questioning

[4] See C Goetze, *The Distinction of Peace: A Social Analysis for Peacebuilding* (University of Michigan Press 2017) where she favours a broad conception of peacebuilding as 'a catch-all term to describe efforts ... to *restore or construct a peaceful society in the wake—or even in the midst—of conflict*' (our emphasis). In our view, this conception of peacebuilding extends to mechanisms and processes aimed at the entrenchment and consolidation of democracy in postconflict societies. In this regard see, eg, CT Call and SE Cook, 'On Democratization and Peacebuilding' (2003) 9 Global Governance 233–46, 235 where the authors see peacebuilding as pertaining to the 'postconflict social and political reconstruction activities aimed at avoiding "a relapse into conflict"'.

[5] See Jeremy Waldron, *Law and Disagreement* (OUP 1999).

[6] J Waldron, 'Participation: The Right of Rights' (1998) 98 Proceedings of the Aristotelian Society New Series 307–37.

whether '*all* political decisions should be made by majoritarian means'[7] and disagrees that 'giving people a say' in the political decision-making of majoritarian institutions is more important than decisional outcomes.[8] Her view is that although the right to democratic participation is valuable in and of itself, it does not negate the centrality of what she refers to as the 'instrumental condition of good government'[9] whereby 'political decision-making mechanisms should be chosen (primarily) on the basis of their conduciveness to good results'.[10] For Kavanagh, such good results lie in securing, amongst other things, 'the dignity of inclusion, respect for people's views, a sense of belonging'[11] but also in ensuring that citizens are able to influence the nature and character of political decisions 'so that they reflect or implement [citizen] views about some aspect of good government'.[12]

While Waldron's focus is largely on the participatory work of legislatures and in the context of a specific attack on judicial review of legislation as being counter-majoritarian, the Waldron–Kavanagh debate resonates strongly with the theme that emerges from our respective chapters. Our view is that the purpose of involving citizens in peacebuilding is not to yield to the views of the citizen majority in Waldron's sense but, rather, to perform an instrumental, good governance function along the lines proposed by Kavanagh. In other words, we argue that procedural values ought not to be applied in a majoritarian or consensus-driven manner, particularly if doing so would undermine the transitional justice project by: (1) impeding necessary action on the part of the state, in the case of Colombia; or (2) coercing the government into acceding to violent demands by citizens, in the case of South Africa. Rather, the key objective of involving the citizenry in transitional justice processes is to encourage greater 'political inclusion' by citizens and, in fact, *all* stakeholders by providing real opportunities to make submissions to such processes. This theme is developed more fully in Section 3 of this chapter.

Considering the Colombian context first, the government's decision to hold a plebiscite to legitimate the 2016 Peace Agreement, which would bring an end to a fifty-year conflict between the government and the FARC-EP, is an apt example of the *undermining* potential of procedural values, and the participation principle in particular.[13] Confronted with the choice of voting either *Yes* or *No* to the terms of the agreement—and in a surprise turn of events—the citizenry voted marginally *against* the agreement. In deciding on the legal status of this outcome, the Colombian Constitutional Court concluded that if the government chose to use

[7] A Kavanagh, 'Participation and Judicial Review: A Reply to Jeremy Waldron' (2003) 22(5) Law and Philosophy 451–86, 457.
[8] ibid 453.
[9] For this Kavanagh (ibid 460) relies on the work of Joseph Raz in *Ethics in the Public Domain: Essays in the Morality of Law and Politics* (Clarendon Press 1994) 117.
[10] Kavanagh (n 7) 451.
[11] ibid 463.
[12] ibid.
[13] Law 1806 of 2016 established the plebiscite.

the plebiscite mechanism to facilitate citizen involvement in the peace process—and the people voted against it—then the popular decision would be binding.[14] In these circumstances, the Court explained that 'the duty of the President of the Republic is to respect this decision and refrain from implementing it as it is'.[15] The Court, however, gave the President a way forward stating that this pronouncement does not 'neutralize [the President's] constitutional obligation to achieve peace (art. 22), and *thus he must pursue other ways of materialising this imperative*'.[16] In light thereof, the government was forced to change parts of the agreement. However, cognisant of the risks of again relying on the plebiscite mechanism to involve the citizenry in the peace process, the government decided to dispense with the participatory requirement entirely by passing the amended agreement *without* involving the Colombian population directly.

The *No* in the plebiscite is a clear example of how a particular conception of citizen involvement within a transitional justice framework can *undermine* peace if a simplistic, majoritarian approach is followed. While it is clear that the views of the Colombian citizens in respect of the peace process and ensuing agreement mattered and ought to have been brought to bear on its terms, the vital point is that a plebiscite was not the appropriate mechanism for doing so. This is because it forced a binary choice between 'Yes' or 'No', which did not allow people to express more nuanced support for some provisions and not others. It also failed to address the fact that some parts of the country were more affected by the conflict than others yet it gave every individual an equal say, thereby allowing those less affected to determine whether those more affected would live in peace. Indeed, what these events show is that a plebiscite is not well suited to the goal of ensuring citizen involvement in peacebuilding and that, in fact, adhering to a political majoritarianism of this kind can actually run counter to the achievement of peace. This is particularly in circumstances where there is an urgent necessity of bringing an end to a long-running and destructive conflict, as the Colombian case shows. In the end, the state may, at times, need to make decisions that run contrary to the views of the majority of the population (or, in the Colombian case, the majority of citizens that participated in the 2016 plebiscite). What was, however, required in the Colombian context was to involve citizens in the peace process through providing them with *qualitative* opportunities to influence the character of the negotiations and subsequent decisional outcomes. Doing so would have given them a sense that they were active and informed participants in the transitional justice project and also, that their views mattered and were genuinely taken into account.

In the South African context, it would be helpful to highlight how an approach that requires government to accede to violent demands made by citizens could

[14] C-379/16 (Colombian Constitutional Court).

[15] C-699/16 (Colombian Constitutional Court), 20.3.

[16] ibid (emphasis added).

undermine rather than *support* long-term peace. Cachalia's chapter, to recap, explores the possible causes driving the high levels of violent protest action in South Africa and in so doing, argues that there is both a substantive component driving the violence (a demand for more equitable allocation of vital state goods and resources) as well as a procedural component (a demand for better quality democratic engagement between citizens and the state).[17] While her chapter's core focus is on the latter procedural aspect, she does give some attention to the ways in which just procedures can advance distributive claims through, for example, better quality decisions that are more likely to lead to just outcomes. Cachalia's argument is not, however, that the government—in extending procedural rights to citizens—must always agree to their substantive demands, particularly where violence becomes the preferred strategy for compelling favourable government action.[18] At times, the government will need to make impartial and, often unpopular, decisions that impact negatively on the allocation of state resources to certain groups and communities.[19] The effect of this is that while the rights of protestors to peaceful protest and democratic expression—as the 'lifeblood of democracy'[20]—must be respected and staunchly defended, the government cannot be strong-armed by citizens seeking to use violence or threats thereof to secure specific distributive outcomes. In fact, acceding to violent demands in these circumstances is likely to counter attempts at entrenching peace and consolidating democracy in the long term, even if doing so can assuage violent action in the short term.

Take, for example, the violent protests in the context of #FeesMustFall. Since 2015, this movement has been driving a sustained campaign for fee-free higher

[17] Her argument in the latter sense is, in essence, that a genuine commitment to procedural justice can encourage better decisional outcomes and a feeling of political inclusion among citizens, which can translate into wider respect for government decisions and deepen the sense of legitimacy in political institutions. This, she argues, is important for assuaging societal tensions and developing a culture of more peaceful and constructive resolution of societal conflict.

[18] In the context of the violence associated with the #FeesMustFall protests at South African universities, see L Lancaster and M Diallo, 'Solving SA's student protests must start with meaningful engagement' *Institute for Security Studies* (7 October 2016) <https://issafrica.org/iss-today/solving-sas-student-protests-must-start-with-meaningful-engagement> accessed 3 October 2022.

[19] As indicated in a recent South African Local Government Association (SALGA) report '*Community Protest: Local Government Perceptions* (2015) <https://www.salga.org.za/Documents/Documents%20and%20Publications/Publications/Community%20Protest%202016%20WITHOUT%20BLEED.pdf> accessed 3 October 2022, '[s]tate resources are finite and the state cannot be expected to provide cradle to grave resource packages amid dwindling natural resources and deepening cyclical downturns in the global economy'. Chaskalson CJ also noted this reality in *Soobramoney v Minister of Health (Kwazulu-Natal)* [1997] ZACC 17; 1998 (1) SA 765 (CC) [11], affirming that the practical realisation of social rights' claims (and the state's obligations for their advancement) are, 'dependent upon the resources available for [particular] purposes, and that the corresponding rights themselves are limited by reason of the lack of resources. Given this lack of resources and the significant demands on them that have already been referred to, an unqualified obligation to meet these needs would not presently be capable of being fulfilled.'

[20] A Habib, 'Understanding violent protest in South Africa and the difficult choice facing leaders' *The Conversation* (8 November 2020) <https://theconversation.com/understanding-violent-protest-in-south-africa-and-the-difficult-choice-facing-leaders-148751> accessed 3 October 2022.

education at tertiary institutions in South Africa. The movement has often included elements of violence over the years by protesting parties, including widespread damage and destruction to property and infrastructure at many tertiary institutions across the country.[21] Following cyclical protests in 2015 and 2016, in late 2017 former President Jacob Zuma announced that, from 2018 onwards, there would be free higher education for first-year students with a combined household income below a certain threshold.[22] This policy position flew in the face of an earlier report by the Heher Commission of Inquiry into Higher Education and Training in South Africa (2017). The Commission found, in short, that there was no capacity within the government for extending free tertiary education to all those unable to finance their education, let alone across the board to all students.[23]

The effect of the former President's announcement was thus to override the Heher Commission's earlier feasibility conclusions and, in so doing, to put in motion a new policy trajectory geared at implementing fee-free higher education for certain income groups. In response, Lancaster and Mouctar have remarked that these violent protests

> set a precedent that it is possible to force the government to concede to demands without negotiation. That is why, unlike the relatively disciplined protests in 2015, we are now increasingly seeing violence in the form of the destruction of property, the intimidation of those who hold different views and death threats.[24]

It is significant to note that the levels of violence pertaining to student fees at tertiary institutions has not abated. This is notwithstanding the implementation of the government's fee-free higher education policy since 2018. In fact, in 2021, the protests again erupted with students demanding immediate and in fact further fee-free related undertakings from government.[25] Compounding this already politically fraught situation has been the perceived militarisation and securitisation of

[21] See, in general, M Langa and others (Commissioned by Centre for the Study of Violence and Reconciliation), '#Hashtag: An analysis of the #FeesMustFall movement at South African universities' (2017) <https://www.csvr.org.za/pdf/An-analysis-of-the-FeesMustFall-Movement-at-South-African-universities.pdf> accessed 3 October 2022.

[22] See, the former President's full statement on fee-free higher education <https://assets.documentcloud.org/documents/4330257/16-December-2017-Chancellor.pdf> accessed 3 October 2022.

[23] The full Heher Commission report is available here <http://www.thepresidency.gov.za/sites/default/files/Commission%20of%20Inquiry%20into%20Higher%20Education%20Report.pdf> accessed 3 October 2022.

[24] Lancaster and Diallo (n 18).

[25] These claims relate to the expungement of pre-2018 historical debt and to address the plight of those that earned above the R350,000 threshold (the so-called missing middle). See, in this regard, F Moosa, 'FMF 2021: Historic debt, the missing middle and free education explained' *Daily Vox* (18 March 2021) <https://www.thedailyvox.co.za/fmf-2021-historic-debt-the-missing-middle-and-free-education-explained/> accessed 3 October 2022.

university campuses and the apparently disproportionate and heavy-handed police response to the student protests in some circumstances.[26]

Overall, these events and the ensuing violence—from a range of actors—have yielded significant political instability in the country and pose a genuine threat to the democratic health and stability of South Africa's transitional justice project. #FeesMustFall is thus one area that requires us to reflect specifically on what procedural approaches could better advance the goals of transitional justice in the context of the violence that has accompanied the student protests in South Africa. Perhaps more dedicated attention ought to be given to promoting deeper political inclusion by improving the overall *quality* of engagement between all stakeholders—students, the government, and universities—as one of the strategies for tempering the violence in this precarious context.

3. The 'Quality' of Citizen Involvement in Transitional Justice: Political Inclusion Not Formal Democracy

In the previous section we considered the purpose of procedural values in *supporting* the peacebuilding processes of South Africa and Colombia. With reference to two concrete examples—the 2016 Colombian plebiscite, and the #FeesMustFall violent protests in South Africa—we sought to show that the objective of involving citizens ought not to be to acquire their agreement, but to facilitate a deeper process of 'political inclusion'. In this section we reflect on the meaning of 'political inclusion' and focus specifically on what state actors (and other decision-making authorities) can do to ensure meaningful citizen involvement in peacebuilding.

Broadly, we argue that inclusion is not about tokenistic[27] or purely formal involvement—in the sense of a box-ticking exercise or a simplistic majoritarian voting procedure—but must rather be viewed as a means of strengthening the overall quality of decision-making by, for instance, creating a culture of listening,[28] information-sharing, and constructive engagement between citizens and the state. Inclusion in this sense is thus about ensuring that citizens have the ability to influence decisional outcomes, even if those outcomes are not ultimately favourable to them.[29] A further aspect of inclusion—which both of our preceding chapters

[26] See, in general, Langa (n 21). See also S Mahomedy, 'Extra-Judicial Engagement in Socio-Economic Rights Realisation: Lessons from #FeesMustFall' (2020) 36(1) South African Journal on Human Rights 49–73.

[27] On the notion of 'tokenistic' engagement, see Mahomedy (n 26), esp 60–66.

[28] This notion of 'listening' made its appearance in South African judgment in *Doctors for Life International v Speaker of the National Assembly* [2006] ZACC 11; 2006 (6) SA 416 (CC) ('*Doctors for Life*') [234] (Sachs J) and has been developed further by scholars. See, eg, M Bishop, 'Vampire or Prince? The Listening Constitution and *Merafong Demarcation Forum & Others v President of the Republic of South Africa & Others*' (2009) 2 Constitutional Court Review 313.

[29] In the South African context, see *Moutse Demarcation Forum v President of the Republic of South Africa* [2011] ZACC 27; 2011 (11) BCLR 1158 (CC) [62]. See further C Hoexter and G Penfold,

highlight—is the importance of information-sharing and in some cases, a duty to justify decisions through giving reasons. While the state benefits from the information and input it acquires from involving citizens in decision-making, it also performs a crucial role in this respect by, for example, explaining the nature and purpose of certain decisions and processes to citizens in a manner that is accessible and understandable to them. In some instances, it will be necessary for the state to further justify—through reasons—why certain policy proposals have been adopted or why the demands of citizens cannot be agreed to. In the remainder of this section we reflect on how information-sharing and justification could have aided real citizen inclusion in the context of the events leading up to the 2016 plebiscite in Colombia, and the seemingly ineffective engagement processes in the #FeesMustFall violent protests in South Africa.

In the context of the Colombian peace process, it is questionable whether the state discharged its obligations in terms of ensuring that the involvement of citizens in the process of drafting the peace agreement was effective and genuinely inclusive, rather than a mere formal exercise. The political context at the time was such that, following decades of violence and conflict, there was deep distrust in government and public institutions and particularly, a sense of despondency with the quality of public participation processes led by the state. It seems that, for this reason, the first version of the agreement—which formed the basis of the Havana negotiations—explicitly acknowledged that peacebuilding required the involvement of the *whole society*. In response, the Colombian government created a mechanism to accept citizen proposals either in person or through electronic means pertaining to the terms of the agreement.[30] It also carried out activities before the plebiscite to publicise the agreement in different parts of the country, trying to shift public perceptions of the state and regain the much-needed credibility that had been lost during the conflict years.[31]

However, in many respects these processes proved to be quite formalistic and impersonal and failed, ultimately, to legitimate the peace agreement—as the 'No' outcome of the plebiscite revealed. This was because, despite these formal opportunities for citizens to comment and give input on the draft agreement, in many

Administrative Law in South Africa (3rd edn, Juta 2021) 502–03. In the Colombian context, see SU-097/17 and SU-011/18 (Colombian Constitutional Court).

[30] Peace agreement, art 6.6 (General Agreement for the Termination of the Conflict and the Construction of a Stable and Lasting Peace), '[i]n order to guarantee the broadest possible participation, a mechanism will be established to receive proposals on the agenda items from citizens and organizations, by physical or electronic means ... It will be possible to make direct consultations and receive proposals on such items, or delegate to a third party the organization of spaces for participation' see, in this regard, <http://www.indepaz.org.co/wp-content/uploads/2013/04/Acuerdo_general_para_la_terminacion_del_conflicto_y_la_construccion_de_una_paz_estable_y_duradera.pdf> accessed 3 October 2022.

[31] M Paula Saffon and V Tacha, 'La participación en las medidas de justicia transicional. Un estudio comparado' (2018) Dejusticia 17–19.

instances, those same citizens were inadequately informed about the nature and purpose of the peace process and were not given reasons that helped them understand why certain political concessions had to be made in the interests of peace. In other instances, they were actively misinformed through the media and the opposition.

For example, one of the common objections to the terms of the agreement was that it was too lenient on guerrilla commanders responsible for war crimes by allowing them to run for public office and that it encouraged impunity by allowing perpetrators to avoid jail time.[32] It would appear that one of the shortcomings in this approach was that the Colombian government had simply presented the terms of the agreement to the citizens and solicited their views but without a further (arguably necessary) step: to engage further with communities based on the feedback it had received. Overall, it may have been more productive for the state to have dedicated time and resources to engaging directly with certain communities to explain and ultimately justify why guerrilla members and commanders would be subjected to the Special Jurisdiction for Peace, rather than the ordinary processes of the criminal justice system. In particular, it seems that in these highly tense circumstances where citizens felt strongly about accountability for past wrongs, a return to communities to justify this concession to guerilla factions was important. Although such an approach would inevitably carry efficiency trade-offs, it would perhaps have bolstered a feeling of inclusion among citizens by demonstrating to them that their views mattered and were taken into account—even if they could not be acceded to, given the priority of securing peace. This may also, in turn, have shifted public perceptions regarding the legitimacy of the peace agreement.

A further problem pertains to the number of instances of misinformation, which may have further accounted for the 'No' outcome in the plebiscite. Examples include rumours in the media relating to significant fiscal reform, impunity for FARC-EP members, and that Rodrigo 'Timochenko' Londoño, the commander of the FARC-EP, would become President.[33] There were also radio reports directed at lower socio-economic groups suggesting that Colombia would follow the economic path of Venezuela, which made many people in the middle and lower classes believe that they would suffer from poverty if the agreement were passed.[34] A final example pertains to a booklet by the Education Ministry to promote greater tolerance in respect of sexual orientation choices. It appears that the 'No' campaign

[32] See Peace agreement, art 3.2.1.2. Political Representation states that 'When the process for the laying down of arms has been finalised, the plenipotentiaries of the FARC-EP at the Negotiation Table (Mesa de Conversaciones) shall formally declare and register at the National Electoral Council the decision to transform into a political movement or party, the act of constitution, its regulations, the ethics code, the ideological platform and the appointment of its officers'.

[33] See, in this regard 'The questionable campaign strategy of the No' *El Espectador* (6 October 2016) <https://www.elespectador.com/noticias/politica/la-cuestionable-estrategia-de-campana-del-no/> accessed 3 October 2022.

[34] ibid.

took advantage of this situation to attract support from certain religious groups by conveying the impression that the agreement threatened the 'traditional family model' in Colombia.[35] These instances of misinformation resulted in citizens being wrongly informed, which impacted on the quality of their understanding of the peace agreement and the process as a whole.

The upshot is that while citizen involvement was an important objective underpinning the negotiation and drafting of the 2016 Peace Agreement, the quality of their involvement was adversely impacted by the fact that many of the opportunities to give input seemed formal and ineffective in light of the lack of proper information, frequent misinformation, and an absence of adequate justification in response to citizen concerns. Perhaps the outcome of the plebiscite would have been different had there been a deeper and better quality understanding among citizens of the purposes and national priorities underpinning the agreement as well as more effort being directed at correcting misinformation.

In South Africa, in the context of the #FeesMustFall protests and the violence that has unfolded across institutions of higher learning, there has been a developing body of research aimed at highlighting the problems with the quality of engagement between key actors—students, universities, and the government—as one of the driving causes of the violence in this contested area.[36] In this regard, Lancaster and Diallo have called for a new approach to address the violence, one that recognises as the first step 'a more empathetic view of protestors' grievances'[37] and which emphasises 'meaningful and respectful engagement'[38] between all actors to mitigate the violence and find a viable and sustainable future solution to the higher education predicament.

In a similar vein, Mahomedy has recently highlighted the trend in post-apartheid politics for citizen involvement in political discourse to be 'tokenistic' in the sense that citizens are formally engaged with but 'their interests and opinions are not meaningfully taken into account when decisions are ultimately made'.[39] In the #FeesMustFall context specifically, Mahomedy relies on empirical information about what has transpired at some universities to highlight the apparently

[35] 'El rol de las iglesias cristianas evangélicas en la victoria del "No" en el plebiscito de Colombia' *BBC* (5 October 2016) <https://www.bbc.com/mundo/noticias-america-latina-37560320> accessed 3 October 2022.

[36] See, eg, Mahomedy (n 26); Lancaster and Diallo (n 18); and Langa (n 21).

[37] Lancaster and Diallo (n 18).

[38] ibid.

[39] See Mahomedy (n 26) 56 (footnotes omitted) where she explain that 'tokenism' includes informing, consultation, and placation. Informing participants of their rights and the various options available to them is important as a first step, but risks being a 'one-way flow of information'. Placation occurs when stakeholders are permitted to have a voice in the decision-making process, but those in power (eg government) have the final word on the legitimacy and feasibility of the decision without really considering stakeholders' opinions. It is thus a façade for engagement, as participants are placated or appeased by the feeling that they have engaged when in actual fact, their opinions and interests are not meaningfully taken into account when making decisions.

pervasive belief among protesting students that 'across universities ... management engaged with [students] on a tokenistic level ... in the sense that the engagement that took place was a façade and did not really have *any impact* on the decisions made' with 'universities being accused of being insensitive and unsympathetic to the protesters and their cause'.[40] She goes on to explain that this resulted in a relationship breakdown between students and university managements which has 'made it difficult for compromises to be reached and resulted in the students resorting to violence'.[41] In some cases, she refers to an outright unwillingness on the part of university management to engage on key issues at all.[42]

In the end, given the deep social marginalisation and inequitable access to education in South Africa (which is a vital tool for future advancement), the demands by protestors raised legitimate and pressing concerns that required ongoing engagement and a carefully calibrated response from university management and the government. On the other hand, there are genuine concerns about the affordability and desirability of totally fee-free higher education.[43] In this difficult context it would be interesting to reflect on whether engagement mechanisms could be used for the specific purpose of information-sharing with a view to empowering protesting students with the 'real facts' surrounding free-fee feasibility in a way that would be accessible and understandable to them. One suggestion, proposed by Lancaster and Mouctar, is to appoint trained mediators 'to chart a way forward for the future of tertiary education in the country'.[44] Perhaps one such role that mediators could play would be to facilitate the more meaningful sharing of information in this context. The objective would be to demonstrate respect and understanding for the financial plight of students and ultimately, to put students in a position whereby they feel empowered, properly informed, and confident that universities and the government are doing all they can to alleviate the hardships being experienced. Such an approach may assuage the ongoing violence and angry responses from students and perhaps pave the way for more constructive future engagement.

4. Conclusion

In this reflection we have sought to develop the notion of 'political inclusion' as a facet of transitional justice by focusing on the *purpose* of involving citizens in the peacebuilding efforts of the state as well as the *quality* of citizen involvement in this

40 ibid 61 (emphasis added).

41 ibid.

42 ibid (footnotes omitted).

43 SM Muller, 'Free higher education in South Africa: cutting through the lies and statistics' *The Conversation* (24 January 2018) <https://theconversation.com/free-higher-education-in-south-africa-cutting-through-the-lies-and-statistics-90474> accessed 3 October 2022.

44 Lancaster and Diallo (n 18).

context. On the *purpose* side, we explored how a 'majoritarian' or 'consensus-based' conception of democracy can *undermine* peace by frustrating the implementation of action necessary for peace (Colombia) or forcing the government to accede to violent demands by citizens (South Africa). The view we have adopted is that the purpose of involvement lies not in always obtaining majoritarian consent for government decisions but rather, to include individuals meaningfully and effectively in deliberative fora as part of a deeper process of democratic consolidation. On the *quality* side, we sought to tease out the principles that are likely to facilitate citizen inclusion and thereby *support* the peacebuilding efforts of our respective jurisdictions. In this regard we focused on what state actors can do to facilitate a feeling of inclusion in peace discourses by highlighting the value of information-sharing, extended engagement mechanisms, and justification on the part of the state or other decision-making authorities. In this regard we reflected specifically on the information deficit in citizen involvement in the Colombian peace process leading up to the plebiscite and in the context of the violence occasioned by #FeesMustFall. It is our hope that through this comparison we can focus attention on ways in which procedural values can best support the consolidation of peace and democracy in South Africa and Colombia going forward.

THEME 8

THE ROLE OF INTERNATIONAL LAW IN ADVANCING TRANSITIONAL JUSTICE

23

South Africa and the International Criminal Court

Perpetuating the Legacy of Overlooking the *Erga Omnes* Obligation to Prosecute International Crimes by Prioritising Peace

Mispa Roux

1. Introduction

The international crimes of genocide, crimes against humanity, and war crimes are considered gross human rights violations, and are universally condemned for their gravity. In terms of international criminal law, it is of interest to all states in the international community as a whole not only to prevent the commission of these gross human rights violations, but also to end impunity by holding perpetrators individually criminally responsible for their crimes.[1] This amounts to an obligation *erga omnes*, and 'all States can be held to have a legal interest in their protection' which is 'universal' in character.[2] Further, the prohibition of genocide, crimes against humanity, apartheid, and racial discrimination, and the basic rules of international humanitarian law form part of customary international law, and are also recognised as having the status of *jus cogens* (peremptory norms).[3]

[1] M Roux, 'The *Erga Omnes* Obligation to Prevent and Prosecute Gross Human Rights Violations with Special Emphasis upon Genocide and Persecution as a Crime Against Humanity' (2012) African Yearbook on International Humanitarian Law 98.

[2] *Barcelona Traction, Light and Power Company, Limited (Belgium v Spain)* 5 February 1970 ICJ Reports 3 (Judgment) [32]–[34] ('*Barcelona Traction*').

[3] Third Report on Peremptory Norms of General International Law (*Jus Cogens*), D Tladi (Special Rapporteur), Report of the International Law Commission, Official Record of the General Assembly, Seventieth Session, 30 April–1 June and 2 July–10 August 2018 (A/CN.4/714) 12 February 2018 ('Tladi's Third Report'); Draft Conclusion 24, Fourth Report on Peremptory Norms of General International Law (*Jus Cogens*), D Tladi (Special Rapporteur), Report of the International Law Commission, Official Record of the General Assembly, Seventy-First Session, 29 April–7 June and 8 July–9 August 2019 (A/CN.4/727) 31 January 2019 ('Tladi's Fourth Report') para 137; Draft Conclusion 23, Fifth Report on Peremptory Norms of General International Law (*Jus Cogens*), D Tladi (Special Rapporteur), International Law Commission, Seventy-Third Session, 18 April–3 June and 4 July–5 August 2022 (A/CN.4/747) 24 January 2022 ('Tladi's Fifth Report'); Draft Conclusion 23, Peremptory Norms of General International Law (*Jus Cogens*): Texts of the Draft Conclusions and Annex Adopted by the Drafting Committee on Second Reading; Identification and Legal Consequences of Peremptory Norms of General International Law (*Jus Cogens*), International Law Commission, Seventy-Third Session, 18 April–3 June and 4 July–5 August 2022 (A/CN.4/L.967) 11 May 2022 ('2022 Peremptory Norms Draft

Mispa Roux, *South Africa and the International Criminal Court* In: *Transitional Justice, Distributive Justice, and Transformative Constitutionalism.* Edited by: David Bilchitz and Raisa Cachalia, with Magdalena Inés Correa Henao and Nathalia Bautista Pizarro, Oxford University Press. © Mispa Roux 2023. DOI: 10.1093/oso/9780192887627.003.0023

'Transitional justice' is a multidisciplinary field that supports societies in coming to terms with decades of systematic gross human rights violations committed by authoritarian regimes.[4] In order to do so, a combination of various mechanisms must be implemented, including 'prosecution initiatives, truth-seeking, reparations programmes, institutional reform or an appropriate combination thereof'.[5] Implementing these mechanisms holistically seeks to achieve the core objectives of transitional justice, namely the establishment of the rule of law, peace, democracy, the protection of human rights, and very importantly, enabling deeply divided societies to reach reconciliation.[6]

South Africa has a history drenched in gross human rights violations. The colonisation of South Africa followed shortly after European explorers' arrival, later developing into apartheid. Apartheid is still universally recognised as a crime against humanity, and is generally defined as consisting of 'policies and practices of racial segregation and discrimination' with the 'purpose of establishing and maintaining domination by one racial group of persons over any other racial group of persons and systematically oppressing them'.[7] The prohibition of apartheid is recognised as a *jus cogens* norm,[8] and the obligation to outlaw racial discrimination is *erga omnes* in nature.[9] Yet, despite the recognition of apartheid as an international crime, it was decided during the negotiated settlement in the early 1990s that 'Nuremberg-style tribunals were simply not a viable political option, given the balance of military and political forces that prevailed at the time'.[10] Criminal prosecution for apartheid as a crime against humanity[11] was forfeited 'for the purposes of effecting a constructive transition towards a democratic order'.[12] The Promotion of National Unity and

Conclusions'). See further *Arrest Warrant of 11 April 2000 (Democratic Republic of the Congo v Belgium)* 14 February 2002 ICJ Reports 137 (Arrest Warrant Dissenting Opinion of Judge van den Wyngaert) [27]–[28]; *Regina v Bow Street Metropolitan Stipendiary Magistrate and Others, Ex Parte Pinochet Ugarte* (No 3) 24 March 1999 House of Lords (2000) 1 AC 147, [174]–[175], [204], [278] <http://www.uniset.ca/other/cs5/2000AC147.html> accessed 2 August 2022.

4 See in general United Nations Approach to Transitional Justice, Guidance Note of the Secretary-General (March 2010) <https://www.securitycouncilreport.org/atf/cf/%7B65BFCF9B-6D27-4E9C-8CD3-CF6E4FF96FF9%7D/TJ_Guidance_Note_March_2010FINAL.pdf> accessed 26 September 2023 ('UN Approach to TJ') 3; RG Teitel, *Transitional Justice* (OUP 1997) 11; K Christie, 'Transitional Justice: Lessons from the Past' (2009) 6 International Studies Journal 171; International Centre for Transitional Justice, 'What is transitional justice?' (2009) <https://www.ictj.org/sites/default/files/ICTJ-Global-Transitional-Justice-2009-English.pdf> accessed 2 August 2022.

5 UN Approach to TJ (n 4) 3.

6 ibid.

7 International Convention on the Suppression and Punishment of the Crime of Apartheid, art II. See further Rome Statute of the International Criminal Court (ICC Statute), art 7(1)(j) and 7(2)(h).

8 Draft Conclusion 23, 2022 Peremptory Norms Draft Conclusions (n 3).

9 *Barcelona Traction* (n 2) [34].

10 Truth and Reconciliation Commission of South Africa, Report, Volume 1, Chapter 5 para 57 <https://www.justice.gov.za/trc/report/finalreport/Volume%201.pdf> accessed 2 August 2022 ('TRC Report'). See further J Dugard, *Confronting Apartheid: A Personal History of South Africa, Namibia and Palestine* (Jakana Media 2018) 144–47.

11 TRC Report (n 10) 94–102.

12 *The Azanian Peoples' Organisation and others v The President of the Republic of South Africa and others* 1996 (4) SA 672 (CC) [32] ('*AZAPO*').

Reconciliation Act instead established the Truth and Reconciliation Commission (TRC). The main objective of the TRC was 'to establish the truth in relation to past events', as well as to achieve 'reconciliation between the people of South Africa and the reconstruction of society'.[13] The Committee on Amnesty could grant amnesty for acts, omissions, and offences 'associated with a political objective committed in the course of the conflicts of the past',[14] and for which the applicant 'made a full disclosure of all relevant facts'.[15] No criminal or civil liability could result after the granting of such amnesty.[16]

Then, in the early 2000s, the South African government seemingly moved away from the argument that international criminal prosecution of international crimes is not 'a viable political option',[17] and played a pivotal role in the negotiations and establishment of the International Criminal Court (ICC).[18] However, in 2015, the South African government started the procedure of withdrawing its membership from the ICC, shortly after its controversial failure to arrest then-President Al-Bashir of the Sudan in accordance with ICC arrest warrants.[19] This event heralded the onset of a very ambivalent, and at times acrimonious, relationship with the Court. Since then the South African government has mainly argued that it considers the obligation imposed by the ICC to arrest persons accused of international crimes a hindrance in its role of promoting 'peace, stability and dialogue' in states 'in which serious conflicts occur or have occurred',[20] and further that it supports

[13] Post-amble of the Constitution of the Republic of South Africa, Act 200 of 1993 (Interim Constitution); Preamble of the Promotion of National Unity and Reconciliation Act 34 of 1995 ('Truth and Reconciliation Act').

[14] Truth and Reconciliation Act, s 20(1)(b).

[15] ibid s 20(1)(c).

[16] ibid s 20(7).

[17] TRC Report (n 10) [57].

[18] South Africa signed the Rome Statute of the International Criminal Court (ICC Statute) on 17 July 1998, and deposited its instrument of ratification on 27 November 2000 <https://asp.icc-cpi.int/states-parties/african-states/south-africa> accessed 2 August 2022.

[19] See further Declaratory Statement by the Republic of South Africa on the Decision to Withdraw from the Rome Statute of the International Criminal Court, United Nations Treaty Collection, reference: CN786.2016.TREATIES-XVIII.10 (Depositary Notification), 19 October 2016 ('SA Withdrawal Notice'); Implementation of the Rome Statute of the International Criminal Court Act Repeal Bill (B23–2016); *The Prosecutor v Omar Hassan Ahmad Al-Bashir* 6 July 2017 ICC-02/05-01/09 (decision under the Rome Statute, s 87(7) on the non-compliance by South Africa with the request by the court for the arrest and surrender of Omar Al-Bashir) (ICC non-compliance decision); *Southern Africa Litigation Centre v Minister of Justice and Constitutional Development* 2015 5 SA 1 (GP) ('*SALC v Minister of Justice*'); *Minister of Justice and Constitutional Development v Southern Africa Litigation Centre* 2016 3 SA 317 (SCA) ('*Minister of Justice v SALC*'); *Democratic Alliance v Minister of International Relations and Cooperation and others* 2017 (3) SA 212 (GP) ('*DA v Minister of DIRCO*'); Withdrawal of Notification of Withdrawal, United Nations Treaty Collection, reference: cn121.2017.treAtieS-XViii.10 (Depositary Notification), 7 March 2017; International Crimes Bill (B37–2017); M Roux, 'Obstacles to the Prevention of Gross Human Rights Violations' (2018) Tydskrif vir die Suid-Afrikaanse Reg/Journal of South African Law 106, 113–15.

[20] International Crimes Bill, Preamble, ss 6, 24, and 28. See further Opening Statement by Adv Michael Masutha, Minister of Justice and Correctional Services, General Debate, Sixteenth Session of the Assembly of States Parties to the Rome Statute, 4–14 December 2017 ('Masutha Statement'). Over the years South Africa's emphasis on the promotion of 'peace, stability and dialogue' in relation to its intended withdrawal from the ICC has gradually transformed into a general official governmental

the notion that senior government officials enjoy immunity in terms of customary international law.[21] Proceedings to withdraw from ICC membership have been halted for the time being, but it is uncertain whether this could safely be interpreted as an indicator that South Africa will comply with its obligations towards the Court.[22]

In this chapter, it will be argued that South Africa's oscillating relationship with the ICC continues to be retrogressive in nature and prioritises, once again, peace over the achievement of international criminal justice. Undeniably, the respective contexts of the negotiated settlement and the current relationship with the ICC are different; however, alarming parallels can be drawn. In the 1990s, *amnesty* for a crime against humanity was preferred as a transitional justice mechanism to ensure peace and stability within South Africa. Currently, a preference is shown for granting *immunity* for international crimes, this time to ensure peace and stability on the African continent and continued good political relations with other states with whom South Africa has strong historical ties. Consequently, several large questions are raised concerning whether one should prioritise peace, or international criminal justice? Should countries prioritise complying with the *erga omnes* obligation to prosecute international crimes, or permitting senior government officials to enjoy personal and functional immunity for committing such crimes? Should we yield to the fear that, unless we bestow immunity on powerful political elites, instead of peace, 'a bloody revolution, sooner rather than later, [will be] inevitable'?[23] Lastly, should a choice even exist, or should we rather be balancing peace and justice as 'mutually reinforcing imperatives'?[24]

policy when it comes to dealing with international crimes. This can be illustrated by two recent examples: first, its failure to cooperate with repeated requests of the Office of the Prosecutor of the International Residual Mechanism for Criminal Tribunals to arrest or locate Fulgence Kayishema, who is charged with committing genocide and crimes against humanity in Rwanda. The second example relates to South Africa's approach to the Ukraine-Russia armed conflict that erupted in February 2022. In an official statement Minister of International Relations and Cooperation, Naledi Pandor, strongly emphasised 'peaceful dialogue', 'mediation', 'negotiation', 'diplomacy', and 'constructive solutions', and stated that South Africa's position is 'non-aligned'. See further Progress report of the Prosecutor of the International Residual Mechanism for Criminal Tribunals, Serge Brammertz, for the period from 16 November 2021 to 18 May 2022, Annex II to the letter dated 19 May 2022 from the President of the International Residual Mechanism for Criminal Tribunals addressed to the President of the Security Council, S/2022/404, 19 May 2022, paras 34–35; Statement by the Minister of International Relations and Cooperation, Dr Naledi Pandor, during the Media Briefing on the Russia/Ukraine Conflict, South African government <https://www.gov.za/speeches/minister-naledi-pandor-russia-ukraine-conflict-8-apr-2022-0000> accessed 1 August 2022.

[21] International Crimes Bill, Preamble, s 3, and Memorandum; *SALC v Minister of Justice* (n 19) [28]; *Minister of Justice v SALC* (n 19) [14], [16], [49]–[50]; and *DA v Minister of DIRCO* (n 19) [3]–[4], [65]–[66].

[22] 'Hansard: The Bill has been withdrawn in accordance with Assembly Rule 334', Parliamentary Monitoring Group, 10 March 2023 <https://pmg.org.za/hansard/36527/> accessed 14 April 2023 ('International Crimes Bill withdrawal').

[23] RJ Goldstone, 'Justice as a Tool for Peacemaking: Truth Commissions and International Criminal Tribunals' (1996) 28 New York University Journal of International Law and Politics 485, 493.

[24] UN Approach to TJ (n 4) 4.

This chapter will engage with these large questions. First, I shall discuss the *erga omnes* obligation to prosecute international crimes and contend that this will require refusing to grant perpetrators of international crimes immunity from prosecution. In Section 3 of the chapter, I will consider the gradual development of the field of transitional justice, specifically by engaging with its three distinct phases as identified by Ruti Teitel.[25] Of specific relevance for this chapter are the second and current phases: the second being characterised by favouring truth commissions and the granting of amnesty over criminal prosecution, whereas the current phase is characterised by a holistic approach that favours the implementation of a wide variety of mechanisms designed to assist in addressing the commission of international crimes. It will become clear in Section 3 that the objective of transitional justice to establish peace alongside justice is, in my view, complementary to the *erga omnes* obligation to prosecute international crimes. The focus will then shift in Sections 4 and 5 to the South African context. It will be shown that the negotiated settlement, which took place during the second phase of transitional justice, is flawed when viewed through a contemporary transitional justice lens, despite the 'hard choices'[26] that made sense at the time to try and resolve the fundamental conflicts in South Africa. Finally it will be shown that South Africa, by not explicitly aligning its foreign policy with the aims of international criminal justice, may lead to a breach of the *erga omnes* obligation to prosecute international crimes as well as the holistic approach that must be followed in terms of transitional justice. The establishment of peace and the achievement of justice should never be seen as a zero-sum game, but as truly a 'mutually reinforcing [imperative]'.[27]

Before delving into these issues, I would like to address how this chapter fits into the larger conceptual framework of this book. In this chapter, South Africa's repeated prioritisation of peace over justice will be critiqued through an international criminal justice lens. Transitional justice and transformative constitutionalism intersect with international criminal justice in that the latter is *one* of the legal avenues through which societies ravaged by gross human rights violations could become reconciled with their legacy, thereby assisting in the creation of a new constitutional democratic order. Other transitional justice mechanisms discussed in the book are illustrative thereof that justice, reconciliation, and accountability will only be achieved through the cumulative implementation of all these various approaches. International criminal justice as a whole includes elements of both retributive and restorative justice: it is retributive in the sense that perpetrators are punished for their crimes, and restorative by way of victim participation in proceedings, as well as various reparation mechanisms. In turn, the different forms of reparation such as restitution, compensation, and satisfaction can all

25 RG Teitel, 'Transitional Justice Genealogy' (2003) 16 Harvard Human Rights Journal 69.
26 *AZAPO* (n 12) [44].
27 UN Approach to TJ (n 4) 4.

be seen to achieve in the domestic setting some measure of distributive justice, whilst symbolic reparation by way of art and memorial museums helps address the society's traumatic history.

2. The *Erga Omnes* Obligation to Prosecute International Crimes

As stated earlier, the obligation to prevent and prosecute the international crimes of genocide, crimes against humanity, and war crimes amount to an *erga omnes* obligation.[28] The ICC has jurisdiction over these crimes, and they are considered 'the most serious crimes of concern to the international community as a whole'.[29] Further, norms of customary international law from which no derogations are allowed are *jus cogens* norms, and include the prohibition of the aforementioned international crimes.[30] *Jus cogens* norms are defined as follows in the Vienna Convention on the Law of Treaties:

> [A] peremptory norm of general international law is a norm accepted and recognized by the international community of States as a whole as a norm from which no derogation is permitted and which can be modified only by a subsequent norm of general international law having the same character.[31]

Both obligations *erga omnes* and *jus cogens* norms reinforce customary international law, specifically because there are significant overlaps between the two:

> [T]o contend that an obligation *erga omnes* may be derogated from would amount to denying its very nature as an obligation designed to protect fundamental values, the respect for which is an interest of the whole international community ... Both the notion of *erga omnes* and that of *jus cogens* aim at the same result, that is, to prevent states from freely disposing of, and disregarding, values safeguarded by international customary rules.[32]

The International Law Commission (ILC) has extensively discussed the concept of *jus cogens* norms in international law since 1966.[33] In 2001, the ILC included the

[28] *Barcelona Traction* (n 2) [32]–[34].

[29] ICC Statute, Preamble and arts 1 and 5.

[30] Draft Conclusion 23, 2022 Peremptory Norms Draft Conclusions (n 3).

[31] Vienna Convention on the Law of Treaties, art 53.

[32] A Cassese, 'The Character of the Violated Obligation' in J Crawford, A Pellet, S Olleson (eds), and K Parlett (assistant ed), *The Law of International Responsibility* (OUP 2010) 415, 417–18.

[33] Commentary to art 50, para 3 at 248 of the International Law Commission's Commentary to the Draft Articles on the Law of Treaties, *Yearbook of the International Law Commission, Volume II, Documents of the Second Part of the Seventeenth Session and of the Eighteenth Session including the Reports of the Commission to the General Assembly* (1966) (A/CN.4/SER.A/1966/Add.1).

concept of *jus cogens* norms in its Draft Articles on the Responsibility of States for Internationally Wrongful Acts,[34] and the Commentary thereto stated that 'those peremptory norms that are clearly accepted and recognised include the prohibitions of aggression, genocide, slavery, racial discrimination, crimes against humanity and torture, and the right to self-determination'.[35] Then, in 2006 the ILC Study Group on the Fragmentation of International Law adopted a document entitled *Difficulties Arising from the Diversification and Expansion of International Law*, which contained its conclusions.[36] In this document, the ILC Study Group recognised that even though it is 'not generally appropriate' to draw up a hierarchical structure of norms and rules in international law, it is true that 'some rules of international law are more important than other rules and for this reason enjoy a superior position or special status in the international legal system'.[37] Topping this hierarchical structure are *jus cogens* norms,[38] followed by article 103 of the UN Charter,[39] the UN Charter in general,[40] obligations *erga omnes*,[41] and, finally, the other sources mentioned in article 38(1) of the ICJ Statute.[42] Specific importance is attached to the correlation between *jus cogens* norms and *erga omnes* obligations: all obligations to prohibit *jus cogens* norms are also *erga omnes* obligations, yet '[n]ot all *erga omnes* obligations are established by peremptory norms of general international law'.[43] Finally, the topic of *jus cogens* norms was included in the ILC's long-term programme of work in 2015,[44] and the international crimes of genocide, crimes against humanity, apartheid, and racial discrimination, as well as the basic rules of international humanitarian law were again pointed out as being 'the most widely recognised examples of peremptory norms of general international law (*jus cogens*)'.[45]

Forming part of the *erga omnes* obligation to prosecute international crimes, is that impunity for perpetrators must be avoided. However, it is also important to balance the principle of the sovereign equality of states with the *erga omnes* obligation to prosecute international crimes. The principle of sovereign equality means

[34] Article 40 of the International Law Commission's Commentary to the Articles on the Responsibility of States for Internationally Wrongful Acts ('ILC Articles on State Responsibility').

[35] Commentary to art 26, para 5 at 208, of the ILC Articles on State Responsibility, *Report of the International Law Commission, Official Records of the General Assembly, Fifty-Third Session*, 23 April–1 June, and 2 July–10 August 2001, Supplement 10 (A/56/10).

[36] Conclusions of the work of the ILC Study Group on the Fragmentation of International Law: Difficulties arising from the Diversification and Expansion of International Law, 58th Session (A/61/10, para 251) 2006.

[37] ibid para 31.

[38] ibid paras 32–33.

[39] ibid paras 35 and 41.

[40] ibid paras 36 and 40.

[41] ibid paras 37–39.

[42] ibid para 31.

[43] ibid paras 37–38.

[44] Report of the International Law Commission, Official Records of the General Assembly, Sixty-Seventh Session, 4 May–5 June and 6 July–7 August 2015, Supplement 10 (A/70/10) paras 21 and 286.

[45] Draft Conclusion 24, Tladi's Fourth Report (n 3) para 137.

that states have to consent to any obligations imposed upon them, in contrast to the *erga omnes* obligation to prosecute international crimes, which is imposed on the international community as a whole irrespective of whether an individual state agrees with the obligation or not.[46] The core of the need to find a balance, is the notion that in public international law, certain principles, norms, rules, and obligations enjoy primacy over others,[47] and states have to adhere to these to comply with public international law. Should senior government officials be granted procedural immunity, as at its most basic this will mean that they will be unaccountable for their conduct? Yet, should they be prosecuted, there is the possibility that it may have a negative impact on the long-term achievement of peace, as was argued in the South African transitional context.

The content and meaning of immunity for international crimes in general,[48] and the customary international law rule on foreign state immunity within national courts in particular, has been the subject of vigorous debate for several years and is yet to be concluded.[49] With regards to immunity at international criminal courts and tribunals, the Appeals Chamber of the ICC held in 2019 that article 27(2) of the ICC Statute enjoys the status of customary international law,[50] whereas the immunity of government officials at the national courts of foreign states has been addressed by the ILC since 1949,[51] and was included in its programme of work in 2006.[52] Further, in 2018 ILC Special Rapporteur Dire Tladi engaged at length with the controversial question of immunity for *jus cogens* crimes,[53] and summarised the prevailing argument by stating that absolute immunity for official governmental acts carried out whilst in office ('immunity *rationae materiae*') does not apply to such crimes.[54] One of the current positions in international criminal

[46] BD Lepard, *Customary International Law: A New Theory with Practical Applications* (CUP 2010) 7.

[47] Conclusions of the work of the ILC Study Group on the Fragmentation of International Law: Difficulties arising from the Diversification and Expansion of International Law, Fifty-Eighth Session (A/61/10, para 251) 2006, Chapter 12.

[48] Draft Conclusion 23, Tladi's Third Report (n 3) paras 121–32, and 160; Draft Conclusion 23, 2022 Peremptory Norms Draft Conclusions (n 3).

[49] Report of the International Law Commission, Fifty-Eighth Session, 1 May–9 June and 3 July–11 August 2006, *Official Records of the General Assembly, Fifty-Eighth Session, Supplement No 10* (A/61/10) Annex A paras 1–13 ('2006 ILC Report'); Eighth Report on Immunity of State Officials from Foreign Criminal Jurisdiction, CE Hernández (Special Rapporteur), Report of the International Law Commission, Seventy-Second Session, 27 April–5 June and 6 July–7 August 2020, 4 July–5 August 2022, (A/CN.4/739) 28 February 2020 ('Hernández Eighth Report'); 2018 ILC Report (n 44) paras 326–30; Report of the International Law Commission, Seventy-Second Session, 26 April–4 June and 5 July–6 August 2021, *Official Records of the General Assembly, Seventy-Sixth Session, Supplement No 10* (A/76/10) Chapter VI 95–133 ('2021 ILC Report'); Current status of the work of the Commission and forthcoming deadlines, International Law Commission (6 June 2022) <https://legal.un.org/ilc/status.shtml> accessed 2 August 2022 ('ILC 2022 Current Status').

[50] *The Prosecutor v Omar Hassan Ahmad Al-Basir* ICC-02/05-01/09 OA2 (Judgment in the Jordan Referral re Al-Bashir Appeal) 6 May 2019, [3]–[4].

[51] 2006 ILC Report (n 49).

[52] ibid para 257.

[53] Tladi's Third Report (n 3) para 113.

[54] ibid para 160.

law is that it excludes immunity for *any* person accused of international crimes, irrespective of the level of seniority of the person, or whether or not the person is still in office or no longer in office.[55] This viewpoint is supported in this chapter, specifically because it is considered to be in line with the *erga omnes* obligation to prosecute international crimes, and granting immunity to a perpetrator would contradict this in its entirety.

The following section will consider transitional justice first from an international criminal justice lens, and thereafter the way in which it transpired in the South African negotiated settlement.

3. Transitional Justice from an International Criminal Justice Lens

Ruti Teitel identifies three phases forming part of the development of transitional justice, or the 'transitional justice genealogy' as she phrases it: the first taking place after the Second World War,[56] the second during political transitions in the 1990s,[57] and finally, the phase we are currently in.[58] The first phase was the 'heyday of international justice': international criminal prosecution was preferred over national prosecutions, and for the first time, the application of public international law extended beyond the consent-based regulation of relations between sovereign equal states to one where it found moral application to individuals that committed international crimes.[59] The second phase was characterised by political transitions from authoritarianism to democracy—where truth commissions were preferred over criminal tribunals, whether international or national, and amnesty over criminal punishment.[60] Decision-making was greatly influenced by the unique political context within a particular state, and transitional justice incorporated restorative and reconciliatory justice mechanisms.[61] The objectives of truth commissions were to heal and rebuild post-authoritarian societies as a whole, with the insertion into the law of moral and theological philosophies around forgiveness, mercy, and redemption, in order to achieve peace and reconciliation.[62] Individual states asserted jurisdiction over human rights violations committed on their territory.[63]

55 *Arrest Warrant* Dissenting Opinion of Judge van den Wyngaert (n 3) [57]; *Al-Adsani v the United Kingdom* Case No 35763/91, Grand Chamber, European Court of Human Rights (Judgment) 21 November 2001 ('*Al-Adsani*') [61].
56 Teitel, 'TJ Geneology' (n 25) 72–74.
57 ibid 75–89.
58 ibid 89–93.
59 ibid 72–73.
60 ibid 76.
61 ibid 77–78.
62 ibid 75–89.
63 ibid 88.

The third transitional justice phase we are currently in, is one where international criminal justice in particular has become 'normalised', and individual criminal responsibility for the commission of international crimes has become a 'routine matter under international law'.[64] Mechanisms implemented in responding to gross human rights violations are balanced and holistic.[65] The most recognisable symbol of the current phase is the ICC, a permanent transitional justice mechanism.[66] The purpose of the ICC is to investigate and prosecute 'the most serious crimes of concern to the international community as a whole', and 'that deeply shock the conscience of humanity'.[67] The principle of complementarity forms a key component of the entire ICC apparatus:[68] the Court will only exercise jurisdiction if a national court with the required jurisdiction over international crimes illustrates its inability or unwillingness to respond.[69] This principle reflects the holistic nature of the current international criminal justice system, as the ICC's jurisdiction is in essence *subordinate* to domestic prosecution: it *complements* national courts' jurisdiction. The Preamble of the ICC Statute explicitly states that prosecution-measures must be taken 'at the national level', and that 'international cooperation' must be enhanced.

The United Nations (UN) interprets transitional justice as the 'the full range of processes and mechanisms associated with a society's attempt to come to terms with a legacy of large-scale past abuses, in order to ensure accountability, serve justice and achieve reconciliation'.[70] Further, 'both judicial and non-judicial processes and mechanisms' are crucial,[71] which include components of 'prosecution initiatives, truth-seeking, reparations programmes, institutional reform or an appropriate combination thereof'.[72] International norms and principles forming the basis for the UN's work on transitional justice consist of international human rights, humanitarian, criminal, and refugee law, as well as the various obligations in terms of these legal frameworks.[73]

The UN recognises that the national political context, unique to a state in transition, is crucial in choosing appropriate mechanisms.[74] In some instances, states 'emerging from years of ... repressive rule may be unable or unwilling to conduct effective investigations and prosecutions',[75] mainly to achieve 'the broader objectives of [the] prevention of further conflict, peacebuilding and reconciliation'.[76]

[64] ibid 90.
[65] ibid 89–93.
[66] ibid.
[67] ICC Statute, Preamble and arts 1 and 5.
[68] ibid.
[69] ibid art 17.
[70] UN Approach to TJ (n 4) 3.
[71] ibid.
[72] ibid.
[73] ibid.
[74] ibid 8.
[75] ibid.
[76] ibid 3.

However, the complete relinquishing of investigations and prosecutions of international crimes is not supported: '[t]he question for the UN is never *whether* to pursue accountability and justice, but rather *when* and *how*'.[77] Therefore, role-players during a transitional period may choose not to prosecute international crimes domestically, but 'prosecution initiatives', whether at international, regional, or local level, must still take place. Thus, the thrust of the current approach to transitional justice is to establish peace alongside justice, and emphasises that individual criminal responsibility is an essential component of transitional justice.[78] That view, in turn, illustrates emphatically that achieving peace is not seen as contradictory but complementary to the *erga omnes* obligation to prosecute international crimes.[79] The next section will illustrate how this is particularly relevant in the South African context, as the opposite view was followed, namely that the prosecution of apartheid as a crime against humanity had to be forfeited in the interest of establishing peace in the country.[80]

4. Transitional Justice in South Africa: The Negotiated Settlement

Transitional justice mechanisms implemented in South Africa in the 1990s successfully served as a 'bridge' between parliamentary sovereignty and racial oppression[81] to a system where the rule of law, democracy, and human rights became entrenched in the Constitution.[82] However, entrenchment in the Constitution does not signify its achievement: transitional justice is of a continuous nature that will take many years to accomplish.[83] In order to achieve the objectives of transitional justice, a complete societal reform is required, signifying that 'South Africa is in a state of permanent transition'.[84]

The framework for the South African transitional justice mechanism was informed by the Post-amble of the Interim Constitution and the Promotion of National Unity and Reconciliation Act. It included concepts such as peace, democracy, human rights, national unity, reconciliation, truth, reconstruction of

[77] ibid 4 (own emphasis).
[78] ibid 7–8.
[79] Tladi's Third Report (n 3) paras 118–19. See further in this regard, Roux, '*Erga Omnes*' (n 1).
[80] *AZAPO* (n 12) [32].
[81] ibid [19] and [48]; Post-amble of the interim Constitution; E Mureinik, 'A Bridge to Where? Introducing the Interim Bill of Rights' (1994) South African Journal on Human Rights 31; Goldstone (n 23); KE Klare, 'Legal Culture and Transformative Constitutionalism' (1998) South African Journal on Human Rights 146; Christie (n 4) 171 and 186; E Doxtader, 'The Quietude of Transitional Justice: Five Rhetorical Questions' (2014) 6 African Yearbook of Rhetoric 24.
[82] Constitution of the Republic of South Africa, Preamble and ss 1, 2, 7, and 8.
[83] *AZAPO* (n 12) [43].
[84] Christie (n 4) 200. See further P Lenta, '*AZAPO*, the TRC and Restorative Justice: A Retrospect' (2005) 20 SA Public Law 335, 355.

society, and forgiveness.[85] The option of a blanket amnesty for apartheid crimes was rejected, and instead made conditional on the 'full disclosure of the truth'.[86] By establishing the TRC, an attempt was made to bring perpetrators face to face with their victims, arriving at and exposing the truth that remained hidden from most ordinary South Africans,[87] in the interests of peace and nation-building.[88]

However, the provision of amnesty was not universally lauded. It was challenged by the applicants in the *AZAPO* case both for its alleged unconstitutionality[89] and for violating the international customary law obligation to prosecute international crimes.[90] The Constitutional Court concluded that amnesty was neither unconstitutional,[91] nor a violation of international law.[92] The Court pointed out that it was 'not a blanket amnesty against criminal prosecution for all and sundry, granted automatically as a uniform act of compulsory statutory amnesia. It [was] specifically authorised for the purposes of effecting a constructive transition towards a democratic order.'[93] In its reasoning, the Court considered 'hard choices'[94] made during the negotiated settlement, and that negotiators were 'entitled'[95] in making 'the historic choice' to favour amnesty over prosecution.[96] Justice Mahomed stated that both liberators and oppressors were victims,[97] and that the

> truth, which the victims of repression seek so desperately to know is, in the circumstances, much more likely to be forthcoming if those responsible for such monstrous misdeeds are encouraged to disclose the whole truth with the incentive that they will not receive the punishment which they undoubtedly deserve if they do. Without that incentive there is nothing to encourage such persons to make the disclosures and to reveal the truth which persons in the positions of the applicants so desperately desire. With that incentive, what might unfold are objectives fundamental to the ethos of a new constitutional order. The families of those unlawfully tortured, maimed or traumatised become more empowered to discover the truth, the perpetrators become exposed to opportunities to obtain relief from the burden of a guilt or an anxiety they might be living with for many long years, the country begins the long and necessary process of healing the

[85] See, eg, in this regard Truth and Reconciliation Act, Preamble and ss 1, 3, 4, 12, 14, 15, 19, 22, 25, 26, 43, 46, and 47B.
[86] Truth and Reconciliation Act, Preamble and ss 3(1)(b) 4(c), 20(1)(c), 36(3)(b) and 36(4); TRC Report (n 10) Chapter 1 para 29.
[87] Christie (n 4) 196–97.
[88] Goldstone (n 23) 488–89; Teitel, 'TJ Geneology' (n 25) 69.
[89] *AZAPO* (n 12) [6], [8]–[15].
[90] ibid [25].
[91] ibid [21], [26]–[32], [38], [48], [50]–[51].
[92] ibid [32].
[93] ibid.
[94] ibid [43].
[95] ibid [50].
[96] ibid [48].
[97] ibid [17].

> wounds of the past, transforming anger and grief into a mature understanding and creating the emotional and structural climate essential for the 'reconciliation and reconstruction' which informs the very difficult and sometimes painful objectives of the amnesty articulated in the [interim Constitution's] epilogue.[98]

Looking back at the *AZAPO* judgment, in particular from a contemporary international criminal law and transitional justice lens, the Court's conclusion was certainly 'not perfect',[99] yet hardly surprising. At the time, transitional justice was informed by the dominant philosophy, adopted by the Court, that amnesty can be granted in the interests of achieving peace, and international criminal justice exchanged for a truth commission.[100] Further, the interim Constitution provided in section 35(1) that a court 'shall, *where applicable*, have regard to public international law applicable to the protection of the rights entrenched in this Chapter'.[101] This contrasts with the obligatory language of the final Constitution, namely that courts, tribunals, and forums '*must* consider international law'.[102] Patrick Lenta stated that '[t]he Court's half-hearted investigation of the question of amnesty in international law ... would seem to indicate that it has made up its mind on the question of amnesty and does not want any contrary norms within international law to interfere with its decision'.[103] With regards to international criminal law, the applicants based their argument for the obligation to prosecute international crimes only on the 'grave breaches' provisions of the Geneva Conventions and Additional Protocols.[104] However, the fields of international criminal, human rights, and humanitarian law have all developed greatly since the 1990s, especially with the establishment of the ICC and various other international ad hoc and hybrid criminal courts and tribunals.[105]

The final report of the TRC echoed the Constitutional Court's *AZAPO* judgment in advancing its reasons for the decision not to establish a 'Nuremberg-style tribunal'[106] to address apartheid as a crime against humanity, and it was also a reflection of the adoption of the dominant approach to transitional justice at the time. First, it was argued that such trials would have threatened the 'miracle of the negotiated settlement [which] would have been overwhelmed by the bloodbath

[98] ibid.
[99] Lenta (n 84) 364.
[100] *AZAPO* (n 12) [16]–[24], [31]–[32], [43]–[48], [50].
[101] ibid [27] (own emphasis).
[102] Constitution, s 39(1) (own emphasis).
[103] Lenta (n 84) 359–60.
[104] *AZAPO* (n 12) [25].
[105] G Waschefort, 'Africa and International Humanitarian Law: The More Things Change, the More They Stay the Same' (2016) International Review of the Red Cross 594; M Roux, 'A New Era for International Criminal Law: Rethinking the Definitions of Crimes Against Humanity and Genocide through the Scope of Its Evolution as an Outgrowth of War Crimes' (2017) South African Yearbook on International Law 80.
[106] TRC Report (n 10) Chapter 1, paras 20–32, Chapter 4, para 18, and Chapter 5 paras 57–59 and 71.

that virtually everyone predicted as the inevitable ending for South Africa'.[107] It was then argued that 'our country simply could not afford the resources in time, money and personnel that we would have had to invest in such an operation',[108] and that '[i]t would have rocked the boat massively and for too long'.[109] A third reason given was the argument that unnecessary constraints would have been placed on the South African criminal justice system,[110] and that trials were not 'the best way to arrive at the truth'.[111] It was lastly argued that a conditional amnesty includes a form of accountability, and that it would be an adequate middle-ground between 'a Nuremberg option and total amnesia'.[112]

As has been argued now, the South African negotiated settlement and TRC were transitional justice mechanisms that took place against the background of Teitel's second phase and, as such, were understandable in their context.[113] South Africa's current oscillating relationship with the ICC is,[114] however, taking place against the backdrop of Teitel's current phase where an *erga omnes* obligation to prosecute international crimes has become normalised,[115] and where peace and justice are regarded as 'mutually reinforcing imperatives'.[116] For the time being, South Africa is still a fully-fledged ICC member state,[117] yet consistently calls for 'diplomacy and dialogue' as 'the only path' to peace during conflict,[118] and is very ambivalent as to whether it would cooperate with the ICC should a request to arrest an accused person be made.[119] This indicates that the question of the relationship between

[107] ibid Chapter 1, para 22.
[108] ibid Chapter 1, para 23.
[109] ibid Chapter 1, para 23.
[110] ibid Chapter 5, para 71.
[111] ibid Chapter 1, para 24. See further Goldstone (n 23) 491–95.
[112] TRC Report (n 10) Chapter 5, para 59.
[113] Teitel, 'TJ Geneology' (n 25) 75–89.
[114] International Crimes Bill (n 19) <https://www.parliament.gov.za/bill/2291658> accessed 1 August 2022.
[115] ibid 89–93.
[116] UN Approach to TJ (n 4) 4.
[117] International Crimes Bill withdrawal (n 22).
[118] 'South Africa's statement in explanation of vote on Ukraine the UN General Assembly Emergency Special Session, International Relations on UN General Assembly Emergency Special Session, South African Government, 2 March 2022, <https://www.gov.za/speeches/south-africa's-statement-explanation-vote-ukraine-un-general-assembly-emergency-special> accessed 17 April 2023; 'Explanation of Vote on the humanitarian resolution in Ukraine on the occasion of the Emergency Special Session of the General Assembly on 24 March 2022', Department of International Relations and Cooperation, 24 March 2022, < https://www.dirco.gov.za/blog/2022/03/24/explanation-of-vote-on-the-humanitarian-resolution-in-ukraine-on-the-occasion-of-the-emergency-special-session-of-the-general-assembly-on-24-march-2022/> accessed 17 April 2023; and 'Explanation of vote on Resolution A/ES-11/L.7 on Ukraine during the 11th UNGA ESS, Thursday, 23 February 2023', Department of International Relations and Cooperation, 23 February 2023, <https://www.dirco.gov.za/blog/2023/02/23/explanation-of-vote-on-resolution-a-es-11-l-7-on-ukraine-during-the-11th-unga-ess-thursday-23-february-2023/> accessed 17 April 2023.
[119] '"We've made it clear that Russia is a friend": Pandor doubles down on SA's Ukraine stance', Q Hunter, News24, 30 March 2023 <https://www.news24.com/news24/politics/government/weve-made-it-clear-that-russia-is-a-friend-pandor-doubles-down-on-sas-ukraine-stance-20230330> accessed 17 April 2023.

justice and peace continues to be of relevance, which may in turn illustrate that it is one of the 'long-term negative consequences to this type of reconciliation politics'.[120] The Implementation of the Rome Statute Act ('Implementation Act')[121] and the withdrawal of the International Crimes Bill could be seen as a reflection that the state is indeed complying with the principle of complementarity which requires states to domesticate international criminal law to enable national courts to adjudicate international crimes, and that it is devoted to avoiding impunity for international crimes.[122] However, the language regularly used by the South African government deeply reflects a prioritisation of peace over prosecution—which has resonances from the negotiated settlement in a different era—and, perhaps alarmingly, suggests a trivialisation of international crimes. The next section will illustrate the way in which the *erga omnes* obligation to prosecute international crimes[123] triggers the question of balancing peace and justice, which is provided for in the South African Repeal Bill of the Implementation Act, as well as the International Crimes Bill. Section 5 will also illustrate that South Africa's opaque relationship with the ICC continues the legacy of prioritising the achievement of peace at the expense of prosecuting international crimes.

5. South Africa's Ambivalent Relationship with the ICC: The Re-emergence of Overlooking the *Erga Omnes* Obligation to Prosecute International Crimes by Prioritising Peace

As mentioned in the introduction, the deterioration of South Africa's relationship with the ICC was triggered by the country's failure to arrest former Sudanese President Al-Bashir when he attended a summit of the African Union between 13 and 15 June. This failure to arrest and surrender an accused person to the ICC was highly controversial, and became the subject of decisions by South African courts[124] and eventually the ICC.[125] Both the High Court and the Supreme Court of Appeal found that the government's failure to arrest, detain, and surrender Al-Bashir to the ICC was in conflict with the Constitution and the Implementation Act, as well as South Africa's obligations in terms of the ICC Statute.[126] The ICC also found that South Africa failed to fulfil its obligations to arrest and surrender Al-Bashir to the Court, but decided not to refer the issue to the ICC Assembly of

[120] Teitel, 'TJ Geneology' (n 25) 84.
[121] Implementation of the Rome Statute of the International Criminal Court Act 27 of 2002 ('Implementation Act').
[122] ICC Statute, Preamble and art 1.
[123] Roux, '*Erga Omnes*' (n 1).
[124] *SALC v Minister of Justice* (n 19); *Minister of Justice v SALC* (n 19).
[125] ICC non-compliance decision (n 19).
[126] *SALC v Minister of Justice* (n 19) [11], [28.13], [31], [34], [37.1], [39]; *Minister of Justice v SALC* (n 19) [113].

State Parties nor to the United Nations Security Council.[127] The reason for the latter decision was particularly 'in light of the fact that South Africa's domestic courts have already found South Africa to be in breach of its obligations under its domestic legal framework'.[128]

South Africa nevertheless declared its intention to withdraw from the ICC, starting the process by depositing its notice of withdrawal from ICC membership with the UN Secretary-General.[129] Shortly thereafter, the South African executive introduced a bill into Parliament repealing the Implementation Act.[130] However, after the three court decisions, the government responded by revoking its notice of withdrawal.[131] This did not mean, however, that South Africa no longer intended to withdraw as state party to the ICC: rather, it was an indication that a different domestic legislative procedure would have to be followed to achieve the same result.[132] The Implementation Act Repeal Bill was withdrawn,[133] and a new bill introduced: the International Crimes Bill. The Bill also set out to repeal the Implementation Act, but its two main objectives were to guarantee immunity from prosecution to incumbent senior government officials,[134] and to enable South Africa to continue to resolve conflicts through diplomacy and dialogue.[135] The then-Minister of Justice and Constitutional Development also discussed South Africa's intention to withdraw from the ICC Statute before the Sixteenth Assembly of State Parties, reiterating that the government is motivated by the

> active role that South Africa continues to play in promoting dialogue and peaceful resolution of conflicts in Africa and elsewhere. South Africa's continued membership to the Rome Statute, as it is currently interpreted and applied, carries with it

[127] ICC non-compliance decision (n 19) [140].

[128] ibid [136], [139].

[129] SA Withdrawal Notice (n 19). ICC Statute, art 127 obliges member states to deposit a written notice with the UN Secretary-General, which will 'take effect one year' after such a deposit is made. However, the withdrawal will not relieve that state of its obligations in terms of the Statute imposed on the state while it was still a member state.

[130] Implementation Act Repeal Bill (B23–2016) (n 19).

[131] Withdrawal of Notification of Withdrawal (n 19). See further for references to these cases nn 124, 125, 126, 127, and 128 and surrounding text.

[132] The main argument for changing the national procedure in withdrawing from the ICC Statute is informed by the Constitution, s 231, particularly sub-s (2): both the National Assembly and the National Council of Provinces have to approve an international agreement by way of resolution before it will be binding on the Republic. Therefore, South Africa's withdrawal from the ICC Statute will only bind the Republic once both the National Assembly and the National Council of Provinces approved hereof by way of resolution. The purpose of introducing the International Crimes Bill is to comply with s 231(4), namely to ensure an international agreement 'becomes law in the Republic'.

[133] 'Implementation of the Rome Statute of the International Criminal Court Act Repeal Bill (B23–2016): Bill withdrawn by the Minister of Justice & Correctional Services in accordance with rule 334 of the Rules of the National Assembly', Parliamentary Monitoring Group, 13 March 2017 <https://pmg.org.za/bill/675/> accessed 15 April 2023.

[134] International Crimes Bill, Preamble and art 3. Immunity is interspersed throughout the Bill though, from the Preamble right through to the explanatory notes. See further Memorandum of the International Crimes Bill, para 2.3.3.

[135] International Crimes Bill, Preamble and art 6.

> the potential risk of undermining its ability to carry out its peace-making mission efforts in Africa, and elsewhere.[136]

The International Crimes Bill lapsed for some time, but was then revived, and it remained 'under consideration' before the South African National Assembly until it was formally withdrawn on 10 March 2023.[137] Although this may indicate a rededication to the achievement of international criminal justice, in practice, the true test will be the way in which South Africa handles requests for cooperation from the ICC. On 17 March 2023, the ICC issued a warrant of arrest against another South African political ally, Russian President Vladimir Putin, for the war crime of unlawfully deporting and transferring children from occupied territory in Ukraine.[138] Shortly thereafter, the Minister of International Relations and Cooperation, Naledi Pandor, issued a statement that legal advice was being sought to establish whether South Africa would be obliged to arrest and surrender Putin to the ICC should he attend a BRICS summit scheduled for August 2023.[139] This is despite the decisions by the South African High Court and Supreme Court of Appeal, as well as the ICC, that very clearly set out South Africa's obligations as a member state of the ICC. At the time of writing it was unclear whether a positive shift has started to take place, or whether continuing political relationships would be prioritised at the expense of international criminal justice.

These events have all been occurring within the context of the current transitional justice phase,[140] and it goes to the core of the question of how South Africa considers the primacy of norms. The government would be taking a retrogressive step in failing to arrest Putin—to a different era of transitional justice—as it readopts its negotiated settlement-era argument of prioritising peace over justice. Further, it is adopting the dominant African geopolitical approach, namely that the denial of procedural immunities and privileges at the national courts of foreign states for international crimes for incumbent senior government officials will be an impediment to establishing peace and stability in conflict-ridden states.[141] This position contradicts the current international criminal law movement of excluding immunity for *any* person accused of committing international crimes,[142]

[136] Masutha Statement (n 20).

[137] International Crimes Bill withdrawal (n 22).

[138] 'Situation in Ukraine: ICC judges issue arrest warrants against Vladimir Vladimirovich Putin and Maria Alekseyevna Lvova-Belova', Press Release, International Criminal Court, 17 March 2023 < https://www.icc-cpi.int/news/situation-ukraine-icc-judges-issue-arrest-warrants-against-vladimir-vladimirovich-putin-and> accessed 17 April 2023.

[139] 'DIRCO awaiting legal opinion before extending an invite to Putin' *SABC News* (24 March 2023) <https://www.sabcnews.com/sabcnews/dirco-awaiting-legal-opinion-before-extending-an-invite-to-putin/> accessed 17 April 2023.

[140] Teitel, 'TJ Geneology' (n 25) 89–93.

[141] Decision on the International Criminal Court, Thirtieth Ordinary Session of the Assembly, African Union, 28–29 January 2018, Assembly/AU/Dec.672 (XXX); Roux, 'Obstacles' (n 19) 115–16.

[142] *Arrest Warrant* Dissenting Opinion of Judge van den Wyngaert (n 3) [57]; *Al-Adsani* (n 3) [61].

specifically because '[i]n practice … immunity leads to *de facto* impunity'.[143] Further, currently, a holistic approach to transitional justice is adopted which assists societies emerging from gross human rights violations[144] through *both* holding perpetrators individually criminally responsible, as well as implementing various other non-judicial mechanisms.[145] It has to be reiterated that prosecution of international crimes is no longer *optional* in terms of the current phase of transitional justice: instead, it is a question of 'when and how',[146] a question of *timing* and *method* therefore.

South Africa's consistent emphasis on promoting peace, diplomacy, stability, and dialogue has gradually transformed into a general official governmental policy when it comes to dealing with international crimes. The impact thereof is that international crimes are trivialised in a number of ways: this evidences the way in which the South African executive and legislature is manipulating legal procedure for political gain: a procedural defence usually only available in a criminal trial to a very limited category of high-ranking government officials[147] is made available to an extremely broad category of persons.[148] To illustrate, in contrast to misleadingly only mentioning 'heads of state' that will enjoy diplomatic immunity in terms of 'customary international law' in the Preamble for committing international crimes, the Memorandum concerning the Bill lists several additional persons who will also enjoy immunity for international crimes.[149] Further trivialisation lies in the fact that the government's purpose appears to be to ensure the continued good political relations between states, particularly on the African continent,[150] but also states with strong 'historical ties' to South Africa such as Russia.[151] Doing so, however, comes at the cost of breaching the *erga omnes* obligation to prosecute international crimes.

South Africa, by becoming a member state of the ICC Statute, clearly supported the purpose of the ICC to 'put an end to impunity for the perpetrators' of 'the most serious crimes of international concern'.[152] South Africa's membership of this first, permanent, international, criminal court complements its own foundational

[143] *Arrest Warrant* Dissenting Opinion of Judge van den Wyngaert (n 3) [34].
[144] UN Approach to TJ (n 4) 4.
[145] ibid.
[146] ibid.
[147] *Arrest Warrant* Dissenting Opinion of Judge van den Wyngaert (n 3) [8]–[33]; Third Report Immunity of State Officials from Foreign Criminal Jurisdiction, CE Hernández, Special Rapporteur, Report of the International Law Commission, Sixty-Sixth Session, 5 May–6 June and 7 July–8 August 2014, Official Records of the General Assembly, Sixty-Sixth Session, Supplement No 10 (A/69/10) Chapter V, paras 111–12.
[148] International Crimes Bill, Preamble, s 3, and Memorandum.
[149] ibid.
[150] ibid Preamble, ss 6, 24, and 28.
[151] See further Minister Pandor hosts the Seventeenth Session of the SA-Russia Joint Inter-Governmental Committee, 30 March 2023, the DIRCOZA YouTube Channel, <https://www.youtube.com/watch?v=jtLESdmOmiY> accessed 13 April 2023.
[152] Rome Statute, Preamble.

constitutional values[153] as well as the state's obligation to 'respect, protect, promote and fulfil' human rights.[154] The act of becoming a member state to the ICC Statute meant that South Africa also pledged that it will 'contribute to the prevention of such crimes',[155] and take steps to ensure its 'effective prosecution',[156] as part of providing a legal remedy to the 'millions of children, women and men [who] have been victims of unimaginable atrocities'.[157]

The ambiguous relationship of South Africa with the ICC is therefore an *especially* serious blow to South Africa's reputation as one of the foremost guardians of human rights, not only on the African continent, but in the international community as a whole. South Africa, by not adopting a clear governmental policy in favour of international criminal justice, is taking a retrogressive step in terms of the *erga omnes* obligation to prosecute international crimes, as well as the rule of law, democracy, and the state's commitment to human rights.[158] When the question of the primacy of norms within the current South African context is examined, the goals of transitional justice have to be reiterated: it cannot be achieved in isolation,[159] and has to be continuously revisited.[160]

6. Conclusion

That South Africans could move from decades of racial oppression and authoritarianism to a democratic society underpinned by the supremacy of a constitution, the rule of law, and the advancement of human rights, is a miraculous and inspiring story filled with hope. It served as a testimony of the resilience of ordinary and great South Africans alike. At the same time, the South African story is an extremely complex, multi-layered and traumatic one. More than twenty years after the official end to apartheid, South Africans are still struggling to come to terms with it. The truth is that an international crime was committed in the country: apartheid was not only committed against South Africans targeted in terms of its racial policies, but the international community as a whole. That 'apartheid' was listed in the ICC Statute as one of the crimes against humanity shows that the drafters thereof recognised the seriousness with which the international community view institutionalised racial oppression. Many 'hard' and 'historic' choices were made during the negotiated settlement.[161] Transitional justice mechanisms implemented in South

153 Constitution, s 1.
154 ibid s 7(1).
155 Rome Statute, Preamble.
156 ibid.
157 ibid.
158 Constitution, ss 1 and 7(1).
159 See Section 1 above.
160 *AZAPO* (n 12) [43]; Christie (n 4); Lenta (n 84).
161 *AZAPO* (n 12) [44] and [48].

Africa in responding to apartheid, in particular the negotiated settlement and the TRC, were certainly not perfect. Viewed through the current transitional justice lens we can accept that granting amnesty for apartheid as an international crime did not conform with the *erga omnes* obligation to prosecute international crimes. With the luxury of hindsight, we can say that many of the 'hard choices' made may very well have been the wrong ones, yet, 'it was a necessary process'.[162]

The ICC and the way in which international criminal justice is carried out is also not perfect, and calls for reform are undoubtedly justified.[163] Continued membership of the ICC should rather be viewed by the South African government as an opportunity of ensuring that international criminal justice is transformed to suit African needs, where peace and justice are 'mutually reinforcing imperatives'.[164] It is an opportunity for South Africa to put its unique stamp on international criminal justice: to incorporate its miraculous and inspiring approach to transitional justice in the 1990s with the *erga omnes* obligation to prosecute international crimes. Transitional justice today involves a holistic approach, with the principle of complementarity at its core.[165] Different ways of serving international criminal justice must be incorporated, whilst being sensitive to the unique and fragile political situation in states emerging from the commission of gross human rights violations.[166]

It is doubtful whether any attempt to revive the International Crimes Bill in its current form would pass constitutional muster. Further, the ILC has considered, and is still considering, various topics that shape the primacy of norms, such as *jus cogens* norms,[167] the immunity of senior government officials at the national courts of foreign states,[168] universal jurisdiction,[169] as well as crimes against humanity.[170] The existing Implementation Act has also not been amended in years to incorporate amendments made to the ICC Statute. Instead of its repeal, this piece of legislation should instead re-commit South Africa to prosecutions for international crimes,

[162] Christie (n 4) 203.
[163] Roux, 'New Era' (n 105) 116–18.
[164] UN Approach to TJ (n 4) 4.
[165] ibid 8.
[166] ibid.
[167] 2022 Peremptory Norms Draft Conclusions (n 3); 2021 ILC Report (n 49) para 91; ILC 2022 Current Status (n 49).
[168] Hernández Eighth Report (n 49) 109–10; ILC 2022 Current Status (n 49).
[169] 2018 ILC Report (n 44) Annex A; ILC 2022 Current Status (n 49).
[170] The ILC adopted the Draft Articles Crimes against Humanity in 2019, and recommended that the General Assembly consider the adoption of a treaty on the basis of its work. At the time of writing the process was still ongoing. See further Report of the International Law Commission, Seventy-First Session, 29 April–7 June and 8 July–9 August 2019, *Official Records of the General Assembly, Seventy-Fourth Session, Supplement No 10* (A/74/10) 34–140; Annex A paras 1–13 ('2006 ILC Report'); International Law Commission's Draft Articles on Prevention and Punishment of Crimes Against Humanity, *Yearbook of the International Law Commission, Seventy-First Session*, A/74/10; General Assembly Resolution 74/187, *Crimes Against Humanity*, 30 December 2019; General Assembly Resolution 74/186, *Report of the International Law Commission on the Work of its Seventy-First Session*, 2 January 2020.

and also include different forms of transitional justice mechanisms, both judicial and non-judicial.[171] Such mechanisms should be holistic and in line with those proposed by the UN, such as 'prosecution initiatives, truth-seeking, reparations programmes, institutional reform or an appropriate combination thereof'.[172] By doing so, South Africa would ensure the genuine entrenchment of the rule of law, democracy, and the obligation to protect human rights, and ultimately advance the reconciliation of a still-deeply divided society.[173]

[171] Teitel, 'TJ Geneology' (n 25) 3.
[172] UN Approach to TJ (n 4) 3.
[173] ibid.

24

Colombia and the International Criminal Court

A Case of Positive Complementarity in Transitional Justice Contexts

Natalia Silva Santaularia

1. Introduction

In December 2016, the Colombian government and the Revolutionary Armed Forces of Colombia—People's Army (FARC-EP) signed a peace agreement.[1] The accord, also known as the Havana Agreement since its negotiation took place in the capital city of Cuba,[2] is undoubtedly a very ambitious one. Not only does it comprise mechanisms to clarify the truth of the facts that occurred during the armed conflict or to prosecute those responsible for grave crimes, it also includes distinctive measures to address the origins of the conflict, such as land ownership or participation in politics. Hence, the establishment of a complex Special Jurisdiction for Peace (SJP)—which investigates and punishes with unusual sanctions the most atrocious crimes committed during the conflict by the Armed Forces or the FARC-EP guerrilla—has been an enormous challenge.

Watching from the city of The Hague, the International Criminal Court (ICC), a permanent international tribunal 'mandated to apply a prevailing international consensus on the obligation to prosecute the most serious crimes',[3] has carefully examined every step taken by the Colombian state in relation to the 2016 Peace Agreement. As a 'watchdog court' whose main goal is to fight against impunity for crimes 'of concern to the international community as a whole',[4] the jurisdiction of the ICC is triggered only if states are 'unwilling' or 'unable' to prosecute the crimes contained in the Rome Statute. Its mandate is essentially based on the principle

[1] Final Agreement to end the armed conflict and build a stable and lasting peace, signed between the government of the Republic of Colombia and the FARC-EP (24 November 2016) <https://bapp.com.co/en/final-agreement-to-end-the-armed-conflict-and-build-a-stable-and-lasting-peace/> accessed 22 September 2023 ('peace agreement').

[2] Cuba is a guarantor of the Colombian peace process.

[3] R Teitel, *Globalizing Transitional Justice* (OUP 2014) 6.

[4] Rome Statute, Preamble, para 4.

Natalia Silva Santaularia, *Colombia and the International Criminal Court* In: *Transitional Justice, Distributive Justice, and Transformative Constitutionalism.* Edited by: David Bilchitz and Raisa Cachalia, with Magdalena Inés Correa Henao and Nathalia Bautista Pizarro, Oxford University Press.
DOI: 10.1093/oso/9780192887627.003.0024

of complementarity, which makes the ICC a court of last resort. The Office of the Prosecutor (OTP) of the ICC conducted preliminary examinations since June 2004 on the situation in Colombia,[5] but on 28 October 2021 it unexpectedly concluded a cooperation agreement with the government of Colombia and closed the examination.[6] Before this happened, the ICC had issued annual reports, visited national entities and organisations, and even submitted an *amicus curiae* brief before the Colombian Constitutional Court. But what has been the role of the ICC in the Colombian transitional justice context, which has developed its own novel mechanisms for justice? Was international criminal law adequately respected by the 2016 Peace Agreement and its implementing legislation? Was the engagement of the OTP in Colombia enough to guarantee its compliance with the Rome Statute? Finally, what should now be expected from the cooperation agreement between the OTP and the government of Colombia?

In this chapter, I will explore the interrelationship between transitional justice at the domestic level—as agreed in the Colombian peace agreement—and the international level—as represented by the Rome Statute of the ICC. I will begin in Section 2 with an examination of the Reports on Preliminary Examination Activities submitted by the ICC on the situation in Colombia, with a special focus on the FARC-EP peace process, the SJP developments, and the OTP's activities in Colombia. Section 3 will detail the controversial aspects of the SJP as identified by the OTP, following a request from the Constitutional Court of Colombia, and the changes made to the law after this intervention. Finally, Section 4 will analyse the dimension of the principle of complementarity that applies to the relationship between the ICC and Colombia, during the preliminary examination and after its closure, while proposing mechanisms to enhance compliance of international criminal law in Colombia.

2. The Situation in Colombia: The Perspective of the International Criminal Court

Political violence, and specially the 'war between guerrillas', has been virtually permanent in Colombian history.[7] For the last forty years, violence from

[5] At the ICC, there is a difference between 'situations' and 'cases': '"Situations" are the object of preliminary examinations and investigations. "Cases" are subsequently initiated by the issuance of a warrant of arrest or a summons to appear by the competent Pre-trial Chamber at the request of the Prosecutor'. See H Olásolo and E Carnero-Rojo, 'The Application of the Principle of Complementarity to the Decision of Where to Open an Investigation' in C Stahn and MM El Zeidy (eds), *The International Criminal Court and Complementarity* (CUP 2011) 402.

[6] Cooperation Agreement between the Office of the Prosecutor of the International Criminal Court and the Government of Colombia, 28 October 2021.

<https://www.icc-cpi.int/sites/default/files/itemsDocuments/20211028-OTP-COL-Cooperation-Agreement-ENG.pdf> accessed 3 October 2022 ('cooperation agreement').

[7] E Pizarro, *Insurgencia sin revolución: la guerrilla en Colombia desde una perspectiva comparada* (TM Editores 1996) 114.

guerrillas has been particularly atrocious. A left-wing armed insurgency still fights against the state while paramilitaries emerged as an organised and armed force in the 1980s. As a result, the conflict has left more than nine million victims, most of them displaced from their homes.[8] The government tried several times to negotiate the end of the internal armed conflict, but many peace agreements have failed since 1982. However, as of 5 August 2002, when Colombia deposited its instrument of accession to the Rome Statute, the OTP has been actively influencing decisions taken by the state to ensure accountability for those responsible for international crimes. Hence, considering that Colombia has been under preliminary examinations by the ICC since June 2004, we can discern two distinct periods: the first is related to the demobilisation process of the right-wing paramilitaries (Section 2A), and the second concerns the peace process with FARC-EP (Section 2B). Without belittling the influence of the OTP during the first period, this chapter will mainly assess the interactions between the ICC and Colombia during the second period in relation to the 2016 Peace Agreement with the FARC-EP and the establishment of a SJP.

A. The International Criminal Court and the Peace Process with the United Self-Defence Forces of Colombia in a Nutshell

It is important to pay special attention to the demobilisation process of the paramilitary group, the so-called United Self-Defence Forces of Colombia (AUC). The 2005 Justice and Peace Law (JPL) established reduced prison sentences from five to eight years in exchange for demobilisation, contributions to establishing the truth, and reparation to victims.[9] Some claim that instead of a negotiated agreement between the government and the AUC, the JPL was imposed on the AUC members and did not produce results for transitional justice in terms of truth, non-recurrence, or full reparation for victims.[10] However, after the ICC Prosecutor's first official visit to Colombia in 2007 and subsequent reports of preliminary examination activities still referring to the JPL, the OTP decided not to open up a formal investigation on the situation in Colombia.

[8] Colombian government, Unit for Victims' Comprehensive Reparation and Care, Unique Victims Register <https://www.unidadvictimas.gov.co/es/registro-unico-de-victimas-ruv/37394> accessed 3 October 2022.

[9] Law 975 of 2005, art 29 <https://www.funcionpublica.gov.co/eva/gestornormativo/norma.php?i=17161> accessed 22 September 2023.

[10] F Barbosa, *¿Justicia transicional o impunidad? La encrucijada de la paz en Colombia* (Ediciones B 2017) 65.

B. The International Criminal Court and the Peace Process with the Revolutionary Armed Forces of Colombia—People's Army

(i) The 2016 Peace Agreement and the Special Jurisdiction for Peace

On 4 September 2012, the official commencement of dialogue with the FARC-EP was announced. Four years later, once the negotiation between President Juan Manuel Santos's government and the armed group was completed, the general agreement was signed on 26 September 2016. On 2 October 2016, a plebiscite took place concerning the agreement which resulted in a narrow vote against it. Parts of the agreement were modified, specifically some aspects related to the SJP,[11] and the peace agreement was finally signed for the second time in the Colón Theatre in Bogotá on 24 November 2016.

The 'Victims' chapter of the peace agreement is the most relevant for this chapter. It includes a system which protects victims' rights to truth, justice, reparation, and non-recurrence, and which is fully integrated throughout the agreement. The components of the system are meant to contribute to the fight against impunity and sanction the most serious violations of human rights and international humanitarian law (IHL), while discovering the truth and providing reparations for the harm caused to individuals and groups. To achieve these objectives, the system comprises both judicial and extra-judicial mechanisms: the Truth, Coexistence and Non-Recurrence Commission, the Special Unit for the Search for Persons deemed as Missing in the context of and due to the armed conflict, the SJP, the comprehensive reparation measures for peacebuilding purposes, and the Guarantees of Non-Recurrence. In order to legally shield the peace agreement, Colombia's 1991 Constitution was modified, and the Legislative Act 01 of 2017, which defined the transitional justice mechanisms, was included in several transitory articles. This was based on a key provision of the Constitution which established peace as a right and a duty,[12] and was designed according to the JPL and the so-called Legal Framework for Peace.[13]

The SJP was conceived as a judicial mechanism of transitional justice created to grant amnesties to those who committed political (and politically-related) crimes,[14] and to impose sanctions on those responsible for atrocious crimes. Having jurisdiction over individuals who participated directly or indirectly in the

[11] For instance, the second peace agreement established that the SJP would be composed only of Colombian judges and prosecutors, excluding the possibility of having foreign judges in the jurisdiction.

[12] 1991 Colombian Constitution, arts 22 and 96(6).

[13] The Legal Framework for Peace was the legislative act which established legal transitional justice instruments in order to advance negotiations with the FARC-EP. It was approved by the Colombian Congress on 14 June 2012.

[14] Law 1820 of 2016 ('Amnesty Law'), arts 15 and 16 <http://es.presidencia.gov.co/normativa/normativa/LEY%201820%20DEL%2030%20DE%20DICIEMBRE%20DE%202016.pdf> accessed 3 October 2022.

armed conflict, the SJP essentially focuses on members of the government forces and the FARC-EP.[15] In its approach, the SJP goes beyond the traditional concept of retributive justice and centres its objectives on the notion of restorative justice, considering that victims and their rights constitute the core of the peace agreement.[16]

(ii) Reports on preliminary examination activities by the International Criminal Court

This subsection will concentrate on crimes within the ICC's jurisdiction committed by the government forces and the FARC-EP, since these are the parties who signed the 2016 Peace Agreement. It will summarise core aspects of the reports issued by the OTP pursuant to its preliminary investigation. These include the views of the OTP on the FARC-EP peace process, the 2016 Peace Agreement, and the SJP mechanism. This section will also outline some of the activities the OTP has been engaging in since 2013 in Colombia.

In its Report on Preliminary Examination Activities of 2013, the OTP referred for the first time to the peace talks between the government of Colombia and the FARC-EP and the six points of the agenda.[17] The Report recalled that there was a *reasonable basis to believe* that the FARC-EP had committed crimes against humanity in the form of murder, the forcible transfer of members of the population, imprisonment, or other severe deprivation of physical liberty, torture, rape, and other forms of sexual violence since 1 November 2002.[18] It additionally referred to war crimes committed by the FARC-EP, particularly murder, attacks against civilians, torture, cruel treatment and outrages upon personal dignity, taking of hostages, rape and other forms of sexual violence, and conscripting, enlisting, and using children to participate actively in hostilities, since 1 November 2009.[19] With respect to state actors, the Report outlined the extrajudicial executions by the military (so-called 'false positives'[20]) as crimes against humanity in the form of murder and enforced disappearances;[21] and highlighted war crimes in the form of murder and attacking civilians, torture and cruel treatment, outrages upon personal dignity, rape and other forms of sexual violence from 1 November 2009 to date.[22] The

[15] Recently, however, in decision TP-SA 1187 of 21 July 2022, the Appeals Chamber of the SJP held that paramilitaries could fall within the SJP's personal jurisdiction <https://drive.google.com/file/d/1kZfKO9cwS06iWiNVZwnFvkOiqNXw1RDo/view> accessed 3 October 2022.

[16] cf Metz, Chapter 2 in this book.

[17] ICC, OTP, Report on Preliminary Examination Activities of 2013, para 123 <https://www.icc-cpi.int/news/report-preliminary-examination-activities-2013> accessed 22 September 2023 ('OTP Report 2013').

[18] ibid para 124.

[19] ibid para 125.

[20] These were deliberate killings of civilians committed by members of the military to present them to the authorities as guerrilla fighters killed in battle. The objective was to bolster body counts and obtain all kinds of benefits (holidays, economic compensations, honours . . .).

[21] OTP Report 2013 (n 17) para 126.

[22] ibid para 127.

OTP also mentioned in the Report that 'pursuant to its *positive approach* to complementarity, the Office has continued to consult with the Government of Colombia in an effort to ensure that any eventual peace agreement is compatible with the Rome Statute'.[23] The OTP conducted two missions to Bogotá, where it gathered and analysed information related to the situation, and held multiple meetings with the Colombian authorities, civil society, and academia. It also participated in public events and roundtables.[24]

In its 2014 Report, the OTP does not refer much to the FARC-EP peace process,[25] but the 2015 Report did introduce a description of the envisaged SJP. The document recalls that the ICC Deputy Prosecutor delivered a keynote speech in Colombia supporting all efforts undertaken during the peace process;[26] and that the Prosecutor expressed her hope that the peace agreement would constitute a *genuine* step towards ending the armed conflict while paying attention to justice as a fundamental pillar of sustainable peace.[27] The 2015 Report finally explained that the peace agreement and its implementing legislation would be analysed, especially 'with respect to the restrictions of liberty in special conditions and the inclusion of State agents'.[28] This meant in the first place that once the peace agreement was signed, the OTP would carefully examine its list of reduced prison sentences and, specifically, its non-prison sanctions. Second, the OTP would check whether the peace agreement included the possibility of state agents appearing before the transitional justice mechanisms and the ways they would be held accountable. This last point was especially important to the OTP because proceedings in Colombia on persons bearing the greatest responsibility within the military hierarchy had been failing.

The following year, the 2016 Report included a specific section where the OTP described the SJP, its personal and subject-matter jurisdiction, and its procedures and sanctions.[29] The OTP expressed the view that it had not formed a final position as to the SJP because it had not been established yet. However, it did pay special attention to the possible lacunae with respect to command responsibility, which

[23] ibid para 131 (emphasis added).

[24] ibid paras 146–50. Taking into account that consultations with national authorities, public discussions, and meetings will appear in all Reports as evidence of OTP activities in Colombia, they are only mentioned once.

[25] See ICC, OTP, Report on Preliminary Examination Activities of 2014, para 108 <https://www.icc-cpi.int/iccdocs/otp/OTP-Pre-Exam-2014.pdf> accessed 3 October 2022.

[26] ICC, OTP, 'Transitional Justice in Colombia and the role of the International Criminal Court', Keynote speech by J Stewart, Deputy Prosecutor of the ICC, Bogotá, 13 May 2015 <https://www.icc-cpi.int/iccdocs/otp/otp-stat-13-05-2015-ENG.pdf> accessed 3 October 2022 ('Stewart's speech 2015').

[27] ICC, OTP, Statement of the ICC Prosecutor on the Agreement on the Creation of a Special Jurisdiction for Peace in Colombia, 24 September 2015 <https://www.icc-cpi.int/Pages/item.aspx?name=otp_stat_24-09-2015> accessed 3 October 2022.

[28] ICC, OTP, Report on Preliminary Examination Activities of 2015, para 167 <https://www.icc-cpi.int/sites/default/files/iccdocs/otp/OTP-PE-rep-2015-Eng.pdf> accessed 22 September 2023.

[29] ICC, OTP, Report on Preliminary Examination Activities of 2016, paras 252–56 <https://www.icc-cpi.int/news/report-preliminary-examination-activities-2016> accessed 22 September 2023.

could hinder the ability of the SJP to '*genuinely* proceed in relation to potential cases which are likely to arise from an investigation into the situation'.[30] Concerning this last point, the Report referred to the statement of the ICC Prosecutor of September 2016, where she welcomed the conclusion of the peace negotiations with FARC-EP and recognised the importance of *genuine* accountability, which includes *effective punishment*.[31]

In the 2017 Report, the OTP identified five potential cases relating to extrajudicial executions allegedly committed between 2002 and 2009[32] and twenty-nine commanding officers who oversaw the divisions and brigades which committed the crimes during the aforementioned period.[33] The OTP remarked that those commanders did have proceedings against them, but 'there is conflicting information about the status of some of the reported cases'.[34] The 2018 Report explained how in relation to proceedings under the SJP, extrajudicial executions committed from 1985 until 1 December 2016 were 'prioritised'.[35] It remarked that the order was based, among others, on the OTP's findings.[36] The Report also highlighted how members of the Armed Forces, including at least five commanders implicated in extrajudicial executions identified as part of the OTP's potential cases, have voluntarily requested to appear before the SJP,[37] and how the SJP had been 'prioritising' cases addressing multiple conflict-related crimes, including forced displacement.[38] Finally, the 2018 Report made clear that as the SJP was then fully operational, the OTP would continue examining developments relating to its regulations, operations, and proceedings, and 'will closely follow individual proceedings that arise from the cases initiated so far, as well as the identification of new cases selected for investigation and prosecution'.[39]

The 2019 Report highlighted that thousands of former members of the FARC-EP and of the Armed Forces signed pledges of commitment ('*actas de sometimiento*') before the SJP and that the SJP had initiated seven 'macro cases' relating to representative conflict-related crimes.[40] The Report stated, importantly, that '[t]he

30 ibid para 257 (emphasis added).

31 ICC, OTP, Statement of the ICC Prosecutor on the conclusion of the peace negotiations between the Government of Colombia and the FARC-EP, 1 September 2016. <https://www.icc-cpi.int/Pages/item.aspx?name=160901-otp-stat-colombia> accessed 3 October 2022.

32 ICC, OTP, Report on Preliminary Examination Activities of 2017, para 131 <https://www.icc-cpi.int/itemsDocuments/2017-PE-rep/2017-otp-rep-PE_ENG.pdf> accessed 3 October 2022.

33 ibid para 134.

34 ibid para 135.

35 ICC, OTP, Report on Preliminary Examination Activities of 2018, para 136 <https://www.icc-cpi.int/itemsDocuments/181205-rep-otp-PE-ENG.pdf> accessed 3 October 2022.

36 ibid para 137.

37 ibid para 139.

38 ibid para 142.

39 ibid para 165.

40 ICC, OTP, Report on Preliminary Examination Activities of 2019, para 94 <https://www.icc-cpi.int/itemsDocuments/191205-rep-otp-PE.pdf> accessed 3 October 2022.

Colombian authorities appear to have made progress towards the fulfilment of their duty to investigate and prosecute conduct amounting to war crimes and crimes against humanity under the Rome Statute, and thereby also addressing the forms of conduct underlying the potential cases identified by the Office'.[41] It finally added that:

> The Office will also seek to conceptualise during 2020 the preparation of *relevant benchmarks* which could enable the Office to complete its preliminary examination, subject to the continued satisfaction of certain conditions, such as: the absence of manifest gaps in the scope of national proceedings or of factors vitiating their *genuineness*, and the imposition of *effective penal sanctions* that serve appropriate sentencing objectives of retribution, rehabilitation, restoration and deterrence.[42]

The last Report before the situation in Colombia was closed in 2021 was submitted in December 2020. It explained how the SJP issued decisions related to the seven macro cases concerning representative conflict-related crimes, ruled on the participation of victims in proceedings, and initiated preparatory activities for the issuance of 'conclusions decisions' ('*resoluciones de conclusiones*'),[43] among others.[44] Furthermore, the Report emphasised that the Colombian authorities, including the SJP, took meaningful steps to address conduct amounting to ICC crimes.[45]

(iii) Interim conclusion

The goal of the preliminary examination is 'to collect all relevant information necessary to reach a fully informed determination of whether there is a reasonable basis to proceed with an investigation'.[46] As we have examined, Reports on Preliminary Examination Activities submitted annually by the OTP were an essential tool to supervise national proceedings in Colombia. These documents summarise progress and setbacks in the prosecution of the crimes over which the ICC has jurisdiction, and which should not remain unpunished. In 2012, peace

[41] ibid para 132 (emphasis added).
[42] ibid para 133.
[43] 'Conclusions decisions' are documents that the Truth and Recognition Chamber of the SJP hands over to the Tribunal for Peace, which is in charge of sanctioning, in cases of acknowledgement of truth and responsibilities. The documents include the identification of the most serious cases and the most representative conduct, the individualisation of responsibilities, the legal characterisation of conduct, the acknowledgements of truth and responsibility, and the sanction project.
[44] ICC, OTP, Report on Preliminary Examination Activities of 2020, para 111 <https://www.icc-cpi.int/itemsDocuments/2020-PE/2020-pe-report-eng.pdf> accessed 3 October 2022.
[45] ibid para 152.
[46] ICC, OTP, Policy Paper on Preliminary Examinations, November 2013, para 2 <https://www.icc-cpi.int/sites/default/files/iccdocs/otp/OTP-Policy_Paper_Preliminary_Examinations_2013-ENG.pdf> accessed 22 September 2023.

negotiations with FARC-EP began. Hence, examining the new transitional justice legislation arising from the peace process and its implementation was a vital task for the ICC.

Since then, the OTP engaged in continuous dialogue with Colombia on the legal framework of the ~~TJ~~ transitional justice system created by the 2016 Peace Agreement to prosecute crimes committed by state forces and the FARC-EP. It was clear from the situation in Colombia that 'despite not having full investigatory powers during preliminary examinations, the OTP is very active during this phase'.[47] This was done, among others, through the annual missions of the OTP in Colombia, which led to meetings with governmental entities or civil society and its participation in public events. In 2018 alone, the OTP conducted three missions to that country.[48] It directly engaged with Colombian institutions such as the Attorney's General Office, the Constitutional Court, and the SJP. This led to visible results in terms of complementarity (from its positive proactive approach). For example, as seen in the 2018 Report, the order of the SJP to 'prioritise' extrajudicial executions was based, among others, on the OTP's findings.

Finally, it should be stated that the OTP was clearly more involved and intrusive in Colombia following the 2016 Peace Agreement. The SJP generated many expectations, and so the OTP carefully analysed the agreement and related legislative developments in light of Colombia's international obligations. In particular, it directly pointed out (for the first time in such detail) the problems and legal gaps in the SJP which are key in terms of accountability for international crimes, to which I now turn in Section 3.

3. Advice from the International Criminal Court: Examining the *Amicus Curiae* Brief from the Prosecutor

International criminal law's relevance in transitional justice contexts has been now, more than ever in Colombia, thoroughly discussed by legal experts.[49] And, although one could argue that the ICC has been the one triggering the debate, Colombia has also done its bit, as will be analysed in the following discussion.

[47] S Warton and R Grey, 'The Full Picture: Preliminary Examinations at the International Criminal Court' (2018) 56 The Canadian Yearbook of International Law 4.

[48] ICC, OTP, Report on Preliminary Examination Activities of 2018, para 161 <https://www.icc-cpi.int/itemsDocuments/181205-rep-otp-PE-ENG.pdf> accessed 3 October 2022.

[49] This is so not only because there was a preliminary examination going on for seventeen years in Colombia, but because ICL is one of the sources which can be directly applied by the SJP when assessing the legal characterisation of facts (see SJP Legislative Act 01 of 2017, transitory art 5) <http://es.presidencia.gov.co/normativa/normativa/ACTO%20LEGISLATIVO%20N°%2001%20DE%204%20DE%20ABRIL%20DE%202017.pdf> accessed 3 October 2022.

A. Action and Reaction: The *Amicus Curiae* Brief of the International Criminal Court Prosecutor

In September 2017, the President of the Colombian Constitutional Court invited former ICC Prosecutor, Fatou Bensouda, to express the OTP's views on the framework implementing the SJP, which was at that moment under constitutional review. The brief was submitted by the OTP in October 2017,[50] and it identified the most troublesome issues from an ICL perspective relating to the SJP Legislative Act 01 of 2017 and the Amnesty Law.

(i) Command responsibility

According to the OTP, transitory article 24 of Legislative Act 01 of 2017 includes a definition of superior responsibility which could lead to impunity. The wording establishes additional requirements for military commanders not demanded by article 28 of the Rome Statute. According to the ICC Prosecutor, the definition of command responsibility departs from customary international law, because it comprises five requirements which are not prescribed by the Rome Statute. The extra requirements included in transitory article 24 of Legislative Act 01 of 2017 are: control over the criminal conduct, commission of crimes within the area of responsibility of the superior, legal and material capacity to send orders, direct capacity to take adequate measures, and 'updateable' knowledge. The OTP expressed its concern about the definition in article 24 of the Legislative Act due to the higher standards required for this mode of liability for military commanders. Accordingly, it found the provision leaves 'impunity gaps' and makes it more difficult to prove such responsibility.

(ii) The definition of 'grave' war crimes

Article 23 of the Amnesty Law allows for amnesties and pardons to be provided for political or related crimes. It added that these benefits would not apply to crimes against humanity, genocide, 'grave' war crimes, or other violent conduct. The same provision established that 'grave' war crimes shall be understood as systematic violations of IHL. In a similar vein, article 46 of the Amnesty Law provided that the waiver of criminal prosecution for state agents would not be available for crimes against humanity, genocide, 'grave' war crimes (again), or other violent conduct.

The ICC Prosecutor argued in the brief that referring to 'grave' war crimes as systematic crimes could imply that amnesties or waivers from criminal prosecutions could be granted to individuals who have committed war crimes that are not systematic, which must be also punished according to the Rome Statute.[51] She

[50] ICC Prosecutor, *Amicus curiae* brief before the Colombian Constitutional Court, 17 October 2017 <http://cr00.epimg.net/descargables/2017/10/21/17135b6061c7a5066ea86fe7e37ce26a.pdf?int=masinfo> accessed 3 October 2022 ('ICC Amicus brief').

[51] ibid para 33.

remarked that the ICC jurisdiction requires that all war crimes included in article 8 of the Rome Statute must be prosecuted, regardless of their systematic or individualised nature.[52]

(iii) The determination of 'active or decisive' participation in crimes

Transitory article 16 of Legislative Act 01 of 2017 establishes that individuals not part of organisations or armed groups ('third parties') who have directly or indirectly contributed to the commission of crimes during the armed conflict will be able to appear before the SJP and to receive special treatment, such as a waiver from criminal prosecution. The provision excluded those individuals who had an 'active or decisive participation' in grave crimes from this beneficial regime.

The concern of the ICC Prosecutor focused, however, on the possibility of there being too broad an interpretation of those criteria ('active or decisive' participation). From her perspective, this could lead to a generalised amnesty being granted to third parties accountable for ICC crimes because it could exclude omissions, among other reasons.[53] Such an interpretation would be incompatible with customary international law. Thus, she called for a clarification of the article's extent to avoid impunity for individuals who made significant contributions to grave crimes, even indirectly or through an omission.[54]

(iv) The implementation of sanctions involving 'effective restrictions of freedoms and rights'

The sanctions the SJP will impose differ depending on at what stage in the process the defendant acknowledges truth and responsibility.[55] 'Special sanctions' will be imposed on defendants who provide exhaustive, complete, and detailed truthful accounts at an early stage in the proceedings. These sanctions, which shall focus on redress and reparations, will consist in the effective restrictions on freedoms and rights whilst having the defendants participate in a series of activities such as infrastructure building and repair programmes in rural areas.[56] They will have a minimum duration of five years and a maximum of eight. If acknowledgement of truth and responsibility is done at a later stage, prior to the ruling, 'alternative sanctions', including the deprivation of liberty in prison for between five and eight years (maximum), can be imposed. Such sanctions will have an essentially retributive nature. Finally, 'ordinary sanctions' of deprivation of liberty in prison from fifteen

[52] ibid para 38.
[53] ibid para 42.
[54] ibid para 48.
[55] In Spanish, the term used to refer to defendants in the SJP is '*compareciente*'. This could be translated as 'the person appearing' before the SJP, which does not have such a negative connotation as 'defendant'.
[56] Peace agreement (n 1) 182–84.

to twenty years will be imposed if there is no acknowledgement of truth and responsibility.[57, 58]

The ICC Prosecutor explained that the Rome Statute does not determine the type or specific length of sanctions that states must impose for international crimes. However, she emphasised that sanctions must support the general goals of ICL, the most important of which is to put an end to international crimes.[59] With respect to *alternative* and *ordinary sanctions*, sentences can be lowered in the context of transitional justice if the individual satisfies conditions that could justify this lower penalty, such as recognising criminal responsibility, guaranteeing non-recurrence, and participating in truth mechanisms, among others.[60] Concerning *special sanctions*, which are the most controversial because they will not be served in prison, the Prosecutor argued that a range of factors will be considered to evaluate whether they are compatible or not with the *genuine* intention to make the convicted individual effectively accountable (such as proportionality in relation to the gravity of the crime or the degree of responsibility of the perpetrator). Moreover, she stated that it will be necessary to analyse if these sanctions comply with the objectives of sentences and if there is a rigorous system to verify compliance with the restrictions on freedoms and rights.[61] It is important to note that the ICC Prosecutor did not per se find that special sanctions were inconsistent with ICL but that whether they are congruent with ICL or not would depend on their implementation.

B. The Colombian Constitutional Court Response

Blatantly disregarding the recommendations expressed by the OTP in its brief would not have constituted an intelligent move on behalf of the Colombian Constitutional Court. However, the four concerns of the OTP were only addressed to a limited extent when the Court undertook its constitutional review of the SJP Legislative Act 01 of 2017 (sentence C-674 of 2017)[62] and the Amnesty Law (sentence C-007 of 2018).[63]

[57] According to the SJP Statutory Law, Law 1957 of 2019, art 20, the intentional non-compliance with any of the conditions included in the Conditionality Regime (providing full truth, reparation to victims, and guaranteeing non-repetition) will result in the loss of all special treatment, benefits, waivers, rights, and guarantees.

[58] SJP Legislative Act 01 of 2017, transitory art 13.

[59] ICC Amicus brief (n 50) para 50.

[60] ibid para 51.

[61] ibid paras 51–52.

[62] Colombian Constitutional Court, sentence C-674 of 2017 <http://www.corteconstitucional.gov.co/relatoria/2017/C-674-17.htm> accessed 3 October 2022 ('Sentence C-674').

[63] Colombian Constitutional Court, sentence C-007 of 2018 <http://www.corteconstitucional.gov.co/relatoria/2018/C-007-18.htm> accessed 3 October 2022 ('Sentence C-007').

(i) Command responsibility

Sentence C-674 of the Constitutional Court addressed the issues concerning the definition of command responsibility arising from transitory article 24 of the SJP Legislative Act 01 of 2017. The tribunal held that, in transitional contexts, the prohibition on impunity requires at least the investigation, prosecution, and sanction of those most responsible for the worst crimes. It referred to the special *margin of appreciation* that exists when designing modes of liability in transitional justice scenarios. It argued that the decisive point is not whether the formula of superior responsibility mirrors article 28 of the Rome Statute, but rather, if this situation leads to impunity. In this respect, the Court detailed the distinct modes of liability which already exist in the national legislation and argued that those could be used to criminalise those cases where a commander's responsibility arises from the breach of his duties to prevent, repress, or submit to the competent authorities the crimes committed or that were about to be committed by his subordinates. In conclusion, the Colombian Court did not declare unconstitutional any part of this article.[64]

(ii) The definition of 'grave' war crimes

As to the notion of 'grave' war crimes, the Court declared unconstitutional the word 'grave' and the expression 'grave war crimes will be understood as systematic violations of IHL', both included in article 23 of the Amnesty Law.[65] In the decision C-007, the tribunal explained that 'grave war crimes' is a category that does not exist in IHL, ICL, or even the Colombian Criminal Code. It argued that the wording of article 23 could lead to misunderstanding and could even open the door to the disregard of the international duty to investigate, prosecute, and punish grave violations of IHL.[66] Hence, the result is that article 23 now does not permit amnesty to be granted for any war crimes in addition to crimes against humanity, genocide, and other crimes listed.

(iii) The determination of 'active or decisive' participation in crimes

In sentence C-674, the Court declared unconstitutional the part of transitory article 16 of Legislative Act 01 of 2017 which included the words 'active or decisive'.[67] The reasons underlying this decision, however, went far beyond the problem the ICC Prosecutor initially found and, in some sense, counteracted the underpinnings of the OTP's intervention. When addressing the question of 'third parties' or non-combatants, the Court established that obliging them to appear before the SJP contravenes the guarantee of natural justice and the principle of legality. Hence, the

64 Sentence C-674 (n 62) consideration 5.5.1.5.
65 Sentence C-007 (n 63) [520]–[521].
66 ibid consideration D7.
67 Sentence C-674 (n 62) consideration 5.5.2.14.

Court emphasised that the appearance before the SJP by 'third parties' would be voluntary—which, in some sense, could reduce accountability. The tribunal based its reasoning on the fact that the SJP was created within the framework of a negotiation between the government and an armed group with the purpose of putting an end to the armed conflict. Besides, it explained that the punitive regime relating to 'third parties' is not defined in the SJP Legislative Act 01 of 2017.[68]

(iv) The implementation of sanctions involving 'effective restrictions of freedoms and rights'

Finally, the Court examined transitory article 13 of Legislative Act 01 of 2017 in sentence C-674. Although it did not declare its unconstitutionality, the tribunal emphasised that the non-compliance with the sanctions imposed by the SJP would result in the loss of the SJP legal benefits.[69] Compliance would be carefully supervised on a case-by-case basis by the SJP. The Court also emphasised that the Legislative Act establishes an independence between the imposition of sanctions and the ability to participate in politics.[70] Hence, the fact of being convicted by this judicial instance does not constitute an inability to run as a candidate for popular election, to hold public office, or to enter into contracts with the state. This has been justified on the basis that political reintegration allows former combatants to defend their ideological, economic, social, and political positions from within the institutional and political system, and not based on illegality and violence. The tribunal drew attention to the fact that sanctions must be subject to a minimum standard which enables compliance with the duty of the state to investigate, prosecute, and punish human rights violations and breaches of IHL, and to guarantee victims' rights and due process. The Court explained that the SJP would determine if the sanctions are compatible with the goals of international law and should thus not lead to impunity. Hence, judges would need to impose sanctions compatible with the appropriate goals of punishment and determine if they are commensurate with the *genuine* intention of bringing perpetrators to justice.[71]

(v) Interim conclusion

The Constitutional Court opened a dialogue with the OTP which paved the way for a fruitful engagement and mutual influence, which is essential in terms of the prosecution and punishment of international crimes domestically. International

[68] ibid consideration 5.5.2.

[69] What losing the SJP legal benefits means in these cases remains unclear. The Court has only stated that the loss of benefits is not the same for any breach of the conditions. This is because the verification of compliance with these commitments must be carried out taking into account the principle of gradualism. Therefore, according to the Court, whoever having received a 'special' or an 'alternative' sanction seriously fails to comply with any of the conditions, will lose the benefits attached to this type of sanctions, which may be replaced by 'ordinary' sanctions.

[70] Sentence C-674 (n 62) consideration 5.3.2.4.3.

[71] ibid consideration 5.5.1.9.

crimes affect the international community as a whole, and the ICC must guarantee that those crimes do not go unpunished. Hence, the system of complementarity is essentially based on the recognition that the exercise of national criminal jurisdiction is a duty of states, which are 'expected to maintain and enforce adherence to international standards'.[72] Through a less coercive and constructive way of intervening in Colombia, the OTP expressed its worry regarding four issues: (i) the 'command responsibility' formula; (ii) amnesty for war crimes which not qualify as 'grave'; (iii) the 'active or decisive' participation criteria of third parties in the conflict; and (iv) the 'effective restriction of freedoms and rights' sanction.

It is virtually impossible to know with certainty how much influence the *amicus curiae* brief had on the Constitutional Court's decisions, since numerous national entities and civil organisations intervened before the Court and exposed the controversial points found in the SJP Legislative Act 01 of 2017 and the Amnesty Law. Nevertheless, the value of the invitation extended to the OTP to express its views in a brief cannot be underestimated. In her introduction, the ICC Prosecutor referred to the 'close working relationship that the Prosecution has with the Colombian State and its national authorities'.[73]

After having compared the content of the *amicus curiae* brief and the decisions of the Constitutional Court, however, it could be stated that the 'impunity gap' the ICC Prosecutor was concerned about was not completely closed. On the one hand, the national court declared the unconstitutionality of two aspects of the SJP legal framework which could result in impunity when applied by judges (Sections 3B(ii) and 3B(iii) of this chapter). On the other, it remains unclear as yet how the SJP will apply the 'effective restriction of freedoms and rights' sanction. Finally, as to the 'command responsibility' formula, it must be stated that the SJP has recently charged members of the Armed Forces with crimes according to this mode of liability, which has been interpreted in compliance with the Rome Statute.[74]

4. The Principle of Complementarity between the International Criminal Court and Colombia

The relationship between the ICC and Colombia has been quite unique. The situation in Colombia was the longest-known preliminary examination of the ICC. During this period, the OTP engaged proactively with the Colombian state, thus

[72] ICC, OTP, Paper on some policy issues before the OTP, September 2003, 5 <https://www.icc-cpi.int/news/paper-some-policy-issues-office-prosecutor> accessed 22 September 2023 ('OTP Paper 2003').

[73] ICC Amicus brief (n 50) para 2.

[74] See Special Jurisdiction for Peace, Truth and Recognition Chamber, Decision 125 of 2021, 2 July 2021 <https://jurinfo.jep.gov.co/normograma/compilacion/docs/Auto_SRVR-125_02-Julio-2021.htm?resaltar=auto+125+de+2021> accessed 3 October 2022.

allowing domestic authorities to understand if their agreements complied with ICL. This is an example of positive complementarity—whereby the ICC influences the decisions of domestic jurisdictions and thus avoids the need to institute a prosecution itself. Indeed, the OTP decided to close the preliminary examination in October 2021 with the signature of a cooperation agreement with the Colombian government. As will be explained, this document constitutes probably the first clear agreement of positive complementarity between a state which is not being formally investigated and the OTP.

A. Negative Complementarity and Positive Complementarity

The principle of complementarity lies at the heart of the ICC. As a permanent international court in charge of attributing criminal responsibility to individuals for international crimes, its main goal is that no crime affecting the international community goes unpunished. In this regard, the principle is a fundamental pillar in the creation of the ICC, as its own founding treaty reveals. Both paragraph 10 of the Preamble and article 1 of the Rome Statute affirm that the ICC shall be complementary to national criminal jurisdictions, and paragraph 6 of the Preamble states that it is the duty of every state to exercise its criminal jurisdiction over those responsible for international crimes.

William A Schabas argues that international and national justice systems function in opposition and to some extent with hostility, which makes complementarity an inherently antagonistic principle.[75] However, Ovo C Imoedemhe affirms that both systems 'should not be deemed to be mutually exclusive'[76] and that without this principle, the ICC could soon become overburdened with referrals by states. The principle of complementarity thus serves the objective of distributing functions and defining the role of the ICC in relation to states. However, the ICC must not affect the competence of states in investigating and prosecuting crimes committed on their own territory. Indeed, complementarity is based on the idea of the national sovereignty of states. This contributes to the efficiency of investigations and prosecutions of grave crimes, since it is more practical and requires less resources to ensure accountability when victims, perpetrators, and evidence are found nearby.

It was not the intention of the parties to create an international court which would be a substitute for national criminal tribunals.[77] In fact, this constituted a

[75] WA Schabas, '"Complementarity in Practice": Some Uncomplementary Thoughts' (2008) 19 Criminal Law Forum 6.

[76] OC Imoedemhe, *The Complementarity Regime of the International Criminal Court* (Springer 2017) 23.

[77] X Fuentes, 'El principio de complementariedad en la práctica de la Corte Penal Internacional' in C Cárdenas and X Fuentes (eds), *Corte Penal Internacional y Jurisdicciones Estatales, El principio de complementariedad* (Legal Publishing 2012) 96.

pre-eminent reason for the wide acceptance of the Rome Statute. Since its origins, the ICC was established to guarantee that states effectively punish the crimes of genocide, crimes against humanity, war crimes, and crimes of aggression. Only if states are 'unwilling' or 'unable' to implement *genuine* criminal procedures will the ICC intervene. The negative side of complementarity, then, 'requires the ICC to refrain from taking the place of states that are already adequately investigating and prosecuting crimes within the jurisdiction'.[78] Thus, the interrelationship between the international and the national criminal jurisdiction could also be defined based on the principle of subsidiarity that works with incentives and sanctions (known as the carrot-and-sticks principle of subsidiarity).[79]

Ultimately, states will want to meet the 'complementarity test'. This test is detailed in article 17 of the Rome Statute, on 'issues of admissibility', which provides a mechanism to ensure negative complementarity.[80] Admissibility, according to article 53(1)(b) of the Statute, is one of the elements to be examined when deciding whether to initiate an investigation. To determine 'unwillingness' of the state in a case, the ICC can consider, for instance, if the proceedings were undertaken for the purpose of shielding the person concerned from criminal responsibility for crimes within the jurisdiction of the Court, or if there has been an unjustified delay in the proceedings.[81] To determine 'inability', the Court shall consider situations of total or substantial collapse of the national judicial system.[82] In essence, 'the admissibility regime of the ICC is embedded in a structure which facilitates *different forms of interaction* between the Court and domestic jurisdictions (i.e. notification, dialogue, consultation)'.[83]

The concept of complementarity evolved to include another function of the Court, namely, to monitor and ensure that national authorities comply with their duty (positive complementarity). This would be achieved by encouraging and enabling states to carry out their primary responsibility.[84] Indeed, the former ICC Prosecutor affirmed in his *Paper on some policy issues before the OTP* of 2003 that: 'The effectiveness of the ICC should not be measured only by the number of cases that reach the Court. On the contrary, the absence of trials by the ICC, as a consequence of the *effective functioning of national systems*, would be a major success'.[85] The principle of positive complementarity has also been associated with the

[78] L Badagard and M Klamberg, 'The Gatekeeper of the ICC' (2017) 48 Georgetown Journal of International Law 666.

[79] G Werle, 'El principio de complementariedad: Una mirada retrospectiva y prospectiva' in C Cárdenas and X Fuentes (eds), *Corte Penal Internacional y Jurisdicciones Estatales, El principio de complementariedad* (Legal Publishing 2012) 79.

[80] Badagard and Klamberg (n 78) 666.

[81] Rome Statute, art 17(2).

[82] Rome Statute, art 17(3).

[83] C Stahn, 'Taking Complementarity Seriously: On the Sense and Sensibility of 'Classical', 'Positive' and 'Negative' Complementarity' in C Stahn and MM El Zeidy (eds), *The International Criminal Court and Complementarity* (CUP 2011) 248 (emphasis added).

[84] OTP Paper 2003 (n 72) 4–5.

[85] ibid 4 (emphasis added).

cooperation and coordination relationship between the ICC and domestic judicial authorities or other actors such as non-governmental organisations (NGOs) and international organisations.[86]

In this sense, Carsten Stahn argues that 'complementarity institutes a legal system under which the Court and domestic jurisdictions are meant to *complement and reinforce each other* in their mutual efforts to institutionalize accountability for mass crimes'.[87] This is the positive dimension of complementarity, which is understood by the OTP as an instrumental or intermediate objective of its activities when affirming that in order to avoid impunity, it will encourage genuine national proceedings.[88]

B. 'Positive' Complementarity Before the Closure of the Preliminary Investigation in Colombia

The SJP legal framework addresses multiple issues a state must decide in the aftermath of an armed conflict, for instance, how to guarantee accountability for international crimes and incentivise the demobilisation of FARC-EP combatants at the same time. Disarmament and the cessation of hostilities in Colombia, hence, go hand in hand with a special jurisdiction which includes benefits, waivers, and sanctions. One general concern before the OTP decided to close the preliminary examination in Colombia was if the state was complying with its duty to prosecute international crimes—this was especially so in relation to the SJP, which was in charge of attributing responsibility to the 'most responsible' members of the Armed Forces and FARC-EP for the 'most grave' crimes. In particular, the OTP was interested in the prosecution of extrajudicial executions, sexual crimes, and enforced displacement, as expressed in its Reports (Section 2B(ii) of this chapter).

After the submission of the *amicus curiae* brief by the OTP, it was clear that Colombia had disregarded its guidelines on the notion of 'command responsibility' and that its application could mostly lead to the impunity of many military commanders accountable for 'false positive' cases (one of the main worries of the OTP[89]). Indeed, since the legislative framework to investigate and prosecute high commanders did not meet ICL standards, it would have been possible to consider Colombia 'unwilling' or 'unable' to *genuinely* prosecute international crimes according to article 17 of the Rome Statute. It was unlikely, however, that the ICC

[86] Badagard and Klamberg (n 78) 688.

[87] Stahn (n 83) 236 (emphasis added).

[88] F Vacas, *El Derecho Internacional ante el Conflicto Armado en Colombia* (Tirant lo Blanch 2015) 354.

[89] ICC, OTP, Situation in Colombia, Interim Report, November 2012, paras 8–10 and especially para 196 <https://www.icc-cpi.int/sites/default/files/2022-09/OTPCOLOMBIAPublicInterimReportNovember2012.pdf> accessed 22 September 2023.

would open a formal investigation on Colombia due to the state's decision to use a definition of command responsibility differing from the customary international law and Rome Statute definition, as long as the SJP found a way to hold accountable those responsible for international crimes, as it has been doing with several decisions delivered in 2021 and 2022 charging members of the Armed Forces with war crimes and crimes against humanity. In fact, there is no obligation for states to implement the Rome Statute exactly as it is[90]—if the law is wrong, the ICC could always intervene through positive complementarity. This is the way it should ascertain that ICL is understood in the 123 state parties to the ICC. If the ICC had opened an investigation in Colombia, however, not only would there have been a risk that the state would withdraw from the Rome Statute, but the peace agreement and the SJP could have been endangered.

As to the system of sanctions established at the SJP, which was the second 'unsolved' problem identified by the OTP in its brief, it directly affects the punishment of all international crimes, not only those committed by the military. It has been argued that national sentencing can be a relevant factor for the complementarity analysis.[91] According to Mark A Drumbl:

> This could be because punishment is viewed as too harsh (i.e. the death penalty, long-term solitary confinement or placement in prisons that fall short of international human rights standards) or too lenient (i.e. community service, house arrest, reparations or apology instead of the internationalized norm of prison incarceration).[92]

In the Colombian case, it could be argued that the three kinds of sanctions the SJP envisages are too gentle for the crimes committed by those bearing the greatest responsibility, especially the sanction consisting of the 'effective restrictions of freedoms and rights'. This indeed was part of the reason many in the population voted against the agreement in the plebiscite. However, it is necessary to understand that the SJP is part of a comprehensive transitional justice system and imposes different sanctions taking into account the procedural stage where the truth was told by those appearing before the SJP. Hence, truth, together with reparation and non-repetition, is a general obligation imposed on all those appearing before the SJP. Additionally, it cannot be forgotten that the system of sanctions was designed as a concession from the government to the FARC-EP to guarantee their demobilisation.

[90] Many states have done so despite the absence of an express obligation to implement the substantive parts of the Statute into domestic law.

[91] H Olásolo, 'Complementarity Analysis of National Sentencing' in R Haveman and O lusanya (eds), *Sentencing and Sanctioning in Supranational Criminal Law* (Intersentia 2006) 40.

[92] MA Drumbl, 'Policy through Complementarity' in C Stahn and MM El Zeidy (eds), *The International Criminal Court and Complementarity* (CUP 2011) 205–06.

Although 'articles 17 and 20 of the Rome Statute consolidate the status of the liberal criminal trial as the idealised way to promote justice in the aftermath of atrocity',[93] it is necessary in my view to go beyond the trial and punishment modalities of the ICC. Transitional justice, as an effort to overcome a past of atrocities and guarantee peace in a violent state, entails the need for local variations that can depart from the classical conception of criminal justice.[94] The SJP may impose a sanction consisting of repairing a public road or building a school in cases where the truth was told at an early stage. As sanctions clearly differ from imprisonment, their acceptance at the ICC would require some flexibility yet, at the same time, this is not a legal impossibility. According to Payam Akhvan, 'making the complementarity principle a practical reality requires meaningful engagement with these messy realities'.[95] Taking into account that the ICC has not developed its standards of punishment when analysing complementarity in its preliminary examinations, it was unlikely that an investigation would be opened on this basis. Besides, it must be remembered that even though the JPL only included reduced prison sentences, the ICC has implicitly accepted its lenient penalties.

It is clear that the two problems identified in the SJP laws are examples of the tension between transitional justice and international criminal law in post-conflict scenarios. The OTP tried to encourage reform of these legislative decisions through its country missions, meetings, and consultations, exercising the positive side of complementarity while Colombia was under a preliminary examination by the OTP. Yet, its activities only had a partial impact, as the Constitutional Court's decisions reveal. Ultimately, understanding the context of transitional justice in Colombia requires bearing in mind that justice cannot be reduced to mere retribution. Restorative justice, as the corollary of scenarios in transition, focuses both on victims' rights satisfaction and resocialisation of combatants, and not only on the punishment of the perpetrator. Therefore, it is important to adopt a broad concept of justice which includes not only sanctions, but also measures to find the truth and guarantee reparations.

C. Positive Complementarity After the Closure of the Preliminary Examination in Colombia

In October 2021, Prosecutor Karim Khan made public his decision to close the preliminary examination and not to open an investigation in Colombia, emphasising the recent progress that had been made before the Colombian national authorities:

[93] ibid 210.

[94] See Theme 1, Chapters 2–4 in this book.

[95] P Akhvan, 'Complementarity Conundrums: The ICC Clock in Transitional Times' (2016) 14 Journal of International Criminal Justice 1059.

> Following a thorough assessment, the Prosecutor is satisfied that complementarity is working today in Colombia. The Government of Colombia, together with the ordinary courts, the Justice and Peace Law Tribunals, the Special Jurisdiction for Peace, civil society and the people of Colombia are to be commended for their resilience and determination in demanding justice and accountability in their quest for peace. The progress made has led the Office to determine that the national authorities of Colombia are neither inactive, unwilling nor unable to genuinely investigate and prosecute Rome Statute crimes.[96]

According to the OTP, the decision not to open an investigation was made on admissibility grounds, that is, by concluding that complementarity is working today in Colombia.[97] Hence, the decision was taken as a result of a profound and serious assessment conducted over seventeen years and 'against the backdrop of the assessment previously conducted and documented in detail by the Office in its situation-specific and annual reports, in its submissions before the Colombian Constitutional Court as well as in key statements setting out the Office's position'.[98] This conclusion is clearly reflected in the cooperation agreement signed between the government and the OTP, which refers to the progress achieved by the judicial authorities in ensuring accountability, including by the SJP.[99]

The ICC Prosecutor stated that the complementarity assessment 'should not, and cannot, be postponed indefinitely pending the completion of all possible domestic proceedings'.[100] On the contrary, the Statute and the jurisprudence of the Court are clear that the assessment of admissibility must be carried out on the basis of the existing facts.[101] In this respect, the decision makes clear that the Prosecutor is strictly applying the principle of negative complementarity under the Rome Statute. The Prosecutor also said that the absence of a preliminary examination does not, however, mean the end of the OTP's engagement with Colombia or its support for ongoing accountability processes. On the contrary, this 'marks the beginning of a new chapter of support and engagement—an example of positive complementarity in action'.[102] In other words, the Prosecutor believes in both sides of complementarity and that the ICC can do its work on the basis of continuing

[96] Press release, 28 October 2021, 'ICC Prosecutor, Mr Karim A. A. Khan QC, concludes the preliminary examination of the Situation in Colombia with a Cooperation Agreement with the Government charting the next stage in support of domestic efforts to advance transitional justice' <https://www.icc-cpi.int/news/icc-prosecutor-mr-karim-khan-qc-concludes-preliminary-examination-situation-colombia#:~:text=On%2028%20October%202021%2C%20in,to%20Colombia's%20national%20accountability%20processes> accessed 3 October 2022.

[97] ICC, PTC I, Prosecution's response to FIDH and CAJAR requests, 6 June 2022, paras 9 et seq. <https://www.icc-cpi.int/sites/default/files/CourtRecords/CR2022_04580.PDF> accessed 3 October 2022 ('Prosecution's response').

[98] ibid para 24.

[99] Cooperation Agreement (n 6) 2.

[100] Press release (n 96).

[101] Prosecution's response (n 97) para 11.

[102] Press release (n 96).

positive engagement with domestic authorities. The closure of the preliminary review makes clear that significant work remains to be done and that national institutions must continue fulfilling their constitutional responsibilities.

The agreement signed with the government of Colombia is perhaps the first major positive complementarity agreement between a state that is not under investigation and the OTP. It has such important provisions as the exchange of knowledge between officials of the ICC and relevant national institutions such as the SJP.[103] This could involve visits by Colombian professionals to the ICC and vice versa, making way for a two-way exchange: it is not only the ICC that will share its latest decisions and best practices, but Colombian lawyers and officials can also explain the innovative development of ICL taking place there. The agreement also provides for the ICC to provide specialised training to explain how ICL should be implemented and applied at the national level. The ICC is also tasked with enhancing the investigative capacity of local authorities to prosecute international crimes through staff exchanges and professional visits to the ICC.

On the other hand, positive complementarity must consist of real initiatives that help to properly implement and apply the Rome Statute in all states. For example, the Colombian Criminal Code does not include crimes against humanity and many of the war crimes listed in the Rome Statute, and this is an obstacle that legal practitioners face every day. It is therefore important that the OTP takes further steps together with Colombia, in order to avoid the possible impunity of high-level officials, third-party civilians, and non-combatant state agents bearing responsibility, as some victim-NGOs have stated before the ICC.[104] The OTP should evaluate the results of its positive complementarity policies in transitional justice scenarios and consider taking measures that have more impact in the understanding and application of ICL at the domestic level.

5. Conclusion

The situation in Colombia has been a clear example of positive complementarity due to the encouragement the ICC has been offering to national proceedings for many years now.[105] Attempts to negotiate with armed groups have existed since the 1980s, and it was only in 2016 when a very ambitious peace agreement with

[103] Cooperation agreement (n 6) 5.

[104] FIDH and CAJAR, 'Request for review of the Prosecutor's decision of 28 October 2021 to close the preliminary examination of the situation in Colombia', 27 April 2022, 18 et seq. <https://www.icc-cpi.int/sites/default/files/CourtRecords/CR2022_03398.PDF> accessed 3 October 2022.

[105] According to Aksenova, 'the interaction between the ICC and Colombian domestic actors can thus be described as a "*dialogical* model"', which 'presupposes *active engagement* of both the transmitter and the receiver of information in the process of constructing the meaning', in M Aksenova, 'The ICC Involvement in Colombia: Walking the Fine Line Between Peace and Justice' in M Bergsmo and

FARC-EP was finally achieved. Arguably, this has in great measure been achieved due to the decision of the ICC to refrain from opening an investigation. As Stahn explains referring to the ICC: 'Initial restraint may be a useful instrument of conflict management in crisis situations, in particular in situations of ongoing conflict. In such situations, it is necessary to coordinate ICC and domestic activities in order to *facilitate peacebuilding and stabilisation initiatives*.'[106]

As analysed in Section 3, the Constitutional Court initiated a discussion with the Court on the SJP legal framework before its application by judges, hence trying to avoid norms which could *prima facie* lead to impunity. This invitation to the OTP clearly constituted a *request for assistance* from Colombia to the ICC to construct a national framework that enables subsequent procedures to prosecute international crimes.[107] Hence, the changes made to the SJP norms after the *amicus curiae* brief are an excellent example of the positive complementarity policy applied in transitional justice scenarios by the OTP. The constructive actions undertaken by the Court when declaring the unconstitutionality of certain provisions showed that an open preliminary examination could arguably be an effective solution to enhance the legal transitional justice framework of a country.

As to the problematic provisions identified by the OTP in its brief that were not modified, it could be argued in the first place that these were points of tensions due to uncertainty regarding the degree of flexibility conceded to domestic authorities within the complementarity regime. This is intensified when the government has just ended negotiations with an armed group and has duties arising from a peace agreement which must be fulfilled at the risk of sparking a new conflict. However, as the SJP has shown, a disposition which in the beginning seemed eventually to lead to impunity, has recently been interpreted in accordance with ICL and the Rome Statute.

A premature intervention of the ICC through the opening of a formal investigation in Colombia could have jeopardised the existence of the SJP and the whole transitional justice system. Now, the closure of the preliminary examination and the signing of a cooperation agreement allows Colombia and the Prosecutor to 'build upon a long lasting, sustainable relationship'.[108] This agreement reinforces and strengthens the commitments of both the OTP and Colombia in the results achieved, in particular by the SJP. This unprecedented agreement creates a new path for positive complementarity outside the preliminary examination. It is to be hoped the commitments included in this document become a reality and do not remain promises existing only on paper.

C Stahn (eds), *Quality Control in Preliminary Examination*, vol 1 (Torkel Opsahl Academic Publisher 2018) 261 (emphasis added).

[106] Stahn (n 83) 266 (emphasis added).
[107] Under the Rome Statute, art 93.
[108] Press release (n 96).

25

Joint Reflection: South Africa and Colombia as Transitional Justice Societies

Mispa Roux and Natalia Silva Santaularia

1. Introduction

Our two contributions illustrate how South Africa and Colombia's international criminal law approach to transitional justice is in some ways similar, but also vastly different. Both countries have had to deal with a past of gross human rights violations due to the apartheid regime in one case, and several armed conflicts in the other.[1] Both have therefore established judicial or extrajudicial transitional justice mechanisms after negotiated settlements to try to achieve peace and reconciliation, and both have had to deal with the peace–justice dichotomy.[2] Finally, it is worth recalling that both South Africa and Colombia are member states of the International Criminal Court (ICC).

2. International Criminal Law and Transitional Justice: Confronting International Crimes in South Africa and Colombia

In South Africa, gross human rights violations were perpetrated for centuries, first during colonialism, and then by the apartheid regime. In the early 1990s, the crime against humanity of apartheid came to a definitive end by way of a negotiated settlement between the African National Congress (ANC) and several

[1] ICRC, Retos humanitarios 2022, Colombia, February 2022. According the ICRC, there are now six internal armed conflicts in Colombia: three between the government and the National Liberation Army (ELN), the Gaitanistas Self-Defence Forces of Colombia (AGC) and the former structures of FARC-EP which did not adhere to the peace agreement, another between the ELN and the AGC. Finally, two other armed conflicts take place between former structures of FARC-EP which did not adhere to the peace agreement and the 'Segunda Marquetalia', and the 'Comandos de la Frontera-EB'. The sixth armed conflict is between the ELN and the EPL. <https://www.icrc.org/es/document/balance-humanitario-colombia-2022-dih> accessed 15 August 2022.

[2] To the current authors, the dilemma is false because peace and justice are mutually reinforcing mandates.

Mispa Roux and Natalia Silva Santaularia, *Joint Reflection: South Africa and Colombia as Transitional Justice Societies* In: *Transitional Justice, Distributive Justice, and Transformative Constitutionalism.* Edited by: David Bilchitz and Raisa Cachalia, with Magdalena Inés Correa Henao and Nathalia Bautista Pizarro, Oxford University Press. © Mispa Roux and Natalia Silva Santaularia 2023. DOI: 10.1093/oso/9780192887627.003.0025

political organisations which led to the establishment of a Truth and Reconciliation Commission (TRC).[3] Colombia experienced crimes against humanity and war crimes during the multiple armed conflicts that erupted between Colombian governmental armed forces, paramilitary armed groups, and rebel armed groups. In 2016, the Colombian national government and the *Fuerzas Armadas Revolucionarias de Colombia—Ejército del Pueblo* (FARC-EP) negotiated to bring the conflict to an end,[4] and adopted the Final Agreement to End the Armed Conflict and Build a Stable and Lasting Peace. The agreement includes, among others instruments, a Special Jurisdiction for Peace (SJP) and a Truth Commission.

3. Truth-telling and Criminal Justice: Mutually Exclusive or Complementary Mechanisms to Achieve Peace and Reconciliation?

Both South Africa and Colombia provided for the concession of a conditional amnesty for political crimes. In South Africa, the TRC was the extrajudicial body in charge of granting it for 'acts, omissions and offences associated with a political objective committed in the course of the conflicts of the past',[5] in exchange for truth-telling.[6] In Colombia, the SJP, a judicial mechanism, can grant amnesty for 'political crimes and crimes related to those'[7] under the requirement to comply with truth, reparation, and non-repetition.[8] In both countries, amnesties were conceived as a key element of a truth and reconciliation process, and Colombia found inspiration in the South African transitional justice system when designing its own. However, the ICC did not exist at the time the South African settlement took place, and amnesty was adopted for all crimes (including international crimes) in exchange for disclosure of all relevant facts. In fact, it was explicitly decided *not* to prosecute apartheid as a crime against humanity in a 'Nuremberg-style tribunal'.[9] Hence, no individual criminal prosecution for grave crimes committed during apartheid could follow if 'full disclosure of all relevant facts' was made.[10] It was argued by proponents of this arrangement that peace was an essential precondition to

[3] See further Post-amble of the Constitution of the Republic of South Africa, Act 200 of 1993 ('Interim Constitution'); and the Promotion of National Unity and Reconciliation Act 34 of 1995 ('Truth and Reconciliation Act').

[4] Final Agreement to End the Armed Conflict and Build a Stable and Lasting Peace, including the Special Justice for Peace, 24 November 2016 <https://www.peaceagreements.org/viewmasterdocument/1845> accessed 26 September 2023.

[5] Truth and Reconciliation Act, s 20(1)(b).

[6] ibid s 20.

[7] Amnesty Law, art 2.

[8] ibid art 14.

[9] Truth and Reconciliation Commission of South Africa, Report, Volume 1, Chapter 5 para 57 <http://www.justice.gov.za/trc/report/finalreport/Volume%201.pdf> accessed 1 October 2020.

[10] Truth and Reconciliation Act, s 20(1)(c).

democracy.[11] This is a clear example of Teitel's second phase in transitional justice ('post-Cold War transitional justice'), which is associated with democratic transition and nation-building.[12]

Colombia's transitional justice system, on the other hand, was established after the Final Agreement and with the ICC examining every step taken by the state. This meant that no 'blanket amnesty' could be conceded[13] and that international crimes had to be adequately prosecuted and punished. Therefore, the transitional justice framework in Colombia properly establishes that amnesty cannot be granted for international crimes (such as torture, extrajudicial executions, or child recruitment).[14] From the sanctions perspective, it is understood that going beyond the traditional concept of retribution is necessary when trying to achieve peace after complex scenarios such as the aftermath of an armed conflict. No armed group will surrender weapons unless there is a certain degree of pardon or some concessions are made on behalf of the government. The question is how much justice is possible without risking the whole negotiation and reconciliation, and when prosecution efforts could be considered 'genuine' by the ICC.[15] Although the ICC does not make clear what kind of punishment for grave atrocities will avoid the opening of a formal investigation, it does give some margin of flexibility to the states in this regard. A broader conception of justice which includes truth and victims' reparation, and which does not necessarily entail prison, might be eventually accepted by the ICC in some post-conflict scenarios. The success of the implementation of various transitional justice mechanisms in Colombia is therefore crucial and will determine if the ICC Prosecution re-opens the preliminary examination which was closed in October 2021.

Ultimately, understanding the context of transitional justice in both societies requires bearing in mind that justice cannot be equated to retribution, and that it does not only consist in the criminal punishment of perpetrators. Restorative justice balances the satisfaction of victims' rights with the re-socialisation of perpetrators, and the adoption of the view that peace and justice are 'mutually reinforcing imperatives'.[16] Therefore, it is important to embrace a broad concept of transitional justice which includes not only individual criminal prosecution, but also measures to find the truth, guarantee reparations, and ensure the non-recurrence of gross human rights violations.[17]

[11] R Teitel, *Globalizing Transitional Justice* (OUP 2014) 56.

[12] ibid 55.

[13] The South African Amnesty Committee was accused of having given a 'blanket amnesty' to ANC leaders.

[14] Amnesty Law, art 23.

[15] ICC Statute, art 17.

[16] United Nations Approach to Transitional Justice, Guidance Note of the Secretary-General (March 2010) <https://www.securitycouncilreport.org/atf/cf/%7B65BFCF9B-6D27-4E9C-8CD3-CF6E4FF96FF9%7D/TJ_Guidance_Note_March_2010FINAL.pdf> accessed 26 September 2023.

[17] Indeed, the cooperation agreement between the Office of the Prosecutor of the ICC and the government of Colombia (October 2021) refers to the 'recent achievements of the transitional justice in Colombia in pursuing the objectives of retribution, rehabilitation, restoration and deterrence'.

4. The *Erga Omnes* Obligation to Prosecute International Crimes and the International Criminal Court

To date, the SJP has conducted hearings to remind perpetrators ('*comparecientes*') of compromises made during negotiations to appear before the special jurisdiction, and has listened to some of their versions about crimes previously selected by the SJP ('*versiones voluntarias*'). In 2021, the SJP issued its first ruling indicting eight FARC leaders for war crimes and crimes against humanity,[18] and later released four decisions charging members of the Armed Forces with national and international crimes.[19] This is one of the reasons why the ICC Prosecution decided to close the preliminary examination concerning the situation in Colombia after seventeen years.[20] Hence, although *a priori* the SJP legal framework did not seem to comply fully with the Rome Statute, as the ICC Prosecutor stated in her *amicus curiae* brief, the SJP is now effectively trying to avoid impunity in practice. Thus, the relationship between Colombia and the ICC can be seen as *sui generis*, with the emergence of a new kind of positive complementarity after the unusually long preliminary examinations which involved the issuing of various annual reports, visiting national entities and organisations, as well as submitting an *amicus curiae* brief to the Colombian Constitutional Court. A new phase in this relationship has been entered recently with the closing of the preliminary investigation and the signing of a cooperation agreement between the ICC Prosecutor and the Colombian government. In our view, the Colombian transitional justice system can be seen to be implemented against the backdrop of a very different ethos than that which was prevalent in South Africa, what Teitel refers to as the current (and third) phase where the *erga omnes* obligation to prosecute international crimes has become normalised.[21] That placed constraints on what Colombia could do in the peace negotiations but also encouraged creativity in the peace agreement with experimentation with different modalities of justice and punishment.

Another example that takes place within this third phase of transitional justice is South Africa's ambivalent relationship with the ICC, resulting from the failure of the government to comply with the duty to cooperate with the Court in terms of the arrest warrant issued for (now former) President Omar Al-Bashir of the Sudan.[22]

<https://www.icc-cpi.int/sites/default/files/itemsDocuments/20211028-OTP-COL-Cooperation-Agreement-ENG.pdf> accessed 3 October 2022 ('cooperation agreement').

[18] Special Jurisdiction for Peace, Truth and Recognition Chamber, Decision 19 of 2021, 26 January 2021 <https://www.jep.gov.co/Sala-de-Prensa/Documents/CASO%2001%20TOMA%20DE%20REHENES/Auto%20No.%2019%20de%202021.pdf?csf=1&e=16bYs0> accessed 27 April 2021.

[19] Special Jurisdiction for Peace, Truth and Recognition Chamber, Decision 125 of 2021, 2 July 2021; Decision 128 of 2021, 7 July 2021; Decision 001 de 2022, 11 July 2022 (Sub-Chamber D and F); Decision 055 de 2022, 14 July 2022 (Sub-Chamber D).

[20] See the cooperation agreement (n 17) which refers several times to the accountability efforts of the SJP.

[21] Teitel (n 11) 89–93.

[22] ICC Statute, art 86.

The ICC Pre-Trial Chamber II decided that South Africa had failed to comply with its obligations under the ICC Statute by not executing the Court's request.[23] The Chamber further decided that a referral to the Assembly of States Parties or the Security Council of the United Nations was not warranted,[24] and explicitly considered it 'of significance that South Africa is the first State Party to seek from the Court a final legal determination on the extent of its obligations to execute a request for arrest and surrender of Omar Al-Bashir'.[25] This situation created an important dialogue which is undoubtedly complex, yet at the same time constructive and also indicating that the relationship between the ICC and South Africa can also be described as being governed by the principle of 'positive complementarity'. In this respect, the South African government's failure to arrest Al-Bashir provided an opportunity to clarify concepts such as immunity and the duty to cooperate.[26]

5. Conclusion—A Vision for the Future: Expanding the International Criminal Court's Role in Developing International Criminal Law

Peace and stability in the African continent have been the values invoked by South Africa when granting *amnesty* and defending *immunity* for gross human rights violations. They have also been claimed by Colombia when negotiating with FARC-EP to end the conflict. Both have taken decisions which have been questioned by the ICC through conversations which shed light and defined the extent of the international duty to cooperate, on one side, and the duty to duly prosecute grave crimes, on the other side. However, the ICC's efforts in terms of joint communiqués and letters to the state, are not as helpful as other actions might be. Measures such as visiting professional residencies at the ICC or the loan of highly qualified personnel to the country should be promoted so that states adequately learn to investigate and punish international crimes. This would be necessary in the stage preceding a formal investigation, but also after a preliminary examination

23 *The Prosecutor v Omar Hassan Ahmad Al-Bashir* 6 July 2017 ICC-02/05-01/09 (decision under s 87(7) of the Rome Statute on the non-compliance by South Africa with the request by the court for the arrest and surrender of Omar Al-Bashir) [123] and [140] ('ICC non-compliance decision').

24 ibid [139].

25 ibid.

26 In 2014 the African Union adopted the Protocol on Amendments to the Protocol on the Statute of the African Court of Justice and Human Rights (the 'Malabo Protocol'), and art 46A *bis* excludes immunity for international crimes for serving heads of state or government. This is in direct contrast to other treaties establishing international criminal courts or tribunals that explicitly provide that no individual will be entitled to enjoy immunity when jurisdiction is exercised over international crimes. See further London Charter of the International Military Tribunal, art 7; Convention on the Prevention and Punishment of the Crime of Genocide, art IV; Statute of the International Criminal Tribunal for the Former Yugoslavia, art 7(2); Statute of the International Criminal Tribunal for Rwanda, art 6(2); and Law on the Establishment of Extraordinary Chambers in the Courts of Cambodia, art 29.

has been closed. Relying only on dialogue does not seem to be working for South Africa and Colombia. If the main goal of the ICC is to strengthen domestic jurisdictions, workshops and training of legal practitioners are essential tools. Hence, we support an expanded role for the ICC whereby it focuses more on the education and empowerment of domestic institutions, instead of mainly exercising its function surrounding prosecutions. This in turn offers a vision of a progressive role for such an international institution in these societies and creates opportunities for the development of international criminal law.

Index

For the benefit of digital users, indexed terms that span two pages (e.g., 52–53) may, on occasion, appear on only one of those pages.

Tables and figures are indicated by *t* and *f* following the page number